Canadian Cataloguing in Publication Data

Campbell, Monica, 1952-
  Profit from pollution prevention

Bibliography: p.
Includes index.
ISBN 0-920668-21-6

1. Waste products — Economic aspects. 2. Recycling
(Waste, etc.). 3. Salvage (Waste, etc.).
  I. Glenn, William, 1952- II. Pollution Probe Foundation.
III. Title.
HD9975.A2C35   363.7'28   C82-094733-4

Profit
from
Pollution
Prevention

A Guide to
Industrial Waste
Reduction & Recycling

by Monica E. Campbell
and William M. Glenn

**with assistance from
Linda R. Pim**

**Published by the Pollution Probe Foundation
under the direction of Monica Campbell.
Pollution Probe, 12 Madison Avenue, Toronto, Ontario, Canada M5R 2S1**

Production Credits

Editing	Karen Englander Rick Wilks
Graphics	Gram Campbell
Design & Assembly	Gram Campbell Larry Rossignol William Glenn
Cover	Larry Rossignol Gram Campbell
Photo Assistance	Jeremy Taylor
Typesetting	Rapid Graphics
Printing	Gagné Printing
Trade Distribution	Firefly Books 3520 Pharmacy Avenue Unit 1-C Scarborough, Ontario Canada M1W 2T8

Many Thanks

Many thanks to the following people whose participation and enthusiasm made this project a meaningful and deeply satisfying experience.

Rebecca Aird
Jenny Baboolal
Rick Beharriell
Carol Brotman
Douglas Campbell
Georgia Campbell
Gram Campbell
Tracy Campbell
Don Chant
David Coon
Gertrude Ewert
Rick Findlay
Jill Fraleigh
Helen Glenn

William Glenn Sr.
Debby Grinstead
Donald Grinstead
Ross Hall
Andrea Howard
Monte Hummel
Colin Isaacs
Marilyn Knox
Robert Laughlin
Judy Liefschultz
Gage Love
Marjorey Loveys
Lorraine Manley
Brian Marshall

Brian Milner
Barry Mitchell
William Mitchell
Vic Niemela
John Ord
Betty Ounjian
Linda Pim
Robert Pojasek
Geoff Rathbone
John Reed
Gail Richardson
Larry Rossignol
Michael Scott
Mike Seward

Glenda Stein
Doug Stewart
John Swaigen
Robin Taviner
Jeremy Taylor
Marjory Thom
Peter Victor
Richard Wietfeldt
Rick Wilks
John Wilson
Anne Wordsworth

About Pollution Probe

The Pollution Probe Foundation was founded in 1969 in response to growing public concern over the deteriorating quality of the Canadian environment. Since that early beginning, hundreds of staff members and volunteers have tackled a host of pollution problems with solid investigation, public education and positive policy advocacy, so that today, Pollution Probe is one of this country's most effective public interest groups.

The organization has been responsible for significant steps forward in alleviating air and water pollution, curbing the generation of solid waste, promoting recycling, adopting better land use policies, educating the public on additives and environmental contaminants in food, and implementing stricter noise controls. Despite past successes, Pollution Probe has always attempted to recognize emerging environmental hazards. It is currently working to develop an effective regulatory programme that will solve the problems of drinking water quality, acid rain, pesticide safety, hazardous waste management, and toxic substances control.

Effective pollution abatement is impossible without an informed public. To this end, Pollution Probe has published books and briefs on a wide range of environmental problems and alternative approaches that will ensure their control. The Probe Post, which addresses current environmental and energy topics, is emerging as one of this country's most respected news magazines in the field.

Demonstration projects that illustrate the practical and economic benefits of Pollution Probe policies have always been a key component of the Foundation's programme. Ecology House, which opened in 1980, effectively argues the benefits of energy conservation, solar heating, and waste and water recycling. In its first year of operation, more than 10,000 people toured the house and came away with a greater understanding of how we can reduce our demands on the world and its shrinking resources.

The Pollution Probe Foundation is an independent registered charitable foundation and needs your support to continue its work. For more information on its projects and a complete list of publications, write to:

Pollution Probe
12 Madison Avenue
Toronto, Ontario
M5R 2S1
(416) 978-6155

About this book

Pollution Probe researchers have been struggling with the problems inherent in the production, use and disposal of hazardous chemicals since the early 70's. In recent years, the technical and economic impediments to safe waste disposal have been augmented by a new and more forbidding obstacle. The inability to site and licence new waste disposal facilities in the face of valid environmental concerns and fierce public opposition have halted a number of proposed projects.

It is axiomatic that the simplest way to get rid of a barrel of industrial waste is to recycle it back into production, or not to generate it in the first instance. Unfortunately, common cant maintains that the technology for such an approach is either unavailable or prohibitively expensive.

The authors of Profit from Pollution Prevention have spent more than a year compiling case histories that disprove these popular misconceptions. It is hoped that this book will inspire industrialists and regulators to investigate these alternatives to traditional waste disposal. If in doing so, the load of hazardous chemicals entering the environment is reduced, we feel our labours will have been well rewarded.

Project Advisory Committee

Many thanks to the Advisory Committee for their unfailing encouragement and assistance in all aspects of the project.

Jack Brooks
Chief Engineer
3M Canada Ltd.

Joe Castrilli
(former) Research Director
Canadian Environmental Law
Association

Dr. Don Chant
Chairman
Ontario Waste Management
Corporation

Thomas Drew
President
D & D Group

Dave Edwards
Waste Management Branch
Ontario Ministry of the
Environment

Rick Findlay
Environmental Protection
Service
Environment Canada

Dr. Ross Hall
Department of Biochemistry
McMaster University

Adele Hurley
Executive Director
Canadian Coalition on Acid
Rain

Brian Milner
President
Chem-Ecol Ltd.

Jack McGinnis
Director
The Is-Five Foundation

Dr. Pamela Stokes
Department of Botany
University of Toronto

Alec Thomas
(former) Acting Chairman
Liquid Waste Carriers
Association

Technical Assistance

Special thanks to Dr. Robert Laughlin and Dr. Robert Pojasek who persevered in reviewing the entire manuscript for technical soundness. In addition, we express our gratitude to the following experts who have reviewed individual chapters of the manuscript for technical accuracy.

Dr. H. J. Campbell
Senior Research Scientist
Textiles & Clothing
Technology Centre

Dr. Peter Cashmore
Assistant Director
Textiles & Clothing
Technology Centre

R. W. Chase
Vice President
Southam Murray Printing

K. R. Coulter
Durham Metal Stamping

Vic Croutch
Department of Materials
Chemistry
Ontario Research Foundation

Thomas Dagon
Environmental Technical
Services
Eastman Kodak Company

Matthew Fyfe
Vice President
Maclean Hunter

Dr. Ross Hall
Department of Biochemistry
McMaster University

Ron Hayter
Director of Environmental
Affairs
Canadian Plastics Society

Dr. G. Henderson
Manager of Technical Affairs
General Foods

Emory Hukill
President
U.S. National Solvent
Recyclers Association

Robert Kreiman
President
Pace International

Dr. Robert Laughlin
Assistant Director of
Environmental Chemistry
Ontario Research Foundation

Jacob Leidner
Department of Materials
Chemistry
Ontario Research Foundation

Alvaro Marchetti
Technical Director
Canadian Paint and Coatings
Association

Brian Milner
President
Chem-Ecol Ltd.

Wilson Mor
Technical Services
3M Photofinishing Ltd.

Richard Mortimer
Textiles, Clothing and
Footwear
Ontario Research Foundation

Dr. Colin McArthur
Department of Chemistry
York University

Jack McGregor
Vice President
Anachemia Solvents Ltd.

Vic Niemela
Director of the Waste
Management Branch
Environment Canada

Dr. Robert Pojasek
Vice President
Weston
Designers/Consultants

David Puska
Assistant Manager
Dry Cleaners and Launders
Institute

Geoff Rathbone
Environmental Protection
Service
Environment Canada

Ronald Turner
Industrial Pollution Control
Division
U.S. Environmental
Protection Agency

Dr. Peter Victor
President
Victor & Burrell

George Wendtland
Assistant Manager
Anachemia Solvents Ltd.

H. F. Yeomans
Technical Manager
Imperial Oil

Funders

We wish to express our gratitude to the Ontario Waste Management Corporation and Environment Canada, each of which contributed one third of the total project cost. In addition, a very special thanks to the Richard Ivey Foundation for their generous donation in the early phases of this project. Many thanks to the following members of the private sector for their financial support in producing this book:

Ariel Computer
Productions Ltd.
B.P. Canada Ltd.
Canadian Pacific Ltd.
Gulf Canada Ltd.

Dr. Donald Chant
Lever Detergents Ltd.
Marion Dewar
D & D Disposal Ltd.
Dr. Gertrude Ewert

Dr. Clinton Kemp
The McLean Foundation
Imperial Oil Ltd.
PetroCanada
The Richard Ivey Foundation

Sunoco Inc.
3M Canada Inc.
Tricil Ltd.
Union Carbide Canada Ltd.
Dr. Peter Victor

Last but not least, we wish to express our deepest appreciation to the hundreds of individuals and companies that continue to support the Pollution Probe Foundation as a whole.

Table of Contents

Pulp and Paper

Solvents

Tanning

Textiles

Waste Management Strategy Information

Introduction

This book documents hundreds of success stories of firms that have turned waste products into financial assets. These businesses have saved money and prevented pollution through a number of improvements ranging from low-cost elimination of leaks to elaborate installations of in-line recycling equipment.

Although most businesses would agree that waste reduction and recovery is an excellent concept, only a small fraction would accept that it is an affordable reality in their plant.

In the past, as the public rallied for waste reduction and recycling, business was fast to respond that it cost more to recover wastes and re-use them than it did to purchase virgin materials. In an era of cheap resources, low energy costs and few regulations governing acceptable means to dump wastes into the ground, business was quite correct in its assertions. Cheap waste disposal took preference over waste prevention as the waste management option of least cost.

As legal requirements for proper waste disposal become more restrictive, and as sophisticated and costly disposal technologies are implemented, the cost of industrial waste disposal will increase significantly in Canada. With the rise in disposal costs, waste reduction and recovery economics will become more attractive than disposal economics in an increasing number of instances. Add to this the upwardly spiralling cost of resources and even marginal recovery technologies may become economically attractive.

It is shrewd for a business of any size to evaluate a waste recovery investment together with the no-action alternative. In many instances, a company would be surprised with the result. This book documents many examples where even a small company profited by investing in pollution prevention.

How to Use This Book

The purpose of this book is to promote pollution prevention through success stories of businesses that have minimized waste and come out ahead. Many opportunities for waste reduction are presented, however because each plant environment is unique, adoption of an isolated waste reduction idea is no panacea to a company's waste problems. Instead, a systematic approach is required.

Begin by reading the entire Waste Management Strategy Information chapter. This chapter stresses the importance of establishing a waste management strategy, starting with a waste survey. Once an inventory of process efficiency and wastes generated has been completed, a waste reduction goal can be determined.

Refer to the appropriate chapters within the "Pollution Prevention Opportunities" section to identify possible alternatives to current practices. In addition, the detailed index in the back of the book should be used to locate specific waste reduction and recovery examples. The index lists entries by subject and company name.

All chapters in the book contain a section entitled "For Further Information". These sections list references, journals and organizations capable of providing additional information.

This book was written to assist primarily small and medium-sized companies, although large companies can also benefit. Small and medium-sized businesses appear to be in a particularly difficult position in managing their hazardous wastes. Unlike larger companies, small companies such as printers, painters and dry cleaners tend not to have the scientific experts or the financial resources to deal effectively with their wastes.

Because of the small production runs involved, small business produces a smaller volume of hazardous waste than large companies, however the small operator frequently produces a large assortment of wastes that may be difficult to recover or dispose properly. In some instances, a small business may not even be aware that it is creating a hazardous waste problem. With technical and financial resources already stretched to the limit, the small operator may find it difficult to keep up on the latest toxicological findings or on new low-waste technologies.

Many of the pollution prevention opportunities identified are based on the experiences of larger companies. However, as recovery economics improve, it is likely that many of the advances made by large companies will be transferrable to the medium-sized and even small-sized operations.

Corporate Environmentalism: How Some Big Companies Turned Environmental Headache Into Profit

In recognizing wastes for what they are — misplaced resources — some companies have sharpened their competitive edge by avoiding pollution at the outset. Exemplary in its pollution reduction efforts, the 3M Company began its Pollution Prevention Pays Programme in 1975 as a means to curtail environmental costs during economic recession. The 3P programme has four basic aspects to ensure the reduction of pollution: product reformulation, process modification, equipment redesign, and recovery of waste materials for re-use.

The experiment paid off. 3M eliminated the equivalent of 75,000 tons of air pollutants, 1325 tons of water pollutants, 500 million gallons of polluted wastewater and 2900 tons of sludge per year.

Total savings from the United States facilities alone netted the company $17.4 million in 3 years. Subsidiary companies overseas reaped an additional $3.5 million.[1] The savings result from improved low-polluting products and processes, as well as reduced spending on conventional pollution control equipment due to pollution avoidance.

Similarly, Union Carbide turned environmental headache into opportunity. Billed as a major polluter in the early 1970s, the company clamped down on the disposal of wastes by marketing them instead.

In 1973, Union Carbide's Surplus Products Group, which finds new markets for process byproducts and wastes, sold over 40 million pounds of materials, recovering almost $1.25 million in cash income and disposal avoidance.

The Surplus Materials Group, which handles excess unused materials, and the Surplus Equipment Group generate an average income of $15 million per year. Every dollar spent by the Investment Recovery Group nets Union Carbide a return of $20 to $25.[2]

Turning an environmental problem into opportunity, Dow Chemical (Canada) and Diversey (Canada) combined research efforts to transform steelmaker's waste dust into a valuable end product. Successful pilot studies resulted in the formation of a joint venture company by Dow and Diversey known as Diversey Environmental Products Limited. In operation since 1974, the plant recycles and eliminates the need to landfill more than 10 million pounds of steelmaker's dust annually.[3]

In addition to providing a commercially useful ferric chloride product, the recycling process created a new market for waste hydrogen chloride. Ferric chloride is sold for use in water purification and waste treatment processes, and is particularly effective in phosphate removal from municipal sewage treatment plant effluents.

This waste exchange effort not only earned Dow and Diversey an Environmental Improvement Award in 1977 from the Chemical Institute of Canada but also earned these companies additional profits while contributing to environmental protection.

And in the United States, the Dow Chemical Company has been under legislative pressure in the past to stem pollution from its many plants. Despite large expenditures on pollution control, the company has found that many pollution control expenditures ended up as very good investments, resulting in a net savings to the company.

Dow's Hemlock plant invested $2.7 million to recover chlorine and hydrogen previously lost to the atmosphere in making silicone, and achieved a savings in operating costs of $900,000 a year. Dow's Midland Division saved $6 million in 3 years on materials previously lost to sewers. Investments at Dow's 14 latex plants are anticipated to cut operating costs by almost $2 million per year.[4]

Monsanto Chemical Intermediates is a newly formed subsidiary of Monsanto Chemicals designed to market the millions of pounds of byproducts resulting from the parent company's chemical synthesis processes. According to Monsanto, these millions of pounds of chemical byproducts represent a potential market of $350 million.[5]

Rising chemical costs have made chemical recovery a shrewd investment for Monsanto, so much so that staff now refer to "byproducts" strictly as "coproducts". Previously, many of these materials were handled by incinerating them, by burning them for fuel value, by deep well injection or by putting them in landfill sites.

Examples of new life given to chemical byproducts include the following. Monsanto's nylon processes and styrene streams yield amine and nitrile streams. One new market for some of the amine streams is as corrosion inhibitors. The "bottoms" left after production of detergent alkylate can be used to make high molecular weight sulfonates, similar to the petroleum sulfonates that some companies manufacture as a primary product.[5]

The experience of big business is telling. Complying with stringent pollution standards has yielded some startling results in the corporate sector. Pollution avoidance expenditures actually enhanced company profits, and with it the rise of corporate environmentalism.

Learning From Other Businesses

By applying pollution reduction and recovery concepts, corporations throughout the world have turned a major expense into a profitable activity. Although the economics are different, the basic principles of pollution prevention are the same in a small company as in a big firm.

Frequently the technology to reduce and recycle wastes is first developed for a big company. The volumes of waste produced are large and the need for clean-up is most pressing. Research and development of waste recovery systems becomes feasible because the potential financial return on the recovered material is very large. With time, the recycling technology becomes scaled down for use even in small and medium-sized businesses. An increasing number of machines designed to prevent pollution are put on the market each year. Instead of piecing together the parts of the puzzle for himself, the small operator can purchase much of the recycling equipment "off-the-shelf".

Another trend in design among equipment manufacturers is to build modular recycling units if the economics justify it. The number of modular units purchased by a company will depend upon the size of the wastestream.

There is much to be learned in pollution control by small companies from their larger counterparts. But even more is to be learned by one industry sector from another. Sometimes, a pollution problem or bottleneck in one industry has already been solved in another industry. Many parallels exist in pollution problems among different industries. It seems plausible that an active information exchange programme may turn up some unexpected solutions to an old problem in another industry.

For example, the concept of replenishing exhausted process baths during photoprocessing has been in operation for years. This same concept is now being applied to research on dye bath re-use in the textile industry. Instead of discharging exhausted dye baths, additional pigments are added to reconstitute the dye bath to its full efficacy.

Whatever the difference between industries, whether big or small, one thing is sure. A company must apply the same ingenuity and know-how to pollution prevention as it does to making its products if it is to survive in an era of rising environmental concern, stiffening competition and rampant inflation.

A Sound Waste Management Programme: Ounce of Prevention Worth Pound of Cure

Any company can benefit both the environment and its financial picture by implementing a sound waste management programme. Economic rewards to be gained from pollution avoidance take hard work, commitment and an understanding that monetary returns may entail some risk. Pollution prevention should not be segregated from other affairs in the company but be integrated smoothly into every phase of the production process. Doing so will enhance productivity, not detract from it.

The availability of cheap landfill sites has acted as a disincentive to the capital expenditure needed to implement waste recovery systems. Now that environmental concerns are closing these hazardous dumps, shrewd businessmen are looking to investing in waste avoidance.

It is important to distinguish between conventional pollution abatement and waste recovery technologies. Conventional pollution abatement such as end-of-pipe treatment technologies generally require the addition of substantial amounts of chemicals and energy to remove the hazardous components from a wastestream (see Figure 1). Typically the resultant sludges are then transported to a landfill site for burial. Instead of eliminating wastes, a water pollution problem is transformed into a potential land pollution problem. The treated wastewater is discharged to a sewer or body of water for further purification or dilution. Conventional pollution abatement is characterized by open-ended systems that use resources once and discard the waste products.

In contrast, waste recovery attempts to achieve closed-loop sys-

Figure 1
Varying Approaches to Waste Management

It is uncommon for industry to discharge its total effluent stream without some pretreatment.

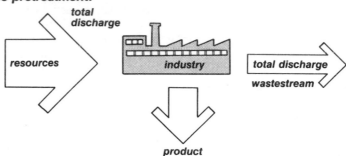

In conventional end-of-pipe waste treatment, large amounts of sludge, slurries and other residual material are generated that require additional disposal.

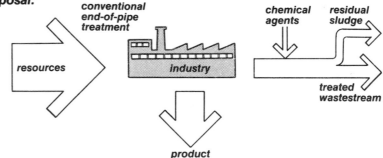

Industries that maximize material and water re-use generate relatively small volumes of wastewater and residuals requiring disposal elsewhere.

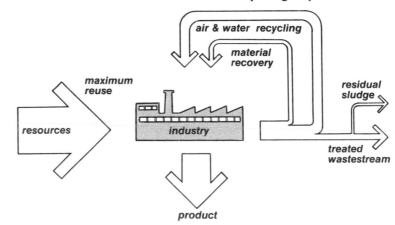

tems in which process wastes are recovered and re-used repeatedly on the premises. Clearly not all wastestreams lend themselves to recycling, particularly if the wastestream contains byproducts of no use to the processor generating the waste. In such instances, a firm may transfer the wastestream for re-use by another industry or alter the production process to minimize the generation of non-reclaimable wastes. Waste recovery is superior to conventional pollution abatement because industry can conserve resources and minimize the volume of waste requiring ultimate disposal.

Land disposal of hazardous wastes is recognized by many as the waste handling method of last resort.[6] In its place, the following hierarchy is gaining greater prominence as the optimal management strategy for hazardous wastes:[7]

1. Reduction
2. Recovery
3. Treatment
4. Disposal

The goal of a waste management system is to utilize the most cost-effective combination of management options to handle wastestreams within the confines of applicable regulations.[8] A scenario involving recovery, treatment and disposal is suggested for handling waste solvents. The solvent is distilled to recover a re-usable fraction. The distillation process leaves a tar-like still bottom which may be incinerated for heat recovery, but which yields an ash requiring further disposal.

Large-scale capital expenditures are by no means the only way to avert pollution. Low-cost measures such as good housekeeping practices, routine checks for faulty and leaking processes, regularly balancing inputs and outputs to identify unusual losses, and making minor process changes all help to minimize pollution in a cost-effective manner. Industry could rapidly eliminate a significant percentage of its current hazardous wastestream through such simple and profitable measures.

1.
Waste Reduction

The ideal solution is to reduce waste at source by changing industrial processes so that waste generation is minimized. Several practices are described that help achieve this goal.

Waste Audit

A first step in any firm's waste reduction programme should be a waste audit. The audit may be performed by a consultant, or by existing staff in response to questions such as:

How much waste is produced?
Which are the hazardous components?
What is the processing efficiency?
What are the costs of disposal associated with each major wastestream?
Are there any leaks or unaccounted material losses?

A waste audit is used to review a company's waste management programme and operating practices. Based on an audit, a company can evaluate options for handling wastes such as comparing the economics of on-site versus off-site waste handling. Audits can identify potential opportunities to reduce waste generation through process changes, product substitutions or recycling measures.[9]

One component of a waste audit is completion of a mass balance (also referred to as a materials balance) which compares resource inputs with product and waste outputs. Small and medium-sized businesses frequently lack detailed information of this type.

Completion of a waste audit may yield surprising information on the quantity of wastes discharged. Such information not only identifies problem areas but can spur company management into fighting the war on waste with new vigour. Once waste areas have been identified, waste reduction goals should be established that can be measured and that are attainable.

Product Reformulation

Although a primary manufacturing company may have the scientific resources and capital to control pollution through closed-loop processing, the sale and transfer of potentially hazardous chemicals to a smaller industry down the line may present environmental problems beyond the control of the small end-user. The secondary manufacturer who inherits product-related pollution problems from a primary manufacturer may have to build costly control facilities to cope with the problem, or find a substitute product. If the secondary manufacturer purchases a substitute product, the primary manufacturer will have lost a market for his product.

Some manufacturers are responding to the plight of the end-user by reformulating their products to minimize pollution problems down the road. An example of this is seen among chemical companies that manufacture polyester resins for use by plastics processors that produce contact moulded items such as bathtubs and boat hulls. During the moulding process, toxic styrene monomer is released into the air. Some chemical producers now manufacture a line of styrene-suppressed resins that reduce styrene loss into the air by 70% compared with nonsupressed systems.[10] Although contact moulding with polyester resins makes up only a tiny segment of the plastics processing industry, it nevertheless provides a useful example of product reformulation by one manufacturer in response to contraints by an industrial end-user.

Substitution

When regulations are enacted that restrict the level of toxic pollutants in the workplace or the environment, industry usually has two recourses. A company can adjust its operation to mitigate pollution through reduction, recovery and treatment, or the company can refrain from using the polluting product at all. Instead, the firm may seek to substitute a low-hazard product for the toxic one.

The replacement of solvent-based products such as paints, inks and adhesives with water-based products is a good example of product substitution. In many instances, the water-borne product is cheaper than solvent-based goods, while meeting or exceeding the specifications set by the users for its particular use.[11]

Solvents vary in their toxicity and environmental effects, however, most solvents share the common characteristic of being highly volatile. Larger companies may choose to meet their fugitive emissions problems by installing vapour recovery systems but for the small industrial user, substitution of water-based products may shape up to be the most cost-effective alternative.

More Efficient Equipment

For the smaller company, a five-digit price tag on waste recycling or treatment equipment may seem prohibitive. Instead, the firm may opt for plant modernization by installing more efficient processing equipment. In response to spiralling energy and feedstock costs, and increasingly stringent pollution regulations, equipment manufacturers have revamped their tools to process better, more quickly, with less pollution and using less energy. In some instances, it may be more affordable for a company to install efficient processing equipment than to retrofit existing equipment for pollution control.

Take the example of the dry cleaning industry. Much of the equipment currently in use was manufactured years before solvent loss and energy conservation were issues. The old models may be responsible for significant leakage of solvents into the workplace and the environment. Nowadays, equipment manufacturers are "building a tighter ship" to minimize solvent loss from the system.

To meet health and environmental regulations, a dry cleaning establishment may retrofit the existing situation by installing ventilation and vapour recovery systems.[12] However, in many instances the more cost-effective solution would be to invest in highly efficient dry cleaning equipment that would eliminate the need for elaborate ventilation systems.

Process Redesign

Industrial processes were designed in an era when productivity and quality were uppermost on the minds of company management. The importance of environmental protection in the last decade has sent process engineers back to the drawing board.

The new attention on resource conservation and minimizing pollution has yielded a wide range of process improvements in every industrial sector. Each plant is its own unique environment and as such requires the commitment of the plant manager to specify the process changes necessary to accomplish waste reduction.

One major process change applicable to many industries involves wastewater recycling. In some situations, wastewater from one operation may be clean enough for re-use as a water input in another part of the plant. Sophisticated separation equipment is now available for many wastestreams which can remove specific constituents for recovery or disposal, thereby leaving wastewater clean enough to be re-used.[13] Given the rising costs of end-of-pipe treatment for discharge to a stream or of pretreatment for discharge to sewers, it may ultimately be cheaper to re-use wastewater rather than simply treat it for discharge.

Process Control

Although a small business may think twice about investing in a capital-intensive recovery system, a business of any size can implement low-cost improvements through process control and come out ahead. When systems in a plant are provided with regulating procedures in processing, the re-sult is process control. Process controls may involve people or may be automatic. In the case of computer-assisted process control, the capital investment may be high although the resulting economic benefits may pay off the capital investment in a relatively short period of time.

Process control measures vary considerably from industry to industry. Process control ensures that unnecessary waste is minimized by ensuring that things are done right the first time. In the printing industry, for example, process control measures can slash paper wastage dramatically by ensuring that the inks, plates and presses are operating at optimum efficiency.[14] A poor printing job may mean that thousands of copies of printed material have to be discarded.

In the photoprocessing industry, implementing process controls means that chemical baths can be replenished in a manner that optimizes print quality and the life of the chemical bath.[15] This not only minimizes print and chemical waste, but also saves money.

Waste Concentration

Some hazardous wastes are so dilute that the cost of transporting them makes inter-industry exchange unfeasible. Oily-water wastes, for example, may contain 70 to 99% water.[16] Although the recovery of oil from the oil-water mixture may be a highly lucrative endeavour, trucking the water component over large distances is not. Commercially available equipment such as ultrafiltration units are available to concentrate the oil fraction from the wastewater.

Waste acids are another wastestream that frequently is very dilute. Some of the larger chemical companies have installed equipment capable of concentrating waste acids to a 95% concentration.[17] Concentrating wastewaters not only makes transportation more affordable but usually enhances the value of the wastestream.

2.
Waste Recovery

Recycling

Companies that generate wastes which are contaminated versions of process in-puts usually can benefit from in-line recycling. In-line recycling refers to the recovery and re-use of process waste back into the same process that generated it. Recycling efficiency is optimum if the recovery equipment is placed at the end of a specific processing sequence, rather than at the combined effluent outflow from the entire plant.

Ion exchange systems used in the electroplating field are a good example of in-line recycling. Although an electroplater may generate a variety of metal-laden wastewaters, metal recycling units placed in-line at the rinse tanks following each metal bath provide optimum and profitable recovery.[18]

Recycling wastes directly for re-use in the same process that generated it offers distinct advantages over the recovery of wastes for use elsewhere. A company should explore the possibility of in-line recycling before making arrangements to transfer wastes to another industry.

By recycling wastes directly on the premises, a firm is able to significantly reduce the purchase of new materials. Newspaper establishments that recycle dirty ink on-site end up with high quality ink and significantly reduced ink charges.[19]

There is another advantage to direct recycling. Take the example of the paint industry. It makes the most economic sense to reclaim the waste paint for its original purpose because industrial paint is custom-formulated for a specific purpose to meet very particular product and performance standards. Recovery economics favour the reclamation of enamel overspray as enamel and primer overspray as primer rather than the recovery of mixed paint sludges as a low-grade primer.[20]

The same holds true for oil and solvent recycling. Oils and solvents tend to be custom blended to meet user specifications. From an energy, materials and cost efficiency point of view, it is usually preferable to remove contaminants from the dirty waste and re-use it in the same process that generated the waste than it does to purify wastes to virgin purity for sale elsewhere. Virgin-purity recycled products may require additional blending and additives to meet customer specifications, a step that is minimized by removing few of these additives in the first place.[21]

Undoubtedly, not all wastes can be recycled directly back into the process. In such instances, the next option to explore is recovery and sale to another industry or professional waste reclaimer.

Waste Recovery

Businesses that generate a waste that is not directly re-usable on-site may benefit by recovering the waste for other uses. The photoprocessing industry, for example, produces a silver-rich wastestream from which the silver can be recovered on the premises and sent to a refiner for purification.[22] The purified silver is sold and re-used by businesses other than photofinishers.

Similarly, plastic wastes may be recovered for other than original uses. Certain plastic wastes that have lived a useful life are recovered and re-used to make construction materials.[23]

Processing of dairy products yields wastestreams rich in starch and nutrients that can be recovered for use in a variety of products including baked goods and animal feeds.[24]

Waste Segregation

Waste segregation is an important concept that is coming into greater use. In the past, when using conventional end-of-pipe waste treatment methods, there was little advantage to be gained from segregating wastestreams. With the new interest in recycling and recovery, keeping wastestreams separate takes on new importance.

A company has the best chance to recover materials if it does not mix in other wastestreams which will contaminate the stream from which it is trying to recover specific substances. The same holds true for energy recovery. A company has the best chance to recover heat if it integrates a hot water wastestream back into the process, rather than mixing it with a cold wastestream.[25]

It pays to segregate toxic wastestreams from other process wastes. Usually, only a small number of wastestreams contains toxic substances. Toxic wastes may require special handling which is usually made easier and cheaper if the wastestream is small. There is no advantage to contaminating relatively innocuous wastestreams with toxic ones.

Another reason for segregating wastestreams is that some wastes may be directly usable by another industry. For example, solvent wastestreams from the electronics industry, which contain only tiny amounts of metals, may be so clean as to be directly usable for wash-up in the paint industry.

Inter-Industry Exchange

For those situations in which on-site resource recovery is not feasible, one company may transfer its wastes to another for re-use. The transfer of wastes from one company to another means that both companies benefit economically from the exchange.

In order for that transfer to occur, the two companies must know of each other's existence. This matching function may be accomplished by a waste exchange programme or through a broker. A waste exchange strives to match waste generators with waste users, thereby linking potential trading partners.

One company may produce a waste continuously for years. The receiving company may use the recycled waste as a raw resource in its manufacturing processes over the years. In such a system, a profitable symbiotic relationship is established that can be expected to continue.

Combine Specific Wastestreams

Most chemical treatment processes used by industry today involve the addition of virgin chemicals including lime, metallic salt cations and sodium hydroxide. The use of virgin chemicals is both expensive and demanding of industry's supply of chemical resources.

Instead of relying solely on virgin chemicals, some industries have learned to precipitate or neutralize one wastestream with another. For example, waste acids from one company may be neutralized with waste alkalis from another company.[26] The blending of wastestreams must be based on a thorough knowledge of the contaminants present in each wastestream and an understanding of how these wastestreams will react. Failure to do so may result in the dangerous release of toxic gases.

3.
Waste Treatment

Those wastestreams remaining after waste reduction and recovery options have been exhausted should undergo suitable treatment. Ideally, waste treatment will render the material completely innocuous. In other situations, waste treatment may only reduce the toxicity of the wastestream or reduce the volume of material requiring ultimate disposal. Unit waste treatment operations are discussed in the chapter Waste Treatment and Disposal Technologies.

4.
Waste Disposal

Even those companies active in industrial waste reduction and recovery may generate a wastestream, albeit small in volume, that requires disposal. Having exhausted reduction, recycling and treatment options, a company may be left with a solid residue containing toxic components that will require disposal in a secure landfill site.

The Special Needs of Small Business: Overcoming the Modernization Hurdle

The Canadian Federal Small Business Secretariat defines small businesses as those with annual sales of $2 million or less.[27] Small businesses constitute 97% of all Canadian enterprises and account for 42% of total employment.[27] In Ontario, small business translates to mean any service business with fewer than 50 employees and any manufacturing enterprise with fewer than 100 employees.[28]

Ontario alone is estimated to generate 45% of the hazardous wastes produced in Canada.[29] Good statistical information on the volume of hazardous wastes generated by small business in Canada will become available in the future.

Wastestreams vary in their economic value and in the costs associated with recovering them. High-value wastes such as silver have been recovered for years.[30] The challenge before industry is to recycle those wastes of low to moderate value for which the feasibility of recovery has been marginal in the past.

There are many reasons why more businesses are not reducing and recovering their wastes. Barriers to recycling are discussed in conjunction with suggestions on how to scale them.

When faced with an external pressure such as material shortages, a change in a by-law or closure of a disposal site, a company may investigate low-waste alternatives. Having made the necessary changes to minimize pollution, the company frequently finds that it was to its economic advantage to do so. By taking the pollution prevention approach, a company usually finds that it saves money when compared to the expenditure that would have been necessary for conventional waste treatment and disposal.

Barriers and Solutions

High Capital Costs

A company must forego the assumption that reducing and recycling its wastes will necessarily entail huge expenditures of capital. Quite the contrary. Before implementing changes in waste handling practices, it is imperative that a modest investment be made to assess the current level of waste production, and assess the potential for low-cost housekeeping measures and process controls in reducing pollution at nominal cost.

Having achieved minor changes to improve process efficiency, a company might implement higher-cost changes such as in-line recycling and the purchase of more efficient equipment. Despite the four- or five-digit price tag associated with such purchases, it must be remembered that these expenditures are investments that yield an economic return once the equipment is paid off.

One aspect that may obscure potential savings through pollution prevention expenditures is the discrepancy between capital and operating cost. Waste recovery and waste disposal activities differ significantly in the relationship between operating and capital cost (see Figure 2).

Firms that routinely transport their wastes for disposal at a specified facility may have low capital expenditures with respect to pollution control and have relatively high operating costs. The operating costs can be expected to increase each year as they keep pace with inflation.

On the other hand, firms that invest in on-site waste recovery may incur relatively large capital expenditures. Operating costs, however, are relatively low, particularly because the value of the recovered materials may more than pay the recovery cost and also contribute to paying off the capital cost.

When identifying a waste management strategy, it is advantageous to compare projected costs, both capital and operating, of the various waste management alternatives. Hastily dismissing waste recycling without sufficient investigation might close a promising opportunity for enhancing profit margins.

Nature of the Wastes and Market Conditions

A number of factors which can influence whether or not economic recovery can be achieved include:[31]

1. Concentration and chemical form of desired material in the waste
2. Degree and nature of the contaminants
3. Cost and availability of virgin raw materials
4. Cost and availability of recycling technology
5. Cost of waste disposal
6. Quality required of recycled material.

There is little control that an individual company can have over market conditions. However, in many instances, control can be placed on the nature of contamination of the recoverable wastestream.

Segregation of the wastestream to be recovered is crucial. For example, in the case of a paint recycler in Illinois, considerable effort was required to encourage the waste generator to keep paint sludge free of extraneous garbage such as cigarette butts and lunch wrappers.[32]

In other instances, wastes may be generated in quantities too dilute to recover economically. Process changes that permit waste concentration may have to be implemented. For example, the recycling of indigo dye in the textile industry requires the installation of a counter-current rinse system to concentrate the indigo wastestream to economically recoverable levels.[33]

Figure 2
Relationship Between Operating and Capital Costs for Waste Recovery and Disposal Options

A company investing in on-site waste reduction and recovery equipment typically incurs high capital costs and low operating charges.

A company that chooses to truck its wastes for treatment and disposal elsewhere typically encounters low capital costs although operating costs are high and escalate with inflation.

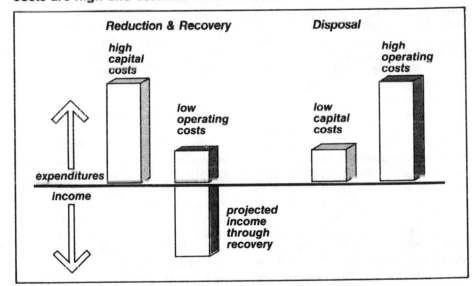

Risks Associated with Leading-Edge Technology

Conventional waste treatment and disposal methods have a distinct edge over most recovery technologies because they are time-tested processes that have been refined over many decades of use. In contrast, many of the separation technologies on which recovery is based have experienced relatively little field testing and implementation.

Skepticism of leading-edge technologies may be based on a lack of guarantees that the technology will work, or in some instances, on reports of unsuccessful implementation in certain situations. Clearly, a processor will stay away from risky investments unless anticipated benefits are very high or risk can be minimized.

This barrier can be minimized if the equipment vendor is pressured to guarantee performance standards, or if the vendor agrees to share in the cost of down time in the event that the new technology fails to operate as anticipated.[8] Businesses should negotiate a contract directly with the vendor to protect their investment. It is in the interest of the vendor as well to offer equipment performance guarantees because such risk-reduction measures may attract more business.

When a small photofinishing lab in Pennsylvania chose to install a rinsewater recovery system, it was one of the first small companies in North America to implement such technology. Instead of purchasing the equipment outright, the lab made a leasing arrangement with the equipment supplier.[34] In the event of performance difficulties, the lab could return the recycling unit without incurring huge financial losses that may have occurred had the equipment been purchased.

Lack of Purity Standards on Recycled Products

Some companies are skeptical of using recycled products because of the lack of purity standards for recycled products. Reputable reclaimers negotiate a minimum purity standard and thereby establish a confident clientele.

Failure to guarantee minimum purity standards, or alternatively, share in the liability of spoiled product batches may impede greater utilization of recycled products. For example, a paint formulator using recycled solvent in new paint mixtures must be assured of a minimal water content in the recycled solvent. Excessive water may ruin a batch of paint. Who bears the costs of the ruined paint? Usually the formulator does.

To counter such economic losses by the user of recycled products, it has been suggested that all off-site vendors be asked to provide the industry with a proper certificate of insurance.[35] It is also desirable to have a tight contract protecting a company's rights. A business and industry trade association could assist in working out a standard contract arrangement for off-site recycling.

Restrictive Specifications for Use of Virgin Materials

The success of any recycling venture depends on the ability of the reclaimer to secure a market for the recycled product. It is a common complaint among reclaimers that industry specifications for manufacturing processes are too restrictive. Product specifications frequently call for the use of only virgin materials.

Although the recycled product may eventually find a use as a low-grade commodity, the selling price may be so low as to discourage significant activity among reclaimers. In the plastics recycling industry, it is common for Canadian plastic scrap to be exported to the United States and Europe where reclaimed materials can capture a higher price.[36]

Recycled products vary in quality, depending on the commodity recycled and the process used. Further investigations are required into whether recycled products can achieve greater acceptance and higher prices in the manufacturing sector.

Attitude: Old Ideas Die Hard

The business world is geared to providing goods and services. Money, materials and time devoted to maximizing goods and services is viewed as a productive, hence profitable endeavour. Money, materials and time spent controlling pollution solely to meet regulations has been viewed as non-profitable.

Small businesses may hang tenaciously to the perception that pollution control competes with productivity. Many presidents of small companies would prefer to take their chances chasing up more business and being assured of additional income than spending the time investigating ways of preventing pollution that, in their estimation, may not be lucrative.

The importance of re-appraising an existing operation for processing efficiency cannot be over-estimated. Allocating staff time or hiring a consultant to enhance system efficiency may result in significant increases in overall profitability through reduced waste.

Another attitude encountered is, "If the existing process works, why change it?" A company may be reluctant to give up existing equipment which is functioning satisfactorily and will not wear out for several more years. However, equipment has a practical lifetime which may have escalating repair and maintenance costs as the equipment gets old. In the recent context of rocketing energy and material costs, equipment manufacturers are constructing highly efficient machinery with operating costs much lower than those designed a decade ago.

An analogy can be made with today's fuel-efficient cars. Despite a high capital expenditure, the rate of return may be higher in purchasing a fuel-efficient model compared with maintaining high operating costs on an old model.

The tendency to retain existing processes because company management knows they work may be countered by the vendor offering a trial period for trying a new process, equipment or material.

For example, one manufacturer of reverse osmosis equipment permits prospective customers to use a demonstration model for a limited period of time without obligation to buy.[37] In the city of Shanghai (China), the highly successful inter-industry waste exchange project is based on trial usage of a wastestream prior to finalizing exchange negotiations.[38]

Lack of Technical and Economic Resources

Another reason more businesses do not install modern closed-loop processing equipment or waste recovery systems is a lack of technical and financial resources among smaller businesses. Whereas large companies retain in-house engineers and outside consultants to keep abreast of waste management programmes, the president of a small company is hard-pressed to complete all the diverse tasks in his harried day. Supervising employees, keeping track of accounts and chasing up new business make for a full day in which environmental protection figures low on the priority list.

Although a company may ultimately hire a consultant to implement any major process redesign, there are many sources of technical information to be tapped at little or no cost. A company can start by contacting relevant trade associations and enquiring about technical and economic information on low-waste technology, the names of appropriate consulting agencies, access to existing government funding programmes, and the latest details on pollution legislation. Each trade association could function as a centralized information office that keeps a registry of waste reduction ideas and exchange opportunities.

Another low-cost source of information on recent advances in pollution prevention are trade journals and newsletters. Some journals are more attuned to pollution issues than others. Inform the editor of specific journals of the value of presenting more articles on waste reduction and recovery opportunities. Keep alert for con-

ferences and workshops in this field.

Consult industry and environment departments within the government for technology transfer assistance. Identify information transfer programmes and publications available through the federal and provincial government. In California, for example, the Department of Health offers free consulting services in waste reduction to industry and links up potential trading partners in a waste exchange.[39]

Other important sources of information are equipment and chemical manufacturers. This advice is often offered free of charge to prospective clients. For example, some suppliers of chemicals to the dry cleaning industry offer helpful on-site advice as to how to minimize solvent loss and minimize occupational risk.[40]

A variety of government agencies offers economic incentives to industry to control pollution. Consult the section on "Funding Programmes" later in this chapter.

Unfamiliarity with Wastes Produced

Many companies, particularly small ones, may not be fully aware of the quantity and degree of hazard of the wastes they produce. Completion of a mass balance which measures material inputs, product and waste outputs may alert a company to a pollution problem. A company might be surprised to identify previously unknown sources of leaks and fugitive emissions, and to realize just how much waste is routinely generated.

Unfamiliarity with Recycling Technology

Companies which lack ample technical experts on staff may be unaware of the latest low-polluting technology. Refer to the sections "Information Centres" and "Organizations and Associations" in this chapter for general information on waste reduction and recovery opportunities.

FOR FURTHER INFORMATION

There are many avenues of self-help open to the business community. The following sections will list some of them. Relatively few of the funding and technical assistance opportunities listed are designed specifically for pollution control efforts, however these programmes can be tapped to assist in minimizing pollution by enhancing processing efficiency.

Funding Programmes

1. Development and Demonstration of Resource and Energy Conservation Technology (DRECT)

The DRECT program provides funds to the private sector to

develop and demonstrate equipment, systems or products designed to recover or otherwise conserve materials and energy through resource recovery. DRECT will pay up to 50 percent of the total estimated costs of an approved project including equipment, buildings, installation, engineering and consulting services.

Contact: National Headquarters

*DRECT Secretariat,
Environmental Protection
Service,
Environment Canada,
Ottawa, Ontario.
K1A 1C8
(819) 997-2057*

Regional Offices

*ATLANTIC REGION
Environmental Protection
Service,
Environment Canada,
5th Floor, Queen's Square,
45 Alderney Drive,
Dartmouth, Nova Scotia.
B2Y 2N6
(902) 426-3593*

*QUEBEC REGION
Environmental Protection
Service,
Environment Canada,
Suite 410,
1550 Maisonneuve Blvd.
West,
Montreal, Quebec.
H3G 1N2
(514) 283-4670*

ONTARIO REGION
Environmental Protection
Service,
Environment Canada,
7th floor, Arthur Meighen
Building,
25 St. Clair Avenue East,
Toronto, Ontario.
M4T 1M2
(416) 966-5840

WESTERN & NORTHERN
REGION
Environmental Protection
Service,
Environment Canada,
8th Floor,
9942 - 108 Street,
Edmonton, Alberta.
T5K 2J5
(403) 420-2577

PACIFIC & YUKON
REGION
Environmental Protection
Service,
Environment Canada,
Kapilano 100 - Park Royal,
West Vancouver,
British Columbia.
V7T 1A2
(604) 666-6711

2. Research and Development Contracts through the Department of Supply and Services

The federal government contracts much of its science and technology requirements to the private sector. Ask the Science Centre of the Department of Supply and Services to send the *Research and Development Bulletin,* a monthly publication listing both solicited and unsolicited proposals that are to be contracted to individual businesses. Submit research proposals that the government may wish to fund under the Unsolicited Proposals for Research and Development category.

Contact: National Headquarters

Science Centre,
Department of Supply and
Services,
Hull, Quebec.
K1A 0S5
(819) 997-2686

Regional Offices

ATLANTIC REGION SUPPLY
CENTRE
Morris Dr. at Akerley Blvd.,
Burnside Industrial Park,
P.O. Box 3000,
Main Post Office,
Dartmouth, Nova Scotia.
B2Y 4A8
(902) 426-3881

QUEBEC REGION SUPPLY
CENTRE
800 Golf Rd.,
Nuns' Island,
Montreal, Quebec.
H3E 1G9
(514) 283-5783

ONTARIO REGION SUPPLY
CENTRE
295 The West Mall,
Suite 200,
Etobicoke, Ontario.
M9C 5A4
(416) 622-8111

MANITOBA REGION
SUPPLY
CENTRE
266 Graham Ave.,
7th Floor, Room 710,
Winnipeg, Manitoba.
R3C 3W6
(204) 949-6114

WESTERN REGION SUPPLY
CENTRE
2nd Floor — Oliver Building,
10225 - 100 Ave.,
Edmonton, Alberta.
T5J 1J9
(403) 425-3702

PACIFIC REGION SUPPLY
CENTRE
3551 Viking Way,
Richmond, British Columbia.
V6V 1W6
(604) 544-6364

CAPITAL REGION SUPPLY
CENTRE
1010 Somerset St. W.,
Ottawa, Ontario.
K1A 0T4
(613) 992-2501

3. Accelerated Capital Cost Allowance Programme (ACCA)

Under this programme, a business may deduct from its income taxes the total cost of pollution control equipment over a two-year period. The tax write-off programme is applicable to equip-

ment or processes installed for the purpose of controlling pollution, and includes energy conservation and monitoring equipment. Although the Department of Revenue does not advise industry on how to obtain advantages from tax measures, it will advise on whether a tax measure is applicable in a particular case.

Contact: National Headquarters

Revenue Canada,
875 Heron Road,
Ottawa, Ontario.
K1A 0L8

District Offices

NEWFOUNDLAND
Sir Humphrey Gilbert Bldg.,
165 Duckworth St.,
St. John's, Newfoundland.
A1C 5X6
(709) 737-5050

PRINCE EDWARD ISLAND
Dominion Bldg.,
90 Richmond St.,
P.O. Box 141,
Charlottetown, P.E.I.
G1A 8L3
(902) 894-5556

NOVA SCOTIA
Ralston Building,
1557 Hollis St.,
Halifax, Nova Scotia.
B3J 2T5
(902) 426-2210

Federal Bldg.
Dorchester St.,
P.O. Box 1300,
Sydney, Nova Scotia.
B1P 6K3
(902) 539-2150

NEW BRUNSWICK
65 Canterbury St.,
Saint John, New Brunswick.
E2L 4H9
(506) 648-4600

QUEBEC
165 Dorchester St. S.,
Quebec, Quebec.
G1K 7L3
(418) 694-3180

50 Couture St.,
Sherbrooke, Quebec.
J1H 5L8
(819) 565-4888

National Revenue Bldg.,
305 Dorchester Blvd. W.,
Montreal, Quebec.
H2Z 1A6
(514) 283-5300

11 Terminus St. E.,
Rouyn, Quebec.
J9X 3B5
(819) 764-5171

ONTARIO
Century Bldg.,
360 Lisgar Street,
Ottawa, Ontario.
K1A 0L9
(613) 996-8340

385 Princess St.,
Kingston, Ontario.
K7L 1C1
(613) 542-2831

New Federal Bldg.,
11 Station St.,
Belleville, Ontario.
M5C 1J7
(613) 962-8611

Mackenzie Bldg.,
36 Adelaide St. E.,
Toronto, Ontario.
M5C 1J7
(416) 869-1500

National Revenue Bldg.,
166 Frederick St.,
Kitchener, Ontario.
N2H 2M4
(519) 579-2230

National Revenue Bldg.,
150 Main St. W.,
Hamilton, Ontario.
L8N 3E1
(416) 522-8671

Federal Bldg.,
32-46 Church St.,
St. Catharines, Ontario.
L2R 3B9
(416) 688-4000

451 Talbot St.,
London, Ontario.
N6A 5E5
(519) 679-4211

185 Ouellette Ave.,
Windsor, Ontario.
N9A 5S8
(519) 252-3611

Federal Bldg.,
19 Lisgar St.,
Sudbury, Ontario.
P3E 3L5
(705) 675-9131

Revenue Bldg.,
201 North May St.,
Thunder Bay, Ontario.
P7C 3P7
(807) 623-2751

MANITOBA
Revenue Bldg.,
391 York Ave.,
Winnipeg, Manitoba.
R3C 0P5
(204) 949-6350

SASKATCHEWAN
1955 Smith St.,
Regina, Saskatchewan.
S4P 2N9
(306) 569-6015

Canadian Imperial Bank of
Commerce Bldg.,
201-21st St. East,
Saskatoon, Saskatchewan.
S7K 0A8
(306) 665-4595

ALBERTA
Government of Canada
Bldg.,
220-4th Avenue S.E.,
Calgary, Alberta.
T2G 4X3
(403) 231-4101

Federal Public Bldg.,
9820-107th St.,
Edmonton, Alberta.
T5K 1E8
(403) 420-3510

BRITISH COLUMBIA
Federal Bldg.,
277 Winnipeg St.,
Penticton, British Columbia.
V2A 1N6
(604) 493-3616

1166 West Pender St.,
Vancouver,
British Columbia.
V6E 3H8
(604) 689-5411

1415 Vancouver St.,
Victoria, British Columbia.
V8V 3W4
(604) 386-2176

4. Industrial Research Assistance Programme (IRAP)

This programme aids industrial research by financing the salary component of approved research and development projects. The IRAP-P programme is geared to larger companies with in-house research capacity. For those firms too small to maintain a viable research effort in-house, IRAP-M will pay the salaries of individuals in other research organizations that are subcontracted to the firm to solve specific research and development problems.

Contact: *National Headquarters*

General Manager,
Industrial Research
Assistance Programme,
National Research Council,
Ottawa, Ontario.
K1A 0R6
(613) 993-0331

REGIONAL OFFICES

NEWFOUNDLAND
Technical Information
Services,
National Research Council
of Canada,
30 Harvey Road,
P.O. Box 4278,
St. John's, Newfoundland.
A1C 6C4
(709) 754-1937

NOVA SCOTIA
Industrial and Information
Services,
Nova Scotia Research
Foundation,
100 Fenwick St.,
P.O. Box 790,
Dartmouth, Nova Scotia.
B2Y 3Z7
(902) 424-8670

Atlantic Regional
Laboratory,
1411 Oxford Street,
Halifax, Nova Scotia.
B3H 3Z1

NEW BRUNSWICK
Management Services,
Research and Productivity
Council,
P.O. Box 6000,
Fredericton,
New Brunswick.
E3B 5H1
(506) 455-8994

PRINCE EDWARD ISLAND
Technical Information
Service,
National Research Council
of Canada,
P.O. Box 2000,
Shaw Bldg.,
73 Rochford St.,
Charlottetown,
Prince Edward Island.
C1A 7M8
(902) 892-0351

QUEBEC
Technical Information
Service,
National Research Council
of Canada,
Suite 215,
2535 Cavendish Blvd.,
Montreal, Quebec.
H4B 2Y5
(514) 482-0651

Technical Information
Service,
National Research Council
of Canada,
1535 Chemin Sainte-Foy,
Quebec, Quebec.
G1S 2P1
(418) 694-3419

ONTARIO
Industrial Productivity
Services,
Department of Engineering,
Ontario Research
Foundation,
Sheridan Park Research
Community,
Mississauga, Ontario.
L5K 1B3
(416) 822-4111 ext. 231

Technical Information
Service,
National Research Council
of Canada,
Suite 910,
789 Don Mills Rd.,
Don Mills, Ontario.
M3C 1T5
(416) 966-5845

Technical Information
Service,
National Research Council
of Canada,
Room 238, Federal Bldg.,
106 Clarence St.,
Kingston, Ontario.
K7L 1X4
(613) 544-1537

Technical Information
Service,
National Research Council
of Canada,
Room 522, Federal Bldg.,
457 Richmond St.,
London, Ontario.
N6A 3E3
(519) 434-4314

Technical Information
Service,
National Research Council
of Canada,
18 Front St., Federal Bldg.,
Thorold, Ontario.
L2V 3Y6
(416) 227-7231

MANITOBA
Technical Information
Service,
National Research Council
of Canada,
1329 Niakwa Rd.,
Winnipeg, Manitoba.
R2J 3T4
(204) 255-9612

SASKATCHEWAN
Industrial Services Division,
Saskatchewan Research
Council,
30 Campus Dr.,
Saskatoon, Saskatchewan.
S7N 0X1
(306) 664-5400

Prairie Regional Laboratory,
110 Gymnasium Rd.,
U. Campus,
Saskatoon, Saskatchewan.
S7N 0W9

ALBERTA
Industrial and Engineering
Services,
Research Council of Alberta,
Terrace Plaza, 4th Floor —
Office Tower,
4445 Calgary Trail South,
Edmonton, Alberta.
T6H 5C3
(403) 438-0666

BRITISH COLUMBIA
Management Services
Division,
B.C. Research,
3650 Westbrook Mall,
Vancouver, British Columbia.
V6S 2L2
(604) 224-4331

Mechanical Engineering
Western Laboratory,
3904 West 4th Ave.,
Vancouver, British Columbia.
V6R 1P5

5. Enterprise Development Programme (EDP)

The purpose of the Enterprise Development Programme is to encourage growth in the manufacturing and processing sectors through financial assistance. The programme is designed to help small and medium-sized businesses that are prepared to undertake innovative, high-risk projects which have good chances of success and attractive rates of return.

Three means of assistance include:
(a) Insurance of up to 90 percent in support of term loans made by private lenders to the business.
(b) Grants, up to 75 percent of eligible costs for research, development and design of the project.
(c) Grants, up to 75 percent of eligible costs, for market feasibility studies, productivity enhancement studies, product development, design, and pollution technology projects.

Contact: National Headquarters
Innovations Secretariat,
Programs Branch,
Department of Industry,
Trade and Commerce,
235 Queen St.,
Ottawa, Ontario.
K1A 0H5
(613) 995-7174

Regional Offices

NEWFOUNDLAND REGION
127 Water St.,
P.O. Box 6148,
St. John's, Newfoundland.
A1C 5X8

NOVA SCOTIA REGION
Suite 1124, Duke Tower,
5251 Duke St.,
Scotia Square,
Halifax, Nova Scotia.
B3J 1N9

PRINCE EDWARD ISLAND
REGION
P.O. Box 2289,
Dominion Bldg.,
97 Queen St.,
Charlottetown,
Prince Edward Island.
C1A 8C1

NEW BRUNSWICK REGION
Suite 642, 440 King St.,
Fredericton, New Brunswick.
E3B 5H8

QUEBEC REGION
P.O. Box 1270, Station B,
Suite 600, 685 Cathcart St.,
Montreal, Quebec.
H3B 3K9

Quebec City Office
Suite 620, 2 Place Quebec,
Quebec, Quebec.
G1R 2B5

ONTARIO REGION
Suite 4840, Box 98,
1 First Canadian Place,
Toronto, Ontario.
M5X 1B1

MANITOBA REGION
507 Manulife House,
386 Broadway Ave.,
Winnipeg, Manitoba.
R3C 3R6

SASKATCHEWAN REGION
Room 980,
2002 Victoria Ave.,
Regina, Saskatchewan.
S4P 0R7

ALBERTA AND
NORTHWEST
TERRITORIES REGION
500 Macdonald Place,
9939 Jasper Avenue,
Edmonton, Alberta.
T5J 2W8

BRITISH COLUMBIA AND
YUKON REGION
P.O. Box 49178, Suite 2743,
Bentall Centre, Tower III,
595 Burrard St.,
Vancouver, British Columbia.
V7X 1K8

6. Regional Development Incentives Programme (DREE)

DREE grants are designed to stimulate industrial growth in slow-growth areas in Canada. Industries that are located or intend to locate in DREE "designated regions" may receive grants and loan guarantees for plant modernization and expansion. Although not intended to fund pollution abatement as such, many plant modernization efforts are eligible, which result in a simultaneous reduction in waste generation. Despite the restructuring of DREE in 1982, and a concomitant name change, programme content and contact telephone numbers listed are anticipated to remain the same.

Contact: National Headquarters

Department of Regional
and Economic Expansion,
200 Promenade du Portage,
Hull, Quebec.
(819) 997-1902

Mailing address:
DREE,
Ottawa, Ontario.
K1A 0M4

REGIONAL OFFICES

ATLANTIC REGION
Regional Office,
14th Floor,
Assomption Bldg.,
770 Main St.,
P.O. Box 1210,
Moncton, New Brunswick.
E1C 8P9
(506) 858-6433

Newfoundland Provincial
Office
90 O'Leary Ave.,
P.O. Box 8950,
St. John's, Newfoundland.
A1B 3R9
(709) 737-4053

Branch Office
P.O. Box 730, Station A,
Goose Bay Airport,
Goose Bay, Newfoundland.
A0P 1S0
(709) 896-2741

New Brunswick Provincial
Office
Armstrong Bldg.,
590 Brunswick St.,
P.O. Box 578,
Fredericton, New Brunswick.
E3B 5A6
(506) 452-3102

Branch Office
Keystone Place,
270 Douglas Avenue,
Bathurst, New Brunswick.
E2A 3Z6
(506) 548-8907

Prince Edward Island
Provincial Office
Confederation Court Mall,
134 Kent St.,
P.O. Box 1115,
Charlottetown,
Prince Edward Island.
C1A 7M8
(902) 892-8551

Nova Scotia Provincial Office
Queen Square, 11th Floor,
P.O. Box 1320,
45 Alderney Dr.,
Dartmouth, Nova Scotia.
B2Y 4B9
(902) 426-7830

QUEBEC REGION
Regional Office
Stock Exchange Tower,
800 Place Victoria,
P.O. Box 247,
Montreal, Quebec.
H4Z 1E8
(514) 283-4160

Quebec Provincial Office
Claridge Building,
Suite 820,
220 Grande Allée E.,
Quebec, Quebec.
G1R 2J1
(418) 694-4670

Branch Offices
690 Sacre Coeur,
Plaza III,
Alma, Quebec.
G8B 6V4
(418) 668-3084

Place de Quebec,
888 3rd Ave.,
Val d'Or, Quebec.
J8P 5E6
(819) 825-5260

320 St. Germain St. E.,
4th Floor,
Rimouski, Quebec.
G5L 1C2
(418) 723-9426

1335 King St. W.,
Suite 401,
Sherbrooke, Quebec.
J1J 2B8
(819) 565-4264

ONTARIO REGION
Regional Office,
7th Floor,
55 St. Clair Ave. E.,
Toronto, Ontario.
M4T 1M2

Northwestern Ontario
District Office
Court Holding Building,
233 South Court St.,
Thunder Bay, Ontario.
P7B 2X9
(807) 345-1381

Northwestern District Office
Royal Bank Tower,
128 Larch St.,
Suite 603,
Sudbury, Ontario.
P3E 5J8
(705) 673-5680

WESTERN REGION
Regional Office
Bessborough Tower,
Room 814,
601 Spadina Cres. E.,
Saskatoon, Saskatchewan.
S7K 3G8
(306) 665-4422

Manitoba Provincial Office
400-3 Lakeview Square,
P.O. Box 981,
Winnipeg, Manitoba.
R3C 2V2
(204) 949-2580

Branch Office
74 Caribou Rd.,
Evergreen Pl.,
Thompson, Manitoba.
R3N 0L3

Alberta Provincial Office
Financial Bldg.,
10621 — 100th Avenue,
Edmonton, Alberta.
T5J 0B3
(403) 425-3325

Saskatchewan Provincial
Office
3rd Floor, 1102 8th Ave.,
Regina, Saskatchewan.
S4R 1C9
(306) 569-6119

Prairie Farm Rehabilitation
Administration, DREE
Motherwell Bldg.,
1901 Victoria Ave.,
Regina, Saskatchewan.
S4P 0R5
(306) 569-5088

British Columbia
Provincial Office
Bank of Commerce Bldg.,
1175 Douglas St.,
Victoria, British Columbia.
V8W 2E1
(604) 388-0198

Branch Office
706 Permanent Tower,
299 Victoria St.,
Prince George,
British Columbia.
V2L 5B8
(604) 562-4451

NORTHWEST TERRITORIES
10th Floor,
Precambrian Bldg.,
P.O. Box 6100,
Yellowknife, Northwest
Territories.
X1A 1C0
(403) 873-6225

YUKON
301—108 Lambert St.,
Whitehorse, Yukon.
Y1A 1Z2
(403) 668-4655

7. Federal Duty Remission Programme

The Federal Duty Remission Programme permits pollution abatement equipment to be imported duty-free if it is not "available from production" from a single manufacturer in Canada.

Contact: Tariffs Division,
Department of Finance,
Ottawa, Ontario.
K1A 0G5

8. Provincial Funding Programmes

Each province has its own business assistance programmes that may contain a component applicable to pollution control expenditures. Contact your provincial department of industry and economic development for information on grant and loan programmes relating to the implementation of low-waste technology.

Contact: Provincial Economic
Development Offices

NEWFOUNDLAND
Department of Development,
Atlantic Place,
Water St.,
St. John's, Newfoundland.
A1C 5T7

PRINCE EDWARD ISLAND
Department of Tourism,
Industry and Energy,
P.O. Box 2000,
Charlottetown,
Prince Edward Island.
C1A 7N8

NOVA SCOTIA
Department of Development,
P.O. Box 519,
Halifax, Nova Scotia.
B3J 2R7

NEW BRUNSWICK
Department of Commerce
and Development,
P.O. BOX 6000,
Fredericton, New Brunswick.
E3B 5H1

QUEBEC
Ministère de l'Industrie,
du Commerce et du
Tourisme,
710 Place d'Youville,
Quebec, Quebec.
G1A 1K9

ONTARIO
Ministry of Industry and
Tourism,
900 Bay St.,
Toronto, Ontario.
M7A 2E1

MANITOBA
Department of Economic
Development and Tourism,
155 Carlton St.,
Winnipeg, Manitoba.
R3C 3H8

SASKATCHEWAN
Department of Industry
and Commerce,
Saskatchewan Power Bldg.,
7th Floor,
Regina, Saskatchewan.
S4P 3V7

ALBERTA
Department of Economic
Development,
Pacific Plaza Bldg.,
10909 Jasper Ave.,
Edmonton, Alberta.
T5J 3M8

BRITISH COLUMBIA
Ministry of Industry and
Small Business
Development,
Legislative Bldg.,
Victoria, British Columbia.
V8V 1X4

YUKON TERRITORY
Department of Tourism
and Economic Development,
Box 2703,
Whitehorse, Yukon.
Y1A 2C6

NORTHWEST TERRITORIES
Department of Economic
Development and Tourism,
Yellowknife,
Northwest Territories.
X1A 2L9

Information and Assistance

Government Information Services

1. Business Information Centres

To obtain further information and clarification on government assistance to business, call your provincial Business Information Centre. The Business Information Centre in any province can be contacted by dialing the operator and asking for Zenith 0-3200 at no charge to the caller. These regional centres can also be called locally:

St. John's	(709) 737-5000
Halifax	(902) 426-7910
Fredericton	(506) 452-3808
Charlottetown	(902) 894-3926
Montreal	(514) 283-8185
Toronto	(416) 369-4941
Winnipeg	(204) 949-6161
Regina	(306) 569-6666
Edmonton	(403) 420-2952
	(also serves N.W.T.)
Vancouver	(604) 666-2014
	(also serves Yukon)

2. ABC Assistance to Business in Canada

The federal government provides a free handbook of business assistance programmes, services and incentives available to Canadian companies. Published in both English and French, the book *ABC Assistance to Business in Canada* is updated on a regular basis.

Contact: ABC Assistance to Business
in Canada,
Ministry of State for Economic
Development,
Ottawa, Ontario.
K1A 1E7

3. The Canadian Institute for Scientific and Technical Information (CISTI)

CISTI provides a general library service to ensure that academic, government and industrial sectors have access to worldwide scientific and technical information at low or no cost. Information requests are received by telephone, telex, mail, courier service and telecopies. Machine-readable files can be accessed throughout Canada and results printed on local terminals.

Contact: CISTI,
National Research Council,
Ottawa, Ontario.
K1A 0S2
(613) 966-5844
Or contact the nearest
regional NRC Office.

4. National Research Council Technical Information Programme (NRC/TIS)

The NRC/TIS programme is the technology transfer component of the National Research Council. This programme is geared to assisting those industries with few technical resources to solve industrial problems. In addition to solving specific problems, NRC/TIS aids in improving productivity, developing new processes, products and markets, reducing costs and increasing profits.

NRC/TIS provides a field service in which engineers and scientists make in-plant contact with clients. The field services are supported by a group of specialists at the NRC/TIS national office in Ottawa.

Contact: Technical Information
Programme,
National Research Council,
Ottawa, Ontario.
K1A 0S3
(613) 966-5845
Or contact the nearest
regional NRC office.

Industrial Research and Development Groups

Numerous industrial research and development institutes and foundations exist in Canada. Contact them directly.

Contact: Atlantic Industrial Research
Institute,
N.S. Technical College,
Halifax, Nova Scotia.
B3J 2X4
(902) 429-8300

Centre for Measurement and
Control of Particles and
Vapours,
McGill University,
Dawson Hall,
853 West Sherbrooke,
Montreal, Quebec.
H3A 2T6
(514) 467-2371

Centre de Recherchers en
Sciences
Appliquées à l'Alimentation,
L'Université du Québec à
Montréal,
Montréal, Québec.
H3C 3P8
(514) 282-6954

Le Centre de Développement
Technologique,
2500 Avenue Marie-Guyard,
Montréal, Québec.
H3C 3A7
(514) 344-4720

Quebec Industrial Innovation
Centre
Ecole Polytechnique,
University of Montreal
Campus,
P.O. Box 6079, Station A,
Montreal, Quebec.
H3C 3A7
(514) 344-4647

Office of Industrial Research,
McGill University,
853 Sherbrooke St. W.,
Montreal, Quebec.
H3A 2T6
(514) 392-4963

Canadian Gas Research
Institute,
55 Scarsdale Rd.,
Don Mills, Ontario.
M3B 2R3
(416) 447-6465

Canadian Industrial
Innovation Centre/Waterloo,
156 Columbia St. West,
Waterloo, Ontario.
N2L 3L3
(519) 885-5870

Canadian Institute of
Metalworking,
McMaster University,
Hamilton, Ontario.
L8S 4K1
(416) 525-9140

Centre for Applied Research
and Engineering Design Inc.,
McMaster University,
Hamilton, Ontario.
L8S 4K1
(416) 522-9140

Centre for Process
Development,
University of Waterloo,
Waterloo, Ontario.
N2I 3G1
(519) 885-1211

Industrial Research Institute,
University of Windsor,
Windsor, Ontario.
N9B 3P4
(519) 253-8862

Office of Research
Development,
University of Ottawa,
Ottawa, Ontario.
K1N 9B4
(613) 231-3282

Ontario Research Foundation,
Sheridan Park,
Mississauga, Ontario.
L5K 1B3
(416) 822-4111

Ryerson Applied
Research Ltd.,
380 Victoria Street,
Toronto, Ontario.
M5B 1W7
(416) 595-5033

Systems Analysis, Control and
Design Activity (SACDA),
University of Western Ontario,
London, Ontario.
N6A 5B9
(519) 679-6570

Waterloo Research Institute,
University of Waterloo,
Waterloo, Ontario.
N2L 3G1
(519) 885-1211

Welding Institute of Canada,
391 Burnhamthorpe Rd. E.,
Oakville, Ontario.
L6J 6C9
(416) 845-9881

Canadian Food Products
Development Centre,
Manitoba Research Council,
210-No. 1 Lakeview Square,
155 Carlton St.,
Winnipeg, Manitoba.
(204) 944-2040

Office of Industrial Research,
University of Manitoba,
Winnipeg, Manitoba.
R3T 2N2
(202) 474-9463

Centre for Research and
Development in Masonry,
207 Sherwood Plaza,
5809 Macleod Trail S.W.,
Calgary, Alberta.
T2H 0J0
(403) 253-6226

Sulphur Development
Institute of Canada,
Suite 830,
Bow Valley Square,
202 6th Avenue, S.W.,
Calgary, Alberta.
T2P 2R9
(403) 265-4220

Associations

Consult trade associations and other applicable organizations for information on pollution prevention opportunities and their implementation. Requests for this kind of information may spur those groups not already concerned with this issue to take it up. The following is a list of associations of general concern. Industry-specific trade associations are listed in the "For Further Information" sections at the back of each of the specific chapters.

Contact: Association of Consulting
Engineers of Canada,
Suite 616,
130 Albert St.,
Ottawa, Ontario.
K1P 5G4
(613) 236-0569

Canadian Association of
Equipment Distributors,
Suite 1411,
130 Albert St.,
Ottawa, Ontario.
K1P 5G4
(613) 233-3474

Canadian Association of
Recycling Industries,
8 Colborne St.,
Suite 602,
Toronto, Ontario.
M5E 1E1
(416) 362-4521

Canadian Centre for
Occupational Health and
Safety,
Health Sciences Centre,
3N25,
1200 Main St., West,
Hamilton, Ontario.
L8N 3Z5
(416) 527-6590

Canadian Chamber of
Commerce,
First Canadian Place,
Suite 3370,
P.O. Box 63,
Toronto, Ontario.
M5X 1B1
(416) 868-6415

Canadian Council of
Professional Engineers,
Suite 401,
116 Albert St.,
Ottawa, Ontario.
K1P 5G3
(613) 232-2474

Canadian Manufacturers
Association,
1 Yonge St.,
Suite 1400,
Toronto, Ontario.
M5E 1J9
(416) 363-7261

Canadian Standards
Association,
178 Rexdale Blvd.,
Rexdale, Ontario.
M9W 1R3
(416) 744-4127

Engineering Institute of
Canada,
Suite 700,
2050 Mansfield St.,
Montreal, Quebec.
H3A 1Z2
(514) 842-8121

Federation of Canadian
Associations on the
Canadian Environment,
(FACE),
1325 Carling Ave.,
Suite 210,
Ottawa, Ontario.
K1Z 8N8
(613) 725-1881

*Federation of Canadian
Municipalities,
No. 1318-112 Kent St.,
Ottawa, Ontario.
K1P 5P2
(613) 237-5221*

*Lambton Industrial Society,
242, A Indian Road South,
Suite 201,.
Sarnia, Ontario.
N7T 3W4
(519) 344-2412*

*National Center for
Resource Recovery,
1211 Connecticut Ave. N.W.,
Washington, D.C.
20036
(202) 223-6154*

*National Solid Wastes
Management Association,
1120 Connecticut Ave. N.W.,
Suite 930,
Washington, D.C.
20036*

*Ontario Waste Management
Association,
1126 Fewster Drive,
Mississauga, Ontario.
L4W 2A4
(416) 624-8353*

Special Waste Reduction and Recovery Projects

1. Canadian Waste Materials Exchange (CWME)

The Canadian Waste Materials Exchange is a country-wide information exchange that informs waste generators and users of waste transfer opportunities through its *CWME Bulletin*.

*Contact: The Canadian Waste
Materials Exchange,
Ontario Research
Foundation,
Sheridan Park Research
Community,
Mississauga, Ontario.
L5K 1B3
(416) 822-4111*

2. Wastewater Technology Centre

The Wastewater Technology Centre is committed to the development and demonstration of new technologies in wastewater

handling. This information is then communicated to industry, municipalities, provincial agencies, universities and consulting engineers.

*Contact: The Director,
Wastewater Technology
Centre,
Canada Centre for Inland
Waters,
Environment Canada,
867 Lakeshore Road,
Burlington, Ontario.
(416) 637-4374*

3. Ontario Waste Management Corporation

Ontario's newly formed Waste Management Corporation is establishing an inventory of waste recovery technologies and identifying recoverable wastestreams.

*Contact: The Chairman,
Ontario Waste Management
Corporation,
60 Bloor St., West,
Suite 707,
Toronto, Ontario.
Phone (416) 963-1162*

4. United Nations Economic Commission Program on Low- and Non-Waste Technology

The United Nations is active in identifying and promoting the use of low-waste technology in industrial processing. At the Non-Waste Technology Conference held in Paris in 1976 under the auspices of the United Nations Economic Commission for Europe (ECE), it was recognized that a first step in promoting low-waste technology was to maintain a register of these technologies that is freely accessible to all industries embarking on pollution prevention programmes.

Contact the ECE regarding its upcoming *Compendium on Low-Waste Technology*. This publication will document many examples of practical application of low- and non-waste technology in major industrial sectors throughout the world. The ECE project emphasizes technological modifications that result in more efficient processing and hence less

waste, as well as advances in waste recovery and exchange.

*Contact: Marvin Rubin,
U.S. Liaison to United
Nations Economic
Commission Program on
Low- and Non-Waste
Technology,
Bureau of Industrial
Economics,
Department of Commerce,
Washington, D.C.
20230*

*United Nations Environment
Program (UNEP),
Liaison Office,
866 UN Plaza,
New York, New York.
10017
(office located at 485
Lexington Avenue)*

*Low- and Non-Waste
Technology Group,
Economic Commission for
Europe,
United Nations,
1211 Geneva 10,
Switzerland.*

*United Nations Environment
Program,
P.O. Box 30552,
Nairobi, Kenya.*

Industrial Waste Prevention: An Assessment and Demonstration Project in the Region of Waterloo

This project is designed to assess the potential for waste reduction in the region of Waterloo. The waste reduction potential will be based on numerous plant visits to establish the on-site feasibility of waste reduction and exchange potential. The project is a joint venture between Resource Integration Systems, the Ontario Research Foundation and Hans Mooij & Associates.

*Contact: Jack McGinnis,
Project Manager,
Resource Integration
Systems,
467 Richmond St. East,
Toronto, Ontario.
M5A 1R1
(416) 366-2578*

6. Great Lakes Basin Commission Study

The Great Lakes Basin Commission is engaging in a major hazardous waste management study, a component of which is devoted to industrial waste reduction and recovery.

Contact: Hazardous Waste
Management Study,
Great Lakes Basin
Commission,
3475 Plymouth Road,
P.O. Box 999,
Ann Arbor, Michigan.
48106
(313) 668-2300

7. Industrial Waste Elimination Research Center (IWERC)

The Industrial Waste Elimination Research Center focuses on waste reduction through process control and modification. Another major thrust of this research body is to develop innovative uses for industrial wastes as resource inputs or as end products.

Contact: Industrial Waste Elimination
Research Center,
Pritzker Department of
Environmental Engineering,
Illinois Institute of
Technology,
IIT Center,
Chicago, Illinois.
60616

8. World Environment Center

The World Environment Center is a non-profit resource service of the United Nations Association of the United States. A recent project culminated in a handbook entitled *Contact: Toxics — Guide to Specialists on Toxic Substances.* This book lists and describes hundreds of experts in industrial processing, hazard identification, resource recovery and other waste management alternatives. Designed initially to plug a reporter into a national network of specialists in the field, this publication is useful to a wider audience.

Contact: World Environment Center,
300 East 42 St.,
New York, New York.
10017
(212) 697-3232

9. California's Hazardous Waste Recycling Programme

The California Department of Health is engaged in a waste recycling programme that actively locates industrial wastestreams whose components might be recycled. The purpose of the free consulting service to industry is to conserve energy and material resources by re-using materials which would normally be disposed, and to reduce the volume of materials going into disposal sites.

Contact: Hazardous Materials
Management Section,
California Department of
Health,
Berkeley, California.
94704
(415) 644-6437

The California Office of Appropriate Technology is active in promoting industrial waste reduction and recovery through policy recommendations and technology assessments.

Contact: Office of Appropriate
Technology,
1600 Ninth St.,
Sacramento, California.
95814
(916) 445-1803

10. N-Viro Systems Ltd. and the University of Toledo

The University of Toledo and N-Viro Energy Systems Ltd. have contributed funds to establish an information centre for assisting in identifying and developing re-usable industrial wastes. Current recycling initiatives are directed to the re-use of kiln dust and fly ash. Future research will focus on sludges resulting from wastewater treatment. Plans include computerizing data and making it available for automated recall.

Contact: N-Viro Energy Systems Ltd.,
3450 West Central Avenue,
Suite 250,
Toledo, Ohio.
43606
(419) 535-6374

Geology Department,
University of Toledo,
2801 West Bancroft St.,
Toledo, Ohio.
43606
(419) 537-2009

11. Battelle's Guidelines for Hazardous Waste Audits

The Battelle Research Institute's Columbus Division has developed guidelines on how to carry out a hazardous waste audit for a company of any size.

Contact: Battelle Memorial Institute,
505 King Ave.,
Columbus, Ohio.
43201
(614) 424-6424

12. New England Workshop Series on Waste Elimination and Recovery

Working through existing trade and business associations, Weston Designers/Consultants are active in initiating workshops and conferences that deal specifically with waste reduction and recovery. The workshops are designed to assist plant engineers and hazardous waste control specialists in achieving more widespread reduction and recovery of specific industrial wastes.

Contact: Dr. Robert Pojasek,
Weston Designers/
Consultants,
Suite 206,
111 South Bedford St.,
Burlington, Massachusetts.
01803
(617) 229-2050

13. World Health Organization

The World Health Organization's Working Group on the Control of Toxic and Hazardous Waste has established "Codes of Good Practice" in the management of hazardous waste. This policy directive stresses the importance of waste elimination and reduction necessary for a sound waste management strategy.

Contact: Dr. Michael Suess,
World Health Organization,
Regional Office for Europe,
8, Scherfigsvej,
DK-2100, Copenhagen O,
Denmark.

References

1. Lehr, L.W. "Pollution Prevention Pays." *Catalyst for Environmental Quality 4(3).*

2. *U.S. Environmental Protection Agency. Waste Exchanges: Background Information.* Office of Water and Waste Management, December 1980.

3. "Ferric Chloride Process Wins CIC Award." *Chemistry in Canada,* Summer 1977.

4. Royston, M. *Pollution Prevention Pays.* Oxford: Pergamon Press, 1979.

5. "They're Getting Gold from Dross." *Chemical Week,* February 4, 1981.

6. Maugh, T. "Burial is the Last Resort for Hazardous Wastes." *Science* 204(22), 1979.

7. Office of Appropriate Technology (State of California). *Alternatives to the Land Disposal of Hazardous Wastes.* Prepared by the Toxic Waste Assessment Group, Office of Appropriate Technology, 1981.

8. Pojasek, Robert. Weston Designers-Consultants, Burlington, Massachusetts. Personal communication, February 1982.

9. "Battelle Develops Technique for Hazardous Waste Audits." *Journal of Coatings Technology,* November 1981.

10. Duffy, M.J. "Reducing Styrene Emission from Unsaturated Polyester." *Plastics Engineering,* August 1979.

11. Mock, J.A. "Water-Borne Paints Cut Auto Costs, Help Reduce Pollution Problems." *Materials Engineering,* May 1978.

12. U.S. Environmental Protection Agency. *Environmental Regulations and Technology for thcleaning Industry.* May 1981.

13. Porter, J.J. and Sargent, T.N. "Waste Treatment Vs. Waste Recovery." *Textile Chemist and Colorist,* November 1977.

14. Hartsuch, P.J. "Less Press Wastes Means Money in Your Pocket." *Graphic Arts Monthly,* January 1980.

15. Mor, Wilson,. Technical Services Department, 3M Canada Inc., Toronto, Ontario. Personal communication, April 1981.

16. "Recycles Cutting Oil Via Ultrafiltration." *Canadian Chemical Processing,* May 2, 1979.

17. "Bofors Introduces New Spent Acid Handling System to North America." *Canadian Chemical Processing,* September 5, 1979.

18. Brown, C. "Recycling Recovered Nickel Salts Can Make Pollution Control Profitable." *Canadian Paint and Finishing,* February 1976.

19. American Newspaper Publishers Association Research Institute. "Ink Reclamation — A Valuable New Process for Newspapers." *R.I. Bulletin* (American Newspaper Publishers Association), May 2, 1979.

20. "Overspray Goes Back to Work." *Industrial Finishing,* January 1981.

21. Milner, Brian. Chem-Ecol Ltd., Cobourg, Ontario. Personal communication, May 1981.

22. Cooley, A.C. and Dagon. T.J. "Current Silver Recovery Practices in the Photographic Processing Industry." *Journal of Applied Photographic Engineering,* Winter 1976.

23. Milgrom, J. "Recycling Plastics: Current Status." In *Conservation and Recycling, Vol. 3.* Oxford: Pergamon Press, 1980.

24. Corning Glass Works. "Hydrolyzed Lactose: New Source of Sweeteners." *Food Engineering,* November 1979.

25. Brandon, Craig. Carre Inc., Seneca, North Carolina. Personal communication, August 1981.

26. Schwarzer, C. "Recycling Hazardous Wastes." *Environmental Science and Technology* 14(2), February 1979.

27. Small Business Secretariat. Department of Industry, Trade and Commerce (Canada). 1981.

28. Ministry of Industry and Tourism (Ontario). *Annual Review.* December 1980.

29. Environment Canada. *The Hazardous Waste Problem: Let's Find Some Common Ground.* 1981.

30. Eastman Kodak Co. *Recovering Silver from Photographic Materials.* Rochester, New York: Eastman Kodak, 1980.

31. Pojasek, R. "Managing Industrial Wastes On-Site." Mimeographed. Burlington, Massachusetts: Weston Designers-Consultants, 1981.

32. Gay, Arthur. Technical Services, W.C. Richards Co., Blue Island, Illinois. Personal communication, August 1981.

33. Leonard, F. Dorr Oliver, Stanford, Connecticut. Personal communication, August 1981.

34. Gentry, Hubert. Gentry Laboratories, Harrisonburg, Virginia. Personal communication, August 1981.

35. Pojasek, Robert. Weston Designers-Consultants, Burlington, Massachusetts. Memorandum to the Business and Industry Association of New Hampshire, February 9, 1982.

36. "Quebec Plastic Recycler Expands to Handle Wire Jacketing Resins." *Eco/Log Week,* December 12, 1980.

37. Osmonics, Inc. *Reverse Osmosis and Ultrafiltration Demonstration Service*. Hopkins, Minnesota: Osmonics, Inc., 1982 (product literature).

38. Ming, Chen. "The Recycling of Waste Acid, Oil and Metal Scrap of the Shanghai Donghai Oil and Chemical Recycling Works." In *Conservation and Recycling*. Oxford; Pergamon Press, 1980.

39. Schwarzer, C. `"The State of California Resource Recovery and Recycle Program for Hazardous Wastes." Presented at the 1979 National Conference on Hazardous Material Risk Assessment, Disposal and Management, April 25-27, 1979.

40. R.R. Street and Co., Oak Brook, Illinois. Personal communication, September 1981.

Pollution Prevention Opportunities

Dry Cleaning

It has been more than a century since dry cleaning had its origin in Paris, France. Since that time, the dry cleaning process, whereby garments are cleaned in a non-aqueous solvent, has witnessed many refinements. Gasoline and carbon tetrachloride have been replaced as dry cleaning fluids by perchloroethylene (perc, and also known as tetrachloroethylene), Stoddard solvent (a petroleum distillate) and fluorocarbon 113.

Soaring solvent prices coupled with forebodings of stricter solvent emission levels have steered dry cleaning equipment manufacturers along a course of closed-loop design and "building a tighter ship". Although the economics clearly favour the new, more efficient and less polluting equipment lines for any dry cleaner about to set up shop, the economics of modernizing existing facilities are more complex. Even so, the potential for recouping lost solvent dollars and preventing pollution by simple low-cost housekeeping measures is large, and in many instances, virtually untapped.

Industry Profile

Dry cleaning establishments include industrial dry cleaners, commercial dry cleaners and coin-operated facilities. The majority of dry cleaning establishments occur within the urban landscape, and as such, fugitive solvent emissions will inevitably impinge on neighbouring shops and homes. Although most dry cleaners recycle the cleaning solvent on the premises, many establishments still vent solvent-laden plant air and dryer exhaust directly into the atmosphere.

Based on a 1977 study by the Department of Industry, Trade and Commerce, 13,800 Canadians are employed in the laundry and dry cleaning industry.[1] Industrial outfits tend to be the largest of the dry cleaning plants, frequently processing 1 million pounds of garments such as uniforms and work gloves each year.[2] In the U.S., 50% of industrial dry cleaners use perc as the cleaning solvent. The rest use either petroleum solvents or fluorocarbons.

Commercial installations range from small neighbourhood shops, which clean clothes on the premises, to large multi-outlet dry cleaning operations which collect soiled clothes from a network of outlets and clean them at a centralized facility. Based on data from the International Fabricare Institute, the typical commercial installation has an annual throughput of 50,000 to 250,000 pounds (23,000 to 113,000 kg) of clothes which undergo dry cleaning.[3]

Industry spokesmen estimate that 75 to 80% of the commercial facilities in Canada use perchloroethylene as the cleaning solvent. Coin-operated dry cleaning facilities typically form part of the self-service laundromat facilities distributed throughout most communities. Most coin-operated dry cleaning machines use perchloroethylene.

Health and Environmental Effects of Dry Cleaning Solvents

Perchloroethylene

Perchloroethylene, in widespread use since the 1950s, is a chlorinated hydrocarbon observed to induce liver cancer in laboratory mice, but not in rats.[4] A preliminary epidemiological study found a higher incidence of

---

Table 1
Average Responses to Inhalation of Perchloroethylene Vapour

Concentration (ppm)	Effect
50	Odor threshold (very faint) to unacclimated. No physiological effect, 8 h.
100	Odor (faint) definitely apparent to unacclimated, very faint to imperceptible during exposure. No physiological effect, 8 h.
200	Odor (definite) moderate to faint upon exposure. Faint to moderate eye irritation (eye irritation threshold, 100-200 ppm).
400	Odor (strong) unpleasant. Definite eye irritation. Slight nose irritation. Definite incoordination, 2 h.
600	Odor (strong) very unpleasant but tolerable. Definite eye and nose irritation. Dizziness, loss of inhibitions, 10 min.
1,000	Odor (very strong) intense, irritating. Marked irritation to eyes and respiratory tract. Considerable dizziness, not likely to be tolerated voluntarily, 2 min.
1,500	Odor (almost intolerable) gagging. Irritation (almost intolerable) to eyes and nose. Complete incoordination within minutes to unconsciousness within 30 min.

Source: Laundry-Cleaning Council, *The Safe Handling of Perchloroethylene Drycleaning Solvent,* Chicago IL, Laundry-Cleaning Council, 1980.

Table 2
OSHA Standards for Occupational Exposure to Dry Cleaning Solvents

| Standard | Concentration (ppm) | | |
	Perchloroethylene	Petroleum	Fluorocarbon
Threshold limit value (no effects below this level)[a]	100	100	1,000
Maximal 8-h time-weighted average	100	500	1,000
Maximal concentration, general	200	NA	NA
Maximal 5-min concentration allowed once each 3 h)	300	NA	NA

[a] *American Conference of Governmental Industrial Hygienists.*

Note: NA = not applicable

Source: Laundry-Cleaning Council, *The Safe Handling of Perchloroethylene Drycleaning Solvent,* Chicago IL, Laundry-Cleaning Council, 1980.

---

death from cancer among dry cleaning workers than among the general population.[5]

Side effects (see Table 1) due to brief over-exposure to perchloroethylene include light-headedness, dizziness, inco-ordination, headache, mental dullness, sleepiness, nausea and an appearance of being drunk. Massive overexposure may cause depression of mental functions, liver dysfunction, unconsciousness, respiratory failure and even death.[6]

Canada, Britain and the United States accept a Threshold Limit Value (T.L.V.) of 100 ppm (8-hour time-weighted average) for occupational exposure to perchloroethylene[7] (see Table 2). Data compiled by the Laundry-Cleaning Council indicate that emissions from poorly operated perc plants may reach or exceed 600 ppm.[8]

NIOSH (National Institute for Occupational Safety and Health) has since recommended that workers not be exposed in excess of 50 ppm for a 10-hour work-day, 40-hour work-week. The 50 ppm limit is still under consideration.[9]

Petroleum Solvent

Petroleum solvent appears to be less hazardous than perc, although it must be recognized that little published data exist on industrial exposure to petroleum solvent vapours. The current OSHA standard of exposure to petroleum solvent vapour is 500 ppm (see Table 2). Symptoms accompanying overexposure to Stoddard solvent include irritation of the eyes, nose and throat, as well as dizziness and headache.

From a health standpoint, petroleum solvent is less hazardous than chlorinated hydrocarbon solvents such as perchloroethylene. However, from an environmental perspective, petroleum solvents are far from ideal candidates as cleaning solvents. Petroleum solvent vapours, like other hydrocarbons, are photochemically reactive and instrumental in producing smog.

Fluorocarbons

Compared to other cleaning solvents, fluorocarbon solvents such as F-113 are least hazardous to human health. OSHA's occupational exposure standard for F-113 vapour is 1000 ppm (see Table 2). However F-113, like other fluorocarbons, is implicated in the destruction of the ozone layer. Destruction of the protective ozone layer is predicted to result in increased incidence of skin cancer. Because fluorocarbons are relatively expensive solvents, solvent

vapour recovery is already widely practised to make fluorocarbon machines competitive with perchloroethylene and petroleum machines.

From a health standpoint, both petroleum and fluorocarbon solvents are less hazardous than chlorinated hydrocarbon solvents such as perchloroethylene. However, from an environmental perspective, neither petroleum nor fluorocarbon solvents is an ideal candidate as a cleaning solvent.

The Dry Cleaning Process and Sources of Wastes

During dry cleaning, garments and solvent are agitated in an enclosed, perforated cylinder called a dry cleaning unit similar to the laundry washing machine.

The garments are then spun in the washer to extract much of the solvent. Used solvent is constantly filtered to remove insoluble impurities. Filtration is followed by distillation to remove the soluble impurities such as oils, fats and greases that were once present in the dirty garments.

During distillation (see Figure 1), the contaminated cleaning

Figure 1
Perchloroethylene Still and Condenser

During distillation, the contaminated cleaning solvent is heated, permitting solvent and water to vapourize. These vapours leave the still and enter a condenser where they pass over water-cooled coil surfaces and condense.

Source: Operating Tips for Better Dry Cleaning, PPG Industries.

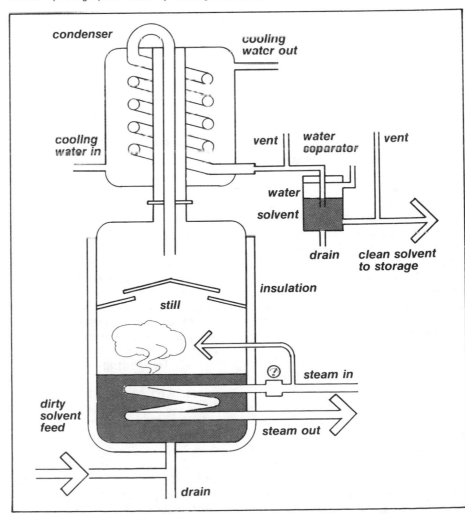

fluid is heated, permitting solvent and water to vapourize. These vapours leave the still and enter a condenser where they pass over water-cooled coil surfaces and condense.[10] Using a separator, water is removed from the solvent-water mixture and discharged to the sewer system. The amount of solvent discharged in the wastewater to the sewer depends upon the effectiveness of the separation tank in separating solvent from the water mixture. However, small quantities of solvent dissolve in water and are discharged with the wastewater. The purified solvent, once free of soap and other impurities, is ready for re-use.

The extracted garments are tumbled dry. During the drying cycle, much of the evaporated solvent is recovered in a condenser and re-used. Depending on the nature of the fabric cleaned, the extracted garments retain up to 45% of the solvent, by weight.[11]

The high cost and potential toxicity of perchloroethylene necessitates that dryer equipment include a reclaiming system. In a reclaiming dryer, solvent vapour given off during drying is condensed, separated from the water fraction and re-used (see Figure 2).

During the drying cycle, circulating heated air carries evaporated solvent to a condenser for reclaiming. After the heated air cycle has finished, the dryer is set to "vent". This opens a flap which allows room air to circulate through the dryer to cool the garments. Vented air is typically released to the outside environment.

In old equipment, this venting process, also known as deodorization, is accomplished by opening the dryer door slightly and venting plant air through the clothes in the dryer.

There are many ways in which solvent can enter both the working environment and the outside environment.

Solvent losses are possible from the transfer and storage of solvents, from leaks and damaged gaskets, and from poor hose connections, couplings and valves.

Solvent is lost to the sewer because of limited efficiency in

Figure 2
Reclaiming Dryer

In a reclaiming dryer, solvent vapour given off during drying is condensed, separated from the water fraction and re-used.
Source: Operating Tips for Better Dry Cleaning, PPG Industries.

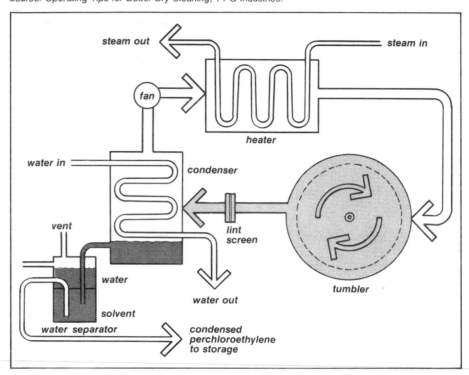

separating solvents from water in the separating process following vapour condensation.

Another potential source of solvent loss concerns disposal of sludge. Filters will contain sludge consisting of filter powder holding a residue. Many plants now use cartridge filtration systems. When the cartridge life is over, most of the solvent is drained before removal.

In perchloroethylene systems, the sludge may be heated and "cooked out" which leaves a dry powder/soil mixture containing small amounts of solvent.

Petroleum solvent systems work similarly, except there is no heat application for solvent removal. Depending on the age of the equipment, wet or dry sludge is removed. In older filters, sludge is deposited on the filter bottom in a wet or slop form. In newer equipment, the solvent is forced from the sludge by air pressure. When the sludge is removed from the filter, it is dried to the point that no liquid solvent remains but the sludge is still moist.

Solvent residue from the distillation unit can emit potentially hazardous vapours or leach into the ground if disposed at a local landfill site. Solvent residue from the distillation unit must be handled as a hazardous waste in the United States.

POLLUTION PREVENTION OPPORTUNITIES

A few years ago when solvent was cheap and emission controls more relaxed, an average of 200 pounds of clothes were cleaned per gallon of solvent used.[7] About 10% of the total solvents used annually escaped to the environment. Now, equipment is available which operates at an efficiency of 1000 pounds per gallon, thereby slashing solvent losses to a fifth of their previous level.[7] The term solvent mileage, used to indicate the pounds of clothes cleaned per drum of solvent, is fast becoming part of every dry cleaner's vocabulary.

There can be little doubt that dry cleaning equipment is becoming increasingly efficient, and as such, is a major force in diminishing environmental pollution from dry cleaning plants. But installing efficient equipment is only half the battle. Despite the lure of high solvent mileage by equipment manufacturers, many operators achieve disappointing efficiencies. Good housekeeping practices to limit fugitive emissions are an integral part of minimizing pollution as well as enhancing company profits.

1.
Good Housekeeping

Total solvent emissions from dry cleaning facilities can vary greatly with operational, maintenance and housekeeping procedures.

A 1980 study by the U.S. Department of Health and Human Services, which examined 20 dry cleaning plants, concluded that gasket and other leaks, solvent retention in garments during unloading, and poor ventilation were common problems.[12] No relationship existed between plant size and solvent mileage (see Table 3). For example, one small plant that processed 600 pounds of fabric a week had a solvent efficiency of 17,000 pounds of fabric per drum of solvent. This approximated the efficiency of a very large plant processing 26,300 pounds of clothes per week. For other plants, solvent mileage hovered at 10,000. Both equipment efficiency and good housekeeping practices figure prominently in achieving high solvent mileage.[15]

It is becoming increasingly apparent that good housekeeping practices can put a big dent in solvent losses, and can do so at a minimum cost. Any company can benefit from a systematic housekeeping routine. It should include daily monitoring of solvent mileage, checking for solvent leaks through the regular examination of gaskets and hose couplings, and paying careful attention to solvent extraction from solid waste residuals such as filters.

Eliminating Liquid Solvent Leaks

The leakage of solvents from worn equipment and hosing may go unnoticed unless the operator routinely checks for signs of solvent loss. Liquid leaks are detectable by sight due to the trace of brown residue left on the lower side of the leak. Locate the leaks and correct promptly by patching the hole or replacing the defective part. Check regularly for liquid leakage in the following areas:[8]

Table 3
Solvent Mileage Versus Plant Size for 15 Existing Dry Cleaning Establishments

Plant Size (pounds of clothes cleaned per week)	Solvent	Mileage (pounds of clothes per drum of solvent)
26,300	perchloroethylene	18,500
19,500	perchloroethylene	7,370
15,000	perchloroethylene	26,000
3,600	perchloroethylene	10,000
2,600	perchloroethylene	9,500
1,370	perchloroethylene	19,800
1,250	perchloroethylene	5,500
650	perchloroethylene	7,200
600	perchloroethylene	17,000
20,700	petroleum solvent	1,095
10,000	petroleum solvent	1,350
2,650	petroleum solvent	1,450
1,813	petroleum solvent	1,400
2,400	fluorocarbon	9,600
1,500	fluorocarbon	25,000

Source: A.D. Little Inc. *Engineering Control Assessment of the Dry Cleaning Industry.* Prepared for NIOSH, October 1980.

This hand-held perchloroethylene sensor is used routinely to monitor the level of vapour emissions. High perc levels at the door may be corrected by replacing worn door gaskets.

Larry Rossignol

- Hose connections, couplings and valves machine.
- Door gasket and seating.
- Filter head gasket and seating.
- Pumps and storage tanks.
- Water separators (solvent lost in water because of poor separation).
- Filter sludge recovery (solvent lost in sludge by improper or incomplete recovery).
- Cartridge filters.
- Distillation unit.
- Divertor valves.
- Saturated lint from lint basket.

Reducing Solvent Vapour Loss

The loss of solvent vapour could go unnoticed for months unless an operator monitors regularly for fugitive emissions. Commercially available low-cost leak detectors can identify leaks before they become large enough to see or smell. Although the unacclimated person should be able to smell vapour levels of 50 ppm, the detection of vapour by smell is not very reliable since acclimation to the solvent odour is rapid.

Some leakage may be due to current operating practices which allow solvent vapour to escape unnecessarily. Plugging leaks and upgrading daily operating procedures in the following ways will minimize fugitive emissions:[2, 13]

- Periodically replace the seals on the dryer deodorizing and aeration valves.
- Repair holes in the air and exhaust ducts.
- Replace faulty gaskets on machine doors.
- Keep containers of solvent closed when not in use.
- Clean lint screens regularly to avoid clogging of the fans and condensers. The operation of the solvent recovery system is impeded if the condensers are caked with lint.
- Open button traps and lint baskets only for as long as necessary for cleaning to avoid residual solvent losses.
- Size the garment load correctly relative to the size of the equipment. Overloading results in incomplete solvent extraction while underloading increases the amount of solvent loss per unit of garment cleaned due to inherent losses in the system.

■ PPG Industries (Pittsburgh, Pennsylvania) are major distributors of dry cleaning solvents that actively promote solvent conservation through an assortment of guidebooks on good housekeeping practices.

■ Since 1970, Dow Chemical (Midland, Michigan), a major producer of perchloroethylene, has provided a free, computerized solvent analysis service for dry cleaners to gauge solvent performance.[14]

■ R.R. Street and Company (Oak Brook, Illinois) provide an on-site trouble-shooting service to dry cleaning plants using Street's products. Local service representatives exist country-wide in both Canada and the United States.[15]

2.
More Efficient Equipment

Nowadays, a dry cleaner about to set up shop can choose from an assortment of highly efficient, low-polluting equipment. Many of the new models hitting the market today are virtually closed-loop systems. Because most of the solvent is retained within the closed system, solvent losses to the environment are minimal.

The closed-loop technology of new dry cleaning equipment extends beyond solvent recovery. Many of the new machines have heat and water conservation loops, resulting in substantial energy and water cost savings. High capital costs become more palatable when the prospective buyer takes into account future savings through reduced operating costs.

New developments in dry cleaning equipment include equipment complete with a carbon adsorption or refrigeration process, and closed-loop equipment. Companies that make closed-loop cleaning units usually make special add-on units to retrofit existing equipment.

Dry-to-Dry Machines

Dry-to-dry machines combine washing and drying functions in a single unit. In contrast, transfer machines consist of a wash unit and a separate drying machine,

This dry-to-dry machine at Embassy Cleaners (Toronto) combines washing and drying functions into a single unit, thereby reducing worker contact with solvent-laden garments.

requiring worker contact with solvent-containing clothes during their movement from the washer to the dryer.

Although all coin-operated perchloroethylene machines are dry-to-dry, many commercial and industrial perchloroethylene facilities still use transfer machines. The shift in use to dry-to-dry machines will result in decreased solvent levels in the work environment.

In contrast to perchloroethylene machines, virtually all equipment designed to use fluorocarbons are closed-loop, dry-to-dry units. The high cost of fluorocarbons prompted early development of closed-loop technology for fluorocarbon systems. Years later, as perchloroethylene costs increased and anti-pollution regulations tightened, equipment designers brought out a line of highly efficient perchloroethylene machines.

"Cold dry" systems are innovation on the horizon. Low temperature drying is an improvement over hot drying because solvent losses are minimized. Furthermore, delicate fabrics can be processed safely and machine seals remain intact longer.

■ When Uni-Rent Ltd. (Whitby, Ontario) bought into an ailing cleaning company in 1977, it was fast to upgrade the facility by replacing an old transfer machine with a Spencer-Mammoth dry-to-dry unit. Worker health and economics both figured strongly in the company's decision.

"I have been told by U.S. sources that perc might cause serious health problems," says Brian Bond, one of Uni-Rent's three co-owners. "I'll take every precaution I can if I have 23 people working here with me."

In 1977, perchloroethylene cost $2.40 a gallon. In the four years since, perchloroethylene has shot up to $6 per gallon.

"There was an incentive to cut solvent losses, especially on the scale that we were using it," says Bond.

Uni-Rent uses 300 gallons of perc a month. According to Bond, if they were still using the old equipment, solvent consumption would be 700 gallons a month. At today's solvent prices, Uni-Rent would be out of pocket an additional $50,000 each year.[16]

Preventative maintenance is part of the routine at this facility. Every morning, all the gaskets and seals in the machines are checked. Ducting and hosing also undergo regular scrutiny.[16] Although Uni-Rent is like many other commercial cleaners that

Uni-Rent is an industrial launderer and dry cleaner specializing in the cleaning of industrial work clothes, gloves, uniforms and rags. A solvent-based cleaning process is used to remove oil and grease from the soiled garments. (1) Cleaned garments are removed from the dry-to-dry machine. (2) Wipers are folded for re-use. (3) The solvent is cooked to separate re-usable solvent from the oil and grease. (4) Dirty oil and grease drain from the solvent recovery system. (5) The waste oil is collected and hauled away by another company.

vent solvent-laden air, the company is looking carefully towards future installation of a carbon adsorption unit to recover solvent vapour from the plant's exhaust air systems. The capital cost of the carbon adsorption units is the major hurdle facing Uni-Rent, but past experience has shown that stopping solvent losses ultimately nets the company a profit.

■ American Permac Inc. (Hicksville, New York) is one equipment manufacturer boasting high solvent mileage due to its built-in carbon adsorption unit and tight machine design. Much of Permac's technology was developed as a result of their experience with highly volatile fluorocarbon solvents.[17]

Other improvements in the Permac equipment that contribute to its high solvent mileage of 30,000 to 50,000 pounds of fabric per drum of solvent include its Sentinel system. The Sentinel system monitors drying time so that drying is automatically extended until the load is completely dry, thereby reducing the movement of solvent vapours into the plant when clothes are removed.[17]

Chemicals and soap are added automatically through closed containers, minimizing solvent loss. Spent cartridges can be dried out within the machine to recover residual solvent before disposal.

■ Frimair (France) recently entered the dry cleaning equipment field when they perfected the integration of a built-in refrigeration unit and a heat pump as a major breakthrough in dry cleaning technology.[18] The machine uses closed-loop technology, does not require outside venting or a carbon-activated reclaimer.

The rate of solvent recovery is accelerated over other systems because condensation is achieved through a built-in freon refrigeration unit with a compressor instead of a conventional water cooling unit.

The rapid speed of the solvent recovery operation permits a longer deodorization phase than other equipment types, without prolonging the length of the cycle. Clothes leave the machine at room temperature, and, according to the equipment manufacturer, are not wrinkled.

The tight design of the equipment ensures that perchloroethylene concentrations remain below a 25 ppm average. In addition to its safety from an occupational health point of view, Frimair points out economic savings compared to open-ended systems. Water costs can be slashed by 50 to 80%, and energy costs by 30 to 50%.[18]

Perc-laden air from the washing machine (unit on the right) and reclaiming dryer (centre unit) are ducted to carbon adsorption units behind.

3.
Emission Control Technology

Many neighbourhood dry cleaning plants and industrial facilities have been in the business for years. Most of the dry cleaning equipment currently in use was purchased years before solvent emissions became a concern. How-

These twin carbon adsorption units permit continuous stripping of perc from solvent-laden air prior to exhausting to the outside environment.

ever, some machines may be costing the owner thousands of dollars each year in lost solvent costs. In some instances, a business might be shrewd to invest in more efficient equipment that promises reduced operating costs in the future.

In other situations, a company may decide to keep its equipment and upgrade it with add-on technologies to meet health and environmental regulations. Two major technologies available to recover solvent vapours from exhausted air are carbon adsorption and refrigeration/condensation. The application of these technologies to perchloroethylene, petroleum and flurocarbon plants is discussed below.

Perchloroethylene Plants

Most perchloroethylene plants use a reclaiming dryer which permits recovery of evaporated solvent during drying. During deodorizing, however, solvent-laden air is typically exhausted directly to the ambient air.

Solvent-laden dryer exhaust can be controlled by carbon adsorption and refrigeration/condensation technologies. Muck stripping and reducing solvent losses from still bottoms are also discussed.

Carbon Adsorption

Carbon adsorption is used to control solvent emissions from air otherwise exhausted directly to the outside of the dry cleaning facility.

Many new equipment designs incorporate carbon adsorption right into the installation. An assortment of carbon adsorption units are currently available that can be retrofitted to accommodate an existing dry cleaning facility.

Most Canadian dry cleaning plants lack carbon adsorbers. In the United States, 35 to 40% of the commercial systems and 50% of the industrial systems use a carbon adsorber for pollution control.[2]

Deodorizing may account for 10 to 50% of the solvent lost in processing every load of garments, depending upon the type of load and other factors.[19] A faulty

damper may permit deodorization to occur unnoticed during the drying cycle, seriously increasing solvent losses.

Exhaust from the solvent storage tanks, distillation unit, muck cooker, dryer condenser and plant ventilation system can all be re-routed to feed into the carbon adsorption unit (see Figure 3). Commercial adsorption units typically contain one carbon cannister which is desorbed once a day. Larger industrial facilities contain dual units to permit simultaneous adsorption and desorption.

During the carbon adsorption process (see Figure 4), the solvent in the incoming air temporarily attaches to the carbon bed. Air cleaned of solvent is exhausted to the outside of the plant. During the desorption, the carbon bed is regenerated by flushing with steam to pick up solvent. Then the steam and solvent vapour undergo condensation and separation.[20] The clean solvent is re-used in the dry cleaning process. Carbon adsorption can remove more than 96% of the solvent in the exhaust stream otherwise vented to the

At Embassy Cleaners (Toronto), numerous floor vents occur at ground level and adjacent to the dry cleaning equipment. Solvent-laden plant air is ducted from these vents to the carbon adsorption units.

This distillation unit is used to purify contaminated liquid perchloroethylene for re-use in the washing process.

Figure 3
Perchloroethylene Dry Cleaning Plant Flow Diagram

Solvent-laden exhaust from the solvent storage tanks, distillation unit, muck cooker, dryer condenser and plant ventilation system can all be routed to feed into a carbon adsorber to remove solvent from the exhausted air.

Source: Perchloroethylene Dry Cleaners — Background Information for Proposed Standards, U.S. Environmental Protection Agency, 1980.

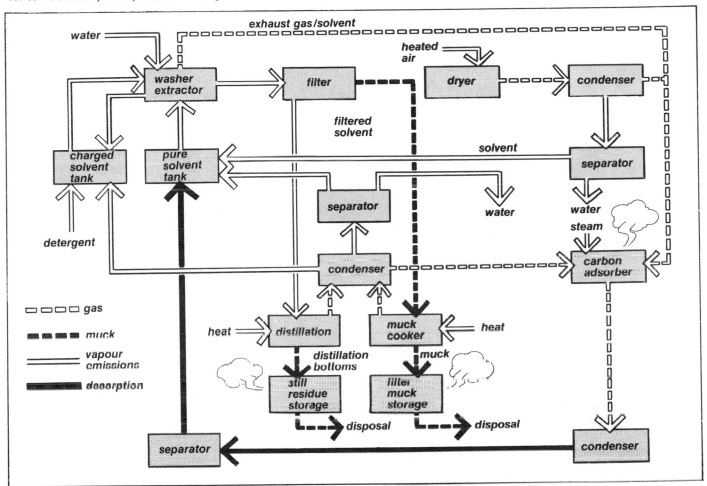

outside.[2]

The 1981 capital cost of a carbon adsorber for a small commercial plant (25-pound machine) is about $5000 (Canadian).[16]

Carbon adsorption is most attractive for the larger industrial dry cleaner, who can actually show a profit from applying this solvent recovery system.[21] Although no profit is shown for the small commercial dry cleaner, the equipment can be operated without significant effect on plant profitability.[8] As solvent costs continue to escalate, the pay-back economics can only improve.

Refrigeration / Condensation

An alternative to carbon adsorption is the refrigeration solvent recovery unit. In the refrigerated condenser system, the stripped air is returned directly to the dry cleaning machine, eliminating the need for external venting ducts. Unlike carbon adsorption technology, the application of refrigeration solvent recovery to perchloroethylene dry cleaners is relatively recent.

Incoming solvent-laden air is cooled by refrigeration to strip it of its solvent (see Figures 5, 6). The temperature of the solvent-laden air is cooled below the dew point of the vapour, causing it to condense. The solvent-free air is returned to the dry cleaning machine, and the condensed vapour drains to a water separator. The recovered solvent is fed into a storage tank for future use and the water from the separator is sewered.

A major advantage of refrigeration units over carbon adsorption systems is that they do not require a costly steam installation to regenerate the carbon. Although capital costs tend to be slightly higher for refrigeration units than for carbon adsorbers, the annual operating costs are less.[8]

■ Perchloroethylene solvent mileage at Model Blue Ribbon Cleaners was already 18,000 pounds per drum with the installation of its Multimatic dry-to-dry cleaning machine. Addition of a refrigerated solvent recovery system, however, boosted solvent mileage to 28,000 pounds of fabric per drum of solvent.[22]

The refrigeration unit has certain advantages over carbon adsorption units. Because many steam, air and water connections are eliminated, the cost of the installation is about a quarter of a conventional adsorber unit. And, because clothes come out of the

Figure 4
The Carbon Adsorption Process

During the adsorption cycle, the solvent in the incoming air temporarily attaches to the carbon bed. During the desorption phase, the carbon bed is regenerated by flushing with steam which in turn picks up solvent. The steam and solvent vapour undergo condensation and separation. The clean solvent is re-used in the dry cleaning process.
Source: Operating Tips for Better Dry Cleaning, PPG Industries.

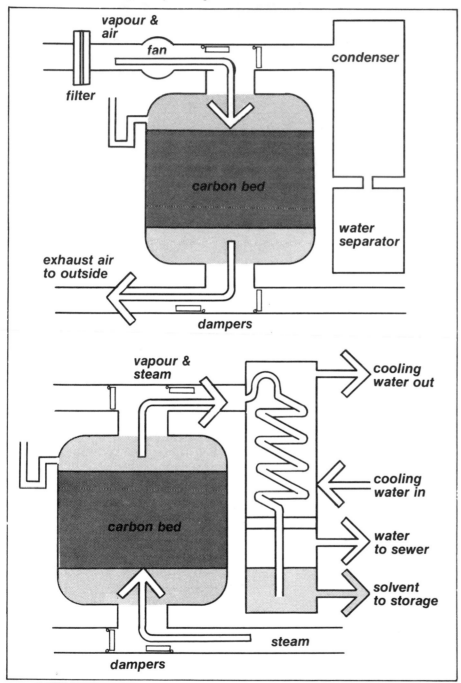

Muck Stripping

One of the most common sources of solvent loss is in the filter sludge, also known as filter muck. Even after 24 hours of draining, filter sludges contain as much as 75% perchloroethylene, or about 3 pounds of solvent for each pound of filter powder.[24]

For some filter types, solvent holdup in the filter sludge can be reduced through air pressure or steam stripping. Some filter bags containing sludge may be dried in a stationary reclaiming dryer to reduce the amount of solvent remaining in the filter before disposal.

Cooking solvent out of regenerable filter materials in a muck cooker can reduce the amount of solvent lost in filter material by 89%.[2]

Most coin-operated and many commercial installations use cartridge filters for filtration. Cartridges can be used where soil loadings are low. Spent cartridges should be drained in their housing for 24 hours before disposal to minimize solvent loss.[25]

Reducing Solvent in Still Bottoms

Residues in the bottom of the distillation unit are also rich in solvent. Proper distillation can reduce the solvent content in the still bottoms to less than 60% by weight.[8] Perchloroethylene content in still bottoms can be reduced to 1% through the use of oil cookers (similar to muck cookers).[2]

Petroleum Plants

Emission control systems suitable for dry cleaning plants that use petroleum solvents include the following: carbon adsorption, condensation, muck stripping, and incineration of still bottoms and dryer exhaust.

Carbon Adsorption

The annual and capital costs of carbon adsorption are considered too great at present for widespread acceptance of this technology by plants using petroleum solvents.[8]

machine cold, a minimum of wrinkling results and the possibility of swales is reduced.

■ The Crown Center Hotel Laundry (Kansas City, Missouri) was ripe for renovation. When an old dry cleaning machine was re-placed with a 75-pound Spencer dry-to-dry machine plus a Spencer Resolver™ (a refrigeration solvent recovery unit), solvent consumption dropped by 75%.[23] So did solvent costs.

When carbon adsorption is used, the technology is similar to that used by perchloroethylene plants. ■ Installation of a carbon adsorption system at a very large dry cleaning plant in Anaheim, California resulted in a 95% reduction of petroleum in the dryer exhaust.

Condensation

Condensation solvent recovery is a relatively new technology for petroleum dry cleaners. Despite its efficiency in reducing solvent emissions and its promising payback, relatively few petroleum cleaners use the system.

The new system is designed to replace conventional dryers. Both the condensation system and the conventional dryer use steam-heated coils to drive off the solvent contained in the fabrics. The major difference is that the condensation solvent recovery unit uses water-cooled coils to condense the solvent vapours.

The petroleum solvent is separated from the water in a separator unit and recovered for re-use. The unit has a 90% efficiency in reduced solvent vapours otherwise exhausted by a conventional dryer.[8]

The capital cost of a condensation solvent recovery unit is enough to make any company president think twice about such a purchase. Solvent recovery dryers sell for three times the price of conventional non-recovery dryers.

A shrewd businessman will look beyond the capital cost and calculate the long-term operating costs of such a venture. Although the capital cost for a 105-pound condensation solvent recovery unit is $15,000 (U.S. dollars in 1981), the first year of operation will net the company a credit of $5000 through reduced solvent costs.[8] Pay-back period to pay off the equipment is 3 years. For the smaller operator, purchase of a 50-pound unit is still an investment, however the pay-back is estimated at 8 years. Both these calculations do not take into account the effects of inflation. In an inflationary economy, recycling becomes even more profitable since the equipment cost is fixed in time while the dividends from the

Spent cartridges heavy with solvent are stripped of solvent in the Cartridge Miser™. The stripped solvent is recovered for re-use.

Larry Rossignol

Figure 5
Solvent Recovery Unit and Dry Cleaning Machine

With the refrigerated condenser system, the air that has been stripped of solvent can be returned directly to the dry cleaning machine, eliminating the need for external venting ducts.
Source: Spencer America Inc., 1982.

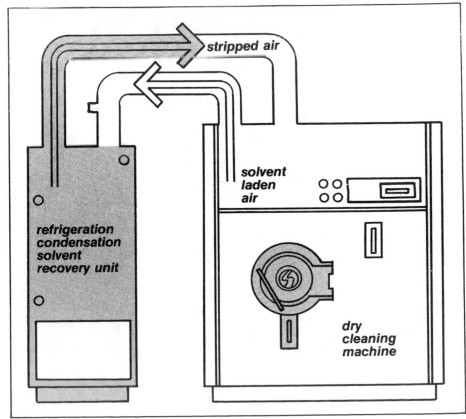

Figure 6
Refrigeration/Condensation System

Low temperature refrigeration is used to strip solvent from the air. As stripping is required for only a few minutes during aeration at the end of each drying cycle, the size of the refrigeration unit is kept to a minimum by using a cold storage system.
Source: Spencer America Inc., 1982.

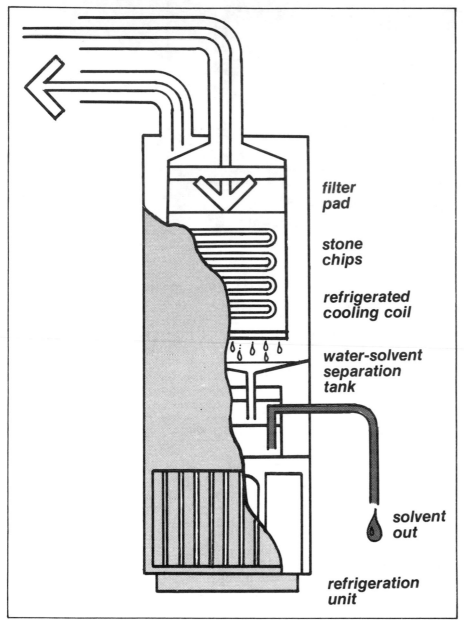

filter pad

stone chips

refrigerated cooling coil

water-solvent separation tank

solvent out

refrigeration unit

oils, lint, dirt, detergent and solvent. In Canada, it is common to landfill this waste. In the United States, land disposal of this waste must be in a secure landfill. A preferable management option is the use of still bottoms as an auxiliary fuel during high-temperature incineration.

Incineration of petroleum-laden dryer exhaust is feasible only if the plant has large on-site steam and heat requirements. Incineration without the benefits of heat recovery tends to be a less economical venture.

Fluorocarbon Plants

Historically, dry cleaning equipment designed to use fluorocarbon solvents was the best designed of the dry cleaning equipment, incorporating built-in controls and maximizing solvent recovery. As the price of other solvents increased, the engineering principles used in fluorocarbon equipment were applied to the design of perchloroethylene and petroleum dry cleaning equipment.

Conclusion

Technological innovation in the dry cleaning industry has moved into high gear, bringing with it an abundance of highly efficient, low-polluting equipment that promises to clean better, more safely and at a lower cost. In many instances, the larger dry cleaning establishments are losing money by not modernizing. The unnecessary loss of solvents, energy and water due to old, inefficient equipment will gradually eat into a company's profit margin.

For the small operator, the capital costs of modernization may be more difficult to overcome. However, in addition to investments in new equipment, there are more affordable measures such as good housekeeping practices that a business of any size can employ to minimize pollution. Good housekeeping practices to limit solvent emissions are an integral part of protecting the environment while enhancing company profits.

recovered materials grow with inflation.

Muck Stripping

During muck stripping, a vacuum assembly presses the filter cake to squeeze out residual solvent. Typically, the dry muck is then sealed in a bag for disposal. A muck stripper is now available that can recover Stoddard solvent for re-use. Solvent is squeezed out of the filter cake at a rate of about 0.3 gallons per pound. One commercially available model can handle 45 gallons of solvent before the muck must be emptied.[8]

Incineration of Still Bottoms and Dryer Exhaust

The wastes left in the bottom of the vacuum still typically contain

FOR FURTHER INFORMATION

Technical Assistance

Various suppliers of dry cleaning chemicals offer technical advice on how to increase solvent mileage.

PPG Industries have produced an informative binder on improving the dry cleaning process. Their publication is entitled *Operating Tips for Better Dry Cleaning* and contains a series of bulletins on the handling and storage of chemicals, solvent efficiency inspection, solvent conservation, carbon adsorption, recovery drying, leak detection and regulations.

Contact: PPG Industries Inc.,
Chemical Division,
One Gateway Center,
Pittsburgh, Pennsylvania.
15222
(412) 434-3131

Associations

Contact your trade association for additional information on pollution prevention opportunities. Many of the following trade associations can provide more information on commercially available recycling equipment, technology transfer programmes, technical experts in the field, existing tax breaks and economic incentives, and upcoming regulations. If such information is presently unavailable, indicate to your trade association the importance of providing information on pollution reduction opportunities.

Canadian Cleaners and Launderers
Allied Trades Association,
Suite 307,
4920 de Maisonneuve Blvd. West,
Montreal, Quebec.
H3Z 1N1
(514) 487-2272

Dry Cleaners and Launderers
Institute,
49 Eglinton Avenue East,
Toronto, Ontario.
M4P 1G6
(416) 481-6881

Institute of Industrial Launderers,
Suite 613,
1730 M Street, NW,
Washington, D.C.
20036
(202) 296-6744

International Fabricare Institute,
12251 Tech Road,
Silver Spring, Maryland.
26904
(301) 622-1900

Laundry and Cleaners
Allied Trades Association,
543 Upper Valley Road,
Upper Montclair, New Jersey.
07043
(201) 744-0090

Journals

The following trade journals carry articles and advertisements on efficienut low-pollution equipment.

CANADIAN CLEANER AND
LAUNDERER,
Canadian Textile Journal
Publishing Company Ltd.,
Suite 307,
4920 de Maisonneuve Blvd. West,
Montreal, Quebec.
H3Z 1N1

AMERICAN DRYCLEANER,
American Trade Magazines Inc.,
500 N. Dearborn St.,
Chicago, Illinois.
60610

AMERICAN COIN-OP,
American Trade Magazines Inc.,
500 N. Dearborn St.,
Chicago, Illinois.
60610

INDUSTRIAL LAUNDERER,
Institute of Industrial Launderers,
1730 M Street, NW,
Washington, D.C.
20036

References

1. Ministry of Industry, Trade and Commerce (Canada). *Occupational Distribution of Employment: Canada and the Provinces*. December 1977.

2. U.S. Environmental Protection Agency. *Perchloroethylene Dry Cleaners — Background Information for Proposed Standards*. Office of Air Quality Planning and Standards, August 1980.

3. Watt, A. and Fisher, W.E. "Results of Membership Survey of Dry Cleaning Operation." *IFI Special Reporter No. 3-1*, January/February 1975.

4. U.S. Department of Health, Education and Welfare. *Bioassay of Tetrachloroethylene*. National Cancer Institute Carcinogenesis Technical Report Series No. 13, 1977.

5. Blair, A. *et al*. "Causes of Death Among Laundry and Dry Cleaner Workers." *American Journal of Public Health* 69(5), May 1979.

6. Laundry-Cleaning Council. "The Safe Handling of Perchloroethylene Dry Cleaning Solvent." *Canadian Cleaner and Launderer*, March/April 1980.

7. Paton, A.J. "Drycleaning Trends." *Canadian Cleaner and Launderer*, March/April 1980.

8. U.S. Environmental Protection Agency. *Environmental Regulations and Technology for the Dry Cleaning Industry*. May 1981.

9. U.S. Department of Health, Education and Welfare. *Recommended Standard for Occupational Exposure to Tetrachloroethylene*. Prepared by the National Institute of Occupational Safety and Health.

10. PPG Industries. "Distillation." *Operating Tips for Better Dry Cleaning*. Pittsburgh, Pennsylvania: PPG Industries.

11. PPG Industries. "Recovery Drying." *Operating Tips for Better Dry Cleaning*. Pittsburgh, Pennsylvania: PPG Industries, August 1973.

12. Arthur D. Little, Inc. *Engineering Control Technology Assessment of the Dry Cleaning Industry*. Washington, D.C.: National Institute for Occupational Safety and Health, October 1980.

13. Hasenclever, K. "How Technology and Detergent Chemistry Can Influence Dry Cleaning Efficiency." *Canadian Cleaner and Launderer*, January/February 1978.

14. "Survey Reveals National Average for Perc Mileage." *Drycleaners News,* August 1980.

15. R.R. Street and Company, Oak Brook, Illinois. Personal communication, August 1981.

16. Bond, Brian. Uni-Rent Ltd., Whitby, Ontario. Personal communication, May 1981.

17. "New Permacs Report High Solvent Mileage." *Canadian Cleaner and Launderer,* September/October 1980.

18. Igual, M. "Frimair Introduces New Line of Dry Cleaning Machines in North America." *Canadian Cleaner and Launderer,* November/December 1980.

19. PPG Industries. "The Carbon Adsorption Process." *Operating Tips for Better Dry Cleaning*. Pittsburgh, Pennsylvania: PPG Industries, October 1973.

20. "Vapor Adsorbers: Principles and Costs." *International Fabricare Institute Bulletin*. Silver Spring, Maryland: International Fabricare Institute, 1981.

21. Fisher, William. International Fabricare Institute, Silver Spring, Maryland. Personal communication, July 1981.

22. Spencer America Inc., St. Louis, Missouri (product literature).

23. "Spencer Saves at Crown Center Hotel." *Laundry News,* June 1980.

24. PPG Industries. "Reclaiming Perchloroethylene from Filter Sludges." *Operating Tips for Better Dry Cleaning*. Pittsburgh, Pennsylvania: PPG Industries, August 1973.

25. "The Drycleaning Filter." *American Drycleaner,* November 1978.

Electroplating

Electroplating is a process whereby an object, usually metallic but sometimes plastic, is coated with one or more relatively thin, tightly adherent layers of some other metal. This is achieved when an electric current is passed through a plating solution and the metallic ions in that solution adhere on one of the electrodes, ideally the product to be plated.[1]

Electroplating is required when the base material, selected for cost or structural reasons, does not possess the ideal surface characteristics (eg. corrosion protection, desired appearance, etc.). A list of the most common plating materials and their uses appears in Table 1.[2]

The Plating Process

During a typical electroplating run, the pieces to be plated are placed on conveyer racks and are dipped in a series of tanks in which cleaning, etching, plating and rinsing solutions are found. The excess process chemical must be removed by rigorous washing after each stage and this action produces large quantities of wastewater contaminated with acids, bases, cyanide, metals, brighteners, cleaners, oils and dirt.

Historically, the major waste concern was the destruction and removal of the more virulent toxics: the cyanide and the hexa-valent chromium. In addition to chromium salts and cyanides, electroplating wastewaters may contain heavy metals, phenols, phosphates, oil and pH fluctuations.[3] It is imperative that batch discharges of these materials are not released to bodies of water or biological sewage treatment plants. The biological floc of a municipal treatment plant can be completely destroyed by the sudden discharge of the toxic effluent of a plating factory.

Relatively small volumes of waste can wipe out the fish life of a large stream. For a plater who thinks in terms of percent solutions in his production facilities, it is sometimes difficult for him to think in terms of parts per million. A 1% solution (a weak solution to a plater) represents 10,000 ppm. A quantity as small as 1 ppm is sufficient to kill fish.[4]

Environmental concerns alone are not the only impetus for examining the wastestream of the electroplating industry. The tough economic conditions of the 1980s require the elimination of unnecessary inefficiency and waste. Rising water costs and water shortages demand reassessment of fresh water supplies. Waste dis-

---

Table 1

Composition of Plating Solutions*

Metal	Purpose	Plating Solutions	Composition of Plating Solutions
Copper	Printed circuit boards, undercoat in decorative finishes.	Plain cyanide	$CuCN$, $NaCN$, Na_2CO_3
		Rochelle cyanide	$CuCN$, $NaCN$, Na_2CO_3, $NaOH$, Rochelle salt
		Copper sulfate	$CuSO_4 \cdot 5H_2O$, H_2SO_4
		Copper fluoroborate	$Cu(BF_4)_2$
Nickel	Bright coating under thin Cr electroplate for decorative, corrosion- and wear-resistance purposes.	Watts	$NiSO_4$, $NiCl_2$, Ni, H_3SO_3
		Sulfamate	$NiCl_2$, $(NiSO_3NH_2)_2$, Ni, H_3BO_3
		Fluoroborate	$NiCl_2$, $Ni(BF_4)_2$, Ni, H_3BO_3
		Chloride	$NiCl_2$, Ni, H_3BO_3
Chromium	Decorative or industrial finishes.	Chromic acid	H_2CrO_4, H_2SO_4 or H_2SO_4, $F-$
Zinc	Protect iron and steel against corrosion.	Cyanide	$Zn(CN)_2$, $NaOH$, $NaCN$, Na_2S_5 or Na_2S_4,
		Noncyanide baths	$Zn_2P_2O_7$, Na citrate, EDTA
Cadmium	Corrosion protection.	Cyanide	CdO, Cd, $NaCN$, $NaOH$, Na_2CO_3
		Fluoroborate	$CdBF_4$, Cd, NH_4CN, H_3BO_3
Lead or lead-tin alloys	Improves solderability, coating properties and performance of steels, Al, Cu, Cu-alloys.	Fluoroborate	Pb, HBF_4, H_3BO_3, glue, resorcinal, gelatin, hydroquinone
Tin or tin alloys	Improve solderability, corrosion protection, antifriction properties.	Sulfate	$SnSO_4$, H_2SO_4, gelatin, B-naphthol
		Fluoroborate	Gelatin, B-naphthol, Sn, HBF_4,
		Halide	H_3BO_3, $SnCl_2$ or SnF_2
Gold	Engineering (switches, semi-conductors), decorative.	Cyanide	$AuCN$, KCN, K_2CO_3, K_2HPO_4, alloy metals
		Acid	$Au(Cn)_3$, $CN-$, citrates
Iron	Rare; for electroformed parts, dies, and cylinder liners.	Chloride	$FeCl_2$, $CaCl_2$
		Sulfate/chloride	$FeCl_2$, NH_4Cl, $FeSO_4$
		Fluoroborate	$Fe(BF_4)_2$, $NaCl$, H_3BO_3

*Data from Jacobsen, Kurt, and Laska, Richard, "Advanced Treatment Methods for Electroplating Wastes." *Pollution Engineering*, October, 1977.

Source: *Industrial Pollution Control: Issues and Techniques*. Van Nostrand Reinhold, 1981.

posal, treatment, and transportation costs are escalating at rates even beyond the increases due to inflation. Furthermore, raw materials, which are present in high volume in the wastes, are becoming increasingly expensive to obtain[5] (see Table 2).

The potential for water and metallic resource recovery in the electroplating field is great, and as yet, virtually untapped. An American study concluded that about 90% of firms use a simple detoxification and disposal treatment on their waste rather than any form of resource recovery. Some firms simply dilute their wastestream and dump it in the sewer system. This means vast quantities of copper, nickel, chromium and zinc are lost every year. For each pound of metal that leaves the plant plated on an automotive rim or piece of galvanized steel, 9 pounds leaves as a sludge in the wastewater stream.[6]

In the United States, about 24,000 tons of metals, worth $40 million, are discarded by electroplaters each year. This total includes over 6000 tons of chromium on essential material used in stress-resistant and heat-resistant alloys for application in jet engines. Chromium is also used for corrosion-resistant alloys and stainless steel. Over 90% of the annual requirements for chromium are filled by Soviet and South African sources. These supplies could be interrupted, leading to a critical shortfall in chromium availability.[7] It is important that industry uses and re-uses chromium as efficiently as possible.

Metal recovery technologies are both tried and proven. A number of progressive firms have used ion-exchange, evaporation, electrodialysis, ultrafiltration and reverse osmosis to reclaim plating metals, additives, cleaners and rinsewater for several years with great success.

An industry consultant estimated that it would be technically possible to recover about 80 to 90% of the copper, 30 to 40% of the zinc, 90 to 95% of the nickel, and 70 to 75% of the chromium presently being trucked as sludge to landfill sites or poured into drains across the country.[6] However, the economics of some of the more innovative recovery technologies favour the larger plater and may as yet be beyond the reach of some smaller firms.

Conventional Waste Treatment

The traditional treatment system for the wastewaters generated by the electroplating industry is based on the addition of chemicals that react with the soluble pollutants to produce insoluble byproducts. These byproducts settle out and are removed as a wet sludge and the water is discharged to the sewers. The diluted sludge is usually thickened before dumping in the most convenient landfill site (see Figure 1).

The chemical additives are an extra expense that must be borne by the operator. Their purchase, handling and storage costs must then be added to the replacement costs of the plating metals they are designed to remove. An additional cost is the disposal cost for the resultant sludge produced.

Either SO₂ gas or sodium trisul-

Table 2
Economic Penalty for Losses of Plating Chemicals

Chemical	Form	Cost (dollars per pound)			
		Replacement	Treatment	Disposal	Total
Nickel	As $NiSO_4$	$ .76	$ .34	$ .17	$1.27
	As $NiCl_2$	1.04	.35	.24	1.63
Zinc cyanide	Using Cl_2 for cyanide oxidation.	1.41	.86	5.00	7.27
	Using NaHSO for cyanide oxidation.	1.41	1.84	5.00	8.25
Chromic acid	Using SO_2 for chromic reduction.	.78	.58	.32	1.68
	Using $NaHSO_3$ for chromic reduction.	.78	.83	.32	1.93
Copper cyanide	Using Cl_2 for cyanide oxidation.	1.95	.86	.25	3.06
	Using NAOCl for cyanide oxidation.	1.95	1.84	.25	4.04
Copper sulfate		.56	.34	.17	1.07

Source: Control Technology for the Metal Finishing Industry: Evaporators. U.S. EPA, June 1979.

phate must be added with an appropriate pH depressant to reduce hexavalent chromium to a trivalent state in which it will precipitate out as a hydroxide. Cyanide in the wastewater can be oxidized to a bicarbonate and nitrogen with the addition of chlorine gas or sodium hypochlorite, but only under high pH conditions.

After further additions of caustic soda or sulphuric acid to neutralize the solution, coagulating agents (such as polymers, alum or ferrous sulphate) are required to increase the formation and settling of the sludges formed in a gravity clarifier.[5]

These systems are known as total waste "destruct" systems. All of an industry's waste is generally pooled and the valuable bath chemicals and the treatment additives are tossed into the ground leaving no option for recovery or re-use — a prime example of throwing the baby out with the bath water. Once such a system is installed, usually at considerable expense, there is often reluctance to make further expenditures on the installation and operation of the new recovery systems.

Unfortunately "destruct" is somewhat of a misnomer. A water pollution problem is simply converted into a (solid) waste disposal problem. The wet toxic sludges produced are becoming less acceptable for land disposal. The metal components may become a major source of ground water contamination. The disposal costs of such sludges are escalating rapidly and the number of sites available for their final deposition is decreasing. Government regu-

Figure 1
Simplified Conventional Wastewater Treatment for Electroplating Wastes

In conventional treatment of electroplating wastewater, chemical reagents are added to react with the soluble pollutants, resulting in the production of insoluble, metal-laden sludge. The wet sludge is dewatered or thickened, and then disposed at a landfill site.
Source: Control Technology for the Metal Finishing Industry: Evaporators, U.S. Environmental Protection Agency, June 1979.

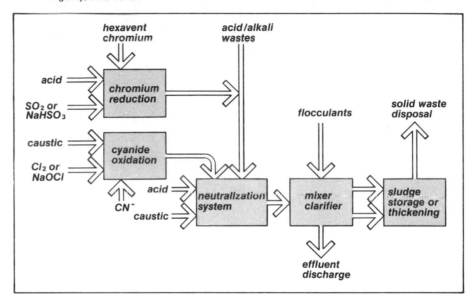

lations may soon require such wastes to undergo further treatment such as encapsulation or solidification subsequent to their disposal in "secure chemical landfills", so as to limit the leaching out of their toxic components. The cost of disposal has increased an average of 500% in the last four years, a trend that will continue as regulators attempt to limit this potential source of drinking water contamination.

New developments in resource recovery technology in the last five years, including efficiency improvements and adaptations that make them attractive to smaller waste generators, offer electroplaters increasingly attractive economic incentives to make the necessary capital investments in recycling.

This chapter will investigate some of the technical advances in resource recovery and a few simple process adaptations that reduce the effluent load and retain valuable plating chemicals in the system.

POLLUTION PREVENTION OPPORTUNITIES

1.
Good Housekeeping and Process Modification

"Just as the failure of medicine is surgery, so then the failure of process is wastewater . . . Perhaps the best perspective is obtained if this word is always both pronounced and spelled *waste* water."[8]

Wastewater costs have increased dramatically in recent years and have expanded to include:

1. Increased cost of water (either produced or purchased).
2. The cost of chemicals lost in the wastewater.
3. Capital for wastewater control facilities and equipment.
4. Operation and maintenance costs (chemicals, labour and

maintenance).

5. Skilled technical supervision.
6. Municipal sewer discharge fees and solid waste disposal.

The net cost of wastewater treatment can be staggering. Superior process technology should be assessed and incorporated whenever feasible before surrendering valuable residues and process water to traditional treatment (flocculation, etc.) and discharge. The first step in revising process efficiency involves an inventory to identify sources of wastewater. Major sources include:

1. Rinsewater —the major component of the wastewater stream. Rinsing is necessary to remove excess process solution or because of the limited tolerance of a particular process solution to a process solution preceding it.

2. Spills, drips, leaks and clean-up wastes.

3. Other accidental losses — those of a large scale not usually accommodated by the process and of great expense because of inherent value, disrupted production and damage liability.

4. Intentional process solution dumps — the disposal of rejected process bath waters is expensive (lost chemicals) and a threat to product quality, which will vary from excellent quality with fresh baths to lower levels with baths that are near to reject. Systems that can maintain the quality of the baths while retaining valuable chemicals from the wastewater stream will safeguard the plater from both these problems.

5. Wastestreams may also be distinguished from process treatment devices (filter cleaning wastes and ion-exchange regeneration wastes) and ventilation collection systems.

For existing plating operations, the measurement of wastewater volumes and a chemical component analysis will be necessary for a waste inventory.

This will allow the selection of the appropriate waste reduction system. The cost of lost chemicals can be calculated and will set the cost parameters for a complete process review with the aim of eliminating, recovering and reducing waste.

Before the installation of any of the complex recovery systems, it is possible for the electroplater to institute a number of line modifications, of minimal capital cost, that may reduce the waste load of his operation. If the manager always keeps in mind that the prime way to limit waste losses is to minimize the toxic contaminants reaching the effluent, some savings are possible. Potential improvements include:[9]

1. Properly designed and racked parts to minimize the drag-out or drag-in of process solutions. For example, a drain station ahead and after an automatic barrel plating line for cyanide-zinc plating will cut the waste treatment chemical cost in half.

2. Counter-current rinsing using at least 3 to 4 overflow tanks where space permits. Chemical losses due to drag-out may be cut almost entirely.

3. Substituting a presently used processing solution with one that contains less toxic materials. For example, corrosive and highly concentrated acidic bright dip solutions, which also generate toxic gases during processing, can be replaced by a solution with no ventilation requirements, and the possibility of metal recovery. Similarily cyanide-containing solutions may be replaced, as can chelated cleaners.

4. Surfactants or other wetting agents can be added to cleaning solutions, anodizing baths or plating tanks to reduce surface tension. By breaking surface tension, the volume of solutions carried out of the tank on a product can be cut by as much as one-half.

5. Superior housekeeping will minimize possible drips, leaks and spills.

6. Maximum drip-time in line operation, possibly in connection with air blow-off. Automatic hoist machinery can regularize and maximize this procedure, holding plated parts for a few moments over the plating bath tank.

Counter-Current Rinsing

After a rack of parts to be coated is dipped in a series of etching and plating solutions, it is immersed in a series of rinse tanks to remove the excess plating solution. Much of the plating material is "dragged out" of the plating bath and removed in the rinsewater. As much as 90% of the chrome plating material is lost into the wastewater stream in this manner, for only the thinnest coat adheres to the treated product.

As the dipped part travels on its automatic hoist down the electroplating line, it is successively washed in cleaner and cleaner rinsewater in a number of rinse tanks (see Figure 2). To conserve water, rinsewater is often added to the system in a continuous flow that is counter to the progress of the hoist. Clean water is added to the last rinse tank and overflows down the row of rinse tanks until the water leaving the first rinse tank contains the greatest concentration of excess chrome or nickel plating solution. Most platers use three to five of these rinse tanks after each plating or etching bath.

Electroplaters have to be exacting with the rinse specifications of a plating run. The proper rinsing of a rack of products, if using only one tank, could require copious amounts of water. The total washwater used is significantly reduced with the addition of each counter-flow rinse tank.

The major saving for both chemical wastewater treatment and recovery systems comes in dramatically reducing the quantity of wastewater that needs treating. The counter-current rinsing system reduces the volume loads that must be handled by recovery or treatment systems. The use of a recovery system offers further savings on reduced sludge disposal costs and a lessened need for new treatment chemicals and replacement plating materials.

For example, a 33-ounce-to-the-gallon bath is rinsed to the excellent standard of 0.001 ounce to the gallon. For a four-gallon-per-hour drag-out (i.e. 4 gal of excess plating material are pulled out of the bath and must be

Figure 2
Counter-Current Rinse System

Counter-current rinsing is used to reduce the total amount of water required to rinse the product. The product is rinsed first in the most contaminated rinse bath, and last in the cleanest bath. Clean water is added to the last rinse tank, which overflows up the row of rinse tanks in a direction opposite to the movement of the product.

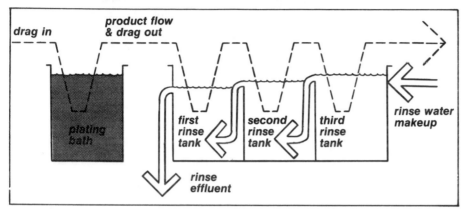

washed clean) the amount of rinsewater required is as follows:

Single rinse tank   132,000 gal/hr
2 tank counter-flow   740 gal/hr
3 tank counter-flow   126 gal/hr
4 tank counter-flow   53 gal/hr
5 tank counter-flow   32 gal/hr

On a standard line there are probably 10 rinse systems following plating and etching baths. By using five rinse counter-flow tanks instead of one, the hourly production of wastewater can be cut from 1.3 million gallons to only 320 gallons. But whether over a million gallons or only a few hundred gallons of wastewater are produced, their total metallic load is identical.

The wastewater from the contaminated first rinse is removed and either directed to a waste treatment facility or to one of the resource recovery units commercially available. Although recovery systems can reduce the overall size and costs of wastewater chemical destruct and clarifier systems, the capital cost savings are not major because of the need to install conventional destruct systems to handle spills, contaminated loads and open cycle washwaters.

■ Six years ago California Electroplating (Los Angeles, California) upgraded their line to minimize their water use and cut down on nickel and chrome drag-

out.[10] The company now has four counter-flow rinses after each plating stage on the line. In the case of the nickel plating operation, the four rinses feed back to a drag-out rinse which feeds directly to the nickel bath itself.

In addition, the firm has installed spray nozzles over each rinse and plating tank to wash drag-out back into that tank. Instead of deionized water, the rinsing rack carrier activates a time switch to pump rinsewater from the neighbouring more dilute tank

through the spray nozzles.

The rinse modifications have dramatically reduced nickel and chromium use and almost eliminated the need to add sulphate and chloride to the nickel bath.

2.
Electrolytic Metal Recovery

Electrolytic metal recovery is finding application with electroplaters, rolling mills, printed circuit board manufacturers, and metal coating firms. It is showing good results in the recovery of gold, silver, tin, copper, zinc, solder alloy and cadmium. The concept is relatively simple — a direct electric current is passed through a metal-bearing solution by means of cathode plates and insoluble anodes. This is essentially the same process that is used in electroplating.

The bath and rinse solutions found in the plant are excellent electrolytes to enhance the process because they contain strong acids, bases or salts that are able to conduct current efficiently. As the current flows from the anode (+) to the cathode (−), the positive metallic ions are attracted to the cathode plate and deposited there. This deposition continues as long

Figure 3
Typical Plating Application

A rinse station recovery system, which circulates rinse through an electrolytic plating recovery cell.
Source: "How to Electrolytically Recover Metals from Finishing Operations," *Industrial Finishing,* April 1980.

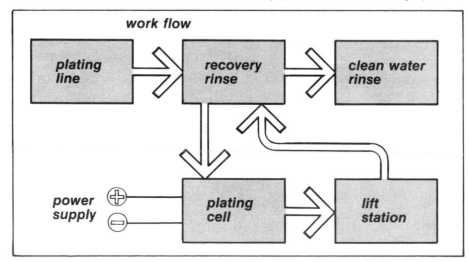

as the current is present and sufficient electrolyte exists[11] (see Figures 3 and 4).

The metal is usually allowed to build up until it reaches a thickness of ¹/₂ inch. The power is shut down and the cathode is removed and rinsed. Then a paint scraper or chisel is tapped with a hammer to loosen the top of the deposited metal plate. Once the top edge has been started, the slabs will peel easily off the cathode. After another cleaning, the cathode can be reinstalled and recovery resumed. The stripping takes about ten minutes.[11]

The metal recovered as a foil, or in some applications as a powder, is as pure as the process solution from which it was lost. It therefore has a high resale value, especially any silver and gold which is recovered.

The most advanced electrolytic cell designs can recover 99% of the metal in rinse solutions, although simpler, cheaper models routinely recover 90 to 95% of available metals.[12]

The technique is not labour-intensive and does not have a large energy requirement. Integrating this system into an existing plating operation is easily accomplished because an existing rinse tank can be converted into a recovery rinse station to feed the metal-containing solution to the cell. Nothing else is needed except for a circulating pump.

■ A Canadian company is at the forefront of electrolytic recovery technology. H.S.A. Reactors Limited (Toronto, Ontario) was incorporated in 1975 to develop the High Surface Area cathode (H.S.A.) based on the research of two British chemists. H.S.A. Reactors now employs nearly 60 people, half of whom are involved in research and development in their laboratory and production facility.[13]

In the H.S.A. system, the first tank after the plating bath becomes a still rinse with its contents continuously circulating through the electrolytic cell (see Figure 5). The drag-out solution enters the reactor where the cyanide is destroyed and the cadmium or other metals are deposited upon the cathode. It is possible to reduce the metallic concentration of the rinsewater to undetectable levels if a large enough reactor is used, although normal recovery runs about 98%. The H.S.A. cathode achieves its high surface area by incorporating a large number of carbon filament mats. These mats collect the metals from the still rinse bath during plant operations.

When operations cease plating, vat solution is drawn from the bath into a separate compartment of the reactor where this solution removes the metal from the cathode by an electrochemical or sometimes chemical process. In

Figure 4
Typical Metal Finishing Application

A metal finishing recovery operation, which circulates the process bath through an electrolytic plating recovery cell.
Source: "How to Electrolytically Recover Metals from Finishing Operations," *Industrial Finishing,* April 1980.

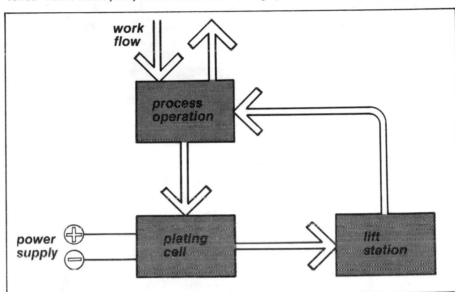

Figure 5
HSA Cadmium Recovery Unit

The pretreatment tank, the first tank after the plating bath, functions as a still rinse with its contents continuously circulating through the recovery unit. Cyanide is destroyed and the cadmium or other metals are deposited on the cathode of the recovery unit. When plating operations cease, cadmium is removed from the cathode using an electrochemical process.
Source: HSA Reactors Ltd., Toronto, Ontario.

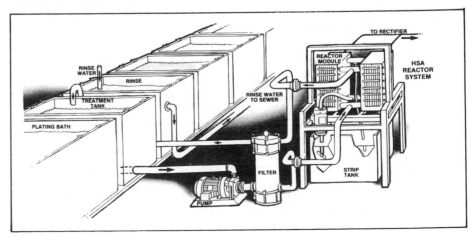

HSA Reactors Ltd.

HSA metal recovery system installed in a typical electroplating facility, showing high surface area carbon fibre recovery module, control box containing microprocessor and strip tank for reclamation of recovered metal.

effect, bath solution is used in a reverse plating operation and the recovered metal is returned to the bath.

■ An H.S.A. reactor was installed at the X-pert Metal Finishing plant (Burlington, Ontario) early in 1981. The X-pert facility was constructed in 1973 to plate a variety of parts including screws, bolts and fasteners. The plant plates zinc, copper, cadmium and tin.

The H.S.A. system was designed to recover cadmium and destroy cyanide. The X-pert staff have noticed "a significant increase in the quantity of material plated per dollar of cadmium input . . . as well as lower cadmium readings." Recent tests have confirmed the H.S.A. reactor is effectively recovering 99% of the cadmium load and destroying most of the cyanide load.[14]

The company still has a few bugs to work out. The rinsing procedures will have to be modified to eliminate some residual contamination that is occurring in the rinse tank. However the company is pleased with the savings realized which are largely due to decreased disposal costs. They are considering adding metal recovery units on the zinc and copper lines.

■ Allied Metal Finishing (Baltimore, Maryland) serves a variety of industrial customers in the Baltimore-Washington area. About 10% of its business is cadmium plating. With American regulators turning their attention to cadmium discharges, a number of platers are getting out of that part of the business. Allied Metal Finishing had a maximum cadmium effluent level of 1.22 ppm. New counter-current water conservation methods were going to raise that concentration even higher.

Vice president Phil Horelick decided to invest in electrolytic cadmium recovery and bought a H.S.A. reactor. The cadmium in Allied's effluent dropped to well below the toughest standards that may be set by the United States Environmental Protection Agency and the company is able to pick up some of the cadmium plating business being discarded by other operators unable to meet the strict limits. Allied is more than pleased with its resource recovery investment. "But the clincher," according to Phil Horelick, "is that (the system) doesn't create any sludge. With the money I don't have to spend on chemicals to create a sludge, and on shipping and landfill fees to dispose of it, I can pay back the cost of the reactor in a year and a half. Maybe less."[15]

■ With the doubling of the cad-

mium plating sales and reduced bills for new cadmium supplies, the pay-back period may be cut even further. One 60,000-square-foot plant contemplating a metal resource recovery installation calculated that such an undertaking would net the company an annual saving of $17,560. Reduced process water and chemical usage would yield an annual savings of $26,060, whereas the cost of the recovery operation is estimated at only $8500.[13]

The most impressive savings result from the reduced waste disposal charges. One pound of metal produces about 21 pounds of "dry waste" in conventional wastewater treatment plants. In the United States, where more stringent disposal regulations are coming into effect, this sludge may cost $100 to $150 per barrel to dispose.[13]

Zinc that used to retail for 10-15¢ a pound now goes for 40-50¢ and the treatment and disposal costs may top $5.00 a pound for the sludge it generates.

It is obvious that a recovery technique that works especially well on cadmium, zinc and copper plating solutions makes economic sense.

■ Ian Heath Ltd. (Birmingham, England) is a silver plating firm. In October of 1979, when the cost of silver was skyrocketing, the firm took advantage of the high prices to install an electrolytic cell for recovering plating silver. The unit paid for itself in eight weeks.[16]

The cell is being marketed under the name Chemelec by BEWT (Water Engineers). The system is a small module containing 12 electrodes of expanded steel mesh (see Figure 6). The unit uses a fluidized bed technique, with rinse solution pumped up through a layer of glass beads. The turbulence created prevents a boundary layer forming around the electrodes and allows the efficient removal of silver from solutions containing as little as 50 ppm of silver.[17]

At Ian Heath, the running rinse tank following the silver plating step was converted to a static drag-out rinse tank and the resultant dilute drag-out solution is recirculated through the adjacent Chemelec cell. At night, the contents of this tank are transferred to an overnight treatment tank and the recovery unit works through the night to recover 99.5% of the silver in the drag-out solution. The cell requires about £1.5 of electricity for each kilogram of recovered silver.

Electrolysis recovery for dilute solutions would not be feasible if it were not for the fluidized bed of glass beads which constantly scrub the surface of the electrode, bringing it fresh solution when the ion concentration has been depleted near the surface.[18] The recovered metal forms a hard deposit on the electrodes, which are manufactured of an inert material. The electrodes are removed at regular intervals and the deposited metal can either be used directly in the plating bath or refined by a metal dealer.

Ian Heath also uses the units on its lines to collect nickel and copper. Gold and cadmium could also be recovered with the Chemelec cell, but not chromium from dilute solutions.

Ian Heath, who electroplate giftware, paid £8000 for their silver recovery cell and anticipate savings of £50-100,000 a year.[19]

The £7000 nickel recovery cell is collecting 14 kg of that metal each week, which is returned directly to the plating tank. The company's £5600 copper recovery unit is capable of retrieving 20 kg of copper a week which is used directly on the plating line.

■ Ecologica Engineering (Macclesfield, England) has developed a continuously operating electrolytic cell, the Eco Cascade™, to recover copper, zinc, silver, nickel and gold from dilute solutions.[20] The unit uses a series of rotating cylinder electrodes within membrane cells. As a solution passes through a series of compartments, up to one-half of the metal content is removed in each. Rinsewaters containing only 100 to 150 ppm of metal can be treated to less than 1 ppm.

3.
Evaporators

Evaporators for material recovery and water re-use in the electroplating field are a proven technology with expanding applications. Quite simply, an evaporator distills rinsewater from the plating line until the chemicals remaining in the wastewater are concentrated to a level that allows their re-use in the plating baths. Because an energy source is needed to evaporate off the excess water, these systems operate most cost-effectively under conditions where the rinsewater is not too dilute. Counter-current rinse systems can be used to concentrate plating chemicals to the point where an evaporator can be used to good effect. The water vapour distilled off and condensed can be returned to the rinse tanks.

While a closed-loop recovery system will maximize the return of valuable plating chemicals to the plating tank, it is possible to reduce the operating and capital costs and still maintain a high recovery rate by open-loop rinsing [21] (see Figure 7). If the evaporator unit is designed to operate with the wastewater from only the first one or two rinse tanks, its evaporative capacity, and thus its capital and operating costs, can be cut nearly in half. Because the open-loop system will not be supplying all the rinsewater for the system, a constant new supply will be required and wastewater treatment will be needed for the contents of the later, more dilute, counter-current rinsewater tanks.

Some of the plating material in the drag-out will be irrecoverably lost as sludge but recovery can still average 90-95% by evaporative treatment. The last rinses will contain 5 to 10% of the metallic plating material and thus require waste treatment before release but the cost of the chemicals for that treatment and the subsequent need for sludge disposal will be drastically reduced.[22]

In the case of a chrome plating operation, the use of sodium metabisulphite for the reduction and subsequent precipitation of

Figure 6
The Chemelec Cell

The Chemelec cell is an electrolytic unit for recovering plating silver. The module contains 12 electrodes of expanded steel mesh.
Source: "Fluidized Beds Offer Savings in Electroplating," *Production Engineer,* July/August 1981.

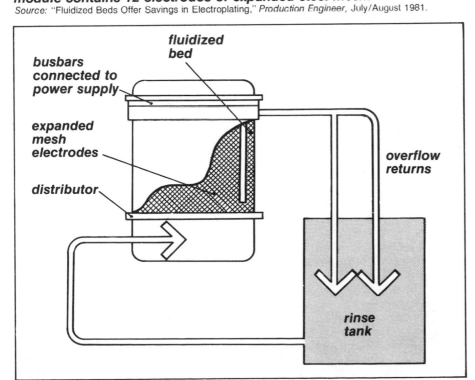

hexavalent chromium can be cut by 90%. In an operation where drag-out of a chrome bath is 3 gal per hour, sludge production is reduced by 162,000 lb (74 tonnes) per year (assuming a 20% by weight solids sludge).

Evaporator Types

Four types of evaporators are in use in the electroplating field. These are: rising film evaporators; flash evaporators; submerged tube evaporators; and atmospheric evaporators.[5]

Rising Film Evaporators

Rising film evaporators use a shell and tube heat exchanger to break the wastewater down into a vapour/droplet mixture. Plating chemicals break down under high temperature. The evaporator applies heat to the wastewater under low pressure conditions (the lower the pressure, the lower the boiling point). The evaporative heating surface is covered by a thin film of wastewater and separates the rinsewater from the steam or hot water heat source. From the reboiler unit, the vapour droplet mixture enters a separator unit from which the water vapour is pulled off, condensed and replaced into the rinse tanks. The concentrated plating solution is continually rerouted through the reboiler unit until it reaches concentrations high enough to allow its return to the plating bath. Depending on the system, this may happen continuously, or the plating solution may collect in a holding tank and be used to top off the bath at periodic intervals.

The rising film evaporator is flexible in terms of operation and offers minimal disruption of the plating operation. The labour requirements are often less than one-half hour per shift and radically reduce the continual need to make up the plating bath.

Flash Evaporators

Flash evaporators are essentially identical to rising film evaporators except in the source of supplementary heat. During plating, the temperature of the plating bath is constantly raised by waste heat generated by the electrolytic process. In a flash evaporator, plating solution from the bath is constantly being recirculated through the separator unit of the evaporator. Because the bath temperature is higher than the low pressure boiling point in the unit, a small portion of the plating solution vaporizes in the separator. Heat is supplied to the wastewater being evaporated and the plating solution drops in temperature and returns to the bath tank.

To save 1 pound of steam, approximately 5 gallons (19 litres) of plating solution must be flash cooled 25°C. This limits the application of flash evaporators to large, high-temperature plating installations.

Submerged Tube Evaporators

Submerged tube evaporators supply the energy for distilling off the wastewater with heating coils immersed in a holding tank of boiling rinsewater. Thus the plating solution is not recirculated continuously through the reboiler unit and the single unit construction reduces the initial capital cost (although not the operating steam requirements).

Atmospheric Evaporators

Atmospheric evaporators require a continual flow of air which is humidified by the wastewater, drawn off and expelled. Because the rinsewater is not captured, and escapes with some of the heat from the evaporator, this system requires about 20% more steam

Figure 7
Open Loop Rinsing

Open loop rinsing utilizes recovery on the most concentrated rinse or rinses, and conventional treatment on the cleanest final rinse. This mode of operation minimizes recovery costs.
Source: "How to Use Evaporative Recovery in Treating Wastes," *Industrial Finishing*, November 1980.

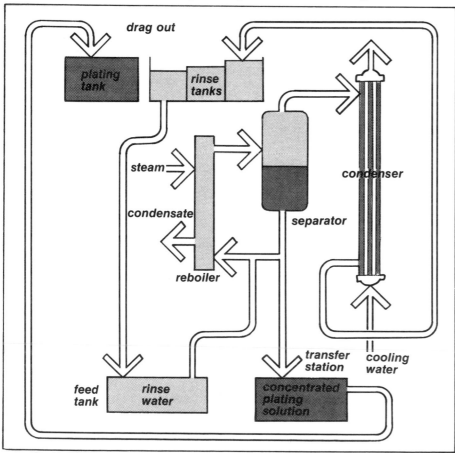

heat than the other systems. It also requires the rinse tanks to be topped up with deionized water to allow proper rinsing and reduce scale build-up in the evaporator. This system does not require a condenser or cooling water system.

Experience with evaporator systems shows that operating and maintenance costs are minimal. Most operations suffer little or no down time. The major expense is the cooling water and heating requirement. Approximately 1.1 pound of steam is needed to evaporate each pound of wastewater, although there appears ample opportunity to recapture and re-use that heat in both the recovery and other plant operations.

It is also possible to reduce steam demand by making use of some of the heat trapped by the vapour in the separator. By using a "double-effect" evaporator system, the heated vapour from the separator is then used to heat rinsewater in a second evaporator unit. The need for a second evaporator and separator raises the capital cost of the system while cooling water (for condensing) and steam costs are cut by 50%. It is possible to reclaim materials from two different plating baths simultaneously using this system.

A mechanical compressor can also remove the need for boilers and condensers. However, its use is limited to alkaline plating solutions. The corrosion caused by acidic solutions would soon render it useless.

An electroplater's competitive edge requires that he maximize the conservation of his materials, energy and water. An operator who cannot efficiently produce a quality product at an acceptable price does not survive.

■ In California, the need to conform to strict limitations on plant effluents and serious constraints on fresh industrial water supplies have placed considerable pressure on electroplaters in that state. Modern Plating (Los Angeles, California) plates steel automotive rims and other automotive parts in a large 75,000-square-foot complex. A four-hoist programmed rack-plating installation can apply a 25-micrometre coat of nickel plus a 0.25-micrometre layer of chromium to 4000 wheel rims each day.[22]

When Modern Plating installed their nickel chromium rack line (at 8000 sq feet; it is the largest on the west coast), they also instituted a water and materials recovery programme. Currently the programme has resulted in the saving of 400,000 gallons of rinsewater a month plus plating chemicals. Future savings are expected to be greater.

Modern Plating maintains a double line of 14-foot-long tanks, 5½ feet deep (solution volumes are usually 1600 gal or 2300 gal). The first row is comprised of facilities for loading, cleaning, acid dipping, required rinsing and three semi-bright nickel plating tanks. A shuttle with a stainless steel drip pan transfers the racks with their loads of rims to the second row with its three bright nickel tanks, two third-layer nickel tanks, two chromium plating tanks and final rinsing, drying and unloading operations.

Modern Plating's conservation programme begins even before the car parts are loaded on the racks to begin the trip down the plating lines. All the parts to be plated are power washed or vapour degreased prior to being brought to the plating department. By this action the lifetime of the presoak cleaner has been extended threefold and rejects are more easily eliminated.

A series of stand counter-flow rinses was installed after nickel and chromium plating to minimize water use and maximize rinsing. To conserve chemicals and reduce the solution carry-over between tanks, the automatic hoist removes a rack of parts and holds still above the process tank for 15 seconds before moving to the next tank. To conserve cleaners and improve rinsing, deionized water is sprayed over the rack of parts as it is removed from each cleaner tank and rinse tank.

Float-actuated pumps automatically transfer rinsewater up to the preceding drag-out tank to maintain the proper solution level in each tank. Drag-out rinsewater from the tanks is constantly being removed and treated in the company's most recent additions to its conservation technology — three evaporative recovery units.

Each 150 gal/hr unit evaporates chromium drag-out rinsewater. The water is distilled off under high temperature and low pressure, and after monitoring for purity, is returned to the final chromium rinse tank (at 147°F). When the remaining chromium solution is sufficiently concentrated, it is drawn off into a storage tank and eventually returned to the chromium plating tanks during weekend maintenance. A 200 gal/hr unit concentrates rinsewater from the nickel rinse tanks. Distilled water from this unit is returned to the final counter-flow nickel rinse tank at about 180 gal. The nickel solution is carbon treated after pH adjustment, sulphur is removed by chemical additions (potassium permanganate and activated carbon), and the settled, treated solution is filtered twice before being restored to the nickel tanks as required.

The entire evaporator system, including two gas-fired boilers, water cooling units, and storage tanks is located outside the plant proper but immediately adjacent to the line.

The distilled water returned to the rinse tanks is already heated to almost 150°F by the evaporator units. The tanks are lined inside and out to reduce heat loss and minimize corrosion and solution contamination. The final rinsing operations are carried out at 90°F (32°C) followed by hot air drying at 110°F (43°C), saving heat energy. Particular attention is also paid to the rack installation to reduce the waste of plating chemicals. Although the operation of the boilers for the evaporation units is a continuing expense, the heat transfer to the rinsing line and the subsequent energy savings in the drying phase helps recover some of the costs.[22]

■ Sommer Metalcraft (Crawfordsville, Indiana) used to consume 150 to 200 pounds of chromium each shift in its custom plating operation. After installing a closed-loop evaporator to allow the recovery of chromium from its

Figure 8
Closed-Loop Evaporator System at Sommer Metalcraft

In addition to recovering waste heat from the chromium plating tank, the evaporator system returns distilled water to the last (fourth) counter-current rinse tank. A continuously operating cation exchange unit removes copper ions and other contaminants from the rinsewater.

Source: "Recovery Pays at Sommer Metalcraft," *Industrial Finishing,* June 1980.

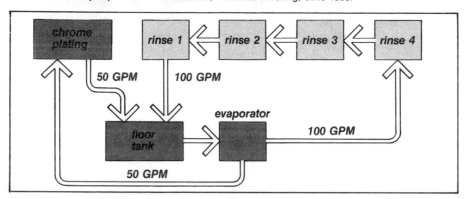

Corning evaporators are sized and specified to meet the particular needs of a company.

rinse tanks, the company uses less than 200 lb of the metal each month. The savings average 8000 lb a month or over $100,000 (U.S.) a year. The cost of the evaporator equipment, obtained from the Plaudler Division of Sybron Corporation, was recouped in the first year of operation.[23]

Sommer Metalcraft paints and plates steel wire to produce products ranging from bird cages to oven racks to novelty items. Its large plating machine not only consumed large amounts of valuable metal but the wastewater treatment facilities and expensive chemical destruct system churned out a large amount of sludge. Over 172,000 lb of sludge a month was an expensive disposal problem.

The closed-loop system returns rinsewater chromium to the chrome plating bath and 100 gal/hr of distilled water to the last (fourth) counter-flow rinse tank (see Figure 8). The closed nature of the system allows a slow build-up of contaminants in the plating bath. Although a continuously operating cation exchange removes positive copper ions, among others, from the rinsewater, not all the contaminants are trapped. The plating bath is decanted after four years' use, and about 500 gallons of residual sludge and bath fluids are disposed.[23]

The evaporator system also recovers waste electrolytic heat from the chromium plating tank. Bath waters are constantly drawn from the plating tank to maintain the bath at a constant level and transfer the waste heat to the evaporation process.

Company officials are impressed with the low maintenance requirements of the evaporator system. In six years of operation, the only unit shut down could have been avoided by stockpiling the proper spare parts. Plating superintendent Dick Stutzman says yearly maintenance consists of replacing one or two pump seals, five or six valve diaphrams and the monthly cleaning of calcium and iron build-up from the condenser.[23]

■ General Plating (Detroit, Michigan) has operated a rising film evaporator unit since 1975. The company, which chrome plates automotive parts, estimates that it has cut its chromic acid costs by 70%. In combination with a cation exchange column, the chromic acid discharge in the wastewater effluent is essentially zero.

As an added bonus, the evaporator also recovers a proprietary mist suppressant used at General Plating. The savings in chromic acid (350 lb/day), treatment chemicals and avoided disposal costs total more than $100,000 a year ($1.70 lb for 172 days).[24]

■ Hudson Bay Diecastings Ltd.

(Bramalea, Ontario) is an automotive parts plating firm. Zinc diecast parts are manufactured inhouse and plated to produce mirror casings, door handles and plumbing hardware. The company was experiencing a heavy chrome drag-out problem with cup-shaped products and blind holes in diecastings.

The two plating lines have been modified with extensive rinsing controls involving countercurrent flows and sprays which are set on timers, activated as parts exit a particular tank.[25]

In 1976 a chrome recovery sys-

tem was installed, consisting of a series of drag-out tanks, a cation scavenger and a Corning evaporator (see Figure 9). The evaporator system allows Hudson Bay to recover plating solutions with concentrations exceeding 70 ounces to the gallon.[24] The firm is presently reclaiming 90% of the chromic acid in the drag-out and returning it to the plating tank. They are now studying possible recovery systems for their nickel and copper solutions.

■ The Ford Motor Company (Saline, Michigan) installed three evaporator recovery units made by Corning Glass Works (Corning, New York) on the chromic and sulphuric acid baths in its plastic preplating line. The system has cut water costs on the rinse baths, returned chromic and sulphuric acid to the etching bath, eliminated sludge disposal and extended the bath life by reducing contamination.[26]

4.
Reverse Osmosis

Reverse osmosis combines physics with modern membrane technology. During the last decade thousands of reverse osmosis (R.O.) units have been used to desalt hundreds of millions of gallons of water throughout the world. A 58 million-gallon-a-day complex started up in 1979 in Saudi Arabia. A 100 mg/day installation is treating agricultural wastewater flowing into the Colorado River. The treatment of electroplating rinsewater has recently come to the forefront and shown excellent results.[27]

Reverse osmosis is based on the principle of natural osmosis. When a concentrated salt solution is separated from pure water by a semi-permeable membrane, the natural tendency is for the water to flow into the concentrated solution until some equilibrium is maintained. If the natural osmotic pressure is overcome by applying external force to the concentrated solution, then water can be made to flow from the salt solution through the membrane to the dilute solution[28] (see Figure 10).

Semi-permeable membranes re-

At Hudson Bay Diecastings Ltd., an automotive parts plating firm, zinc diecast parts are manufactured and plated in-house.

The Corning evaporator (centre cylinder) allows the company to recover chrome plating solutions for re-use.

Figure 9
Corning Evaporator Recovery System

This open loop flow diagram shows the general arrangement for partial recovery of plating solutions. Changeover to total recovery of drag-out involves only minor piping changes. Recovery requires the removal of contaminants. In the case of chrome solutions, a small cation exchanger is adequate for the removal of contaminants.
Source: Corning Glass Works Ltd., Corning, New York.

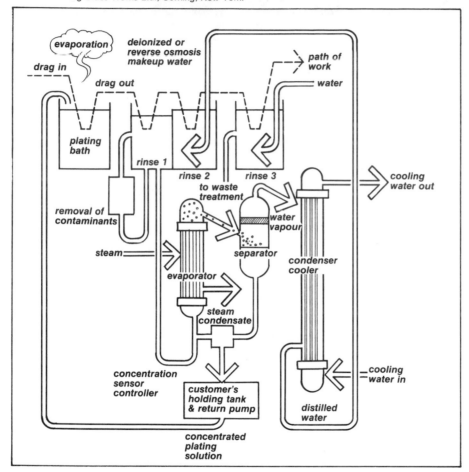

sist the movement of most dissolved minerals and organics. Either the molecules do not fit through the membrane pores or they are actively repelled by the composition and structure of the membrane. Membrane technology has been carried out by the National Research Council of Canada since the early 1960s. Much of the original work on cellulose acetate was done there. In recent years, new membrane materials such as polyamide, polyfurane and polysulfone have increased the applicability of R.O. to new wastewater streams.[29]

R.O. has been successfully used on the rinsewater from a number of electroplating baths. These include Watts nickel, nickel sulfamate, copper pyrophosphate,
nickel fluoroborate, zinc chloride, copper cyanide, zinc cyanide and cadmium cyanide. Chromic acid and high pH cyanide baths are not readily amenable to R.O. treatment.[2]

The R.O. treatment is an attractive option to electroplaters. The units are relatively small and the energy needed to concentrate a solution is about 200 times less than that needed for evaporation.[29] The product water usually contains less than 10% of the dissolved solids present in the wastewater stream, so this product can be returned directly to the last rinse tank.[27] The concentrate is replaced in the plating bath.

The operation and manpower requirements of R.O. are usually
limited to monitoring feedstock and effluent quality. Attention to these parameters will prevent membrane fouling and increase membrane life. The clogging of the membrane with suspended solids, organic brighteners or wetting agents may be significant in some operations, although reverse cycle and counter-current procedures have been developed to minimize this. Platers must be prepared to develop the skills necessary to ensure R.O. operates at its maximum efficiency.

A prime advantage of R.O. technology is that not only are metals recovered for return to the bath but all the other additives as well. However, this does not allow the mixing of three or four different types of nickel baths with different additives, for example.

One analyst has identified four reasons why reverse osmosis systems are not more widely used in the electroplating field:[30]
(1) The chemical limitations of available membranes have made many applications impractical.
(2) The absence of clearly defined federal regulations on waste discharge.
(3) The failure of R.O. system manufacturers to aggressively promote the economic benefits of the process, to provide test data on various applications and to offer total treatment systems.
(4) The normal reluctance of potential customers to purchase a new or "unproven" technology.

This analyst foresees a time when there will be a place for reverse osmosis to be a part of virtually every total waste treatment system.

■ Electrohome Ltd. (Kitchener, Ontario) manufactures a line of reverse osmosis equipment for water purification and water treatment based on cellulose acetate membranes.

The system uses a series of 1.5-metre-long cylindrical modules containing a number of fibreglass tubes supporting the membrane. More modules can be connected to the pump and control system depending on the volume of rinsewater needing treatment.

An Ontario electroplater using the Electrohome system previously lost 11 kilograms of plating

Figure 10
Tubular Reverse Osmosis

By applying external pressure to a concentrated salt solution, water can be made to flow from the salt solution through the semi-permeable membrane to the dilute solution.

Source: "Reverse Osmosis," *Water and Sewage Works*, Reference Issue, 1979.

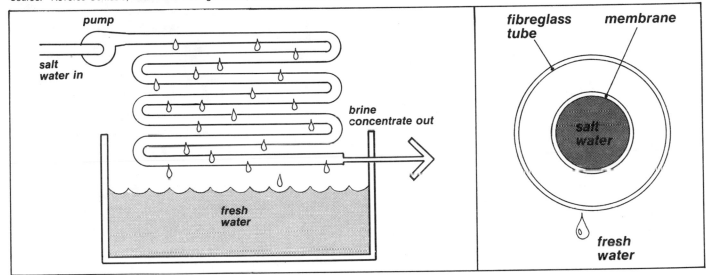

metals and 1 litre of brightener each operating day. The cost of the lost nickel sulfate, nickel chloride, brighteners and rinsewater totalled $23 a day and over one hundred kilograms of sludge were generated for disposal.[29]

The installation of an R.O. unit cost the firm $16,000 and entailed operating expenses, primarily membrane replacement, of $6.30 a day. The unit was able to recover virtually all of the lost chemical for the bath unit and 90% of the water from the 260-litre-per-hour feed stream. The unit was thus able to pay for itself in 20 months and eliminated the need for costly destruct treatment systems and waste disposal.

■ Teijin Ltd. (Japan) has begun manufacturing reverse osmosis equipment utilizing some of the newly developed membrane material.[29] Polybenzimidozolone (PBIL) significantly extends the range of acidity and temperature the units can be exposed to. The tolerance to pH ranging from 1 to 12 allows the membrane to be cleaned more readily and may extend the lifetime by avoiding clogging. Clogging is the main limitation of the R.O. process. The Teijin equipment has already been used to handle nickel plating rinsewater.

5.
Ion Exchange

Ion exchange technologies have been used for nickel recovery on electroplating lines for some time.[31] Ion exchange can also be used for concentrating the chemical contaminants in rinsewaters and anodizing baths, and produces, as a byproduct, deionized water, which can be used in rinse tanks or for preparing new plating solutions. For example, when rinsewaters from a chromium plating line are passed through an ion exchange column, the chromium chemicals can be reclaimed by backwashing the anion column. At the same time, impurities such as trivalent chromium, copper, zinc, nickel and iron can be trapped and removed in the anion column. These contaminants can be backwashed out and resulting concentrated solution can be sent to the waste treatment centre.[32]

The ion exchange system allows the reconcentration of valuable chemicals and the re-use of the rinsewaters. Using ion exchange, it is possible to remove, for instance, the aluminum from a chromic acid anodizing bath and avoid the need for the periodic

disposal of the bath waters.

The basis of the ion exchange system is the ability of certain resins to act on ion solutions and selectively replace some of their own ions with ions from the solution. The process is essentially cyclic. The solution being treated passes through the resin until its absorption capacity is exhausted. Then the resin is regenerated by another chemical that replaces the ions given up by the ion exchange process, converting the resin back to its original composition.[33]

For the processing of nickel plating rinsewater, the process would be as follows. The rinsewater would be pumped through a cation exchanger operating on the hydrogen cycle where the nickel ions are exchanged. The water then passes through an anion exchanger operating on the hydroxide cycle, where the remaining anionic components are exchanged and the purified water recycled to the rinse system (see Figure 10, Waste Recovery Technologies Chapter).

The cation exchanger is regenerated with sulphuric acid and a concentrated solution of nickel sulphate is eluted with a residual of sulphuric acid. The anion exchanger is regenerated with sodium hydroxide and the spent regenerate is discharged as waste.[31]

Since ion exchange units are susceptible to fouling by certain organic compounds including oil, some wetting agents and organic brighteners, it is often necessary to insert a carbon filter into the system to intercept these materials from the rinsewater before it enters the ion exchangers. Normally, parallel ion exchange systems are employed. This set-up allows one system to be backwashed while the other is on-stream.

New developments in fast-cycling, small bed ion exchange systems, moving bed ion exchange columns and reciprocating flow ion exchange have done much to reduce the space requirements and increase the versatility and capacity of the technique. Because ion exchange does not recycle organics, one unit can handle several different organic nickel plating baths. This is the system's major drawback as well. The spent regenerate with its load of sodium, chloride, sulphate, borate and organics is discharged as waste. This is not as serious a constraint as it may seem. The major expense in making a nickel plating bath is the nickel salt. Boric acid is responsible for about 4% of the total cost, organics 5% and nickel over 90%. Thus a system which can reduce new bath costs by 90% and cut sludge production by 98% is an enormous improvement over conventional precipitation methods.

■ Eco-Tec Limited (Toronto, Ontario) has taken the ion exchange concept and adapted it to fill the needs and budgets of smaller electroplating firms. Their system, the Reciprocating Flow Ion Exchanger (RFIE) is based on a very short ion exchange column which operates on a very short cycle of flow, regeneration and washing. Traditional units could take more than two hours to absorb ions fully, segregate them and regenerate the resins. The RFIE goes through the whole cycle in a matter of minutes. It is also much smaller and hence more affordable. In the RFIE system, the resin is regenerated long before it reaches saturation. This reduces the cycle time and takes advan-

tage of the very high initial ion exchange rates. The short bed also allows the use of very fine resins that maximize the surface area and minimize flow problems such as maldistribution and channelling.[34]

RFIE also takes advantage of counter-current regeneration which is designed to keep the lighter fluid on top. In cation regeneration, the sulphuric acid is pumped into the resin bed in a direction opposite to which the bed was loaded. The regenerate effluent containing a high concentration of nickel, for instance, can be returned to the plating tanks. After the nickel concentration has peaked, tap water is admitted into the top of the bed to push back the entrained regenerate solution down the column.

The nickel remaining in the solution re-exchanges back into the resin and the sulphuric acid is pushed back into the acid reservoir.[34]

■ The advantages of the Eco-Tec system have not escaped the notice of electroplaters. Plastics CMP Limited (Peterborough, Ontario) has opened a new $4 million plastics plating facility for molding, electroplating and painting parts for the automotive industry.[35] Almost 10% ($375,000) of the new plant cost was for Eco-Tec's PARR (Pollution Abatement via Resource Recovery) system. An end-of-the-pipe disposal system would have cost more than $1 million, with a $250,000 annual operating budget.[36] Resource recovery seemed the logical choice. The CMP plant covers 74,000 square feet and can produce 4000 square feet of plated plastic an hour. Chrome, copper and nickel plating are carried out on the automated hoist lines.

Using the Eco-Tec recovery equipment, CMP is able to return about 92% of the treated wastewater to the plating operation for re-use. The remainder of the liquid goes to sludge processing where even more water is removed by another anion-cation exchange system. Only about 2 to 3% of the treated wastewater is released to the sewers. The metal content is only 1.5 ppm.

Ion exchange returns almost

An atmospheric concentrator is used in conjunction with the chromic acid recovery unit.

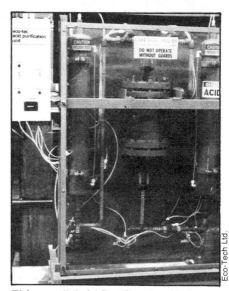

This small Acid Purification Unit continuously removes metallic salts from contaminated acid, permitting re-use of the acid in the strip bath tank.

The installation of Eco-Tech's recovery equipment at this plating plant for plastic automotive parts permits the recycling of chrome, copper and nickel ions, as well as waste rinsewater. The chromic acid recovery unit is in the foreground; the nickel salt recovery system is in the centre.

The unit at the left is used to recover copper salts from the first rinse tank. Cylinder to right is an activated carbon filter used to remove dye-type additives.

Nickel salt recovery unit is in the back left. The tank heater in the foreground is unrelated to the recovery system.

The water recycle unit purifies contaminated rinsewaters for re-use. The ion exchange resin is contained in the 3-inch-high resin beds on top of the frame.

The size of the conventional waste treatment system is considerably smaller than if no residue recovery systems were installed. Residual wastes are precipitated, separated in the sludge clarifier to the left, and dewatered in the filter press at the right.

99% of the chrome, copper and nickel in the first rinse tank to the plating baths, helping to reduce sludge volumes fifty-fold. Environmental control officer Roy Druce says, "I'd hate to think what it would cost us to get rid of this material without this equipment." Nitric acid recovery is also being practised.

Looking at the value of the recovered material and water re-use alone, the PARR system has a pay-back period of about two years. Other, smaller systems can pay for themselves in as little as eight months.[31]

Nitric acid is used by electroplaters in a variety of metal etching, stripping and pickling baths. With time, these baths become contaminated with dissolved metal oxides and the build-up of the metallic ion impurities inhibits the effectiveness of the pickling process. Evenually, the bath must be discarded, despite the fact that it still contains an appreciable amount of free nitric acid.

This cycle of progressive ion build-up and bath disposal is both inefficient and expensive. Caustic soda is needed to neutralize the bath water and new nitric acid must be used to make up the new solution. The chemical cost is approximately 50¢ a litre.[37]

In addition, the etching quality varies according to the level of contaminants in the bath and is optimum only after the etch has been regenerated. The dumping of large volumes of nitric acid also poses certain difficulties. The load may exceed the capacity of a "flow-through-type" waste treatment facility and the neutralization of a full-strength base can be dangerous because of the large amounts of heat released. Even if the treatment system can handle the flow, it will not be able to contain the nitrate ion which will pass right through. Finally, there is the labour needed to pump out the old bath and make up the new one with the associated down time for the line.

■ Ion exchange technology can offer a cost-effective solution to this myriad of headaches. Eco-Tec Ltd. markets an Acid Purification Unit (APU) that utilizes their Reciprocating Flow Ion Exchange process.[37] A resin has been developed that will collect the acid and reject the metallic contaminant.

The operation entails two stages. First, spent acid is drawn out of the bath and forced by air pressure through the resin. The acid is absorbed into the resin particles and the metallic salts pass through and are collected at the top of the unit. The second stage entails the flushing of tap water into the top of the resin bed, which displaces the absorbed acid. The purified acid is collected at the bottom of the bed and returned to the bath (see Figure 11). Valves can be installed on the feed and product lines of each of the baths on the line so that the acids can be purified from each in turn by the one APU. The Eco-Tec system, in operation on a nitric acid copper/nickel rack-stripping process, recovered more than 98% of the free nitric acid in the feed. Table 3 illustrates the savings in reduced chemical neutralization and acid replacement costs that are possible using ion exchange. Acid recovery and effluent nitrate control are achievable with a pay-back period of less than one year.[37]

6.
Ion Transfer

Two American plating companies have invested in ion transfer systems to allow the closed-loop recovery of chromium from their operations.[38]

■ Advance Plating Co. (Cleveland, Ohio) has purchased two units and is considering a third. Advance attached one unit to the flow of its automatic rack machine that plates chromium onto small diecastings.

■ A second recovery system is installed on a nickel/chromium Cyclemaster machine. Reliable Plating Works (Milwaukee, Wisconsin) connected its unit to an automatic hoist line that plates chromium onto napkin, paper towel and toilet tissue dispensers.

■ Both companies are using the Innova Chrome Napper™ ion transfer system, marketed by the McGean Chemical Company (Cleveland, Ohio). The unit consists of a number of ion transfer cells. Each cell consists of a stainless steel mesh cathode which makes up the outside of the cell, lined on the inside by a half-inch-thick polyester-based membrane. This membrane encloses the anode compartment which contains a platinum-plated titanium anode.

When the switch is thrown, a pump draws rinsewater into a tank containing the cells. A rectifier supplies 25 Vdc across the cell electrodes, causing the chromate and sulphate ions to pass through the membrane and enter the anode compartment. The clean

Figure 11
Ion Exchange Acid Purification

In the first stage, spent acid is adsorbed into the resin particles of the acid purification unit and the metallic salts pass through the unit. In the second stage, the resin is flushed with tap water to displace the adsorbed acid. The purified acid is returned to the baths.

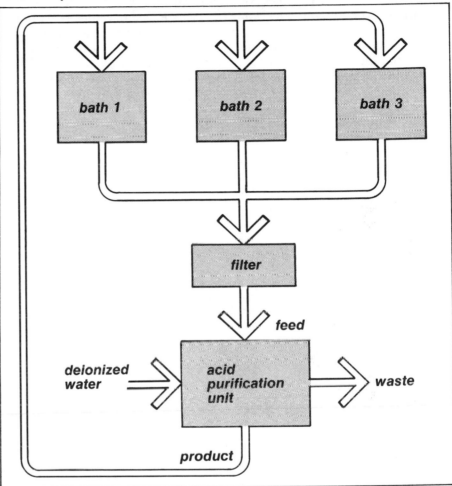

rinsewater overflows the ion transfer tank and returns by gravity to the original rinse tank on the line. The anolyte is drained periodically from the anode compartments and transferred as needed to the chrome acid plating tank.[39]

The Advance Plating and Reliable Plating installations are slightly different due, in part, to the different volume capacity of rinse tanks in the two plants. Figures 12 and 13 illustrate the set-ups in the two plating lines.

Despite the differences in execution, management at both plants are equally pleased with the recovery results:

(1) Chrome use has been reduced by 80 to 90%. Reliable Plating used to consume 45 kg of chromic acid a week. Since the installation of the Chrome Napper™ unit, Reliable uses only 5.6 kg a week.

(2) Water use has dropped 99%. Rinsewater use on Reliable's chromium line dropped from 53,000 litres a day to 379 litres a day. This is what is needed to make up evaporative, plating and drag-out losses.

(3) The U.S. Environmental Protection Agency's chromium discharge limits are easily met and sewer discharge fees have been eliminated. Also, there is no cost associated with chemical destruct systems or sludge disposal because these services are not needed.

(4) The system is easy to operate, requires little maintenance

and has low power requirements ($50 per month). The supplier guarantees the cell membranes for two years.

(5) Product quality is enhanced because of the increased purity of the final rinse.[5]

Finally and perhaps most importantly, the savings in chromium replacement and reduced water requirements have amortized the capital costs of the ion transfer units that were installed in October 1980, for approximately $15,000 apiece.

Waste Matching

Two researchers have developed a system for Third World electroplaters to neutralize their highly toxic chromic acid waste using an ubiquitous solid waste — the rusty tin can.[40]

The electroplater with chromic acid waste is faced with either a capital intensive recovery operation or an expensive chemical destruction process. Hexavalent chromium (Cr^{6+}) must be reduced to the trivalent form (Cr^{3+}) by the addition of SO_2, sulphite, or sulphide so that it will precipitate out as a hydroxide. The solution is then neutralized with sodium bicarbonate. The operation must be carefully monitored with expensive laboratory equipment. This equipment is often beyond the means of small Third World operators.

E.A.R. Ouano and F. Arellano have suggested that the rusting reaction of iron can cause the reduction of other metals.[40] They postulated that if chromic acid was passed through a stack of rusted cans, while the iron and tin oxidized to the ferrous and stannous states, Cr^{6+} would be reduced to Cr^{3+}. ($Cr_2O_7^{2-} + 2Fe + 14H^+ \longrightarrow 2Cr^{3+} + 2Fe^{3+} + 7H_2O$).

The chromic acid solution, in test runs, had to be held in the pile of heavily rusted cans for at least 24 hours. The cans were consumed after six or seven cycles. However the pile could simply be topped up and limestone was as effective as and cheaper than sodium bicarbonate for neutralizing the solution.

The researchers say the tin can treatment would save a considerable sum in lab equipment. The materials cost would be less than 50% of the sum required for conventional treatment chemicals. It would also aid poorer countries in safeguarding water quality and removing another source of rusting solid waste.

Spills

Despite the best laid plans, no resource recovery and treatment process can be 100% effective. There is always the possibility of a large, possibly catastrophic, accidental release of process chemical and the certainty of routine leaks, drips and spills.

Positive protection against an accidental loss to the sewage system or the plant environment, or a concentrated surge of contaminants through the treatment/recovery process must be planned for and installed. The toxicity of the materials used routinely in electroplating and the possibility of producing highly poisonous gases due to the mingling of incompatible material from concurrent mishaps requires that all spilled materials be confined to the plant. They should be kept segregated,

Table 3

Economic Evaluation for Nitric Acid Recovery[a]

Costs	30,000 L/yr (7,500 gal/yr)	120,000 L/yr (30,000 gal/yr)	200,000 L/yr (50,000 gal/yr)
Approx. APU cost	$ 9,400	$11,300	$ 18,400
Previous neutralization cost[b]	$ 7,575	$30,300	$ 50,500
Previous acid cost	$ 8,775	$35,100	$ 58,500
Total previous cost	$16,350	$65,400	$109,000
Annual savings[c]	$ 9,810	$39,240	$ 65,400
Pay-back period (months)	11.5	3.5	3.4

[a] Based on 4,000 hr/yr operation; bath held at 50 per cent of spent bath.

[b] Cost of caustic soda; excludes costs of solids separation, disposal and labour.
Costs for neutralization and replacement of acid lost due to dragout also are excluded because they will accrue in any case.

[c] The overall efficiency of acid recovery by APU is 60 per cent.
Operating costs, including those for compressed air, electricity, and resin replacement, are negligible.

Source: "Recovery of Nitric Acid from Solutions used for Treating Metal Surfaces" *Plating and Surface Finishing*, February 1980.

according to type, until they can be handled by on-site technology or off-site contractors.

Segregated pit collection areas should be maintained. These collection systems should not be automatically vented to the waste treatment/recovery equipment to prevent possible overloads. It is also important that these containment areas be kept reasonably clean to maximize the possibility of valuable material recovery and re-use.

For established platers, it is not always possible to build a collection system of adequate volume around each process bath and rinse installation. One operator managed to overcome this difficulty by installing a second tank inside the process tank with only a one-inch clearance between the two, then providing a drain from the original tank to a nearby collection pit.

The separation of incompatible wastestreams with adequate capacity to overcome all contingencies is essential if the plater is to safeguard both his employees' health and his investment in expensive chemicals.

Sludge

It is relatively easy now to determine the right mix of coagulants and flocculants, and the optimum parameters of temperature and pH that will guarantee the effective precipitation of the soluble and insoluble components of an aqueous wastestream. The experience of sewage treatment engineers and chemists gives the industrial engineer a wealth of data to draw on. Indeed, much of the pioneering work in industrial waste exchange has been aimed not at recycling or re-using wastes as raw material for another industry, but in finding compatible garbage streams that will neutralize each other.

But obtaining a sludge material from an electroplating wastestream is far simpler than disposing it. Disposal becomes a difficult and expensive problem. The sludge is composed principally of the hydroxides of the various metals used in the plating process

Figure 12
Reliable Plating Chrome Recovery

Reliable Plating circulates water from final rinse in counterflow rinse network. A hot rinse after the final rinse speeds parts drying time. Large rinse tanks eliminate need for equalization tank to help balance flow rates.
Source: "Ion Transfer Recovers Chrome," *Industrial Finishing*, March 1981.

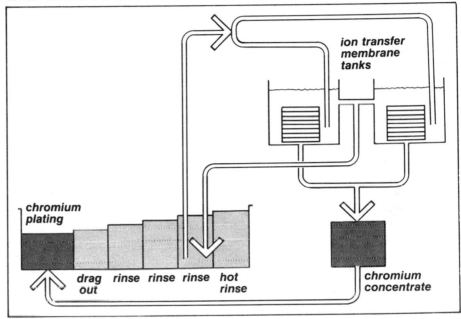

Figure 13
Advance Plating Chrome Recovery

Advance Plating circulates water from rinse tank to ion transfer membrane tanks and back. An equalization tank helps to balance water flow to correct for very small size of rinse tank. Chromium concentrate collects in carboy for transfer back to chromium plating tank.
Source: "Ion Transfer Recovers Chrome," *Industrial Finishing*, March 1981.

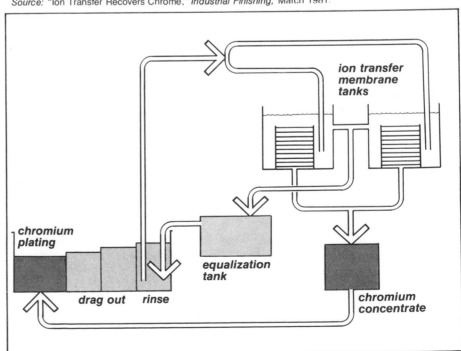

plus the salts and additives needed for effective plating and the polymers and coagulants added for their removal. All are gelatinous and exceedingly difficult to dewater. The sludge may also contain scrap from the product plated, and paints, solvents and oils used in its preparation for plating. Dirt may get into it as well.

Sludge from the clarifier of a waste treatment system may contain only 2 to 4% solids. Dewatering processes can increase the content to 20%. The sludge will not dewater easily beyond 20% unless it freezes. In areas with severe winters, sludge ponds shallow enough to freeze solid may have some use, but the space required is generally prohibitive. For example, a copper-nickel-chromium electroplater with a production capacity of 1000 sf/hour of parts and a drag-out of 5.4 gallons per hour will generate 19,700 gallons of 8% sludge *each week*.[8]

At present this material is disposed in municipal landfill sites from which it is often free to leach out into the environment. A secure chemical landfill site on land with the proper geology and drainage patterns, with the proper leachate collection technology and pre-treatment facilities, would significantly enhance the containment of sludges. At present, however, no such site exists in Canada and, when and if such a facility is designed and approved, the disposal costs for its use will far exceed those presently borne by electroplaters.

It may be that electroplating wastes, as they are presently constituted, will not be included in the list of acceptable wastes for land-fill. One expert maintains that if a 20% sludge is dumped in a landfill site resulting in depths of 2 feet or more, that area will remain unstable forever.[8]

Since the sludges generated by plating are far richer in metal than any ore, the day may come when waste material is mined for its metallic lode. Until that time, the options for alternative sludge disposal are limited to fixation (locking the soluble components up in chemical strait jackets in which they will stay put), encapsulation (actually coating the material with a permanent seal) or re-use. The more promising or advanced techniques are listed in the Fly Ash and Sulphur chapter. The recovery of valuable materials from sludges is discussed in more detail in the Tanning chapter.

Generally, however, the most effective way to recover material from a sludge is not to produce that sludge in the first place.

Conclusion

Resource recovery and waste treatment must shake the stigma of being separate and unusual activities and take their rightful places with the other economic facets of good business. The plater can then begin to effectively manage the resources that are presently wasted. It is important that the responsibility for treatment not be segregated from the other technical affairs of the electroplating shop. The treatment plant designer should be familiar with the operation and finances of the entire operation. The mainte-nance and handling of the treatment process should also be the responsibility of those who routinely make the decisions on the handling and routing of materials into the plating process. When it is realized that the production of quality plated products includes the effective use and conservation of all the raw materials, then the smooth integration of, and necessary innovations in, the treatment process will occur.

The technology is available and the economics are growing more favourable for the smooth integration of resource recovery into the electroplating field. One motivation is environmental protection and avoidance of the unsanitary waste disposal techniques of the past. Although these sentiments may be shared by industry, it is important that the business community recognize the financial opportunities inherent in pollution prevention.

Finally, it is not sufficient to merely make the necessary investment in waste treatment/resource recovery. The field is a young and growing one, and will require vigorous dedication to innovation and development. Without the proper aggressive supervisory attention, any installation can deteriorate and eventually become counter-productive. Although tough new effluent controls and rising costs are strong incentives to controlling waste residues, unless the management and staff look on resource recovery as a viable business proposition, it is doomed to wasteful ineffectiveness.

FOR FURTHER INFORMATION

Associations

Contact the following trade associations for additional information on pollution control technologies and equipment. These trade associations can assist you directly or point you in the right direction for more information on commercially available recycling equipment, technology transfer programmes, technical experts in the field, economic incentives and upcoming regulations. If your association ranks pollution prevention low on their priority list, express your interest in this area.

American Electroplaters' Society:
Canadian Branches (In 1982)

Ottawa Branch
P.O. Box 399, Station A,
Ottawa ,Ontario.
K1N 8V4
(613) 728-5854

Montreal Branch
c/o MacDermid Chemicals Ltd.,
2737 Lewis A. Amos Street,
Lachine, Quebec.
H8T 1C3
(514) 613-1862

Toronto Branch
68 Burnhamthorpe Crescent,
Etobicoke, Ontario.
M9A 1G7
(416) 255-1371

Western Ontario Branch
1961 E.C. Row,
Windsor, Ontario.
N8W 1Y6
(519) 547-1471

American Electroplaters' Society,
1201 Louisiana Avenue,
Winter Park, Florida.
32789
(305) 647-1197

National Association of Metal
Finishers,
One Illinois Center,
111 East Wacker Drive,
Chicago, Illinois.
60601
(312) 644-6610

Association for Finishing Processes,
One SME Drive,
Box 930,
Dearborn, Michigan.
48128
(313) 271-1500

Society of Automotive Engineers,
400 Commonwealth Drive,
Warrendale, Pennsylvania.
15096
(412) 776-4841

National Metal Decorators
Associations,
435 N. Michigan Avenue,
Chicago, Illinois.
60611
(312) 644-0828

Journals

CANADIAN PAINT AND
FINISHING,
Maclean-Hunter Ltd.,
481 University Avenue,
Toronto, Ontario.
M5W 1A7

CANADIAN CHEMICAL
PROCESSING,
Southam Business Publications Ltd.
1450 Don Mills Road,
Don Mills, Ontario.
M3B 2X7

CANADIAN RECYCLING MARKET,
c/o Venture Publications Ltd.,
223A McLeod Street,
Ottawa, Ontario.
K2P 0Z8

INDUSTRIAL FINISHING,
Hitchcock Publishing Co.,
Hitchcock Building,
Wheaton, Illinois.
60187

PLATING AND SURFACE
FINISHING,
American Electroplaters'
Society,
1201 Louisiana Avenue,
Winter Park, Florida.
32789

METAL FINISHING,
Metals and Plastics Publications Inc.,
Hacensack, New Jersey.
07601

PRODUCT FINISHING,
Sawell Publications Ltd.,
127 Stanstead Road,
London, England.
SE 23 1JE

References

1. Glasstone, Samuel. *The Fundamentals of Electrochemistry and Electrodeposition.* Palisade, New Jersey: Franklin Publishing Company, 1960.

2. Sell, Nancy J. "Metals Finishing." In *Industrial Pollution Control: Issues and Techniques.* New York: Van Nostrand Reinhold, 1981.

3. Zievers, James F. and Novotny, Charles J. "Curtailing Pollution from Metal Finishing." *Environmental Science and Technology,* March 1973.

4. Ontario Ministry of the Environment. "Metal Industries: Manufacturing, Working, Finishing." Chapter XII in *Control of Industrial Wastes in Municipalities.* Industrial Wastes Branch, Ontario Ministry of the Environment, 1977.

5. U.S. Environmental Protection Agency. *Control Technology for the Metal Finishing Industry: Evaporators.* Industrial Environmental Research Laboratory, U.S. Environmental Protection Agency, Report No. EPA 625/8-79-002, June 1979.

6. U.S. General Accounting Office. *Industrial Wastes: An Unexplored Source of Valuable Minerals.* Controller General's Report to the Congress of the United States, May 15, 1980.

7. "Waste of Chromium Could Become Critical." *Canadian Recycling Market,* March 6, 1981.

8. Graham, A. Kenneth. "Wastewater Control and Treatment." Chapter 11 in *Electroplating Engineering Handbook, 3rd Edition.* New York: Van Nostrand Reinhold, 1971.

9. Stewart, F.A. and Lancy., L.E. "Pollution Abatement, Material Conservation and Recovery, Part III: Methods of Effluent and Waste Treatment." *Metal Finishing,* March 1981.

10. "Tough Decision: Upgrade." *Industrial Finishing,* June 1981.

11. Lewis, T.A. "How to Electrolytically Recover Metals from Finishing Operations." *Industrial Finishing,* April 1980.

12. Hutt, M.J. "Effluent Treatment in the Metal Finishing Industry, Part II." *Product Finishing,* May 1980.

13. Davies, John. "Metal and Water Need Not Be Money Down the Drain." *Canadian Machinery and Metal Working,* April 1981.

14. Environment Canada. "X-Pert Metal Finishing." In *Environment Short Course on the Metal Finishing Industry.* Environmental Protection Service, Environment Canada, November 3-4, 1981.

15. HSA Reactors Limited. *Effluent Treatment Problem Solvers.* Rexdale, Ontario: HSA (product literature).

16. "Waste Recovery: Chemelec's Silver Lining." *Chemistry in Britain,* March 1981.

17. "Fluidized Beds Offer Savings in Electroplating." *Production Engineer,* July/August 1981.

18. Murphy, John. "Why Metal Recovery is Well Worth Its Weight . . . in Silver." *Engineer,* February 12, 1981.

19. "Silver Spearheads Metal Recovery Market." *Processing,* March 1981.

20. "Electrolytic Cell for Treatment of Metal Bearing Liquids." *Environmental Pollution Management,* March/April 1979.

21. Hartley, Howard S. "How to Use Evaporative Recovery in Treating Wastes." *Industrial Finishing,* November 1980.

22. Atimion, L. "A Program of Conservation, Pollution Abatement." *Plating and Surface Finishing,* March 1980.

23. "Recovery Pays at Sommer Metalcraft." *Industrial Finishing,* June 1980.

24. Bhatia, Salim and Jump, Robert. "Metal Recovery Makes Good Sense!" *Environmental Science and Technology,* August 1977.

25. Environment Canada. "Hudson Bay Diecastings." In *Environment Short Course on the Metal Finishing Industry.* Environmental Protection Service, Environment Canada, November 3-4, 1981.

26. Schrantz, J. "Closed-Loop Waste Treatment System Saves Chemicals." *Industrial Finishing,* July 1976.

27. Keller, Robert A. "Reverse Osmosis." *Water and Sewage Works,* Reference Issue, 1979.

28. Mattair, Robert. "Closed Cycle Treatment of Electroplating Rinses by Reverse Osmosis." In *Proceedings: Closed Cycle Operations by Industry.* Delaware River Basin Commission, September 1972.

29. "Recovering Ni/Cr from Plating Wastes." *Canadian Chemical Processing,* February 1978.

30. Cartwright, Peter S. "Reverse Osmosis and Ultrafiltration in the Plating Shop." *Plating and Surface Finishing,* April 1981.

31. Brown, Craig. "Recycling Recovered Nickel Salts Can Make Pollution Control Profitable." *Canadian Paint and Finishing,* February 1976.

32. Steward, F.A. and Lancy, L.E. "Pollution Abatement, Materials Conservation and Recovery, Part IV: Chemistry of Effluent and Waste Treatment." *Metal Finishing,* April 1981.

33. Steward, F.A. and Lancy, L.E. "Pollution Abatement, Materials Conservation and Recovery, Part III: Methods of Effluent and Waste Treatment." *Metal Finishing,* March 1981.

34. Eco-Tec Limited. *Reciprocating Flow Ion Exchange — What It Is.* Toronto, Ontario, Eco-Tec (product literature).

35. "Model Plant for Plastics Painting — Decorating." *Industrial Finishing,* Febraury 1980.

35. McCormick, R. and Brown, C.J. "Pollution Abatement System Recovers Process Chemicals." *Modern Power and Engineer,* February, 1981.

37. Brown, C.J. *et al.* "Recovery of Nitric Acid from Solutions Used for Treating Metal Surfaces." *Plating and Surface Finishing,* Febraury 1980.

38. "Ion Transfer Recovers Chrome." *Industrial Finishing,* March 1981.

39. "Bumper Plater Recovers Chromic Acid with New Process." *Plating and Surface Finishing,* April 1980.

40. "Chrome Wastes: Tinpot Technology." *Chemistry in Britain,* April 1981.

Fly Ash & Sulphur

This book is essentially a guide dealing with resource recovery options for small and medium-sized businesses, an aid to help them deal with their liquid industrial waste problems. This chapter, however, discusses primarily large corporations, smelters and power companies, and the way they can handle bulk solid wastes like sulphur and fly ash. This may appear, at the least, incongruous and perhaps even irrelevant, but it has been included for several reasons.

Other solid wastes — paper, glass, metals — have received a tremendous amount of coverage in the technical, popular science and recycling literature. It was thought that here was a chance to bring to a wider audience some material which is usually showcased only in slightly obscure journals. Decision-makers and regulators, waste generators and future consumers may not have been exposed to many of the recent innovations in the sulphur and ash fields. Simple information exchange is a valuable end in itself.

These are also stories of industries which are being forced to deal with waste products in vast, previously unheard of quantities (in the case of sulphur trapped in air pollution control equipment) or wastes which can no longer simply be dumped in unregulated landfills (in the case of fly ash). Their reactions to these new challenges are of interest to anyone who has to face a new waste disposal problem. And their responses hold lessons for us all. In some instances they have turned to technologies that were discarded years ago as unfeasible, inappropriate or unprofitable. New situations make a reappraisal of ideas that have sat on the shelf for decades a rewarding experience.

In other instances the solution has required the questioning and rethinking of established concepts. If someone had not wondered whether their residuals would not make better cement than the products already available, new uses for sulphur or fly ash

would not have been developed. Their success stories are essentially object lessons that prove the need for imaginative research and innovation — lessons applicable to industries of every size.

The recent history of sulphur and fly ash research is a history of firms and individuals who were not willing to accept the status quo — the established way of doing things — but went out and looked for a better way. And having found it, fought to have it gain acceptance, to find new markets among the consumers of older, established products and lines and, where no market existed, to create one.

Finally, this chapter illustrates the need for co-operation, not only among the new byproduct generators and their markets but government co-operation as well. Many of the innovations in this section will realize their full potential only with active government support. This is important not only in aiding research and testing, but in rewriting standards and procurement contracts, in providing the necessary transportation infrastructure and, perhaps most importantly, in effective public education and coordination.

And that is why this chapter is here.

FLY ASH

The great billowing cloud of black smoke which accompanies the burning of coal was perhaps the most recognizable symbol of the new industrial age. With the awakening of modern environmental concerns, the smokestack and its plume of black ash became the target of some of the first regulatory controls. Eventually a wide array of technologies was developed and employed to rid the skies of dirt. Today, electrostatic and mechanical precipitators, cyclone separators, baghouses and scrubbers of various makes and designs are routinely removing as much as 99.5% of the solids that formerly went up the stack. This collected material is fly ash and typically represents about 70% of the solid waste generated by coal combustion. The remaining 30% is composed of heavier and coarser bottom ash and boiler slag.

The United States, with its heavy reliance on coal-fueled thermal electric power, generated some 70 million tons of fly ash, bottom ash and boiler slag in 1978.[1] Of this material, only 24% was reclaimed for further use and 76% was disposed. By 1990, the ash industry in the U.S. predicts that the burning of 816 million tons of coal by utilities will generate 113 million tons of fly ash and approximately 50% of it will be utilized in byproducts.[2] The Cana-

dian situation is not nearly as bright, although Canadian researchers have done a great deal of pioneer work on potential fly ash uses.[3,4] Still, according to a Canadian government scientist, "many other countries are making far better use of materials such as fly ash ... Fly ash is a key byproduct where development and marketing activities should foster a demand based on (the) positive research and applications in many countries."[5]

Most of the coal used in Canada is burned in thermal generating stations to produce electricity or consumed in the manufacture of steel. Canadians burned more than 30,000,000 tonnes of coal in 1980, generating power and 2.7 x 10^6 tonnes of fly ash. This fly ash is composed of spherical particles, ranging in diameter from 1 to 150 microns.

The proportion of material trapped is a function of the type of collection equipment employed; mechanical collectors remove only the coarser fractions of the material while electrostatic precipitators are capable of trapping the finest sized particulate. The fly ash is made up of a number of chemical compounds and glasses that are formed from silicon (SiO_2), aluminium (Al_2O_3), ferrous (Fe_2O_3), calcium (CaO) and magnesium oxides (MgO). Those

ashes formed by burning subbituminous coals contain more CaO and less Fe_2O_3 than those from bituminous varieties.[4]

Unburned carbon will also be present; the amount is dependent on the combustion conditions of the boiler and operating procedures of the plant. The ash may also contain varying trace amounts of heavy metals and radioactive compounds. The degree to which these are present will determine the necessary precautions (often expensive precautions) that need to be taken to ensure safe and permanent disposal, if disposal is the option chosen by the generator.

Dumping fly ash may not be the most advantageous approach, however; this material also exhibits strong pozzolanic properties, properties which make it suitable as a constituent of concrete.

Pollution Prevention Opportunities

1.
Cement Substitute

A pozzolan is a siliceous or siliceous and aluminous material which in itself possesses little or no cementitious value, but which will, in finely divided form and in the presence of moisture, chemically react with calcium hydroxide at ordinary temperature to form compounds possessing cementitious properties.[6] In other words, it is a silica form that will make cement when mixed with lime and water. With cement, a lot of crushed aggregate material, including in some instances slag and coarse ash, and water, concrete can be made.

In a landfill site, fly ash may be slowly leached of its trace contaminants which may, in turn, pollute the water table. As concrete, it can be used for a more constructive purpose. And if fly ash is ever classified as hazardous waste, the charges for its disposal could reach $50 to $100 a ton. On the other hand, its sale as a commercial byproduct should help offset the capital, operating and maintenance costs of the utilities' or industrial boilers' pollution abatement costs. Before fly ash can be incorporated into concrete, it has to be collected. It must be kept segregated from the other solid waste from the boiler; if combined with bottom ash, boiler slag and scrubber sludge, it becomes impossible to recover the fine material for cement production.

■ Lakeview Generating Station (Mississauga, Ontario), a 2400-megawatt plant, produces some 400,000 tons of ash per year. A pilot plant was installed to collect the ash for use in cement. The raw ash was first separated into coarse and fine fractions with a low velocity air separator. The coarse material was screened and passed through a magnetic separator to remove, respectively, the unburned carbon and iron particles.

The magnetic component makes up about 9% of the total and contains 60% iron. The remaining coarse material can be used as a light-weight aggregate.[3]

The finer ash, with an average particle size of about 10 microns, can also be treated for carbon removal and then serve as a suitable cement substitute. Cement is normally made up of a mixture of limestone, silica, sand, clays and iron ore. Baked at high temperatures in huge rotary kilns, it is then ground and mixed with a small amount of gypsum. The resultant material is a fine gray powder commonly known as Portland cement. Portland is a generic name for an inorganic cement which will harden when mixed with water.[7]

The pozzolanic fraction of the fly ash contains oxides of silicon (40-45%) iron (9-18%), aluminium (14-16%) and calcium (3-4%). This material can be mixed with Portland cement in concentrations up to 35% by weight. When examined under an electron microscope, there is considerable reaction between the fly ash particles and the lime-rich matrix. The web-like calcium silicate hydrate fibres help bind the cement and aggregate to form a durable and high-strength concrete. The fly ash can be either blended with Portland cements or used directly as an admixture in concrete as a partial replacement for the Portland cement.

As a part of the composite that makes up concrete, fly ash plays a role as a fine aggregate and as the cementing agent that bonds the material together. Table 1 shows the types of cement that can benefit from fly ash substitution.

The substitution of fly ash indeed offers a number of benefits for the purchaser and user of concrete. Of prime interest is the cost. A plant that processes fly ash would cost only a fraction of one that produces cement.[8] The burning and grinding of Portland cement is an energy-intensive operation which is avoided almost entirely by fly ash substitution. In 1979, a detailed report produced by the U.S. Department of Energy at-

Table 1

The Substitution of Fly Ash for Portland Cement

ASTM Cement Type	Purpose	Substitute Fly Ash
I	General Purpose	Yes
II	Moderate sulphate resistance and heat of hydration	Yes
III	High early strength (28 days)	Could be used, but would defeat the purpose of type III cement
IV	Low heat of hydration	Yes
V	High sulphate resistance	Yes

tempted to quantify the possible energy savings. The report, *The Potential for Energy Conservation through the Use of Slag and Fly Ash in Concrete,* anticipated that, "with consumer participation and a willingness on the part of industry to foster the use of blended cements or admixtured fly ash concretes wherever suitable, it is reasonable to expect that 40% of the annual United States cement consumption could be satisfied by these materials."

The 40% substitution (based on a 20% fly ash or 30% blast furnace slag intermixture), if instituted in 1976, would have equalled savings of 16.3% of the energy required over the base year 1972.[8]

Product quality is the second major concern and it is here, surprisingly, that the byproduct recovery comes into its own. The use of fly ash in concrete in many cases enhances the final product. The U.S. federal government now requires procuring agencies using appropriated federal funds to purchase material composed of the highest percentage of recovered materials that is practical. On November 20, 1980, the U.S. Environmental Protection Agency issued guidelines designed to encourage the use of cement and concrete containing fly ash.[7]

Based on many years of intensive testing, the advantages of fly ash concrete can be summarized as follows.

First, greater ultimate strength. Although there is a longer curing time needed for fly ash cement, after 28 days the concrete will equal or better any typical Type I cement. After 56 days the strength will be superior in almost all cases. The Chicago Committee on high-rise buildings writes, "The use of a good quality fly ash . . . is a must in the production of high strength concrete".[4] In Chicago, the Sears Tower, John Hancock Center, Standard Oil Building, Water Tower Place and River Plaza all offer mute testimony to that conviction.

Second, improved workability. The addition of fly ash, made up of glassy spherical particles, improves the pumpability, handling, placing and finishing of fresh concrete.

Third, reduced water consumption. Because the fly ash mixture is easier to handle, less water has to be mixed into the concrete. This results in less drying shrinkage and less cracking.

Fourth, lower heat of hydration. Since less heat is generated during the hydraulic reactions after the addition of water, there is less thermal cracking. This is particularly beneficial in the pouring of large masses of concrete in dams, retaining walls and foundations.

Fifth, increased sulphate resistance. The increased resistance to sulphate attack is one of the most important aspects of the behavior of fly ash in concrete.[4] Sulphates in the soil and ground water or in the form of air-borne salts cause cracking and the eventual disintegration of concrete. The fly ash forms stable cementitious compounds with components of the concrete which are then unavailable for reaction and combination with the invading sulphates. Perhaps for much the same reasons, fly ash increases the durability of concrete in seawater.

Finally, reduced alkali-aggregate reactions. Alkalis which are formed during cement hydration may react destructively with certain aggregates to provoke expansion and cracking of the concrete. Fly ash gets there first, so to speak, and reacts to form stable compounds with the alkalis before they get a chance to be disruptive.

Fly ash does have to be carefully analyzed and controlled to give an optimum performance as a Portland cement substitute. The new user should become familiar with information on mixing and preparation and make sure the fly ash obtained has the properties needed to ensure good concrete. It is also important to remember that fly ash cements require an extended curing time and have an increased demand for an air entraining agent. But with the proper information and normal precautions, fly ash can offer a superior concrete.

Fly ash cement is already being used with impressive results. The U.S. Army Corps of Engineers has been using the material for

dam construction for a number of years. The Georgia Department of Transport has poured over 3 million cubic yards of fly ash concrete pavement and road shoulders since 1975.[7] A dam on the South Saskatchewan River used fly ash as a replacement for fine aggregate because of its resistance to sulphate attack and increased strength.[4]

Australia's BMI Ltd., which markets fly ash in the United Kingdom, is test marketing fly ash cement in the United States now. It is using material obtained from Appalachian Power's new 2900-megawatt plant in West Virginia. If the test is successful, BMI plans to build a multi-million-dollar collection and storage system in the U.S.[9]

In Fargo, North Dakota, fly ash concrete was used to construct the base of a 1450-foot test strip of road. Fly ash replaced 80% of the Portland cement used in the concrete slab. The road was topped with a two-inch asphalt wearing course. The project was cost-competitive with standard bituminous concrete bids and surpassed the compressive strengths called for in the specifications.

Duane Heley, inspector on the job, thinks there could be considerable savings achievable on a large scale job. "But our real aim is to get a superior product at equal cost while using waste material and local aggregate and reducing dependence on bituminous materials."[5] The Fargo choice of fly ash over bituminous also had profound energy savings. The 1000 cubic yards placed saved the 30,000 barrels of oil required for the bituminous mix plus another 6000 for processing and transport.

2.
Fly Ash Aggregate

The aggregate in concrete makes up three-quarters of the final bulk. The solid wastes from coal combustion can do much to replace the dwindling local supplies of gravel normally used for this purpose. Furnace clinker and bottom ash may be used as light-weight aggregates for making concrete blocks.[10]

Fly ash also makes a suitable light aggregate, and although only small amounts are presently being used for this purpose, its carbon composition offers an energy saving advantage which should increase its role. The fly ash is mixed with water and formed into pellets using either a revolving cone disc or drum, or by extrusion. Sometimes alkali is added to improve the pellets' resistance to mechanical or thermal shocks. The pellets are then fused into a cake form by sintering at temperatures between 1150 and 1200°C. The carbon in the fly ash supplies the needed heat to evaporate the water in the pellets and bring them to a sintering temperature. This improves the energy efficiency of the process and reduces the fuel requirement.

The cake is then broken to obtain the crushed aggregate. As these aggregates have good shape, strength and moderate water absorption, they are suitable for producing light-weight concrete blocks and structural light-weight concrete.[10]

In the next 20 years more cement will be poured than is already in place. The pozzolan market alone has more than doubled in the last three years. For the next 20 years, industrial nations will be turning increasingly to coal to supply process heat and generate electricity, particularly as gas and oil climb in price and are designated for use as vehicular fuels and chemical raw materials. This means a lot of fly ash will be looking for a home.

It seems only logical that this "waste material", which appears economically and structurally superior to Portland cement, will have an increasingly larger role to play. The concerns of cement companies will have to be allayed, but it is hoped that positive test results now available will prove the economic viability of the production and marketing of blended cements. Fly ash suppliers will have to ensure quality control measures and maintain a standard product, but the advantages far outweigh these problems. According to an American cement industry analyst, with the antici-

pated rise in cement demand, the industry has the opportunity to ease its capital requirements and optimize its fuel use through the ambitious development of blended cement production."[8]

Producers of fly ash and slag are going to prefer long-term contracts if they are to guarantee a supply of consistent quality product. Such an arrangement may require intermediary brokerage operations that will ensure the year-round availability of adequate stocks and provide a buffer between the steadily operating producer and the vicissitudes of the construction markets. It is hoped that this function could be undertaken by private interests, although it may require public intervention, perhaps in the form of a Fly Ash Marketing Board.

With care, fly ash cements will find a home among the traditional construction materials. It would give heart to industrialist and environmentalist alike (indeed some people may fill both roles) to know that every new concrete edifice was also a monument to resource recovery.

3.
Road Base

Although fly ash makes an effective cement substitute, there will be some cases where the fly ash produced does not meet the qualities needed for good concrete, or sufficient local markets do not exist to utilize all the fly ash produced. In these cases, there still exist opportunities for use that are alternatives to landfilling. Fly ash can be utilized as a road bed material, loose aggregate or even soil stabilizer.

The U.S. Environmental Protection Agency conducted a four year study to investigate the feasibility of using fly ash and coal mine waste as a road base.[11] The fly ash played the role of a stabilizing agent, filling the voids in the coal mine refuse and neutralizing the acidity produced from the rock. The coal mine waste served as the load-bearing aggregate. Coal refuse is accumulating in the U.S. as

a result of environmental measures aimed at limiting the impurities in fuel.

Mining, crushing and washing tend to concentrate impurities in this material, leaving it highly toxic and difficult to handle.[11]

The fly ash acted to plug the holes in the road bed and prevent the passage of water through the mine waste, which could leach out toxic compounds. Fly ash offers excellent compacting qualities and the test results, from a mixture of 25% fly ash and 75% mine refuse, showed almost no water discharge from the bed.[11] The toxic level in the collected groundwater "represented *almost negligible* (EPA's emphasis) pollutant loads because of the small volume of the discharge". Needless to say, fly ash would work as well with a less toxic load-bearing aggregate.

■ The heavy metals and other toxic components in some ashes would normally make that material unsuitable for a road bed material. Nippon Kokan (NKK) (Japan) has developed what is hoped may be the answer.[12] Municipal waste in Japan is incinerated and landfilled, requiring both a great deal of valuable land and constant vigilance against the leaching of heavy metals out of the disposal site. NKK has a practical and pollution-free system in operation to melt down and solidify the municipal waste ashes. The resultant slag reduces the ash volume by one-third to one-half and chemically encapsulates the harmful heavy metals.

The firm is now investigating the suitability of the slag as a road base material. They have recently built an experimental road on the grounds of their Keihin Works' Ohgishima complex.

The NKK melting system also has the advantage of separating out the metal component of the waste due to differences in specific gravity. The reclaimed metals can then be used in steel making.

■ N-Viro Energy Systems (Toledo, Ohio) are involved in a similar project in which they mix fly ash, cement kiln dust and aggregate to provide a strong base for highway construction.[13]

4.
Soil Stabilizer

Research on fly ash has also established its usefulness as a soil stabilizer.[14] The ash from sub-bituminous coal burned in Wyoming can effectively stabilize clay and sand soils. Adequate mixing and rapid compaction are necessary to make the process successful.

5.
Clean Fill

Finally, there are a number of processes available that depend on additives that stabilize and harden wastes which can then be used as clean fill or road filler. Dravo Corporation's (Pittsburgh, Pennsylvania) Calcilox and Conversion Systems Incorporated's "Poz-o-tec" for sludges[16] and EWR's (Waterbury, Connecticut) Kayset for metal hydroxide wastes[16] are two examples. This type of system may be effective, but should be investigated only after other by-product or re-use avenues prove fruitless. They do not offer the producer any return, and entail an additional disposal cost. If no other use can be found they do limit the release to the environment of potentially hazardous waste.

6.
Metal Recovery

The metallic components of fly ash — aluminium, titanium and iron, among others — are beginning to attract the attention of North American researchers. The contaminants that help make fly ash a difficult disposal problem also make it attractive as a potential ore body. Fly ash contains up to 20% aluminium oxides, 20% iron oxides and 1% titanium.[17] George Burnet of Iowa State University estimates that the treatment of the entire fly ash output of the United States in 1978 would have supplied 90% of the alumina and 100% of the titanium oxide imported by that country in a year.[17]

In the Ames Laboratory at Iowa State, Dr. Burnet has developed a process that recovers up to 90% of the aluminium present in fly ash. A pelletized mixture of fly ash, limestone and soda ash is sintered at 1200°C to form a soluble aluminate compound. This is leached out with dilute sodium carbonate leaving a residue (mainly dicalcium silicate) which is a suitable ingredient in Portland cement. As a substitute for limestone in the original sintering process, waste cement kiln dust also gives equivalent results.

The Iowa research team has also used high-temperature chlorination of fly ash to vapourize volatile metal chlorides. This method retrieves 80% of the aluminium and 76% of the titanium but the work is still in a preliminary stage.

■ The Oak Ridge National Laboratory (ORNL) is also testing a metal recovery system, known as Calsinter.™ The ORNL process involves heating the fly ash to 1200°C along with a mixture of limestone and gypsum. Sludge from a wet limestone flue gas desulphurization unit (a "scrubber") could be used instead of virgin limestone and gypsum. After heating, the mass is leached with sulphuric acid to recover more than 98% of the aluminium and 90% of the other metals.[18]

The Calsinter™ process yields the aluminium in the form of aluminium chloride which aluminium companies could convert directly without any complicated intermediate stages.

Special energy-efficient electrolyte cells developed by Alcoa can convert aluminium chloride to aluminium. Ronald Canon of ORNL's chemical technology division is concerned that the reagents for the process are too expensive to make the technique commercially viable.[17]

The ORNL is also working on an extraction based on a one-step leach of fly ash with strong hydrochloric acid. Although this system seems to have commercial potential, it recovers only 45% of the available metal.

■ Scientists at Memphis State University, Tennessee, in conjunction with the Tennessee Valley Authority (TVA) are also working at a cost-competitive way of reclaiming aluminium and iron from fly ash.[17,19] The ash is pre-conditioned with a sodium hydroxide solution (caustic soda), filtered and leached with hydrochloric acid. The metals in the leached solution can then be separated. Iron is recovered either by electroplating or precipitation and the titanium must be stripped from the aluminium before the latter can be used by the aluminium companies. The Memphis State team is working its way from lab-scale tests to pilot plant and eventually to a full-scale commercial facility. They say "everything we have now shows it will be cost-effective from both an energy standpoint and a dollar standpoint".[17]

While metal recovery has not been ensconced in a full-size commercial operation, many think it is only a matter of time. While other sources of titanium, aluminium and iron do exist, none of those mining enterprises offer the economic and environmental bonus of eliminating a major waste disposal problem. The by-product market may be too variable to guarantee that these extraction methods remain consistently competitive, but the cost of dumping is guaranteed to do nothing but escalate at a rapid rate. When added into the economic equation, metal recovery makes sense.

7.
Scrubber Absorbent

Fly ash is being used by one enterprising utility to help control another serious pollutant, sulphur dioxide.

■ The Clay-Boswell Power Plant (Cohassett, Montana) uses fly ash in a $20-million wet scrubber for a 500-megawatt generator. Fly ash is removed from the gas stream and the resulting slurry is used as an alkaline reactant to remove sulphur dioxide in a spray-tower absorber. By eliminating the need for precipitators, construction costs are halved in this operation compared to conventional lime or limestone scrubbers. Additional savings of about $1 million per year are realized in operational costs because no reagents need to be purchased.[20] Handling problems with the produced slurry may increase operating costs to some degree.

8.
Mineral Wool

Glass and Ceramics International (California) is working on a project to assess the feasibility of producing a mineral wool from fly ash and cement kiln dust. The coal ash from the Southern California Edison power plant and kiln dust from California Portland Cement Inc. are being combined into a mineral product that resembles rock wool. The two waste materials are ground, screened, chemically characterized, mixed in varying proportions, melted and then cooled by placing them in aerated water.

9.
Soil Nutrient

And finally, a number of research efforts have been directed towards the disposal of fly ash on agricultural land.[21,22] Fly ash as a soil nutrient requires much more investigation but it seems promising. The ash can be a source of boron, selenium, potassium, zinc, sulphur, molybdenum and phosphorus. Some soils show deficiencies of these elements, and because molybdenum and selenium are often found only sparingly in forage crops, they have to be added in diet supplements. Test plots on soils amended with soft coal fly ash show vegetable and forage crops do absorb these trace nutrients. The concern remains that they may also absorb harmful levels of heavy metals and other toxics present in the ash. Although this has not proven to be a serious problem as yet, the work is still continuing.

10.
Recovery Advantages

Fly ash, unlike sulphur, has no monetary value at present and is not competing with producers of "virgin fly ash" for part of an established market. The future of byproduct fly ash is the future of possibilities: cement replacements or supplements, aggregate or road bed material, soil stabilizers or even nutrients, metal recovery or mineral wool.

According to *Mining Engineering,* the success of programmes using ash in an environmentally sound manner depends on knowledge. "Basically, the process is one of informing the producer that he has a versatile, valuable product and convincing the user the material can be economically placed without sacrificing the quality of the end product. Along the way changes will have to be made in time-honoured specifications to permit their expanded use."[2]

Even if fly ash fails to return a significant profit to its producer, the development of these possible uses should prohibit the expensive disposal of ash into the increasingly scarce landfill sites across North America. New disposal regulations in the United States (RCRA) are forcing utility executives to take a long look at their waste practices. It is no longer possible to indiscriminately dump ash; alternatives must be supported. An effective ash marketing programme will come only with the active commitment of the top level of utility management.

SULPHUR

The acrid odour of burning sulphur inspired both the fire and brimstone visions of hell evoked by religious zealots and the labours of the early alchemists in their quest to transmute dross into gold.[23] While fundamentalist preachers are still with us, alchemy has fallen upon hard times. However, researchers have not entirely abandoned the dream of turning waste sulphur products into financial assets.

The cleaning of fuels and ores and the scrubbing of stack gases result in the accumulation of vast quantities of sulphur compounds. In lieu of disposing these wastes, the technology is being developed to turn them into concrete, protective coatings, asphalt extenders, fertilizers and gypsum. The economic return can do much to offset the cost of the sulphur dioxide pollution abatement that must be borne by refineries, smelters and power companies.

Under natural conditions, solid sulphur is a yellow, powdery, crystalline material, lacking cohesion and with little practical use as a structural material.[24] But sulphur is a complex element, the atoms of which can combine in a number of ways to form different molecular patterns and crystals.

All solid sulphur melts around 120°C but due to a polymerization process that transforms the standard ring structure of the atoms into long-chain molecules, at 160°C the liquid undergoes an increase in viscosity. By rapid cooling, a "plastic sulphur" product can be obtained. This plastic sulphur exhibits good compressive and tensile strength but these properties fade after several hours as the molecular structure reverts to that of the brittle, nonflexible natural solid sulphur.

In the last ten years, a number of additives has been developed that allows "plastic sulphur" to retain its advantageous properties. Polymeric polysulphides, thiols and olefinic compounds are being used to preserve or enhance the polymer links in the sulphur and retard the return to the crystalline sulphur form.

Pollution Prevention Opportunities

1.
Sulphur Concrete

Because sulphur is available in vast quantities[24] (see Figures 1 and 2), much of the research on its utilization has been directed towards formulating new materials for the construction industry. The demand for concrete in particular has been growing in recent years and now at least three sulphur concrete products have entered the commercial market place.

The mixing of molten sulphur with hot aggregate to form concrete has been attempted for more than a century. However, the practice did not gain widespread acceptance until the 1930s with the development of efficient additives, usually thiokols. Sulphur concretes were used in electrolytic vats and acid storage vessels until they were replaced by newer and more economical plastic products.

The availability of vast new supplies of low-cost sulphur has reawakened interest in sulphur concretes and two western Canadian firms have brought products on the market.

Sulphurcrete™ is the patented brainchild of Sulphur Innovations Ltd. (Calgary, Alberta) and is now widely used in the west. The additive, an unsaturated resinous hydrocarbon polymer, is added to a mixture of sulphur and aggregate to produce a durable acid-resistant concrete. No water is used in the production of sulphur concretes. Sulphurcrete™ has been used to build highway medians, parking curbs and factory floors, and also to repair highways and pipelines.

In Calgary, all the traffic signs are firmly embedded in sulphur concrete and in Trail, British Columbia, a large plant run by Cominco is replacing all its flooring with the material. While regular Portland cement would corrode under the acidic conditions in the big lead and zinc refining facility, the Sulphurcrete™ floors have held up well for three years. The Sulphur Development Institute of

Figure 1
Western World Sulphur Stockpiles

Source: "Sulphur Materials," *Chemistry in Canada,* September 1981.

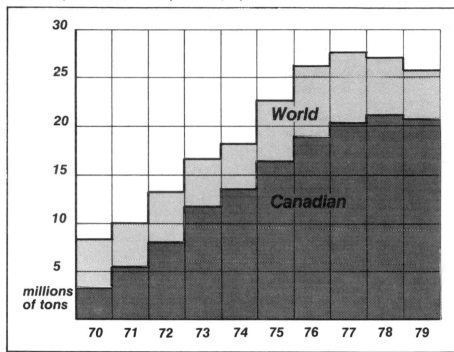

Figure 2
World Sulphur Production 1970-79

Source: "Sulphur Materials," *Chemistry in Canada,* September 1981.

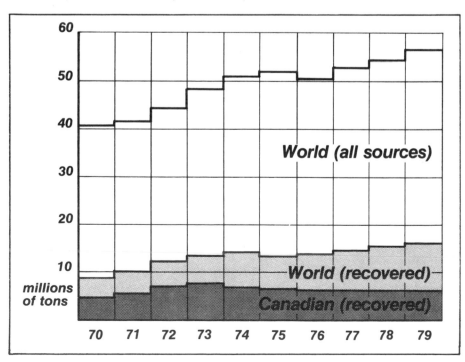

Figure 3
Comparison of Mix Proportions for Sulphur Concrete and Portland Cement Concrete

Sulphur replaces Portland cement and water to act as the binding agent in concrete mixtures. Sulphur concretes offer improvements in acid resistance, strength and setting time. They also can be used over a wider range of air temperatures.

Source: "Sulphur Concrete: Understanding/Application," Concrete International, October 1981.

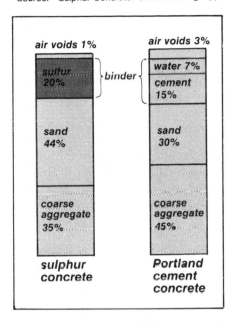

Canada (Calgary, Alberta) with its patented Sudicrete™ product, was also involved in the Cominco project.

Sulphur concretes can be used to form concrete blocks for residential or industrial construction or poured directly into cast forms on the building site. Because the sulphur must be heated above 120°C a standard ready-mix concrete truck must be fitted with propane heaters and insulated to allow transport to the construction site. An asphalt plant, with minor modifications, is suitable for preparing sulphur concretes.

In sulphur concrete (see Figure 3), sulphur is substituted for Portland cement and water to act as a binding agent.[24] As with fly ash concretes, sulphur concrete has shown some very positive qualities in comparison with traditional concrete mixtures.[25]

Sulphur concretes' tensile, compressive, flexural and fatigue strengths are generally greater than those of ordinary Portland cement concrete. The use of diffe-

rent modifying additives makes available a wide range of strength/flexibility combinations. Fatigue resistance, for instance, at various high loading levels can range 10 to 30 times greater than that of conventional concretes. Table 2 shows the range of performance possibilities achievable with the Sudicrete™ concretes.[25]

Sulphur concretes show excellent resistance to deterioration from a wide range of acids and salts. They offer additional protection against the ravages of environmental pollution, from acidic precipitation to road salts, and the

highly corrosive acids and salts used by chemical industries and food manufacturers. Industrial floors, unless protected with costly acid brick or asphalt overlays, can begin to break down in a matter of months. Sulphur concrete floors under the same chemical assault have remained in good condition since their installation in 1978.[24] Table 3 lists some of the chemicals to which sulphur concretes are resistant.[25]

Sulphur concrete sets very rapidly with full strength achieved within 24 hours.

Sulphur concrete can be used year-round and placed successfully in below-freezing temperatures. Unmodified sulphur mixes showed a high degree of thermal expansion which led to internal stress and fracturing. New additives developed by the Sulphur Development Institute of Canada (SUDIC) and the U.S. Bureau of Mines and Minerals now produce concretes that adequately pass the ASTM C666 freeze/thaw test. SUDIC reports the example of

Table 2
Comparison of Structural and Physical Properties of Sulphur Concrete and Portland Cement Concrete

Property	Portland cement concrete	Sudicrete HS	Sudicrete SF
Density, Kg/m^3	2400	2335	2280
Air Voids, %	10	1-10	2-12
Compressive Strength, MPa	34.5	31-55	17-24
Modulus of Rupture, MPa	3.7	5-10	2-4
% of Compressive Strength	10.8	12-20	12-20
Tensile Strength, MPa	3.5	3-8	3-8
% of Compressive Strength	10	10-20	10-20
Modulus of Elasticity, GPa	28	30-40	7-20
Coefficient Thermal Expansion, per °C (x 10^6)	11	8-35	8-35
Thermal Conductivity W/(m.°C)	1.6	0.4-2.0	0.4-2.0
Water Absorption, %	3	0-15	0-1.5

Source: "Sulphur Concrete: Understanding/Application," Concrete International, October 1981.

Sulphur Development Institute

Sulphur concrete is easily produced in a conventional asphalt batch-plant, with only very few modifications.

Sulphur Innovations Ltd.

Batch-type portable asphalt plant used in the production of Sulfurcrete.™

1.7-ton sulphur concrete weights used in pipeline construction that were manufactured in temperatures as low as -40°C.[26]

There is a maximum temperature range to which sulphur concretes can be exposed before either they begin to melt and lose all strength (softening and rapid creep begin above 80°C), or, in the presence of hydrocarbons, they begin to generate hydrogen sulphide gas (149°C). However, this "deficiency" can prove very useful at times. There is never any loss of unused material; because melting does not change the chemical properties of the mix, left-over

concrete can be remelted and recycled into the next day's batch. And unlike Portland cement, which must generally be poured within an hour of mixing, sulphur concrete can sit all day in molten form.

The economics of sulphur concrete hinge inexorably on the economics of sulphur. Sulphur concrete can be batched, mixed, transported, placed and finished using conventional and existing asphalt and concrete equipment. One firm modified a used ready-mixed concrete truck and an abandoned kiln to produce sulphur concretes to supplement

other concretes used in construction and maintenance work. The total cost was less than $50,000.[26] Since the use of sulphur as a substitute for Portland cement does not require the creation of expensive new facilities, the major impediment to mass acceptance is the rising cost of delivered sulphur.

2.
Sulphur Protective Coatings

Sulphur coatings have been developed by the U.S. Bureau of Mines and the Chevron Chemical Co. (San Francisco, California), in co-operation with the Sulphur Development Institute of Canada.[24] These coatings improve the resistance of conventional building materials to chemical attack and other stress. Because sulphur exhibits good adhesive properties and, with the addition of the proper additives, allows sufficient flexibility to absorb the stress and movement of the base structure, these protective coating formulations can be used in a wide variety of situations.

■ The U.S. Bureau of Mines, with the Southwest Research Institute, used a coating mixture to replace mortar in the construction of one building. A formulation of 86% sulphur, 9% dicyclopentadiene and a 5% mixture of talc and fibreglass was sprayed on both sides of the walls of the structure built of mortarless blocks. The surface bonded walls are far stronger than those constructed with conventional mortar and have stood up well to several years of harsh climatic extremes and even one tornado.

■ Chevron's Sucoat™ material has found a wide range of users. Different mixtures have been used to coat the walls of reservoirs, canals, silage pits and chemical plants, applied to concrete floors and used as a base for artificial turf.

The protective properties of sulphur can be sprayed over other construction materials or mixed right in with them, impregnating cements or even fabrics. Mixing

Table 3

Partial Listing of Those Acids and Salts to Which Sulphur Concrete is Resistant

Acids	*Salts*		*Other*
Sulphuric acid	Ammonium sulphate*	Copper chloride	Food wastes
Hydrochloric acid	Ammonium chloride*	Copper sulphate*	Animal wastes
Nitric acid (to 50%)	Sodium chloride*	Nickel sulphate	Some vegetable oils
Acetic acid	Magnesium sulphate*	Nickel chloride	Sea water
Butyric acid	Zinc chloride*	Ferric chloride*	Saturated lime (20°C)
Lactic acid	Zinc sulphate*	Ferric sulphate*	Some hydrocarbons
Hydrofluoric acid	Calcium sulphate*		
Phosphoric acid			
Silage acids	*Saturated		

Source: "Sulphur Concrete: Understanding/Application," *Concrete International,* October 1981.

sulphur with normal Portland cement increases its compressive and tensile strength while making it more resistant to acid corrosion. The development of this application has been carried out since 1971 by the Canadian Centre for Mineral and Energy Technology (CANMET).

■ Fabrics, particularly polypropylene, can be impregnated with sulphur and additive mixtures to produce flexible or rigid lining materials. Thames Polytechnic and the French firm Elf Aquitaine have both developed processes to this end. Elf Aquitaine's product, Sodovia, has been used to line a storm reservoir outside Paris to produce a small lake of 83,000 square metres.[24]

Redi-mix unit equipped with insulating shroud to transport hot mix.

3.
Asphalt Extenders

The oil embargo of 1973-74 by OPEC has spurred western nations to fervently increase research into materials that will extend or replace petroleum-based products. Asphalt is one such material which is expected to be in increasingly short supply. New technologies that allow heavy crude fractions to be cracked to produce gasoline may accelerate the anticipated shortages.[27]

The search for a sulphur-asphalt binder began more than a hundred years ago[24] and Texas Gulf had obtained patents on formulations of sulphur-extended

Because of the high resistance of sulphur concretes to many corrosive materials, sulphur concretes are particularly suited to roadway structures such as curbing and median barriers which are often exposed to corrosive salts.

asphalts by 1939.[28]

But wartime shortages of sulphur delayed the practical application of the research until plentiful supplies of cheap asphalt were threatened in the 1970s. Since 1973 the Sulphur Development Institute of Canada has been working with Gulf Oil Canada (and their SAM system), Shell Canada (Thermopave™) and the engineering firm of R.M. Hardy and Associates. The U.S. Federal Highway Administration has also been working with the Southwest Research Institute in San Antonio to develop an asphalt replacement material, Sulphlex.™

Asphalt extenders have had a long research history but in the last several years, different formulations have had wide use in a number of roads in Canada, the United States, Europe and the Middle East.[24]

When sulphur is mixed with hot asphalt, it becomes highly dispersed through the blend and upon cooling reverts to its crystalline form. But up to 14% of the sulphur will react with the molecules that make up asphalt. These reactions, most likely with the olefin links, greatly resemble those found between sulphur and the additives in the sulphur concrete mixes. Greater strength, flexibility and a rapid set time are once again the

qualities sulphur can bring to road paving materials.

Road building and repair jobs with the Gulf Canada sulphur-asphalt-module (SAM) prove that despite obstacles in the form of sulphur supply, price and temperature, the method cuts road cost.[29] Experience with the SAM system has encompassed contracts requiring both full-depth road beds and resurfacing work under a wide range of climatic conditions.

At the batch plant, liquid sulphur is pumped out of a tanker into the SAM. The module pre-blends the sulphur and asphalt prior to mixing in the pugmill. The SAM produces up to 80 tons per hour of binder at a 40 to 50% sulphur-to-asphalt mix by weight. Scheduling is an important consideration to the contractor because the infrastructure necessary for the firm delivery of liquid sulphur is not yet in place. Temperature is also a major concern. Mixing must be carried out below 149°C to prevent the production of dangerous hydrogen sulphide gas. "Hydrogen sulphide in small concentrations can be metabolized, but in higher concentrations it quickly can cause death by respiratory paralysis. It is insidious in that it quickly deadens the sense of smell".[30] The sulphur asphalt hot mixes cannot be stored

overnight in surge bins because of gas production.

As of spring 1981, there had been 23 tests of the SAM process including five projects in Ontario.[31] The key to success, according to David Bean of Gulf's Mississauga Research Center, have been good communication and scheduling. The contractor must dovetail his mixing with the arrival on site of SAM and the liquid sulphur. Although western sulphur supplies can be economically transported to the east, "The real problem is that there are no trucks and terminals to facilitate distribution. It's tricky for the contractor."

■ Miller Paving (Unionville, Ontario have completed three sulphur-asphalt jobs in that province. The firm recently finished a two-kilometre stretch of high-traffic-volume road in Metropolitan Toronto. They did experience some difficulty in obtaining a ready supply of liquid sulphur and eventually had to rely on a source in nearby Buffalo, New York. They did not have any problems with the technology, however. There were no odour problems and the work crew, using traditional paving equipment, found no noticeable difference working with the sulphur-asphalt mixture.

While Miller Paving was showing the system was practical, the Metro Toronto roads and traffic department was enjoying the economic benefits. With asphalt selling for between $180 and $200 a tonne, the SAM reduced the material costs by over $5000. Greater savings would be possible by increasing the sulphur content from 40 to 50%, and efficiencies due to economies of scale could be reaped from larger projects. While not yet committed to the sulphur-asphalt mixes (the municipality wants several more years of experience to evaluate performance), officials are encouraged. Chief engineer Tom Johnson says that tight money is forcing road builders to look at innovative technology. "We're not just falling back on tried and true methods. Now we're being pushed to look for solutions."[29]

Warm weather in Toronto usu-

Sulphur extended asphalts make use of molten sulphur to replace up to 40% of the asphalt in paving binders, thus extending asphalt supplies.

Sulphur Development Institute

ally means a softer penetration grade asphalt is unacceptable. An 85-100 grade is used to reduce rutting. But sulphur additions increase the asphalt's stability, giving the soft grades greater strength in the summer and allowing a more flexible material for cold weather work.

Beyond increased versatility for new road work, sulphur-extended asphalts are also amenable to recycling. The Ontario Ministry of Transportation and Communications successfully recycled 28 tonnes of sulphur asphalt pavement near the town of Renfrew in 1980.[31]

■ Asphalts Associates Inc. (East Peoria, Illinois) is using sulphur-extended pavements and realizing additional savings, by making it with solid sulphur.[32] They melt the sulphur in their asphalt plant rather than depending on more expensive liquid sulphur sources. Liquid sulphur sells at about $120 a ton or $50 more expensive than solid forms. The firm believes the sulphur extended pavements save about $1.50 a ton compared to asphalt and the economics will continue to improve as the price disparity between the two substances increases.

Sulphur asphalts have also been developed by the National Research Council of Canada (NRC) and Shell Canada.

■ The Division of Building Research of the NRC in Ottawa has patented a sulphur asphalt product designed for pothole repair.[33] Field tests in Winnipeg, Manitoba, and St. Laurent, Quebec have shown positive results; potholes repaired in the spring of 1979 and 1980 stood up through the vigours of winter while those filled with conventional material did not survive.[33]

The formulation is produced at a plant developed by the Ontario Research Foundation. The composite is solidified and fragmented before being transferred to the repair site. There it is remelted in a portable, heated kettle. The composite is thrown in the pothole and, because it develops strength while it is cooling and solidifying, it is self-compacting. The product bonds well to the road base and cools in less than half an hour.

Unused material can be remelted and re-used.

The rapid set time is extremely important. Like sulphur concretes, which can also be used for road patching,[25] the NRC mix allows pavement repairs to be made on heavily travelled streets in a minimum of time. Potholes can be filled and the highway almost immediately opened to traffic during any time of the year.

■ Shell Canada's Thermopave™ product has a higher sulphur-to-asphalt ratio than the Gulf system. Asphalt normally makes up about 6% of a highway paving mix with the remainder various forms of aggregate.[28] Thermopave™ is approximately 13% sulphur, 6% asphalt and 81% sand.[24] Because of the high sulphur content the mixture is very fluid when molten. A modified Mix-Paver is used to lay the material, but no rolling is required to compact it.

4.
Asphalt Replacements

Sulphlex™, a product of the U.S. Southwest Research Institute (San Antonio, Texas) goes one step beyond the sulphur asphalt mixtures by totally eliminating the need for asphalt. The selection of specific additives gives a sulphur binder an array of flexibilities that ranges from a malleable asphalt-like substance to the rigid concretes discussed earlier. Sulphlex™ contains approximately 60-70% sulphur and 10-15% each of dicyclopentadiene (or mixed cyclodienes), dipentene, vinyl toluene and coal tar.[24]

It compares favourably with asphalt in regard to ductility, softening point and penetration, and there is little difficulty in processing it. Both asphalt and Sulphlex™ are heated to 120°C before paving.[27] A major concern with the acceptance of Sulphlex™ is the rising price of sulphur. According to Douglas M. Bernard of the U.S. Federal Highway Administration, "to be economically competitive with asphalt, sulphur has to be half the cost, since the specific gravity of sulphur is half that of asphalt," and 25 to 50% more must be used.[28]

At present, in the small quantities used, the additive plasticizers used in Sulphlex™ are extremely expensive, making it uncompetitive with standard asphalt hot mix.[32] The potential market, if sulphur is affordable, is fantastic. In the United States, 23.6 million tonnes of asphalt are used each year, while elemental sulphur production was only 9.3 million

Paving with sulphur extended asphalt. A few modifications of the plant are required to produce sulphur extended asphalt, but transport, paving and rolling operations are carried out as usual.

Stockpile of sulphur in Alberta (usually 99.9% pure or better).

Sulphur Innovations Ltd

tonnes. Consumption, mainly for fertilizer production and industrial use, was 12 million tonnes. The sulphur for road building must come from pollution control, and possibly, synfuels production.

In 1980, Sulphlex™ was to be tested on public highways in Texas, North Dakota, Nebraska, Pennsylvania, Arizona, Georgia and Florida. A test strip on the SWRI grounds has performed well since 1979. Sulphlex is still several years away from commercialization, but if and when it is ready for wide-scale application, it should supply both an alternative to scarce petrochemical products and a ready market for a major byproduct of pollution abatement equipment.

5.
Sulphur Production

The existing sulphur market is dominated by the production of phosphate fertilizers. About 60% of the total sulphur consumption is diverted to this enterprise. The sulphur is converted to sulphuric acid and used to treat phosphate rock to produce wet process phosphoric acid. Phosphoric acid, in turn, is used to produce a variety of fertilizers including regular, triple super phosphate and diammonium phosphate.[34]

The remaining sulphur market is mostly for sulphuric acid, the workhorse of industrial production. The three major consumers are non-fertilizer chemical producers (8%), petroleum refiners (6%) and metal miners (6%). The remaining 20% goes into a wide variety of products including rubber, explosives, pulp and paper, water treatment, etc. Their markets are, by and large, temporarily stagnant, reflecting the present recessionary traits of the economy in North America.[3]

Sulphur sources to meet these markets are divided primarily between natural sulphur-bearing formations which are mined using the Frasch steam process, and sulphur recovered from industrial operations through refining processes or air pollution control programmes. In 1979 western world brimstone production by type was:[35]

Frasch Sulphur 8,460,000 tonnes

Recovered Sulphur :

Natural Gas	11,073,000 tonnes
Oil Refinery	5,293,000 tonnes
Coke Oven Gas	25,000 tonnes
Power Plants	28,000 tonnes
Tar Sands	180,000 tonnes
Coal Gasification	—
Native Refined	170,000 tonnes

TOTAL 25,229,000 tonnes

Non-brimstone sources of sulphur recovered from pyrites (4,160,000 long tons) and smelter gases (6,100,000 long tons) accounted for 10,495,000 tons for a grand total of 36 million tons of sulphur.[36]

The other form of sulphur produced in great quantities and not included in these totals is sulphur dioxide. This gas is spewed forth from the smoke stacks of power plants, smelters, refineries, sour gas plants and tarsand operations by the millions of tonnes in Canada each year. Provincial air pollution legislation has largely been geared to ensuring that these emissions do not have a detrimental effect on local ambient air quality. Sulphur dioxide at high concentration kills vegetation, damages buildings, and can be the cause of respiratory ailments ranging from emphysema to bronchitis, with fatal effect.

The favoured strategy for controlling these gases has been termed the dilution solution. It entails building tall smokestacks which force the pollutant gases high into the atmosphere. In theory, they are to disperse and scatter so that by the time the gases drift back to earth they are in such low concentrations that the earth's natural assimilative capacity can absorb them without ill effect. Unfortunately, this has not been the case. The sulphur gases are instead suspended in the upper atmosphere for several days during which time, under the influence of water vapour, oxygen and the sun's rays, they undergo a complex chemical transformation. When they finally return to earth, hundreds of kilometres from their source, they do so as dilute acid. This is the acidic precipitation that is proving the scourge of North America's lakes, forests, historic monuments and wildlife.

While new air pollution regulations in this country are recognizing this problem[37] (with major ramifications for the future supply of recovered sulphur products), the problem of long distance air pollution is anything but recent.

6.
Fertilizers

Sulphur gases from Cominco's large Trail smelter in British Columbia were arousing the ire of U.S. farmers back in the 1920s. The year 1929 proved to be a landmark year for effective environmental control, for that year saw both the introduction of international air pollution control legislation and the installation of the first 25-ton-per-day sulphuric acid plant at the Trail smelter.[38]

The negotiations for equitable transboundary air pollution legislation have continued to this day and are presently the centre of controversy between forces in Ottawa and Washington. The Cominco acid plants have also continued in operation and are now the basis of a highly successful fertilizer and chemical sales division which accounts for almost one-quarter of Cominco's sales.[38]

Two years after the acid plant began converting the offensive gases from the lead sintering and zinc roasting operations into acid, the production of ammonium sulphate and ammonium phosphate fertilizers began. Fifty years later, Cominco is one of Canada's largest fertilizer suppliers. The original fertilizer facility at Warfield, near Trail, cost $10 million and continually grew through the 30s, mid-60s and was extensively modernized in the mid-70s. During the Second World War, an ordnance grade ammonium nitrate plant was added and converted to fertilizer production after hostilities had ended.

The Warfield phosphate plant treats about 900 tons per day of phosphate rock brought in by rail from the United States and requires 790 tons of 93% sulphuric acid each day to do the job. The ammonium sulphate plant also draws its sulphur product from the sulphuric acid plant at the smelter. In addition, Cominco operates plants at Kimberley, B.C. (an iron sulphide roasting plant, a sulphuric acid plant, and a phosphate fertilizer plant), Calgary, Alberta (three fertilizer operations), and Carseland, Alberta (a modern

ammonia-urea plant). The Carseland plant also boasts a zero discharge water management system. Process water is largely cleaned and recycled although some used water containing trace amounts of urea and ammonia is used to irrigate 1650 acres of cultivated land.

The Cominco success story is not simply one of a firm that had the good fortune to discover its waste to be a valuable byproduct. The viability of its chemical fertilizer operation required hard research, daring innovation and aggressive salesmanship. Cominco did not simply enter an established fertilizer market; it created it through diligent product development and public education. Table 4 shows the impressive list of "firsts" the smelter firm has contributed to the fertilizer industry.[38] Other firms have retorted

that they "are not in the sulphur business" but in the metals business or the power business or whatever. Cominco recognized they were pouring a valuable component of their sulphur-rich Sullivan ore up the stack and onto their down-wind neighbours. Although they were a smelter firm, if hard work would turn an air pollutant into an economically attractive venture, they were willing to enter the fertilizer business, or any other.

When Cominco first contemplated the manufacture of fertilizer back in 1927, there was no large, untapped market waiting for them. A few regions in British Columbia used fertilizers, mostly on specialty crops, and there was some small consumption in the United States. Cominco scientists with the co-operation of government, universities and industry,

Table 4

Cominco's Contributions to the Nitrogen Fertilizer Industry

1931	First production of ammonium sulphate fertilizer in western Canada.
1941	First petrochemical plant in North America to use natural gas for the manufacture of ammonia.
1945	First commercially successful prilling in the world of ammonium nitrate for fertilizer use.
1954-55	Introduction of anhydrous ammonia into the western Canadian market.
1960	First production of urea in western Canada.
1963	First commercial scale drum granulation of ammonium nitrate in the world.
1965	First commercial scale drum granulation of urea in the world.
1965-66	Introduction of nitrogen solution fertilizer to the western Canadian market.
1967-68	First production in the world of large urea granules for aerial application to forested land.
1969	First commercial production in Canada of granular ammonium nitrate-sulphate fertilizer.
1973	First manufacture in Canada of a dust free homogeneously conditioned granular urea.
1975-76	First to demonstrate that granular urea is a satisfactory carrier for certain wild oat control chemicals and other herbicides.
1976	First commercial production of granular urea-ammonium sulphate fertilizer analyzing 40-0-0-6.
1981	First commercial production of homogenous granular urea-sulphur fertilizer.

Source: "Cominco Fertilizers: Fifty Years of Innovation and Growth," *Canadian Mining Journal*, May 1981.

had to undertake large-scale field testing programmes to prove the value of field and forest fertilization. Once that was completed, an education programme had to be launched to introduce farmers to the practice.

Cominco engineers even developed an attachment for grain drills that would deposit the proper amount of fertilizer with the seeds at planting time. This is indicative of the diversification and imagination a smelting company went through to turn farmers' anger over air pollution into a profitable industrial activity.

■ Agri-Sul Canada has also entered the fertilizer derby by producing a fertilizer supplement for sulphur-deficient soils from sulphur derived from natural gas processing. This firm treats elemental sulphur, breaks it down into granular form from which it is quickly converted by bacteria into sulphate. Agri-Sul's process mixes molten sulphur with other ingredients into a slurry, which is cooled into a solid slate. The material is ground and either loaded into bags or shipped in bulk.[39] The fertilizer supplement has found consumers on the Canadian prairies and in the United States, Europe and Australia.

7.
Flue Gas Desulphurization

The use of fossil fuels, primarily coal, to supply energy to both industrial and residential consumers is on the upswing. The rapidly escalating cost of fuel oil, the public opposition to new nuclear power plants and the already efficient use of most of the available hydraulic capacity is forcing power companies to turn to coal to supply future increases in power demand. Although energy conservation has done much to reduce the growth in consumption, American utilities still plan to convert from oil and natural gas, or build from scratch, 271 coal-fired electrical generating plants in the next ten years.[2] Canadians have seen plans unveiled for new plants in the Atlantic provinces,

Table 5
Flue Gas Desulphurization in the United States

Status	Number of Units	Capacity (MW)
Operational	46	16,054
Under construction	43	17,297
Planned		
Contract awarded	20	10,690
Letter of intent signed	3	1,960
Requesting or evaluating bids	5	3,100
Considering FGD	27	13,406
TOTAL	144	62,507

Source: Flue-Gas Desulfurization Technology, U.S. National Research Council, 1980.

Alberta, Ontario and British Columbia. These stations will be a major addition to the North American atmospheric loadings of acid gas. But all the news is not black, for this is one pollution problem for which an abatement technology with a proven track record already exists.

Flue gas desulphurization units (FGD), or scrubbers as they are more commonly known, have been in development and operation for years.

■ Indeed, the London Power Company began the operation of a scrubber at its plant on the bank of the Thames in the 1930s. The British scrubber operated at 95% efficiency for 40 years.

A power company, hunting for the ideal scrubbing system to control its sulphur dioxide emissions, has a wide range of technologies to choose from: wet limestone, dry scrubbing, dry injection and electron beam systems are all being marketed. As for end products, utilities can pick among equipment that produces sulphur, sulphuric acid, gypsum or some non-saleable sludge material.

There are no scrubbers operating as yet on Canadian power plants although U.S. utilities are gaining a certain amount of exper-

tise in the field (see Table 5).[40] Ontario Hydro, in the spring of 1981, announced what will be Canada's first acid gas control programme to incorporate scrubbers.[37] By 1986, flue gas scrubbers will be installed and in operation on two of eight 500-megawatt units at the Lambton Generating Station. These scrubbers will remove 90% of the sulphur dioxide emitted from the units and will utilize a wet limestone system that produces a sludge requiring landfill disposal. Most wet limestone systems generate 2 to 3 tons of sludge for each ton of SO_2 they remove.

Ontario Hydro maintains that the wet "throwaway" systems are the state of the art for FGD. During an earlier investigation of the available technologies, Hydro found that marketing firms for equipment capable of producing a saleable byproduct were unable or unwilling to offer performance guarantees that met with Ontario Hydro's satisfaction.

The trend towards the disposal systems is also marked in the United States, where, of the firms operating, constructing or planning FGD installations, 70% had opted for the wet limestone throwaway variety, 24% were undecided and less than 6% had chosen types that would yield saleable byproducts.[41] It is estimated that by 1990 only 3.6% of the U.S. plants will be operating recovery systems.

Despite the preponderance of the swing towards throw-away systems in the United States and Ontario, there have been good results and extensive experience gained with FGD byproduct recovery systems in Europe and Japan. As sulphur prices escalate, there will be greater incentive to take the risk on "unproven" technologies in the hopes of offsetting the high cost of scrubber installation and operation through byproduct sales.

Of perhaps greater importance is the decreasing amount of land available for, and increasing costs associated with, waste disposal. It is estimated that a typical 1000-megawatt utility plant will require 400-700 acres for disposal of ash and flue gas over a lifetime of 30 years (depending on the type of coal and regional locations).[42] Disposal costs may range as high as $50 to $100 a ton.[1] Financial burdens such as these should spur utilities to look at byproduct recovery systems. Of course the prime consideration must remain the efficiency of the chosen system in removing air pollutants from the flue gases. According to R.C. Rittenhouse, associate editor of *Power Engineering*, "The lure of a little pocket money possibly to be gained from future (byproduct) sales should not take priority over the primary function of the air pollution control system in selection."[43] This is certainly sound advice but it must be remembered that the economic rewards to be gained from innovative pollution control mechanisms take hard work, commitment, and the understanding that monetary return almost always entails some risk. If turning dross into gold simply required the installation of packaged, accepted, proven technology, there would be no need to write these case studies; they would be common knowledge. If firms were unwilling to take a calculated risk on technologies that had compelling though not conclusive evidence to support them, then industrial development would slowly grind to a halt. There is an opportunity for the vendors of pollution abatement systems to assume a degree of risk through performance guarantees or other contractual arrangements.

In a press release for a 1979 Environmental Protection Agency report *Sulphur Oxides Control Technology in Japan,* based on a fact-finding mission to study FGD systems, former EPA chief Douglas Costle writes, "Application of scrubber technology in Japan has generally preceded that in either the U.S. or Canada. This is in part due to the concentrated nature of Japanese industry and its proximity to population centres. But perhaps, more importantly, Japanese executives in general have shown a stronger commitment to installing scrubbers and making them work."[44]

The most common FGD system is the wet scrubber. This equipment removes SO_2 with between 70% and 90% efficiency and has a high reliability based on years of experience. The performance of the system depends on variables such as the pH of the scrubbing liquor, the liquid-to-gas ratio, the gas residence time, the pressure drop across the system, and the gas velocity. Most wet scrubbing systems incorporate the throw-away technology of calcium-based scrubbing. They require huge amounts of limestone which is contacted with SO_2 in an absorption vessel to produce a wet sludge. This sludge is composed of 15 to 35% solids which are primarily calcium sulphite and calcium sulphate. This is the material which normally requires disposal, but a number of system modifications have been developed which help circumvent this expensive problem.

The Davy Saarberg-Hoelter (Davy S-H) FGD process offers an SO_2 removal efficiency reaching 98%, eliminates liquid waste and produces an acceptable gypsum byproduct.[45] It also does much to alleviate scrubber scaling and plugging.

The lime-based wet scrubbing process was first demonstrated in Germany in 1974 and has been available in North America since 1978 through Acres Davy McKee (Rexdale, Ontario). It uses a clear alkaline solution (rather than the more commonly used slurry) as a washing fluid to trap SO_2. This takes place in a Rotopart™ absorber where the flue gas combines to form a water soluble intermediate, calcium bisulphite.

In the next on-line stage, forced oxidation, using ferric chloride as an oxidation catalyst, converts the calcium bisulphite into gypsum-calcium sulphate dihydrate.

The wash then has to be replenished with calcium, in the form of slurried lime, to replace those ions consumed in the formation of gypsum. At this point the pH is adjusted, and formic acid, and if necessary hydrochloric acid, is added.

In the final step, the gypsum crystals are separated out in a thickener. The filtrate is recirculated through the thickener and the clear overflow is returned to the Rotopart™ absorber to pick up the next load of sulphur. The washing fluid continues to flow through this closed-loop system, eliminating liquid waste.

The gypsum crystals can be processed into a quality gypsum grade for resale to wall board producers or sold for use in cement manufacturing. The important considerations for profitable byproduct marketing are gypsum quality and transportation costs. To be a saleable product, the gypsum's quality must meet the requirements of the user. This is dependent on the coal quality, contaminant removal and scrubbing system chosen. But the producers of gypsum products are interested in power plant derived stocks. The U.S. firm, National Gypsum Co., has accepted the material from at least four scrubbing systems as being of suitable quality,[43] so markets are available.

High quality gypsum was bringing between $2 and $7 (1981 Can. $) a short ton. Byproduct sales of power plant gypsum are thus feasible only when the transportation costs are not excessive when the power plant is close enough to the gypsum market to allow the byproduct to compete with natural sources. If markets are not available and stacking is required, the product from the Davy S-H scrubber requires only 60% of the land necessary for sulphite sludge disposal.[45] Unlike sludge disposal, there is no need for a settling pond.

When faced with local sulphur dioxide pollution problems, North American regulators opted for a control strategy which led directly to acid rain. In attempts to control acid rain, there is no reason to accept a new solid waste disposal problem on the grounds of necessity or expediency. There are alternatives.

■ Research-Cottrell (Somerville, New Jersey) also is marketing a calcium sulphite oxidation stage in their SO_2 scrubber systems.[15] The firm has contracts to engineer and supply systems that produce commercial grade gypsum for a 425-megawatt station owned by Tampa Electric and a 150-megawatt unit operated by the Muscatine Power and Water Company in Iowa.

Oxidation occurs on-line in the Cottrell system. This is carried out in one of the absorber loops in the Double Loop™ desulphurization process where the optimum pH (4 to 5.5) conditions exist. After oxidation, the gypsum sludge is settled out in hydro-cyclones to a minimum of 60% solids. The larger crystals of calcium sulphate settle out first. Vacuum filters further concentrate the material to at least 80% solids.

A commercial gypsum product is then produced using a technology developed with a West German wall board manufacturer, Kanauf. The characteristics of the scrubber product which are its calcium sulphate dihydrate content, chloride ion count and particle size, make it suitable for use in gypsum products and cement.

■ The demonstration unit at Northern Indiana Public Service Company's Mitchell station uses a Wellman-Lord sulphur dioxide recovery system to generate concentrated sulphur dioxide.[43] An Allied Chemical sulphur producing system is operated by that firm on the tail end of the system. The output has been going to Allied's nearby acid plant and as of October 1980 the power company was

realizing $64 a tonne in sales.
■ The Public Service Company of New Mexico uses a similar system to the one used by Northern Indiana Public Service to market sulphur, sodium sulphate and sulphuric acid.[43] Two 325-megawatt units on the San Juan plant produced 7066 tons of sulphur worth $423,000 (U.S.), and 31,726 tons of sodium sulphate worth about $350,000, in 1980. A 472- and a 476-megawatt unit will produce sulphuric acid to supply a uranium processing plant 150 miles away.
■ Avco/Ebara (Greenwich, Connecticut) uses an innovative electron beam scrubbing system to remove 95% of the SO_2 and 85% of the nitrogen oxides while producing a byproduct which is saleable as a fertilizer supplement.[46] The E-beam system also costs 40% less than conventional systems. After the fly ash has been removed from the flue gas, the gas is cooled and ammonia is added. The gas is then transferred to a reactor chamber where electron beams convert the sulphur and nitrogen oxides to

ammonium sulphate and ammonium nitrate. The dry powder is removed and compacted into granules for sale. The clean gas leaves the system hot enough to be exhausted to the atmosphere without reheating.
■ A system marketed by Peabody International (Stamford, Connecticut) removes the need for expensive limestone purchases by using captured fly ash from the same plant to snare the sulphur dioxide in the flue gases.[46] The system removes fly ash with a wet venturi scrubber and the resultant slurry is then used in an adjacent spray tower absorber to remove SO_2. Although operating and maintenance costs are slightly higher than in other processes, capital costs are lower and there is no need to buy alkali.
■ There are a number of processes available to transform scrubber wastes into building aggregate. I.U. Conversion Systems (Horsham, Pennsylvania) market a pozzolanic stabilization reaction process.[15] A lime-based reagent is added to scrubber sludge and fly

Figure 4
Impact of Sulphur from Coal

The impact of pollution control measures will significantly affect the amount of sulphur available over the next 10 years. If acid gas abatement programmes require sulphur recovery from power plant and smelter stack gases, then millions of tons of sulphur may come onto the North American market.

Source: "Sulphur Supply and Highway," *Highway and Heavy Construction*, July 1981.

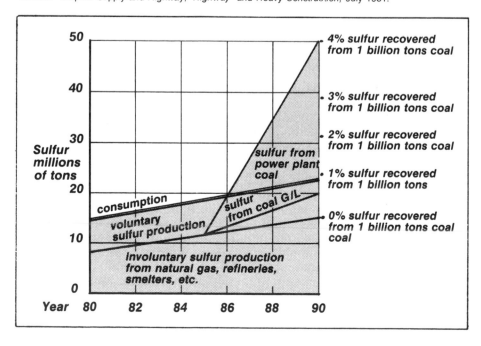

ash to create a mineral product suitable for road base building. A company director explains, "It is a very old technology. The Romans used similar know-how to build the Appian Way. They mixed volcanic ash with lime to make a paving material."[15] I.U. Conversions is also investigating solidifying the waste into block form to build an artificial reef off Long Island.

Sulphur Marketing

The last decade has been a decade of expanding possibilities for sulphur: sulphur concretes and sulphur protective coatings, sulphur asphalts and asphalt replacements, fabric and concrete additives, fertilizers and soil supplements, gypsum and aggregate, acids and salt cake and elemental forms. The potential markets for sulphur byproducts are growing constantly.

During that same ten years, the initiative to control and finally contain sulphur dioxide air emissions has gained impetus and acquired the technical expertise to make it effective.

On one hand a growing number of uses for sulphur, on the other a potentially vast supply of captured sulphur wastes (see Figure 4).[47] The markets must be matched with the producers, with two provisos. First, the producer must be willing to capture and process a good quality sulphur byproduct. Second, the economics of sulphur must be good enough to make the necessary transportation network available while still allowing the new sulphur uses to remain price-competitive.

One sulphur analyst remarked that it is almost impossible to write about sulphur markets and trends; information is hopelessly out of date before the ink is dry. What is indisputable is that sulphur prices have been rising rapidly in recent years. In 1970, sulphur sold for $20 a ton and even dropped as low as $5 a ton at Canadian processing plants.[48] By 1981, spot prices in Florida markets reached $140 a long ton;[36] other world markets paid $200 per long ton. Alberta producing plants

were getting more than $100 a metric ton for offshore sales to some of 40 different countries.[48]

The sulphur demand is presently outstripping supply and much of the traditional sources of sulphur, from Frasch mined sources and natural gas proces-

sors, are going to meet the demands of fertilizer producers and other longtime industrial customers. The Canadian producers of acid (see Table 6)[49] have well established markets waiting for them and increased production will probably be earmarked for

Table 6
Canadian Producers of Sulphuric Acid

Company	Location	Nameplate capacity (kilotonne/year)
Alcan Smelters & Chemicals*	Jonquière, Que.	78
Allied Chemical Canada	Valleyfield, Que.	140
Border Chemical	Transcona, Man.	150
Brunswick Mining & Smelting*	Belldune, N.B.	125
Canadian Electrolytic Zinc	Valleyfield, Que.	120
Inco†	Copper Cliff, Ont.	865
C-I-L†	McMasterville, Que.	60
C-I-L†	Courtright, Nobel, Ont.	**
Canadian Titanium Pigments*	Varennes, Que.	47
Cominco	Trail, BC	440
Cominco*	Kimberley, BC	280
Du Pont Canada†	North Bay, Ont.	**
Esso Chemical Canada*	Redwater, Alta.	515
Falconbridge Nickel	Sudbury, Ont.	320
Gaspe Copper Mines	Murdochville, Que.	245
Gulf Minerals*	Rabbit Lake, Sask.	45
Inland Chemicals	Ft. Saskatchewan, Alta.	200
Inland Chemicals	Prince George, BC	35
International Minerals & Chemical	Pt. Maitland, Ont.	250
Sherritt Gordon Mines*	Ft. Saskatchewan, Alta.	190
Sulco Chemicals	Elmira, Ont.	35
Texasgulf Canada†	Timmins, Ont.	205
Western Co-operative Fertilizers*	Calgary	360
Western Co-operative Fertilizers*	Medicine Hat, Alta.	190
Total capacity, 1980		4,930

*Primarily for captive use
**Byproduct acid for sale
†Marketed by C-I-L

New capacity planned or under construction:

Texasgulf	Timmins completion late '81	200
Western Co-operative Fertilizers	Medicine Hat replacing existing unit in 1981	397

Source: "Canada Strong in Sulphuric Acid," *Canadian Chemical Processing*, October 1980.

those same users. Over the next ten years, the supply will scarcely meet the demand and one study forecasts that by 1990, there will be a shortfall of six million tonnes a year in available sulphur.[50] The huge stockpiles in Alberta, estimated at almost 19 million tons,[48] face exhaustion over the next decade despite expansions. New sources in Poland, the USSR and the Middle East are threatened by continued domestic upheaval.

Conclusion

Canada has been a world leader in developing new uses for sulphur. Research in this country is yielding sulphur-based products that do not simply get rid of excess sulphur but offer new and improved products that could compete with traditional materials on the basis of properties and performance.[51] It is vitally important that this intensive research and development now begin to pay back dividends. The other powerful research nations, West Germany, Japan, the United States, all depend on pay-back to fuel research, and national implementation programmes to keep the economic and employment benefits within the country.

Canada has a number of large sulphur dioxide emitters: smelters, power plants, refineries, natural gas and tarsands plants. Economic incentives, coordination and the development of an efficient distribution network would guarantee that the Canadian sulphur product developments achieve practical application. Both private and public initiative and co-operation will ensure that present air pollution problems can be transformed into the raw material for cheaper, more durable highways, more versatile concretes, resistant building materials and more productive farmland. Researchers have designed the yellow brick road; now all we have to do is follow it.

OTHER SOLID WASTES

Sulphur and fly ash byproducts are not the only examples of unconventional waste utilization that could have been chosen for this chapter. The glass industry has been experimenting with novel raw materials. Rice husk ash, bagasse ash (from a sugar factory), blast furnace slag and open hearth furnace slag have been used to manufacture inexpensive glass products.[52] The glass from waste proved to be more durable than standard soda-lime-silica bottle glass and showed desirable thermal expansion and working characteristics. More importantly, it proved to be a cheaper way to produce glass containers, construction panels, fibres and foams.

There has also been a great deal of investigation into blast furnace slag cements.[53,54] The history of slag cement stretches back to the last century and they achieved wide use in Germany during World War II. Now the products are fighting to gain a place in modern construction practices. In the United States, 26 million tons of slag were produced in blast furnaces in 1976; of that only 1.6 million tons were granulated and of any potential value to the cement industry. In Hamilton, Ontario, the Standard Slag Cement Company has proven blast

Table 7
Solid Wastes of Potential Use in the Construction Industry

Class 1	Class 2	Class 3
Blast furnace slags	Phosphate slag	Gold tailings
Fly ash	Copper slag	Copper tailings
Sulphur	Cement kiln dust	Lead-zinc tailings
Steel slag	Quarry waste	Coke breeze
Boiler slag	Mine refuse	Foundry sand
Bottom ash	Slate waste	Ceramic and refractory wastes
Nickel slag	Bark and sawdust	Resin
Demolition wastes	Fluorspar tailings	Lignin
Colliery spoil	Tires and rubber	Potassium salt mine wastes
Oil shale residue	Zinc slag	Pyrite cinders
Taconite tailings	Lead slag	Waste glass
China clay sand	Mixed ash	Waste plastics
Iron ore tailings	Incinerator residue	Cellulosic
Pyrolysis residue		

Class 1 — Wastes and byproducts of maximum potential. They possess the best properties either in their naturally occurring, processed or combined form, or have a record of satisfactory performance.
Class 2 — Wastes and byproducts requiring more extensive processing and/or where properties are not as adequate as those in Class 1.
Class 3 — Wastes and byproducts showing less promise than Classes 1 and 2, and recommended for use only in isolated situations.

Source: "Utilization of Wastes and Byproducts as Construction Materials in Canada," *Conservation and Recycling* 2(1), 1978.

furnace slag can be a successful cement replacement.[5] The slag can substitute between 25 and 65% of the Portland cement in concrete mixes and offer cost savings of 10 to 30%.

The total investment for facilities to granulate and grind slag are about one-half of that for a new Portland cement plant and the fuel needed to dry slag is less than one-tenth of that required to fire the most efficient cement kiln.[53]

Canada is also an innovator in the development of a process of direct pelletization of slag to produce a light-weight aggregate. The small pellets are used for slag cement and the large for aggregate. Among the advantages of the process are its low capital costs, time- and space-saving features, water conservation, gas control and high product quality.[5,54] This system, an invention of National Slag Limited (Hamilton, Ontario), is being copied throughout the world.

Blast furnace slag has been used to produce a durable glass ceramic product, Slagsitall, in the Soviet Union. Government pressure to increase industrial waste recycling has resulted in the development of Slagsitall, a building and insulator material that shows excellent chemical and wear resistance.[55] When formed into sheets or tiles, the ceramic can be used as wall cladding or industrial flooring. Installation costs are also claimed to be lower.

Steel slag can be used in asphalts. It is highly stable and offers a high degree of skid control. Indeed it "is the most skid resistant aggregate available in southern Ontario."[5] The price of steel slag asphalt concrete mixes is comparable to conventional mixes.

Lead and zinc slags can be used as raw materials for ceramic tile manufacture. Trial runs using a 60% zinc slag substitution produced high quality tiles that met all specifications. An economic analysis of the substitution shows potential fuel savings of 7% and raw material savings of 32%.[56]

The diligent student of waste re-use literature has to come to one conclusion: you can make concrete out of anything. Russian researchers report that adding 0.5% mycelial wastes from penicillin manufacturing (with 0.1% calcium chloride and 0.5% calcium carbonate) to fine-grained concrete results in a construction material with enhanced bending and compression strengths.[57] The report doesn't mention if disease resistance is increased.

Other work has utilized recycled waste glass for insulation and "glasphalt",[58] reclaimed concrete,[10,59,60] cement kiln dust, tires, asphalt,[61,62,63] chrome slags,[64] and sawdust.[10] Table 7 lists those wastes that the Organization for Economic Co-operation and Development deems of potential use in the construction field.[5]

The major constraint on the use of many of these materials, particularly as a replacement for aggregate or other low-cost building supply, is transportation costs. Transportation contributes about 35% of the total cost of aggregate, which limits competition from wastes to those within 30 to 50 km of the job site.[5]

According to J.J. Emery, the other limiting factors in a waste product's acceptance as a construction material are "the inherent variability of many wastes, current economic conditions, agency conservatism and obsolete specifications and industry structures."[5] The sulphur and fly ash case studies illustrate how these obstacles are being overcome and the extent of the work that still has to be done.

FOR FURTHER INFORMATION

Associations and Research Institutes

Sulphur Development Institute
of Canada (SUDIC),
1702 Canada Trust Building,
505 3rd Street S.W.,
Calgary, Alberta.
T2P 3E6
(403) 265-4220

The British Sulphur
Corporation Limited,
Parnell House,
25 Wilton Road,
London SW1 V1NH, England.
01-828-5571

Sulphur Innovations Limited,
3015 58th Ave. S.E.,
Calgary, Alberta.
T2C 0B4
(403) 279-2720

National Ash Association,
1819 H Street N.W.,
Washington, D.C.
20006
(202) 659-2303

Sulphur Institute,
1725 K Street N.W.,
Washington, D.C.
20006
(202) 331-9660

Southwest Research Institute,
6220 Culebra Rd.,
San Antonio, Texas.
78284
(512) 684-5111

National Asphalt Pavement
Association,
6811 Kenilworth Ave.,
Riverdale, Maryland.
20840
(301) 779-4880

Asphalt Recycling and Reclaiming
Association,
Suite 1200,
1000 Vermont Ave. N.W.,
Washington, D.C.
20005
(202) 628-4634

Association of Asphalt Paving
Technologists,
155 Experimental Engineering
Building,
Minneapolis, Minnesota.
55455
(612) 373-2518

American Concrete Institute,
P.O. Box 19150,
Redford Station,
Detroit, Michigan.
48219
(313) 532-2600

National Slag Association,
300 South Washington Street,
Alexandria, Virginia.
22314
(703) 549-3111

Journals

JOURNAL OF THE
AMERICAN CONCRETE
INSTITUTE,
P.O. Box 19150,
Redford Station,
Detroit, Michigan.
48219

ROCK PRODUCTS,
Maclean Hunter Publishing
Corporation,
300 W. Adams Street,
Chicago, Illinois.
60606

ENGINEERING NEWS-RECORD,
McGraw-Hill Building,
1221 Avenue of the Americas,
New York, New York.
10020

HIGHWAY AND HEAVY
CONSTRUCTION,
Circulation Department Manager,
666 Fifth Ave.,
New York, New York.
10103

CONCRETE INTERNATIONAL,
American Concrete Institute,
P.O. Box 19150,
Redford Station,
Detroit, Michigan.
48219

References

1. "The Continuing Disposal of Fly Ash." *Electric Power Research Institute Journal,* March 1980.

2. "Fly and Bottom Ash." *Mining Engineering,* May 1980.

3. Mills, R.H. "Fly Ash — Pollutant or Pearl?" In *Engineering Forum.* Faculty of Applied Science and Engineering, University of Toronto, February 1974.

4. Berry, E. and Malhotra, V.M. "Fly Ash *for Use in Concrete —A Critical* Review." *Journal of the American Concrete Institute,* March/April 1980.

5. Emery, J.J. "Utilization of Wastes and Byproducts as Construction Materials in Canada." *Conservation and Recycling* 2(1), 1978.

6. "Standard Specifications for Blended Hydraulic Cements." In *1975 Annual Book of ASTM Standards, Part 13.* Philadelphia: American Society for Testing and Materials, 1975. ASTM C595.

7. "Guideline for Federal Procurement of Cement and Concrete Containing Fly Ash." *Federal Register* (U.S.) 45(226), November 20, 1980.

8. Grancher, R.A. "Slag and Fly Ash in the Industry's Future." *Rock Products,* November 1979.

9. "Australian Firm to Market Fly Ash as Concrete Additives." *Chemical Week,* November 14, 1979.

10. Ramachandran, V.S. "Waste and By-Products as Concrete Aggregates." *Canadian Building Digest,* April 1981.

11. U.S. Environmental Protection Agency. *Utilization of Fly Ash and Coal Mine Refuse as a Road Base Material.* Industrial Environmental Research Laboratory, U.S.E.P.A., August 1979 (Report No. EPA-600/7-79-122).

12. "Waste Ash as Road Bed Material." *Environmental Pollution Management,* May/June 1981.

13. Campbell, Moni. *Hazardous Waste Reduction and Reclamation.* Toronto: Pollution Probe at the University of Toronto, March 1981.

14. "Fly Ash for Soil Stabilizer." *Biocycle,* May/June 1981.

15. "Scrubber Users Want a Home for Waste." *Chemical Week,* May 14, 1980.

16. "Converting Hazardous Waste into a Road Filler." *Chemical Week,* August 12, 1981.

17. "The Fly Ash Route to Metals Will Get a Pilot Test." *Chemical Week,* October 1, 1980.

18. "Oak Ridge Develops Ways to Recover Aluminum from Coal Fly Ash." *Chemical Week,* October 31, 1979.

19. "Metal Recovery from Fly Ash Will Get a Tryout." *Chemical Week,* July 30, 1980.

20. "Fly Ash Saves $1 Million in Wet Scrubber System." *Engineering News Record,* October 23, 1980.

21. "Trace Element Absorption on Soil Amended with Soft Coal Fly Ash." *Biocycle,* March/April 1981.

22. Adriano, D.C. *et al.* "Utilization and Disposal of Fly Ash and Other Coal Residues in Terrestrial Ecosystems: A Review." *Journal of Environmental Quality* 9(3), 1980.

23. Friend, J. Newton. *Man and the Chemical Elements, 2nd. Edition.* New York: Scribner, 1961.

24. Currell, B.R. and Parrett, F.W. "Sulphur Materials." *Chemistry in Canada,* September 1981.

25. Pickard, S.S. "Sulphur Concrete: Understanding/Application." *Concrete International,* October 1981.

26. Saxon, R.T. "Use of Sulphur Concrete in the Metallurgical/Fertilizer Industry." *Sulphur-81* (Sulphur Development Institute of Canada), Calgary, May 1981.

27. "Sulphur May Pave Way for Yellow Brick Road." *Chemical Week,* August 15, 1979.

28. "Sulfer: Paving Material Down the Road." *Chemical Week,* June 18, 1980.

29. Hancock, N. "What to Expect on Sulphur/Asphalt Jobs." *Engineering and Contract Record,* March 1981.

30. Weast, Robert C. (ed.) *Handbook of Chemistry and Physics, 56th. Edition.* Cleveland: CRC Press, 1975.

31. Wilson, D. "Scheduling, Good Communications Key to Success." *Engineering and Contract Record,* March 1981.

32. "Sulfer Makes Paving Inroads." *Engineering News Record,* September 25, 1980.

33. "Sulphur-Asphalt for Pothole Repair." *Chemistry in Canada,* February 1981.

34. "Sulfur's Future Hangs on Phosphates." *Chemical Week,* October 14, 1981.

35. British Sulphur Corporation Limited. *Marketing Study for Byproduct Sulphuric Acid Produced by Canadian Non-Ferrour Smelters.* Supply and Services Canada Contract No. OSQ77-00279, May 1979.

36. Eckert, George F. "Sulphur: Inventory Reductions and Higher Prices Prevail." *Engineering and Mining Journal,* March 1981.

37. Ontario Hydro. *Acid Gas Control Program Status Report.* May 31, 1981.

38. Pabst, M. "Cominco Fertilizers: Fifty Years of Innovation and Growth." *Canadian Mining Journal,* May 1981.

39. "Fertilizer Supplement for Sulfur-Deficient Soils." *Industrial Finishing,* July 1978.

40. National Research Council (U.S.). *Flue-Gas Desulfurization Technology.* Washington, D.C., 1980.

41. U.S. Environmental Protection Agency. *Utility Flue Gas Desulfurization Survey.* U.S.E.P.A. Report No. EPA-600/7-81-012a, 1981.

42. U.S. Environmental Protection Agency. *Sulfur Emission Control Technology and Waste Management.* U.S.E.P.A. Report No. 600-9-79-019, May 1979.

43. Rittenhouse, R.C. "Waste: Sell or Throw Away?" *Power Engineering,* March 1981.

44. U.S. Environmental Protection Agency. *Sulfur Oxides Control in Japan.* U.S.E.P.A. Report No. EPA-600/9-79-043, November 1979.

45. "Desulfurization Process Eliminates Liquid Waste." *Eco/Log Week,* September 12, 1980.

46. "Acid Rain Spurs Scrubber Research." *Modern Power and Engineering,* February 1981.

47. Dale, John M. "Sulfur Supply and Highways." *Highway and Heavy Construction,* July 1981.

48. Yackulic, George. "Alberta Sulfur Industry Leaps from Slump." *The Globe and Mail* (Canada).Mar 2, 81.

49. "Canada Strong in Sulphuric Acid." *Canadian Chemical Processing,* October 1980.

50. "Shortage by 1990 Forecast for Sulphur." *Toronto Star,* October 20, 1981.

51. Hyne, J.B. "Sulphur." *Chemistry in Canada,* June 1979.

52. Samdani, S. and Laxmikantham, A. "Use of Industrial Agricultural Wastes for Making Glasses." *American Ceramic Society Bulletin* 57(11), 1978.

53. Gee, K.H. "Slag Cements Make Sense!" *Rock Products,* April 1979.

54. Spellman, L.U. "New Generations of Slag Cements Show Promise." *Rock Products,* February 1980.

55. Scholes, Stafford, "Blast Furnace Slag — Wastes to Build On." *New Scientist,* July 26, 1973.

56. Carr, Dodd S. "Utilization of Lead and Zinc Slags in Ceramic Construction Products." *Conservation and Recycling* 3, 1980.

57. Karpukhim *et al.* "Complex Additive to Concrete Based on Mycelial Wastes from Antibiotics Production." *Zhim-Farm Zh* (USSR) 13(12), 1979; Abstract: *Chemical Abstracts* 92, 115363, 1980.

58. Low, N.M.P. "Innovative Building Materials Developed from Recycled Waste Glass." *Canadian Research,* April 1981.

59. "Recyclers Beat the Clock." *Engineering News Record,* November 6, 1980.

60. "D-Cracked Concrete Pavement Recycled for Less." *Highway and Heavy Construction,* April 1981.

61. "Asphalt Pavement Milled and Recycled on Same Project." *Highway and Heavy Construction,* August 1981.

62. "In Place Recycling Cuts Paving Cost, Time." *Highway and Heavy Construction,* June 1981.

63. "Hawaii Places First Recycled Asphalt." *Highway and Heavy Construction,* April 1981.

64. "Chrome Aggregate Used in Place of Limestone." *Highway and Heavy Construction,* August 1981.

Food Processing

Few industries create as much waste as the food processing industry.[1] Growing, harvesting, processing, preserving, transporting and consumption activities all reject part of the original produce and toss it on the refuse heap. It is estimated that only 20 to 30% of the vegetable plant is utilized for human consumption.[2] That means 70 to 80% of the organic material is discarded somewhere along the path from field to dinner plate.

Much of the waste is generated by the processing industry. For instance, between one-half and two-thirds of the fruits and vegetables produced in the United States are commercially processed, and this proportion is increasing. During canning, as much as 40% of the raw vegetables are discarded as waste.[3]

"In many cases these wastes are often not used in the final saleable product because of size, shape or blemish, but remain high in nutritional value. Much of this material is currently being carted to a landfill site or incinerated. Ideally they should be recycled into the food production system to preserve their maximum nutritive and economic value."[4]

Table 1
Cannery Liquid Wastes

	Items canned					
Composition of Wastes	Beans	Corn	Peas	Spinach	Cherries	Pears
Waste volume, (gal per case)	26	25	25	20	40	51
Suspended solids, ppm	60	980	2,800	3,500	20	310
BOD, ppm	240	3,000	2,400	6,000	750	450
pH	7.6	6.5	7.0	7.0	6.2	

Character of wastes: Organic, suspended and soluble; dirt and grit

Source: Science and Engineering for Pollution Free Systems, Ann Arbor Science Publishers Inc., 1975.

Waste Characteristics

For the most part, food processing wastes do not present a difficult disposal problem. They seldom possess highly toxic or potentially hazardous properties, but they are characterized by their overwhelming volumes, seasonal variations and high biological oxygen demand (BOD). Their organic nature usually ensures that they are readily biodegradable, but when released into a water course, "the oxygen demanded by microorganisms degrading (this) material results in anoxic conditions, anaerobic decay, the evolution of foul-smelling and toxic gases, and the loss of higher life forms."[5]

Food wastes generally contain significant amounts of carbohydrates and other soluble organic materials, a high organic suspended solids content, and a low concentration of nutrient elements such as nitrogen and phosphorus. BOD levels are thus very high and can swamp the capacities of conventional sewage treatment plants. The BOD from apple processing reaches 19,000 ppm; from beets, 6500 ppm; from snap beans, 2200 ppm; and from sauerkraut, 40,000 ppm. In comparison, domestic sewage ranges between 200 and 300 ppm.[3] One litre of potato juice has the pollution potential of the daily wastes excreted by one person.[2] If, however, the grease, fats and proteins were collected for byproduct uses, the BOD could be reduced by 80%, the suspended solids by 65%, and the grease levels by 95%. Tables 1, 2 and 3 illustrate the volumes and nature of the wastes produced by the processing of meat, dairy and vegetable products.[6,7]

Seasonal variation is extreme in food processing wastes, particularly fruits and vegetables. Most of the processing of a crop occurs over a few months, because of crop availability and the deterioration of food quality during extended storage. This results in high flow

Table 2
Slaughterhouse and Packing House Wastes

Type of Waste:	Suspended solids ppm	Organic nitrogen ppm	BOD ppm
Killing floor	220	134	825
Blood and tank water	3,690	5,400	32,000
Scalding tub	8,360	1,290	4,600
Meat cutting	610	33	520
Gut washer	15,120	643	13,200
Sausage department	560	136	800
Lard department	180	84	180
Byproducts	1,380	186	2,200

Character of wastes: Organic, contain grease, hair, flesh, blood

Source: Science and Engineering for Pollution Free Systems, Ann Arbor Science Publishers Inc., 1975.

rates and exceptionally high BOD loading rates for a short period each year. These heavy loads may exceed the capacity of both the plant's water treatment facilities and the regional sewage system. The California peach and prune canning industry is a good example of this food waste characteristic. Figure 1 shows the rapid increase in BOD that follows summer harvesting.[5] Turkey processors operate only about 100 days a year — October, November and December. Their effluent flow patterns follow a similar pattern.[6]

If these wastewaters are contained and treated by typical tail-end systems, tremendous amounts of sludge are generated. In the United States, the food industry generates an estimated 650,000 tons of sludge a year (on a dry weight basis).[9] Over 3 billion gallons of wastewater are generated annually in the processing of the 34 varieties of fruits and vegetables packed in New York State.[3] Tomato canning alone results in the accumulation of approximately 5 million tonnes of waste each year. This represents a squandered food source; that tomato waste contains almost 100,000 tonnes of protein and 400,000 tonnes of carbohydrates. If that material could be reclaimed

for human consumption, it would provide the total caloric requirements for 2.5 million people and the minimum protein needs of a population of 5 million.[2]

Robert Baker expresses the opinion that it would be cheaper to supply more food by preventing waste than by increasing primary production.[10] If losses could be reduced by 30 to 50%, the available food supply would increase by 15% without having to hoe a single new acre.

Wastewaters are not the only sources that should be investigated for product recovery. Baker lists a number of other avenues that could be explored; at least 8% of all the bread produced stales before it ever reaches the consumer (and is thrown away); many fish are rejected either because they are boney or have names with negative connotations, like sucker or crappie. About 80% of fish harvested from the Great Lakes are killed and returned to the water; a quarter of all fruits and vegetables spoil and are discarded between harvest and the time they reach the consumer; the necks and giblets of broiler chickens are almost always discarded by the consumer along with the plastic bag they come in. Although meat strippers are used on poultry neck

Figure 1
Yuba City Water Reclamation Plant (Wastewater Flow and BOD Load)

The seasonal variation in waste loadings from a food processing plant is clearly shown in this data collected in a Yuba City water reclamation plant. The California peach and pear harvest immediately preceded the great jump in BOD.

Source: "Treatment of Wastewater from Food Processing and Brewing," *Chemistry and Industry,* July 4, 1981.

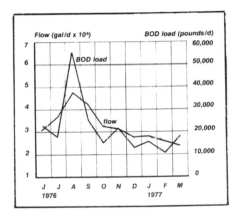

Table 3
Solid and Liquid Wastes Generated During Processing of Food

Processed Food		Total solid waste (g/kg)	Liquid volume (m³/kg)	BOD$_5$ (mg/kg)
Vegetable	Kale	16	0.004	11,000
	Spinach	20		11,000
	Mustard greens	16		10,000
	Turnip greens	15		9,000
	Collards	13		8,000
	Potatoes	66	0.012	44,000
	Peppers (lye peel)	65	0.020	33,000
	Tomatoes (lye peel)	14	0.010	
Dairy	Cheese whey		9.000	270,000
	Skim milk		0.070	1,500
	Ice cream		0.080	3,000
Meat	Red	0.440	25,000	14,000
	Poultry	0.270	50,000	13,000
	Eggs	0.111		

Source: "Maximizing Efficiencies in the Food System: A Review of Alternatives for Waste Abatement," *Journal of Food Protection,* March 1980.

and back pieces to produce chicken and turkey rolls, if the deboned necks and giblets were further processed, 787 million more pounds of edible poultry meat would be produced in the United States each year.

The consumer is also responsible for the growing mound of wasted food. Arizona researchers spent two years picking through garbage cans before reporting that 9 to 10% of a family's total food resources end up in the trash as permanent leftovers.[10] Cornell University investigators peg the waste total at closer to 15%.[10]

As inefficient as the system is in North America, in Third World countries, the losses are significantly higher. Insects, rodents, moulds, bacteria, spillage, bruising, excessive peeling or trimming, immature fruits and vegetables, inadequate drying equipment for grains, poor transport and refrigeration equipment, primitive processing and poor marketing all take their toll.[11]

Waste Inventory

It is the goal of every food processor to achieve the maximum efficiency in his system as long as he can show it is cost-effective. He wants to produce the greatest amount of quality product at the lowest cost. This is also the most efficient approach for controlling waste. By minimizing inefficiencies at each step in the food processing system, waste can be eliminated and significant improvements can be made in the recovery of a final saleable product or byproduct.

Once it is recognized by senior management that food wastes are a valuable resource, it is necessary to begin to devise a control programme which will reap the greatest benefits while reducing the effluent loadings. The first step must be through inventory of the flow of material through the process operation. Robert Zall of Cornell University's Department of Food Sciences (Ithaca, New York) has devised a simple series of questions to be answered:[12]

(1) What is being lost to the sewers?

(2) How much (of whatever it is) is being lost?
(3) What is the composition of the material being lost?
(4) Can the loss be stopped?
(5) Can the loss be reduced?
(6) If the lost material could be intercepted before it goes to the sewer, could it be used?

Often the answers to these questions offer the obvious, commonsense solution to waste control, a solution that might have been overlooked in the rush to install aerobic water treatment facilities and lagoon systems. It is most effective to assign one individual to the task of tracking material as it flows through the various processes of the plant. Liquid waste and food fragments should be identified — "materials unaccounted for and missing in action" — and the operations that generate these wastes should be pinpointed. The data needed to build a complete flow sheet of resources would include raw materials, ingredients, process chemicals, service materials, cleaning compounds, water consumption, sewage volume and energy use.

The next step is to collect representative samples of the waste produced by each process stage and conduct a complete analysis. On the basis of the laboratory findings, it should be possible to assign each component of the effluent stream both a unit cost value and a pollutant loading priority. When these figures are plugged into the regular cost accounting systems, their economic importance can be gauged against other plant operations.

There are two major advantages to this approach. First, it gives solid, quantitative data on the extent of raw material wastage and the potential for recovery. When the full extent of the problem is known and can be seen in economic terms, then recycling and byproduct marketing options start to appear attractive. Second, plant personnel begin to look at waste as a process stream rather than an odious nuisance. As one plant manager who performed this exercise commented, "Waste truly becomes a real identity to you when you personally measure the stuff by the bucketful."[12]

The spinoff of this new appreciation of the possibilities of waste is a greater awareness by employees of how they handle raw materials and process chemicals. As Robert Zall writes, "A good deal of evidence indicates that plant personnel are motivated to reduce waste once they know their work can be evaluated by the amount of waste they allow."[12]

Recovery Potential

It is obvious that the potential for recovery is enormous, as is the opportunity to reduce effluent volumes. Not all the industry's waste is going down the drain. This chapter will look at more than thirty examples of resource recovery and re-use projects that are reclaiming marketable products and improving line efficiency.

Indeed, agricultural activities were spawning ground for the recycling industry. Long before the development of a written language, crop, animal and human wastes were being returned to the soil to boost its fertility. Recycling could well be the world's oldest profession.

Today, some 40% of the vegetable and fruit processing plants are using land disposal to help rid themselves of their waste disposal problems.[9] Spray irrigation is returning the nutrients from some cannery washwaters to the land. Brewery sludge is being composted and spread. Whey can be used as a soil builder. Tomato pomace is being processed with corn to provide animal feed. Sludges are incinerated to increase their nitrogen concentration and used as fertilizer. Bagasse and coconut husks are spread between plant rows to suppress weeds and conserve moisture. Other sludges are used to provide food for carp on fish plantations.

The use of wastes as a source of animal food and fertilizer has received the lion's share of investigators' attention. Now, rising fuel costs are focusing a great deal of research on using organic wastes as the raw material for ethanol,[13,14], methanol[15] and oil.[16] These byproducts could be used in the processing plant to supply needed process heat and reduce fuel charges or be sold to a growing market looking for alternative energy sources.

The optimum use for food wastes would be to recycle them back for human consumption. A process change that increases the yield of the manufacturing operation is the most effective way of doing this. Table 4 lists some examples of the returns such process changes offer.[7]

Ultra-filtered milk, which retains proteins normally lost to whey, would boost the return to cheese makers by 16 to 20%. New peeling techniques and the use of various surfactants are more efficient than the old abrasion technology and applicable to a wider variety of fruits and vegetables. The enzymatic treatment of meat before the animal is slaughtered results in more tender meat cuts and less waste due to inferior meat quality. Some of the case studies in this chapter will examine other process modifications that increase yields.

The second approach to reclaiming wastes is to use them as a base for byproduct development. One of the major problems in recovering proteins or other valuable products from effluents is the dilute nature of food industry wastewaters. Effective water conservation methods are available for both

reducing the volume of the effluents and making the soluble organic material and suspended solids more accessible. Some of the approaches being used successfully are described near the end of this chapter.

Much of the organic material in the wastewater consists of carbohydrates. This can serve as a substrate for microbial protein production. With the proper nutrient addition, single cell protein (SCP) can be grown on the waste

---

Table 4

Technologies Which Result in Increased Yield and Decreased Waste Production

Industry	Subclass	Process	Increased yield
Meat	Beef	Protein-enzyme tenderization	39%[a]
Dairy	Cheese	Ultrafiltration	16-20%
Fruit and vegetables	Peaches	Lye peeling	Marginal
	Pears	Lye peeling	Marginal
	Potatoes	Lye peeling	12-40%
	Pimiento peppers	Lye peeling	30%
	Apples	Lye peeling	6%

[a] The increase in yield quoted here is an increase in meat acceptable for dry heat cooking from 29% in a conventional carcass to 68% in a Pro Ten carcass.

Process modifications can greatly increase yields and coincidentally reduce waste.

Source: "Maximizing Efficiencies in the Food System: A Review of Alternatives for Waste Abatement," Journal of Food Protection, March 1980.

Table 5

Protein Yields from Conventional Crops and from Crop Byproducts

	Yield of Protein (Kg/ha)		Fungal protein from			
	Seed	Leaf protein	leaf juice	leaf fibre	maize cobs	TOTAL
Maize: Conventional crop	352	—	—	—	—	352
Combined with waste recovery	352	300	110	1290	80	2132
Peas: Conventional crop	400	—	—	—	—	400
Combined with Waste recovery	400	625	125	1366	—	2546

About half of the available protein is lost in the processing of maize and peas. When combined with the potential fungal protein that could be grown, the protein yield could be increased five-fold.

Source: "Recycling Food Wastes," Compost Science/Land Utilization, November/December 1979.

and harvested by filtration or centrifuging. SCP can be used as an animal feed supplement, or a source of food protein. Anaerobic fermentation can also be employed to produce ethanol or alcohol as well as SCP.

SCP is not yet available as a human food source. There is still some uncertainty as to its safety, due to its nucleic acid content. A great deal of work is still needed to prove both its safety and its economic viability before SCP hits the dinner table.

The growing of SCP has been accomplished using many wastes including whey, citric acid waste, lye peeling effluents, cellulosic wastes, coconut water, rice straw[7] and potato washwater.[2] By combining the protein collected by coagulation in the washwater and that derived by SCP growing on the crop residues, the yield of protein per unit of growing area

can be increased six-fold (see Table 5).[2]

The recovery of protein for human consumption is still in its infancy. There is a great deal of work still to be done on the taste, odour, texture and appearance of protein additives to make them palatable to consumers. There is also the problem of toxic contaminants in some of the waste-streams; solanine in potato protein concentrates, alfatoxin in peanuts and erucic acid in rapeseed (canola) oil. But advances are being made every day and will continue to be made as long as adequate funding is being accorded food research and development.

The two keys to a successful waste byproduct sales programme in the food processing industry are economics and regulation. The relative efficiencies of a number of potential technologies make sci-

entific obstacles a component of the economic decision-making process. How to do the best for less.

Of perhaps greater concern are marketing and regulatory considerations. "It is becoming more apparent that the regulatory review and analysis of a proposed project is more important than the economic evaluation."[17] The limitations of what can be placed in a food product, how it must be labelled, and how it can be advertised may kill a potentially cost-effective recovery process before it gets off the ground. It is not within the purview of this book to analyze the regulatory criteria, but it is important for any food processor to work closely with both his legal and marketing staff to ensure that any re-use or byproduct utilization scheme is both possible and practicable.

POLLUTION PREVENTION OPPORTUNITIES

The case studies in this chapter are drawn from the experiences of food processors in Canada, the United States, New Zealand, France and England, and include both commercial installations and pilot plant studies.

1.
Dairy Products

About 80% of the milk that goes into cheesemaking is converted to whey, or about 1000 gallons of whey for every 2000 pounds of cheese produced. This whey carries with it an enormous BOD. It would take 1800 people to create the waste load of that 1000 gallons of whey and it would take most of the oxygen dissolved in over 4.5 million gallons of water to accommodate its breakdown.[12]

The methods that cheese producers have used to address the whey disposal problem encompass a wide variety of technical options: ultrafiltration, evaporation, re-

verse osmosis, centrifuging, distillation, ion exchange and land disposal. Every year in Canada, 1.5 million tons of whey (representing 90,000 tons of sugar, essential amino acids and other nutrients) are left over from the milk used in cheese making.[18] The variety of approaches industries have used to control this high-BOD waste product is an excellent illustration of the economic potential made possible and the flexibility afforded by resource recovery in the food processing industry.

■ Twin Dakotas Dairy (Pollock, South Dakota) found a dam had created a brand new recreational lake on the water course it used to dump its wastewater in. The plant produces 30,000 gallons per hour of whey-laden wastewater in the conversion of some 250,000 to 300,000 lb of milk into cheddar cheese each day.[19]

Twin Dakotas chose ultrafiltration (UF) to separate and recover the valuable components in its wastes and produce an effluent compatible with water sports. The

whey coming from the cheese vats is first screened and centrifuged to remove fat traces and then repasteurized to kill any acid-type bacteria and deactivate the rennet enzymes.

Ultrafiltration concentrates the protein-bearing fraction to 34% protein (dry weight). Evaporators further concentrate the material to 42% solids before it is spray dried. Hot water from the evaporators is re-used for boiler feed water.

The "permeate" side of the UF unit discharges a liquid rich in lactose and ash. This material is currently being landfilled but Twin Dakotas is planning to convert this stream to yeast and alcohol in a fermentation unit.[19] This alcohol can supplement the plant's fuel supply.

The efficiency of the UF system is even better than anticipated: installed as a 20,000-gallon-per-hour unit, it is now operating at 30,000 gph. It is also processing whey from other cheese makers in the area.

One of the complaints critics of ultrafiltration have voiced is that the common breakdown of membranes causes subsequent problems with quality control. Twin Dakota's UF equipment is produced by Dorr-Oliver, (Stamford, Connecticut). "When a filter cartridge ruptures, the cloudiness of protein pollution in the permeate (lactose and ash) line calls it to the operator's attention. A check of delivery tubes from individual cartridges quickly locates the one that must be replaced. The system has been designed so that a ten-minute shutdown allows replacement of the segment that has been ruptured".[19]

The protein recovered is now being marketed by the dairy as a nutritional supplement. As it is derived from a food manufacturing operation, it is suitable for human consumption. The firm is also investigating concentrating its byproduct to 60-90% protein for use as a replacement for caseinates and egg whites.

■ Millions of pounds of cheese whey are generated as a byproduct of cheese manufacturing. Ultrafiltration of the whey byproduct yields a recoverable protein residue, but also a secondary polluting byproduct known as whey permeate. Although whey permeate is rich in lactose sugar, this form of sugar has no value as a commercial sweetener.[20]

Corning Biosystems (Corning, New York) have developed a lactose hydrolysis unit to convert the lactose in the whey into the commercially valuable sweeteners glucose and galactose. In doing so, Corning Biosystems is doing away with the whey permeate disposal problem, while at the same time finding a new market for cheese production byproducts. The glucose and galactose resulting from Corning's lactose hydrolysis unit has a ready market as a sugar replacement in bakery goods, ice cream, chocolate and fruit drinks.[21]

■ France's Rhone-Poulenc Industries is developing an alternative to ultrafiltration (UF) with the commercial use of ion exchange technology for whey protein recovery.[22] Rhone-Poulenc claims ion exchange recovers 100% of the

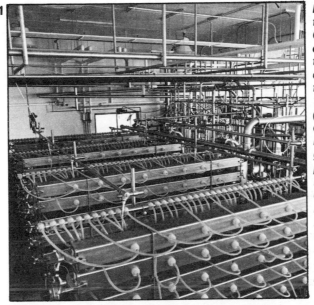

Dorr-Oliver Iopor Ultrafiltration installed at Lugano Cheese in Monroe, Wisconsin. (1) System is used to produce whey protein concentrates and has a feed capacity exceeding 1,000,000 pounds per day. (2) Four-stage Whey Processing System. Access to membrane cartridges is gained by removing end plate via the hand wheel. Membrane replacement can be made in a few minutes. (3) Dorr-Oliver Iopor 40-Cartridge Ultrafiltration Station. Horizontal tube leaching to section of recirculation pump is heat exchanger which is used to maintain process temperature.

Dorr-Oliver Incl.

proteins in whey and can concentrate the purified protein solution to 90% pure, compared to ultrafiltration purities which range from 35 to 80%.

Furthermore, the firm says ion exchange is cost-competitive with UF at concentrations up to 35%; beyond that, ion exchange costs less to operate.

Ion exchange is based on the principle that an electrically charged molecule, like a protein/amino acid, has an affinity for an electrically charged substrate. The charge on the desired compound can be adjusted by the manipulation of the pH of the protein solution. Rhone-Poulenc has developed a substrate for its ion exchange equipment which maximizes protein recovery and allows the collection of different protein fractions for different end uses.

The new substrate, trade-marked Spherosil,™ is made up of porous silica microbeads. They are rigid, stable and able to selectively adsorb protein in large quantities and eventually yield up pure un-denatured products.

The basic ion exchange process involves the use of the Spherosil™ beads in a column and consists of four stages (see Figure 2).[22] First, adsorption: whey feed stock is passed through the column where the proteins are adsorbed, electrically trapped and bound to the ion exchange beads. Second, washing: the de-proteinized solution remaining in the column is washed out with one or two column-volumes of water. Third, elution: reagents (hydrochloric acid for anion columns, ammonia for cation columns) remove the entrapped proteins, and sanitize the column to make it ready for re-use. Fourth, washing: after elution, the column is washed again with one or two bed-volumes of water to remove any solution remaining in the column. The column can then be immediately re-used.

Complex solutions (such as whey) containing several different proteins can be treated by two columns in series: One column contains the anionic exchanger, the other the cationic exchanger. Proteins can thus be fractionated one from another (see Figure 3).[22]

Figure 2
Acid Whey Protein Adsorption

Whey protein is trapped on the porous microbeads that make up the cationic exchange column. The column is then washed, and reagents are flushed through it to remove the recovered protein.
Source: "Recovers Whey Proteins of 90% Purity," Food Engineering, April 1981.

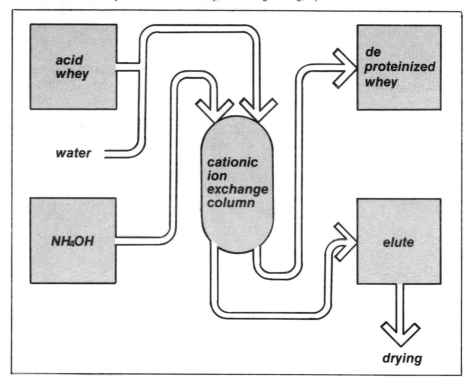

Figure 3
Two-Column Sweet Whey Protein Adsorption

Most of the protein is collected in the anionic exchange column, but 7 to 10% of the proteins are cationic and their recovery requires a second column.
Source: "Recovers Whey Proteins of 90% Purity," Food Engineering, April 1981.

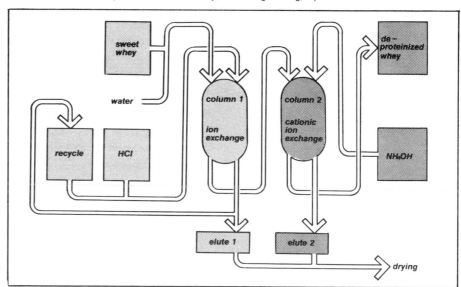

The process can also be adapted for purifying the soluble proteins in skim milk, and the vegetable proteins from solutions of soy, rapeseed, press cakes, lucerne and residual starches from potato starch production. By adjusting the pH and temperature conditions, the desired proteins can be selectively adsorbed in the ion exchange columns while the impurities are not. The fixed proteins can then be removed (eluted) with a solvent solution, either a mineral or organic acid or a mineral base.

The whey resulting from cheese or casein production can come in one of two forms: sweet whey with a pH of about 6.3, and acid whey with a pH of 4.5. Acid whey processing requires the use of only one ion exchange column since all the protein will adhere to the base in the cationic ion exchanger.

Sweet whey protein recovery requires two columns. Most of the protein can be collected in the anionic ion exchanger but about 7 to 10% is cationic and will adsorb in the second column.

The first commercial operation of chromatographic ion exchange went into protein recovery production in October 1980 at Bel Dairies (Sable, France). The plant recovers 1000 pounds of protein a day (150 tons a year) from 100,000 litres.

When skim milk is processed through the Spherosil™ material, casein, due to its large molecular structure, is not adsorbed in the beads or retained in the column. After protein separation, the remaining solution contains all the casein, lactose and mineral salts found in the original skim milk. This solution can be used to make cheese identical to that produced with whole milk, but without the extended draining time.

The operating costs of the ion exchange equipment are presented in Tables 6 and 7.[22] This information was gained from two years of operating three French pilot plants. A commercial scale-up assumes a 90% yield and a whey protein content of 5.5 grams per litre.

■ The management of the Wapsie Valley Creamery (Independence, Iowa) was fighting for its financial

Table 6
Extraction Costs: Acid Whey Protein

Whey Capacity (lb/day)	200,000	500,000	1,000,000
Protein Production (lb/day)	990	2,475	4,950
Initial Investment Cost			
Hardware	$300,000	$483,000	$680,000
Spherosil™	140,000	301,000	561,000
Total	$440,000	$784,000	$1,241,000
Annual Operating Cost			
Fixed Cost			
Depreciation 12%	$30,000	$48,300	$68,000
Interest	23,000	37,000	52,600
Insurance 2%	6,000	9,600	13,600
Variable (300 days)			
Labour	20,000	38,500	38,500
Utilities:			
Power	10,000	15,150	22,500
Water	4,200	6,300	9,000
Expendables:			
Spherosil™	70,000	151,000	281,000
HCl	800	2,000	4,000
NH3	1,800	5,400	10,800
Trypsine	2,000	9,800	10,000
Maintenance	4,000	4,800	6,800
Total Operating Cost	$171,800	$327,850	$516,800
Total Annual Production (lb)	297,000	742,500	1,485,000
Extraction Cost/lb	$0.57	$0.44	$0.34

Source: "Recovers Whey Proteins of 90% Purity," *Food Engineering*, April 1981.

life in 1978. Its effluent discharge was right on the edge of tightening state and federal pollution control standards for BOD and Total Suspended Solids (TSS) and the firm was facing the prospect of paying high municipal sewage penalties or building its own wastewater treatment plant. But the greatest hurdle the cheesemaker had to overcome was the rapidly escalating cost of energy.[23]

Wapsie Valley Creamery, in addition to producing Cheddar and Colby cheeses, processes whey into lactose and protein products for sale to baby food manufacturers and other food and feed producers. Whey is evaporated, and the concentrate is run through crystalizers, centrifuges and dryers to obtain lactose and a 26% high-protein ingredient.

The local public utility had completely cut off the supply of

natural gas to the creamery during the bitterly cold winter of 1978/79. The firm was forced to buy oil to fire the boiler that produced steam for the evaporators and switch to propane to fuel its dryers. Its energy bill jumped 2.75 times.

"We reached the point where, if we didn't do something, we weren't going to do anything", said Wilbur C. Nielsen, general manager. "In other words, we would have been out of business."[23]

In the summer of 1978, Wapsie Valley installed a new evaporation system utilizing thermal vapour recompression (TVR) with a maximum heat exchange surface. The capital costs were high and the firm anticipated a long 8- to 9-year pay-back period.

Wapsie Valley Creamery eliminated its original two-effect evaporator system. The old system concentrated 21,000 lb of whey an hour from a 6% solid to a 40% solid. With no vapour recompression, the steam efficiency of the system was only 0.9:1 (i.e., one pound of steam vapourizes 0.9 pound of water).

The company called in Wiegand Evaporators Inc., the U.S. subsidiary of the West German parent firm, to design, partly manufacture and install the new three-unit system.

The first unit, a five-unit pre-evaporator, concentrates the cheese whey from 6% solids to a 50% solid with a steam efficiency of 7.25:1. The second unit, a single-effect high concentrator, further concentrates the whey to 60% solids with a steam efficiency of 1.9:1. The steam efficiency of the total system is almost 7.5 times better than the creamery's original equipment.

The third new unit is a two-phase vacuum cooler that can handle material from either the pre-evaporator or the high concentrator and cool it to as low as 45°F.

The company could have opted for mechanical vapour compression rather than the TVR system but local electricity prices (5¢ per kilowatt-hour) were too high to make it competitive. Although new MVR designs offer comparative energy efficiencies, the capital cost requirements are still somewhat greater.

The performance of the new system has been impressive. The reduction of TSS and BOD by 80% placed the company's effluent well below both present and anticipated limits and has saved them the cost of building and operating expensive wastewater control facilities. The evaporator also includes a clean-in-place (CIP) capability designed by Wiegand Inc. After a day's operation, the system automatically shifts to a potable water rinse, caustic wash and acid cycle. In 2.5 hours the equipment is neutral and ready to go. Reclaim tanks reduce the cleaning consumption to less than 10 gallons of 50% caustic and 10 gallons of 50% acid per day.

The system has also doubled Wapsie Valley's whey feed capacity from 21,000 to 40,000 lb per hour or 650,000 lb per day. Before

Table 7
Extraction Costs: Sweet Whey Protein

Whey Capacity (lb/day)	500,000	1,000,000
Protein Production (lb/day)	2,475	4,950
Initial Investment Cost		
Hardware	$ 537,000	$ 756,000
Spherosil™	534,000	1,058,000
Total	$1,066,000	$1,814,000
Annual Operating Cost		
Fixed Cost		
Depreciation 12%	$ 53,700	$ 75,600
Interest	41,700	58,500
Insurance 2%	10,700	15,100
Variable (300 days)		
Labor	38,500	38,500
Utilities:		
Power	20,250	30,000
Water	8,400	12,000
Expendables:		
Spherosil™ QMA	247,500	495,000
Spherosil™ XOB	17,000	34,000
HCl	4,000	8,000
NH₃	2,000	4,000
Trypsine	9,800	12,000
Maintenance	6,000	7,600
Total Operating Cost	$459,550	$730,300
Total Annual Production (lb)	742,500	1,485,000
Extraction Cost/lb	$0.61	$0.53

Source: "Recovers Whey Proteins of 90% Purity," *Food Engineering*, April 1981.

installation, the creamery couldn't process all the whey it produced itself; the excess was used as fertilizer by local farmers, where regulation permitted. Now the company is able to process all its own product plus the whey from nearby cheese companies.

The new units also increase the range of whey products and process services Wapsie Valley can offer its customers. Liquid whey concentrate at 40 to 50% solids can be pulled from the evaporators to be used as food additives or feed supplements. Liquid whey at 55 to 62% solids can also be sold from the high concentrator. But the bulk of the business will still be dried and powdered lactose and protein products produced by straight-through whey concentration in both units and further treatment down the process line.

Energy savings, the prime reason for the changeover, have also been dramatic. Whereas the

company used to need 10,000 lb of steam to concentrate 21,000 lb of whey per hour, it now uses only 5400 lb of steam to process 40,000 lb of whey to 62% solid. Twice as much product at half the cost. The increase in whey concentrations also improves the capacity of other drying and processing equipment down the line.

The new system saves the firm 12,000 lb of steam each operating hour. Using energy costs in 1978, Nielsen calculated savings of $43.80 an hour or $788 per 18-hour day.

It would be conservative to assume monthly savings of $15,000. Since the company calculated these figures, rising energy costs and, of course, savings have almost doubled again.

The energy crisis prompted Wapsie Valley Creamery to make the substantial investment for the energy efficient multi-effect evaporators and thermal vapour recompression system. Fortunately Wapsie Valley's investment has paid off handsomely. The energy efficient evaporator has almost doubled whey production, cut energy requirements in half and reduced BOD, TSS and ammonia in the effluent by 80%. The rapid soaring of fuel prices alone has cut the pay-back on the equipment to between only three and four years.

Wapsie Valley has shown that pollution abatement solutions can be included in process design improvements to the benefit of both. A more efficient system becomes a cleaner system and a wasted and expensive effluent becomes a valuable resource.

■ The University of Guelph (Guelph, Ontario), aided by grants from the Ontario Ministry of Agriculture and Food, has been working with modern membrane technology to concentrate the dilute whey into protein-rich cattle feed. Professor D.M. Irving of the University's food science department says, "The method is simple and energy efficient. We can now increase the concentration to 20% (solids) at a cost of no more than half a cent a gallon of whey."[18]

The lactose component of whey can make up to 65% of the solids. This sugar, which resembles cane sugar, is hampered in its commercial applications by its low sweetness, poor solubility and a tendency to form large, sharp crystals that are unacceptable in some foods. The Guelph researchers have used yeast to break the lactose down into sweeter, more soluble forms: glucose and galactose. These sugars could find a ready, lucrative market in soft drink manufacturing, among others.

The food science department has also developed a process to convert whey protein into cheese spread. "We already have a beautiful product," Professor Irving says. A pilot project has proven the commercial viability of the process and it is only a matter of time before waste whey will be diverted from the sewers to the supermarket shelves.[18]

■ It seems everybody is working on making something from cheese wastes; where there's a will, there's a whey. Andrew Peng, Ohio State University, has developed a method to combine cheese whey with equal amounts of soybeans to produce a curd for about 10¢ a pound.[24] But one pound of whey with a dash of water, a pinch of salt and an equal measure of soybean serves up 14 pounds of curd. The curd can be used in puddings, pie fillings and non-dairy yogurt.

■ The recent improvements in membrane separation technology and energy efficient evaporators make possible the production of marketable high-grade protein concentrates and lactose from the waste whey generated by the cheese and dairy industries. The lactose component, except for relatively small amounts processed into pure form or into lactose hydrolysates (used as industrial sweeteners), has not found itself a plentiful and profitable supply of customers.

Now, Carbery Milk Products Ltd. (the Irish subsidiary of Express Dairy Foods of London, England) has developed a fermentation/distillation process to turn that lactose into saleable alcohol products.[25]

A full-scale operation in Ballineen, Ireland now converts 600,000 litres of whey into 2600 litres of proof alcohol (57.1% alcohol by volume) each day, seven days a week. That is enough alcohol to produce 4600 bottles of vodka a day.

The potable spirit market offers the greatest rate of return to Carbery, but the process is also adaptable to producing lower grades of alcohol for use as surgical spirits or even as a component of automotive fuel blends.

In 1976, Carbery began to examine the wealth of laboratory and theoretical data that had been developed on whey-to-alcohol conversions. The correct distillation and fermentation conditions were selected and a suitable yeast found. By May 1978 a six-column unit was put in commercial operation. Ultrafiltration techniques are used to separate the protein and lactose components of the whey and the lactose is then treated to derive various alcohols.

The Carbery process is seen as a breakthrough for both those seeking to solve a whey effluent disposal problem and manufacturers of alcohol products searching for new sources of raw materials. Canadian regulations, however, require that alcoholic beverages be derived from spirits, so that any domestic whey distillation and fermentation facility would be forced to supply more sober markets.

■ Manco Dairy products in Dauphin, Manitoba produces 70,000 lb of cheese whey daily. The company now pays a hauler to truck the waste material from the plant; the sewage treatment system of the rural municipality cannot deal with the high BOD load. Limited amounts are spread as fertilizer on farmers' fields; the majority is dumped in sloughs.

Now the municipality is looking at the waste material as a possible dust suppressant on rural roads. Although the whey is 95% water the residual butter fat is sufficient to keep the dust down.[26]

Manitoba environment officials agree the material could be used on the province's by-ways but express concern over its excessive use. "The whey will evaporate in about a day, but if puddles are left they begin to smell," says waste hauler Stan Pavlin.

There may be more efficient uses of a protein-rich resource than the control of dirt on the highway, but if whey replaces the PCB-contaminated road oils now being employed, then it is preferable, at least until more efficient recovery methods are installed.

2.
Meat and Fish Processing

■ The Swift Canadian Company packinghouse (Lethbridge, Alberta) had a big problem with the BOD, suspended solids and hexane extractables in its effluent.[27] Its treatment plant could not meet the municipal effluent requirements and the company was forced to pay an extra $120,000 a year surcharge, on top of the normal monthly service charge.

Swift also had a solution, but a solution with a formidable price tag. An electrocoagulation unit to recover fats and oils from its wastewater would bring it in line with the regulatory agencies. The equipment is made by Dravo Lectro Quip (Neville Island, Pennsylvania) and would cost $400,000; big money, even in Alberta.

Swift decided to go ahead and now produces high quality tallow from the recovered contaminants, which brings in revenues of $181,000 a year and eliminates the surcharges to the Metropolitan Sanitary District of Lethbridge. Big problems, big solutions and big returns.

The Swift plant slaughters 500 to 600 head of beef each eight-hour shift. It has its own rendering facilities, a blood recovery system and it trucks out paunch content material, (PCM). In July 1979, it installed the first industrial electrocoagulation system: a system that uses sulphuric acid instead of a metallic coagulant like alum[27,28] (see Figure 4).

Electrocoagulation is an electrolytic technology. Using sulphuric acid at a concentration of 300 ppm, the pH of the wastewater is adjusted to the point where the average surface charge of the particulates in the effluent is zero (zero zeta potential). Zero zeta is achievable at a pH of about 4.0 to 4.5 and the addition of an anionic polymer ensures the process is reproducible.

At zero zeta, the particulates coalesce and the electrolytic micro-bubbles interact with them to form a stable solid-gas composite. This composite floats to the surface of the electroflotation basin. The floating solids are then skimmed off and the remaining water can be discharged. The skimming volume is about 0.4% of the effluent volume and contains 10 to 25% solids.

The dwell time in the coagulation/flotation basin is about 45 minutes. During this time, the BOD of the treated effluent drops from 900 to 209 ppm, and the suspended solids from 520 to 58 ppm.

The system is able to handle 404 gal per minute over a 16-hour day and requires 966 lb of sulphuric

Figure 4
Electrochemical Treatment of Food Processing Wastewaters

Wastewater treatment system uses an electrocoagulation cell to produce micro-bubbles. Particles in the washwater accumulate around the bubbles, then float to the surface in the electroflotation cell.
Source: "Electrochemical Water Treatment Removes Suspended Fats, Proteins," *Food Engineering*, March 1979.

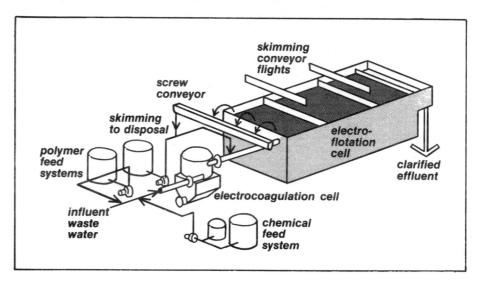

acid, 6.5 lb of the polymer and 644 lb a day of sodium hydroxide to raise the pH of the wastewater back to 6.5 prior to discharge into the sewage treatment system. The skimmers remove 3200 lb of oils and fats a day that produce tallows and cracks worth $726.71. The expense of running the system, including chemicals, electricity, labour and maintenance is $315.60 a day. The savings in avoided surcharges total about $400 a day for a net savings of about $800 a day before depreciation and interest.[27]

The working capital requirements on the original investment come to $20,000 a year over the life of the project. Assuming a 250-day working year, the income and savings exceed the total project costs by $180,000 a year.

The advantages are obvious: clean effluent; a cheap process chemical (sulphuric acid) eliminates the need for metallic coagulants; without coagulants, skimming volumes are reduced and rendering is simpler and cheaper; and marketable tallow is produced. Swift Canada has turned a pollution liability into a commercial asset.

■ Swift and Company (Grand Island, Nebraska) was another packinghouse that invested in electrolytic equipment to solve their wastewater treatment problems.[28] The firm had experimented with screens, dissolved air flotation and sedimentation basins without success before purchasing a Lectro-Clear system from Dravo (see Figure 4).

The process, which combines electrolytic action with trivalent coagulant additions, has reduced BOD to between 60 and 150 ppm, suspended solids between 70 and 140 ppm and hexane extractables to between 5 and 60 ppm. Among other advantages of the system, sludge particle size is minimal and efficient operations can be performed in cold water. The only drawback of the system is the use of the trivalent coagulant which makes reprocessing of the skimmings difficult.

■ A New Zealand meat packer went over 12,000 miles to find the waste recovery system it needed.[29] Southland Frozen Meat Limited could not meet the new water standards for the effluent it discharged into the nearby Mataura River. It was not possible to build a

Dravo's Lectro Clear™ Process is a waste separation system combining electrocoagulation, electroflotation and sludge processing.

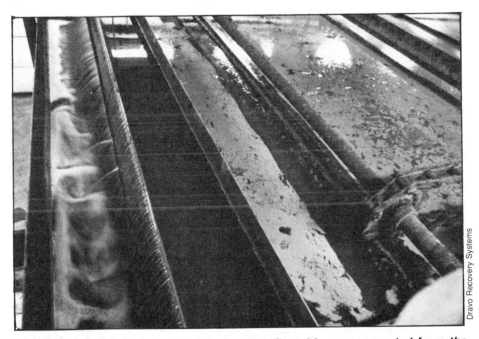

In the electroflotation basin, floc and other floatables are separated from the treated water.

Figure 5
Southland's Wastewater Treatment System

Southland Frozen Meat Limited in New Zealand is using the Danish-built Aminodan system to recover protein byproducts and animal fats. Coagulators, filter presses and a rotary dryer produce a dry cake animal feed, the sales of which have reduced the firm's waste treatment costs to almost nothing.

Source: "Wastewater Byproducts are New Source of Income for New Zealand Meat Packer," *Meat Processing*, June 1981.

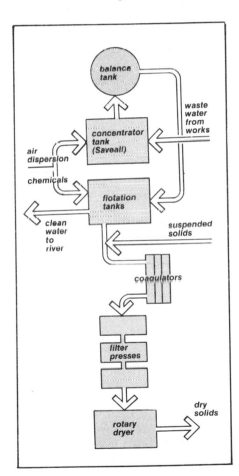

standard anaerobic lagoon treatment; there was no room close to the plant and it was too expensive to pipe the waste over two miles to the closest available site.

In 1977, Southland found the answer in a $1.6 million automated treatment system proposed by Aminodan Technologies of Skagen, Denmark (see Figure 5).[29] The Danish process was guaranteed to reduce BOD by a minimum of 70% (and often 80 to 85%), fat by a minimum of 90% (and up to 99%) and suspended solids by a minimum of 80 to 85%. This kind of efficiency would satisfy the pollution control regulatory agency, The Southland Catchment Board.

The system also had to be able to deal with a heavy load of wastewater and be flexible enough to respond to great variations in flow. Southland slaughters up to 12,800 lambs a day on four chains plus another 400 beef, operating an average of 200 days a year (the plant closes from July through October for lambing season). The Southland operation at its peak produces 370,000 gallons of effluent an hour.

But according to Southland's supervising engineer, Owen Paris, the equipment had to do more than purify the plant's effluent. "Since we realized that a wastewater treatment system of that capacity would require a major capital investment, the concept of capturing a usable byproduct became an important consideration.

The Aminodan machinery offered the recovery option and facilitated the recovery of a protein byproduct. After two years of animal feeding tests, Southland was able to conclude the recovered byproduct "produces comparable nutritional results when used as a supplement (about 10%) to meat and bone meal in poultry feeding trials."[29] The company believes it can sell the product at comparable prices as well. Meat and bone meal is currently selling for $250 a ton in New Zealand. At present the Aminodan system is producing 5 tons of byproduct a day with a 44% protein content. In addition, about $720 worth of fats are also being recovered each week. The revenue from the byproduct sales will cover about 80% of the system's annual operating costs.

The Danish engineers decided to use Southland's existing 100,000-gallon "save-all" bin as a concentrator tank and add a flotator to its surface to improve fat collection by 50%. An air dispersion system has also been added to the collector tank to force more of the suspended solids to the surface.

The effluent then flows to a balance tank for pH adjustment. The 30,000-gallon unit can also handle flow surges. From the balance tank, wastewater can then flow to any one of twelve 30,000-gallon flotation tanks. Chemical coagulants and further air dispersion is added to force more of the protein and fat to the surface where it is automatically scraped off. Any or all of the twelve units can be in operation at one time to respond to variations in plant operations.

The recovered material (about 10% solids) is pumped through a bank of nine steam coagulators and then conveyed to three belt-type filter presses resulting in a dry cake of 30 to 40% solids.

Further drying in a rotary disc dryer removed all the remaining moisture, save about 8%. Other Aminodan installations in poultry and fish processing plants heat the reclaimed sludge to melt the fat and then centrifuge to remove the protein dry matter and oil. Reclaimed oils can be used in many products, from paints to margarine.

The system has been operating since March of 1978. The daily operating expenses total $1650 and include $495 a day for water, steam and electricity, $615 for chemicals and $540 for labour and maintenance. Although the pollution control equipment has yet to turn a net profit for the firm, the effluent can be discharged to the river at almost no daily cost to Southland.

■ The greasy wastes from a chicken processing plant are being effectively handled by dissolved air flotation units. The collected fat and proteins are then sold to a renderer. When the Rocco Farm Foods Co. (Edinburg, Virginia) doubled its production to 90,000 chickens a day it was forced to add the flotation unit to meet U.S. Environmental Protection Agency regulations.[30]

The oily wastes are screened and introduced and mixed with the effluent under pressure. When the mixture is piped into the flotation chamber, air bubbles are formed and adhere themselves to the contaminants in the wastewater. The greasy scum that forms on the surface is scraped off by rotating pivoted arm skimmers and collected for resale to the renderer.

The resultant sludge, when dried, contains 16.6% protein, 72.6% fat and 3.4% ash. The effluent is then treated in standard wastewater lagoons. The flotation unit has reduced the BOD and suspended solids content of the water by 40-60%, making further treatment more effective and reclaiming a saleable byproduct.

■ A research team at Cornell University has taken a commercial process from the soybean industry and used it to reclaim protein from clam wastewater. The clam processing business produces a heavy wasteload, posing some real environmental difficulties. The wastes generated by shucking and eviscerating tend to spoil rapidly and are heavy in turbidity and BOD.

The Cornell scientists took clam washwater from a commercial plant in Greenport, New York. The clam washwater is essentially a dilute protein solution and constitutes more than 50% of the organic load in the plant effluent.[31] Protein recovery would be a major contribution towards pollution abatement in the industry.

Soybean processors are already using an acid precipitation technique to recover proteins. The clam washwater was subjected to an equivalent process. Sulphuric acid was added to reduce the pH of the fluid to 4.0. After mixing, the protein component precipitated to the bottom of the reaction vessel and could be removed by centrifugation.

The process recovers about 41% of the protein in the effluent. This protein can then be sold as an addition to poultry and livestock feeds, to offset the costs of abatement. The recovery system also reduces the oxygen demand of the

Table 8
Paunch Content Material (PCM)

	Average Wet Weight of raw PCM per animal (Kg)	BOD (mg/litre)
Cattle	27.0	50,000
Sheep	2.7	30,000

Source: "Utilization of Paunch Content Material by Ultrafiltration," *Process Biochemistry*, March 1980.

wastewater by 63% and the turbidity by 75%.[31]

Like all the condemned, cattle and sheep on the way to the slaughterhouse are allowed one last meal. After they have shuffled off these mortal coils and their remains are turned into hamburger, the meat processor must deal with paunch, or first stomach contents of this final repast. The paunch content material (PCM) can be a tricky waste disposal problem. Consisting of partially digested grass and a high water content (90 to 95%), the PCM is rich in BOD. Furthermore, this undigested material is not readily handled by a bacteriological treatment facility. "For some reason bugs do not like PCM."[8]

At present, the processor slits the paunch and the contents are "wet dumped". The fibrous material is often separated from the liquid component on a vibratory screen and further dewatered after mixing with other solid plant waste on another screen or in a desludger. The fluids are discharged to the drains or the wastewater treatment plant and the solid residue, with a 60 to 70% moisture content, is hauled away for land spreading or disposal. The process has several major drawbacks: 80% of the BOD in the PCM is soluble; the wastewater from the plant becomes heavily contaminated and expensive to treat; it is also carrying off the organic component with the marketable potential. Land-spreading the fibrous residue requires large areas suitable for burying the PCM, areas hopefully close enough to the plant to preclude heavy transport costs. Finally, there have been some reports that the fibre does not break down readily after burial.

■ A researcher at the Meat Industry Research Institute (Hamilton, New Zealand) has developed a method of dealing with PCM that yields saleable protein and a fuel source.[37] Using ultrafiltration techniques, researcher T. Fernando estimates byproduct sales and energy savings can cut waste disposal costs by at least 50%.

Fernando's process entails collecting the PCM without adding any water and then separating the liquids with a press or a decanter centrifuge. The liquids, with 60 to 80% of the available protein, are concentrated in an ultrafiltration unit, and the residue is used as fuel. The concentrate from the UF unit closely resembles cheese whey (in protein, amino acid com-

Figure 6
Paunch Content Material Processing

A proposed system to turn paunch content material into animal feed and fuel would also reduce effluent BOD by 95%. A centrifuge and ultrafiltration equipment are the keystones of the process.

Source: "Utilization of Paunch Content Material by Ultrafiltration," Process Biochemistry, March 1980.

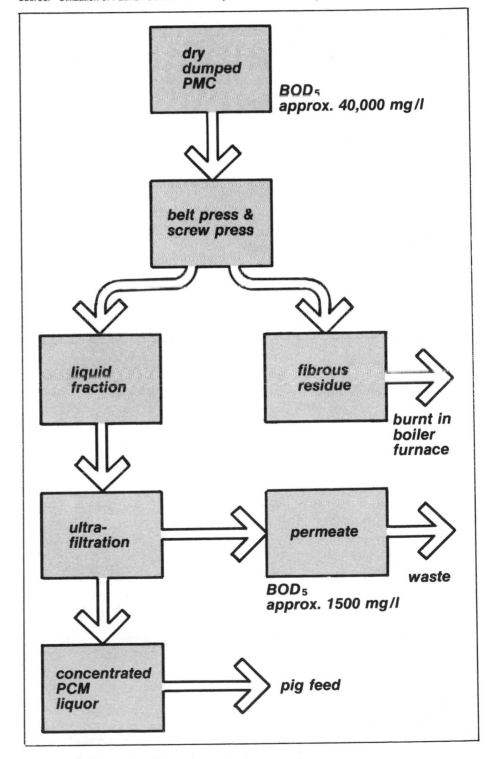

position) and is suitable for pig feed (see Figure 6).[32]

An economic analysis of the process shows the cost of PCM disposal would decrease by over 50% a year. A plant that processes 1000 cattle or 5000 sheep a day, 225 days a year would have approximately 9000 tonnes of PCM to get rid of annually. At $8 to $10 a tonne, the processor would have waste disposal bills of $72,000 to $90,000 (N.Z.) a year.

The capital costs of installing the belt press, screw press, conveying system, ultrafiltration unit and a heat exchanger (for sterilization) would total $95,500. The annual operating cost including the capital cost (at 12% over 4 years) and labour, electricity and membrane replacement, would be $62,920. The sale of protein and the use of the PCM residue as fuel would return to the firm $26,560, leaving a net deficit of $36,360 a year or about $4.00 a tonne of PCM. Increases in the fuel costs, displaced by using PCM residues, would make Fernando's process even more attractive.

But in the final analysis, PCM recovery and re-use will probably not generate a net profit. Not all firms are able to make enough money from their pollution control programmes to recoup capital investment, cover operating costs and still generate income. Some will have to settle for cutting their waste disposal costs dramatically, increasing their efficiency and recover a usable resource. Not a bad deal, really.

■ An Oklahoma researcher, D.M. Farmer, has turned to the sun in an attempt to remove the excess water from paunch content material (PCM).[33] Farmer developed a pilot plant solar dryer that, even during a chilly Oklahoma November, can reduce the moisture in PCM from 80% to 30% in five days.

The system is run by a concentrating solar collector that is adjusted every two to three weeks to be perpendicular to the noon-time incident solar radiation. "During high insolation the system was operated as a solar still: during periods of low insolation, drying was done by a silica gel desiccant regenerated with air that was heated to 40°C by a concentrating air collector."[33]

■ Egg albumen in the wastewaters of egg-breaking plants is a recoverable protein that Dennis Sievers, University of Missouri, intends to reclaim.[34] Sievers is developing a process to separate the albumen, to be used for refeeding purposes, and reduce the BOD of plant effluent.

The protein in the wastestream is coagulated by heating the effluent to 75°C and reducing the pH to 4.5 by the addition of acid. This produces a light and unstable floc that must be dewatered to recover the coagulated protein. Sievers is continuing his work at the Department of Agricultural Engineering, University of Missouri.

3.
Vegetable Processing

The introduction and immediate popularity of convenience foods has been a boon to the food processor. It's now his job to make your cole slaw, cut your french fries, slice your beans. But instead of only a blemish or two to cut out and toss in the trash can, he has tons of rejected material to deal with every day.

■ Urschel International Ltd. (Leicester, England), a manufacturer of high-speed cutting equipment, deals with firms that slice, dice and chop for a living. They have developed some processing expertise that puts more food on the consumer's plate, and less in the garbage.[35]

French fry producers use a wide variety of potato stock. As the season progresses, they have to deal with more and more spuds plagued with blemishes, damage and eyes. Even after effective peeling, trimming and stripcutting, a significant percentage of the raw fries have some evident discolouration. Urschel developed a transverse slicer to utilize this unacceptable product. After cross cutting to produce commercially acceptable diced potatoes, the material is passed through a colour-sorting machine that rejects the discoloured dices. This leaves a high percentage of perfect dices that can be used in potato croquettes or hashbrowns.

The makers of French-style sliced beans have had to handle the waste resulting from cutting. Whenever the natural protective coat of a vegetable is cut open, there are going to be seeds released and the leaching out of other plant material during cooking or processing. Although these losses can be minimized by adjusting the slice thickness, some waste will still result. If collected, the bean material can be reduced to a smooth paste using a microcutting tool. This paste can be used as a soup base or as an ingredient in geriatric or baby food.

The companies which shred cabbage to make cole slaw or other salads usually remove the core of the plant which must be discarded. Urschel recommends using a dicer with a julienne assembly that produces a 4 mm (3/16 in) shred. This machine is capable of turning the whole cabbage, including the core, into tasty cole slaw. It can also process slightly frost-damaged plants without any visible damage in the final product.

Potato chips must be one of the most popular snack foods available. But while a chip that is thin and crispy may be popular with the consumer, it is a producer's nightmare to pack in a little bag. The brittle chips often fragment in the packaging machines making an unattractive and unmarketable product — a possible waste. It is also difficult to pack the correct weight of product in each bag, so extra chips have to be used.

One manufacturer has investigated reducing this fine material to a paste and transforming it into a snack biscuit.[35] Others have looked at ways of reclaiming the oil contained in the waste chips (up to 35% by weight). The chip bits can be reduced to a slurry and the oil extracted in a commercial centrifuge. It is important that the microcutting of the chip waste is done so as not to produce too viscous a slurry. Extraction of the oil is difficult from a thick paste.

Imaginative thinking is the key to reducing wastes. It is important to draw ideas from other fields, other processes — concepts that may offer the ideal solution to a particular problem. One company faced with the waste of this crumbly potato chip material held a think tank session.[36] While trying to visualize packaging operations that had optimal efficiency, one executive noted how easy it was to pack wet leaves lightly together; dry leaves were much more intransigent. The company tried packing chips in a wet and pliable state but found they became overly brittle after drying in the package and crumbled away. Their work, however, resulted in the development of chip paste, used to produce chips of uniform size and shape. The product is packed in rigid cylinders and can be found in virtually every North American variety store. Imaginative thinking has eliminated a major process waste and helped carve out a significant portion of the American snack market for a company that tried to do something a little differently.

■ The processing of corn for freezing or canning constitutes a major source of organic water pollution. Researchers at the United States Department of Agriculture (Berkeley, California) have completed pilot studies on a new method of separating corn kernels from the cob that reduces the BOD in the effluent by up to 80%.[37,38]

Normally, sweet corn is cut from the cob, leaving about 20%, and sometimes as much as 50%, of the corn attached to the cob. These wastes are presently sold as cattle feed. The cutting also opens the tip of each kernel. This allows some of the contents of the kernel to leach into the process waters and get lost in the plant effluent.

The new Berkley process essentially rubs the corn, intact, off the cob. The husks are removed and the ears split lengthwise. The ears, starting at the split, are pressed up against a rotating rubber cylinder, and slowly rotated as the kernels are removed. A small stream of water is sprayed against the rotating drum surface to wash away juices formed during the contact. Also, heated air is blown along the surface to evaporate water and maintain the necessary friction needed for efficient removal.

The pilot testing has been carried out using two representative commercial sweet corns commonly grown in the northwest U.S. for canning and freezing. An experimental strain, a glumeless cultivar that holds the kernels less lightly to the cob, was also used, although the research team does not anticipate new corn strains will be necessary to ensure the success of the new system.[37]

A taste test panel brought in to sample the processed corn preferred the new product, comparing it to "corn on the cob" flavour. It is not unusual to find process changes that increase production by reducing waste; after all, that is the purpose of efficiency. It is encouraging to find a way that also makes food taste better.

■ Chicago meat packing companies used to make the claim that they were able to use every part of the pig but the squeal. The advertising for ADM Foods (Cedar Rapids, Iowa) claims it goes one better where corn is concerned.[39]

Because corn is one of the least noisy vegetables, it is difficult to dispute ADM's blurb, but they do produce a bewildering range of products from a kernel of corn.

The starch is used in foods, paper making, adhesives, textile weaving, charcoal briquettes, pharmaceutical tablets, etc.

The starch can also be converted to sweeteners like corn syrup, dextrose, and high fructose corn syrup. These are used in baby foods, bakery products, soft drinks, tobacco, chewing gum, fruit drinks, ice cream, jams, peanut butter, vinegar, breakfast foods, wine, processed cheese, olives, mashmallows and medicines.

The liquid dextrose can be fermented to produce alcohols which can be used in gasohol. During the process the carbon dioxide that is generated can be captured to put the fizz in carbonated soft drinks or used in refrigeration.

The germ of the kernel yields oil that is used in cooking oils, margarine, mayonnaise, salad dressings and shortening. For every bushel of corn processed for sweeteners or alcohol, enough oil is captured to make two pounds of margarine.

The proteins and hulls of the kernel are used to make gluten meal or gluten food. These are prime ingredients of animal feed mixtures. The soluble portions of the kernel are also used for feed. The bushel of corn mentioned above will also yield enough fibre and protein to feed three broiler chickens to market weight.

Not all foodstuffs offer the same versatility and range for by-product manufacture. And with corn there is still room for improvements in process efficiency, as the following Amaizo corn syrup case study shows. But it should be the goal of all food processors to maximize the utilization of all the available organic matter in the harvest. Good resource management is good pollution control.

■ An American corn syrup processor has saved itself $6.6 million since September 1975 by changing to a granular activated carbon (GAC) purification system that recovers more product and reduces wastes. The Amaizo (American Corn Products Company) corn processing plant (Hammond, Indiana) grinds more than 25 million bushels of corn a year to produce starches, animal feed and 10 different grades of wet and dry syrups.[40]

About 60% of the corn processed is destined to reach the marketplace as corn syrup. The carbon system is designed to produce a water-white coloured syrup by removing colour contaminants. The company had previously been using a powdered activated carbon (PAC) in its three, 40 foot-high, pulse bed adsorption columns. The PAC material was destined for disposal with its burden of adsorbed organics after a single use.

Since switching to the GAC system, manufactured by Calgon Corp. (Pittsburgh, Pennsylvania), Amaizo has cut wash water use, increased syrup recovery, raised quality and reduced waste. The granular carbon can be used several times; each day about 25,000 lb of GAC is reactivated and mixed with 1000 lb of virgin carbon to be returned to the adsorbers.

Carbon removed from the adsorbers is treated in "sweeting off tanks", where syrup is displaced with water. A slow wash with hot water recovers additional sugar that is trapped in the pores of the GAC. This water and sugar is returned to the untreated syrup stream. The saving in washwater is approximately 33% (from 20,000 gal to 13,000 gal).[40]

However, the improvement in product quality is the advantage that the GAC system has over PAC, which excites the management of Amaizo. It has proved to be both more economical and more efficient. According to Stanley Kulka, manager, "Since start-up of the system, we have been producing more and better quality syrup, with fewer operating problems and at a much reduced cost."

The powdered carbon system had a number of quality control problems resulting in underdosing and poor colour or overdosing and wasting of the carbon. "We're achieving high levels of syrup quality in regards to colour, flavour, and odour", says Kulka. "With granular activated carbon, we don't play guessing games".

Amaizo is also pleased with the dependability of their new system. Greater efficiency means less down time, less filter washing and fewer rejected batches. The side effect of replacing old equipment is often an associated increase in reliability, the reliability that comes with new machinery and fewer attendant mechanical breakdowns. The result is fewer spoiled product runs and fewer mistakes to flush down the drain.

■ Vince Farms (Norwalk, California) bought a stainless steel stationary screen and now collects an extra 4500 to 5000 lb of vegetable cullage and trimmings a year.[41] The Vince Farms operation processes 80 million lb of vegetables (about 85% carrots) a year. Peel and scrap have always been collected for resale as dairy cattle feed, but a lot of the smaller scraps were escaping in the plant's wastewater.[42]

In 1977, Vince Farms mounted a coarse-mesh, slotted stationary screen above the feed collection hopper. The wastewater from the carrot processing lines is pumped to the headbox. Solids are retained on the face of the cycloid screen (curve of quickest descent) and

slide down the face into the hopper. The four-foot wide screen can handle flows of up to 900 gallons per minute, and is used to process the wastes from two shifts a day, six days a week.

The extra organic material collected and sold as feed paid off the cost of the screen within the first year. Vince Farms has also been able to avoid paying higher sewer surcharges.

A once-a-day cleaning with a high alkaline compound and steam equipment to remove carrot build-up on the screen is all the maintenance required.

■ The concept of a sauerkraut plant that produces 10,000 gallons of brine a day may seem, at first thought, to pose a greater hazard to digestion than to the environ-

trucked to the plant, shredded, salted and placed in a fermentation vat. To pack as much cabbage in the vat as possible, about 3000 gallons of brine are withdrawn to be disposed. After the cabbage has effected its transformation into a German delicacy, much of the remaining brine, minus the small amount packaged, is discarded. Of 100 tons of cabbage entering the plant, more than 30 tons are trimmed off as solid waste and 20 tons more are dumped with the brine.[43]

It may be possible in the future to use new strains of cabbage, high-dry-matter hybrids, which will reduce the amount of brine by 75%, but these are still in the development stage.

In the meantime, the Geneva

Figure 7
Aerobic Treatment of Sauerkraut Waste with a Food Yeast

The waste brines from sauerkraut production can be treated with a food yeast to yield an animal feed protein while cutting BOD by 90%.
Source: "Reducing Wastes in Sauerkraut Plants," *New York's Food and Life Sciences* 10(1), 1977.

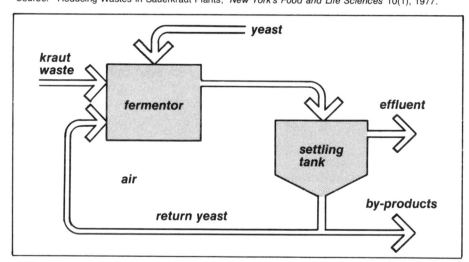

ment. However, while most vegetable wastewaters can be handled without major mishap by a standard lagoon treatment plant, sauerkraut brine requires special precautions. It has a high salt and high acid content and is particularly rich in BOD. While domestic sewage has a BOD of only 200 to 300 ppm, sauerkraut waste ranges as high as 40,000 ppm.

Not only is the brine rich in undesirables, but it also contains a lot of wasted food. During sauerkraut manufacturing, cabbage is

Experiment Station in New York State has developed a yeast digestion process that is being used commercially in three New York plants to treat 5000-10,000 gal of strong brine a day.[43] The waste brine is treated in a fermentor with the food yeast *Candida utilis*. When the yeast cells have settled to the bottom, the remaining liquid can be treated in the local waste treatment plant. While some of the yeast is returned to the fermentor to begin eating the next batch, the remainder can be a valuable source of protein (see Figure 7).[43]

The waste from 100 tons of cabbage will yield up to 800 pounds of dry yeast. This yeast is about 45% protein, rich in vitamin B and an excellent source of invertase, an enzyme widely used in the food industry. Although the potential of byproduct recovery has not been realized yet, the process is still being investigated. Single cell protein (SCP) is another area of research that may offer some advantages.

What has been shown in New York is that reductions in BOD (over 90% in 24 hours), nitrogen (75%) and phosphorus (90%) are indeed achievable. Effluent cleaning and protein production are meshing together in New York State.

It has been suggested that the most common nutritional deficiency disease in the world is protein-calorie deficiency. Although this is not a severe problem in Canada, many countries are going to be looking for new and unconventional protein sources. Researchers at the Ohio Agricultural Research and Development Center (Wooster, Ohio) believe they have a prime candidate: tomato seeds.

Tomato seeds contain approximately 29% crude protein. They also constitute the majority of tomato pomace, the residue of the processing industry. Most of the processed tomatoes are transformed into liquid products; juice, catsup, paste and puree. The peels, seeds, trimmings and culled fruits can end up in a landfill site, or more likely, in a sewage treatment plant, after the screening out of the large lumps. Protein recovery from the seeds would radically reduce the waste load of the processing plant and, if drying could be accomplished cheaply, constitute a net source of income.

The Ohio scientists used commercial tomato cultivars and removed the seeds from the rest of the pomace by microchopping in a Waring blender and screening. After drying, the seeds were ground and defatted before protein analysis (see Table 9).[44] The team decided tomato seeds would prove an excellent source of lysine, which is an amino acid used to fortify bread. The tomato seeds contain about 13% more lysine than soy protein, the present major source.[44]

The team also discovered that the protein content of green tomatoes, usually left to rot in the field, is equivalent to ripe fruit and could offer another untapped resource. If, for example, solar drying could reduce the energy requirements, tomato processors have the opportunity to reduce BOD and expand their product range, cost-effectively.

■ In March 1977, the Geo. Bassett Holdings Company gave financial approval to set up a plant to recover yeast by a fermentation process. The raw material was to be the effluent from its candy company in Sheffield, England. As much as 10% of the sugars used in a confectionery factory can be lost in the wastewater.[1,45]

The feasibility of the process was proven in a pilot plant which produced 5 kg of a protein product over a three-month period. Since that time, the pilot operation has determined the optimum fermenting conditions. The company decided to go ahead with the project.

A commercial scale fermentation plant has now been completed by Farrow Effluent Engineering in conjunction with Tate and Lyle Research. The two most highly loaded effluent streams have been disconnected from the domestic sewer system and piped to the treatment plant where the carbohydrates are fermented in a

---

Table 9

Amino Acids in Tomato Seeds Versus Other Foods

	Egg	Soy Flour	Cow's Milk	Tomato red stage	Opaque 2 corn
Isoleucine	6.6	4.7	6.4	4.4	3.4
Leucine	8.8	6.6	9.9	2.6	9.1
Lysine	6.4	5.8	7.8	6.6	4.8
Phenylalanine	5.8	5.7	4.9	3.9	4.5
Tyrosine	4.2	4.1	5.1	3.4	4.0
Cystine	2.4	0.9	0.9	0.2	1.7
Methionine	3.1	2.0	2.4	0.1	2.1
Threonine	5.1	4.0	4.6	7.8	4.0
Tryptophan	1.6	—	1.4	—	—
Valine	7.3	4.2	6.9	4.6	5.1

Dry weight basis, g/100 g protein

The amino acids available in discarded tomato seeds could be used as food additives, supplementing those derived from soy and other sources.

Source: "Protein Content and Amino Acid Composition of Protein of Seeds from Tomatoes at Various Stages of Ripeness," *Journal of Food Science*, March/April 1980.

25-cubic-metre unit by the yeast *C. utilis*.

The yeast is dried and offered for sale as animal feed. Bassetts used to face annual disposal surcharges of nearly £9000. The reduced effluent charges due to the operation of the new fermentation plant and the revenues from the sale of the yeast feed should recover the plant's capital cost in four or five years. After that, the plant will be operating at a profit.

The natural colour of food is liable to change considerably over time. The addition of dyes or food colours to processed food helps to maintain its appearance and improve its marketability. Artificial dyes, manufactured from coal tars, have traditionally been used for this purpose. Recent reports of negative health effects and growing consumer concerns may limit the future acceptability of some of the artificial colour additives. Natural plant pigments, particularly those derived from process wastes, may supply alternatives.

■ Researchers at the University of Massachusetts have been extracting the pigment from wine grape skins.[46] The pomace obtained from a commercial winery in California was treated with various solvent-acid combinations to obtain anthocyanins. Anthocyanins (or Acys for short) impart the red and blue colours to many fruits and vegetables and many sources of Acy have been suggested. Grapes may be the obvious answer. There is little chance of short supply since grapes are the single largest fruit crop in the world.[26,46]

The Massachusetts team, under lab conditions, found citric acid and methanol offered the best extraction results, although alcohol extraction procedures would require special precautions to prevent atmospheric alcohol build-up in a commercial operation. If it was decided to use water as an extractant, acetic acid gave the best results. The team envisages a continuous counter-current flow procedure used commercially, although solvent recovery and economic viability still need to be demonstrated in pilot operations.

■ Meanwhile, a team at the University of Wisconsin has completed studies of Acy extraction

from commercial cranberry pulp wastes generated from the processing of juice.[47] The scientists believe the pigment collected could be used in the colouring of cranberry cocktail, cherry pie fillings and other processed foods.

The researchers removed the colourant with solvent, separated it with an appropriate membrane in an ultrafiltration system and concentrated the Acys with reverse osmosis and vacuum equipment. The reverse osmosis procedure purified the product as well as removed excess water. The combination of reverse osmosis and vacuum distillation has already been used to concentrate maple syrup and dairy products.[47] The two units have a definite advantage in energy efficiency achieved over the use of vacuum processes alone.

Although the pilot project achieved only a 50% yield of pigment, the team believes that percentage would be substantially increased in a large-scale operation. Future improvements in membrane technology would certainly improve the economics of the procedure further.

The pigments in food processing wastes are not, in general, hazardous in an effluent flow. They can, however, cause an aesthetic problem when wastes are disposed in local water bodies. It is more important, though, that wastestreams are looked at as a resource rather than as a nuisance. Utilizing them as a source of alternative food additives is an excellent example of this philosophy.

4.
Wastewater Control

In the United States in 1976, approximately 653 million pounds of leafy greens and broccoli were processed, requiring 2.5 billion gallons of water. Between 70 and 90% of the wastewater generated by the industry came from the initial washing of the vegetables. Now researchers in Virginia have developed a washing system using water circulation and some novel mechanical features that can cut water requirements to one-fifth of

what used to be needed.[48]

■ During a study on a commercial processing plant, the team found their system produced a slightly cleaner product, trapped more organic material from the wastewater effluent and had a pay-back period of *only six days*. Traditionally, producers use, in order: a dry tumbler for the removal of loose soil and small particles, hand inspection belts and from one to four wet washers. These washers may be fed with water taken from the blanched product cooling flume introduced through a single perforated pipe (no sprays) below the water level at the head of each washer.

The Virginia team redesigned the conventional washers and tumblers to create high recirculation rates within the system and provide hydraulic agitation to supplement the mechanical agitation. The new process consisted of two modified immersion washers in series, each with a settling tank and filter for cleaning the water during recirculation. Fresh makeup water was sprayed on the vegetables as they were lifted from the second washer. Excess water from the second settling tank reverse flowed into the first tank providing the only hydraulic link between the two washing subsystems. The excess water from the first tank overflowed to a drain.

The settling tanks were specially designed to trap organic material and remove it from the effluent. The water from the washing drums, along with dirt and organic matter, was collected in a sump and pumped to a moving filter belt above the input to the settling tank. The belt, made of a very fine mesh, monofilament plastic, allowed the water to percolate through to the tanks while the grit and organic material was carried on to a separate container and removed with a blower. Thus most of the organic wastes could be kept separate from the washer effluents.

The initial cost of a conventional system from the manufacturer was $12,000. The annual fixed costs for owning it, including depreciation, interest, taxes and insurance would be $1656 per year. The Virginia system has a higher capital cost, $16,000 and would thus have fixed costs of $2208 or $552 more a year.

However, when it comes time to include the operating costs of the two systems, the advantages of a low-flow, low-polluting alternative become dramatically evident. The researchers calculated that the traditional system, handling 1360 kg of spinach and turnip greens an hour would have a daily operating cost of $251.15. This included electric power, water, sewer charges, sewer surcharges based on waste strength, repairs and labour. The comparable figure for their recirculating system was only $158.38 or $92.77 a day less.[48]

With six days of operating each season, the system would pay for itself, and then operate at an economic advantage for the following months the processing plant was in operation.

It is true that all process modifications won't yield such spectacular results. But when a relatively simple design can cut water use by 80%, improve effluent quality and clean produce better, with a six-day-a-year pay-back period, there is real incentive to rethink the traditional way of doing things.

■ The industry that handles the food we eat must be meticulous in its house cleaning. This applies particularly in the way it "washes its dishes", the vats, pots and cookers used in food processing. J. J. Saunders (Cheesemaking) Ltd., (Emborough, England) was spending a lot of time and effort cleaning the stainless steel vats used for agitating the milk in its operation.[49] They were also producing a large quantity of dirty washwater that needed to be treated.

The four, 2500-gallon capacity vats contain the cheese product until the pressing stage. After the whey and product are drained off, the vats are left covered with scum, baked on during the cooking process. The clean-up crew were forced to tackle these deposits with scrapers and hoses, a long and arduous job which required both a lot of muscle and a lot of water.

In an effort to bring this operation into line with an otherwise highly efficient plant, the firm contracted a high-pressure water equipment manufacturer, Flexian Hydraulics (Salisbury, England). Flexian outfitted Saunders with a high-pressure unit fitted with two guns capable of exerting a water pressure of 1000 psi. In addition to cleaning the agitation vats, the pump and nozzles are being used to clean everything from the floors to the milk tanker trucks. The firm even installed a second unit at a nearby piggery. The pigs

Figure 8
Prototype Vegetable Washing System

Counter-current water flow is the only hydraulic link between the two washing settling tanks in this prototype vegetable washing system. The innovative process reduces water use by 80% and pays for itself in only six days.

Source: "A Comparison of Single Use and Recycled Water Leafy Vegetable Washing Systems," *Journal of Food Science*, March/April 1979.

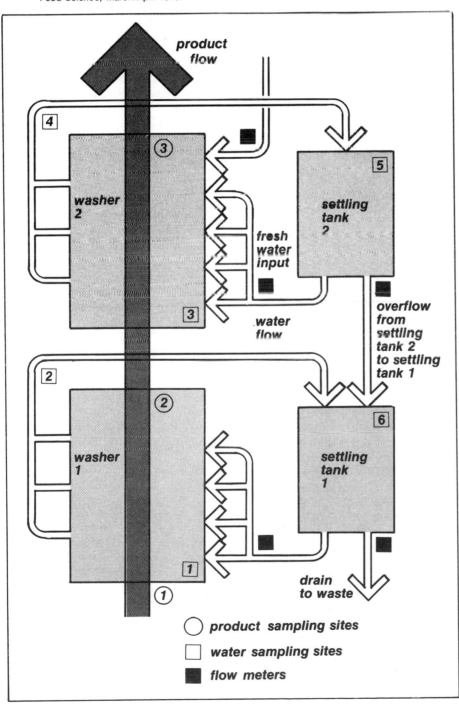

product flow

washer 2

fresh water input

settling tank 2

water flow

overflow from settling tank 2 to settling tank 1

washer 1

settling tank 1

drain to waste

○ product sampling sites

☐ water sampling sites

■ flow meters

already utilized the waste whey from its cheesemaking as a food supplement. Saunder's high-pressure hose can clean the pens out in under two hours.[49]

The results in saved water and manpower have been impressive. The dirty vats are now being cleaned in half the time taken by hand and the water consumption has dropped by two-thirds. J. J. Saunders Ltd. has learned it pays to let the water do the work.

■ The capture and recovery of food from waste rinsewater used in plant clean-up can save an appreciable amount of raw material from disappearing down the drain. The Agropur cheesemaking plant (Granby, Quebec) recovers the equivalent of 25,000 litres of milk each day by treating its rinsewaters.[50] The first rinse from the tanker transports, transfer lines, holding tanks, separators and pasteurizers is treated in evaporators to separate the milk product and recycle the water. The rinsewater can be re-used up to seven times for wash-up purposes.

The Agropur plant is one of Canada's largest and most modern milk processing facilities. A producer of specialty cheeses and other dairy products, the firm has a capacity of 315 million litres of raw milk annually. The rinsewater recovery programme is responsible for keeping more than 2% of that capacity from ending up as part of Granby, Quebec's pollution load; about 7 million litres of potential contaminants become cheese instead.

Agropur also installed milk recovery on its air pollution control line. When milk powder is manufactured by a spray process, the raw milk is atomized and dried on cushions of hot air, some of which is lost to the outside environment. The Quebec plant is able to recover most of this air-borne milk, turning a profit and mollifying its neighbours at the same time.

Conclusion

Food producers and processors can no longer be simple tillers of soil or hawkers in a marketplace. The complexities of modern agriculture and the great deal of capital involved make a keen business mind more important than a strong back. Like all businessmen, the food producer has tried to maximize the value of his food output and minimize the costs incurred. This has resulted in the development of thousands of new food products, products consumers have come to relish and rely on.

As food handling shifted from the control of the farmer and entered the sphere of the corporate world, its adverse effects on the environment have grown more serious. When the processing wastes from vegetables were left in the fields, the impact was often beneficial; the nutrients returned to the soil. But the modern processor faces food quality problems that are not found in a farmers' market.

"While a housewife peeling a carrot at her sink might accept a small blemish, she would hold up her hands in horror if she saw the same blemish in a frozen package or can," explains J. M. Dalgleish, an engineer with Imperial Foods Ltd. "Since natural produce is not always perfect, the food processor is faced inevitably with ruthless discard from his main line."[45] Bruised, diseased and deformed food all join the organic waste load of the plant to form a single effluent that can strip the oxygen from a river or choke a sewage treatment plant.

Most of the wastewater generated by the food industry is currently being handled by municipal sewage treatment plants or treated on-site by systems that closely resemble them. The aerobic and anaerobic digestion facilities, with their familiar lagoons and sludge handling units, are based on the proven engineering technologies designed to treat human waste. This expertise is readily adaptable to breaking down the high-BOD organic wastes, and the resultant sludges can be spread on agricultural land or trucked to incinerators or landfill sites. The equipment is available and the costs can often be absorbed by a large firm but, as is often the case, this popular approach can prove to be neither economical nor practical in a business context.

Imaginative approaches that recognize the market value of present wastes have the potential of solving an effluent problem and earning revenue. Simple process changes that reduce the waste load to complex new technologies that generate valuable byproducts are all being tested and incorporated into plants of companies that look on waste as a resource to be exploited.

Whether it be a better method to peel peaches, an advanced ultrafiltration technique to concentrate whey protein, or the development of new microorganisms to produce single cell protein, recycling and recovery of food can be feeding a hungry planet (and turning a profit). The firms that stick to the old ways will be paying an ever-increasing amount to the sewage plant or landfill operator to dispose an important raw material.

FOR FURTHER INFORMATION

Associations

Brewers Association of Canada,
Suite 805, 151 Sparks Street,
Ottawa, Ontario.
K1P 5E3
(613) 232-9601

Canadian Dairy and Food
Industries Supply Association,
R.R. #1,
Bradford, Ontario.
L0G 1C0
(416) 939-2545

Canadian Food Processors
Association,
Suite 1409, 130 Albert Street,
Ottawa, Ontario.
K1P 5G4
(613) 233-4049

Canadian Frozen Food Association,
Suite 1409, 130 Albert Street,
Ottawa, Ontario.
K1P 5G4
(613) 233-9400

Canadian Institute of Food Science
and Technology,
46 Elgin Street,
Ottawa, Ontario.
K1P 5K6
(613) 233-8992

Canadian Meat Council,
5233 Dundas Street West,
Islington, Ontario.
M9B 1A6
(416) 239-8411

Grocery Products Manufacturers of
Canada,
Suite 101, 1185 Eglinton Ave. East,
Don Mills, Ontario.
M3C 3C6
(416) 429-4444

The National Dairy Council of
Canada,
Suite 704, 141 Laurier Ave. West,
Ottawa, Ontario.
K1P 5J3
(613) 238-4116

Food Processing Machinery and
Supplies Association,
Suite 700, 1828 L Street N.W.,
Washington, D.C.
20036
(202) 833-1790

Institute of Food Technologists,
Suite 2120,
221 North LaSalle Street,
Chicago, Illinois.
60601
(312) 782-8424

National Food Processors
Association,
1133 20th Street N.W.,
Washington, D.C.
20036
(202) 331-5900

Journals

FOOD ENGINEERING,
Chilton Company,
Chilton Way,
Radnor, Pennsylvania.
19089

FOOD MANUFACTURING,
Morgan-Grampian (Process Press)
Ltd.,
30 Calderwood Street,
Woolwich,
London SE18 6QH, England.

FOOD PROCESSING,
Putman Publishing Company,
301 E. Erie Street,
Chicago, Illinois.
60611

FOOD PROCESSING INDUSTRY,
IPC Consumer Industries Press
Ltd.,
40 Bowling Green Lane,
London EC1R ONE, England.

FOOD TECHNOLOGY,
Institute of Food Technologists,
Suite 2120,
221 North LaSalle Street,
Chicago, Illinois.
60601

FOOD TECHNOLOGY IN
AUSTRALIA,
Council of Australia Food
Technology Association Inc.,
44 Miller Street,
North Sydney, Australia.

JOURNAL OF FOOD SCIENCE,
Subscription Department,
Institute of Food Technologists,
Suite 2120,
221 North LaSalle Street,
Chicago, Illinois.
60601

NEW YORK'S FOOD AND LIFE
SCIENCES,
400 Robert's Hall,
Cornell University,
Ithaca, New York.
14853

References

1. Walker, Godfrey. "Optimising Waste Recovery." *Food Processing Industry*, June 1979.

2. Knorr, Dietrich, "Recycling Food Wastes." *Compost Science/Land Utilization*, November/December 1979.

3. Robinson, W.B. "Our Wasted and Underused Food Resources." *New York's Food and Life Sciences* 11(4), 1978.

4. Jones, H.R. *Waste Disposal Control in the Fruit and Vegetable Industry*. Park Ridge, New Jersey: Noyes Data Corporation, 1973.

5. Fuggle, Roger W. "Treatment of Wastewater from Food Processing and Brewing." *Chemistry and Industry*, July 4, 1981.

6. Krofchak, David and Stone, N. *Science and Engineering for Pollution Free Systems*. Ann Arbor, Michigan: Ann Arbor Science Publishers Inc., 1975.

7. Moon, Nancy J. "Maximizing Efficiencies in the Food System: A Review of Alternatives for Waste Abatement." *Journal of Food Protection*, March 1980.

8. Jones, H.R. *Pollution Control in Meat, Poultry and Seafood Processing*. Park Ridge, New Jersey: Noyes Data Corporation, 1974.

9. "An Organic Industrial Waste Survey." *Compost Science/Land Utilization*, September/October 1978.

10. Baker, Robert C. "The Problem of Food Waste." *New York's Food and Life Sciences* 11(2), 1978.

11. Bourne, M.C. "Wasted Food in Developing Countries." *New York's Food and Life Sciences* 11(4). 1978.

12. Zall, Robert R. "Waste Misplaced." *New York's Food and Life Sciences* 11(4), 1978.

13. "Canora Site of Ethanol Plant." *Toronto Star,* January 22, 1982.

14. Morris, Charles E. "Cuts Energy Costs in Half for Ethanol Production." *Food Engineering,* February 1981.

15. Lane, A.G. "Methane from Anaerobic Digestion of Fruit Waste and Vegetable Processing Wastes." *Food Technology in Australia,* May 1979.

16. "Tangerines a Gas: Car Firm." *Toronto Star,* January 21, 1982.

17. Goldenfield, Irving H. "How to Utilize Waste and Not Get Into Trouble with Regulatory Bodies." *Food Technology,* June 1978.

18. "When They Put Whey to Work." *The Engineering Times,* April 20, 1981.

19. Streeter, Robert R. and Forwalter, John. "Ultrafiltration of 30,000 lb/hr of Whey Eliminates Waste Problem." *Food Processing,* September 1979.

20. Corning Glass Works. *Whey: A Problem Becomes An Opportunity.* Corning, New York: Corning Biosystems, Corning Glass Works, 1979.

21. Corning Glass Works. "Hydrolyzed Lactose New Source of Sweeteners." *Food Engineering,* November 1979.

22. Morris, Charles E. "Recovers Whey Proteins of 90% Purity." *Food Engineering,* April 1981.

23. Morris, Charles E. "Twice as Much at Half the Price." *Food Engineering,* June 1980.

24. "Whey Up." *Biocycle,* January/February 1981.

25. "Alcohol from Whey, the Carbery Process." *Food Technology in Australia,* February 1980.

26. Blicq, A. "Dauphin Toys with Idea of Whey as Dust Fighter." *Winnipeg Free Press,* June 1, 1981.

27. Smith, Lorne C. "Recovers Fat and Oil Worth $181,000/yr." *Food Processing,* September 1980.

28. "Electrochemical Water Treatment Removes Suspended Fats, Proteins." *Food Engineering,* March 1979.

29. "Wastewater Byproducts are New Source of Income for New Zealand Meat Packer." *Meat Processing,* June 1981.

30. "Treatment System Removes BOD, Suspended Solids 40-60%." *Food Processing,* September 1980.

31. Hang, Y.D. *et al.* "Isolation and Chemical Evaluation of Protein from Clam Waste Water." *Journal of Food Science,* July/August, 1980.

32. Fernando, T. "Utilization of Paunch Content Material by Ultrafiltration." *Process Biochemistry,* March 1980.

33. Farmer, D.M. *et al.* "Paunch Drying with Direct Solar Energy Supplemented by Solar Regenerated Dessicant." *Transactions of the American Society of Agricultural Engineers* 23, 1980. Abstract: *Journal of the Water Pollution Control Association, June 1981.*

34. "Engineers Tackle Energy and Wastewater Problems." *Food Engineering,* April 1980.

35. "The Hidden Profit in Waste." *Food Processing Industry,* June 1979.

36. "You're Smarter Than You Think." *Reader's Digest,* October 1981.

37. "More Corn: Less Pollution." *Food Technology in Australia,* April 1979.

38. Robertson, G.H. *et al.* "Yield, Effluent Reduction and Organoleptic Incentives for Intact or Unit-Kernel Sweet Corn." *Food Technology,* August 1977.

39. ADM Foods (advertisement). "Using Everything But the Squeal, as Applied to Corn." *Food Technology,* May 1981.

40. "Granular Carbon Decolorization Saves Corn-Syrup Processor $6.6 Million." *Food Engineering,* July 1981.

41. Garratt, Frank *et al.* "Recovers an Extra 4500-5000 lb Cattle Feed from Trimmings and Culls." *Food Processing,* September 1980.

42. Frederic, W.R.L. *et al.* "Solids Separation/Water Re-Use System Removes 16 Tons of Soil Daily." *Food Processing,* September 1980.

43. Hang, Y.D. "Reducing Wastes in Sauerkraut Plants." *New York's Food and Life Sciences* 10(1), 1977.

44. Brodowski, D. and Geisman, J.R. "Protein Content and Amino Acid Composition of Protein of Seeds from Tomatoes at Various Stages of Ripeness." *Journal of Food Science,* March/April 1980.

45. "Losses are Too High, Conference Is Told." *Food Processing Industry,* January 1979.

46. Metivier, R.P. *et al.* "Solvent Extraction of Anthocyanins from Wine Pomace." *Journal of Food Science,* July/August 1980.

47. Woo, A.H. *et al.* "Anthocyanin Recovery from Cranberry Pulp Wastes by Membrane Technology." *Journal of Food Science,* July/August 1980.

48. Wright, M.E. *et al.* "A Comparison of Single Use and Recycled Water Leafy Vegetable Washing Systems." *Journal of Food Science,* March/April 1979.

49. "High Water Pressure Cleans Cheese Vats." *Food Processing Industry,* May 1981.

50. Bhagat, Teresa. "Energy Savings and Pollution Control Ensured by Latest Technology." *Water and Pollution Control,* April 1981.

Oil

Waste oils offer a tremendous recycling potential. An important, dwindling natural resource of great economic and industrial value, oil products are a cornerstone of our modern industrial society. Petroleum is processed into a wide variety of products: gasoline, fuel oil, diesel oil, synthetic rubber, solvents, pesticides, synthetic fibres, lubricating oil, drugs and many more[1] (see Figure 1).

The boilers of American industries presently consume about 40% of the used lubricating oils collected. In Ontario, the percentage varies from 20 to 30%.

Road oiling is the other major use of collected waste oils. Five to seven million gallons (50-70% of the waste oil collected) is spread on dusty Ontario roads each summer. The practice is both a wasteful use of a dwindling resource and an environmental hazard. The waste oil, with its load of heavy metals, particularly lead, additives including dangerous polynuclear aromatics and PCBs, is carried into the natural environment by runoff and dust to contaminate soils and water courses.[2]

The largest portion of used oils is never collected, but disappears into sewers, landfill sites and backyards. In Ontario alone, approximately 22 million gallons of potentially recyclable lube oil simply vanish each year.

While oil recycling has ad-

Figure 1
Petroleum Products

The petroleum distillation process produces a wide range of different oil products. The mixing of these various fractions with their individual additives in a waste collection system would make their subsequent re-refining impossible.
Source: The Way Things Work, Simon and Schuster, 1967.

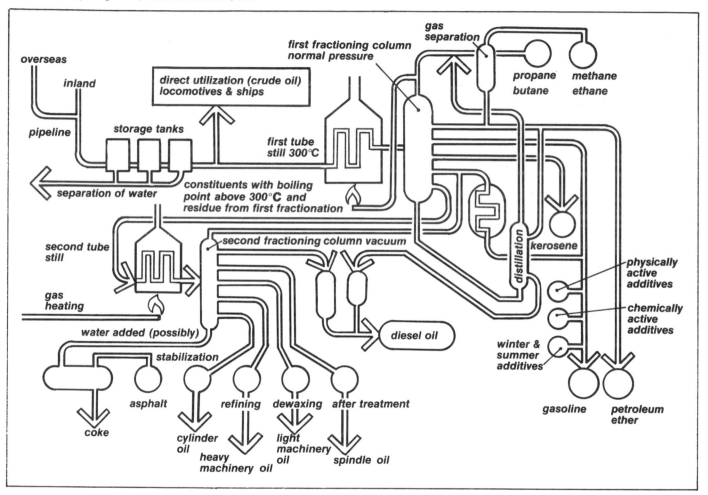

vanced in Europe to the point where much of what is available is collected (50% in Germany, 30% in France), North America lags somewhat behind. Canada recycles between 2 and 10% of its potentially recyclable oils. There is much room for improvement.

It is certainly possible to increase this figure, and by doing so pass on considerable savings to industry and reduce our import-dominated balance of payments.

One researcher believes it is feasible, using presently available re-refining technology, to cut our demands for virgin lubricating oils by 40%.[3] One hundred tonnes of lubricating oil or virgin raffinates will yield a further 80 tonnes of recycled lubricating oils, if 60% of oil is repeatedly collected after use and re-refined with a 75% efficiency.[3]

The same oil could conceivably be recycled five times to accumulate that 80-tonne recycling return.

This untapped potential would advance Canada a little further along the road to energy independence. It also offers economic rewards to those individuals and firms who are presently flushing down sewers or dropping in landfill sites millions of gallons of this valuable resource each year.

The establishment of an efficient collection system (backed by the proper legislative incentives) would allow all the present and proposed recycling operations to remain viable.

Industry can begin with good housekeeping. Occasionally oil is deliberately dumped, more often it is spilled accidentally, or it steals away insidiously and unnoticed as a hydrocarbon vapour loss. These losses, which result from leaks in pipes or tanks, process exhausts, etc., not only cause air pollution problems but can waste appreciable amounts of energy. British Petroleum Limited (BP) in the United Kingdom has installed a portable data logging system to cut these losses. Sensitive to hydrocarbon levels of 0.1 ppm, it is possible, with a ring of six sensors, to identify the positions of major emissions, leading to the ultimate location of individual leaks with portable detailed scans.[4]

Pollution Prevention Opportunities

1.
Re-Refining

The re-refining of used or spent oils is nothing new. In the United States, re-refining peaked in the 1960s, when some 150 refineries produced about 300 million gallons of reclaimed oil every year. But largely through inequitable taxation provisions, oil recycling lost its profitable edge over the refining of virgin stocks. According to the Association of Petroleum Re-refiners, by 1980, only 10 companies were left in the business, producing merely 100 million gallons annually in the United States.[5]

Now, the development of new re-refining technology, linked with rapidly escalating oil prices, has put new life into the enterprise.

Economically, re-refining makes good sense. "It is cheaper to re-refine rather than refine lubricating oils because one, the cost of crude is so high today and two, it takes fewer refining steps because the lubricating components are present already in the waste oil," said Stan Abraces, president of Northern Oil Limited (Quebec).

And from an energy conservation standpoint, re-refining offers substantial benefits. A Teknekron study for the U.S. Environmental Protection Agency showed net savings of about 20,000 Btu per gallon of lubricating oil re-refined over production of the same amount of lubricating oil from crude, assuming in both cases that all products other than the produced lubes are burned as fuel.[6]

Four types of oil can be re-refined: crankcase oils, industrial lubricants from machinery and process operations, turbine oils from aviation and hydraulic oils. The contaminants include water, cleaners, organic solvents and the metallic solids from oxidation and wear. Only those oils that have been exposed to extremely high temperatures or have been mixed with incompatible substances[7]

(including different oils, see Table 1) cannot be restored to their original specifications.

Although a number of small Canadian firms has been tapping these supplies for many years, they are soon to be joined by the giants in the oil field. Projects worth over $50 million have been announced and are in various stages of development.[8] If all are completed, Canada will have a capacity to re-refine a further 180 million litres (42 million gal) of waste oils each year.

■ Mohawk Oil has opened a North Vancouver facility to handle 18 million litres per year and is proposing another plant in Alberta to process a further 18 to 36 million litres.

■ Turbo Resources Ltd. is planning a 45-million-litre facility at its proposed new condensate refinery north of Calgary.

■ In Ontario, Shell is constructing a 36- to 45-million litre plant in Toronto and Imperial Oil is planning an equivalent facility somewhere in the southwestern section of the province.

■ Lubrimax Inc. has opened Quebec's first plant to recycle used industrial oil. The plant in St.

Table 1
Products of Petroleum Distillation

Fraction	Molecular Size Range	Boiling-point Range (°C)	Typical Uses
Gas	C_1-C_5	-164 to 30	Gaseous fuel
Petroleum ether	C_5-C_7	30 to 90	Solvent, dry cleaning
Straight-run gasoline	C_5-C_{12}	30 to 200	Motor fuel
Kerosene	C_{12}-C_{16}	175 to 275	Fuel for stoves, diesel and jet engines
Gas oil or fuel oil	C_{15}-C_{18}	Up to 375	Furnace oil
Lubricating oils	C_{16}-C_{20}	350 and up	Lubrication
Greases	C_{18}-up	Semisolid	Lubrication
Paraffin (wax)	C_{20}-up	Melts at 52-57	Candles
Pitch and tar	high	Residue in boiler	Roofing, paving

The distillation of crude oil results in a wide variety of petroleum fractions. Many of the re-refining techniques employ a distillation stage to duplicate this process, but the contamination of waste oils with additives still requires that disparate and incompatible wastestreams be kept separate.

Source: Seager, S.L. and Stoker, H.S. *Chemistry: A Science for Today*, 1973.

Lazare uses a European process to reclaim 7 million litres of oil a year. The company intends to extend its operations in the province to recover "all 35 million litres of industrial oil used in Quebec annually".[9]

Acid/Clay

■ A typical, traditional small operator is Breslube Enterprises (Breslau, Ontario) which has been operating for four years. Like most established firms, Breslube uses an acid/clay re-refining process. In its first year of operation, Breslube recycled 1 million gallons of oil; by 1981, the company was processing 4 to 5 million gallons and still had the capacity to handle another million gallons.[10]

Joe Chalube, president, is competing for his supplies with road oilers and those who burn waste oil as a supplementary fuel. Approximately 2 to 3 million gallons are burned each year in Ontario as a fuel blend for the production of Portland cement. The new Shell and Imperial Oil refineries will place further competitive demands on available stocks.

At present, Breslube pays gas stations 8¢ a litre for used oil (about 20% of the cost of virgin oil). The company can reprocess the oil, sell it at less than the going price for new oil (about 10 to 20¢ less) and *still* make a profit.[10]

Unfortunately, the standard acid/clay method for re-refining spent oils has several drawbacks. This technique depends on treatment with sulphuric acid. The process produces about 15 tonnes of acid tar for every 100 tonnes of waste oil treated. Also an after-treatment with Fullers earth (a variety of claylike materials which absorb oil and grease) is essential and yields a further 5 tonnes of high sulphur oily sludge. These residues are difficult and expensive to dispose and a potential hazard to the environment.

More and more chemical additives are being added to oil base stocks. The re-raffinate obtained may be higher in sulphur, chlorine and some metallic substances than equivalent virgin raffinates, which might affect re-use.

Figure 2
The PROP Process

The PROP re-refining process produces high yields and low waste volumes. The chemical treatment step removes metal contaminants, while the hydrotreating process removes inorganics, sulphur, nitrogen, oxygen and chloro compounds as well as H_2S, NH_3 and HCl. The re-refined oil is identical to virgin stocks.
Source: "Spotlight Falls on Recycling Plants," Oilweek, June 9, 1980.

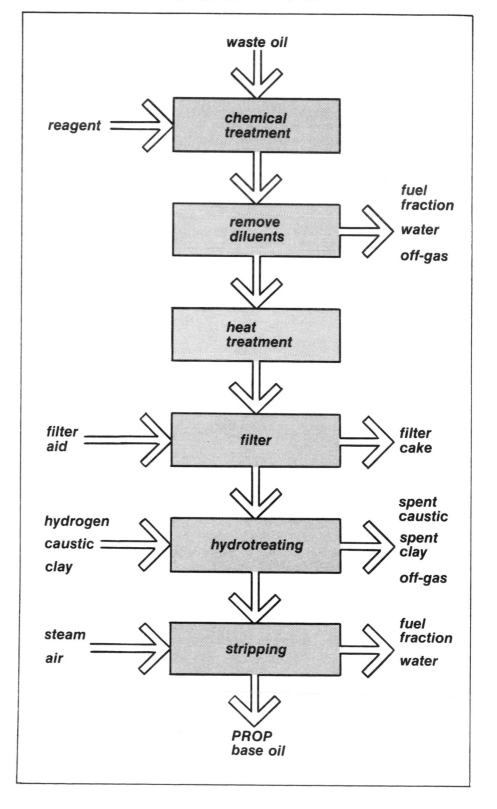

And finally, the acid/clay process has relatively high operating costs. Private operators using this system may have difficulty competing for their share of the waste oil supplies in the advent of large new plants using more advanced technologies springing up across Canada.

Hydrotreating

■ Philips Petroleum has developed a re-refined oil process (PROP) which combines hydrotreating with chemical demetallization to produce 90% yields of base oil. This compares with the 40 to 50% yields achievable with the acid/clay process. Philips is offering turn-key plants — fully engineered, prefabricated plants with provisions for installation and start-up. These plants have a 2- to 10-million-gallon per-year capacity and come with a guarantee that the re-refined product will match virgin oils.

Plants have been sold to Mohawk Lubricants (Vancouver), Shell Canada (Toronto), The State of North Carolina (Garner, North Carolina) and Clayton Chemical (St. Louis, Missouri).

PROP is essentially a two-stage process[8] (see Figure 2). Demetallizing is carried out with the addition of diammonium phosphate (DAP). This results in the formation of metallic phosphates which have a very low solubility and are removed by filtration. Water and lighter ends of the fuel diluent are taken off by progressive increases in temperature and decreases in pressure. This procedure removes 99% or more of the ash-forming material in the waste oil and the filter cake collected for disposal is two or three times less than what is removed in the acid/clay process. This filter cake has a near-neutral pH and under some conditions may be suitable for disposal on agricultural land, used as landfill or as an asphalt extender.

The second stage is hydrotreating. The oil is heated, mixed with recirculating hydrogen, percolated through a guard bed of clay and hydrotreated over a conventional nickel-molybdate catalyst.

The hydrogen removes H_2S, NH_3 and HCl; the clay bed removes inorganics; and hydrotreating takes out the sulphur, nitrogen, oxygen and chloro compounds. Sulphide-spent caustic is a by-product of the hydrotreating step. It may have a secondary market with leather tanners and paper makers.

The resultant oil stream is identical to that produced by primary refineries. Fractionation separates the light and heavy oils which can be mixed with various additives to make some 30 to 40 types of specification lubricating oils.

Material costs, including the DAP, amount to 11.5¢ (U.S.) per gallon (3¢ per litre) of spent oil. The re-refining process takes only a few hours as opposed to days required for older techniques.

The PROP system can remove the usual types of contamination that will occur in service stations and fleet garages. Water, engine coolant, anti-freeze and small amounts of brake fluid can all be handled. However, it is impossible to mix oils of differing viscosities with the high-viscosity automotive lubricating oils and expect to get an end product that meets industry standards.

■ The North Carolina PROP installation has operated for more than a year. The re-refined oil has successfully passed rigorous engine performance specifications and meets much of the demand for oil by the state and local governments for their vehicles.

■ Mohawk Lubricants has contracts with Philips for the first commercial application of the PROP process. Planned to open in the spring of 1981, but since delayed, the North Vancouver facility cost $10 million and has a capacity of 4 million gal (18 million litres) annually. Mohawk has added a fractionator to produce both light and heavy stocks to provide greater flexibility for blending.

■ The collection of waste oil feedstock is the responsibility of another Mohawk Oil subsidiary, Waste Oil Salvage Company (WOSCO). In British Columbia there is currently a potential waste lube oil supply of 46 million

litres (10 million gal) of which 30 million litres (6.6 million gal) are collected annually mostly for burning or road oiling.[8]

The Mohawk facility, when operating at capacity, has the potential of supplying 25% of B.C.'s lube oil demand.

WOSCO's six-truck collection fleet serves service stations, equipment dealers, industrial plants and transport companies on Vancouver Island and the lower mainland. In addition to a depot at the PROP facility, Mohawk is planning facilities in Cranbrook, Kamloops and Prince George.

Do-it-yourself oil changers in B.C. use 2.7 million litres of oil annually. WOSCO encourages motorists to bring their used oil to selected locations in exchange for coupons redeemable on anything sold at Mohawk outlets.

■ Shell Canada has also contracted for a $20 million PROP facility capable of re-refining 10 million gal of lubricating oil annually.[11]

The Shell plant will be operated by a wholly owned subsidiary, Canada Oil Company. General manager Dave Fisher is concerned about future sources of lube oil supply. Canada Oil is purchasing spent oil from Newfoundland to Saskatchewan. Supplies brought in from the United States are charged 12% duty by the federal government, a situation that reduces the profitability of the recycling operation.

Fisher would like to see a remission of the federal duty as well as the implementation of a deposit on lubricating oils. Motorists would be charged a small deposit on each quart which could be refunded when they return the used oil.

Vacuum Distillation

■ West German chemists have developed a new method of re-refining waste lubricating oils that is being distributed worldwide by Leybold-Heraeus (Hanau, West Germany) under the trade name Recyclon.[3]

Since 1977, a complete pilot plant with a daily capacity of 1000 kg has been in operation in Bern, Switzerland. Spent oil processed

Figure 3
The Recyclon Process

The West German Recyclon process entails three major steps. First, impurities are removed, then the reaction products are removed by evaporation and finally, the distillate is separated into various oil fractions by vacuum distillation.

Source: "Recyclon — A New Method of Re-refining Spent Lubrication Oils Without Detriment to the Environment," *Conservation and Recycling* 3(2), 1979.

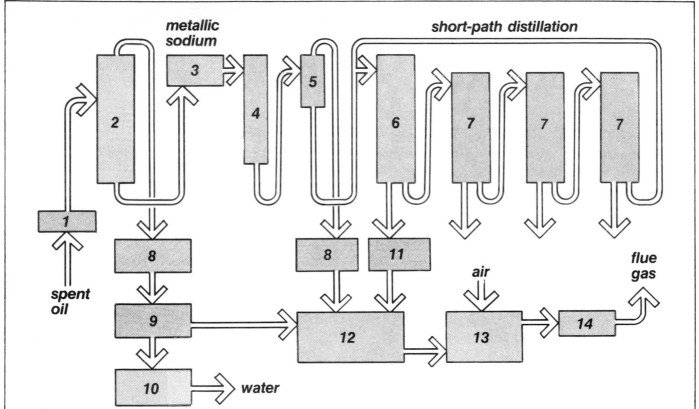

(1) filter (2) dehydration gasoline extraction (3) dispersing agent (4) mixer (5) flasher (6) total evaporation (7) fractions 1, 2, 3 (8) condensate (9) separation tank (10) neutralizer (11) residues (12) mixing and storage tank (13) furnace (14) electric filter

by the system yields approximately 30% by weight fuel oils and 70% re-raffinates. The re-raffinates are of excellent quality and compare favourably in comparison quality testing with virgin oils.

The preliminary planning of a complete re-refining plant with a 250,000-tonne annual capacity shows waste oils could be re-refined at costs below 70% of the market values of re-raffinates.

The Recyclon process is a three-step operation[3] (see Figure 3). First, spent oil is filtered, dehydrated and treated with approximately 1% metallic sodium to precipitate all impurities and decomposing agents; second, the reaction products formed are removed through the total evaporation of the lubricating oil by means

of a special product-preserving, thin-film, short-path distillation under a vacuum of less than one millibar; and third, the distillate obtained is separated into lubricating oil fractions of various viscosities by means of vacuum distillation.[3]

The highly viscous residue from the total distillation is combined and blended with low-boiling-point substances from the pre-treatment to produce a heating fuel with a 7% ash content. This high-Btu fuel can be burned in furnaces equipped with the proper air pollution control equipment. About 25% of the heating energy is used in the re-refining process; the rest is available for other uses.

■ Raffinerie Elf Feyzin is an oil refinery in France. Seizing a business opportunity, the refinery in-

vested 11 million francs to set up a waste oil recovery operation. Sales from reclaimed oil products soon covered operating costs as well as yielded a net profit of more than 5 million francs each year. Costs for disposing of an equivalent amount of waste oil would have been 2.5 million francs each year.

Evaporator/Clay

■ Midland Oil Refineries (England) collects most grades of industrial oils, including cutting and lubricating oils, from customers in minimum quantities of eight 45-gallon drums or 500-gallon bulk tanker loads.[13]

Midland uses a Phaudler Wiped Film Evaporator in place of the sulphuric acid treatment in the traditional acid/clay re-refining process. Waste oil is evaporated inside a stainless steel tube while steam flows through the outer heating jacket. The distillate condenses and is collected while the residues are left to flow down the inner tube to the bottom of the evaporator, aided by a mechanical wiper to prevent fouling of the heating surface.

Similar units are available for solvent recovery by Raywell Process Plants (Stratford, East London, England).

Midland reclaims used oils at a cost of up to 50% less than that of new oil.

While hydrotreating technology, modern distillation and other innovations have drastically reduced the sludge waste loads of the new re-refineries, many of those companies involved still rely on landfilling and incineration of wastes.

■ Berk Associates Inc. (Pottstown, Pennsylvania) has pushed material recovery from the re-refinery process one step further. They have pioneered the use of residue from oil re-refinery operations for roof coating applications.

2.
Oil Cleaning

The advantage of oil cleaning over conventional re-refining is that additives to not have to be replaced in order to bring the oil back to specification. It is essential, however, that used dieselube or industrial oils are not contaminated with other waste oil stocks. Strict segregation is required. The process will not work on mixed oils, particularly if the dieselube is collected along with lubricating oil from gasoline engines.

■ Petroleum Recycling Services Ltd. (Toronto, Ontario) uses a simple settling, filtration and vacuum evaporation system to return used oil to new oil standards for about one dollar a gallon.[12] Escalating oil prices and environmental concerns have doubled their business each year since its inception in 1975.

Waste industrial oils are received in drums and bulk by Chem-Ecol, an Ontario recycler.

Petroleum Recycling operates three mobile units with hourly recycling capacities up to 600 gallons. These units can treat oil in company-heated settling tanks or be hooked directly into the machinery to recycle oil without any shutdown period necessary.

Petroleum Recycling's services are in great demand by users of refrigeration oils. Since mid-1978, the oil fields mining the base stock have been rationing their dwindling supplies at 50% of requirements. Synthetic equivalents are available at $20 a gallon. The Toronto re refiner is still recycling these oils at $1 a gallon.[12]

■ Six years ago, British Rail's Scientific Services Branch began investigating ways of extending the lifetime and reducing the maintenance costs of the engine lubricating oil filters of their diesel electric locomotives.[14] The crankcase of a locomotive holds 140 gallons of dieselube and if this is seriously contaminated with water, fuel oil or other material, it can cause expensive trouble.

The scientific staff began centrifuging used dieselube to remove 7 to 10% of the contaminants of the dirty oil with the aim of extending filter life with no risk to the engines. A pilot plant was built at Inningham.

With the advent of steeply rising oil costs, the researchers began looking for a chemical that when added to the used dieselube would combine with or absorb pollutants and convert them into a form that the centrifuge would remove. Eventually a blend of coagulants was found that gave the desired results. This process has been carried out at Inningham ever since.

British Rail was able to test the recycled oil on their own engines. By careful inspection at each service or overhaul, it was impossible to find any evidence of increased wear between these and engines running on new dieselube. Nor was there any increase in oil consumption or in service failures.

British Rail dubbed their new process Dieselclene and are realizing savings of up to 50% on lubricating oil costs.

The Dieselclene process is being marketed under an agreement with Sunclex Limited (White Horse Lane, Canterbury, Kent, England). Sunclex was set up seven years ago to provide an oil laundering service to industry. It handles hydraulic, cutting, quench and refrigeration oils.

Sunclex estimates Britain uses 100,000 tonnes of potentially recyclable dieselube each year. "Based on today's market prices, Dieselclene will show savings of $10 million a year within the next 2 years".[14] Sunclex plans to operate 12 plants in the United Kingdom and Ireland to handle dieselube plus other industrial oils.

At Chem-Ecol (from left to right, top row), (1) The waste oil undergoes initial separation into oil (upper) and water (lower) fractions. (2) The oil is heated to decrease its viscosity, ensuring easy movement through the small-diameter piping. (3) Sludge collects in a rectangular trough from the initial cleaning phase. (bottom row) (4) A vacuum heater is employed to remove residual water in the oil. (5) The oil is then filtered under pressure through a series of perforated metal plates layered with diatomaceous earth. (6) After filtration of a batch of oil, the dirt-laden diatomaceous earth is removed and replaced with clean material. (7) The filter press is seen at the left.

2

Monica Campbell

3

Monica Campbell

6

Monica Campbell

7

Monica Campbell

Sunclex expects its customers to come from transport companies, bus companies, plant hire companies and any other concern operating a number of diesel engines.

■ Chem-Ecol Limited (Cobourg, Ontario) is a small, well-established, independent oil recycling operation specializing in custom recycling of industrial oils (hydraulic oils, transformer oils, etc.).[15]

The operation at Chem-Ecol is a good example of small business 'imagineering". Six years ago, when Chem-Ecol was being put together, the company president scavenged junk yards for components for his system. Material for the vacuum heater, for example, were bought for $2000 from a scrap dealer. The replacement cost today would top $50,000.

The plant is designed to process over 1 million gallons of waste oil per year and return them to the company of origin at one-half to two-thirds the cost of new oil. Chem-Ecol uses the dehydration clay method to separate oil from water and then processes and replenishes the oil with the required additives.

3.
On-Site Separation

■ Monsanto Ltd. expects to save $10,000 a year, and the Abu Dhabi Marine Areas Operation Company (ADMA-OPCO), when operating at full capacity, will save $2 million a year. They both are separating valuable raffinates from their wastewaters using an oil/water separator developed by the Fram Company.[16,17]

The separator, originally designed to treat oil-laden bilge water on ships, consists of a series of vertical and horizontal corrugated plates. Oil droplets coalesce and rise to the underside of the oleophilic polypropylene plates. Eventually the oil passes through weep holes to the upper surface where it is collected by a skimmer[16,17] (see Figure 4). The filter was adapted to industrial situations where solid contents of the wastewaters could be as high as

Figure 4
The Fram Oil/Water Separator

The Fram oil/water separator uses a series of vertical and horizontal plates to force oil to the surface of the unit, where it is skimmed off.
Source: "Effective Methods for Difficult Effluents," *Processing*, December 1980.

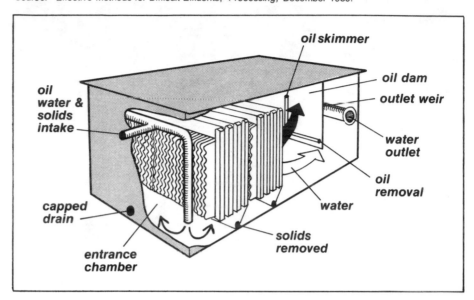

1000 ppm and oil droplet size varies considerably. A computer simulation programme allows for a precise calibration of the plates to maximize recovery from a specific wastestream.

Monsanto's works at Newport (United Kingdom) use the filter to recover expensive phosphate ester plasticiser from a process wash effluent. The plasticiser content of the waste dropped from 240 to 30 ppm. The three Fram separators in Abu Dhabi, installed at a cost of $500,000, treat wet crude oil. The oil content of the water drops from 1000 to 50 ppm.

■ Waste oil skimmed from the hot strip mill of the Iron and Steel Industrial Corporation (ISCOR) Works (Vanderbijlpark, South Africa) had until recently defied the best attempts of both the local and the imported oil re-refining and dewatering technologies.[18]

New developments by the firm in mechanical skimming and chemical processing have resulted in the recovery of waste oil with an insignificant solids content and a water content of less than 1% (down from a high of 60%). This has saved the country foreign exchange and the company thousands of rand. The present recovery of 40,000 litres of oil a

month could save the firm over $100,000 a year.

At the same time, the removal of oil from the water discharged into the water circulation system decreases the fouling of tanks and filters and increases the quantity of water available for re-use.

An improved automatic floating skimmer and baffle plate removes floating emulsion. An airlift tank displaces emulsion to the main storage tank above the scale pit with considerably reduced mixing, which facilitates the following separation process. A patented chemical is added, which coagulates solids which settle out and leave a clear oil to float up.

ISCOR is now recovering 95% of the oil in the original skimming and this high-viscosity raffinate is an excellent base for re-refining.

■ A West German company near Hanover receives up to 150 cubic metres of waste oil each week from a car manufacturing firm. The oil is steam-heated and introduced into an Alfa-Laval decanter centrifuge which removes dirt and metal clippings from the slurry.[19] A trip through a high-speed, disc-type separator produces a water-free oil which is sold to a local power station. The centrifuging of oil slurries and sludges not only offers saleable heating oil, but it reduces sludge disposal volumes five-fold, offering additional economic incentive.

The same equipment to clean the oil from the dross of new cars can reclaim the oil from soiled clothes. A firm that specializes in the loan and cleaning of industrial overalls and cloths recovers 5000 litres (1100 gal) a day which is used in their own boilers.

Oil contaminated washwater is chemically treated (sulphuric acid and ferric chloride) and air floated. The oil is skimmed off and sent through the decanter and disc-type centrifuges. The resulting oil is clean enough for boiler use. In effect, the dirt runs the washing machine[19] (see Figure 5).

■ Budd Automotive (Kitchener, Ontario) produces between 10,000 and 15,000 gallons of wastewater each day.

The firm manufactures automobile frames. The coiled steel used must be oiled prior to forming and then washed clean before welding. The water from the industrial washers and die-washing equipment, along with cutting fluids, is heavy with oil, grease, and solids.[20, 21]

In 1976, the firm purchased an ultrafiltration system from Electrohome (London, Ontario) to recover the oil used in the press shop. Electrohome's system is custom designed for each application and as such can be scaled down for use by even small businesses. By re-using oils it had previously discarded and by avoiding a costly shutdown of the washers every two weeks, the pay-back period for the equipment is short. Electrohome estimates their system will pay for itself within a year.

Budd's wastewater is also treated with a system designed by King Technology Limited (Barrie, Ontario) to reduce BOD (Biological Oxygen Demand) by 90% and suspended solids by 99%. The process, combining electrostatic and electrolytic principles with chemical pH adjustments[22] (see Figure 6), reduces Budd's sludge production appreciably.

Figure 5
The Alfa-Laval Centrifuge System

The Alfa-Laval centrifuge system has been used to reclaim oil from the waste slurry of a car manufacturer and the washwater of an industrial apparel cleaning firm.
Source: "Spinning Out the Value of Waste Oils," *Process Engineering,* May 1981.

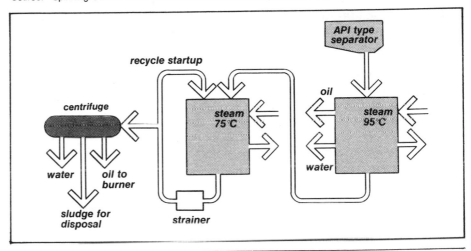

Figure 6
Typical Continuous Flow Electro-Chemical Waste Treatment Process

Budd Automotive has installed a King Technology treatment system to reduce both its BOD and TSS by more than 90%.
Source: King Technology Ltd. (Barrie, Ontario), product literature, 1981.

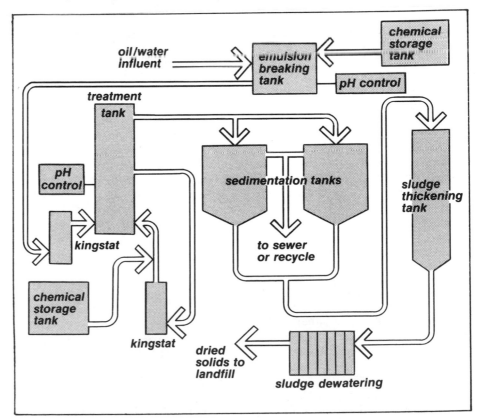

4.
Packaging

Another prime source of expensive waste in an oil marketing system is packaging.

■ Henderson's Minit Dispensers Ltd. (Winnipeg, Manitoba) are out to reduce excessive packaging in the marketing of quarts of motor oil. The company's resident inventor has pioneered a syringe-like self-serve oil dispenser. By designing a re-usable dispenser to transfer oil directly into a car engine, the need for a metal quart can has been eliminated. The consumer saves 30 to 35% of the cost of the oil by doing away with excessive packaging.

Dispensing units, which sell for under $200, have been purchased by Canadian Tire (Ontario) and two large Winnipeg dairies.

Conclusion

The recovery and re-use of waste oil is both technically and economically feasible. Waste oils are of significantly high economic value to make conventional disposal practices such as landfilling a non-lucrative alternative. Instead, prudent businesses are looking to oil recycling as the preferred option.

FOR FURTHER INFORMATION

Associations

Contact the following associations for additional information on waste oil reclamation opportunities. These associations may identify a re-refiner or oil cleaning operation in the vicinity.

Canadian Petroleum Association,
Suite 625, 404-6th. Ave. S.W.,
Calgary, Alberta.
T2P 0R9
(403) 269-6721

Independent Petroleum Association of Canada,
7th. Floor, 707-7th. Ave. S.W.,
Calgary, Alberta.
T2P 0Z2
(403) 290-1530

Petroleum Recovery Institute,
3512 33rd. Street N.W.,
Calgary, Alberta.
T2L 2A6
(403) 282-1211

Petroleum Association for the Conservation of the Canadian Environment,
Suite 400, 130 Albert Street,
Ottawa, Ontario.
K1P 5G4
(613) 236-9122

Association of Petroleum Re-refiners,
Suite 913,
2025 Pennsylvania Ave. N.W.,
Washington, D.C.
20006
(202) 833-2694

National Petroleum Council,
1625 K Street N.W.,
Washington, D.C.
20006
(202) 393-6100

American Petroleum Refiners Association,
607 Ring Building,
1200 18th. Street N.W.,
Washington, D.C.
20036
(202) 331-7081

American Petroleum Institute,
2101 L Street N.W.,
Washington, D.C.
20037
(202) 457-7000

Independent Refiners Association of America,
Suite 1000,
1775 Pennsylvania Ave. N.W.,
Washington, D.C.
20006
(202) 466-2340

Journals

The following journals carry occasional articles on new developments in waste oil recovery.

OILWEEK,
Maclean-Hunter Ltd. (Calgary),
200-918-6th. Ave. S.W.,
Calgary, Alberta.
T2P 0V5

CANADIAN CHEMICAL PROCESSING,
Southam Business Publications Ltd.,
1450 Don Mills Rd.,
Don Mills, Ontario.
M3B 2X7

CHEMICAL WEEK,
McGraw-Hill Inc.,
1221 Avenue of the Americas,
New York, New York.
10020

PROCESS ENGINEERING,
Morgan-Grampian
(Process Press) Ltd.,
30 Calderwood Street,
Woolwich,
London SE18 6QH, England.

PROCESSING,
IPC Industrial Press Ltd.,
33-40 Bowling Green Lane,
London EC1R ONE, England.

ENVIRONMENTAL POLLUTION MANAGEMENT,
Polcon Publishing Ltd.,
268 High Street,
Uxbridge,
Middlesex UB8 1UA, England.

RECOUP,
Venture Publications Ltd.,
223A McLeod Street,
Ottawa, Ontario.
K2P 0Z8

References

1. *The Way Things Work*. New York: Simon and Schuster, 1967.

2. Rudolph, Mark. "Road Oiling: An Example of Environmental Mismanagement." *Alternatives* (Friends of the Earth Canada), Spring 1980.

3. Fauser, F. and Ritz, W. "Recyclon — A New Method of Re-refining spent Lubrication Oils Without Detriment to the Environment." *Conservation and Recycling* 3(2), 1979.

4. "Environmental Management Practice: Data Loggers Help to Locate Pollution Sources." *Environmental Pollution Management*, March/April 1980.

5. "Lube Oil Recycling Tries for a Comeback." *Chemical Week*, September 24, 1980.

6. Rudolph, Mark. *System of Recovery and Reuse of Used Lubricating Oils: A State of the Art Study*. Waste Management Advisory Board, Government of Ontario, August 1978.

7. Seager, Spencer L. and Stoker, H. Stephen. *Chemistry: A Science for Today*. Glenview, Illinois: Scott, Foresman and Co., 1973.

8. "Spotlight Falls on Recycling Plants." *Oilweek*, June 9, 1980.

9. "Quebec to Recycle Used Industrial Oil." *Toronto Star*, November 24, 1981.

10. Campbell, Moni. "Oil's Well That Ends Well." *Probe Post*, September 1981.

11. Lush, Patricia. "Shell Builds $20-Million Oil Recycling Plant." *The Globe and Mail* (Canada), July 3, 1981.

12. "Mobile Oil Recycler Growing Fast." *Recoup*, May 15, 1980.

13. "Recycling Boosts Profits and Saves Resources." *Process Engineering*, May 1980.

14. "Recycling Used Diesel Lubricating Oil." *Environmental Pollution Management*, May/June 1980.

15. "Oil Recycling Neglected." *Probe Post*, September/October 1978.

16. "Effective Methods for Difficult Effluents." *Processing*, December 1980.

17. "Waste and Product Oils Recover Cash." *Processing*, May/June 1980.

18. "Oil Recovery from Hot-Strip Mill Skimmings." *Environmental Pollution Management*, September/October 1980.

19. "Spinning Out the Value of Waste Oils." *Process Engineering*, May 1981.

20. Edur, Olev. "Electrochemical Process Clarifies Wastewater at Auto Parts Plant." *Materials Management and Distribution*, March 1981.

21. "Recycles Cutting Oil Via Ultrafiltration." *Canadian Chemical Processing*, May 2, 1979.

22. King Technology Limited, Barrie, Ontario. (Product literature) 1981.

Paints & Coatings

Technological innovation in the paint industry has moved into high gear, bringing with it a complex array of new paints and sophisticated methods of applying them. In response to spiralling energy and feedstock costs, and increasingly stringent pollution regulations, North American paint manufacturers and equipment suppliers have revamped their tools to coat better, faster, with less pollution and using less energy.

Not only has operating efficiency improved, but in many cases operating costs have dropped. Yet despite the abundance of commercially available low-polluting equipment options, widespread implementation of such low-waste technologies lags several steps behind.

There can be no question that modernization in any painting facility will cost money. However, because many expenditures in pollution prevention will result in increased painting efficiency, such expenditures can be viewed as an investment that yields an economic return, rather than as just a drain of money.

In many of the smaller businesses, the company president may find himself repairing equipment and training staff as well as drumming up business and keeping the accounts in order. Given the stresses of daily life in a small business, it is sometimes difficult to take the time to assess the efficiency of the company's processes. It must be recognized however, that if a company is not maximizing its processing efficiency, the resultant waste can cut deeply into company profits.

A first step in pollution prevention taken by any company, no matter how small, is to assess the overall efficiency of the existing processes. This can be determined by comparing raw material inputs with product and waste outputs. If the quantity of product and known waste outputs do not match the material inputs, it indicates that some materials are escaping unnoticed from the company's operation. This is particularly troublesome in coatings operations which use solvent-based paints and solvent degreasing systems. Because solvents evaporate readily at room temperature, a company may unwittingly lose thousands of dollars worth of solvents to the atmosphere each year.

Many improvements in process efficiency are readily affordable by even small businesses. For example, industrial painters employing conventional air atomized spray equipment would be surprised to realize that as little as 30% of the paint sprayed actually reaches the target object.[1,2] Installing electrostatic spray equipment will more than double the efficiency of paint transfer, as well as save the company money through reduced paint costs and disposal charges.[1]

In other instances, the capital cost of new equipment is beyond the financing capabilities of small business. In such instances, small businesses would benefit through well-placed tax breaks and technology transfer programmes.

Improving the rate of paint transfer to the target object goes a long way in minimizing the amount of paint sludge requiring ultimate disposal.

Another strategy to keep paint overspray out of the landfill site is to recycle it. Some paint formulators will recycle paint for their clients. For large and medium-sized companies, the economic pay-back is increased by recycling overspray directly on the premises.[3]

The need for compliance with environmental and health regulations in North America has triggered the paint industry to develop several non-solvent coating systems. Water-borne paints that replace solvent-borne paints are doing so at a profit in many instances. Coating innovations such as powder coating and electrodipping virtually eliminate the production of paint sludge. UV-curable paints both eliminate solvents and significantly reduce energy costs.

In the future, the paint industry may well have to grapple with two major challenges. One is to continue to identify and substitute less hazardous constituents for many of the coating products currently in widespread use. The second challenge is to lessen the dependence on petrochemical feedstocks and shift to a manufacturing system based on renewable resources. In the meantime, the paint industry must be encouraged and assisted to install existing, commercially available equipment to minimize environmental pollution.

Industry Profile

The Canadian paint industry, also known as the coatings industry, includes paint manufacturing

---

Table 1

Types of Products Made by the Paint and Coatings Industry

Architectural Coatings (applied on-site)

Interior water-borne
Exterior water-borne
Interior solvent-borne
Exterior solvent-borne
Architectural lacquers

Industrial Coatings (factory applied)

Automotive finishes
Truck and bus finishes
Other transportation finishes, e.g. aircraft, railroad
Marine coatings, including off-shore structures
Appliance finishes
Wood furniture and fixture finishes
Wood and composition board flat stock finishes
Sheet, strip and coil coatings on metals
Metal decorating, e.g. can, container and closure coatings
Machinery and equipment finishes
Metal furniture and fixture coatings
Paper and paperboard coatings
Insulating varnishes
Magnet wire coatings

Special Purpose Coatings

Industrial maintenance paints — interior, exterior
Metallic paints, e.g. aluminum, zinc, bronze
Traffic paints
Automobile refinish coatings
Machinery refinish coatings
Marine refinish coatings
Aerosol paints
Roof coatings
Multicolor paints

and paint application. The terms *paints* and *coatings* are used interchangeably in many cases. In the past, when paints were applied predominantly by brush or with a spray gun, the term *paint* was preferred. More recently, with the development of new coating methods such as electrodeposition and powder coating, the term *coating* is gaining wider usage.

Statistics Canada identifies 150 Canadian companies involved in the manufacture of paint in 1978,[4] over half of which are located in Ontario.[5] The industry is characterized by relatively small companies. Almost half the Canadian plants have fewer than 50 employees, while 7% have more than 100 employees.[4] There is a tendency for paint formulating plants to be located in urban centres, close to consumers.

The number of companies involved in the application of paint is more difficult to identify because many paint operations are embedded in a larger manufacturing operation. Paint application operations are distinguished as architectural or industrial. The architectural category includes on-site painting of homes, offices and other buildings (see Table 1). Industrial application includes the painting of automobiles and other vehicles, appliances, furniture, pre-coated building materials, metals, packaging and machinery. By 1978, industrial consumption of paint had surpassed domestic uses.[7]

Sources of Waste

Paint Manufacture

The manufacture of paints and coatings consists of mixing various raw materials in batch operations. Raw materials include pigments, pigment extenders, solvents, resins or vehicles, and miscellaneous additives. The manufacture of pigments, solvents and other paint components is carried out by the chemical manufacturing industry, which is characterized by complex and large scale chemical synthesis processes.

Because the formulation of paints is essentially a mixing and

Figure 1
Total Wastes Generated by U.S. Paint Manufacturing Industry (non-aqueous metric tonnes per year)

American researchers estimate that only 25% of the total wastes produced by paint formulators contain potentially hazardous components. Furthermore, the hazardous constituents within the hazardous wastestream comprise only 0.2% of the total wastes produced by the industry.

Source: *Assessment of Industrial Hazardous Waste Practices, Paint and Allied Products Industry, Contract Solvent Reclaiming Operations, and Factory Application of Coatings,* U.S. Environmental Protection Agency, September 1978.

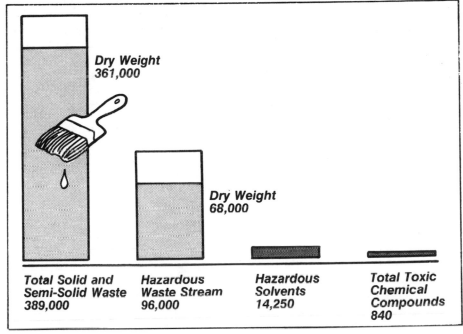

blending process, the major source of liquid waste results from equipment clean-out. Other major sources of waste include raw materials packaging, solids from air pollution control equipment and spoiled batches of finished product. Based on 1974 data, American researchers estimate that only 25% of the total wastes produced by paint formulators contain potentially hazardous components.[6] Furthermore, the potentially hazardous constituents within the wastestream comprise only 0.2% of the total wastes produced by the industry (see Figure 1). It becomes apparent that the most cost-effective way to manage the hazardous waste component is by keeping the potentially hazardous wastestream as concentrated and separate as possible from other more innocuous wastestreams.

Paints can be either solvent-based or water-based, and equipment clean-out procedures will vary accordingly. Paint plants clean solvent-based formulation tanks and equipment with solvent or with a hot caustic solution. Contaminated solvent is handled in different ways. It may be collected in drums for disposal or incineration. Some paint formulators reclaim the solvent on-site or send it to a professional solvent reclaimer for cleaning. In some establishments, a formulator will recycle used cleaning solvent as part of the formulation of the next paint batch.

Water-based paint tanks are cleaned by washing with water or a caustic solution. The wastewater is collected in holding tanks and treated before discharge, discharged directly into a sewer or receiving stream, collected in drums and landfilled, re-used in the next paint batch or re-used in the washing operation.

It is estimated that 90% of the solid wastes produced by paint manufacturers consists of raw materials packaging, including paper bags, plastic containers and metal drums.[6] Although the containers are innocuous in themselves, they may contain an ounce or more of potentially hazardous pigments or other toxic substances that cling to the packaging.

Paint formulators typically use pigments in powder form. Pigment dust trapped by filter bags in plant ventilation systems is a source of small amounts of potentially hazardous waste. Where such equipment was installed, 5 pounds of dust were collected for every 1000 gallons of paint produced.[6]

The quantity of waste derived from spoiled batches, spills, out-of-date stock and other discarded products will vary from plant to plant. The quantity disposed is not usually related to production, but rather to housekeeping, production scheduling and the degree of care used by the operators.[6]

Paint Application

One of the major sources of pollution during paint application is from solvent-borne paints, which typically contain 60 to 80% solvent by volume. As the paint dries, all of the solvent evaporates and becomes a potential air pollution and health problem. The United States Environmental Protection Agency estimated in a recent study that 60.7 billion kilograms of volatile organic compounds are emitted annually from stationary sources in the United States. The paint application industry accounts for 10 to 15% of this total output.[7] Only 1 to 2% of the solvent emissions produced by the paint industry result from the paint manufacturing sector. The remaining 98 to 99% is emitted at the point of application.[7]

Another significant source of waste is from paint overspray, clean-out equipment and paint packaging which may yield waste solvents, pigments and other constituents. Paint formulations may include potentially hazardous constituents such as xylene, toluene, methylene chloride, cadmium, lead, zinc, chromium and cobalt.[6]

Health and Environmental Concerns

The variety in paint colours and formulations seems endless. With more than 1500 pigments to choose from,[8] and an even greater number of solvents, resins, fungicides, and other additives to mix in, scientists are just scratching the surface in understanding the health effects of many of these compounds. The John Hopkins University School of Public Health (Baltimore, Maryland) and the International Brotherhood of Painters and Allied Trades (Washington, New York) are currently investigating potential health hazards associated with coatings and solvents.[9]

Because of the lag time between commercialization of a new paint formulation and verification of its health effects on paint applicators, potentially hazardous coatings may be in current use. As the hazard is identified and verified, the paint manufacturing industry responds by replacing a hazardous ingredient with a less hazardous chemical. Usually, however, many years elapse between the entry of a new formulation to the market place and verification of its negative impact on people exposed to it.

Many industrial paint facilities still use manually operated spray guns which atomize the paint into a very fine spray. By inhaling the fine paint mist, the worker is doubly at risk because of inhalation of both solvent vapours and potentially toxic constituents in the paint itself. Painters exposed to solvent-based paints for long periods of time show symptoms of toxicity such as dizziness, headache, blurred vision slurred speech and impaired memory.[10,11,12]

Solvents are of environmental concern because many of them are photochemically reactive, resulting in smog formation. Regulatory pressure to reduce solvent content in paint coupled with increasing solvent costs has accelerated the development and implementation of non-solvent coating systems.

POLLUTION PREVENTION OPPORTUNITIES

Paint Manufacturing

Two major strategies to abate pollution in the formulation of paint are more exacting blending operations, and more efficient equipment clean-out procedures. The computer is emerging as a viable and cost-effective tool in assisting even smaller companies to blend new formulations with a minimum number of spoiled batches.

1.

Computer Assistance

Unlike many other small businesses, the paint formulator keeps on hand hundreds of different raw materials and intermediates required to mix custom-specified batches of paint. And, unlike other small businesses, finished product wastes due to spoiled batches and colour mismatches are much higher than for other manufacturing sectors where quality control can be more predictable.

To assist in making a complex job simpler, increasing numbers of Canadian paint manufacturers, from small to large, are installing computer capacity to enhance everything from colour matching, to controlling raw materials inventory. By taking the guesswork out of colour matching, a company not only reduces the quantity of spoiled batches that needs to be disposed, but also saves company time, money and raw materials.

A computer can determine pigment volumes required in a new formulation, or can colour match to an existing shade. And, for those pigments identified to be potentially toxic and threatened by regulation, a computer can select a suitable pigment replacement. By programming in pigment cost, the computer can come up with the cheapest pigment combination while maintaining product quality.

A computer can optimize scheduling of production sequences so as to minimize equipment clean-out needs. A computer can also assist in reworking a spoiled batch into something marketable by recording its composition and indicating what ingredients need to be added to make it saleable. Because the computer can be programmed to keep track of the raw materials and finished goods inventory, it can reduce the frequency of having to dispose of out-of-date warehouse stock. The increased efficiency in formulating paints means that a company can reduce its stock of raw materials and finished goods, a proposition welcomed particularly by smaller operations.

■ Some medium-sized firms such as Kelcoatings (London, Ontario) have been using computers for formulation and batch costing for some time. Others, including XYZ Paints (Cambridge, Ontario) are planning major investments in computer capability.[13]

■ For large companies such as C-I-L Paints (Toronto, Ontario) and Sico Inc. (Montreal, Quebec), computers are invaluable in both the lab and accounting office.[13] Keeping track of raw materials and price data on a daily basis, as well as optimizing production scheduling, is just one more way to survive in a competitive market while minimizing pollution.

2.

Equipment Clean-Out

Many of the smaller paint plants still clean portable mixing tanks and paint drums by hand with strong solvents.[14] Use of solvents is not only potentially hazardous to worker health, but is costly as well.

From both an economic and safety perspective, it is more desirable to use a high pressure alkali cleaning system than solvents. Although a number of commercial systems are available, an adequate system can be installed by plant maintenance personnel without too much expense, according to Alun Morris of the L. V. Lomas Chemical Company (Toronto, Ontario).[14] Before cleaning the mixing tank, as much wet paint should be removed as possible to minimize contamination of the washing solution. Wet paint clinging to the container walls during paint transfer can be wiped free using a rubber squeegee.

Caustic cleaning solution is stored and heated in a special tank (see Figure 2). The hot caustic solution is pumped under pressure to the tank to be cleaned. A rotating jet or spray nozzle system shoots cleaning solution against the walls, top and bottom of the mixing tank. When the cleaning operation is complete, the dirty caustic solution is filtered through a straining unit and returned to the storage tank for re-use.[14] The paint mixing tank is then rinsed with hot water.

The system can be modified to wash 5-gallon pails and 45-gallon drums by inverting them over a spray nozzle. By installing an air micro-switch that would open an air-operated valve only once the container is inverted over the spray nozzle, operator safety is enhanced. A drain pan located beneath the cleaning area collects waste cleaning solution for re-use.[14]

Although alkali cleaning solutions do not present the same

chronic and cumulative threats to health as solvents, their caustic nature dictates use of proper safety equipment such as goggles, face masks and protective clothing.

Industry spokesmen suggest that caustic cleaning solution is recycled among many of those plants that use this cleaning method. Waste rinsewater, on the other hand, is typically sewered. Some paint formulators successfully re-use waste rinsewater in the production of water-based paints without impairing paint quality.[6] Such water recycling applications are rare.

■ According to a study of the United States paint manufacturing industry by Burns and Roe Industrial Services Corp. (Paramus, New Jersey), if the 800,000 gallons of wastewater produced daily by the entire paint manufacturing industry in the United States were treated by conventional chemical precipitation and settling, it would yield a sludge volume of 120,000 gallons per day.[15]

On the other hand, if 80% of the wastewater generated is recycled industry-wide, this would shrink the total wastestream to 160,000 gallons per day.[15] This assumes that 20% of the total wastewater volume would be incompatible for re-use because of colour and formulation restrictions.

Recycling wastewater is anticipated to be the cheapest treatment option because it greatly reduces the volume of wastewater requiring costly chemical precipitation and sludge disposing procedures.

Figure 2
Caustic Recycling During Equipment Clean-Out

Hot caustic cleaning solution is pumped under pressure to the tank to be cleaned, where a spray system shoots the cleaning solution against the walls of the mixing tank. When the cleaning operation is complete, the dirty caustic solution is filtered and returned to the storage tank for re-use.

Source: "A Tank Cleaning System for the Small Paint Plant," *Journal of Coatings Technology,* September 1979.

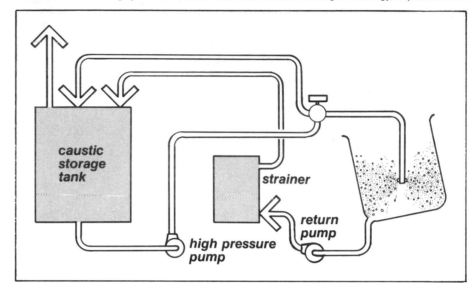

Paint Application

It has been decades since industrial painters foresook the paint brush for more modern methods such as spray painting. Although the development of the spray gun did much to escalate productivity and enhance the quality of painted finishes, it also unleashed a Pandora's box of problems. In addition to potential health hazards posed by inhalation of atomized paint, the question of what to do with the millions of gallons of paint sludge generated annually continues to plague the paint industry.

By spraying paint onto an object, as little as 30% of the spray reaches the target object. The rest, known as overspray, commonly ends up in a barrel at a landfill site. This dilemma has the industry pursuing several strategies to minimize the quantity of waste paint requiring disposal. The major thrust is in improving the efficiency of paint application. Another strategy is to maximize the re-use of paint overspray and wastewater.

A third direction is to substitute less hazardous materials, namely to reduce or eliminate the solvent component of paints. It must be recognized, however, that some of the non-solvent coating systems contain potentially hazardous components such as isocyanates which are considered to be of even greater hazard than conventional solvent-borne systems.[16,17] Research into substitution of less hazardous pigments and other constituents is still in its infancy, but can be expected to accelerate as health hazards associated with existing components are identified.

Although technological innovation in the paint industry has come a long way, it still has some way to go. In the meantime, however, pollution reduction and company profits can be maximized by implementing some of the proven technologies now commercially available.

One thing is clear. Unlike the 1940s and 1950s when solvent-borne alkyd resins ruled supreme, no single coating type will capture the entire coatings market. In an age of cost cutting and greater environmental awareness, industrial finishers will have to make their selections in terms of end-use requirements and conditions specific to their own operations.[18]

1.
New Coating Types

Paintmakers are tackling the solvent problem by formulating coatings with substantially less or no volatile organic solvents. Low solvent and solvent-free paint systems include high-solids emulsion paints, two-part catalyzed systems that convert fully to film, and solution types made of pre-polymers, co-solvents and water [19, 20] (see Figure 3).

Conventional paints are composed of three basic components: a film-forming binder consisting of resins or drying oils; a volatile organic solvent or water to maintain fluidity; and a pigment system containing colouring, opacify-ing materials and various extenders. Conventional solvent-borne paints contain 60 to 80% volatile organic solvents.[21]

Water-Borne Coatings

Water-borne paints contain substantial amounts of water, with up to 80% of the volatiles being water.[22] The polymers used can be dissolved, dispersed or emulsified.

By 1977, Canadian sales of water-based paints exceeded those of oil-based paints (see Figure 4). Prior to 1977, solvent-borne paints were the predominant coating type.

Water-borne industrial coatings consist of alkyd, polyester, vinyl acetate, acrylic and epoxy vehicles. Water-borne coatings are supplied as baking finishes as well as air-dry formulations. No major equipment changes are necessary to apply water-borne rather than solvent-borne coatings for most paint application methods. Electrostatic spray equipment, however, must be modified to handle water-based paints.[16]

Some car manufacturers are particularly advanced in their use of water-borne coatings for engine application and prime coating where traditionally a solvent-borne coating was used. One of General Motor's California plants has a water-borne coating system in full operation.[16] Similarly, the General Motor's plant in Oshawa (Ontario) uses electrodeposition to apply a water-borne coating.

■ Unlike conventional solvent systems in which overspray is difficult to collect for recycling, water-borne coatings can be recovered and re-used. Overspray from a water-borne coating goes into solution in the water wash curtain in the spray booth. The solution can then be concentrated to the point where it is a paint again, and can be re-used. Although not in commercial use yet, one major auto manufacturer is designing a spray booth to recover water-borne paint overspray and re-use it.[16]

■ The Caterpillar Tractor Company's new engine-painting facility (Mossville, Illinois) minimizes air pollution and conserves energy.[23] The use of water-borne coat-

Figure 3
Organic Solvent Emissions from Various Coating Types

In recent years, regulatory pressure has been placed on the coatings manufacturer to reduce the organic solvent content in new paint formulations. This has resulted in coatings which are much higher in solids content.

Sources: *Coatings Industry Introduction to Air Quality,* Canadian Paint and Coatings Association, 1981.
Controlling Pollution from the Manufacturing and Coating of Metal Products, U.S. Environmental Protection Agency, 1977.
"How to Figure Potential Emission Reductions for High-Solids Coatings," *Industrial Finishing,* November 1979.

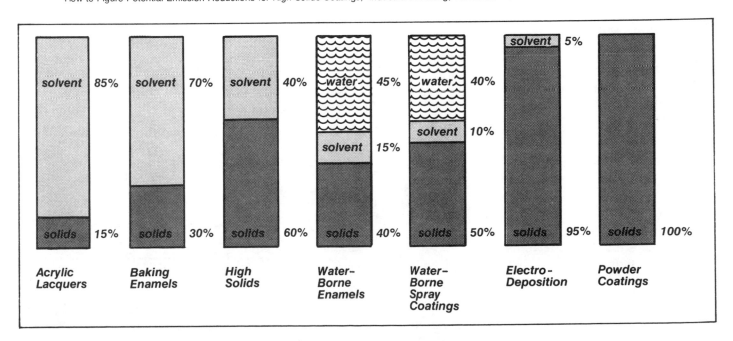

Figure 4
Shift in Canadian Paint Production (in millions of gallons)

Prior to 1977, solvent-borne paints were the predominant coating type. By 1977, sales of water-based paints exceeded those of oil-based paints.

Source: "Industry Statistics: Real Growth Lags But Paint Dollar Value Continues to Rise," *Coatings Magazine*, March/April 1981.

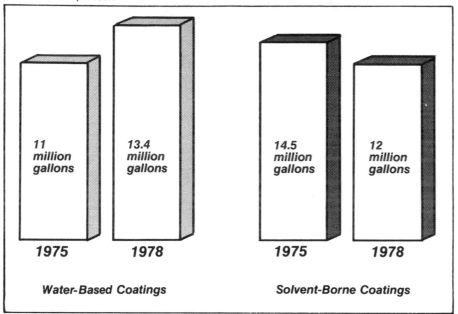

11 million gallons	13.4 million gallons	14.5 million gallons	12 million gallons
1975	**1978**	**1975**	**1978**
Water-Based Coatings		**Solvent-Borne Coatings**	

ings holds down air pollution while a low-temperature drying oven saves energy. Unlike solvent-based systems, the hot air in the drying oven used to cure water-borne paints can be recirculated, keeping heating costs down. Other advantages of the waterborne painting operation are reduced fire hazards[24] and insurance costs.

High Solids Coatings

High solids coatings can actually deliver more than double the usual amount of paint compared to conventional low solids or waterborne paints.[22]

The resins used in many coatings are not suitable for one component high solids coatings because as the resin solids are increased, the finish becomes very viscous, making application difficult. To achieve the required viscosity, the resin is kept dispersed as discrete particles. Known as non-aqueous dispersions, these coatings achieve a 30 to 60% solids content.[20]

Two Component Catalyzed Coatings

Catalyzed polyurethane coatings contain 80% or more solids by volume. They are two component systems produced by the reaction of isocyanates and hydroxyl compounds, and as such need no organic solvent. The automotive industry has been exploring the use of polyurethane to replace solvent-borne acrylic lacquers and enamels used for topcoating. But isocyanates represent highly toxic materials which would require the industry to install costly and complex robots to spray autos.[8]

Radiation-Curable Coatings

Radiation-curable coatings contain no organic solvents and are 100% solids.[8] Reactive monomers are applied to a surface which is then subjected to high-energy radiation such as ultraviolet (UV) light. Radiation-curable coatings now command about 12 to 15% of the curable coatings market, and are expected to capture 20% by 1985 as equipment and formulations improve.[8]

■ In the UV curing process, special photo-initiators such as thioxanthones, acetophenone derivatives and benzoin ethers are activated by photons to provide free radicals for the polymerization reactions.

In the electron beam (EB) process, a thin coating is applied to a substrate and heated by a stream of electrons which polymerizes the coating instantly.

The infrared (IR) system is based on a thermal cure process, unlike the UV and EB systems in which the curing is based on a photochemical reaction. Electrical consumption for IR is high, 20 to 50 times higher than for EB, and 10 to 20 times higher than used for UV systems.[8] The advantage of using the IR process is its ability to cure thermally-sensitive coatings and difficult shapes.

■ Degussa Ltd. (Burlington, Ontario) has developed a painting system that eliminates the need for an organic solvent. The new technology involves a liquid prepolymer and mixture of reactive thinners (acrylates) that are cross-linked by radiating with UV light.[25] Unlike conventional solvent systems, the "solvent" in the Degussa system does not evaporate but rather becomes part of the surface coating. This solventless coating technology is well-suited for painting steel, chipboard, laminates, cardboard and polystyrene.[26]

Powder Coatings

Powder coatings are 100% solids, frequently composed of hybrid polyester epoxy or polyurethane powder.[20] The powder is sprayed on to the target object and baked at high temperatures to fuse the individual particles to form a continuous film. Resultant coatings can be very hard and resistant to corrosion. Because the powder does not set until it is baked, it is possible to recycle virtually all the overspray.

2.
Increasing Paint Transfer Efficiency

Paint transfer efficiency refers to the percentage of paint applied that actually reaches the target object.[27] Paint transfer efficiencies for different application methods are listed in Table 2.

Spray Painting

Conventional Air-Atomized Spray Painting

At present, air-atomized spray painting is still the most wide-spread coating technique. A jet of compressed air impinges on the paint stream which subsequently atomizes the paint and propels it forward (see Figure 5). In its simplest form, an operator manually directs a hand-held gun. Automatic units are available in which the fixed gun is turned on and off as an object moves automatically in front of the paint spray.

Conventional spray painting using the air-atomized method has the lowest transfer efficiency of any of the coating methods currently available. Typically only 30 to 50% of the paint reaches the target.[27] The other 50 to 70% of the spray is collected as overspray and incinerated or landfilled.

Pressure-Atomized Spray Painting

In airless spray painting, paint is forced through the nozzle at a high enough pressure to propel the paint spray forward (see Figure 6). Such a system is an improvement over air-atomized painting because 65 to 70% of the spray reaches the object.[27]

Electrostatic Spray Painting

In electrostatic spray painting, the object to be painted is grounded. The gun nozzle is given the opposite charge, thereby charging the atomized paint as it leaves the gun. Because the charged paint particles are attracted to the opposite charge on the object being painted, overspray is greatly reduced (see Figure 7). In air-atomized electrostatic coating, 70 to 85% of the paint reaches the target. For pressure-atomized electrostatic coating, 85 to 90% of the paint coats the object.[27]

Users of electrostatic equipment point to the high quality and uniform coverage of this painting method. Where paint is deposited on the surface of the object, the charge in that area is reduced and ultimately changed to the charge of the gun. This repels additional paint which instead is attracted to areas not adequately covered.

■ The W.C. Walberg Company (Downers Grove, Illinois) provide manual and hand-held electrostatic spray paint equipment that cuts paint consumption by at least 50% over conventional systems. After 30 years in the business, Walberg says, "Most firms resist spending money to solve pollution

---

Table 2
Expected Transfer Efficiency of Various Painting Methods

Painting Method	Transfer Efficiency
Air-atomized, conventional	30 to 60%
Air-atomized, electrostatic	65 to 85%
Pressure-atomized, conventional	65 to 70%
Centrifugally-atomized, electrostatic	85 to 95%
Roll coating	90 to 98%
Electrocoating	90 to 99%
Powder coating	90 to 99%

Source: Calculations of Painting Wasteloads Associated with Metal Finishing. U.S. E.P.A., June 1980.

Figure 5
Air-Atomized Spray Painting

A jet of compressed air impinges on the paint stream which subsequently atomizes the paint and propels it forward.

Source: Calculations of Painting Wasteloads Associated with Metal Finishing, U.S. Environmental Protection Agency, June 1980.

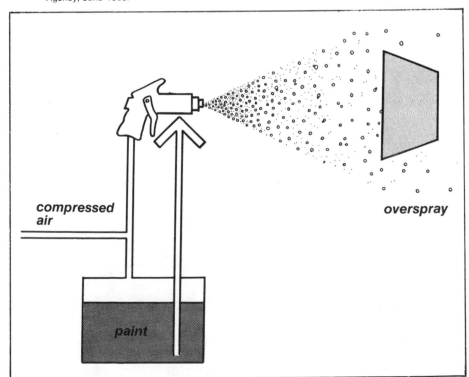

Figure 6
Pressure Atomized Spray Painting

In airless spray painting, paint is forced through the nozzle at high enough pressure to propel the paint forward.
Source: Calculations of Painting Wasteloads Associated with Metal Finishing, U.S. Environmental Protection Agency, June 1980.

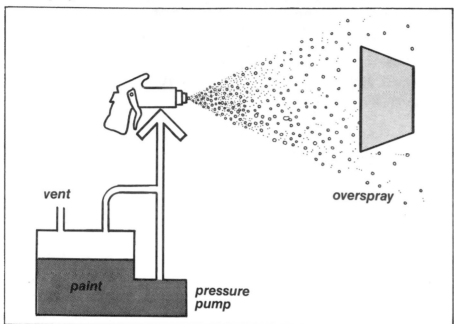

Figure 7
Electrostatic Spray Painting

The object to be painted is grounded and the paint is given the opposite charge. Overspray is greatly reduced because the paint is attracted to the opposite charge on the object being painted.
Source: Calculations of Painting Wasteloads Associated with Metal Finishing, U.S. Environmental Protection Agency, June 1980.

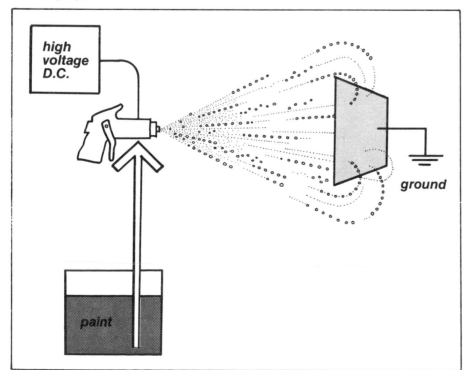

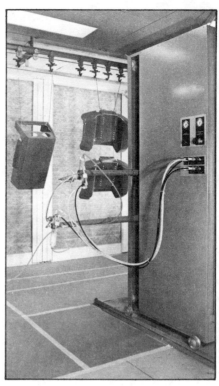

Automatic electrostatic spray system. A simple plug-in connection brings high voltage to the gun for high-solids or other high resistance paints. Water-borne paints require no direct high voltage connection to the gun since it is applied directly to the fluid supply system.

problems but do not hesitate to spend money if they can recover the investment in a short period of time. We don't sell a system unless the pay-back period is less than two years."

According to Walberg, the plastics and wood industries are still spraying with conventional spray equipment. Non-conductive items such as wood and plastic can be sprayed electrostatically if conductive water-borne coatings are used. But this would necessitate a shift away from conventional solvent-borne paints, a shift the industry has been reluctant to make.

■ Flexsteel Industries (Dubuque, Iowa) changed from a conventional air spray to an electrostatic finishing system at its furniture plant.[28] In doing so, the company reduced overspray by 40% and saved itself $15,000 a year in new paint costs. Pay-back for the Binks (Chicago, Illinois) manual electrostatic equipment is estimated at less than two years.[29]

Manufacturers of electrostatic spray guns vary in the methods used to atomize and direct the spray. In one equipment type, the centrifugal force of a rapidly rotating bell moves the paint to the open end where it passes through an electrostatic field and emerges as a charged, atomized spray. Centrifugal atomization has the highest transfer efficiency of commercial spray paint equipment, achieving efficiencies of up to 95% transfer.[26]

Another variation of electrostatic spray equipment is the spinning disc type. Spinning disc type electrostatic spray units offer several advantages over air atomized spray guns, particularly in transferring difficult-to-disperse high solids paints. Atomization with speed as occurs in spinning disc spray units breaks the paint particles down finer than air-atomization, and also directs more paint onto the target object.[27]

■ High-speed electrostatic bells and discs are currently the leading edge of spray paint technology, especially where high solids coatings are involved. De Vilbiss (Chicago, Illinois) make an ultra high-speed rotary atomizer (electrostatic bell) that can handle water-borne and two-component coatings as well as high solids coatings.[30] The Turbodisk™ (electrostatic disc) manufactured by Ransburg (Cooksville, Ontario) is well suited to handle high solids paints and water-borne coatings. For those companies shifting from solvent-borne paints to high solids paints, Ransburg make a unit that can be retrofitted onto existing disc systems for improved atomization of the more viscous high solids coatings.[30]

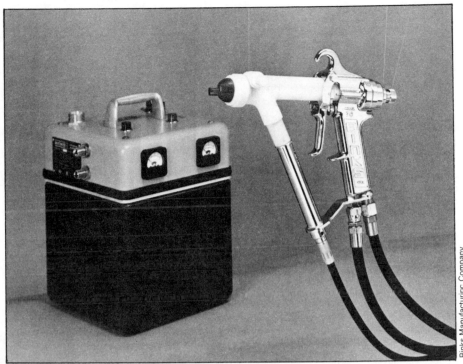
Electrostatic hand gun system.

Binks Manufacturing Company

Ultra-high-speed rotational atomizer.

The DeVilbiss Company

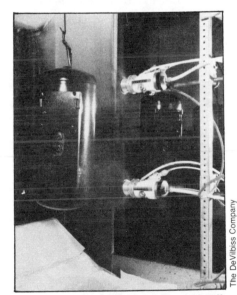
Two rotary atomizers electrostatically apply a liquid coating to compressor tanks.

The DeVilbiss Company

Paint Arrestors

No matter how efficient the spray gun, some overspray will result. Spray operations should be confined to a spray booth with an exhaust fan and a filter to trap spray drift. The most commonly used paint arrestors are filter-type arrestors. However, paint-laden filters require constant replacement and disposal.

If spraying more than 10 gallons of paint a day, filter-type paint arrestors require daily changing.[31] At a 1981 cost of $1 per filter, an industrial painting company can expect to spend $3000 per year just to change filters on a 10-foot-wide spray booth. At that rate, a company could pay for a sophisticated water wash spray booth within three years on the filter savings alone.[31]

Some self-winding fabric filters trap paint particles so efficiently as to permit recirculation of 80% of the air within the spray booth. By recirculating plant air, costs of heating the plant are significantly reduced during winter months.[1]

Another product available to collect overspray involves coating the inner surfaces of the spray booth. When a layer of waste paint has accumulated on the coating, the coating is peeled off along with the waste paint and replaced with a new coating. Paint overspray collected in this manner is not amenable to recycling, and tends to be discarded at a landfill site.

■ One promising paint arrestor is the water wash type in which a curtain of water cascades over a series of baffles (see Figure 8). Stray paint impinges on the water curtain and drains to a paint separator. The paint and water mixture is then separated so that the clarified water can be re-used. Ultrafilt Inc. (Troy, Michigan) manufacture a water/sludge separator which recirculates the collection water for re-use.[32] According to Waste Technology Inc., designers of the Ultrafilt™ unit, it is just a question of time before the same range of water/sludge separators becomes available to the small operators that is now available to the larger companies.[33]

■ At the Oshkosh Truck Corporation (Oshkosh, Wisconsin) heavy specialty trucks are assembled and spray painted. Paint-laden air from the giant spray booth is purified by water swirling through 14-inch Venturi tubes. Water drains from each tube to a large holding tank. The water is then circulated through two electrostatic water treaters which make the overspray paint float for easy removal by skimming. Because the water is kept clean enough to be drained without additional treatment, the Oshkosh Truck Company benefits financially by avoiding additional capital investment in a wastewater treatment facility.[34]

Roll Coating

Roll coating, also known as coil coating, is a process in which the coating is applied to a roller and transferred to the object by rolling contact, thereby limiting its application to flat or flexible surfaces (see Figure 9). Roll coating can apply paint to one side only, or both sides simultaneously.

Roll coating requires the use of high viscosity paints, and as such contains few or no organic solvents. Transfer efficiencies are very high, ranging from 90 to 98%.[27]

■ Hunter Douglas of Canada Ltd. (Montreal, Quebec) manufactures and finishes aluminum siding for homes and office buildings. Pollution is kept to a minimum by using

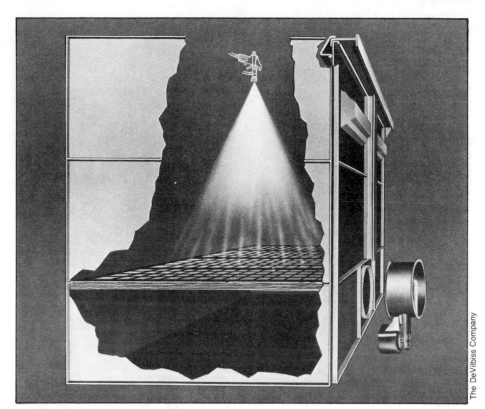

Paint arrestor spray booth catches and retains overspray in arrestor type filters.

Electrostatic spray operation using water wash spray booth to catch and retain overspray.

water-borne rather than solvent-borne paints in 85% of its coil coating operations. According to company management, the water-based coatings have superior performance to most of the solvent-based types.

In addition, Hunter Douglas has recently installed a new pretreatment system to eliminate effluent problems during pretreatment. The new pretreatment is a chrome-phosphate type which is dried in place in an infrared oven, thereby eliminating the need for an acidified rinse and treatment of associated waste rinsewater.[35]

Electrocoating

Electrocoating, also known as electrodeposition, is a dip method for applying a water-borne coating to metal by electrically coagulat-

Manual "non-electrostatic" operation using water wash spray booth and gas convection drying oven.

ing paint solids onto the surface to be coated.[16] The operation more closely resembles the electroplating of metal than it does painting, and is applicable to coating long runs of objects.

The paint resin and pigment, which is dissolved or suspended in water, is given a charge. An electrical current is passed through the bath, causing the charged paint particles to migrate by a process known as electrophoresis towards the surface to be coated. The coating coagulates on the surface to be coated, and much of the water is squeezed out by a phenomenon known as electro-osmosis.

The coated object emerges from the paint booth with a tightly adhered, slightly tacky coating. After a water rinse to remove excess coating, the object undergoes heat curing in a conventional drying oven.[27]

Electrocoating can be 90 to 99% efficient in paint usage. Although electrocoating paint formulations may cost 10 to 25% more than conventional coatings, electrocoating can save money because of its excellent ability to cover and penetrate into corrosion-sensitive areas. A single electrocoat layer may substitute for a conventional two-coat system.[16]

■ The electrocoating system's high transfer efficiency is due in part to closed-loop rinsing (see Figure 10).

Loose paint particles in the rinse water can be recycled back to the coating tank, thereby bumping transfer efficiency from a 50 to 80% range to a 90%-plus range.[16]

■ The Fisher Body plant (Lansing, Michigan) has drastically cut solvent emissions from its car painting facility by switching to electrocoating. In the old, solvent-borne finishing system, car bodies underwent a 15-minute oven-dry-off following pretreatment washing. This was to ensure a dry substrate prior to application of the solvent primer.[36]

■ The new painting system does away with this dry-off stage. Because the electrocoating paint is itself water-based, car bodies can move directly from pretreatment to the coating tank. By eliminating the intermediate drying stage, a considerable amount of energy and money is saved. As solvent costs continue to soar, the economics of water-borne systems such as electrocoating look more attractive every day.

Ultrafilt™ Suspended Sludge Separator. The fibreglass separator tank is positioned on an 8 x 10 foot elevated platform. Sludge pump and sludge hopper are located below the platform.

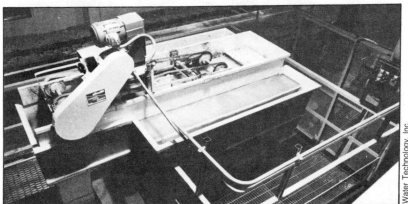

The paint sludge enters the middle section where "doctor" blades on variable speed skimmer sweep sludge out of the water into the hopper below.

Figure 8
Water Bath Paint Arrestor in Spray Booth

Spray paint impinges on a curtain of water— cascades created by water falling over a series of baffles. The paint and water mixture can be separated, permitting re-use of the water.
Source: *Calculations of Painting Wasteloads Associated with Metal Finishing,* U.S. Environmental Protection Agency, June 1980.

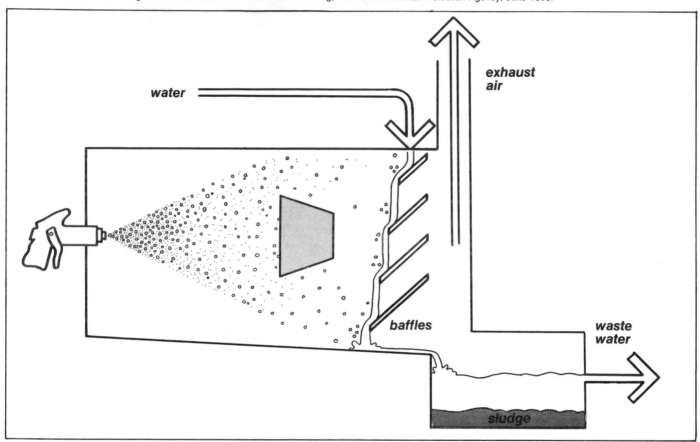

Figure 9
Roll Coating

The paint is applied to a roller and transferred to the object by rolling contact. Roll coating can apply paint to one side only, or both sides simultaneously.
Source: *Calculations of Painting Wasteloads Associated with Metal Finishing,* U.S. Environmental Protection Agency, June 1980.

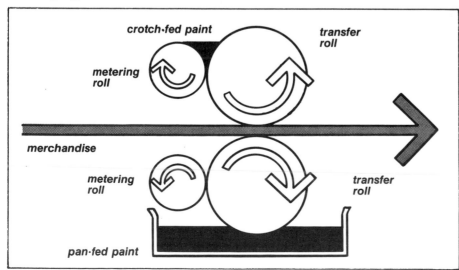

■ Furniture makers can both reduce pollution and increase productivity by switching to electrodeposition coating techniques. La-Z-Boy (Dayton, Tennessee) has raised its production of metal sofa bed mechanisms eight-fold since installing an electrodeposition paint line. Increasing productivity has meant a savings in labour and maintenance costs.[37]

Sputtercoating

Sputtercoating is a process where a thin metallic deposit is sandwiched between two organic coatings to give an object a metallic appearance (see Figure 11). The sputtercoating process most closely resembles a spray paint operation, however the finished product resembles an object that has been electroplated. Metals that are applied by sputtering include chromium, silver, gold,

Figure 10
The Electrocoating Process

Electrocoating can be 90 to 99% efficient in paint usage. The high transfer efficiency is due in part to closed-loop rinsing. Loose paint particles in the rinsewater can be recycled back to the coating tank.

Source: *Calculations of Painting Wasteloads Associated with Metal Finishing*, U.S. Environmental Protection Agency, June 1980.

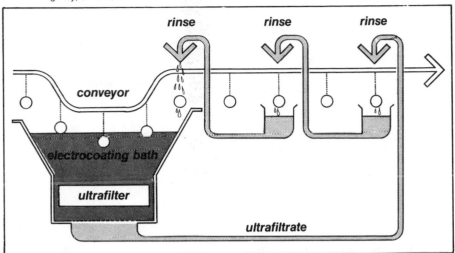

Sputtercoating: ISC 800 sputtering system produces thin (approx. 500 angstrom) metal film on furniture corner.

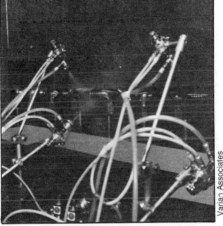

Chain On Edge coating system produces base or topcoat over irregular shapes.

Linear Pass reciprocating spray system produces base or topcoat at 5-15 feet/minute.

Ultraviolet Curing Station is capable of fully curing topcoat in seconds.

brass, bronze, aluminum, copper, stainless steel and rhodium.

■ According to Robert Rainey, operations manager at Varian's Advanced Industrial Coating Operation (Florence, Kentucky), sputtering is a physical phenomenon that was discovered in the 1880s as a failure mode in high-voltage vacuum tubes. The metal from the cathode of the tube would "sputter" away and end up as a build-up on the glass enclosure.[38]

"It wasn't until the mid-1900s that this *problem* was converted to a useful tool for the formation of thin films," says Rainey.[39]

Until the 1970s, sputtering technology application was hampered by the slow rate at which the metal layer could be deposited. Since then, the development of high-rate magnetron sputtering sources has increased metal deposition rates 30-fold to a level compatible with rapid production needs.[38]

The resulting metal layer is very thin, typically ranging from 500 to 1000 angstroms in thickness. Because thin coatings reduce the quantity of metal used, production costs are shaved accordingly. In addition, sputtering consumes only one-third of the energy required in conventional electroplating.[39]

The base coat, the first layer to be applied, functions to level and seal the substrate as well as

Figure 11
Structure of a Sputtercoat

The sputtercoat is composed of an organic base coat, a very thin metal layer and an organic top coat which functions to protect the metal layer.

Source: "Sputtercoating: A Production Reality," *Plating and Surface Finishing*, April 1981.

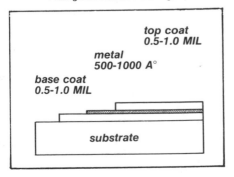

improve the adhesion of the metallic layer. Frequently, the base coat is 100% solids UV-curable paint that is spray-applied. Conventional solvent-based paints are used only if required by the product specifications. UV-curable paints offer an advantage over the more conventional air-dry or bake-dry paints in that they significantly reduce energy requirements.

Depending on the product specifications, the top coat may vary from solvent-borne urethanes to UV-curables. Rainey concedes that problems still exist with UV-curable topcoats in view of their poor adhesion to the metal film. Improving the performance standards of low-polluting topcoats is just one of the challenges that Varian Associates hopes to solve in the coming decade.

Varian's Florence plant, which opened late in 1980, will apply a metallic finish using the sputter-coating technique to appliances, furniture and plumbing components fabricated of plastic. The types of plastic to be coated at the new plant will centre mainly on acrylonitrile-butadiene-styrene (ABS) plastics and some polypropylene plastics. Varian Associates has demonstrated that other sputterable plastics include polystyrene, nylon, phenylene-oxide-based resin, polycarbonate, acrylic, thermoplastic, acetal and polyurethane.[40]

According to Rainey, sputter-coating economics might not be as good today as more conventional painting methods, but it is generally competitive with electroplating. Unlike electroplating which is a proven technology, sputter-coating is a newcomer to the finishing world.

Rainey speculates that in five years, sputtercoating will be two times cheaper than electroplating.[39] Unlike electroplating, which requires complex and costly pretreatment steps to prepare the substrate for plating, the sputtercoating process is relatively simple.

Powder Coating

In the powder coating process, specially formulated fusible paint

Small parts in the load zone, background is the spray booth and far right hand side background is the oven.

Cabinets — upside down on the conveyor at the unload zone.

powder is applied to the object to be coated and fused to its surface by heat curing in an oven. At most modern installations, powder is applied by an electrostatic spray method to keep the powder on the surface of the target object until it can be fused. Because powder coatings are 100% solids, they present no solvent emission problems during curing. Another significant low-pollution aspect of powder coatings is that they are easily recycled. Operating costs are lower than for conventional liquid paint lines because of reduced material, labour and energy requirements.[41]

■ Moyer Diebel (Jordan, Ontario) has recently upgraded the small paint line at its vending machine manufacturing plant. In a spirit of modernization, Moyer Diebel chose an automated powder coating operation.

"We were very hesitant when we first considered going to powder because it represented something of a leading edge technology. Being on the leading edge is not a very comfortable position to be in," says George Perdue, vice president of manufacturing.

According to Perdue, the capital cost of the automated powder system and the automated conventional liquid system were virtually the same. At the time of the installation, Moyer Diebel paid $280,000 for its new powder line manufactured by Interrad International, about $5,000 less than for a liquid paint line. The real savings result from the reduced energy consumption, reduced material costs, and reduced maintenance costs. The powder system is costing Moyer Diebel about 15% less in operating costs than a comparable liquid system.[41]

At Moyer Diebel, the majority of parts coated are steel. Some aluminum and stainless steel parts are coated as well. Before the parts can be coated, they must be washed to permit proper adhesion of the paint. Steel parts usually have a thin protective film of oil on the surface which must be removed before painting. Since the company installed its powder line, the previous four-stage washing system has been reduced to a three-stage process.

Perdue says, "We were surprised to find that the powder coating stuck on easier and with less cleaning. The upshot is that it is cheaper to pre-clean surfaces to be powder-coated because fewer cleaning cycles are needed."

For Moyer Diebel, reducing the total volume of wastewater generated by reducing the number of cleaning cycles is a significant benefit. The company's rural location means that no sewer is available to accept their wastewater. The wastewater from the washing process is recycled for re-use as washwater. Sludge and residual

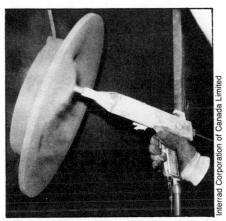

Manual dry powder electrostatic spray gun.

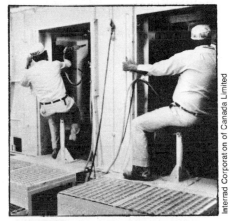

Dry powder electrostatic touch-up booth on automatic appliance line.

Twin air bell powder booth and reclaim unit.

wastewater are hauled away by a disposal company.

Once the parts have been moved automatically through the three-stage wash system and dry-off oven, the parts are ready to pass through an enclosed spray booth.

Several spray guns automatically spray coat the part with a positively charged powder, allowing the powder to adhere to the metal until baking. A manual touch-up using hand operated electrostatic guns follows immediately to coat inaccessible areas.

The excess powder that does not adhere to the object falls to the bottom of the paint booth onto a moving belt. The belt carries the excess powder to a vacuum system which collects and transports the overspray to the filter units. Once the overspray has been filtered to remove dirt, metal bits and clumps of paint, the powder is returned to the feed hopper for re-use.[42]

Only 40 to 50% of the powder sprayed stays on the target object, however the highly efficient overspray recycle system means that almost all of the 5000 pounds of powder used each month is actually used in coating the parts.

"Because the recovery rate of overspray is about 99 percent, we don't accumulate barrels of paint sludge," says Perdue.

The powder-coated parts are then moved to a gas-fired oven which cures the paint for a durable finish. Although powder baking requires an oven temperature of 400° to 425°F, about 20°F higher than for a liquid system, the overall energy efficiency is much higher.[42] According to Perdue, the new powder line requires 35% less energy than a conventional system.

"We used to have to exhaust hot air from our baking ovens because it was laden with solvents," says Perdue. "Now we get excellent energy conservation because the hot oven air is filtered and recycled immediately instead of exhausted. The energy savings are especially tremendous in the winter."

There is no doubt in Perdue's mind that the economics of powder are best for those applications that do not need many colour changes. Powder coating technology does have a relatively wide range of application, particularly in the appliance industry, the outdoor furniture industry, or as a base coat in the automotive industry.

Colour change takes about three hours to accomplish. This is done by manually sweeping down the walls of the booths and switching spray gun hoses to the hopper containing the other colour. The powder that is brushed from the walls and air-purged from the spray guns is then recycled back into the system.[42] Unlike conventional liquid paint systems which generate large volumes of wastewater and sludge during a colour change, changing colour for a powder system is sludge-free.

■ The W.C. Woods Company Ltd. (Guelph, Ontario) has been in the powder coating business for more than ten years. The company can powder-coat its freezers in any of four colours, and it is about to install another powder coating system with greater multi-colour capacity.[43] According to company management, the real benefits of the powder coating system are often hidden. The benefits are the things that are not required, such as no solvents to worry about, no sludge to dispose of, and no need for heat or air make-up.

■ Marshall Industries Ltd. (Rexdale, Ontario) manufactures a wide range of wire products from patio furniture and dishwasher racks to grocery shopping carts. PVC and nylon are the predominant powders used to coat the metal objects. When the company started using powder coatings in 1963, it was one of the first in Canada to use this technology. Company management claims that the economics of powder coating will only improve with time as the cost of competing finishes such as conventional wet coating and electroplating continue to escalate.[44]

■ The USI Agribusiness Plant (Atlanta, Georgia) installed a powder system to paint its poultry feeding equipment, egg collectors, and environmental control equipment. Design and installation assistance was imported from Torrid Oven Ltd. (Mississauga, Ontario), with spray equipment by Volstatic Equipment Division of Canadian Hanson (Toronto, Ontario).

The coating applied is a hybrid polyester epoxy designed to replace porcelain enamel used in the past. Advantages of the polyester epoxy coating include its excellent

corrosion and abrasion resistance. Company management claims that no solvent system would approach the finish and durability achieved with their powder coating operation.[45]

3.
Recycling Overspray

With paint sludge disposal costs in an upward spiral, and paint and solvent costs following suit, some businesses are turning to recycling paint overspray as one buffer against high overhead.

In the United States, paint sludge (overspray) is classified as hazardous waste, and as such is causing industrial painters some very expensive headaches. Disposal costs for a drum of paint sludge have jumped as high as $200 per drum in parts of the United States, up 100-fold since the $2 charge in the early 1970s.[46]

One chronic problem with recycling overspray is that the paint dries and becomes unworkable as a new paint. Recycling is most efficient if the drying or curing factor can be minimized. Many of the new paint formulations and innovative coating methods enhance paint recovery opportunities. For example, in radiation curing and powder coating methods, the coating that is applied will not cure until it is put through a special curing cycle. Hence, it becomes technically possible, and in many cases economically necessary to recycle overspray.

■ 3M (St. Paul, Minnesota) redesigned a spray booth to eliminate excessive resin overspray and to recycle the overspray back into the project. In doing so, the 3M company avoided wasting 500,000 pounds of resin a year as unused spray. With a capital investment of $45,000, the company turned its finances around to net themselves an annual saving of $125,000.[47]

■ The W.C. Richards Company (Blue Island, Illinois) has been recycling overspray for more than 30 years. According to Bill Richards, company president, the recycling of paint overspray is hardly a breakthrough in new

technology. Quite the contrary.

"It was a war-time crisis which forced us to develop the technology. As supplies improved and prices dropped in the 1950s and 1960s, industry gradually drifted back to the use of virgin materials. We put recycle on the back shelf, but today's battles against inflation and environmental deterioration are forcing a return to an already proven technology," says Richards.

The W.C. Richards Company's own history of paint recycling has its roots in scarcity and necessity. Back in 1946 when the firm still manufactured toys, red enamel paint was in such short supply that Richards, in desperation, attempted to reclaim the sludge from spray booths. The experiment met with such success that other manufacturers requested Richards to recycle their paint wastes. Seizing a business opportunity, the company abandoned its toy line and plunged into the paint formulating and recycling business.[46]

More than 30 years later, business is still booming, although the company is once again shifting its direction. In the past few years, the firm recycled about 1 million gallons of sludge a year, mainly from the appliance and automotive industries. At present, however, they are cutting back on the quantity of paint they accept for recovery. Instead, the company is assisting businesses in on-site recovery. The Blue Island plant has about 100 employees, more than 30 of which are technical people who consult other companies on how to recycle overspray.

Technical director Arthur Gay explains, "Nowadays we are more interested in licensing other companies to use our recycling process to reclaim their own paint wastes. We want to teach people to do it for themselves."

The technical consultants will tell a company if it is economically feasible to recycle its paint sludge. In addition, the consultants will provide the design and specifications for the on-site construction of the paint reclamation system, as well as train operators to use the new equipment.[48]

What is industry's reaction to

paint sludge recycling? "They think it's a great idea but they want someone else to do it for them!" exclaims Gay.

Why not continue to recycle paint instead of teaching other companies how to do it? Both Richards and Gay suggest many reasons why paint recycling makes most sense when done on-site by the company that generates the sludge.

Paint designed for a production line should be re-used as paint for that same production line because that paint is already tailor-made for those specific demands. To find another customer with the same specification is very difficult. It makes more sense to reclaim primer sludge as primer, and enamel sludge as enamel, than to reclaim mixed sludges as primer.[46]

Another argument in favour of on-site recycling is that the sludge can be reclaimed soon after it is generated, while it is still fresh. The fresher the sludge, the greater the yield of reclaimed paint.[48]

According to Gay, air-dry paint systems give a much smaller yield of reclaimed paint than do bake systems. The overspray of bake-type paints remains in the liquid unpolymerized form, unlike air-dry paints which quickly polymerize and form a skin. Typically, 80 to 90% of the paint sludge of an air-dry system can be reclaimed. For a bake system, 97 to 99% of the paint sludge can be recycled.

On-site recovery offers another advantage over hauling the paint sludge to an outside reclaimer by eliminating freight and handling costs. In the United States, any movement of hazardous wastes off a company's premises must be accompanied by multiple forms designed to track the location of these substances. Recycling paint on-site eliminates the paperwork necessary to comply with the manifest system.

The psychological effect of having a company deal with its own wastes on-site appears to be a favourable one. Gay laments the difficulties his own company has had in obtaining consistently clean paint sludge, free of cigarette butts, lunch leftovers

and other garbage.

"There is the human element. People have been treating this stuff as garbage for so long that it is hard to get them to collect it and keep it clean when they know it goes off their premises. It would be easier to keep the overspray clean if it were treated every day right at that facility. It is a continual education process at the plant," says Gay.

But what are the economics of sludge recovery? How small a company can benefit?

"If a company generates 100 drums (5000 U.S. gallons) of sludge a month, it is worthwhile to recycle paint. Even with 50 drums it might be worthwhile," says Gay.

Typically, industrial paints sold for $8 to $14 a gallon in the United States in 1981. By recovering paint on-site, the recycled paint cost only $3 to $5 per gallon. If the sludge is hauled off-site for re-claiming, the cost of the reclaimed product may reach $7 per gallon, still well below the price of virgin paint.[48]

The economics of recovery are sound. Given that a company generates only 100 drums (5000 U.S. gallons) of sludge a month, assume that 80% or 4000 gallons are reclaimed at a cost of $7 per gallon. If the virgin product sells for $12 per gallon, the monthly savings in paint costs alone would be $20,000. Add to this the more than $3000 saved each month by avoiding sludge disposal costs and the economics become even more promising.[48]

The W.C. Richards Company suggests that most types of paints can be recovered, including alkyds, acrylics, lacquers and epoxy esters. The company has been successful in recycling many of the new high solids formulations and some water-borne formulas.

In the sludge recovery process, the first step is to re-dissolve everything that is soluble in the sludge. Some of the paint sludge will remain in its polymerized form as lumps. The next step is to filter out or centrifuge the non-soluble lumps. Essentially all the pigment is saved. Some binders, resins, solvents or other ingredients are added to bring the paint back close to its original condition.

Although the W.C. Richards Company is not the only company involved in paint recycling, its approach is somewhat unusual. By putting paint recycling back in the hands of those who generate the sludge, the company hopes to help win today's battle against inflation and environmental deterioration.

■ The Clyde Paint and Supply Company (Clyde, Ohio) is another company which recycles paint overspray from other businesses. The company accepts paint from automotive paint lines. The paint is reconditioned and returned to the automotive companies for use as a primer coat.[33]

■ In Britain, Leigh Analytical Services Ltd. have come up with a new use for difficult-to-dispose-of paint sludges. Leigh, which specializes in waste treatment and recovery, have developed a novel means of converting waste paints, tars, oil sludges and latex into a homogeneous solid form. The solidified material, which has an energy content similar to brown coal, can be easily stored, transported and then burned as a solid fuel.[49]

4.
New Directions in the Paint Industry

The coatings industry is not alone in its heavy dependence on petrochemicals. The plastics, adhesives, pesticide, ink, organic dyes, solvents, automotive, appliance and textile industries all depend on a steady and affordable supply of petrochemicals. This was not always the case. Prior to the 1940s, the manufacturing sector had to look to the forests and fields for many of its raw materials.

The boom of the petrochemical industry in the 1950s provided such a predictable and cheap supply of petrochemical-based polymers as to edge other competitors out of the market. Polyester replaced cotton, natural dyes were substituted by synthetic dyes, and plastic invaded markets previously held by the paper industry. A similar change swept the paint industry.

Historically, the paint industry has been a large user of renewable resources. Prior to the 1950s, soybean and linseed oil were the workhorses of alkyd resin technology. Alkyd resin technology yielded paints which were readily solvent in turpentine. The use of renewable raw materials such as turpentine, soybean and linseed oil has declined slowly but steadily since the 1950s. This decline can be attributed in large part to the increased availability of petrochemical-based acrylics and other polymers currently in use by the paint industry.

If petroleum resources were suddenly restricted through some calamity, could the coatings industry remain in business? According to the Renewable Resources Committee of the Chicago Society of Coatings Technology, the answer is "yes", but the renewables-based technology would be 30 to 50 years behind the types of coatings the industry is capable of producing today.[50]

There is a vast potential of renewable raw materials from natural sources available to the coatings industry (see Table 3). Numerous plant species exist which produce hydrocarbons suit-

able for chemical processing and energy uses, while others can yield specialized oils and chemical feedstocks. Cellulose and starch can provide new polymer types or they can be converted to basic alcohols for the synthesis of many of the required chemicals.[50]

One major source of material and energy resources available to industry is organic waste. Corn cobs and oat hulls are two agricultural wastes that can be used to produce the chemical intermediary furfural. Furfural can undergo further processing to yield a range of solvents usable by the coatings industry.[50]

Table 3

RENEWABLE RESOURCES FOR THE COATINGS INDUSTRY

There are several sources of renewable raw materials that are usable by the coatings industry. Some of the natural materials listed, such as turpentine and linseed oil, can be used relatively directly with little additional processing. Other materials, such as forestry and agricultural wastes can undergo complex chemical reactions to yield resins, polymers and binders important in the manufacture of paints.

Source: "Renewable Resources for the Coatings Industry" *Journal of Coatings Technology.* November 1981.

Traditional Agricultural Feedstocks Used by the Paint Industry

Soybean Linseed	Prior to the 1950s, alkyd resin technology was based on soybean and linseed oil. Since the 1950s, paint production shifted to petroleum-based acrylics and other polymers.
Castor bean	Castor bean oil is an important source of hydroxy substituted fatty acids currently used in the coatings industry.

Alternative Agricultural Feedstocks

Crambe (Crambe abyssinica)	Crambe has an extremely high erucic acid oil content. Crambe can be grown in the desert.
Jojoba (Simmondsia chinensis)	Jojoba seeds contain 50% oil by weight which is made up of fatty esters. This oil is a good substitute for sperm whale oil.
Buffalo gourd (Cucurbita feotidissima)	The seed oil contains 60% linoleic acid and 22% oleic acid. When the oil is formulated to a protective coating, it exhibits properties between those of linseed oil and soybean oil.
Vernonia anthelmintica	This species of plant produces seeds containing 30% of an oil which is rich in vernolic acid.
Guayule	The Guayule is a small shrub that grows in semi-arid regions of the world. The stems and branches yield a natural latex used in the production of rubber. The resinous material in the latex, and the seed oil are believed to be suitable for the production of paints.
Euphorbia	Euphorbia is a plant native to semi-arid areas. Like guayule, the euphorbia plant produces a natural latex potentially usable by the paint industry.

The Synthesis of Chemicals and Polymers from Agricultural Feedstocks

Soybean	The unsaturated fatty acids from soybean can be used in the production of polyamides and polyesters for coatings and adhesives. It is also applicable to urethane technology.
Linseed Safflower	Linseed and safflower acrylates and methacrylates have been synthesized and incorporated into emulsion polymers.
Corn cobs Oat hulls	These agricultural wastes can be used to produce furfural and other related compounds. Furfuryl alcohol, furan, tetrahydrofurfuryl alcohol and tetrahydrofuran are all excellent solvents.
Corn Sorghum Wheat Potato and other plants abundant in starch	Starches are a valuable renewable raw material for the coatings industry because of their use as paint thickeners, absorbents, sizes, adhesives and flocculants.

Wood Feedstocks

Wood resins and saps	Trees have traditionally furnished the coatings industry with turpentine, resin, pine oil and dipentine.
Cellulose	Cellulose can be used to produce cellulosic film formers such as nitrocellulose and cellulosic thickeners for latex paints.
Wood waste	Conversion of wood waste to methanol could become a source of many coatings resins such as epoxies, polyesters, phenolics, vinyl resins and others.

Similarly, starches from agricultural wastes are valuable raw materials for the coatings industry because of their application as paint thickeners, absorbents, sizes, adhesives and flocculants. The cellulose in forestry and wood waste can be used to produce cellulosic film formers such as nitrocellulose and cellulosic thickeners for latex paints.[50]

There are many renewable materials that potentially could supply the chemicals and fuel of the paint industry. Some renewable materials have been used widely in the past and the technology to use them is well known. In other instances, years of intensive research are required to produce high quality coatings from renewable materials. Furthermore, the cultivation and harvesting of the resource base requires careful and longterm planning to ensure a sustainable yield. The time to plan for the future is now. Creative chemical engineering and strong government support are needed to shift industry from its petrochemical dependence to a manufacturing system based on renewables.

Conclusion

The paint industry has blossomed with technological innovations in the last two decades despite the hurdles presented by tightening health and environmental regulations. No longer content with open-ended processes, equipment engineers are designing several paint application systems that are virtually closed-loop systems.

Those businesses well on the road to closed-loop processing through solvent re-use, wastewater recycling and recovery of paint overspray are finding that eliminating waste not only protects the environment but also enhances company profits.

For smaller businesses, the challenge to reduce pollution may be more formidable than for the larger companies. Scarce financial resources and technological expertise will make the small operator reluctant to divert any company time or money to control pollution when the same resources could be spent on soliciting more business or making more product. It must be recognized, however, that failure to minimize waste can cut deeply into company profits. Furthermore, in the face of stringent anti-pollution regulations, failure to abate pollution can threaten the future survival of a business.

Many of the smaller and medium-sized firms do not have sufficient access to technical expertise and financial resources necessary to reduce the amount of wastes requiring off-site disposal. Accessibility to expertise and funding must be improved if the small business sector is to improve its manufacturing processes.

There is a need to provide economic incentives that promote waste reduction and recovery above and beyond conventional pollution abatement. Incentives and regulations must be structured to make waste recycling a cheaper option than waste burial. Failure to do so will impede rapid modernization and the minimization of pollution in the manufacturing sector.

FOR FURTHER INFORMATION

Air Pollution Control

The Canadian Paint and Coatings Association has completed a pollution control guidebook for the coatings industry entitled Introduction to Air Quality. The guidebook provides cursory information on air pollution, Canadian regulatory activity, coatings technology and pollution control equipment and procedures. This association also provides information on waste management and occupational health issues.

Contact: Canadian Paint and
Coatings Association,
Suite 825,
515 St. Catherine St. W.,
Montreal, Quebec.
H3B 1B4
(514) 285-6381

Solvent Recycling

The National Association of Solvent Recyclers (NASR) in the United States has completed a narrated slide presentation on solvent recycling. Solvent recycling is applicable to many industries including the paint industry. No solvent recycling association has been formed to date in Canada, although some Canadian solvent reclaimers belong to the American association.

Contact: National Association of Solvent Recyclers,
1406 Third National Building,
Dayton, Ohio.
45402
(513) 223-0419

Health Hazards Associated with Paint Application

Increasing attention is being paid to painter health problems in the United States. In Canada, occupational hazards associated with painting have not surfaced as an issue to the same degree is in the United States. The International Brotherhood of Paints and Allied Trades is active in investigating potential health hazards associated with the application of paint.

Contact: Health and Safety
Director,
International Brotherhood of Paints and
Allied Trades,
1750 New York Ave., N.W.,
Washington, D.C.
20006
(202) 637-0700

Safe Industrial Use of Radiation-Curable Coatings

The U.S. National Paint and Coatings Association has produced the publication Safe Handling and Use of Ultraviolet/Electron Beam Curable Coatings to assist operators in the safe use of radiation equipment. Chapter titles include Handling and Application Guidelines, Industrial Hygiene and Safety, Toxicology Testing, and Biological Safety Evaluation.

Contact: National Paint and
Coatings Association,
1500 Rhode Island Ave.
N.W.,
Washington, D.C.
20005
(202) 462-6272

Associations

Contact the following associations for information on low-waste technologies and equipment. These trade associations can assist you directly, or point you in the right direction for more information on commercially available recycling equipment, technology transfer programs, technical experts in the field, existing tax breaks and other economic incentives, and upcoming regulations.

Encourage those associations which rank pollution control low on their priority list to direct more attention to pollution prevention. Preventing pollution can benefit both the business community and the environment.

The following list identifies primarily national associations in Canada and the United States. It is not uncommon for Canadian companies to belong to American associations. Contact the national associations and ask if a local chapter is in operation near your business.

Canadian Paint and
Coatings Association,
Suite 825,
515 St. Catherine
St. West,
Montreal, Quebec.
H3B 1B4
(514) 285-6381

National Paint and Coatings
Association,
1500 Rhode Island Avenue, N.W.,
Washington, D.C.
20005
(202) 462-6272

Federation of Societies for
Coatings Technology,
Suite 830
1315 Walnut St.,
Philadelphia, Pennsylvania.
19107
(215) 545-1506

Chemical Coaters Association,
Box 241,
Wheaton, Illinois.
60187
(312) 668-0949

Canadian Painting Contractors
Association,
Suite 218,
85 Ellesmere Road,
Scarborough, Ontario.
M1R 4B9
(416) 444-7958

International Brotherhood of
Painters and Allied Trades,
1750 New York Avenue, N.W.,
Washington, D.C.
20006
(202) 637-0700

National Association of
Solvent Recyclers,
1406 Third National Building,
Dayton, Ohio.
45402
(513) 223-0419

Journals

Numerous excellent publications are currently available in both Canada and the United States. The journals listed below frequently contain articles that relate to improving paint transfer efficiency, energy and materials conservation, and waste recovery. These journals also carry an assortment of advertisements by manufacturers of low-waste paint application and recovery equipment.

COATINGS MAGAZINE,
86 Wilson St.,
Oakville, Ontario.
L6K 3G5

CANADIAN PAINT AND FINISHING,
Maclean-Hunter Ltd.,
481 University Avenue,
Toronto, Ontario.
M5W 1A7

JOURNAL OF COATINGS
TECHNOLOGY,
Federation of Societies for
Coatings Technology,
Suite 830,
1315 S. Walnut St.,
Philadelphia, Pennsylvania.
19107

INDUSTRIAL FINISHING
Hitchcock Publishing Co.,
Hitchcock Building,
Wheaton, Illinois.
60187

AMERICAN PAINT &
COATINGS JOURNAL,
American Paint Journal Co.,
2911 Washington Avenue,
St. Louis, Missouri.
63103

FINISHING INDUSTRIES,
Wheatland Journals Ltd.,
157 Hagden Lane,
Watford, Herts,
England.
WD1 8LW

THE PAINTERS AND
ALLIED TRADES JOURNAL,
International Brotherhood of
Painters and Allied Trades,
1750 New York Avenue, N.W.,
Washington, D.C.
20006

References

1. Walberg, Arvid. A.C. Walberg & Co., Downers Grove, Illinois. Personal communication, August 1981.

2. Aldorfer, D.M. and Praschan, E.A. *Preliminary Report on Transfer Efficiency of Water-Borne Enamel.* General Motors Transfer Efficiency Task Force. April 24, 1979.

3. Gay, Arthur. W.C. Richards Company, Blue Island, Illinois. Personal communication, July 1981.

4. "Industry Statistics: Real Growth Lags But Paint Dollar Value Continues to Rise." *Coatings Magazine,* March/April 1981.

5. Environment Canada. *Characterization of Industrial Wastes Generated in the Manufacture of Organic Coatings, Pharmaceuticals and Medicinals.* Solid Waste Management Branch Report EPS 3-EC-77-1, February 1977.

6. Scofield, F. *Assessment of Industrial Hazardous Waste Practices, Paint and Allied Products Industry, Contract Solvent Reclaiming Operations, and Factory Application of Coatings.* Prepared for the U.S. Environmental Protection Agency, September 1978.

7. "Industry Now Leads in Paint Usage." *Canadian Chemical Processing,* June 6, 1979.

8. "New Mixes Meet Air-Quality Tests." *Canadian Chemical Processing,* June 6, 1978.

9. "Painting Health Hazard Claimed by U.S. Unions and Study Groups." *Coatings Magazine,* May/June 1981.

10. Elofsson, S.A. *et al.* "Exposure to Organic Solvents." *Scandinavian Journal of Work and Environmental Health,* No. 6, 1980.

11. Arlien-Soborg, P. *et al.* "Chronic Painters' Syndrome." *Acta Neurologica Scandinavica,* No. 60, 1979.

12. Selikoff, I.J. *Investigations of Health Hazards in the Painting Trades.* Washington, D.C.: National Institute for Occupational Safety and Health, December 1975.

13. "Computers are Like Having Another Staff in Laboratory." *Coatings Magazine,* May/June 1981.

14. Morris, A. "A Tank Cleaning System for the Small Paint Plant." *Journal of Coatings Technology,* September 1979.

15. Dawson, R.A. "Sludge Management in the Paint and Coatings Industry." *Sludge,* September/October 1979.

16. Mock, J.A. "Water-Borne Paints Cut Auto Costs, Help Reduce Pollution Problems." *Materials Engineering,* May 1978.

17. Marchetti, Alvaro. Canadian Paint and Coatings Association, Montreal, Quebec. Personal communication, February 1982.

18. "No Single Coating Expected to Sweep the Market." *Coatings Magazine,* November/December 1980.

19. Marchetti, Alvaro. "New Wave." *Coatings Magazine,* November/December 1900.

20. Canadian Paint and Coatings Association. *Coatings Industry Introduction to Air Quality.* Montreal, Quebec, 1981.

21. U.S. Environmental Protection Agency. *Controlling Pollution from the Manufacturing and Coating of Metal Products: Metal Coating Air Pollution Control.* Environmental Research Information Center, U.S. E.P.A., 1977.

22. Niemi, B. "How to Figure Potential Emission Reductions for High-Solids Coatings." *Industrial Finishing,* November 1979.

23. "Meeting Tough Mandates." *Industrial Finishing,* February 1981.

24. Newman, R.M. and Dobson, P.H. *Evaluation of Fire Hazard of Water-Borne Coatings.* Prepared for the National Paint and Coatings Association, Washington, D.C., December 1977.

25. "Solvent-Like Prepolymers Could Save Oil-Based Coatings from Oblivion." *Canadian Chemical Processing,* March 21, 1979.

26. Degussa (Canada) Ltd. *Radiation Curing*. Burlington, Ontario: Degussa (product literature).

27. Brewer, G. *Calculations of Painting Wasteloads Associated with Metal Finishing*. Industrial Environmental Research Laboratory, U.S. Environmental Protection Agency, June 1980.

28. "Compliance with OSHA Standards Offers Furniture Maker Opportunity to Modernize Finishing System and Reduce Costs." *Industrial Finishing,* May 1979.

29. Santillo, Sam. Flex Steel Industries, Dubuque, Iowa. Personal communication, July 1981.

30. "New Paint Technologies Bring New Spray Systems." *Coatings Magazine,* May/June 1981.

31. "Filter Cost Rising Fast, What's Alternative?" *Coatings Magazine,* March/April 1981.

32. Water Technology Inc. *Ultrafilt™ Suspended Sludge Separator: A New Technology in Paint Sludge Removal*. Troy, Michigan: Ultrafilt Inc., 1979 (product literature).

33. Morr, Allen. Water Technology Inc., Chicago, Illinois. Personal communication, July 1981.

34. "Oshkosh Truck Paint Booth Saves Energy." *Industrial Finishing,* May 1979.

35. "New Pretreatment System Ends Effluent Problems." *Coatings Magazine,* May/June 1981.

36. Schrantz, J. "Fisher Body's New Painting Facility." *Industrial Finishing,* November 1979.

37. "New Techniques Increase Production." *Industrial Finishing,* April 1979.

38. Rainey, R.M. "Sputtercoating: A Production Reality." *Plating and Surface Finishing,* March 1981.

39. Rainey, Robert. Varian Associates Inc., Advanced Industrial Coating Operation, Florence, Kentucky. Personal communication, July 1981.

40. Rose, B.A. "Sputtering Advances on Target-Zero." *Industrial Finishing,* April 1981.

41. Perdue, George. Moyer Diebel, Jordan, Ontario. Personal communication, July 1981.

42. "New Line Slashes Coating Time, Provides Large Savings." *Coatings Magazine,* September/October 1980.

43. "Powder Line So Good Woods Planning Another." *Coatings Magazine,* September/October 1980.

44. "Used Powder Since '63, Marshall Now Has Five Lines." *Coatings Magazine,* September/October 1980.

45. "Porcelain Replaced in Innovative Hybrid Epoxy Line." *Coatings Magazine,* September/October 1980.

46. "Overspray Goes Back to Work." *Industrial Finishing,* January 1981.

47. Ling, J.L. "Making Cleanup Pay." *Environment,* April 1980.

48. Gay, Arthur. W.C. Richards Company, Blue Island, Illinois. Personal communication, August 1981.

49. "Perspectives: Solid Fuel from Sludge." *Chemistry in Britain,* May 1980.

50. Chicago Society for Coatings Technology. "Renewable Resources for the Coatings Industry, Part I: What and Where." *Journal of Coatings Technology,* November 1981.

Photography

In the old days when Hollywood immortalized Charlie Chaplin in silent film, little attention was paid to polluting discharges from the processing of film. Posterity remembers Chaplin for his humour, not for the pollution associated with film making.

The motion picture and photographic processing industries have made great strides in pollution reduction since those early, stardust days. Two decades ago, most small film processors across the country would not have thought twice about flushing spent developers and fixers down the nearest sewer.

Things have changed since then. In 1962, the price of silver was 90 cents U.S. per Troy ounce. In 1967, the United States government removed its price restraints on silver, then worth about $1.25 per ounce, permitting silver prices to respond to market demand and speculative buying.[1]

One year later, silver prices had doubled and many of the photographic processing labs not already reclaiming silver were well into recovering silver from their process wastewaters. In 1979, silver prices rose to $9 per Troy ounce and then rocketed to an unprecedented $40 per Troy ounce in 1980.

It is clear that the impetus to recover silver from process waters was an economic one, not an environmental one. Whatever the motive, the fact remains that silver recovery benefits both the environment through improved water quality, and business by putting more silver in the company vault.

The escalation in silver prices did much to steer the film industry along a course of pollution prevention. Along with the knowledge that silver recovery fetched higher profits came the awareness that recycling process chemicals and washwaters might further enhance profit margins. For example, desilvering of exhausted fix solutions meant that recovered fix could be re-used to replenish process fix.

The photofinishing industry is exemplary in its pollution prevention research. Researchers in the field were fast to realize that maximizing re-use of process baths and wastewaters would ultimately be a superior approach to the more conventional one of precipitating out the most hazardous chemicals and discharging the rest. Turning water pollutants to sludge may help confine wastes, but it does little to eliminate them. Instead, conventional pollution abatement methods tend to shift a water pollution problem to a land pollution problem.

More than a decade of active research in maximizing waste re-use in photofinishing has resulted in the availability of a growing selection of recovery equipment and retrofit design options. Commercially available equipment is capable not only of recovering silver, but also of regenerating spent fix, bleach, bleach-fix and developer process baths using individual closed-loop systems. The use of recycling technology in photographic processing requires care in monitoring to guarantee consistent product quality.

Refinement in re-use technology allows many of the dilute contaminants in waste rinsewaters presently discharged to sewers to be recovered economically by medium-sized businesses. Future technology developments may see further scaling down of equipment to be economically attractive to even very small photoprocessing plants.

However, as with any pollution reduction strategy, some aspects will yield a greater economic return per unit of investment than others. The industry is now realizing that implementing pollution abatement technologies that it once viewed as a drain on the organization, or at best marginally profitable, have resulted in some unexpected applications and benefits. The pursuit of maximum re-use technologies in the film industry is rife with examples of unexpected financial and environmental benefits.

Closed-loop technologies such as developer re-use and rinsewater re-use are far from widely implemented in North America. It may be the direction in which the film industry is headed, but attainment of this target is still years away.

Just a decade ago, most companies would have turned a deaf ear to equipment manufacturers extolling the virtues of waste recycling. Process chemicals were relatively cheap, emission regulations were lenient, and disposal costs were rock-bottom.

In today's penny-pinching climate, however, an increasing number of businesses are reappraising the value of the waste chemicals slipping down the drain. Today's attention to waste is all the more critical in the face of escalating chemical, energy, water and waste disposal costs.

No one can deny that pollution control costs money. Although pollution prevention makes good economic sense, it is an investment that may require substantial expenditure on recovery equipment. The hurdle facing most small and medium-sized businesses is overcoming the capital costs of modernization. Technical assistance is not inexpensive either.

Despite the availability of off-the-shelf recycling equipment for the photofinishing industry, the degree of implementation of recovery technology is limited.

Manufacturers of recovery equipment lament the hard-sell necessary to convince firms to purchase recycling equipment.

Economic incentives such as well-placed tax breaks are key in steering industry along a course of pollution prevention and resource conservation. Economic incentives are particularly important for small and medium-sized companies that cannot afford the capital costs of recycling equipment. The industry must be encouraged and assisted to apply the same ingenuity to pollution prevention as it does to product processing.

During the past several years, many of the largest laboratories adopted recycle techniques such as colour developer regeneration and the use of ion exchange for removing silver from washwaters. These laboratories were able to adopt these techniques because they had employees with the technical skills required to operate the units successfully and found recycling to be economically beneficial.

Smaller processing operations do not usually have personnel that are trained to successfully regenerate and re-use many of the processing solutions. This situation need not continue. Photofinishers in the field must be encouraged and assisted to apply the same know-how and commitment to pollution prevention as they do to ensuring print quality.

Photoprocessing and the recovery of wastewaters is an exacting science requiring considerable knowledge and analytical capability by the staff. Suppliers of photographic materials and waste recovery equipment provide a variety of useful publications on the subject of waste handling. In addition, it may be advantageous to offer technical assistance programmes to small operators currently lacking expertise in this area.

The success stories that follow show how some photographic processors have minimized pollution while maximizing profit margins.

The Photofinishing Process and Sources of Wastewater

Wastes of Concern

The photographic processing industry includes a large number of diverse establishments processing a wide range of films and papers. The processing of colour

Table 1

Ions or Compounds that May Be Found in Processing Solutions for Black-and-White and Colour Processing*

Type of Solution and pH Range	Concentration Range in Grams per Litre		
	10 to 100	1 to 10	less than 1
Prehardeners, Hardeners and Prebaths pH 3 to 10	Sulfate Acetate	Formaldehyde Aluminum Trivalent Chromium Succinaldehyde Formaldehyde Bisulfite Sequestering agent Carbonate ion	Antifoggant (for example, 5-nitrobenzimidazole nitrate)
Developers pH 9 to 12	Sulfite Borate Phosphate Carbonate Sulfate	Bromide Developing agents (hydroquinone or KODAK Color Developer Agent CD-3) Coupling agents (in KODACHROME process) Sequestering agent Hydroxylamine Diethylhydroxlamine Benzyl alcohol Hexylene glycol Citrazinic acid, sodium salt Ethylenediamine Polyethylene glycols	Thiocyanate Iodide Antifoggant Tertiary butylamine Borane Citrate
Stop Baths pH 2 to 4	Acetate Sulfate	Aluminum Borate Citrate	
Permanganate Bleaches pH 1 to 2	Permanganate Sulfate	Aluminum	
Ferricyanide Bleaches pH 5 to 8	Ferricyanide Ferrocyanide Bromide Sulfate	Bicarbonate Nitrate Phosphate Borate Polyethylene Glycols Thiocyanate	
Dichromate Bleaches pH 3	Bromide Acetate	Aluminum Dichromate Sulfate	
Clearing Baths pH 5 to 10	Bisulfate Sulfite		Hydroquinone
Reversal and Reversal Auxiliary Baths pH 8 to 13		Borate Sequestering agent	Potassium borohydride Tertiary butylamine Borane Nonanoyl hydroquinone

(continued)

(continued)

Type of Solution and pH Range	Concentration Range in Grams per Litre		
	10 to 100	**1 to 10**	**less than 1**
Fixing Baths pH 4 to 8	Chloride Thiosulfate Ammonium	Aluminum Bisulfite Sulfite Bicarbonate Borate Acetate Bromide Silver thiosulfate complex Ferrocyanide Formalin Sequestering agent	
Neutralizers pH 5	Bromide Sulfate Hydroxylamine	Acetate	
Stabilizers pH 7 to 9	Formaldehyde	Zinc Sulfate Phosphate Citrate Benzoate Sequestering agent	Wetting agent
Sound-Track Fixer or Redeveloper pH 13	Ammonium Iodide Sulfite Thiosulfate Hydroquinone Formalin	Thickening agent Hexylene glycol	
Monobaths pH 10 to 11	Thiosulfate Developing agent Sulfite	Bromide	
Viscous Solutions	Thickening agents (Other constituents similar to non-viscous solutions)		

*Relates to Kodak Products

Source: Eastman Kodak Company, *Disposal of Photographic Processing Wastes,* 1969.

print films and paper, colour slide films and colour movie film far exceeds that of other types of film and paper. Typically, only 10% of a commercial photo processor's business involves black and white processing. Other users of photography such as hospitals processing x-ray films and printing plants processing graphic arts films are not considered part of the photofinishing industry. Nevertheless, the processors of photographic materials in laboratories, hospitals, industry and graphic arts firms can benefit from many of the pollution prevention strategies used by the commercial photofinisher.

A photofinishing lab may discharge a large number of chemicals in its effluent stream due to the variety of films and papers processed (see Table 1). Two substances of environmental concern found in photofinishing effluents are ferrocyanide and silver. Also of concern but not as widespread are cadmium and chromium. Chromium is found in certain bleaches and cadmium is known to occur in select developer solutions.[2]

Ferrocyanide in streams can slowly undergo conversion to free cyanide in the presence of sunlight and oxygen over a period of several weeks.[25] Ferrocyanide appears to have no serious effect on activated sludge treatment systems and passes through the plant with little or no change.[26]

Ammonium salts, trisodium phosphate and sodium nitrate, present in a few photographic processing solutions, are undesirable because they are nutrients for plants and algae. Research has been underway to minimize the use of phosphates and nitrates in processing.[26]

Many of the chemicals present in photographic processing effluents are readily biodegradable, however, some are not (see Table 2). Although a municipal treatment plant having secondary treatment can treat combined wastewaters containing a low flow of photoprocessing effluents, the non-biodegradable fraction may accumulate in the treatment plant sludge. Contamination of sludge with certain materials such as silver and ferrocyanide detracts from the use of municipal sewage sludge as an agricultural soil amendment.

The Photofinishing Process

Many commercial photofinishers use continuous processing machines to develop film and to print standard-size photographs. Film passes through a sequence of baths including developer, bleach, fixing agent (fix) and stabilizer (see Figure 1).

A similar process is used in the processing of prints, although the types of chemicals and number of baths may differ. Many of the waste reduction and recycling technologies applicable to film processing are also applicable to the processing of prints. Wastewater effluents from paper processing tend to be greater in volume than from film processing due to the larger size of prints relative to negatives. Over the past years, the trend has been to simplify colour processing by reducing the number of process baths required.

Most commercial installations replenish exhausted developer with a make-up solution. The flow rate of the make-up solution into the developer bath exceeds the rate of developer carry-over (chemical that adheres to the film) as the film moves to the next bath.

Table 2
Biodegradability of Chemicals Used in Photographic Processing

Rapid Bio-degradation	Slow Bio-degradation	No Bio-degradation
Acetate	Developing Agents	Phosphate
Benzyl Alcohol	Citric Acid	Bromide
Hydroquinone	Ammonium Salts	Ferrocyanide
Sulfite	Glycols	Borate
Thiosulfate	Hydroxylamine Sulfate	Nitrate
	Formalin	
	Formic Acid	

Source: "The Biological Treatment of Photographic Processing Effluents". *Information for a Cleaner Environment.* Eastman Kodak, 1975.

Frequently, this next bath is a wash bath. Developer chemicals are lost to the washwater and overflow pipe, both of which are discharged to the sewer.

Bleaching assists in removing silver halide from the film. Concentrated replenisher bleach is added continuously to the bleach bath. Overflow from the bleach bath and wash bath result in bleach loss to the sewer, although the re-use of bleach overflow is common among large processing laboratories.

In the fixation process, un-

Figure 1
General Photo Processing Steps

This diagram shows the steps used in the processing of film at the typical photo processing lab. Most labs currently recover silver from the used fix solution. Few labs recover silver from the washwater after the fix. Similarly, few labs other than very large ones recycle spent developer, bleach and fix solutions.

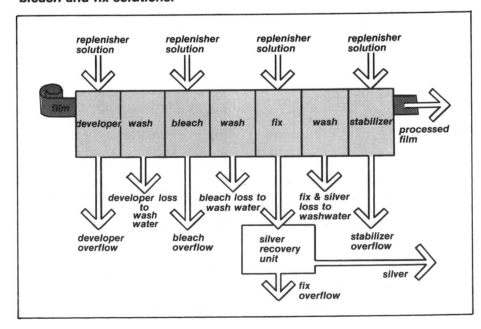

wanted silver halide is converted to a soluble compound that can be removed from the film. Hence, the greatest percentage of recoverable silver in the entire photofinishing process is found in the fix. The most commonly used fix compounds are sodium thiosulfate and ammonium thiosulfate. Concentrated fixing agent is added to the fix bath, and the overflow routinely passes through a silver recovery unit. Residual silver and fix chemicals from the silver recovery operation typically are sewered in smaller plants and recycled in larger plants.

Subsequent processing of the film is varied, but usually includes stabilizing operations. Concentrated stabilizing chemicals are added to the process bath. Stabilizing chemicals typically are lost to the sewer via washwater and process bath overflow.

The use of replenisher chemicals greatly enhances the life time of process baths, and hence reduces chemical loss compared to simply discarding exhausted process solutions. Even so, in the absence of closed-loop technologies to re-use the major process baths, a photofinishing lab typically discharges sizable amounts of chemicals.

Chemical re-use in the photofinishing industry, as in any industry, is most cost-effective if individual process solutions are reconstituted, rather than com-

Figure 2
Recycling Potential in Photo Processing

Commercially available recycling equipment exists that makes it possible to re-use spent developer, bleach, bleach-fix and fix process solutions. Equipment is also available to recover the dilute amounts of silver present in the washwater after the fix bath.

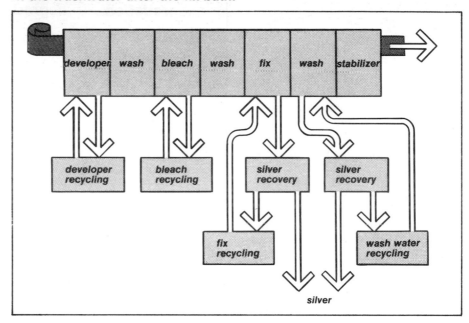

bining all the wastestreams and then trying to reclaim the mixture. Re-use of individual wastestreams is a technological challenge in itself because each process bath becomes somewhat contaminated with interfering chemicals from the previous process bath. Good housekeeping practices that keep individual process baths as uncontaminated as possible are a prerequisite to the successful recycling of process and rinse baths. Figure 2 indicates the recycling potential in film processing.

POLLUTION PREVENTION OPPORTUNITIES

1.
New Black and White Film Systems

The flux in silver prices has the film industry pursuing a new strategy — taking silver out of the picture altogether. Some companies are substituting less toxic metals such as bismuth to function as the image carrier in the film. Along with taking silver out of the film, some companies are experimenting with film processing sys-

tems that will significantly reduce the need for wet processing, thereby minimizing water pollution from film processors.
■ Agfa-Gevaert (West Germany) has developed a black and white film that contains no silver. Instead of silver, the metal layer is bismuth. According to Agfa-Gevaert, several metals are suitable for making film. What is needed is a substance that is sensitive to light, retains a latent image for subsequent development, and has a comparatively low evaporation temperature. Bis-

muth is suitable as a silver substitute because it is readily available, cheap, and one of the least toxic of available metals.[5]

The negative film is composed of a photo-resist layer on a polyester film base. The outer layer of the photo-resist emulsion reacts with light and exposes the bismuth layer.[5] Although standard chemicals for processing such film include organic solvents, Agfa-Gevaert has produced its own alkali-soluble resist layer for the negative film. Because waste alkalis are easier to handle than organic solvents, smaller graphic arts labs will be in a better position to process these films and treat the wastewater than if they required solvent baths.

■ Energy Conversion Devices (ECD), a small firm in Troy, Michigan, has invented a non-silver film for contact and duplication use in graphic arts. According to Stanford Ovshinsky, company president, this film known as Rapi-Lux™ is less expensive than silver halide films and not subject to the same fluctuations in the price of silver. Exposure and processing time is reduced by 75% over conventional silver film.[6]

Energy Conversion Devices are also experimenting with a non-silver film that does not require chemical baths to develop it. Instead, the film can be developed by heating, thereby eliminating polluting wastewaters.

■ Xonics Incorporated (Van Nuys, California) in conjunction with Agfa-Gevaert (West Germany) are experimenting with an x-ray film that completely eliminates the need for silver. The silverless x-ray film is being tested in German and Belgian hospitals, and will soon be available for commercial use.

■ Ilford (Ciba-Geigy) still uses silver in its black and white film, however, it has developed a process by which nearly all the silver can be recovered when the film is developed.[7] Unlike most black and white film, Ilford's new process requires no silver to form the image in the negative. Silver granules form the image in conventional black and white film. With Ilford's system, the image is composed entirely of a dye and the remaining silver is bleached away and recovered. An additional benefit in using a dye substitution process is that Ilford is now able to obtain very fine-grain images with high-speed film. This is not possible with conventional silver-based film.

Although much research and engineering talent is currently directed to rethinking conventional processing of film, major commercial penetration of alternate systems such as water processing or heat processing systems is several years away for black and

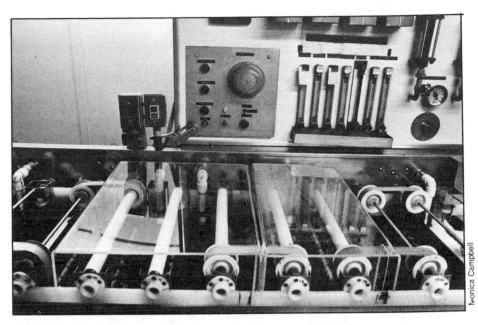

Process bath replenishment gauges (back wall) ensure that chemical make-up is optimum. This minimizes unnecessary losses of chemicals to the sewer.

white products and even further away for the complex colour photographic products processed by commercial photofinishers. In the meantime, many other cost-effective waste reduction and re-use options are available for conventional film processing labs.

2.
Good Housekeeping and Low-Cost Process Changes

Good in-process control is a significant pollution abatement technique for all types of photographic processing. Good housekeeping involves a low-cost, systematic review of the efficiency of existing processes, as well as preventative maintenance to spot potential leaks and spills before they happen.

Materials Balance

Embarking on a review of existing process efficiencies may include completion of a materials balance. A materials balance compares process inputs with process outputs. The difference helps identify the quantity of materials discharged in the wastewater. For

example, periodic analysis of fix wastewaters will indicate whether unexpected quantities of silver are draining down the sewer.

Because photofinishers demand a high quality product, there is a tendency among some companies to overcompensate by using more chemicals than necessary to develop and print pictures. Excessive chemical use not only increases the strength of the wastestream, but also pinches the pocket book. Taking care to accurately add and monitor chemical replenishment of process baths will save money in the long term by saving total chemical costs.

Another area where a low-cost investment can yield considerable savings concerns improving water use efficiency. Because a principle use of water in photofinishing is in the washing of photographic material, more efficient rinse techniques will greatly reduce the total volume of wastewater that is treated on-site or discharged to a sewer.

Counter-Current Washing

Two major functions of washing are to reduce processing solution contamination and to ensure long-term stability of the photographic image. Wash tank configurations include parallel tank and

Figure 3
Counter-Current Rinsing

The basic concept of counter-current rinsing is to use the water from previous rinsings to contact the film at its most contaminated stage. Fresh water enters the process at the final rinse stage, at which point much of the contamination has already been rinsed off the film. The greater the number of counter-current rinse stages, the less total water is required. A decision on the number of counter-current stages required must be balanced against space allocation and the capital cost of the rinse tanks.

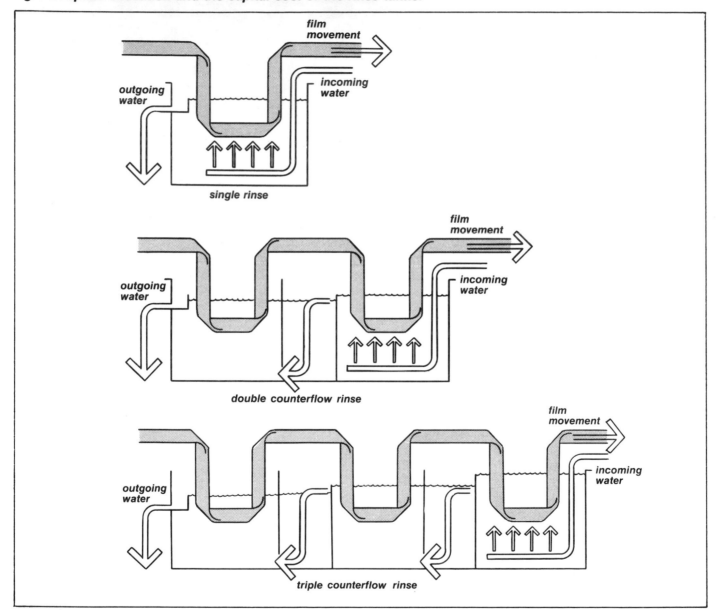

counter-current wash systems.

In a parallel system, fresh water enters each wash tank and effluent leaves each wash tank. In the counter-current system, fresh water enters the final wash tank near the exiting film, each of the wash tanks overflows into the preceding wash tank, and the effluent leaves the first tank near the entering film (see Figure 3).

Where space permits, tank re-design to convert an existing wash system to a counter-current system will pay off because of reduced water use and costs. A two-stage counter-current system can be one hundred times more efficient when compared to washing in a single deep tank with the same total volume of washwater.[8]

Squeegees

Squeegees perform an invaluable function in reducing chemical carry-over on film and paper moving from one process bath to the next, by wiping off excess liquid (see Figure 4). Typically, squeegees reduce chemical carry-over by 50%.[9] By minimizing chemical contamination of process baths, the total quantity of replenisher chemicals required is drastically reduced. It is advisable to place squeegees at the exit points of each different process bath for all continuous processors.

Figure 4
Operation of a Squeegee

A squeegee wipes excess liquid from the moving photographic material. By reducing chemical carry-over, the lifetime of the process bath is enhanced, reducing the total quantity of wastewater discharge.

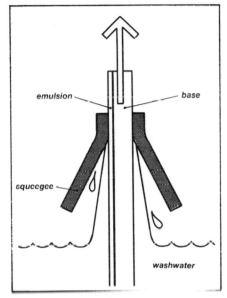

The earliest form of wiper blade squeegee was a rubber blade which began to deteriorate after only a few days of operation.[8] Good housekeeping dictates regular inspection of the squeegee apparatus to ensure its optimum effect. Polyurethane blades are more resistant to chemical deterioration and may be preferred to rubber blades. Other squeegee types are available and should be investigated as possible improvements to an existing system (see Table 3).

Water Consumption

Water consumption can be greatly reduced if the water is shut off when no film is being processed. Or, a solenoid valve can be installed to automatically reduce water flow when film processing stops.

Some photofinishing labs, upon reappraising the efficiency of the rinsing process, have come to the conclusion that their rinse system may be overdesigned for some uses of the finished product. Reductions in the total volume of washwater used may be possible without impairing photo or film quality. Assessment of the degree of rinsing must be based on testing to determine whether the photographic product is relatively stable over time. Insufficient rinsing may lead to premature loss of a high quality image.

Every film processor can wage his own low-cost war on water waste. In the example that follows, most of the water savings were obtained through simple equipment readjustments. Hence a low-capital investment yielded significant savings.

■ Palo Alto is a city in a semi-arid region of California. It has been the home of the Eastman Kodak Color Print and Processing Lab for several decades. Residents of Palo Alto joke about the origin of California's nickname: with an average annual rainfall of 13 inches, the fields are golden brown by July — hence the nickname "The Golden State".

In 1968, Kodak embarked on its water conservation programme. In that year, the Kodak lab consumed 130 million gallons of water at a cost of $48,300. Years later, John Motch of Kodak[10] said, "That was a lot of water, a lot of dollars and a lot more of both than really necessary for our operation, but in those days we were just waking up to water waste, and like many others, we had many wasteful operations."

By 1976, consumption was trimmed back 70% to 40 million gallons, despite a significant growth in business. The $26,000 water bill for 1976 was close to half the 1968 level. Motch estimates that if consumption had continued at the 1968 level, Kodak's water bill would have been an additional $273,000 over the 8-year period.

When northern California's drought extended into its second year in 1977, Kodak was faced with a mandatory requirement to cut back water consumption by another 28%. Kodak did even better. By the end of 1977, they were well below the ration level and had almost halved the 1976 consumption level.

Among the measures used to streamline water wastes were the following. Leaks and running hoses were attended to and "water awareness" became the watchword among employees. Stand-by flows were reduced to a minimum. By measuring actual process wash rates, many control valves were found to be over specification and so valves were adjusted accordingly. At first Kodak reduced the flow rate for the stop wash. Then it was decided to recycle water from the final wash to supply the stop wash.

Motch feels that Kodak's programme was not startling. Rather, it was based on sensible housekeeping and conservation, rather than on "big technology" that might or might not have been economical.[10]

3.
Silver Recovery from Process Baths

It is rare to find a photofinishing lab that does not recover silver from spent fix. Although most labs recover silver, recovery efficiencies vary depending on the type of recovery method used.

There is more than just the lure of high economic returns prodding photofinishers to recover silver. The fact that silver is a scarce resource is added incentive in increasing the scope of silver recovery practices.

In 1973, it was estimated that photographic materials were one of the largest industrial uses of silver in the United States, accounting for 48 million Troy ounces of silver or 25% of total consumption.[11] This represented 10% of the total world consumption of 480 million Troy ounces. New production of silver mining accounted for 240 million Troy ounces, approximately half the silver used. The deficit has been supplied by silver recovery.

Three major sources of recoverable silver in the photoprocessing industry include exhausted fixes and bleach-fix, film scraps and unexposed paper, and waste washwater following fixes and bleach-fixes.

Because the image in black and

Use of squeegees (centre) minimize chemical carry-over from one processing tank to the next.

At 3M Photofinishing Lab, film scraps and expired papers are desilvered prior to disposal.

Table 3
Squeegee Types

Squeegee	Areas of Application	Specific Use	Advantages	Dis-advantages
Air-Knife	Noncritical applications; perforated films general	Cross over squeegee; sometimes final squeegee	Convenient to use; good for perforated films; inexpensive, low maintenance	Requires compressed air; not used for wide films
Venturi	High machine speeds; critical drying applications; soft emulsions that cannot withstand contact with polymeric blades	Final squeegee before impingement drying or before sound application	Highly effective	Requires compressed air; possible frequent minor maintenance; critical adjustment; cannot be used for wide films; practical limitation approximately 70mm wide products
Rotary Buffer	Applications more critical than the air-knife and less critical than the Venturi; high speeds	Lubricators (coats even layers of lubricant on motion-picture films); final squeegee	Self-cleaning easy maintenance; handles wide film webs	Large size; power required (less than Venturi); buffers require replacing
Polyurethane Blade	General, except for narrow film widths or soft emulsions	First choice for many applications because of cost and simplicity used between tanks and as final squeegee	Simple to install; no external power, inexpensive, little maintenance	Perforations not squeegeed; may scratch soft emulsions; may be cut by edges of polyester films
Belt turn-around and soft-core roller	General; for slowspeed transport of wide films where tracking is not a problem	Wide sheet films and paper	Allows selfthreading of film and paper; less frictional drag; squeegee aids in transporting film	Requires external power; less effective at high speeds; tracking may be a problem with long lengths of wide film

Source: "Reducing Wash Water Consumption in Photographic Processing." *Journal of Applied Photographic Engineering.* September 1976.

white products is composed of silver, not all the silver is removed to the process baths and washwaters. Although the quantity of silver remaining in the film or print depends on the exposure, as much as 80% of the silver may be removed from the emulsion.[11]

In colour products, the final image consists of dyes. Essentially all emulsion silver is removed in the process solutions. Colour films

Table 4

Quantity of Silver Potentially Recoverable from Processing Solutions and Scrap Photographic Materials

Film Type	Name	Troy ounces per 1000 Square Feet		
		In Solutions	Unprocessed Scrap	Processed Scrap
Amateur and Professional Colour Films	Kodacolor II	20.8	20.8	None
	Reversal Process K-14	15.2	15.2	None
Amateur and Professional Black-and-White Films	Medium Speed ASA 125	5.2	29.8	14.9
	High Speed ASA 400	7.8	13.5	21.7
Professional and Photo-finishing Papers	Prints from colour negatives	2.3	2.3	None
	Prints from B&W negatives	1.2	2.4	1.2
Motion Picture Film	Colour negative film	22.2	22.2	None
	Colour negative print	5.7	5.7	None
	B&W negative	11.6	17.8	6.2
	B&W print	4.8	9.6	4.8
Graphic Arts Film and Paper	Film 50% exposure	5.5	11.0	5.5
	Paper 50% exposure	1.7	3.5	1.7
Phototypesetting Films and Papers	RC paper 10% exposure	3.8	4.2	0.4
	Films 10% exposure	12.8	14.2	1.4
Micrographic Films	Colour Camera Microfilm	13.7	13.7	None
	B&W Duplicating Negative Image	2.1	3.7	1.7
Radiography Films and Papers	Medical film (average values)	9.8	20.4	9.2
	Conventional industrial film	29.3	48.9	19.6
Aerial Films	B&W negative	6.1	12.2	6.1
	Colour negative	20.4	20.4	None

Source: Eastman Kodak Company. *Potential Silver Yield from Kodak Photographic Products.* 1981.

yield 3 to 4 times as much recoverable silver in process baths as do black and white films[12] (see Table 4).

Previously, colour processing involved separate bleaching and fixing operations. In recent years, many colour processes use a one-bath bleach-fix process to both bleach the silver and solubilize it in one solution.

The four basic methods used to recover silver are metallic replacement, chemical precipitation, electrolytic plating, and ion exchange. Of these, metallic replacement and electrolytic plating are in the most widespread use.

Metallic Replacement

Metallic replacement occurs when a metal such as iron contacts a solution containing dissolved ions of a less active metal such as silver. The dissolved silver, present as a thiosulfate complex, reacts with the iron and settles out as a sludge.

■ Kodak markets a Chemical Recovery Cartridge based on the metal replacement principle. Overall silver recovery efficiency ranges from 60 to 90% with a properly maintained system. The Kodak cartridge is a five-gallon plastic drum filled with steel wool. Exhausted fix is allowed to circulate through the drum. A simple test using indicator paper tells when it is time to replace the cartridge.[13]

The Kodak cartridge is a low-tech, low-cost option that can be used by even a single photographer operating out of his basement. The small-time operator may choose to make his own silver recovery unit by putting steel wool in a plastic container and adding spent fix.

Larger companies routinely use the Kodak cartridge as a back-up system to collect overflow from the electrolytic recovery units. A major drawback of metallic replacement systems is that the resultant silver sludge is of low purity. Hence refining costs to purify the silver to re-usable form are much higher than for electrolytic units. Recovery costs are also much higher for cartridge desilvering than for electrolytic recov-

---

Table 5

Comparison of Silver Recovery and Refining Costs for Cartridge versus Electrolytic Desilvering*

	Cartridge ($ per Troy, oz)	Electrolytic ($ per Troy oz)
Recovery	$0.34	$0.04
Refining	0.60	0.10
Assay	0.05	0.02
Total	$0.99 + shipping	$0.16 + shipping

*Does not include amortization of the capital investment.

Source: "A Review of Electrolytic Silver Recovery for the Regeneration of Bleach — Fix Solutions." Journal of Applied Photographic Engineering. Summer 1979.

---

ery (see Table 5). Furthermore, because iron goes into solution to replace the silver complex, the iron ultimately ends up in the sewer, adding to the discharge emanating from the lab.

Chemical Precipitation

Silver may be precipitated from fixes and washes using a variety of chemical products. Sodium sulfide will precipitate the silver in preparation for filtering and recovery. Organic polymer flocculants promote coagulation and make settling practical.

■ Ventron Corporation (Beverly, Massachusetts) manufacture a specially formulated product known as Vensil™ which may be used directly for the recovery of silver from spent fix. The main ingredient, sodium borohydride, is reputed by the manufacturer to be an efficient reducing agent capable of reducing ionic silver directly to metal. Some photofinishing labs express reluctance at using such a product because of their difficulties in controlling exhaust fix acidity. If the fix is too acidic, the Vensil™ is destroyed rapidly by the competing side reaction of hydrolysis to give boric acid and hydrogen.

Electrolytic Recovery

Probably the most promising silver recovery technique for even small photofinishing labs is electrolytic recovery. During elec-

The Kodak Chemical Recovery Cartridge contains steel wool on a core.

Use of clear tubing makes it possible to monitor cartridge exhaustion — a dark red effluent indicates exhaustion, however use of indicator paper is more accurate.

3M's electrolytic Silver Savers are installed in-line at various locations to receive spent fixer solutions for desilvering.

trolytic recovery, a controlled direct electrical current is passed between two electrodes (a cathode and an anode) which are suspended in the fix solution. Silver is deposited on the cathode in the form of silver plate with a purity close to 99%. The cathodes are removed periodically and the silver is chipped off.

■ The 3M Photofinishing Lab (Toronto, Ontario) is one of many Canadian companies to recover silver electrolytically from spent fix. What distinguishes this facility from some of the other processors in the country is the systematic approach taken to prevent pollution.

John Howse, production manager, cites three strategies used to abate pollution. "One, we use commercially available pollution abatement equipment. Two, our staff scientists design and implement pollution reduction equipment to meet specific process requirements. In putting together our own equipment, we save money compared to buying it all 'off-the-shelf'. Three, we hire outside consultants to redesign our process for improved efficiency and pollution abatement."[14]

3M has designed its own silver recovery unit called the Silver Saver to function as its workhorse for in-plant silver recovery operations.

Because they discharge into the city sewer system, 3M must meet the municipality's BOD (biological oxygen demand) and silver limit. In the case of Toronto, the

Large desilvering tank.

Overflow tanks collect excess fixer.

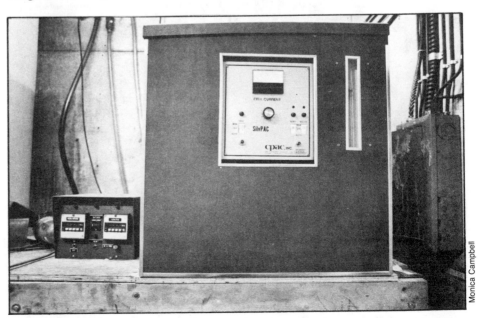

This automatic, commercially available, electrolytic silver recovery unit is also in use at 3M Photofinishing.

Monica Campbell

Tailing units operating on the metallic replacement principle collect residual silver from the electrolytic desilvering process.

municipality adopts the 10 ppm United States EPA guideline for maximum silver discharges. At present, 3M discharges only 5 to 6 ppm of silver to the city sewer.[15]

Spent fix is circulated through the Silver Saver which by electrolysis causes 98% pure silver to be deposited on a central cathode rod. The Silver Saver is placed in-line to remove silver continuously from recirculating fix. An advantage of this in-line system is that the silver concentration in the processing bath is kept very low, thereby reducing the amount of silver carried out with the fix into the wash tanks.

The Silver Saver is an example of in-house "imagineering". Instead of buying costly commercial units, 3M designed and built its own simple recovery units from "bits and pieces of pipe and plastic." At its Toronto plant alone, 3M recovered $600,000 worth of silver in 1980. Little more than a decade ago, all of this silver would have been lost to the city sewers.

"We are aiming for a closed-loop system in which we recover silver from both process and washwaters, as well as regenerate all process solutions," says Wilson Mor of 3M.[15] "We are ahead of many film processors in Canada by doing it now instead of being forced into it later through stricter emission control laws."

■ A number of silver recovery cells with self-contained power supplies have hit the market. One commercially available unit, manufactured by CPAC (Leicester, New York), is a fully automated batch-type or continuous recovery unit. Although more costly than "home-made" systems, CPAC units make economic sense in even relatively small labs. Pay-back period, which depends on the quantity of film processed, ranges from several months to two years.

■ A very simplified, low-cost version of electrolytic silver recovery applicable to the small user is the Silver Magnet™ produced by the TMW Corporation (West Bend, Wisconsin). According to TMW, most of the 200 million Troy ounces of silver thrown away each year are lost through sources which mistakenly consider silver recovery in small quantities uneconomical.[16] SRS (Silver Recovery Systems Inc. of Edmonton, Alberta) is one silver refiner who sells and reimburses customers for the silver recovered from a Silver Magnet.™

4.

Bleach, Bleach-Fix and Fix Re-Use

From the standpoint of better environmental protection, ferricyanide bleach has been replaced in some colour processes by a combined bleach-fix solution consisting of a ferric EDTA complex as the oxidizing agent and a thiosulfate as the fixing agent. However, because of its high oxygen-demanding property and relatively high cost, effective regeneration of the bleach-fix solution is of economic concern in colour processing labs.[17]

Environmental Reclamation Ltd.

The Silver Magnet™ is designed to electrolytically recover silver from used hypo and fixer solutions generated by the low-volume user.

In the past, ferricyanide bleach was widely used in colour processing to convert developed metallic silver and bromide to silver bromide that may be removed by fixer in a subsequent process bath. During this conversion of silver, the ferricyanide is changed into ferrocyanide and leaves the process as overflow. In the past, ferrocyanide overflow from a processing machine was allowed to pass untreated to the sewer, however, in recent years, the regeneration of ferricyanide bleach has become more desirable for both economic and environmental reasons.[18]

Although some colour processes have been switched successfully to the environmentally less harmful iron-complexed bleaches and bleach-fixes, these alternative bleach-fixes have not met with widespread use in processing Kodachrome, Ektachrome and certain professional motion picture films.[19] As long as the potentially toxic ferricyanide bleaches remain in use, it is advantageous to recover and re-use these chemicals, rather than discharge them to the environment.

Bleach Recycle

Four methods exist to regenerate spent ferricyanide bleach. These are ozone oxidation, electrolysis, use of persulfate salts, and use of liquid bromine.

Ozone Oxidation

Use of ozone oxidation to regenerate spent ferricyanide bleach depends on the production of ozone gas. Although this method is simple to operate, it requires the purchase of relatively costly ozone generators.

In a continuous processor, the film or paper moves from the bleach bath to a wash bath and on to the fix bath. Effective recovery is enhanced by keeping the ferricyanide concentration in the wastestreams as high as possible within the tolerance of the process. Counter-current fixes and washes can significantly reduce the total volume of solution while maintaining process quality. The dilute rinsewater containing ferricya-

Figure 5
Ozone Oxidation for Ferricyanide Bleach Recycle

Ozone generators produce ozone gas to function as the oxidation agent which regenerates the spent ferricyanide bleach. In addition, ion exchange columns are used to concentrate the dilute rinsewater containing spent ferricyanide bleach to a level that permits regeneration.
Source: CPAC Inc., Leicester, New York.

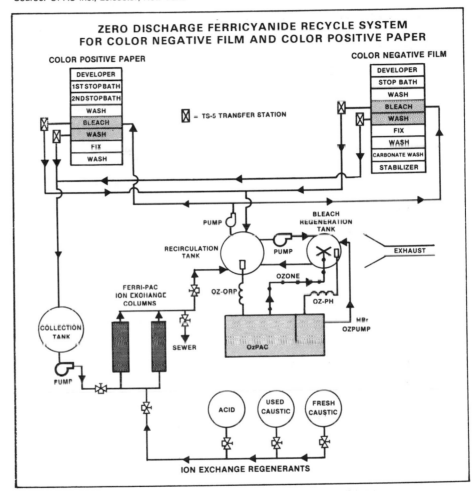

nide bleach may then be put through a commercially available ion exchange column to concentrate the ferricyanide to the point at which it may be added to the regeneration tank. The overflow from the ferricyanide bleach tank is controlled directly and regenerated.

■ CPAC (Leicester, New York) provides a unit known as the OzPac™ (see Figure 5). The OzPac™ unit is based on ozone oxidation to regenerate spent bleach. Bleach regeneration by the ozone method can reduce the effluent ferrocyanide concentration by about 90%[20].

Although such bleach recovery equipment constitutes a signific-

ant capital investment, it is just that, an investment. Unlike conventional destruct systems, bleach recovery will eventually pay off equipment costs through savings in new chemical costs.

Electrolysis

During the electrolytic regeneration of spent bleach, an electrical current is applied to the ferrocyanide overflow. The solution is converted from non-active ferrocyanide to active ferricyanide, generating byproducts of hydroxide and hydrogen gas. By separating the hydroxide from the ferricyanide solution and adding to it a solution of hydrobromic acid, the essential bromide and water replenishment is made, completing the requirements for an active regenerated bleach.

Generally not all the fix can be re-used. With some processes, attempts to re-use as little as 50% of the desilvered fix along with new fix have resulted in serious stains on the sensitized product unless proper precautions are taken such as sulfiting the replenisher solution. It is this sort of adverse interaction with the sensitized product that causes some processing laboratories to avoid using certain recycling techniques.

Some laboratories prefer to use an in-line electrolytically desilvered system. The in-line system continuously desilvers the fix in the tank and allows the use of a reduced replenishment rate for the fix. It may be necessary to modify the replenisher solution by adding additional sulfite before this system can be used successfully.

Residual silver in the electrolytically desilvered fix can be captured using a metallic replacement cartridge. This secondary silver recovery step is known as tailing.

■ CPAC (Leicester, New York) manufactures an electrolytic silver recovery unit for the closed-loop desilvering of fix. By maintaining the silver concentration in the processor tank at 1 ppm or less, fix activity is maximized. Such a continuous system for removing silver from the fix bath allows a 50 to 90% reduction in fix replenishment, reducing the cost of new chemicals added accordingly (see Figure 6).

■ The Nash Cell, by Eastman Kodak (Rochester, New York), is a small piece of equipment composed of a bundle of carbon welding rods suspended within a canister. The carbon rods function as the anode. The anode is surrounded by a diaphragm which is resistant to a highly alkaline environment. The cathode is made of a perforated metal cylinder positioned around the diaphragm.

Exhausted ferricyanide bleach is pumped into the bottom of the canister, and rises upward past the anode until it overflows through a central weir pipe. Con-

Conversion of spent bleach (ferrocyanide) to ferricyanide occurs at the anode rods.

The Nash Cell electrolytically regenerates exhausted ferricyanide bleach for re-use.

version of spent bleach to active ferricyanide occurs at the anode rods. The Nash Cell assembly can be set up to add hydrobromic acid to the recirculated bleach in quantities equivalent to the generation of byproduct hydroxide. In this manner, a batch of bleach overflow can be regenerated to replenisher strength with the required amount of bromide already included.[18]

Use of Persulfate Salts

The most common method used to regenerate ferricyanide bleach

Figure 6
In-Line Electrolytic Silver Recovery and Fixer Recycle

By continuously removing silver from the exhausted fix, a portion of the desilvered fix can be re-used. This allows a significant reduction in the quantity of new fix that must be added to replenish the fix bath.
Source: CPAC Inc., Leicester, New York.

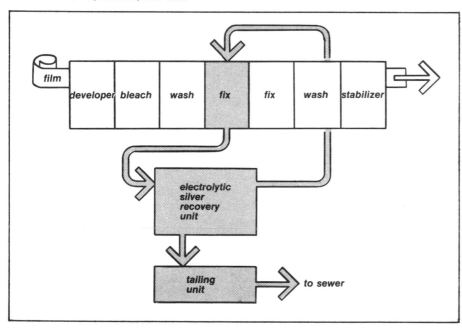

film | developer | bleach | wash | fix | fix | wash | stabilizer

electrolytic silver recovery unit

tailing unit → to sewer

is based on the addition of persulfate salts. Although the technique is economical and makes use of relatively safe chemicals, it is less efficient than the electrolytic and ozone oxidation methods.

After several regenerations with persulfate, the ferricyanide bleach becomes saturated with sulfate. The build-up of sulfate reduces bleaching efficiency, fouls piping and pumps, and may require the elevation of ferricyanide to higher concentrations in an attempt to maintain adequate bleaching.[18]

Use of Liquid Bromine

The use of liquid bromine to regenerate ferricyanide is very efficient and provides the bromine ions required for bleaching. A major drawback of this method is the potential hazard associated with the handling of liquid bromine.

Bleach-Fix Recycle

Electrolytic System

Most of the techniques used to recover silver from fix can also be applied to bleach-fix solutions. However, unlike recovery from fix, silver recovery from bleach-fix must be done in a batch system — closed-loop recovery is not possible.[21] In general, the electrolytic desilvering of bleach-fix allows for greater re-use of the bleach-fix chemicals from the bleach-fix overflow than does the use of metallic replacement cartridges.

Colour paper processing frequently uses a bleach-fix solution containing ferric EDTA. Regeneration of the bleach-fix includes three steps. First, the silver is recovered. Then, the iron EDTA complex must be oxidized back to ferric EDTA so that it will again be able to bleach. Lastly, certain chemicals lost through carry-over must be added to bring the solution up to replenisher strength.[11]

The CPAC electrolytic silver recovery system automatically collects, desilvers and aerates the bleach-fix for re-use. Aeration of the desilvered bleach-fix is important because it permits all the iron

in solution to be oxidized from ferrous EDTA to ferric EDTA. This not only restores the efficacy of the bleach-fix, but also minimizes cyan dye loss which could occur when residual ferrous EDTA reduces cyan dye to leuco dye.

If a laboratory were extremely careful and always maintained a high enough sulfite concentration in the bleach-fix being desilvered, the resultant solution would not cause adverse effects during its re-use. However, failure to ensure that the electrolytic regeneration was operating properly could result in a serious stain problem. If sulfite levels dropped, benzyl alcohol carried over from the developer could be oxidized to benzaldehyde, interact with chemicals in the colour paper and form a yellow stain.

The oxidized bleach-fix is then regenerated by chemical addition

and re-used as replenisher. Many continuous processing labs have two consecutive bleach-fix tanks. Bleach-fix flow may be countercurrent or co-flow. A countercurrent flow is preferable because only 7% of the silver is lost to washwaters. In the co-flow arrangement, 20% of the silver is lost to the washwaters, even when squeegees are used on the processor.

Ion Exchange

Ion exchange resin technology has been applied to the regeneration of bleach-fix process baths. Although earlier research suggested that resins did not have enough adsorption capacity for practical use, a small scale pilot application demonstrated resin technology to be feasible.[17]

Bleach-fix overflow from the processing tank is passed through

---

Figure 7
Bleach-Fix Re-Use Based on Ion Exchange

Bleach-fix overflow from the processing tank is passed through an ion exchange resin column to separate the silver complex. The desilvered overflow is re-used as replenisher solution. The silver adsorbed to the ion exchange resin is eluted and recovered electrolytically.

Source: "Regeneration of Ferric-EDTA Thiosulphate Bleach-Fix Solution by Anion-Exchange Resins," *Journal of Applied Photographic Engineering,* Spring 1976.

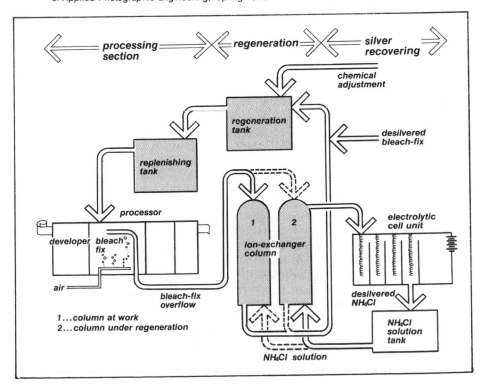

1...column at work
2...column under regeneration

an ion exchange resin column to eliminate the silver complex in the overflow (see Figure 7). The desilvered overflow is collected, sent to the replenisher tank after proper pH adjustment and concentration of component chemicals, and re-used as the replenisher solution.[17]

The column containing the ion-exchange resin to which silver is fully adsorbed is treated with a suitable eluting solution to dissolve the adsorbed silver out of the resin. The resin is thus regenerated and is ready for re-use.[17]

Despite prototype development, ion exchange resin technology is not a commercial success in the re-use of bleach-fix to date.[22]

Highly Concentrated Bleach-Fix Replenishment

The use of highly concentrated bleach-fix replenishment is an alternative strategy to bleach-fix recycle systems. Introduced to the trade in 1978, the alternative bleach-fix system does not re-use spent bleach-fix. Instead, the system strives to minimize the generation of spent process chemicals. Known as bleach-fix NR, the system uses a more concentrated replenisher solution and reduces the rate of replenishment by 75%. This type of bleach is currently used by approximately 80% of photofinishers.[22]

Although the bleach-fix NR is not regenerated, the ultimate loss of chemicals to the environment is slightly less than with a regenerated system.[22] Additionally, the bleach-fix NR system can be utilized by almost any laboratory of moderate productivity without encountering problems of interference with photographic paper.

By following the bleach-fix NR with a counter-current low-flow wash, photofinishers are able to collect in a very small volume approximately 98% of the totally available silver[22] (see Figure 8). The bleach-fix NR and low-flow wash mixture can then be electrolytically desilvered from a level of 3 to 4 grams silver per litre down to as low as 50 mg/L of silver. If this were done, between 93 and 95% of the totally available silver could be recovered in the form of

Figure 8
Bleach-Fix NR and Low-Flow Wash with Electrolytic Silver Recovery

The use of highly concentrated bleach-fix replenishment minimizes the generation of spent process chemicals, reducing the rate of replenishment by 75% over more conventional systems.
Source: Eastman Kodak, Rochester, New York, 1982.

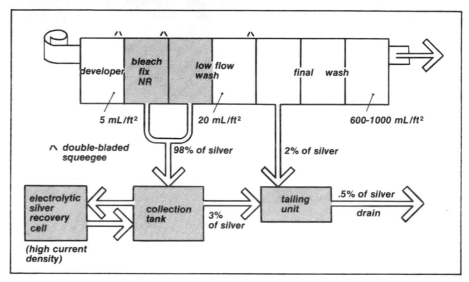

electrolytic plate. An additional 3 to 5% could be recovered by tailing the bleach-fix NR low-flow wash mixture through a recovery cartridge.[22]

5.
Developer Re-Use

Technologies for bleach, bleach-fix and fix recycle are already in limited use, but for colour developer, the most expensive processing solution, recycling technology came into wider prominence recently.[23] Although developer recycling technology was first applied in the early 1950s, it did not become economically feasible to apply it until the last five to seven years once the price of organic chemicals escalated.

During development, silver halide salts in the emulsion such as silver bromide are reduced to elemental silver. Bromide ions are subsequently released into solution with the corresponding oxidation of the developing agent. During colour processing, the oxidized developing agent reacts with the dye couplers to form visible colour dye in the emulsion.

Colour developer overflow from a continuous processing machine cannot be used directly as a replenisher because it contains a high concentration of halide salts and decomposition products that have undesirable photographic effects.[24]

Before spent developer can be re-used, the bromide ions must be selectively removed and the concentration of the developing agent must be increased.

Two major directions currently taken to recycle developer are developer re-use by ion exchange resins, and developer re-use by electrodialysis. Commercially available units exist for both technologies.

Ion Exchange Systems

Ion exchange developer recycling systems depend on strongly basic anion exchange resins. Equipment needs are simplified by doing batch processing of the spent developer.

A specific volume of colour developer is passed through the resin and stripped of the bromide ions. The ion exchange bed is regenerated by passing an acidic eluting solution through it, restoring capacity for subsequent bromide removal (see Figure 9). With time, resin efficiency decreases as the resin surface becomes blocked with oxidized byproducts in the spent developer. However, commercial systems in use for more than a year show no sign of reduced resin efficiency yet.[25]

Once the bromide ions are removed, the solution is analyzed. New chemicals are added to bring the solution up to replenishment specification. Because carry-over accounts for 17 to 30% of the replenisher volume used, fresh replenisher must be mixed into the recycled developer to maintain the processing volume.[23]

Laboratories that utilize developer regeneration are laboratories that use bulk chemicals and have analytical facilities available. Although some equipment manufacturers may advertise that analytical facilities are not needed, many laboratories claim that it is advantageous to have them. It is the smaller processing firms that tend to lack suitable technical expertise and analytical services to ensure adequate quality control on developer recycling operations.[22]

■ Winnipeg Photo (Winnipeg, Manitoba) is a large, family-owned company that has been in the photoprocessing business for 52 years. Winnipeg Photo has been recovering silver since the 1940s, and has been recycling spent ferricyanide bleach since 1974.

"We didn't wait for the city to impose its effluent standards. We're way ahead of them," says Mark Erlichman, vice president and co-owner. "There is no question that our efforts are paying off, both in terms of reduced operating costs and those more intangible benefits such as reduced pollution."

Winnipeg Photo has recently installed a CPAC colour developer recovery machine. The 1981 capital cost of $65,000 (Canadian) is expected to be paid off in 2 years through reduced chemical costs. According to Erlichman, even if the pay-back period was 10 years, his company would find it a feasible investment.[26]

New premixed developer costs

CPAC's DeveloperPac™ is a single column ion-exchange unit that removes bromide ions from used developer solutions, permitting re-use of exhausted developers upon replenishment.

the company $2.13 per gallon. At 82¢ per gallon, the cost of regenerating used developer is only a fraction of new chemical costs. By recycling 85% of their developer chemistry, Winnipeg Photo have not only cut their monthly chemical bill, but also reduced their burden on the local sewage system.[26]

Electrodialysis Systems

Electrodialysis is another emerging technology in developer re-use. An electrodialyzer consists of cation-exchange membranes stratified alternately, with a pair of electrodes installed at both ends. By applying a suitable direct current voltage, anions and cations in the developer solution compartments are attracted toward the electrode of the opposite charge. In the case of developer recycling, only halide ions such as bromide must be accumulated and eliminated, leaving other ions in the developer undialized. Not all developers are compatible with electrodialysis.

■ At the Shizuoka TV Station (SBS) in Japan, a Fuji FDR-TV Developer Recycling Unit is used successfully to recycle used developer in the processing of colour TV film. The commercially available system is a very compact machine with no requirement for analytical work.[27]

■ Colorcraft (Rockford, Illinois) is a medium-sized photofinishing lab that installed a production prototype developer recycling unit manufactured by the Snook Cor-

Figure 9
Colour Developer Re-Use by Ion Exchange

Spent colour developer is passed through an ion exchange resin to remove bromine ions. The bromine-free developer solution is analyzed, replenished and re-used in developing.

Source: "Colour Developer Recovery by Ion Exchange," *Photo Lab Management,* November/December 1980.

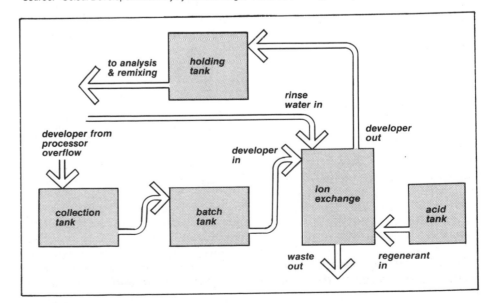

poration (Los Gatos, California). Known as the Rotex Developer Regeneration System ™, this developer recovery unit is based on the electrodialysis principle.[28]

At Colorcraft, the chemical bill used to include charges for buying 40,000 gallons of new developer each year. With the installation of the developer recycling unit, developer consumption has dropped 80%. With developer costs hovering at $1.50 per gallon, Colorcraft will save close to $50,000 on new developer costs this year.

Colorcraft personnel noted an unexpected benefit.

"We're not sure why, but the developer recovery system enhanced the quality of the developing process," says Lee Raiford, technical supervisor at Colorcraft.

Raiford speculates that the improved quality of the developing process may be due to improved stability in the developer chemistry.

The company used to buy premixed developer in 75-gallon batches. Developer composition may have varied from batch to batch. By recycling developer onsite, Colorcraft feels it has better control of its developer chemistry.[29]

6.
Silver Recovery From Washwater and Washwater Re-Use

Even with the installation of an efficient electrolytic silver recovery unit, most photofinishers lose 10% of the total recoverable silver to the sewer via carry-over into the rinse baths. Justification for recovering dilute silver concentrations from washwaters is two-fold. One, the value of the reclaimed silver will provide an economic return on the capital investment. Two, removing silver and other impurities from the used washwater will permit its re-use, adding to the return on the investment. Also, pollution loadings on the local sewer system will be minimized.

But with water costs as low as they are in Canada, water conser-

This Osmonics Osmo™ machine is for recovery of the photographic fixer wastestream at a large publishing firm. The wastestream contains silver and thiosulfate.

This Osmo™ unit handles 20 gpm of fixer rinsewater to reclaim silver and recycle water. The system operates at 90% recovery on sodium thiosulfate solution.

vation in itself does little to spur the advancement of water re-use technology. One of the more influential events that triggered research into water recycling systems was the United States legislation set in 1972 by the Federal Water Pollution Act. Amendments to this act set a "zero discharge" goal for American industry by 1985.

The zero discharge approach requires industrial processes to be closed systems with no pollutants released to the environment. Although the zero discharge approach provides a useful framework in which to concep-

tualize pollution abatement strategies, industry has hotly contested both the technological and economic feasibility of such a mandate.

Industry prefers to think of the zero waste target in terms of waste reduction and maximum re-use. The concept of zero waste technology has been softened over the years. One aims for zero and hopes to get close to it. The residual waste is frequently so expensive to remove that it becomes questionable whether it is worth the cost. But it must be recognized that the quantity of residual waste can be reduced drastically over its level of even just a decade ago.

There can be little doubt that strong environmental legislation or other constraints such as resource shortages have steered industry along a direction that it would not have taken in the absence of these constraints.

"Often in the course of industrial research, a production tool is grudgingly designed because of a problem, bottleneck or regulation that has impacted the efficiency of operations. Once accepted, these production tools often find a number of unexpected applications and provide ever increasing economics in the operation," says Robert Kreiman, president of Pace International (Culver City, California). "The ion exchange system for recycling photographic washwater is one of those tools."

Ion Exchange Technology

Ion exchange technology is making inroads in recovering dilute silver concentrations from rinsewaters, thereby preparing the waste rinsewater for re-use.[30] The basic cycle in anion exchange system consists of an exhaustion step, whereby the silver thiosulfate is selectively removed from the solution, and a regeneration step, where the silver complex is eluted from the column in a minimum volume of solution (see Figure 10). The eluted silver is then in a high enough concentration to be plated out in the same type of recovery unit used to recover silver from spent fix.

Associated with the two basic steps are various backwashes and rinses. The backwashes remove particulate matter such as gelatin that collects on the resin bed. Rinsing is generally a downflow operation that removes the excess regenerant before the next exhaustion step.[31]

Commercially available ion exchange systems are capable of recovering 90% of the remaining 10% of the silver normally sewered with the waste washwater. Because the ion exchange system can remove iron EDTA and other multivalent anions found in the photographic washwater, the washwater can be re-used for rinsing provided adequate con-

trols are available to monitor product quality. If ferrocyanide is present, a separate ion exchange system must be used to remove the ferrocyanide before strong base anion resins are used to remove the silver thiosulfate. The resin has such a strong affinity for ferrocyanide that it cannot be removed by regeneration, and consequently poisons the resin. In the case of iron EDTA, there is no problem because iron EDTA is easily stripped off the resin in the regeneration process.

To prevent a build-up of salt in the recycled rinsewater from residual ions, it is advisable to bleed in 10% fresh water. Even so, total water consumption is reduced by 65% when recycling waste washwater. Also, because the waste washwater is recycled continuously, it retains much of its heat, requiring less energy to heat it to its process temperature of 90°F than does cold city water. By recycling rinsewaters, the total energy bill for heating process waters is reduced by 40 to 45%.

The following case studies show how washwater recycling paid off for some photofinishers.

■ Business was booming for Deluxe Motion Picture Laboratories in Hollywood. So was the amount of pollution. By the mid 1970s, Deluxe Labs was discharging about 300,000 gallons of waste washwater per day into the Los Angeles district sewers. This was equivalent to the daily wastewater requirements of a city of 5000.

Faced with tightening regulations on the quantity of metals and BOD (biological oxygen demand) discharged to the sewer, Deluxe's research department, somewhat reluctantly, decided to tackle the problem placed before them. Their task was to clean up waste washwater before it was dumped into the sewer, and recover enough silver to assure cost recovery.

Although ion exchange technology for removing heavy metals from dilute aqueous solutions had been known for years, no one had found a method for applying it

Figure 10
Silver and Water Recovery System for Waste Washwaters

During the exhaustion step, silver thiosulphate is removed from the dilute waste washwater, enabling re-use of the washwater. In the regeneration step, the silver complex is eluted and recovered electrolytically.
Source: "The Long Road to Zero Discharge," *Photographic Processing*, April 1979.

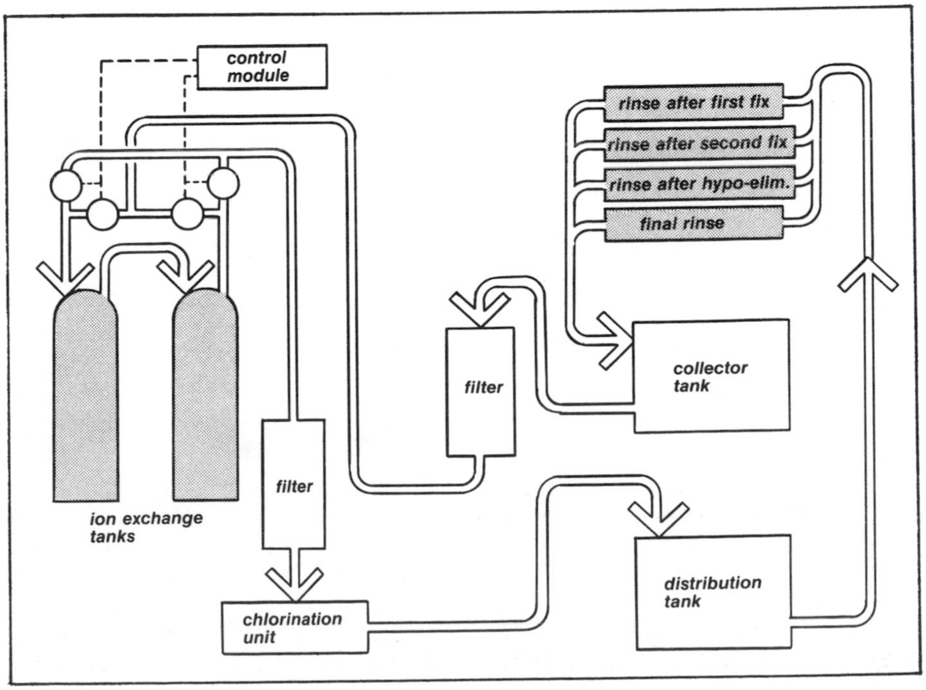

economically. Problems resulting from clogging of the resin filter with photographic gelatin, and the inability to regenerate expensive resin for re-use thwarted the cost-effectiveness of ion exchange technology for washwater from the film industry. Since then, scientists at Deluxe have solved both problems, providing a basis for filing three patents.[32]

■ The successful pilot project at Deluxe Labs led to the installation of a second test system at the Keith Cole Photofinishing Lab (Redwood City, California). These two pilot projects demonstrated conclusively that ion exchange technology was feasible for cleaning wastewater from both photographic and motion picture processing to meet local discharge limits.

California is famous for its sun and beaches. What is less well known is that parts of California are highly vulnerable to drought. When a serious drought hit northern California, scientists at Deluxe Labs were sent back to the drawing board. Everyone agreed that great progress had been made in cleaning up the film industry's wastewater. The question was then posed: could the technology be pushed a few steps further to make the wastewater pure enough for re-use?

The success was astonishing. By purifying the wastewater for re-use, Deluxe Labs were able to reduce water use by 62%. Since the water was still hot when recirculated, 42% less energy was required to heat the incoming water. In addition, 90% of the silver residue in the washwater otherwise lost to the sewer was recovered.

■ What started out to be a solution to an in-plant problem was so successful as to become a marketable product. The technology developed at Deluxe Motion Picture Labs is now being marketed by Pace International (Culver City, California). The Canadian distributor is Lisle-Kelco Ltd. (Downsview, Ontario).

"Thus, equipment designed initially to solve a problem had begun to serve a much broader purpose and had generated some unexpected economies," says Robert Kreiman (Pace International) of the ion exchange system for recycling photographic washwater. "Furthermore, in an inflationary economy, conservation always pays since the conservation system cost remains fixed at today's price while the pay-back grows with inflation."

■ The Gentry Photography Lab (Harrisonburg, Virginia) is located just beyond the area serviced by sewer lines. For years, this small colour lab discharged its photo washwater into a septic system. A jurisdictional change now made that discharge illegal.

It was a no-win situation. The Department of Health made discharge to the septic system illegal, and the Sanitation Department was unwilling to provide a costly sewer connection. Faced with the unwelcome prospect of closure, Gentry Labs chose instead to install a Pacex™ 15 (manufactured by Pace International) water recycling system still new to the market. In addition to protecting the environment, Gentry Labs have reduced their water bill by 60%, their heating bill by 40% and enhanced their profits on silver recovery by close to 10%.[33]

Designed to process up to 15 gallons of washwater per minute, the Pacex™ 15 is small enough for use by more than 90% of North American film labs, according to Kreiman.[34]

In 1982, Pace International made available an even smaller water recycling system designed for mini-labs, litho and x-ray installations with photographic washwater flow rates of 5 gallons per minute or less. The six-foot-tall system occupies a floor area less than 2 by 3 feet.

7.
Closed-Cycle Systems

Although photofinishers are gradually recycling more of the individual process baths and washwaters, few companies have

This Pacer™ Water Recycling unit removes silver from photographic washwater by ion exchange.

maximized re-use opportunities. PCA International (Matthews, North Carolina) is one company that has.[35]

■ PCA prides itself in being the world's largest portrait photographer, and in its estimation, one of the cleanest. A large part of PCA's success was its systematic approach to achieving zero discharge and maximum chemical recycling.

By following a carefully orchestrated set of stepping stones towards a zero discharge goal, the company found itself ahead of United States EPA requirements (see Figure 11). According to a company spokesman, by 1978, PCA was four years ahead of the federal EPA schedule of Best Available Technology requirements.

At that point, PCA recycled 90% of the water used each day, slashed its expenditures on waste treatment in half, recovered close to 100% of its silver, and extracted enough ammonia from waste process chemicals to fertilize much of its 57-acre site.[36]

Seven out of a total of 11 processing solutions are either partially or totally recycled.[36]

A CPAC electrolytic silver recovery unit is used to recover 90% of the silver in colour negative film fix. By installing the silver recovery unit in-line, fix replenishment is reduced by 70%.

Ferricyanide bleach used to process the colour film is reclaimed through oxidation via an ozone generator.

Silver is reclaimed from the colour paper bleach-fix, and the bleach-fix is recovered for re-use.

An ozone generating unit is used to oxidize residual chemicals in the wastestream that are not recycled for re-use. Treating wastewater with the ozonation unit reduced both COD and BOD levels by almost 90% compared to levels before installation.[37]

Used developer solution is collected and unwanted byproducts are removed by ion exchange. The processed developer is then pumped to a mixing station where it is analyzed and adjusted before re-using.[36] Mixing and reconstituting process chemicals is computer-assisted.

Excess water and chemistry

Figure 11
PCA's Stepping Stones to Zero Discharge

Source: "A Zero Discharge Wastewater Treatment System" *Environmental Science and Technology,* September 1978.

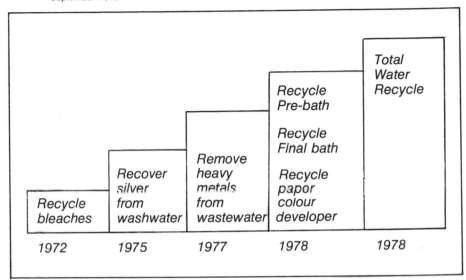

that is not re-used is combined ultimately into a wastestream which typically contains 2% solids. Use of a three-stage evaporation system boils off the liquid, leaving a paste. The paste, which contains silver, is sent to a refinery for silver recovery.

The evaporated water is condensed and put through an ion exchange process to remove ammonia. The clean water is then ready for re-use.[36]

8.
Off-Site Silver Recovery

Most photofinishing firms invest in on-site silver recovery systems. Many institutions, however, such as hospitals, medical labs, schools and government agencies that are involved in developing their own pictures choose not to recover silver on the premises. In many instances, the volume of waste fix generated does not merit the capital investment in sophisticated recovery equipment. In response to this business opportunity, some small firms have sprung up to tap these potential sources for silver recovery.

■ The Electro-Medical Equipment Company (Toronto, Ontario) is one of several establishments in Canada which assist small businesses in setting up a silver recovery programme. This company installs and monitors silver recovery systems, as well as arranges for the refining of collected silver.

Unlike some companies, Electro-Medical does not buy the fix or scrap outright, but instead pays a percentage of the market value of the silver recovered. According to company president Peter Cotnam,[38] there is no minimum amount of fix or scrap that has to be collected before silver recovery is economically feasible.

■ Multi-Cell Recovery Systems (Willowdale, Ontario) is another of many small businesses able to sustain itself on other people's wastes. Scrap film including x-rays are usually purchased outright. The desilvering process is a closed-loop system. Film is immersed in a ferricyanide bath to pull silver off the film into solution. The silver in solution is then electrolytically recovered through a commercial silver recovery unit. The ferricyanide bath is recycled and replenished.[39]

Although the desilvering operation is virtually pollution-free because it is a closed-loop system, Multi-Cell's owner Mel Kay ponders over the desilvered film base that is taken to a landfill.

"We are creating as much pollution, albeit non-hazardous pollution, as we sought to eliminate," laments Kay. "I end up with one ton a week of waste polyester material. The fabric manufacturers don't seem to want it."

Clearly, there is opportunity for yet another intermediary business to reclaim a waste.

Conclusion

The potential for waste reduction and recovery is great in the photofinishing industry. Despite the abundance of tried and proven recycling equipment, many small and medium-sized companies continue to dispose much of their process chemistry down the sewer. In some instances, a small firm may not be aware of the latest commercially available equipment capable of minimizing polluting discharges, however the barriers to waste recovery generally tend to be more complex.

Years ago, medium-sized companies would have been right in their claims that process bath recycling was beyond their financial means. Today, in the face of stricter environmental controls and escalating processing costs, waste recycling is slowly becoming the cheapest pollution control option for many wastestreams.

Even so, recovery equipment costs may present an unwelcome hurdle to the smaller operator facing high borrowing charges in today's harsh economic climate. If progress is to be made in preventing pollution, it will require the commitment of company management to identify the means of minimizing pollution, and perhaps more importantly, to direct a concerted and well-informed effort at maintaining successful in-plant recycling. Photographic processing and pollution control are exacting sciences that demand technical know-how to achieve a high-quality product. Despite specific problems faced by individual firms, it is generally true that modern technologies designed to avoid pollution or maximize re-use constitute an investment that yields an economic return. In an inflationary economy, recycling pays since the recycling equipment cost remains fixed at today's prices while the dividends from chemical recovery grow with inflation.

FOR FURTHER INFORMATION

Associations

Contact the following trade associations for additional information on pollution control technologies and equipment. These trade associations can assist you directly or point you in the right direction for more information on commercially available recycling equipment, technology transfer programmes, technical experts in the field, existing tax breaks and economic incentives, and upcoming regulations.

Canadian Photographic Trade
Association,
Suite 200, 3500 Dufferin Street,
Downsview, Ontario.
M3K 1N2
(416) 635-5040

Society of Photographic Scientists
and Engineers,
Box 1740, Station B,
Mississauga, Ontario.
L4Y 1R8

National Association of
Photographic Manufacturers,
600 Mamaroneck Avenue,
Harrison, New York.
01528
(914) 698-7603

Society of Photographic
Scientists and Engineers,
7003 Kilworth Lane,
Springfield, Virginia.
22151
(703) 642-9090

Association of Professional
Color Laboratories,
3000 Picture Place,
Jackson, Michigan.
49201
(517) 788-8146

Society of Motion Picture and
Television Engineers,
862 Scarsdale Avenue,
Scarsdale, New York.
10583
(914) 472-6606

Journals

Numerous excellent trade journals are currently available in both Canada and the United States. The journals listed below frequently contain articles that relate to improving process efficiency, conserving water, and recycling chemistry. These journals also carry an assortment of advertisements by manufacturers of recycling and other pollution abatement equipment.

PHOTO MARKETING,
36 Yonge St.,
Suite 110,
Toronto, Ontario.
M5E 1G3

PHOTOGRAPHIC PROCESSING,
PTN Publishing,
250 Fulton Avenue,
Hempstead, New York.
11550

PHOTO LAB MANAGEMENT,
PLM Publishing Inc.,
P.O. Box 1700,
1312 Lincoln Boulevard,
Santa Monica,
California.
90406

SMPTE JOURNAL,
Society of Motion Picture
and Television Engineers,
862 Scarsdale Avenue,
Scarsdale, New York.
10583

JOURNAL OF APPLIED
PHOTOGRAPHIC ENGINEERING,
Society of Photographic Scientists
and Engineers,
7003 Kilworth Lane,
Springfield, Virginia.
22151

PHOTOGRAPHIC SCIENCE AND
ENGINEERING JOURNAL,
Society of Photographic
Scientists and Engineers,
7003 Kilworth Lane,
Springfield, Virginia.
22151

PHOTO SCIENTIST,
Rochester Institute of Technology,
1 Lomb Memorial Drive,
Rochester, New York.
14623

Publications by Kodak

The Eastman Kodak Company produces a wide selection of publications on waste treatment and recovery for photographic processing labs. The following is a partial list of relevant publications:

Analysis, Treatment and Disposal of Ferricyanide in Photographic Effluents — A Compendium. Publication No. J-54.

Potential Silver Yield from Kodak Photographic Products. Publication No. J-10A.

Recovering Silver from Photographic Materials. Publication No. J-10.

The Kodak Silver Recovery Program. Publication No. J-8.

Directory of Silver Services. Publication No. J-10B.

Contact: Kodak Canada Inc.,
3500 Eglinton Avenue West,
Toronto, Ontario.
M6M 1V3
(416) 766-8322

Eastman Kodak Company,
343 State Street,
Rochester, New York.
14650
(716) 274-4000

References

1. "They're Taking Silver Out of the Picture." *Chemical Week,* February 20, 1980.

2. Davies, L. *et al.* "Summary of EPA Effluents Guidelines Study of Photographic Processing Industry." *Journal of Applied Photographic Engineering,* September 1979.

3. Burdick, G.E. and Lipschuetz, M. "Toxicity of Ferro- and Ferricyanide Solutions to Fish, and the Determination of the Cause of Mortality." *Transactions of the American Fish Society* 78, 1949.

4. Dagon, T.J. "The Biological Treatment of Photographic Processing Effluents." In *Information for a Cleaner Environment.* Kodak Publication No. J.-46, 1975.

5. "Germans' Second Take in Silverless Film." *New Scientist,* February 23, 1981.

6. Energy Conversion Devices Inc. Rapi-Lux™ (product literature), Energy Conversion Devices Inc., Troy, Michigan.

7. Ortner, E.H. "The Coming Era of Photography Without Silver." *Popular Science,* December 1980.

8. Fields, A. "Reducing Wash Water Consumption in Photographic Processing." *Journal of Applied Photographic Engineering,* September 1976.

9. "Profitable Chemical Management." *Photo Lab Management,* November/December 1980.

10. Motch, J.F. "Cost-Effective Water Conservation." *Journal of the Society of Motion Picture and Television Engineers,* September 1979.

11. Cooley, A.C. and Dagon, T.J. "Current Silver Recovery Practices in the Photographic Processing Industry." *Journal of Applied Photographic Engineering,* Winter 1976.

12. Eastman Kodak Co. *Potential Silver Yield from Kodak Photographic Products.* Eastman Kodak Co., Rochester, New York, 1981.

13. Eastman Kodak Co. *Silver Recovery.* Eastman Kodak Co., Rochester, New York, 1980.

14. Howse, John. 3M Photofinishing Lab, Toronto, Ontario. Personal communication, April 1981.

15. Mor, Wilson. 3M Photofinishing Lab, Toronto, Ontario. Personal communication, April 1981.

16. TMW Corporation. Silver Magnet™ (product literature). TMW Corp. West Bend, Wisconsin.

17. Iwano, H. *et al.* "Regeneration of Ferric-EDTA Thiosulfate Bleach-Fix Solution by Anion-Exchange Resins." *Journal of Applied Photographic Engineering,* Spring 1976.

18. Kleppe, J.W. and Nash, C.R. "A Simplified Electrolytic Method for Ferricyanide Bleach Regeneration, *Journal of the Society of Motion Picture and Television Engineers,* April 1978.

19. Cooley, A. "Regeneration and Disposal of Photographic Processing Solutions Containing Hexacyanoferrate." *Society of Photographic Scientists and Engineers,* Spring 1976.

20. Dagon, T. "Processing Chemistry of Bleaches and Secondary Processing Solutions and Applicable Regeneration Techniques." *Journal of Applied Photographic Engineering,* Winter 1976.

21. Thompson, E.E "Profitable Chemical Management." *Photo Lab Management,* March/April 1980.

22. Dagon, T.J. Environmental Technical Services, Eastman Kodak, Rochester, New York. Personal communication, February 1982.

23. Barbo, B. "Color Developer Recovery by Ion Exchange." *Photo Lab Management,* November/December 1980.

24. Kleppe, J.W. "The Application of an Ion Exchanges Method for Color Developer Reuse." *Journal of Applied Photographic Engineering,* Summer 1979.

25. Medenbach, Paul. CPAC Inc., Leicester, New York. Personal communication, August 1981.

26. Erlichman, Mark. Winnipeg Photo, Winnipeg, Manitoba. Personal communication, August 1981.

27. Tashiro, M. *et al.* "Application of Electrodialysis to Developer Reuse in ME-4 Process." *Journal of Applied Photographic Engineering,* Fall 1979.

28. Wood, David. Snook Corporation, Los Gatos, California. Personal communication, August 1981.

29. Raiford, Lee. Colorcraft, Rockford, Illinois. Personal communication, August 1981.

30. Cooley, A. "Ion-Exchange Silver Recovery for Process EP-2 with Nonregenerated Bleach-Fix." *Journal of Applied Photographic Engineering,* August 1981.

31. Mina, R. "Silver Recovery from Photographic Effluents by Ion-Exchange Methods." *Journal of Applied Photographic Engineering,* October 1980.

32. Kreiman, R.T. "The Long Road to Zero Discharge." *Photographic Processing,* April 1979.

33. Gentry, Hubert. Gentry Laboratories, Harrisonburg, Virginia. Personal communication, August 1981.

34. Kreiman, Robert. Pace International Corporation, Culver City, California. Personal communication, November 1981.

35. Rissmann, E.F. *et al.* "Evaluation of the Published Literature in the Water Reuse/Recycle Area." In Cooper, W.J. (ed.) *Chemistry in Water Reuse, Volume 1.* Ann Arbor, Michigan: Ann Arbor Science Publishers, Inc., 1981.

36. "A Zero Discharge Wastewater Treatment System." *Environmental Science and Technology,* September 1978.

37. Diagnault, L, "Pollution Control in the Photoprocessing Industry Through Regeneration and Reuse." *Journal of Applied Photographic Engineering,* Spring 1977.

38. "Hard Cash for Your Waste." *The Graphic Monthly,* April 1980.

39. Kay, M. Multi-Cell Recovery Systems, Willowdale, Ontario. Personal communication, April 1981.

Plastics

A decade ago, when a manufacturer brought a new product to the marketplace, the factors uppermost in his mind were costs, competition and consumer acceptance. Things have changed since then. Business savvy must be augmented by an understanding of the impact of that product on scarce resources, and the burden it places on ecological systems.

This holds particularly true for the plastics industry. It is not enough to claim that plastic products are inert and relatively innocuous, and therefore of no threat to the environment. Although the plastics processing industry is probably one of the less polluting stages in the manufacture of a plastic polymer, it is one stage of many that transform petroleum crude and natural gas to a plastic consumer object. The first stages of petroleum transformation, which are carried out by the chemical industry, not the plastics processing industry (see Figure 1), require complex and potentially toxic synthesis reactions to produce the resins that later comprise most plastics.

The production of resins tends to be the most energy intensive and potentially polluting aspect of plastics synthesis. Typically, 85 to 95% of the energy content of the plastic end product resides in the resin. This includes the energy of the petroleum feedstocks used to manufacture the resin. An additional 5 to 10% of the energy content is used in fabrication of the resin into a plastic object.[1]

From an energy and materials conservation point of view, the most wasteful disposal option is to landfill plastic scrap and post-consumer waste. More conservationist methods of dealing with plastic waste include recycling into alternate products, recovery of materials, and incineration for heat recovery.

Burning plastic wastes as fuel saves some energy, however, recycling plastic wastes into a fabricated product will frequently double the energy savings. For example, 1000 pounds of high-density polyethylene has a fuel value of 20 million Btu but recycling 1000 pounds of polyethylene wastes into a fabricated product will save as much as 39 million Btu — an average energy saving of 88%.[1] Materials recovery has the added advantage of minimizing the volume of resins and accompanying wastes that are produced in the manufacture of plastic products.

In today's energy- and environment-conscious society, many businesses recognize that material re-use of a plastic waste is a more profitable utilization of a petroleum-based product than incineration or landfill. An increasing number of businesses are opting for on-site recycling of homogeneous plastic waste. If the capital cost of such equipment is unaffordable, plastic scrap can be sold to a professional reclaimer.

Although the plastics processing industry recycles the majority of homogeneous scrap generated in the manufacturing process, large volumes of heterogeneous industrial waste remain as a potential recycling resource. Heterogeneous scrap recovery from mixed plastic wastestreams is technically more difficult and economically less attractive because the wastestream is composed of a variety of plastic types and contaminants.

Recent developments in plastics recycling technology may enhance the feasibility of recycling mixed wastes collected from industrial and domestic users. High resin prices and the increasing cost of waste disposal will continue to

Figure 1
The Plastics Industry

Source: *Canadian Plastics Statistical Yearbook 1981*, Society of the Plastics Industry of Canada.

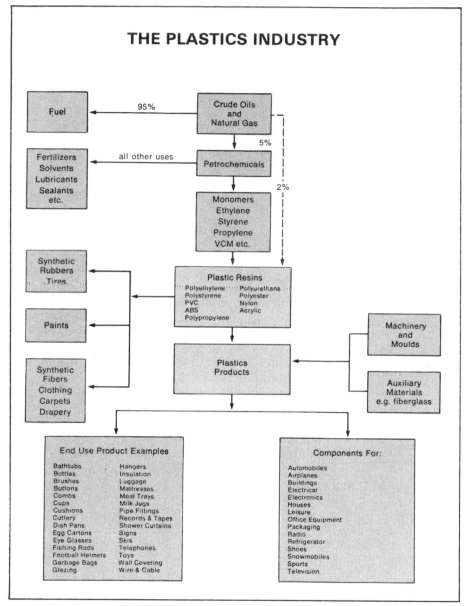

stimulate material recovery. Even so, the recycling of plastic waste will not reach its full potential until the cost of recovery becomes competitive with the disposal option. The recycling examples in this chapter introduce the technological advances that have been made in the recovery of plastic waste.

Another strategy for reducing plastic waste is to install modern, highly efficient processing machinery and techniques.[2] Some advances are still in the development stage. Others are commercially viable operations that have

netted the user increased profits while minimizing pollution.

Plastics Processing Industry Profile

Plastics are made up of molecules with long chains of linked atoms, generally referred to as macromolecules or polymers. The production of resins, which function as the raw material for the plastics processing industry, is characterized as belonging to the chemical industry. The plastics processing industry transforms resins and other materials into plastic forms for consumer and industrial use.

The four major activities that make up the plastics processing industry are compounding, fabricating, converting, and reprocessing.[3] Compounding is the process of mixing the polymer with additives and colorants. Fabricating refers to the process of transforming the resulting compound or uncompounded polymer to a finished or semi-finished plastic product. In the converting process, the fabricated plastic product is decorated, printed, cut or otherwise altered for completion. Reprocessing is the process of converting scrap plastic to a useful material.

Typical processing methods include extrusion, injection molding, thermoforming and blow molding. At present, plastics are derived almost exclusively from petrochemical sources such as oil and natural gas.

Canada's plastics processing industry consists of 1400 establishments representing a wide range in company size. Sixty percent of Canadian firms have annual sales of less than $1 million. Companies with sales of $2.5 million or more account for 73% of the total industry sales and for 60% of total industry employment. The plastics industry is concentrated in Ontario and Quebec. In 1976, about 66% of the total plastics processing work-force was employed in Ontario, 24% in Quebec, and the remaining 10% distributed throughout the rest of Canada.[4]

In 1972, the Canadian plastics industry consumed about 1.8 billion pounds of plastic resins. In 1980, resin consumption had increased to 2.8 billion pounds per year.[5]

Description of Plastics

Plastics fall into two principal categories, thermoplastic and thermosetting. Thermoplastics are converted by suitable heating, forming and cooling. Because thermoplastics can be reheated, melted and reformed, it is possible to recycle them repeatedly. Virtually all packaging is thermoplastic.[6]

In Canada, the four plastics used most frequently are polyethylene, polyvinyl chloride, polystyrene and polypropylene[7] (see Figure 2). These four plastic types are all recyclable thermoplastics.

Thermosetting plastics are set into permanent shape when heat and pressure are applied to them during forming. Typical thermoset plastics include the phenolic and urea plastics used in electrical sockets, plastic laminates and crockery. Generally, reheating will not soften thermosetting plastics. Although the technology has been developed in recent years to recycle thermoset plastics, it is still relatively rare to recycle these plastics. Some thermosetting resins such as phenolics are recycled by grinding and re-using them as fillers in virgin material.[8]

There are approximately 35 major groups of plastics in commercial use, and each of these groups may include several similar types.[9] Each plastic type has particular physical and chemical qualities that make it suitable for a given commercial application. Table 1 identifies 17 common plastic types and applications.

About one-third of plastic resin consumption has a life expectancy of less than 2 years[10] and usually ends up at a landfill site. Plastics with short lifespans include plastic packaging and disposable consumer goods. Examples of long life-cycle plastic products include tiles, wiring, insulation, furniture, appliances and automobiles.

Packaging and disposable serviceware accounted for 30% of the total plastic resin consumption in 1975, and building and construction uses accounted for 19%[4] (see Figure 3).

Figure 2
Canadian Resin Markets

Polyethylene, polystyrene, polyvinyl chloride and polypropylene make up more than half of all the plastics in use in Canada.

		Domestic Demand 1980 (1000 metric tonnes)
LDPE	Low-density polyethylene	310
PVC	Polyvinyl choride	180
HDPE	High-density polyethylene	165
PS	Polystyrene	117
PP	Polypropylene	93
ABS	Acrylonitrile Butadiene Styrene	42
	Polyester (unsaturated)	25
	Other	427
	Total	1359

Source: Society of the Plastics Industry of Canada, 1981.

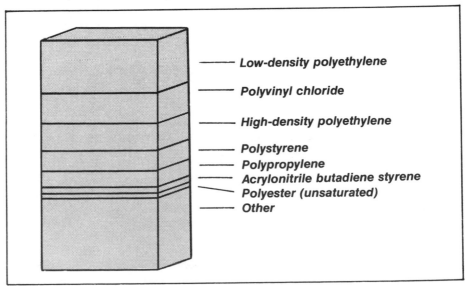

- Low-density polyethylene
- Polyvinyl chloride
- High-density polyethylene
- Polystyrene
- Polypropylene
- Acrylonitrile butadiene styrene
- Polyester (unsaturated)
- Other

Table 1

Major Plastic Groups and Typical Applications

Plastic	Type	Typical Applications
ABS Acrylonitrile-butadiene-styrene	Thermoplastic	Telephones, appliances, pipes, fittings
Acetal Resin	Thermoplastic	Gears, bearings, bushings
Acrylic	Thermoplastic	Outdoor signs, window glazing
Alkyd	Thermoset	Enamels, paints, lacquers, light switches
Cellulosics	Thermoplastic	Blister packs, photographic film
Epoxy Resin	Thermoset	Adhesives, protective coatings
Melamine	Thermoset	Dinnerware
Polyamide (nylon)	Thermoplastic	Gears, electrical and electronics products
Phenolic	Thermoset	Automobile distributor caps
Polycarbonate	Thermoplastic	Air conditioner housings, glazing
Polyester	Thermoset	Boats, truck bodies, bathtubs
Polyethylene	Thermoplastic	Milk jugs, dry cleaning bags, detergent bottles, garbage bags
Polypropylene	Thermoplastic	Safety helmets, battery cases automotive trim, carpeting
Polystyrene	Thermoplastic	Coffee cups, housewares, insulation
Polyurethane	Thermoset Thermoplastic	Automobile seat cushioning, insulation
Polyvinyl (includes PVC)	Thermoplastic	Upholstery, floor tiles, pipes, housesiding
Urea	Thermoset	Stove knobs

Source: *Types and Properties of Plastics*, Society of the Plastics Industry of Canada.

Sources of Pollution

Two potential areas of pollution in the plastics processing industry are air pollution during processing, and solid plastic waste generated on-site.

In general, the plastics processing industry does not use large amounts of water, nor does it generate large amounts of wastewater. Hence, water pollution problems are relatively small.

Plastic wastes become a poten-tial disposal problem when certain plastics are incinerated. Once the plastic product has completed its useful life, it is referred to as post-consumer waste. Post-consumer waste is not a problem of the plastics processing industry, however it is useful to discuss potential problems associated with industrial scrap and post-consumer waste together.

Air Pollution During Processing

Air pollution problems presented by the plastics processing industry consist primarily of removing processing chemicals such as solvents, softeners and plasticizers from plant exhaust air streams. In a few instances, air pollution problems may arise when the monomer (reactant) is highly volatile and escapes during transfer, drying or curing in the plastics forming process.

One potential source of air pollution in plastics processing is fabrication with polyester resins. Polyester resins make up less than 2% by weight of the total amount of plastics used in Canada (see Figure 2). Although polyester resins take up only a small corner of the plastics market, some of the polyester processing methods still in use present potential health and environmental problems to the smaller operator. Contact molding and spray gun application may result in significant on-site styrene emissions during the manufacture of polyester products. Various closed-mold processes are available which result in lower styrene emissions than contact-mold methods.

Another instance of a potential air pollution problem in plastics processing concerns those companies which use phenolic resins. As with polyester resins, phenolic resins comprise a relatively small segment of the plastics market. Low-molecular-weight phenolic resins in particular can evolve considerable amounts of phenols either by themselves or in products incorporating them.[3] The production and use of phenolic adhesives may yield an air pollution problem from the release of volatile phenols.

Although polymerized plastics tend to be relatively inert and innocuous, they may contain residual monomers and other constituents that are potentially harmful to human health. Under normal use, these constituents remain locked up inside the plastic and are of relatively low hazard.

The volatilization of certain toxic monomers has been reason for environmental and health concern in the last decade. For example, during the synthesis of PVC plastic, vinyl chloride monomer undergoes a polymerization reaction in which the monomers link up to form a polymer. If the synthesis reaction is incomplete, residual vinyl chloride monomers remain in the plastic. If the PVC is not stripped properly of its volatile monomers, it is possible that vinyl chloride will escape during pro-

Recycling of garden hose scrap is one example of plastics reclamation of industrial processing wastes. String and plastic are ground, the fluff is removed, and the plastic regrind is re-used to form the black inner part of new hoses.

Figure 3
Consumption Pattern of Canadian Plastics Resins — 1976

Source: Department of Industry, Trade and Commerce (Canada), 1976.

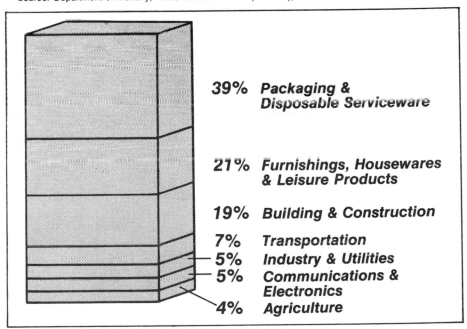

39% Packaging & Disposable Serviceware

21% Furnishings, Housewares & Leisure Products

19% Building & Construction

7% Transportation

5% Industry & Utilities

5% Communications & Electronics

4% Agriculture

cessing. Because vinyl chloride is a known carcinogen and highly toxic, the manufacture of polyvinyl chloride has been upgraded considerably by the chemical industry over the past years to ensure that vinyl chloride emissions are virtually eliminated during plastics processing and utilization.[11]

Solid Waste

The three main sources of plastic waste are the plastics industry, other industrial sources, and household and commercial garbage.

The Plastics Industry

Despite the continuing advances in processing efficiency of new equipment, most plastics processing plants generate some plastic waste. Plastic waste may result from spoiled batches, extruder start-up waste, edge trim and other trim procedures. Frequently, the plastic scrap is homogeneous (one type of plastic), uniform and uncontaminated, making on-site recycling an affordable reality for many companies. In on-site recycling, a small percentage of clean scrap is added to virgin resin and processed into product. If too large a quantity of scrap is added, the finished product may not meet design specifications because of reduced strength, increased brittleness, loss of chemical resistance and mechanical properties. Plastics vary in their sensitivity to degradation during processing.

Industrial Sources

Industrial plastic wastes are plastics that have completed a useful life. Examples of plastic waste from industry include used photographic film cartridges from the film processing industry, plastic jackets on wire and cable, upholstery and other plastic car parts from the automobile wrecking industry, industrial packaging materials and computer tapes.[10]

In some instances, plastic waste from industrial sources is relatively clean and homogeneous whereas in other instances the waste requires cleaning and separating from the contaminating fraction. Although recycling of industrial plastic waste does occur, the potential for recycling exceeds the current rate of plastics recovery from these sources. Much of the industrial plastic wastestream is still disposed in landfill sites with municipal garbage.

Household and Commercial Garbage

Household and commercial plastic waste, also known as postconsumer waste, includes packaging, disposable products, toys, fabrics and household objects that have completed their useful life. Unlike industrial wastes, domestic plastic waste is contaminated

and mixed with many types of plastics. Generally, the mixed and contaminated nature of domestic garbage makes its material recovery technically difficult and expensive. However, in several instances, the potential for recycling is great. For example, returnable packages such as plastic beverage bottles provide a large, homogeneous source of waste for which recovery may make economic sense.

At present, plastic waste from the domestic sector is landfilled or incinerated. The incineration of plastic and other combustible plastic wastes provides auxiliary heat that may be used by power generating stations and district heating systems. Plastic wastes typically make up 4% of domestic garbage.[3]

Potential Pollution from Incineration

Controversy exists regarding the effect of incineration of plastics on the environment. Although a significant portion of domestic waste contains relatively harmless plastics such as polyethylene, the incineration of other components of garbage may contribute to air pollution and ash disposal problems.

When a high percentage of certain plastics is incinerated, the burning process may yield potentially toxic gases. For example, the burning of PVC generates hydrogen chloride gas. The incineration of urethanes produces hydrogen cyanide. Imperfect burning of plastics produces soot. Specially designed incinerators have to be used when the plastic content is high to protect the equipment against corrosive damage from combustion products such as hydrogen chloride, ammonia, sulphur oxides and nitrogen oxides.

Plastics are more than simple chains of monomers. An assortment of chemical additives is used in the production of plastics to impart the final object with specific characteristics such as fire resistance, strength, durability and colour[12],[13],[14] (see Table 2). The toxicological effects and incineration end products of many of these additives are not well understood

at present. For example, the controversy continues in North America about the effect of cadmium on the environment when cadmium-stabilized or cadmium-pigmented plastics are incinerated.[12] Some research scientists report that cadmium-containing plastics emit toxic cadmium oxide fumes to the atmosphere when burned.[15] In Sweden, the use of cadmium in plastics has been eliminated. The incineration of significant amounts of PVC which contain lead and cadmium additives will yield an ash that contains lead and cadmium.[16] Incinerator ash rich in toxic metals requires special and often costly disposal.

Table 2
Chemicals and Additives in Plastics

Additive	Purpose	Some compounds in use
Flame Retardants	Flame retardants are added to plastics to yield products that will ignite and burn with greater difficulty than untreated plastics. Current research efforts include minimizing the toxic smoke and gas associated with the burning of plastics, particularly as it relates to unexpected fires in buildings.	• Aluminum trihydrate (ATH) • Organic phosphates • Antimony oxides • Organic halogen compounds • Boron compounds
Heat Stabilizers	Heat stabilizers are used to ensure product durability. Heat stabilizers are important additions to heat-sensitive polymers that undergo relatively high temperatures to soften them during fabricating operations.	• Liquid organotin compounds and tin mercaptides • Barium/cadmium concentrates • Barium/zinc additives
Lubricants	The principle function of lubricants is to decrease the viscosity of the resin melt and to control resin-to-melt friction during plastics processing. These additives also lower the die swell of extrudates and promote surface gloss.	• Metallic stearates • Waxes, fatty acids and mineral oil • Silicones • Molybdenum salts • Polyfluorocarbons
Plasticizers	Plasticizers are added to polymers such as PVC to make them soft and flexible. Plasticizers are also used to improve melt processibility and toughness of rigid plastics such as cellulose esters and ethers, and in a variety of specialized applications.	• Phthalates • Adipates • Phosphates • Epoxy • Polyesters
Antioxidants	Antioxidant additives are required in the stabilization of ABS, polypropylene, polyethylene and polystyrene plastics. These additives may be free radical scavengers (primary oxidants) or peroxide decomposers (secondary antioxidants).	• Primary antioxidants such as butylated hydroxytoluene (BHT) • Secondary antioxidants such as dilauryl thiodipropionate and tris phosphite • Phosphite/phenolic blends

Additive	Purpose	Some Compounds in Use
Ultraviolet Stabilizers	UV (ultraviolet) stabilizers function to prevent degradation of plastics by UV radiation such as occurs in sunlight. Many organic UV stabilizers tend to migrate to the polymer surface.	• Hindered amine stabilizers • Zinc oxide and nickel complexes • Benzophenones and benzotriazoles • Carbon black • Phosphite co-stabilizers
Blowing Agents	Blowing agents are used in the production of cellular plastics such as foamed insulation, and plastic film, sheet and pipe obtained by extrusion.	• Fluorocarbons • Chemical blowing agents (CBA) such as azodicarbonamide and sulfone hydrazide • High temperature blowing agents (HTBA)
Colorants	Colour is added to achieve the desired colour of the final product. Colour may be compounded into the resin and sold as such. In other instances, the end-user blends the appropriate amount of dry colour powder with resin and produces the final colourpart. Nowadays, colour is frequently added as pellet concentrates or direct-feed liquids to minimize occupational exposure to colorants .	• Titanium dioxide • Carbon black • Inorganic colorants such as iron oxides, cadmium, chromium, lead, nickel and molybdate • Organic colorants such as as phthalocyanines, nigrosines and others
Fillers and Reinforcements	Fillers are added to plastics to reduce the quantity of high-cost plastics required in the final product. Reinforcing fillers such as fibreglass and graphite give additional strength to the plastic product.	• Non-reinforcing fillers include calcium carbonate, silicas, clay, talc, carbon black and fly ash • Reinforcing fillers include fibreglass, graphite and cellulose
Organic Peroxides	Organic peroxides are used as curing and cross-linking agents for polymers such as unsaturated polyesters and polyolefins. Their purpose is to initiate cross-linking, and in doing so decompose. These peroxides are not present as such in the finished product unless in minor residual amounts.	• Benzoyl peroxides • Methyl ethyl ketone peroxides • Peresters and dialkyl • Peroxides

Additive	Purpose	Some Compounds in Use
Impact Modifiers	Impact modifiers may be added to plastics to enable plastic products to withstand stronger impacts and still remain intact. For example, rubbery polymers are added to PVC and other thermoplastics to produce products with improved impact resistance.	• Styrene-butadiene polymers • Chlorinated polyethylenes • Ethylene vinyl acetate copolymers • Calcium carbonate
Antistatic Agents	The use of antistatic agents in plastics is of growing concern to electronics, computer and aerospace applications where electrostatic damage can result in costly defects. The increasing miniaturization of electronics components, for example makes them even more susceptible to static electric charges.	• Internal antistats • Ethoxylated alkylamines • Metal flakes such as aluminum • Surface modifiers including silanes and titanates

Sources: References 12, 13 and 14.

POLLUTION PREVENTION OPPORTUNITIES

1.
Air Pollution: Suppression of Fugitive Emissions

Since plastics processors rely on chemical manufacturers for their raw materials, they sometimes inherit problems from the chemical industry over which they have little control. Although the chemical manufacturer may have the scientific resources and capital to control pollution through closed-loop processing during the manufacture of materials, the sale and transfer of potentially hazardous materials to a smaller industry down the line may present environmental problems beyond the control of the small end-user.

Whereas a larger company might afford sophisticated ventilation systems and pollution abatement equipment to minimize air pollution from volatile manufacturing processes, a small operator would be hard-pressed to control air pollution on-site. Stringent pollution regulations for the workplace and environment may have the unwanted effect of forcing the smaller operator out of the market.

Serious air pollution problems are restricted to a relatively small portion of the plastics processing industry. This fact should not detract from the seriousness of the air pollution problem in those small plants where it does occur. The pollution prevention examples that follow show how styrene emissions can be minimized in a cost-effective way during the manufacture of polyester products.

■ Some chemical manufacturers are responding to the plight of the end-user by making special chemical formulations that promise to minimize pollution problems down the road. The Ashland Chemical Company (Dublin, Ohio) is one such company. Ashland produces a line of styrene-suppressed resins which can assist a plastics processor to reduce styrene emission during the production of polyester products such as bathtubs and boat hulls.

Based on the principle that any liquid evaporates only at the surface, the suppressed resin system is chemically designed to keep styrene below the surface of the polyester while both are still in the liquid state. Styrene losses can be reduced by 70% compared to non-suppressed systems.

Contact molding is still the most widely used application technique for unsaturated polyester resins which contain styrene because of its adaptability in the production of large plastic components.[17] The need for an open mold, coupled with the high ratio of surface area to mass, results in an unavoidable release of styrene monomer to the atmosphere.

According to Michael Duffy, corrosion chemist for Ashland,

in-plant styrene levels can be reduced through efficient exhaust systems to meet worker exposure levels, however this would only shift an indoor pollution problem to the outside.[18]

The current threshhold limit for styrene in the workplace is 100 ppm per 8-hour day, however the United States Occupational Health and Safety Administration is talking of reducing this to 50 ppm. Given restrictions on styrene emissions into the environment, Duffy is doubtful that many of the smaller and older plants can afford to keep up in the costly struggle to abate styrene emissions using conventional means.[18]

The Ashland line of supressed resins ensures reduced styrene loss to the internal plant atmosphere and to the surrounding environment. Although suppressed polyester resins are somewhat more expensive than unsuppressed ones per unit volume, their use produces definite cost savings because more of the styrene becomes part of the finished product instead of being volatilized.[17]

According to Duffy, without suppressant about 1900 pounds of styrene are lost per 40,000-pound tank wagon, while with it only 500 pounds of styrene are lost.[17] This enables the plastics processor to manufacture more parts per load of resin, thereby reducing total materials costs.

■ Material substitution with a less polluting formulation is one way for the small operator to reduce styrene emissions. Another way is to modify the resin application technique.

A polyester applicator typically uses a spray gun to deposit the polyester resin in a layer against a mold. The operation resembles spray painting and occurs in a ventilated spray booth. By reducing frontal velocities for spray booth and application areas, a polyester spray operation can reduce styrene emissions while saving energy and money.

Under normal operating conditions, a considerable amount of heat used to cure the resin and heat the plant goes straight out the exhaust stack. When exhaust booths are operated at 100 feet per

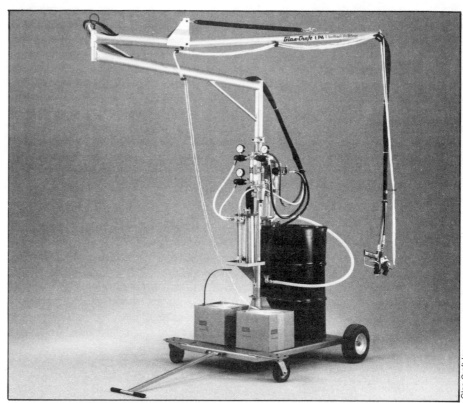

This Low-Pressure-Airless fibreglass spray equipment by Glas-Craft is designed to minimize overspray and volatile organic emissions over more conventional spray-up systems.

minute frontal velocity, the energy needed to heat outdoor air from 20 to 65°F for a small (4 foot square) spray booth for an 8-hour day amounts to about 10 gallons of fuel oil.[19]

The consumption of polyester resins for spray gun applications was estimated to be 330 million pounds in the United States in 1976. About half of this was styrene, and about 4% of this styrene evaporated during application, a loss of 6.5 million pounds.

The styrene monomer is estimated to leave the ventilation system at an average concentration of 700 ppm. At this rate, 37 billion cubic feet per year of make-up air is going through the industry's heaters and out the exhaust fans.[19]

If exhaust velocities can be safely reduced to 25 feet per minute, energy losses would be reduced by 75%. This represents a potential savings of 13.5 million gallons of fuel oil yearly at a 1980 value of $13.5 million.[19]

By reducing exhaust velocities from 100 to 25 feet per minute, the reduction in styrene loss to the environment is estimated to save the industry an additional $1.6

million in materials cost.[19]

■ Glas-Craft, a division of Ransburg Corporation (Indianapolis, Indiana) recently started marketing a new spray gun that permits plastics resins to be atomized at pressures as low as 250 psi, thereby substantially reducing overspray and styrene emissions. The system, known as LPA (low-pressure atomization) is also available in a retrofit kit to convert most airless and air-atomized systems. Resin overspray is reduced by 25% over conventional spray guns.[20]

2.
Plastics Recycling

The majority of plastics in use in Canada can be recycled. Plastic processors are in the best position to recycle plastics because they are assured of relatively clean, homogeneous and continuous sources of scrap.

Although the plastics processing industry, and to some degree other industrial sectors, contributes to the recycling of much plastic scrap, the domestic scrap market in Canada remains virtually untouched as a source of re-usable plastic.

The amount of scrap generated by a plastics processor can be surprisingly large. A 400-ton injection machine, for example, having a 24-ounce shot capacity and running two cycles a minute can produce about half a pound of reclaimable scrap each minute, assuming sprues and runners account for about 15% of the shot weight. Adding a reject weight of 5% to the sprue and runner weight, one 400-ton machine can produce up to 600 pounds of scrap in a 15-hour day. At an average price of 45¢ per pound of resin, that means $270 per day worth of scrap resin, or $80,000 to $90,000 worth of scrap are generated per year from just one machine. Investing $10,000 to $30,000 in a granulator means that a company can pay off equipment costs in a few months by recycling about 98% of the plastic scrap.[21]

While the practice of discarding plastic wastes in an landfill site can be viewed as a relatively "safe" disposal option, it is a waste of both material and energy resources. Recycling plastics into fabricated products saves some 85 to 95% of the energy of a typical plastic package. This includes the energy of the petroleum feedstocks used to manufacture the resin[1] (see Table 3). Furthermore, by recycling plastics, this reduces the quantity of resins that needs to be produced by the chemical industry, and hence reduces the total quantity of pollution produced compared with pollution generated when manufacturing virgin plastic from petrochemicals.

While it is true that simply burning plastic wastes as fuel saves energy, recycling these wastes into a fabricated product will frequently double the energy savings. For example, 1000 pounds of high-density polyethylene has a fuel value of 20 million Btu, but recycling 1000 pounds of polyethylene wastes

Table 3
Energy Savings in Recyling Various Plastics

End Product	Energy Content (%)	
	Resin	Fabrication
PVC 1/2 gal. container	85	15
HDPE 1 gal. container	90	10
LDPE 1 gal. produce bag	94	6
Polystyrene meat tray	83	17

Source: J. Milgrom. "Recycling Plastics: Current Status". *Conservation and Recycling* Volume 3, 1980.

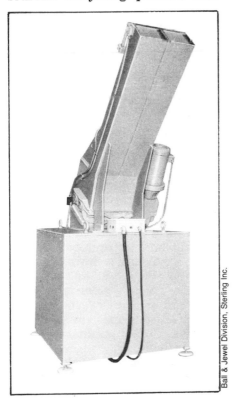

Ball & Jewel Division, Sterling Inc.

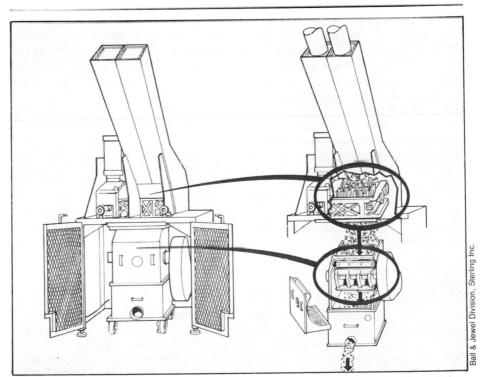

Ball & Jewel Division, Sterling Inc.

As the scrap pipe is shredded (primary size reduction), the pieces fall directly into the granulator below for final size reduction.

◄——— The Ball and Jewel Shred-Buster™ is an energy efficient, two-stage granulator suitable for recovery of tough plastics such as extruded PVC or ABS pipe.

into a fabricated product will save as much as 39 million Btu. This represents an 88% saving in energy consumption.[1]

Recycling by Plastics Processors and Reprocessors

Some raw material suppliers have an in-house capability to recycle off-grade or reject material which they produce.

Within the processing segment of the plastics industry, many of the larger companies have in-house facilities for reclaiming and recycling their scrap, trim, or reject plastics. Plastics recycling by a plastics processor usually involves the blending of in-house scrap back into the processing cycle. As much as 30% of the finished saleable product has been through processing at least twice.[10]

If an in-house recycling facility does not exist, clean homogeneous scrap is sold to a well-established secondary materials industry which reprocesses this material back into a form usable by the processing segment of industry.[10] In such cases, the recycled scrap is made into slightly lower-grade plastic, usually for uses other than its original use. It pays even the smaller plastics processor to carefully evaluate the economics of his particular situation. Contrary to current assumptions, a small processor may discover that the cost of hauling waste plastic for outside recovery is far in excess of the cost of purchasing in-house reclaiming equipment.

An assortment of plastic recycling equipment is currently available to both in-house recyclers and the secondary plastics recycling industry. According to some suppliers of reclamation equipment, industrial recycling of plastics came to the forefront with the 1974 oil crisis, a time of resin shortages and price hikes. As chemical companies provided more materials in the post-crisis years, the push for high reclamation ceased.[22]

Plastics recycling or reprocessing involves operations which transform the scraps into reusable pelletized or granular form.

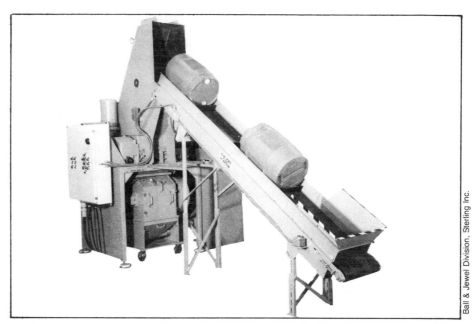

Bulky scrap such as plastic drums are conveyor-fed to the upper shredding chamber. After primary size reduction, the scrap is reduced to granule form in the lower grinding chamber.

Ball & Jewel Division, Sterling Inc.

A chopper or guillotine may be used to reduce large chunks into small pieces that can be fed into a granulating machine. The granulated scrap is then blended with other additives, or fed directly to an extruder where it is pelletized or diced. Film scrap is often made into confetti and similarly fed directly into an extruder. Manufacturers of chopping and grinding equipment are continuously trying to improve the energy efficiency of plastics processing equipment. Energy efficient machinery promises to shave hundreds of dollars off equipment operating costs.

The professional reclaimer is prone to encounter contaminated and mixed wastes. Screens and magnets are used to remove contaminants such as wood, paper, garbage, dirt and metal. Generally, the professional reclaimer processes one type of plastic at a time to ensure a relatively homogeneous product. However, it is not uncommon to accept relatively small lots of coloured scrap from various sources. Usually, small lots of scrap are mixed in a blender before being extruded and pelletized. If a variety of coloured wastes are processed together, carbon black may be added to the blend and sold as a secondary resin.

Some professional plastic re-

claimers accept scrap from a processor and return it to the original user for a fee in a granulated or pelletized form ready for normal processing.

In the past, the principle difficulty in recycling plastics was that they are generally not compatible with each other.[3] Using different plastic types can result in a product that appears striated. Perhaps more serious is that the physical properties of the product also suffer. Even so, despite reduced strength and durability, a large potential market exists for lower grade recycled products. Some uses include flower pots, coat hangers, door mats and fences.

Some plastic types withstand reprocessing and limited mixing better than other plastics. A volume of 15% polypropylene can be mixed with polyethylenes without causing serious problems. Similarly, a mixture containing up to 15% polyethylenes and the remainder polypropylene is a usable combination. Polystyrene, on the other hand, tends to be very sensitive to contamination with other polymers.[3]

Recent advances in plastics recycling technology are expanding the possibilities for recycling mixed plastics. Although many of the innovations are still in the prototype stage, some are com-

Defective golf ball cores are one of numerous items recycled by Custom Cryogenics.

mercially available and in use in other countries. The examples that follow are of homogeneous plastic scrap recycling.

■ When Ontario dairies converted to metric packaging in 1980, they had more than complex arithmetic to contend with. Replacing the old-fashioned quart milk container with the litre model meant more than changing the packaging. It has meant that the durable, polyethylene milk crate had to undergo a size reduction as well.

Instead of throwing out a sizeable quantity of obsolete plastic crates, Custom Cryogenics (Toronto, Ontario) recovered plastic milk crates and reprocessed them into metric-sized crates to meet the needs of the now metric milk packaging.[5]

■ Aclo Compounders Inc. (Cambridge, Ontario) recycle homogeneous thermoplastic scrap from a variety of industrial sources. Types of wastes reclaimed include milk crates, battery case scrap, bottle scrap and polypropylene textile scrap. According to Aclo Compounders, a knowledge of resin additives and compatibility are important to the plastics reclaimer. Certain problems such as brittleness can be corrected during compounding through the use of resin additives.[23]

■ Advance Waste Recycling (Toronto, Ontario) is a plastics recycling company that currently handles contaminated plastic wastes from a variety of industries. According to Paul Lawson, company manager, his company

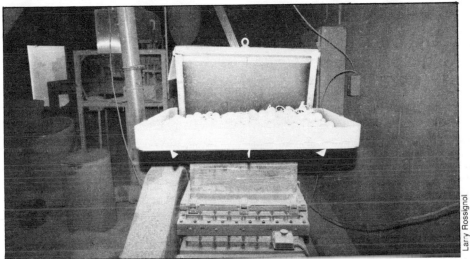

Golf balls undergo initial size reduction to pellets in a granulator.

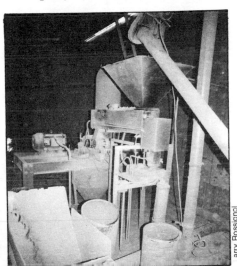

The plastic pellets are fed into a hammermill in which the plastic is cooled by liquid nitrogen.

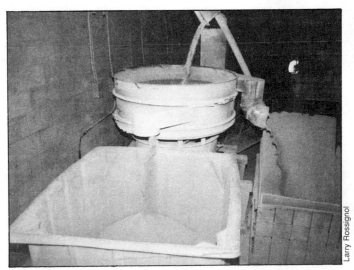

The crushed plastic is screened to separate debris and coarse plastic from the finely granulated material.

The coarse plastic material is fed back into the hammermill for further grinding.

would be interested in obtaining household waste plastic collected by citizens' conservation groups.[24] Although the segregated collection of glass, cans and newspapers does occur in some areas, household plastic wastes are not collected in Canada.

■ Recent technological innovation has resulted in the ability of the plastics processor and reclaimer to recycle thermoset plastic scrap. Hull Corporation (Hatboro, Pennsylvania) is one equipment manufacturer that provides the necessary equipment to recycle thermoset scrap such as phenolic plastics.

The plastic scrap passes through a series of hammer mills and granulators which reduce the scrap to a fine granulation. A set of screens ensures that the regrind is of the proper size. The regrind is blended precisely with a pre-selected ratio of virgin resin. Generally, 10 to 15% recycled resin can be added to the virgin phenolic resin without having detrimental effects on the physical properties of the molded product. However, in some heat resistant grades of phenolic resins, the physical properties of the final product may be impaired if the recycled resin content exceeds 5%.[25]

The recycling machine is equipped with a dust collector to trap dust generated during grinding. Included also is a gas purifier similar to a catalytic converter used on cars. This purifier operates at about 700°F to eliminate the gases produced during the high–temperature grinding action.[25]

Although the capital cost of the recycling machinery may be significant, molding shops using high volumes of thermoset resins save money through reduced resin costs and waste disposal charges.

■ Rather than simply accepting a high percentage of scrap from their machinery, today's sophisticated processors first do everything they can to minimize the generation of scrap. Mold-Masters Ltd. (Georgetown, Ontario) have designed a melt conveying system to fill the demand for better and

The Hull Recycler provides the thermoset industry with a fully automatic method of re-using all types of thermosetting resin scrap such as rejected parts, runners and sprues.

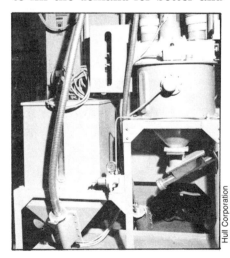

Scrap is pulverized, atomized and mixed with virgin material in predetermined proportions, ranging from 5 to 40% regrind. The pulverizing unit is equipped with dust collector, sound arrestor, gas purifier and safety nitrogen gas blower.

more efficient injection molding of thermoplastics. By using a melt conveying system, the plastics molder can minimize cycle time, reduce energy consumption, abolish the production of sprues and runners, lower reject rates and thereby drastically reduce the amount of plastic scrap generated.[26]

■ A.C. Hamilton Ltd. (Toronto, Ontario) is one of Canada's largest suppliers of plastic reclamation equipment, selling granulators, flash gatherers, grinders, conveying systems and compounding extruders and pelletizers.[22]

■ One new machine helping to spur interest in regrinding is an industrial shredder by Zeus Inc. (Italy) that replaces expensive granulators in the 75 to 150 horsepower range. The new shredder uses 10 horsepower, and cuts plastic of any size into small chunks which are then fed into a 30 horsepower granulator. The machine operates at a third of the cost of large grinders, making it a more feasible investment for smaller shops.[22]

Plastics processing equipment manufacturers are now marketing extruders with a larger-diameter conical intake than normal size extruders. This eliminates the grinding process, as processors can densify and extrude all in one operation.[22] Most equipment manufacturers still recommend a certain degree of size reduction in film scrap to maximize extruder efficiency.

■ Rapid Granulator Inc. (Rockford, Illinois) has developed a new granulator that reportedly enables processors to reclaim any kind of scrap — tough bulky parts, large purgings, large diameter pipe, bottles, fibres and film — with relatively low power consumption.[27]

■ When Sweetheart Plastics (Conyers, Georgia) sought to cut energy consumption at its thermoformed packaging plant, the company was hoping for a 10% energy savings. By switching to a more efficient, two-stage granulator design, horsepower requirements for scrap regrinding were slashed by 80%, and yielded an astonishing power cost saving of $46,000 per year.[28]

■ The Automated Scrap Recycle System (ASR) is a patented system by Process Control Corporation (Atlanta, Georgia). This equipment functions to recycle film and sheet scrap directly to the extruder, thus increasing production efficiency and eliminating the expense of repelletizing.

According to the manufacturer, the system will handle very high scrap percentages and still produce high quality film.[29] Cost savings have been estimated for an operation that produces 600 pounds of clear sheeting each hour. Assume that virgin plastic which is used to make high quality film costs 57¢ per pound. Assume also that 10% of the plastic used becomes plastic scrap and that 90% becomes product. Process Control Corporation claim that a plastics processor which invests in the on-site recycling equipment will save $68,000 per year compared to what it makes by repelletizing scrap at a cost of 5¢ per pound and selling it as a downgraded product worth 45¢ per pound.

■ The Plastcompactor (available through Canadian Plastics and Rubber Machinery Ltd., Mississauga, Ontario) is a scrap recovery unit designed to recover fibre (such as polyester and nylon), film (such as polyethylene and polypropylene), foam (such as expanded polystyrene), and sheet plastic.[30]

An ASR™ Refeed Machine is shown mounted on a blown film extruder. Ground edge trim and roll scrap is compacted and combined with virgin pellets for extrusion.

Process Control Corporation

Plastic scrap is cut into small pieces and moved to a compaction chamber. Here, the material moves through two discs. One disc is stationary, the other is rotating, thereby generating heat through friction. This action brings the material to a fluxing point — not melted as it would be if it were an extruder. From here, the material is cut at a second granulator, resulting in a free-flowing high-density granulate ready for re-use.[30] Savings result over conventional systems because no extra heating is required since the compaction is achieved through frictional heat.

■ The use of chrome-plated plastic in the automobile and appliance industries has plastic processors confronting a new recycling chal-

lenge — how to recycle a metal-plastic hybrid.

The Ford Motor Company currently produces 14 million pounds per year of chrome-plated plastic parts in the manufacture of exterior automotive grills for cars and trucks. In the process, 1.2 million pounds per year of unusable chrome-plated materials have been scrapped at considerable cost to the company.[31] Ford's Saline (Michigan) plastics plant has since installed a recovery system to reclaim its chrome-plated ABS plastic scrap. Developed in co-operation with the Process Control Corp. (Atlanta, Georgia), Ford has applied for a patent on the process and will make the system available for licensing.[31]

The recovery system involves

feeding defective automotive grills into a grinder (see Figure 4). The grinder contains a pre-crusher which breaks up the parts into smaller pieces and feeds them into the grinder which subsequently reduces the scrap to half-inch pieces. A magnetic drum separator removes the larger pieces of metal that have been split off during grinding. The remaining metal and scrap goes through a cryogenic feeder. Liquid nitrogen cools the scrap to almost freezing, creating stresses which cause additional metal to splinter off.

The scrap moves to an impact mill which reduces the scrap to a coarse powder. The powder passes through another magnetic drum separator designed to remove the

Figure 4
Chrome-Plated Plastic Recycling Operation

Chrome-plated plastic scrap is broken into increasingly smaller pieces. A magnet is used to remove metal from the plastic fraction. When the grinding and magnetic separation processes are completed, the plastic powder is 99% free of metal and can be re-used in the injection moulding operation.

Source: "Now You Can Reclaim Chrome-Plated Scrap," *Plastics Technology*, September 1979.

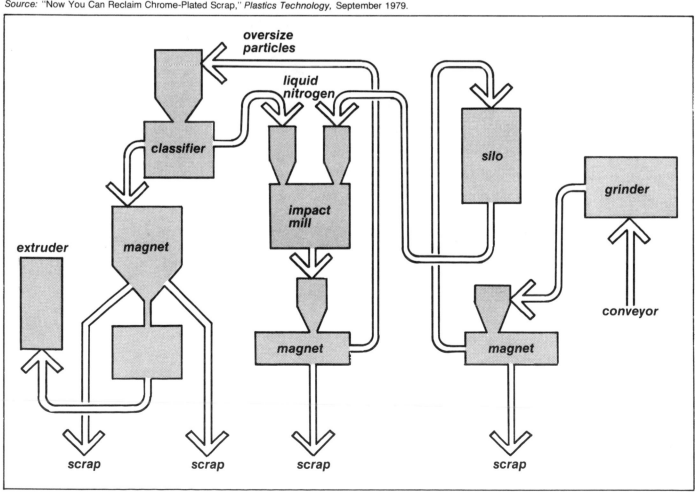

remaining metal from the powder. The separated ABS powder is 99% free of metal and used as regrind in the plant's injection molding operations. The metal scrap is sold to an outside reclaimer.

Because of the potential problem from the dust and fine powders inside the plant, the whole reclaim system is designed as a closed system. According to Ford, the operating costs are quite low. Operating costs include an operator's salary, $5000 per year in energy costs and the cost of liquid nitrogen.[31]

Recycling Contaminated Plastic Scrap and Resin

Industrial users of plastic are sometimes confronted with the problem of plastics that have become contaminated with oil and other liquids. Usually such plastics suffer the unwelcome fate of disposal at a landfill site, bearing the owner not only the cost of lost materials but also disposal costs.
■ B&K Recycling Industries (Cranford, New Jersey) feel they offer a unique service to industry in that they accept contaminated plastic scrap, clean it, shred it and return it to the owner for a fee.

It is a business that B&K got into two years ago, more or less by accident. According to Gerry Blumenfeld, president and co-owner, his company used to be a wholesale dry cleaner. When a large company came along with the unusual request of asking B&K to clean a big lot of contaminated plastic, B&K tackled the problem and have been in the business ever since.[32]

The plastic cleaning process resembles a dry cleaning cycle or laundry cycle. Some plastics are cleaned using organic solvents, however most plastics are washed in water at a temperature of 180°F. B&K have the equipment to grind plastic, but they also accept ground plastic for cleaning.

Shell Kaylie, vice president and co-owner, says B&K can make scrap usable at a cost often below the market price of virgin material. Once reclaimed, the plastic may be ground for use in powder coatings, or may be remelted for casting or molding materials. The firm's 1980 fees ranged from 75¢ a pound for 25,000 pound lots to 45¢ a pound for 250,000 pound lots.[33]

At present, the economics favour the cleaning and recycling of contaminated scrap whose going commodity price is significantly higher than the cost of recovery. This rules out cheap plastics such as polyethylene. As resin prices continue to escalate, it may become feasible to recycle the cheaper range of contaminated plastics.

According to Blumenfeld, teflon at $30 per pound is one of the most expensive resins in use. So expensive that industry finds it in their economic interest to hire B&K to remove machine oil from teflon turnings, flakes and chips so as to permit the recycling of teflon wastes.[33]

Another big market in plastics recycling is the recovery of nylon tire cord, which is also very costly. Depending on the value of the plastic, B&K receive shipments of waste plastic from all over the country. According to Kaylie, his company fills a need and a service. By putting contaminated resins back in circulation, one pound of oil used to manufacture virgin materials is saved for every 2 to 3 pounds of resin recycled.

Recycling Mixed Plastic

Most polymers are incompatible and do not adhere well to each other. It is this property that has plagued past efforts to recycle mixed plastic wastes. Generally, as more plastics contaminate the mixture, the resulting recycled product has inferior physical properties compared with relatively pure plastics. Nevertheless, technological innovations are im-

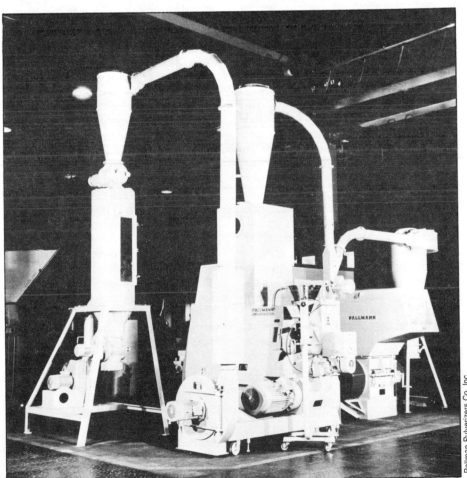

The Pallman Plast-Agglomerator continuously produces free-flowing plastic granules for re-use from agglomerated thermoplastic films, fibres and foam waste. Suitable plastic wastes include polyethylene, polypropylene, polystyrene, PVC, polyamide, polyester and ABS materials.

proving the recycled product when a mixed stock is used.

■ Scientists at the Polytechnic Institute of New York have developed a simple laboratory method using light analysis to determine when different plastics are mixing at the molecular level. The technique involves marking the two different polymers in the mixture with light-sensitive chemicals. Adsorption by one polymer will lead to emission of a colour characteristic of the other, indicating that molecular mixing has occurred. The technique can indicate how much the polymer chains are entangled, and hence how high the quality is of the recycled product.[34]

■ Mitsubishi Petrochemical (Japan) has developed a special molding machine, known as the Reverzer, that recycles mixed thermoplastic plastic wastes containing up to 20% non-plastic materials such as paper waste. Incoming wastes include LDPE film, PVC bottles, polystyrene egg boxes, plastic beakers and other domestic waste.

In the Reverzer process, the plastics are ground, blended and fed to a melter cone where the compressed material is subjected to friction and sheer stresses between the rotating cone and the outside wall. The molten material is passed to an injection molder where the product is formed. Adding sand, paper or glass fibre improves the stiffness. Typical products made by this method include fence stakes, posts, irrigation drain pipe, cable reels, park benches and road drains.[6] A Mexican company recently purchased a Reverzer to make cable drums.

■ In Britain, the quantity of post-consumer waste far exceeds the amount of mixed and contaminated waste plastics generated during manufacture. Post-consumer waste plastics in that country average 1.8 billion pounds annually, resulting in an active interest in the recycling of these wastes.

In the early seventies, Regal Packaging Ltd. (Britain) developed a process for producing plastic sheets and wall boards up to 20 mm thick from waste plastics. The mixture of waste plastics, which contains primarily polyolefins, is granulated, deposited on to a moving belt and fused in an oven. The fused sheet can be compression-molded into a variety of products. A limited amount of contaminants such as paper, metal, glass and sand can be incorporated into the plastic sheet.[35]

■ Plastic Recycling Ltd. (Worcester, Britain) operates a continuous process based on fused sheet technology. The product is a 4-foot by 8-foot mixed plastic board with a surface coating of polyethylene, usually in black, which is used in pig pens, cow sheds and chicken houses.[35]

■ In France, plastic packaging wastes accounted for 1.2 billion pounds of the country's garbage in 1976. The PVC mineral-water bottle alone contributed 175 million pounds of waste plastic. Since then, France has launched several programmes to recycle waste PVC bottles. Waste plastic is retrieved through at-source collection systems and by mechanical separation procedures from municipal garbage. The recovered bottles are transferred to reprocessing firms which clean the wastes and produce a secondary resin used to manufacture sewer pipe, drainage pipe and cable sheathing.[35]

■ In the United States, General Motors, Ford and Chrysler use a mixture of waste plastic materials for trunk mats. The mats are made by shredding fabric, vinyl and urethane cushion foam scraps, and binding this mixture with PVC resin.[1]

■ In Germany, concrete and plastic waste mixed to provide the base material for highway foundations was observed to increase the life of the roadway.[1]

Recycling of Industrial and Domestic Waste Plastic

Although the plastics industry recycles most of the relatively homogeneous scrap generated in the manufacturing process, large volumes of the more heterogeneous waste generated by industry as a whole remain as a potential recycling resource. Examples of industrial wastestreams for which recycling has been demonstrated to be economically and technically feasible include PVC-coated upholstery scrap, PVC and polyethylene wire insulation scrap, and film packaging scrap. These industrial plastic wastes are frequently generated in large enough quantities to justify collection and recycling. Except for a few isolated examples, much of these plastic wastes still find their way to a landfill site rather than to a professional reclaimer.

Almost no materials recovery of plastics from mixed household waste occurs in Canada at present. Many factors impede the recycling of post-consumer waste. Obstacles to plastics recovery include:

- The unfavourable economics of collecting and transporting relatively small amounts of plastic wastes from many sources is a barrier in recycling household plastic waste. Although at-source separation of plastic waste may make the greatest economic sense, no such programme has been initiated because the markets for heterogeneous plastic waste are scarce.

- Segregation of waste plastics by resin type is difficult since the identification of plastics is difficult. There are over 700 different grades of polyethylene alone.[3]

- High purity specifications and virgin plastic requirements make it difficult for Canadian reprocessors to find a local market for recycled plastics. Contaminated plastic wastes to be shipped to European and American markets due to a scarcity of lucrative Canadian markets.

- Although the technology for recycling mixed wastes is advancing in other countries, in many instances these developments are not yet commercially available or in use in Canada.

Some collection of homogeneous household plastic wastes such as plastic beverage bottles does occur in Canada. Alberta, for example, collects and sells its PET (polyethylene terephthalate) beverage bottles to an American recycler for material re-use. To date, however, materials recycling of household plastic remains virtually untapped in Canada.

Wire and Cable Scrap Recycling

The insulating plastic casing on wire typically contains a mixture of PVC and polyethylene polymers. Companies that recycle plastic wire scraps use processes that separate the mixture into relatively pure polyethylene and PVC compounds.

■ Produits Jalisson (Chambly, Quebec) is a small plastics recycler which has recently expanded its operations to recycle waste wire-jacketing resins from Northern Telecom. Northern Telecom strips the copper from the wire fragments and sends it to a refinery for purification.

According to Jacques Giguer of Produits Jalisson, the ground plastic jackets received from Northern Telecom contain 55 to 60% polyethylene and the rest is PVC. The plastic scrap also contains residual copper and aluminum. Because most customers require pure plastics, the two polymers are segregated and sold as a good-grade non-virgin material suitable for injection molding and extrusion.

According to Giguer, many plastics processors can save money by buying reclaimed plastic for low grade uses. For example, the going rate for polypropylene is about 55¢ per pound for virgin material. Produits Jalisson can sell reprocessed polypropylene at 35¢ per pound.[36]

Canadian plastics recyclers rely heavily on export sales to American and European customers because domestic specifications for many plastic products require virgin material.[37,38] Recycled plastics sold domestically tend to be processed into low-grade plastic products such as plastic clothes hangers.[36]

■ Chem-Ecol (Cleveland, Ohio) reprocesses segregated PVC insulation wastes on a toll basis. The reclaimed product is used primarily for low-voltage automotive wiring.[1]

■ Ore Corporation (Fort Wayne, Indiana) recovers polyethylene

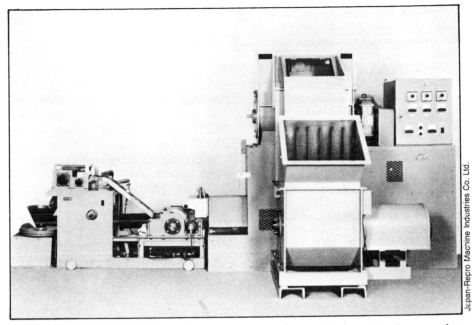

The FS-type plastics recycling machine by Japan-Repro is capable of recovering and pelletizing bulky wastes, foam polystyrene, polyethylene wastes, blow-moulded bottles and crushed film scraps.

Japan-Repro Machine Industries Co. Ltd.

from wire scrap. The reclaimed polyethylene is compounded with carbon black and sold to molders and extruders which fabricate automotive parts, irrigation pipe and plant pots.[1]

■ Bell Labs, Western Electric and the Nassau Recycle Corporation have developed new recycling technology to reclaim PVC despite the diverse and large amounts of contaminating materials in the scrap. The cost of reclaimed PVC (26¢ per pound) is estimated at two-thirds less than virgin plastic.[39]

The recycled PVC is used as sheathing to cover new buried telephone cables and central office cable. Because of the addition of stabilizers, plasticizers, fire retardants and lubricants, the recycled PVC is fire retardant, bends at sub-freezing temperatures, resists tears, and is expected to keep its flexibility for at least 40 years.[39]

Polypropylene Recycling

■ Although industrial recycling of polypropylene is not new, the addition of fly ash is. General Motors wants to put to good use the 200 thousand tons of fly ash that it generates each year in coal-fired power houses. By mixing fly ash into polypropylene in

the manufacture of radiator fan shrouds and air conditioning cases, the fly ash additive not only colours the plastic black as desired, but also enhances the plastic's mechanical properties.[40]

Polystyrene Recycling

■ The Free-Flow Packaging Corporation (Redwood City, California) processes industrial polystyrene scrap into spaghetti-like dunnage. This company has a plant in Europe that similarly uses recycled polystyrene.[1]

■ In Japan, where government regulations forbid the introduction of plastic beverage containers unless at least 90% of the containers can be recycled, the impetus to recycle is strong. The common practice of delivering yogurt in polystyrene containers to the home generates a large source of waste plastic. These containers are recycled into a number of non-food products.[1]

■ Japan Repro (Tokyo, Japan) has introduced commercially available equipment that can convert worthless expandable polystyrene scrap into pellets with a resale value of 20¢ per pound. The equipment manufacturer is represented in the United States by Uniglobe Kisco (White Plains,

New York). Available in various sizes, the systems employ one to three extruders to continuously densify, strand and pelletize from 150 to 1300 pounds of expandable polystyrene scrap per hour. The recycled polystyrene pellets retain good gloss and melt flow, though tensile properties suffer slightly.[41]

PET Recycling

PET (polyethylene terephthalate) is rapidly emerging as another significant source of plastic waste in North America.

Since its introduction as a 2-litre bottle, the PET bottle proved to be the fastest selling new container in the history of the American soft drink industry, accounting now for 16% of the soft drink container market. By 1979, bottle sales numbered close to 2 billion, however, less than 20% of the bottles sold were recovered and recycled.[42]

Although the PET bottle is in use in eight of Canada's ten provinces, there are no plants in Canada that recycle PET. Ontario and Saskatchewan have refused to accept the PET bottle for environmental reasons.

Alberta operates a deposit system in which a customer receives a 30¢ refund for bringing in a used PET bottle. Alberta then sells its PET bottles to a PET recycler in South Carolina.[42]

PET can be re-used directly by blending it with a virgin stream and reforming, or by grinding it into small pieces for use as a filler material. Both of these methods are economically viable operations currently in use in Europe and the United States.

A third technology in PET recycling involves the reduction of the monomer components in PET, and the subsequent re-use of these chemical feedstocks. At present there are no commercial facilities involved in this type of chemical reduction and recycling in North America, although pilot projects do exist.

Monomer regeneration by polymer decomposition can be expected to increase in the future as the economics become more attractive. Once monomers have been regenerated, processing

them into new plastics is equivalent to using virgin materials.[43] Applying chemical recovery technologies to plastics recycling may substantially enhance re-use applications of waste plastics.

■ Wellman Industries (Johnsonville, South Carolina) is one plastics recycler which re-uses waste PET. The company shreds the baled waste PET plastic, separates the plastic from the paper labels and metal closures and regenerates the washed material, mixed with polyester textile waste, into fibre products such as industrial filter medium.[44] Consumer products using the regenerated fibre include life jackets, pillows, sleeping bags, puffed jackets and vests.[42]

Several difficulties face PET bottle recyclers. Because PET bottles come in green or clear, there is a need to separate the two bottle types if the recycler wants to get an optimum price for the reclaimed product. Another problem in some countries but not in Canada concerns the foreign materials in PET waste including the metal ring from the cap closure and the non-PET plastic base. The high density polyethylene base must be removed from the rest of the bottle, adding energy and labour costs to the recovery process.

A third problem confronting the PET recycler is obtaining an adequate supply of plastic waste. In the absence of rigorous bottle collecting measures, such as mandatory deposit systems, the PET bottle has only a remote chance of ending up at a recycling facility.

■ Eastman Chemicals (Kingsport, Tennessee) has demonstrated the possibility of producing thermoset polyester resins from used PET containers. Thermoset polyester is a resin that cannot be softened by heating once it has been formed into a finished product. Typical uses of thermoset polyester are in the manufacture of boat hulls and storage tanks.[42]

■ Goodyear Tire and Rubber Company (Akron, Ohio) shows that empty PET bottles can be recycled economically into fabric, small auto parts, carpeting, home insulation and other products.

Twelve half-gallon polyester

soft drink bottles provide enough fabric for a pair of trousers. An automobile steering wheel can be produced from 20 half-gallon PET bottles, 45 and 50 feet of clothes line can be fabricated from 12 bottles. According to Goodyear, the cost of recycling PET for these uses is considerably less than manufacturing them from virgin materials.

■ The Michigan Technological University (Houghton, Michigan) has developed technology that can economically recover valuable chemicals such as terephthalic acid (TPA) and ethylene glycol from used PET bottles.[43] The patent for this recovery process is available for licence. The researchers at MTU estimate payback period of the recycling system at less than three years.[46]

The recovery process starts with the grinding of the waste bottle (see Figure 5). The ground plastic is slurried with water recycled from the distillation column and pumped to the PET reactor. Ammonium hydroxide, used as the base for saponification, is added and the reactor is heated to 400°F.

Saponification, essentially a reversal of the polymerization process, unzips the PET to produce diammonium salt of TPA and ethylene glycol.

The entire mixture is cooled and filtered. Filtering removes most of the impurities such as aluminum, paper, polyethylene, pigment and the polymerization catalyst. The saponification products, diammonium salt of TPA and ethylene glycol, are soluble in water and pass through the filter.

Addition of sulfuric acid to the filtrate causes the TPA to precipitate, permitting its recovery by filtering. The recovered TPA is 99% pure.

The filtrate, which contains ethylene glycol, is stripped of ammonia. The ammonia is recycled for re-use in the PET reactor. The remaining ethylene glycol and water mixture is distilled so as to separate the ethylene glycol.[47]

The income generated through the potential sale of the TPA and ethylene glycol exceeds the operating expenses. Pay-back period on the capital expenditure is estimated at 2.7 years based on a

Figure 5
The Hydrolysis of PET

Waste plastic is ground, slurried with water recycled from the distillation column and pumped to the PET reactor. Ammonium hydroxide and heat are added to the reactor to unzip the plastic polymer, yielding ethylene glycol and diammonium salt of TPA. Some additional processing results in re-usable, high-purity ethylene glycol and TPA.

Source: "Petrochemicals from Waste: Recycling PET Bottles," *Chemical Engineering,* December 1, 1980.

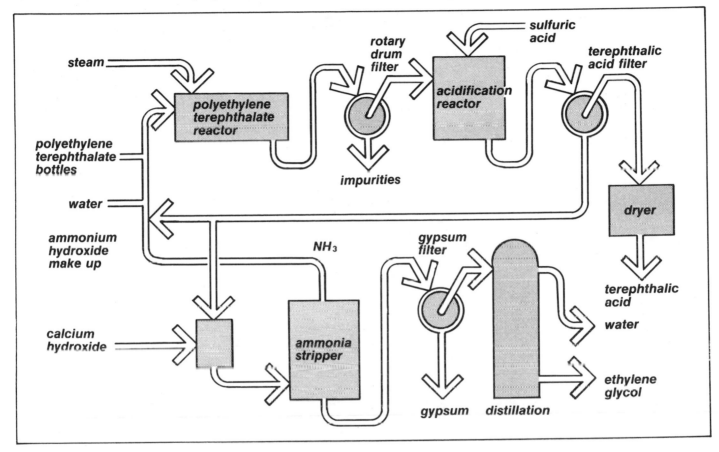

PET processing volume of 6 million pounds of plastic scrap per year.[46]

According to researchers at MTU, the system can recover TPA from polyester photographic and x-ray film, recording tapes, old clothes and other polyester products.[46]

Chemical Recovery By Pyrolysis

Pyrolysis, which is the use of flameless high temperatures to break down organic compounds, is a means of disposing solid wastes including plastics. Since pyrolysis does not involve incineration, it minimizes potential air pollution. In addition, pyrolysis offers possible recovery of chemicals or synthetic gas for use in the production of methane or higher hydrocarbons.[3]

Pyrolysis holds promise as a recycling method for plastics which not only reduces the volume of waste, but from which valuable chemicals and fuel-grade products can be recovered.

■ Investigations of pyrolysis by the United States Bureau of Mines and other organizations have led to the conclusion that pyrolysis of plastic wastes may be economically attractive because more by-product fuel gas is generated than is needed to supply heat for the reaction.[3]

Research for the Bureau of Mines demonstrated that the pyrolysis of PVC yields hydrogen chloride, a liquid condensate, a char and off-gases. About half of the weight of virgin PVC resin is hydrogen chloride, but the addition of plasticizers and fillers dilutes this amount.

The hydrogen chloride may be recovered for chemical re-use as hydrochloric acid. The char, liquid condensate, and off-gas all have fuel value. The char from waste PVC, which makes up about 45% of the original waste volume, contains volatile matter, fixed carbon, ash and water. The liquid condensate, about 10 to 15% of the original sample, contains benzene, toluene, xylenes and a heavy oil. The off-gas, about 10 to 20% of the original sample, contains water, methane, ethane, propane and butane. The PVC waste which underwent test pyrolysis contained about 30% hydrogen chloride by weight.[3]

Pyrolysis has been used to recover hydrogen chloride and heat from waste wire insulation jackets. Liberated hydrogen chloride reacts with the residual aluminum and copper metal to form metal chlorides that remain in the char fraction.

Pyrolysis has been demonstrated to be technologically feasible in the regeneration of styrene monomer from waste polystyrene. The waste polymer is fed into a reaction vessel for thermal degradation into monomers (see Figure 6). Other plastics for which pyrolysis technology has been applied include polyurethanes, polyolefins and mixed plastic wastes.

Conclusion

Soaring resin costs and waste disposal charges have the plastics processing and recycling industry pursuing pollution prevention strategies with new vigour. Equipment manufacturers are responding to the call for greater material and energy efficiency by designing a range of machinery that minimizes the production of scrap during processing, and that recycles unavoidable plastic wastes.

The plastics processing and reprocessing industries have been active in the recovery of homogeneous scrap in the last decade. The same is not true for mixed plastic waste. In the past,

Figure 6
Pyrolysis of Waste Polystyrene

The waste polystyrene is fed into the pyrolysis reactor. Nitrogen is used as the inert carrier gas and fed to the reactor at a temperature of 1230°C to provide a degradation temperature of about 600°C. The effluent from the reactor passes through heat exchanger and refrigeration units. Cooling of the effluent stream to about 20°C removes all but 0.6% of the styrene monomer from the gaseous nitrogen. The effluent stream goes to a phase separator and an inhibitor is added to the liquid monomer before it is pumped to the product storage tank. The nitrogen carrier gas is recycled for re-use in the process.

Source: M. Sittig, *Pollution Control in the Plastics and Rubber Industry,* Noyes Data Corporation, 1975.

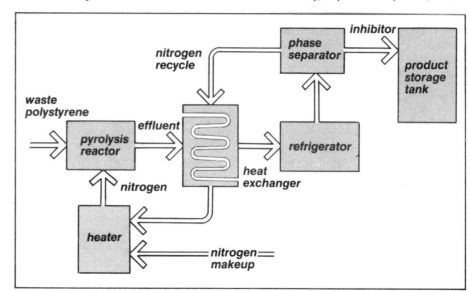

the recycling of mixed plastic wastes was viewed as technically unfeasible and economically unattractive. Technological advances in the recovery of mixed and contaminated wastes promise to make a larger segment of the plastics wastestream available for recovery.

FOR FURTHER INFORMATION

*For additional developments in plastics recycling, refer to the book entitled **Plastics Waste: Recovery of Economic Value** by Jacob Leidner. Published in May 1981 by Marcel Dekker, this book covers sources, separation techniques, primary, secondary and tertiary recycling, energy recovery and disposal techniques. The author currently works in this field at the Ontario Research Foundation in Mississauga, Ontario. Phone (416) 822-4111.*

Journals

Many excellent journals exist that contain articles on low-waste plastics processing and on plastics reclamation. In addition, these journals carry numerous advertisements and new product information on more efficient processing technologies.

CANADIAN PLASTICS,
1450 Don Mills Road,
Don Mills, Ontario.
M3B 2X7

CANADIAN CHEMICAL
PROCESSING,
1450 Don Mills Road,
Don Mills, Ontario.
M3B 2X7

PLASTICS ENGINEERING,
14 Fairfield Drive,
Brookfield Center,
Connecticut.
06805

PLASTICS DESIGN &
PROCESSING,
Lake Publishing Corporation,
700 Peterson Road,
Box 159,
Libertyville, Illinois.
60048

PLASTICS TECHNOLOGY,
Bill Communications Inc.,
633 Third Avenue,
New York, New York.
10017

ADHESIVES AGE,
Communication Channels Inc.,
6285 Barfield Road,
Atlanta, Georgia.
30328

JOURNAL OF ELASTOMERS
AND PLASTICS,
Technomic Publishing Co. Inc.,
265 Post Road West,
Westport, Connecticut.
06880

Associations

Contact the following associations for information on low-waste processing technologies and reclamation equipment. These trade associations can assist you directly, or point you in the right direction for more information on commercially available recycling equipment, technology transfer programmes, technical experts in the field, professional plastics recyclers, upcoming legislation, existing tax breaks and other economic incentives.

Encourage those associations which rank pollution control low on their priority list to direct more attention to pollution prevention. Preventing pollution can benefit both the business community and the environment.

The following list identifies primarily national associations in Canada and the United States. It is not uncommon for Canadian companies to belong to American associations. Contact the national associations and ask if a local chapter is in operation near your business.

Society of the Plastics
Industry of Canada,
Suite 104,
1262 Don Mills Road,
Don Mills, Ontario.
M3B 2W7
(416) 449-0444

Society of the Plastics Industry,
355 Lexington Avenue,
New York, New York.
10017
(212) 573-9400

Society of Plastics Engineers,
14 Fairfield Dr.,
Brookfield Center,
Connecticut.
06805
(203) 775-0471

Plastic and Metal Products
Manufacturers Association Inc.,
225 West 34th St.,
New York, New York.
10001
(212) 564-2500

National Association of
Plastic Fabricators,
1701 N. St., N.W.,
Washington, D.C.
20036
(202) 223-2504

Canadian Association of
Recycling Industries,
8 Colborne St.,
Suite 602,
Toronto, Ontario.
M5E 1E1
(416) 362-4521

National Association of
Recycling Industries,
330 Madison Avenue,
New York, New York.
10017
(212) 867-7330

References

1. Milgrom, J. "Recycling Plastics: Current Status." In Conservation and Recycling, Vol. 3. Oxford, England: Pergamon Press, 1980.

2. Von Hassel, A. "RIM Machinery and Materials Evolve Toward Higher Productivity." Plastics Technology, November 1981.

3. Sittig, M. Pollution Control in the Plastics and Rubber Industry. Park Ridge, New Jersey: Noyes Data Corporation, 1975.

4. Department of Industry, Trade and Commerce (Canada). A Report by the Sector Task Force on the Canadian Plastics Processing Industry, (A. G. Moeton, Chairman), 1976.

5. Hayter, R. Society of the Plastics Industry of Canada, Don Mills, Ontario. Personal communication, November 1981.

6. Porteous, A. Recycling Resources Refuse. New York: Longman Inc., 1977.

7. Society of the Plastics Industry of Canada, Don Mills, Ontario. Data for 1979.

8. Leidner, Jacob. Ontario Research Foundation, Mississauga, Ontario. Personal communication, November 1981.

9. Plastics Industry Council. *Types and Properties of Plastics.* Don Mills, Ontario: Society of the Plastics Industry of Canada.

10. Plastics Industry Council. *Resource Recovery from Plastic Wastes.* Don Mills, Ontario: Society of the Plastics Industry of Canada.

11. Lauber, Jack. Toxic Materials Section, New York State Department of Environmental Conservation, Albany, New York. Personal communication, April 1981.

12. "Chemicals and Additives 1981." *Plastics Technology,* July 1981.

13. Seymour, R.B. *Additives for Plastics: Volumes 1 and 2.* New York: Academic Press, 1978.

14. Hall, F. "Additives 1981 — The Key to Cost-Effectiveness." *Plastics Engineering,* May 1981.

15. "The Case for Cadmium Debate." *Plastics Engineering,* July 1980.

16. Leidner, J. "Plastic Waste — Recovery of Economic Value." In *Reclaim Plastics — Minimize It, Utilize It.* Proceedings of the Regional Technical Conference of the Ontario Section of the Society of Plastics Engineers, October 14, 1981.

17. Duffy, M.J. "Reducing Styrene Emission from Unsaturated Polyester." *Plastics Engineering,* August 1979.

18. Duffy, Michael. Ashland Chemical Company, Dublin, Ohio. Personal communication, July 1981.

19. Hauser, R.L. "Polyester Sprayup is not Spray Painting." *Plastics Engineering,* June 1980.

20. "Low-Pressure RP Spray System Is Said to Minimize Overspray." *Process Engineering News,* May 1981.

21. Balos, J. "Minimizing and Reclaiming Plastic Scrap." In *Reclaim Plastics — Minimize It, Utilize It.* Proceedings of the Regional Technical Conference of the Ontario Section of the Society of Plastics Engineers, October 14, 1981.

22. Hutchinson, M. "One Man's Garbage is Another Man's Gold." *Canadian Plastics,* August 1980.

23. Winter, D.C. "Reclamation of Five Homogeneous Polymers." In *Reclaim Plastics — Minimize It, Utilize It.* Proceedings of the Regional Technical Conference of the Ontario Section of the Society of Plastics Engineers, October 14, 1981.

24. "Recycling: Prospects Look Good Despite Some Market Slowdowns." *Eco/Log Week,* December 4, 1981.

25. Abbot, E. "Thermo-sets: Efficient Use and Recycling." In *Reclaim Plastics — Minimize It, Utilize It.* Proceedings of the Regional Technical Conference of the Ontario Section of the Society of Plastics Engineers, October 14, 1981.

26. Gellert, J. "Efficient Materials Usage With Melt Conveying Systems." In *Reclaim Plastics — Minimize It, Utilize It.* Proceedings of the Regional Technical Conference of the Ontario Section of the Society of Plastics Engineers, October 14, 1981.

27. "New Granulator Rotor Eats Anything But Doesn't Gobble Energy." *Process Engineering News,* March 1980.

28. El-Amin, H. "Energy Efficiency: Don't Overlook Big Savings Potential." *Plastics Technology,* October 1981.

29. El-Amin, H. "In-House Film Scrap Reclaiming: What Your Options Are." *Plastics Technology,* February 1981.

30. Maclean, S. "Plastics Observe Conservation Ethics — Energetically." *Canadian Plastics,* May 1980.

31. Von Hassel, A. "Now You Can Reclaim Chrome-Plated Scrap." *Plastics Technology,* September 1979.

32. Blumenfeld, G. B&K Recycling Industries, Cranford, New Jersey. Personal communication, July 1981.

33. "A Recycler Saves Plastics Producers Two Jobs." *Chemical Week,* August 20, 1980.

34. "NSF Develops Method to Determine Recyclability." *Materials Engineering,* July 1978.

35. Milgrom, J. "An Overview of Plastics Recycling." In *Reclaim Plastics — Minimize It, Utilize It.* Proceedings of the Regional Technical Conference of the Ontario Section of the Society of Plastics Engineers, October 14, 1981.

36. Giguer, Jacques. Produits Jalisson, Chambly, Quebec. Personal communication, August 1981.

37. "New Recyclers for Plastics." *Canadian Chemical Processing,* February 13, 1981.

38. "Quebec Plastic Recycler Expands to Handle Wire Jacketing Resins." *Eco/Log Week,* December 12, 1980.

39. Nassau Recycle Corporation, Gaston, South Carolina. Information release, 1980.

40. "There's Fly Ash in My Polypropylene." *Materials Engineering,* July 1978.

41. "Continuous Reclaim System Pelletizes PS Foam Scrap." *Plastics Technology,* October 1981.

42. "PET Bottles in Canada." *Recoup,* August 15, 1980.

43. Barna, Bruce. Michigan Technological University, Houghton, Michigan. Personal communication, March 1981.

44. Wellman, Gregory. Wellman Industries, Johnsonville, South Carolina. Personal communication, April 1981.

45. Mion, Leslie. Goodyear Tire and Rubber Company, Akron, Ohio. Personal communication, July 1981.

46. Barna, B.A., Johnsrud, D.R. and Lamparter, R.L. "Petrochemicals from Waste: Recycling PET Bottles." *Chemical Engineering,* December 1, 1980.

47. Johnsrud, D.R., Barna, B.A. and Lamparter, R.L. *PET Bottle Recycling.* Houghton, Michigan: Center for Waste Management Programs, Michigan Technological University (mimeographed).

Printing

Printers and publishers have come a long way since Johann Gutenberg, reputedly the first European to print with movable type, set a milestone in the history of communications with the production of the first printed Bible. In those days, the printing process was painstakingly slow and labour intensive compared to automated presses of the 1900s. Since the early Gutenberg days, innovation in the printing industry was characterized by the push for high-speed availability of the printed word.

In the 1980s, technological innovation is racing ahead at dizzying speeds. With the introduction of lasers, computers, satellites and even robots into the printing trade, innovation continues to run at top speed. Despite the abundance of electronic media in our daily lives, industry spokesmen suggest that the print media will continue to be with us for a good many years.[1]

To complement the printed word, electronic information storage systems have been developed that reduce weighty tomes of paper and ink into snippets of coded film. The Battelle Institute Laboratories in San Francisco, for example, has developed a new optical recording system which can record the entire Encyclopaedia Britannica on a square centimeter of photosensitive materials, creating tiny dots by laser exposure.[2] Although the intent of such miniaturization is to grapple with the problem of burgeoning files and book-laden library shelves, it is probable that associated pollution from paper production and ink application is reduced significantly.

The communications revolution carries with it its own set of environmental and social problems that are not the topic of this chapter. Rather, this chapter wishes to emphasize the astonishing ability of industry to forge ahead in processing and product improvement. In the past, innovation in the printing industry was designed to cut labour and improve productivity. A new variable has been added to innovation in recent years — that of minimizing pollution.

Government regulations calling for cleaner air, cleaner waterways and fewer contaminants around us have spurred the printer and inkmaker to provide a range of process improvements and new products that promise to minimize pollution. In many instances, reducing the generation of pollutants and recycling wastes whose production is unavoidable has resulted in unexpected savings to the company. The theme of this book is that pollution prevention is profitable. Although much progress has been made in preventing pollution, there is much more to be done in this field.

As in most other industrial sectors, the largest printing companies and newspapers tend to be in the best position to minimize pollution. Large companies have the technical resource people to identify and correct possible sources of pollution. Furthermore, large companies are better suited financially to invest in more-efficient, less-polluting equipment, and to install on-site recovery systems such as solvent reclaimers and ink recyclers. The sheer volume and economic value of wastes that can be recycled by a large company points to short pay-back periods on recovery equipment expenditures.

As waste reduction and recovery gains greater prominence in industry as a whole, manufacturers of recovery equipment will be assured of a strong market for their wares. In many instances, manufacturers of recycling equipment market machinery only for large volume users. As waste disposal and material costs continue to escalate, waste reduction and recovery technologies can be expected to be scaled down for application by smaller and medium-sized businesses. Although the pay-back period may be much longer for a smaller company than a larger one, the expenditure in waste reduction and recovery equipment is an investment all the same. Once the equipment has been paid off, the income from waste recovery will continue to accumulate.

Pollution prevention makes any company a two-time winner — once through reduced disposal costs and once through the reduced costs in the purchase of raw materials. Perhaps the greatest hurdle facing smaller businesses today in minimizing pollution is the lack of financial and technical resources to accomplish modernization. Well-placed tax incentives and modernization programmes can do much to assist the smaller operator in helping to protect the environment.

Industry Profile

The printing industry, also known as the graphic arts industry, covers a wide range of functions including the printing of advertising materials, business forms, books, newspapers, magazines, stationery, packaging and an assortment of consumer goods.

Based on 1976 census data, Canada's commercial printing industry consists of more than 2200 shops employing almost 50,000

Figure 1
Distribution of Printing Establishments Based on Number of Employees

For example, 64% of the total number of commercial printing establishments in Canada have fewer than 10 employees.
Source: Department of Industry, Trade and Commerce (Canada), 1976.

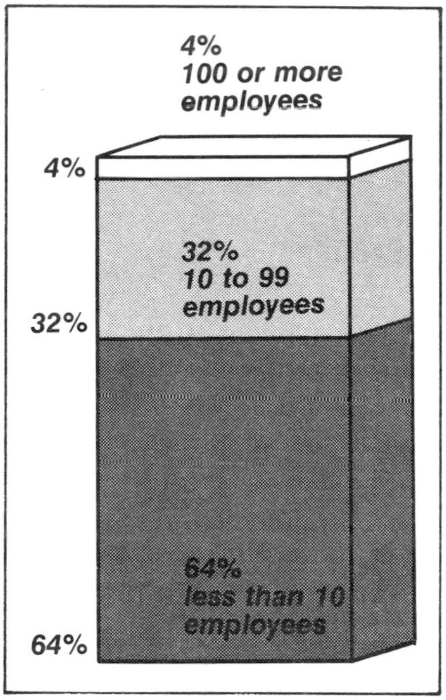

4%
100 or more employees

4%

32%
10 to 99 employees

32%

64%
less than 10 employees

64%

Table 1
Canadian Printing Industry Structure (1976)

Number of employees	Establishments		Total employment	
	Number	%	Number	%
Less than 10	1452	64	4587	10
10-99	728	32	19657	42
100 or more	82	4	22559	48
Total	2262	100	46803	100

Source: Industry, Trade and Commerce. *A Report by the Sector Task Force on the Canadian Commercial Printing Industry*, 1976.

people.[3] This figure does not include integrated printing facilities in organizations such as banks, insurance companies and government, commonly referred to as "in-house" printing plants.

The printing industry is characterized by many small businesses with an annual sales volume hovering at $600,000 in 1976. About 65% of these companies had fewer than 10 employees (see Figure 1). Although only 4% of the companies had more than 100 employees, this group alone employed almost half the printing industry (see Table 1).[3]

The American printing industry shows a similar pattern. In 1981, the industry included 50,000 individual companies, only 4% of which had more than 100 employees.[4,5]

The bulk of Canada's printing plants are clustered in urban centres. Seventy-five percent of Canada's printing companies, employing 85% of the industry, are located in Ontario and Quebec.[3]

Process Overview

The purpose of a printer is to duplicate a given image repeatedly on specified materials. Printing is essentially a two-phase operation. In phase one, the printer makes a plate or negative copy of the original artwork. In the second phase, the plate is inked and applied to paper or other materials.

Any discussion of the printing industry must start with a look at printing inks. Until the mid 1880s all printing inks remained virtually the same, containing lampblack dispersed in linseed oil.

The explosion of the petrochemical industry has brought more than 2000 dyes, pigments and intermediates to the vats of ink formulators. A major ink maker may, in turn, brew more than a million distinct formulations to meet printers' needs.[6]

The printing industry is dependent on the ink formulating industry, which in turn is dependent on the petroleum industry to provide it with dyes and pigments, resins, ink oils and solvents. In fact, more than 80% of the ink industry's raw materials are derived from petroleum.[6] As oil prices reach dizzying heights, the printing industry is fast to feel the pinch.

Inks have three component parts: pigments, which yield colour; resins, which act as carriers of the pigment and permit it to attach to an object; and solvents, which dissolve resins and make the ink workable.

All three components are derived from the refining of crude oil (see Figure 2). Carbon black, the work-horse of the pigment series, is produced exclusively from petrochemicals, as are the solvents and other organic pigments.

Non-petroleum based components include pigments such as lead, mercury, cadmium, cobalt, chromium and nickel. Some resins are derived from trees.

The major printing processes are letterpress, lithography (also known as off-set), gravure and flexography (see Table 2). About two-thirds of the industry's processes are letterpress or lithography systems[7] (see Figure 3). Other less frequently used processes include screen printing (also known as serigraphy), electrostatic printing and ink jet printing. Each of these printing processes has its own ink requirements and hence generates its own particular blend of pollutants.[8]

The letterpress process was once the most widely used printing process. Its application includes commercial printing, magazines, newspapers, books, containers, folding boxes and bags. It is expected that the American trend of declining letterpress use is occurring in Canada also. In letterpress printing, the image carrier (printing plate) is inked and the resulting image is transferred to the paper under pressure.

Figure 2
Printing Ink Raw Materials Produced from Crude Oil

Source: "Why Printing Ink Prices Are Going to Skyrocket," *Canadian Printer and Publisher,* June 1980.

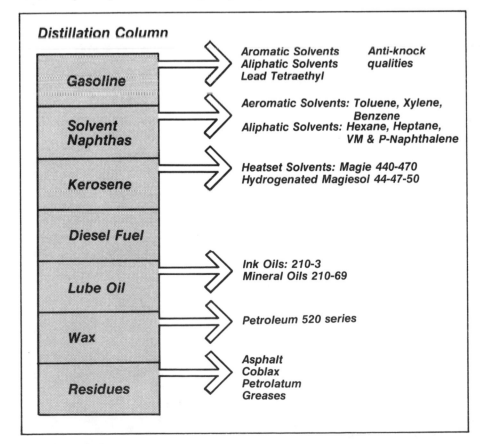

In off-set lithography, the printing areas of the image carriers are distinguished from the non-printing areas by means of chemical treatment. The chemical treatment consists in the dampening of the plate with a liquid known as the fountain solution. Fountain solution is water-based and is in continuous contact with lithographic inks during printing. Unlike letterpress inks, waste litho inks contain water. Waste ink recovery may entail separating the waste ink from the water and recycling only the ink. Or, it is possible to put a chemical into the waste ink to emulsify the water with the ink and keep it in suspension.

The printing industry generates three major categories of potentially hazardous pollutants: process chemicals from platemaking and phototypographic processing; solvents, particularly from vapourization during ink drying and equipment clean-out; and waste pigments and other ink additives.

Table 2

Description and Application of Major Printing Processes

Process	*Description*	*Application*	*Ink Type Used*
Letterpress	Image transferred under pressure directly to paper from an inked plate.	Magazines Newspapers Books Stationery Advertising	Oil-based inks
Lithographic (Off-set)	Indirect printing using an intermediate element (blanket) between image carrier and paper.	Magazines Newspapers Books Stationery Advertising Containers	Oil-based inks Some UV curables
Flexography (Anilox)	Direct transfer of an image from an inked flexible plate, frequently used on a rotary press.	Packaging	Alcohol-borne inks Water-borne inks
Gravure	Printing method based on photography and photomechanics, capable of reproducing continuous tone pictures.	Art books Greeting cards Advertising Packaging	Solvent-borne inks Some water-borne
Silkscreen	Ink is pressed through unblocked part of porous screen where it forms the printed image.	Greeting cards Decalcomanias Banners Signs Fabrics Wall paper Ceramics	Solvent-borne Some UV curables

POLLUTION PREVENTION OPPORTUNITIES

1.

Housekeeping and Process Control

Although a small business may think twice about investing in a capital-intensive recovery system, a business of any size can implement low-cost improvements in housekeeping and come out ahead. Systematically improving process controls means better quality printing, less materials waste and improved profits.

In earlier days when paper and ink prices were low, the average printer was more concerned with quality improvement and customer satisfaction than pollution and minimizing waste. High ink and paper costs in conjunction with increased difficulty in disposing of waste has changed all that. In this harsh economic climate, a printer cannot afford to ignore ways of reducing process spoilage and waste.

A first step in any successful trouble-shooting programme is to identify problem areas.[10] The importance of keeping accurate records of printing runs — both good and poor quality — cannot be overemphasized.[11] Monitoring information should also include the lot of the paper run, the inks, the blankets and their age, and the pH of fountain solutions. Completion of a waste inventory may yield surprising information showing unexpectedly large volumes of wastes. Such information not only identifies problem areas but also spurs the printer into fighting his war on waste with new vigour.

Company management must be committed to the project if a waste reduction programme is to be successful. It is necessary for the company to know where it stands in terms of waste production so that it can keep track of progress. Once waste areas have been identified, goals should be established that can be measured and that are reachable.

War On Waste

When systems in a plant are provided with regulating procedures to achieve uniformity of printing, the result is process control.[12] Process controls are not necessarily automatic and may involve people. The object is to solve production problems systematically and thereby avert pollution.

Adoption of pollution prevention strategies does not mean that a printer has to forego product quality. Quite the contrary. Equipment is available that serves the dual purpose of cutting spoilage and improving the quality of the product to satisfy even the fussiest clients.

■ One function of the technical services group at the Graphic Arts Technical Foundation (Pittsburg, Pennsylvania) is to perform technical plant audits.[12] Plant audits can pinpoint problems that occur when process controls are not adequate. These problems include press mechanical faults, faulty materials, poor image fit on press, improper ink and water balance, water fountain pH out of control, variable dot size during a run, lengthy makeready time, exces-

Figure 3
Trends in Distribution of Printing Processes (U.S.)

American industry spokesmen forecast a significant increase in the use of gravure processes and a decrease in letterpress methods. At present, lithography and letterpress processes dominate the printing industry.

*Projected value

Source: "New Developments in Printing in the United States, Featuring High Speed Non-Silver Films," *Professional Printer,* July 1977.

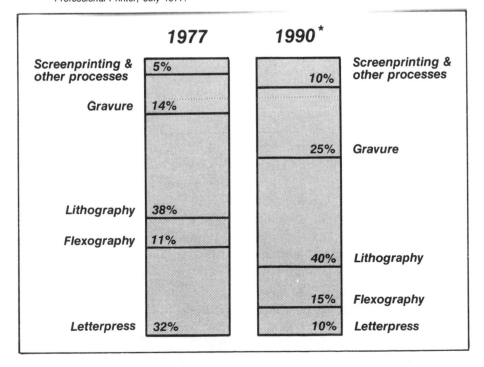

	1977	1990*	
Screenprinting & other processes	5%	10%	Screenprinting & other processes
Gravure	14%	25%	Gravure
Lithography	38%	40%	Lithography
Flexography	11%	15%	Flexography
Letterpress	32%	10%	Letterpress

sive plate remakes, and dirty conditions in the plant.[13] These are things that a plant can control.

■ The Oxy-Dry Corporation (Elk Grove Village, Illinois) is one of several equipment manufacturers that offers a line of anti-waste press accessories. The company manufactures an electronic system that detects web breaks in web offset printing. Web breaks are detected in a non-contact fashion that will not smear ink nor crease the web, thereby reducing potential waste. The company also produces an automatic ink leveller which maintains the desired ink level in the fountain for optimum inking conditions. This prevents ink waste or ink spoilage around the press.[14]

■ For many years, Crosfield (Chicago, Illinois) has produced high-accuracy control equipment for web fed presses. A recent addition, the Pressdata 190 waste system, provides a means of monitoring press performance. The company claims that on a press printing 40,000 copies per hour for 40 hours a week, the savings in paper alone would ensure paying off the capital cost of the equipment in one year. If total printing costs are considered — ink, presstime and labour — the savings would be even more dramatic.[14]

■ Prior to the waste reduction programme at the *St. Petersburg Times* (St. Petersburg, Florida), this newspaper office wasted 4.4%

of the total newsprint used. By 1980, eighteen months after the waste programme started, paper waste dropped to 2.4% and resulted in a total savings of $168,000.[15]

■ There are other big time winners in the paper chase. Slashing paper waste at Judd & Detweiler saved the company $300,000 in paper costs in 1979. McGraw-Hill Publications (New York, New York), in one printing plant alone, saved $200,000 a year by cutting back on paper waste.[16]

Print Quality Control

The book market has blossomed lately with a selection of

Table 3
Print Quality Control Resources

Publication	Author	Description	Where available
Practical Steps to Quality Printing	Kodak	Contains a flow chart of production steps where a quality control check is needed and tells how to do it	Contact nearest Kodak representative
Practical Steps to Customized Quality Control	Kodak	Audio-visual material available to medium-to-large printing plants	Contact nearest Kodak representative
Quality Control Techniques for Phototypesetting Film	Louis Laurent	Details quality control in phototypesetting	The National Composition Association, 1730 North Lynn St., Arlington, Virginia 22209
GATF Production Quality and Control Devices	Graphic Arts Technical Information	Describes quality control devices to assist the entire printing process	GATF, 4615 Forbes Ave. Pittsburgh, Pennsylvania 15213
Preventative Quality Control: Sheetfed Pressroom	Graphic Arts Technical Information	Describes techniques to prevent problems in sheetfed printing	GATF, 4615 Forbes Ave., Pittsburgh, Pennsylvania 15213
Test Images for Printing	Graphic Arts Technical Information	Includes test images comercially available in printing	GATF, 4615 Forbes Ave., Pittsburgh, Pennsylvania 15213

guidebooks to assist the printing industry in enhancing process control and cutting waste.[17] Businesses of any size will benefit by investing in some of the books listed in Table 3.

Conserving Photosensitive Materials

Phototypography is any photo-mechanical printing process in which photographs are reproduced in relief for use with type. Because phototypography involves the use of photosensitive substrates, phototypographers use large quantities of silver which eventually are washed down a drain in the absence of a silver recovery programme. The recovery of silver and processing wastewater is discussed in the photography chapter.

Although the technologies of tomorrow include silver-free methods such as substitution with photopolymers, or the adaptation of digital and video technology to the graphic arts, such upcoming technologies are of little solace to the average printer and photo-typographer of today who is stuck with present equipment and limited resources in an era of stiffening competition and rampant inflation.[18]

What follows are a few tips on how to minimize waste at the typesetting stage. These suggestions are by no means a panacea for all shop ills nor a prescription for making a million. Rather they outline simple procedures for cutting back on waste that many shops have heard before but too few have put into practice.[18]

- Plan camera work to utilize every square inch of the film and use the most economical size of film suitable for the job.
- Point out to customers the savings possible if the art is properly prepared for the minimum number of shots and is submitted on boards with minimum margins.
- Use photosensitive paper or film of the proper width to conserve materials.

Publication	Author	Description	Where Available
Catalogue	Graphic Arts Research Center	Free annual catalogue of services	Rochester Institute of Technology, 1 Lomb Memorial Drive, Rochester, New York 14623
Quality Control Bibliography	Graphic Arts Research Center	Contains abstracts of articles on quality control in the graphic arts	Rochester Institute of Technology, 1 Lomb Memorial Drive, Rochester, New York 14623
Quality Control For the UPC Symbol	Prof. A.D. Rickmers	Aimed at the printer of packaging materials	Rochester Institute of Technology, 1 Lomb Memorial Drive, Rochester, New York 14623
Quality Control Manual	Flexographic Technical Association	Quality control for flexographic printers	The Flexographic Technical Association, 95 West 19th St., Huntington Station, New York 11746
Quality is Free	Philip Crosby	General book on managing quality for profit	McGraw-Hill Publishers

Source: "Quality Control Guides to Improve Your Profit", *Canadian Printing & Publishing*. October 1980.

- Check photosensitive film and paper storage areas to see if the materials are stored in a manner conducive to economical and efficient use. Some shops waste up to one-fourth of their photosensitive materials because of inefficient work and storage habits.
- Save all scraps of exposed and obsolete photosensitive materials for silver recovery.
- Apply on-site silver recovery units to process wastewaters. Smaller shops might consider processing wastewater in a cooperative arrangement with other businesses.

2.
Reducing Pollution in Platemaking

In conventional platemaking, the paste-up material is photographed using silver halide film. A press plate is made based on the information in the film. The process generates wastewater streams that are rich in silver and other process chemicals.

Reclaiming silver can go a long way in abating pollution and recouping film costs for even the smallest outfit. New options are now becoming available to platemakers that are reputed to be both cost-competitive and less polluting than conventional platemaking. Silverless platemaking systems, a relative newcomer to the field, are undergoing further refinement to enhance commercialization. By eliminating the use of silver, price fluctuations and costs can be reduced, as can the production of silver-bearing wastestreams during plate processing.

Most platemaking systems currently in use are characterized by the need for chemical reagents to process the plate. Design changes in platemaking systems are resulting in systems in which the "chemistry" is in the plates rather than in the processing baths. While this technology is still new, some commercially available applications now exist. One intent of the new technology is to minimize the quantity of chemicals required

and waste chemicals generated by the platemaker. In some instances, only tap water is required to process the film and plate.

■ Napp Systems (San Marcos, California) has produced a non-silver system for the printing and graphic arts industries. The system makes use of acrylic fibres impregnated with carbon black.[19] The system is revolutionary in that it requires only tap water to process the film. In doing so, the need for chemical developers is eliminated.

■ Although not common, water-developed off-set plates are not unheard of. S.D. Warren (Boston, Massachusetts) markets several paper-based plates that are water developed, though these are intended for small run lengths of 5000 to 25,000.[20]

■ 3M (St. Paul, Minnesota) is refining its new Hydrolith™ plate for the printing industry. The Hydrolith™ plate is a major advancement in lithographic platemaking because it requires only water to process the aluminum off-set plates.[21] The plate is capable of runs up to 60,000 impressions.

The structure of the Hydrolith™ plate consists of three layers of coatings over an aluminum base plate (see Figure 4). The three coatings include a patented Hydroguard™ treatment over the

---

Figure 4
Composition of the Hydrolith™ Plate

The Hydrolith™ Plate is composed of three coatings over an aluminum base. The photopolymer coating is similar to that of other 3M off-set plates but water, rather than chemicals, releases the nonimage areas from the aluminum base.

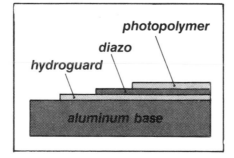

aluminum base, a diazo sensitizer coating and a photopolymer top coat with water-soluble properties.[20] Before developing, the surface of the plate is water resistant. Once normal developing action begins, however, the surface becomes hydrophilic and all the unimaged coating is dissolved.

In the early days of product testing, Midwest Business Forms (St. Paul, Minnesota) agreed to use the prototype plate in test production work.[20] Midwest Business Forms was pleased with the results and even more pleased that 3M kept supplying free developer. It was not until the end of the production experiments that 3M revealed the contents of the developer — only tap water.

■ For large printing offices, 3M has designed an automatic platemaking system to produce press-ready off-set plates directly from paste-up, bypassing the need for silver halide film. The Pyrofax™ system, which operates in normal room lighting, eliminates the need for plumbing and film developing, thereby reducing wastewater treatment needs. This system has already been installed in some off-set and direct litho newspapers worldwide which are banking on their investment to pay off in the long term.

3.
Minimizing Pollution Associated with Inks

Ink Description

Toxicologists are finding growing evidence to substantiate their long-felt malaise regarding the health effects of exposure to many of the pigments currently in use. Some of the pigments identified to date that pose potential hazards include carbon black, lead chromate, molybdate, cadmium, benzidenes, mercury sulfide, phthalocyanide and toluidines. The task of systematically identifying potentially hazardous pigments is enormous and still in its incipient stages.[22]

As scientific research verifies serious health problems with select ink components, ink formulators tend to substitute constituents that are believed to be less hazardous. In the absence of a comprehensive screening process to establish which chemicals currently available on the chemical market are safe, it is probable that ink makers will have to accommodate continual substitution of certain ink components as advances in toxicological testing document new health problems. Waste ink is designated hazardous because it contains a mix of known and potentially toxic compounds.

In many printing processes, excess ink is collected in a drip pan underneath the press. The collected ink may include dirt, grease from the equipment, fragments of paper and dried globs of ink. Most companies still pay to have this unwanted ink carted away. The technology is available to recycle waste letterpress, lithography or Di-Litho inks.[23] Several newspapers across North America are helping both the environment and their pocket book by giving waste ink a second debut.

Conventional inks may contain as much as 90% solvent. In water-borne inks, at least 75% of the volatile component must be water, and must not contain more than 25% solvents.[5] High-solids inks refer to inks which have a solids content of at least 60%.[5] UV-curable inks are polymer-based and require UV light to set the polymer.

The majority of printing inks in use in Canada are still solvent-based. They can contain up to 90% solvents, which evaporate upon drying the ink.[24] Small print shops, if they have a ventilation system at all, vent solvent-laden air to the outside environment. Some of the larger printing establishments invest in on-site solvent recovery or incineration.[25]

In addition to solvent emissions in the air, the printing process yields contaminated solvents generated during equipment clean-up. This liquid wastestream can be taken to a professional solvent recycler for clean-up, or may be recovered on-site. Either option may be well within even a small printer's economic reach. If solvents are in liquid form, reclama-

tion will be cheaper than other disposal options. But for low concentration vapour emissions escaping into the environment, the cost of solvent vapour reclamation may be too high for the small operator because these vapours must be first condensed to liquid form. Once liquid, the waste solvent may be sent to an outside recycler for purification. Additional information on minimizing pollution from solvents is reviewed in the solvents chapter.

Given the high capital cost of solvent vapour recovery systems relative to a small shop's investment capability, on-site reduction of solvent emissions appears to be a dead-end for most small businesses. A new trend promises relief to small business. Ink manufacturers are working on getting the solvents out of ink. Three directions taken in pursuit of this goal are the development of water-borne inks, high-solids inks, and ultraviolet (UV)-curables.

These directions parallel the ones taken by the paint and adhesives industries, both of which are under regulatory and economic pressure to reduce solvent emissions. Unlike the paint industry, the printing industry is finding success more elusive.

Water-Based Inks

Water-based inks have had difficult beginnings. Unlike their precocious cousins, the water-borne paints and adhesives, water-based inks have yet to get off the ground.

One factor stifling the development of water-based inks is that they require more energy to dry than do solvent-borne inks.[26] Ink manufacturers are responding by formulating water-based inks at much higher than conventional ink strength so that as little ink (or water) as possible need be used. Lowering the water content by increasing the solids reduces energy requirements during drying.[26]

Another difficulty is shutting down presses for short periods of time. Although water is the solvent for water-borne ink when it is in the liquid form, it is not a

solvent for dried ink film. This makes it difficult to shut down a press during gravure printing and then have a start-up where the dried ink or drying ink is soluble in the wet ink.

Water-borne inks have made their greatest penetration into gravure and flexographic printing processes. Flexography is already replacing letterpress in book printing and could become a serious competitor to letterpress and even lithography in the newspaper field.[18, 27] Flexography is expected to penetrate other publishing areas such as newspaper inserts and low-budget magazines. Based on the projected increase in use of both gravure and flexographic processes in the future, it is anticipated that water-borne inks will make substantial in-roads in future ink markets.

To date, water-borne inks find their greatest application in flexographic printing on paper substrates, such as folding cartons, corrugated containers and paper cups.[5] Water-based inks are also available that adhere to less porous surfaces such as polyethylene, polypropylene, foil and polycoated paper.[28] Although water-based ink technology does not have the benefit of years of research and application as do solvent inks, the recent legislative pressure in the United States to curtail solvent emissions is likely to spur the formulation of high quality water inks in the future (see Table 4).

Water-borne inks attract only limited commercial use for the gravure process. The situation is changing. United States Environmental Protection Agency requirements to limit solvent volume to 25% or less in rotogravure printing inks has the industry taking another look at water-borne systems.[5] This equates to a reduction in solvent emissions of 70 to 75% from inks during the drying process.

■ Stuart Klein of Cello Corporation (Havre de Grace, Maryland) says, "Water for gravure will inevitably become a reality. As solvent prices soar, the cost advantage of water inks will increase. And plant insurance rates can be reduced drastically when water-

Table 4
Comparison of Properties: Water-Based and Solvent Inks

Properties	Water-based in 1979	Water-based in 1982
Economics	Equal	Superior
Print Quality	Equal	Equal
Ease of Handling	Superior	Superior
Air Pollution Abatement	Superior	Superior
Drying	Slower	Slower
Adhesion	Inferior	Equal
Gloss	Inferior	Equal
Raw Material Availability	Equal	Superior

Source: "Propose Water-Based Inks as Answer to Meeting EPA Pollution Guidelines." *Graphic Arts Monthly*. September 1979.

based inks are used exclusively."[26]

Klein, whose company produces a water-borne gravure ink called Cellocryl™ feels that environmental pollution is the main reason for water conversions, coupled with increasing solvent costs and decreasing availability.

Klein is quick to point out, however, that water-borne ink technology still is not perfected. Cello's research team is taking aim at drawbacks of water-borne inks compared to solvent-based inks. Problems besetting water-based inks include energy intensive drying, low gloss, pigment dispersability, equipment shutdown and start-up, and paper curl.[26]

Taking solvents out of ink solves only half the problem. There still remains the question of pollution from what is left in the ink — the pigments and other additives.

"Wastewater coloured with pigment will pollute rivers and streams, so it requires careful disposal," says Klein. "We know of some ink manufacturers who are actually precipitating their wash water and recycling it while filtering out the pigment sludge. This sludge can then be disposed of as solid waste, recycled back into inks, or possibly used as a filler."[26]

■ Although letterpress and off-set printing methods have been traditionally reserved for the production of newspapers, flexography (also called anilox) has recently invaded the newspaper pressroom. One optimistic report on the virtues of flexography comes from *The Oregonian* newspaper (Portland, Oregon) which claims a reduction in newsprint waste of 25% since field testing the anilox inking device.[29] Newspaper industry spokesmen envision a time in the future when the industry can change over from solvent inks to water-based inks once drying problems have been eliminated.

■ The Newspaper Printing Corporation (Nashville, Tennessee), agent for the *Nashville Banner* and *The Tennessean,* is the first North American pressroom to retrofit an existing letterpress unit to a flexographic process.[30]

Unlike the previous letterpress unit, the flexographic process uses water-based ink. The decision to switch to flexographic printing was based on the desire to improve the quality of the paper and to reduce operating costs. Test runs to date have been very successful. The conversion project is being pioneered by Flex-O-Line Inc. (Portland, Oregon).[30]

Larger companies may choose to meet their fugitive emissions problems by installing on-site solvent vapour recovery systems. But for the small printer or ink formulator, water-based inks may shape up to be the best alternative.

UV-Curable Inks

Ultraviolet-curable (UV-curable) inks are making in-roads into the printing industry as a viable substitute to solvent-based systems. UV-curable printing systems minimize polluting solvent emissions during ink drying and conserve energy compared to more conventional systems.[31]

The ink chemistry is based on an epoxy acrylic resin system with low molecular weight acrylates.[32] Although UV inks have eliminated the volatile solvent portion of the ink, the chemicals used to formulate the ink are potentially as toxic as other ink components. UV-curable inks are frequently described as "non-polluting" by both manufacturers and users, however, this attribute is in reality a misnomer. UV inks might not contribute to air pollution from volatile organics, but they might pollute land and water as any other commercial ink if disposed in the environment without proper precautions.

In conventional printing based on solvent-borne inks, the wet ink is set by driving off solvents with heat or high velocity air drying. This is an energy intensive process that results in substantial solvent emissions into the air.

UV inks depend on polymerization rather than drying to set the ink. Exposure to intense UV light sets off a chain reaction (polymerization) in the UV-liquid-film that results in solidification. The liquid resin film immediately becomes a solid with the full amount put down as liquid remaining on the final dried product[32] (see Figure 5).

UV inks and curing technology are available for many applications including narrow web letterpresses, silk screen tag and label presses, high-speed web off-set presses, litho printing on non-absorbent substrates such as plastic, foil or coated sheets, and for printing plastic or aluminum containers.[31, 33]

When a printer decides to change from a solvent-based ink to a water-based ink, conversion costs are relatively low. The ink is changed, not the equipment. In contrast, for conversion to a UV

Figure 5
UV-Cured Printing

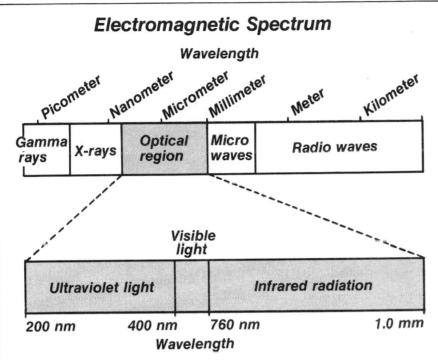

Electromagnetic Spectrum

Wavelength

Picometer · Nanometer · Micrometer · Millimeter · Meter · Kilometer

| Gamma rays | X-rays | Optical region | Micro waves | Radio waves |

Visible light

Ultraviolet light | Infrared radiation

200 nm — 400 nm — 760 nm — 1.0 mm

Wavelength

The UV portion of the spectrum causes curing. Visible light extends from violet to red providing colours we are able to see.

In UV-cured printing, exposure to intense UV light sets off a chain reaction in the liquid film that results in solidification.

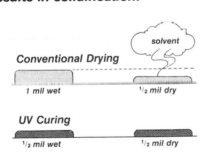

Conventional Drying
solvent
1 mil wet   ½ mil dry

UV Curing
½ mil wet   ½ mil dry

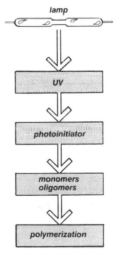

lamp

UV

photoinitiator

monomers oligomers

polymerization

Conventional drying drives off solvents so initial laydown is reduced by more than 50%. Since UV has no solvents, chemicals in the coating cure instantly with no loss of film thickness.

Source: Fusion Systems Corporation, 1980.

printing system, the printer must change not only the ink but also the equipment. Nevertheless, a large printing establishment may find it more profitable to install a UV-curing system, complete with new equipment, than to continue using existing printing equipment and simply changing to a water-based ink.

Pacing the new interest in UV-curable inks, designers continue to transform their machines into more efficient and compact equipment. Several machine suppliers now manufacture multi-colour, in-line printing/curing systems for the screen printing process. Typical applications include printing onto plastic bottles and aluminum cans.[34]

■ The Adolph Coors Company (Golden, Colorado) is one company that switched to a UV-curable system. Although more famous for its beer, Coors also make the 3.2 billion aluminum cans that contain their beer.

Why change to a UV-curable system?

"We had to do it because of air pollution laws," says Paul Le Fevre, supervisor of Packaging Research and Development. "But within that framework we could select the technology type we wanted, so we chose UV-curable inks."[35]

Le Fevre describes the following printing process used at Coors. Cans are fed to the printer and placed over a steel mandrel. The mandrel is spun, permitting the can and mandrel to contact a rubber blanket which has the reverse image of the decoration to be printed (see Figure 6).

As the contact is made, the image is transferred by rolling contact to the rotating can. The blankets are re-inked as the blanket wheel rotates and each blanket contacts each of four printer plates. Ink images from the four plates are transferred, in registration, to the blanket. After the cans are inked, the rotating mandrel wheel carries them over the over-varnish roll where each can receives a layer of clear UV-curable coating over the wet inks.[36]

The cans then move to the cure oven which is a compact rectangular cabinet nine feet high, four feet wide and two feet deep. Six UV lamps (Fusion Systems) cure the ink transferred to the cans. The lamps are mounted three on each side with parabolic reflectors facing them. The reflectors direct radiation which does not fall on the can back toward the opposite side (see Figure 7).

UV-curing ovens are under close scrutiny in the United States to minimize worker exposure to deflected UV radiation.

How do performance and economics of the UV system compare to a conventional heat-cured system?

Le Fevre feels that the UV

system gives equivalent print quality to that of conventional thermal cure systems. Although Coors has no difficulty with its colour match, Le Fevre speculates that other companies printing a large variety of labels may have problems because not all pigments can be used with the UV system. Ink gloss is inferior compared to that of polyester-thermally-cured ink, however Coors is satisfied with its product.[35]

One user of the in-line screen printing/drying system contends that his UV system gives better detail in the final impression than conventional systems. This is because UV systems require finer-mesh screens, and because the ink will not dry up on the screen and cause clogging.[34]

For companies setting up shop for the first time, the economics are in favour of UV systems instead of conventional heat dry systems. However, companies that already have a conventional thermal drying system may feel reluctant to incur new equipment costs, and so may opt for a water-based ink.

Coors gambled with a UV system, and is pleased with the result. Although UV inks cost 20% more than polyester thermal cure inks, energy costs to cure UV ink are 60% less than for a conventional gas-fired oven.[35]

The UV oven at Coors has eight feet of can-conveying chain versus 120 to 150 feet for a thermal oven. Less chain means less energy is required to power the chain. It also means that the size of the curing oven is drastically reduced.

Capital costs for a UV-curing oven are 50% of those for a thermal oven. Installation costs are much less for a UV oven because its small size permits it to be factory assembled, unlike a thermal oven which must be assembled on-site.[36]

UV-curable inks seem to have licked the solvents problem. The cost and energy savings compared to conventional systems seem very promising. But, as with any new technology that surfaces, its impact on human health and environmental well-being must be assessed on more than just a single class of pollutants, such as sol-

Figure 6
Beer Can Printer

Cans are fed to the printer and placed over a steel mandrel. The mandrel is spun, permitting the can to contact a rubber blanket which has the reverse image of the decoration to be printed.
Source: The Adolph Coors Company, Golden, Colorado.

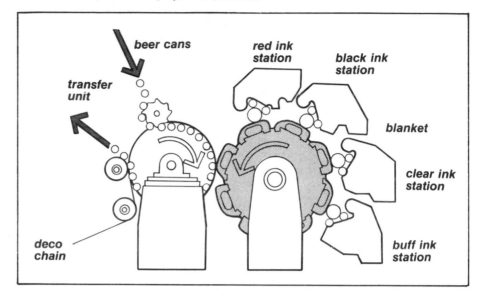

vents. Future trends may see simplification of ink formulations, and substitution with less hazardous constituents.

4.
Recycling Waste Ink

The successful recycling of waste ink in the newspaper business erodes the myth that recycled products are second rate in performance to virgin products. Quite the contrary. Newspapers that have installed ink recycling systems to avoid the increasing costs and difficulties of waste disposal are not only saving money but also ending up with better ink.[37]

Although today's emphasis on cost cutting has spurred some newspapers to recycle, such establishments remain rare. Typically, waste ink is still drummed and hauled away for burial in a landfill site.

■ Several commercially available ink recovery machines have hit the market since the *Milwaukee Journal and Sentinel* (Milwaukee, Wisconsin) developed one of the first in-house ink recycling sys-

tems in 1973. By 1979, the Milwaukee newspaper was saving more than $40,000 a year by recovering 54,000 gallons of waste ink.[38]

■ Charleston Newspapers (Charleston, West Virginia) is another newspaper company that employed in-house expertise to design an ink recycling unit. Both colour and black ink are collected, filtered and mixed with additives as needed to ensure that the reclaimed ink is of proper viscosity.[39]

■ Although some newspapers have the engineering talent and research time to design their own ink recovery systems, many prefer to purchase commercially built units such as the Semler Waste Ink Recovery System (Franklin Park, Illinois).

Commercial ink recycling units can recover off-set, letterpress and Di-Litho inks. Off-set inks are more viscous than letterpress inks, making them more difficult to pump and filter. However, by raising the temperature of off-set inks in the recycling unit, they become less viscous and as easy to filter as letterpress inks.

Because virtually all newspaper ink is oil-based, commercially av-

Figure 7
UV Curing Oven

The beer cans move through a compact curing oven. UV lamps are mounted three on each side with parabolic reflectors facing them. The reflectors direct radiation which does not fall on the can back toward the opposite side.
Source: The Adolph Coors Company, Golden, Colorado.

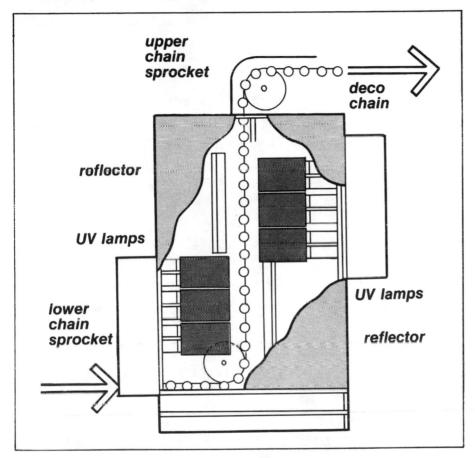

posed at a dumpsite, but because 80% of the ink is recycled, the amount of ink reaching landfill is substantially reduced.[37]

Max Repton of the *Star's* production department says, "When we first installed the recovery unit, we found that we went through a lot of filters. By installing our own pre-filtering system, we could make our rough and fine filters last much longer, and thereby reduce our operating costs."

The filtered ink is often better than new ink received from manufacturers. The recycling process produces an ink with smoother flow properties, better absorbency, faster drying characteristics and smaller, more uniform particle size.[40]

In the first eight months of operation of the ink reclaimer, the *Toronto Star* recovered 260,000 pounds of waste ink, replacing new ink costing over 15¢ per pound. This saved the *Star* $40,000 in new ink costs, and dropped disposal costs to a fraction of the previous level.[38]

Although the $28,000 equipment and installation price tag reflects a considerable capital expenditure, the pay-back economics were so good that the ink reclaimer paid for itself in only six months.

■ Semler Industries also manufacture a portable unit to reclaim ink directly from the press fountain. Newspapers may clean press fountains by circulating ink from the fountain through the ink reclaimer and directly back into the fountain again. Or the newspaper may choose to completely drain a fountain, clean the fountain, and then pump filtered ink back into the fountain tray.

■ The *Minneapolis Star and Tribune* (Minneapolis, Minnesota) invested $4000 in a portable fountain cleaner in 1977. Eighteen ink fountains are cleaned weekly with the portable ink recovery unit.

Danny Cruger, special project foreman with the *Minneapolis Star* estimates that 80% of the ink is recovered, thereby significantly reducing new ink costs. But the real savings, according to Cruger, are the reduced wage overhead.[41]

ailable recovery units such as Semler's are geared to the re-use of oil-based inks.[23]

"At present, our equipment does not handle water-based inks," says Warren Braun of Semler Industries, "but we feel confident that should water-based inks jump into the foreground, we could develop the capacity to reclaim them."

■ The *Toronto Star* installed a Semler waste ink reclaimer in 1978 in response to increasing difficulty in disposing its waste ink. Prior to 1978, the *Star* was paying $15,000 a year to dispose of its ink in a nearby landfill site. When the provincial Ministry of the Environment closed the dump the newspaper had been using for waste ink disposal, the *Star* was faced with the expensive proposi-

tion of hauling its waste to a dump 200 miles away.[38]

Instead, the *Star* opted for a pre-manufactured ink reclaimer, becoming the first Canadian newspaper to undertake this type of recycling programme.

Drip pans underneath each printing press collect waste ink. Colour and black ink are mixed and reclaimed together. The ink is pumped out of the drip pans with a portable machine and drained down a chute which feeds into the reclaimer on the floor below.

The unit is operated two to three times per week on a batch treatment basis. The ink passes through a series of specially designed rough and then fine filters which trap any particles larger than 75 microns in diameter.

The ink-laden filters are dis-

(1) Succession of printing presses at the Toronto Star. (2) Drip pans underneath each printing press collect waste ink. (3) The Semler waste ink reclaimer filters the ink to trap any particles larger than 75 microns in diameter. (4) Ink-laden filters are drained of excess ink which is collected for recirculation in the reclaimer. (5) Both rough and fine filters are used. Cloth wipers used in cleaning up are sent to an outside reconditioner and returned clean to the Toronto Star for re-use.

Prior to installing the portable fountain cleaning and reclamation equipment, it required more than 20 people per week to clean the 18 fountain trays of the presses, at an annual cost of $400,000. Use of the portable cleaner so simplified the process as to slash costs to $25,000 per year, including wages.[38]

The technology to recycle newspaper ink was first developed for large businesses, however, equipment manufacturers are now providing recovery units for smaller businesses as well. Semler industries is now marketing an off-set recovery system designed especially for small newspaper printing companies.[23]

5.
Dirty Rag Recycling

The printing business can be a dirty business. Personnel require an abundance of rags to clean ink and solvent off the presses and themselves. Numerous small firms exist that clean dirty rags for a fee and return them to the company of origin for re-use.

■ Uni-Rent (Whitby, Ontario) is a small Canadian company that recycles dirty rags laden with inks and solvents. Although business is good for Uni-Rent, Brian Bond, one of the company owners, laments that it is still cheaper to buy a disposable cleaning product than to recondition cloth rags.[42]

Says Bond, "The cost of cleaning a wiper (cloth rag) is 5 to 7¢. The cost of replacing a comparable area of rag with a disposable product is 25% less, so the economics favour disposal."

The *Toronto Star* (Toronto, Ontario) is one of several companies that sends its inked rags for reconditioning by Uni-Rent. Rags are cleaned in washing machines, using special detergents and a water-wash system. The wastewater from the cleaning cycle is put in separator tanks to let the sludge settle out. The clarified wastewater, which meets municipal effluent guidelines, is put down the sewer.

Conclusion

Controlling pollution in the printing industry is a difficult task. The large number of processes and products in use by this expansive industry sector results in the generation of many diverse wastestreams.

Nevertheless, some companies have been successful in stemming pollution from solvents and waste inks. These are by no means the only sources of wastes but they are significant ones for which continuing innovation is promising cost-effective solutions.

An important step in any pollution prevention strategy must be an honest examination of the types and quantities of wastes that each particular company generates. In many instances, a firm embarking on such a waste audit would be shocked to discover just how much waste is actually generated that in many instances can be averted. Any firm, no matter how small, can minimize pollution and benefit financially by taking some time out of a hectic schedule to plan a systematic programme for improving process efficiency and reducing waste.

Top. At Uni-Rent, dirty rags contaminated with inks, solvents and grease are reconditioned by cleaning in washing machines.   Left . Cleaned cloth wipers previously contaminated with ink.

FOR FURTHER INFORMATION

Associations

Contact the following trade associations for additional information on pollution control technologies and equipment. These trade associations can assist you directly, or point you in the right direction for more information on commercially available recycling equipment, technology transfer programmes, technical experts in the field, existing tax breaks and other economic incentives, and upcoming regulations.

Encourage those associations which rank pollution control low on their priority list to direct more attention to pollution prevention. Preventing pollution can benefit both the business community and the environment.

The following list identifies primarily national associations in Canada and the United States. It is not uncommon for Canadian companies to belong to American associations. Contact the national associations and ask if a local chapter is in operation near your business.

Graphic Arts Industries
Association,
Suite 906,
75 Albert St.,
Ottawa, Ontario.
K1P 5E7
(613) 236-7208

Council of Printing Industries
of Canada,
Suite 808,
159 Bay St.,
Toronto, Ontario.
M5J 1J7
(416) 362-2528

Technical Association of the
Graphic Arts,
P.O. Box 3064,
Federal Station,
Rochester, New York.
14614
(716) 475-6662

American Institute of Graphic Arts,
1059 Third Avenue,
New York, New York.
10021
(212) 752-0813

National Association of Printers and
Lithographers,
780 Palisade Avenue,
Teaneck, New Jersey.
07666
(201) 342-0700

Graphic Arts Technical Foundation,
4615 Forbes Avenue,
Pittsburg, Pennsylvania.
15213
(412) 621-6941

International Association of
Photoplatemakers,
552 W. 167 St.,
South Holland, Illinois.
60473
(312) 596-5111

Canadian Daily Newspapers
Publishers Association,
Suite 214,
321 Bloor St. East,
Toronto, Ontario.
M4W 1E7
(416) 923-3567

American Newspaper Publishers
Association,
The Newspaper Center,
11600 Sunrise Valley Dr.,
Reston, Virginia.
22091
(703) 620-9500

Gravure Research Institute
22 Manhasset Avenue,
Port Washington,
New York.
11050
(516) 883-6670

Canadian Printing Ink
Manufacturers Association,
Box 294,
Kleinburg, Ontario.
L0J 1C0
(416) 851-1118

National Association of
Printing Ink Manufacturers,
550 Mamaroneck Avenue,
Harrison, New York.
10528
(914) 698-1004

Journals

Numerous excellent publications are currently available in both Canada and the United States. The journals listed below frequently contain articles that relate to improving process efficiency, energy and materials conservation, and waste recovery. These journals also carry an assortment of advertisements by manufacturers of recycling and other pollution prevention equipment.

CANADIAN PRINTER AND
PUBLISHER,
Maclean Hunter Ltd.,
481 University Avenue,
Toronto, Ontario.
M5W 1A7

ANPA R.I. BULLETIN,
American Newspaper Publishers
Association,
Research Institute,
Box 598,
Easton, Pennsylvania.
18042

AIGA NEWSLETTER,
American Institute of
Graphic Arts,
1059 Third Avenue,
New York, New York.
10021

BRITISH PRINTER,
Maclean Hunter Ltd.,
30 Old Burlington St.,
London, England.
W1X 2AE

EDITOR & PUBLISHER,
Editor & Publisher Co. Inc.,
575 Lexington Avenue,
New York, New York.
10022

PACKAGING PRINTING,
American Publishing Co.,
401 N. Broad St.,
Philadelphia, Pennsylvania.
19108

References

1. Chapman, B. "Focus on New Products for '81." *Graphic Arts Monthly,* January 1981.

2. "The Things I Hear." *Canadian Printer and Publisher,* November 1980.

3. DesMarais, P. *The Canadian Commercial Printing Industry: A Report by the Sector Task Force.* Department of Industry, Trade and Commerce (Canada), 1976.

4. Lofquist, W.S. "Pollution Abatement Costs and Expenditures by the U.S. Printing and Publishing Industry." *Printing and Publishing,* Winter 1980/81.

5. George, H.F. "The Challenges of the Eighties in Coatings and Graphic Arts." *Journal of Coatings Technology,* March 1981.

6. Hendershof, H. and Browne, B. "Why Printing Ink Prices Are Going to Skyrocket." *Canadian Printer and Publisher,* June 1980.

7. Bruno, M.H. "New Developments in Printing in the United States, Featuring High Speed Non Silver Films." *Professional Printer,* July 1977.

8. Mooij, H. and Law, C. *Characterization of the Industrial Wastes Generated In the Manufacture of Adhesives and Printing Inks.* Prepared for the Environmental Protection Service, Environment Canada, September 30, 1975.

9. Puttergill, N. "Graphic Reproduction Developments." *Professional Printer,* September/October 1979.

10. Ingram, P. "Reducing Waste." *Professional Printer,* May/June 1980.

11. Hartsuch, P.J. "GATF Features Seminar on Process Controls for Printing." *Graphic Arts Monthly,* September 1980.

12. Hartsuch, P.J. "Process Control for Higher Productivity is Subject of R & E Council Seminar." *Graphic Arts Monthly,* January 1981.

13. Lee, L.K. "Common Problems Plague Pressmen; Scumming, Piling, Dot Gain, Blinding, Are Hazards that Can Be Overcome." *Graphic Arts Monthly,* February 1981.

14. "Press Accessories: Keys to Spoilage Control." *Graphic Arts Monthly,* August 1981.

15. "Waste Incentive Program Fosters Staff Awareness." *Editor and Publisher,* January 10, 1981.

16. Hartsuch, P.J. "Less Press Waste Means Money in Your Pocket." *Graphic Arts Monthly,* January 1980.

17. White, I. "Quality Control Guides to Improve Your Profits." *Canadian Printer and Publisher,* October 1980.

18. Palmer, C. "Conserving Photosensitive Materials." *Graphic Arts Monthly,* May 1980.

19. "Film System Needs No Silver, Darkroom or Chemical Developers." *Chemical Week,* April 9, 1980.

20. Deaver, J. "Water: Pollution-Free Plate Developer." *Graphic Arts Monthly,* November 1979.

21. 3M Company. Hydrolith™. St. Paul, Minnesota: 3M Company (product literature).

22. Markle, R.A. *et al.* (Batelle's Columbus Laboratories). *Potentially Toxic and Hazardous Substances in the Industrial Organic Chemicals and Organic Dyes and Pigments Industries.* Prepared for the Office of Research and Development, U.S. Environmental Protection Agency, March 1980.

23. Braun, Warren. Semler Industries Inc., Franklin Park, Illinois. Personal communication, August 1981.

24. Whittenberg, Henry. Canadian Printing Ink Manufacturers Association, Kleinburg, Ontario. Personal communication, July 1981.

25. Teale, J.M. "Fast Payout from In-Plant Recovery of Spent Solvents." *Chemical Engineering,* January 31, 1977.

26. Klein, S. "Water-Based Inks Merit Another Look, Researcher Says." *Graphic Arts Monthly,* May 1980.

27. Bruno, M.H. "New Trends in the Printing Industry in the USA." *Professional Printer,* September/October 1979.

28. O'Keefe, R.M. "Propose Water-Based Inks as Answer to Meeting EPA Pollution Guidelines." *Graphic Arts Monthly,* September 1979.

29. Owen, E.H. "Flexographic Printing, Inserting Draw Top Interest at Conference." *Canadian Printer and Publisher,* July 1981.

30. "Flexo Test Underway at Nashville Papers." *Editor and Publisher,* December 5, 1981.

31. Matthews, John. Fusion Systems™ Corporation, Rockville, Maryland. Personal communication, July 1981.

32. Fusion Systems™ Corporation. *Fusion Systems Ultraviolet Curing.* 1980 (product literature).

33. Matthews, J. "UV Curing in Packaging." *Radiation Curing,* August 1979.

34. Rogers, M. "Decorating, Printing and Finishing in the '80's." *Plastics Technology,* November 1980.

35. Le Fevre, Paul. Adolph Coors Company, Golden, Colorado. Personal communication, August 1981.

36. Le Fevre, P.H. *UV Cure of Two-Piece Can Decoration.* Presentation to the Metal Decorators Association, 1981.

37. Repton, M. Production Department, Toronto Star, Toronto, Ontario. Personal communication, April 1981.

38. American Newspaper Publishers Association Research Institute. "Ink Reclamation — A Valuable New Process for Newspaper." *R.I. Bulletin* (American Newspaper Publishers Association), May 2, 1979.

39. "Ink Recycling System Put into Operation." *Editor and Publisher,* January 19, 1980.

40. Spolsky, M. "Newspaper Inks Get Second Debut." *Probe Post,* July/August 1979.

41. Cruger, D. *Minneapolis Star and Tribune,* Minneapolis, Minnesota. Personal communication, August 1981.

42. Bond, Brian. Uni-Rent, Whitby, Ontario. Personal communication, June 1981.

Pulp & Paper

There is no denying that the pulp and paper industry is one of the mainstays of Canada's economy. It is the leading manufacturing industry in Canada in terms of value of shipments, employment and exports. It remains the dominant economic force in the Atlantic region, Quebec, and to a slightly lesser extent, British Columbia. When one looks beyond the aggregate totals, it is also plain that for many towns across the country it is the only source of income and the sole reason for those communities' existence. Pulp and paper production is a $3 billion a year enterprise and the employer of over 85,000 Canadians.[1]

There is also no denying that pulp and paper is the major source of water pollution in Canada. The Quebec Ministry of the Environment has completed a study that shows the pulp and paper mills of that province produce as much pollution as 14 million people (which is two and a half times the population of the province). The industry consumes 3 million cubic metres of water each day, equivalent to the entire flow of Quebec's largest river, the Montmorency. The waste treatment activities of Quebec mills require nutrients equal to one-third of all the chemical fertilizers used by Quebec farmers in one year. And the result of all this activity? Only one of the mills tested was able to pass ministry toxicity tests, two-thirds fail the federal suspended solids requirements and half are not in compliance with biochemical oxygen demand (BOD) limits.[2]

The picture is no better in Ontario, where the industry is responsible for 80% of all the soluble organic material and 60% of the suspended solid matter discharged directly into that province's lakes and rivers.

It is certainly not difficult to uncover a wealth of information on the industry. Over the last ten years, it has maintained a high profile in both the technical journals and the daily headlines — mercury pollution in the English-Wabigoon River system (Ontario), spruce budworm controls and other insecticide spraying programmes, logging practices in provincial parks, reforestation deficiencies, the loss of competitive standing in world markets, and the dire need for modernization. The industry is continually

in the centre of controversy.

When it comes to pollution abatement, the story is equally complex. There are dozens of examples of waste control technologies. The industry trade journals devote much of their space to examples of both innovative and traditional waste control practices. The urgent need to increase efficiency in uncompetitive and aging mills has been coupled with a concurrent realization of environmental problems. The rush to find solutions has resulted in millions of dollars of research and hundreds of millions of dollars of new construction.[3]

The rewards, if the programmes are successful, will be great. Few industries deal with a raw material so rife with possible applications. The humble tree is a complex chemical factory. Starting with just the rudimentary materials of carbon dioxide, water and sunlight, it builds simple glucose sugars into complex structures.

Cellulose is the basic building block and starch is the storage material. Cellulose is polymerized into complex chains which bond together with lignin to form fibres. A piece of dehydrated wood is a chemist's delight; 40 to 50% cellulose, 20 to 25% lignin, the rest made up of minerals, tanning agents, fats, oils, resins, carbohydrates, hemicellulose and a host of other substances.[4] With this chemical raw material, a wide variety of industries can be fueled. Figure 1 illustrates the range of products that are based on wood — fabrics, glue, food coatings, chemicals and, of course, paper.[4]

Environmental Impacts

The relative complexity and versatility of wood is both its glory and its nemesis. The complex systems devised to turn trees into paper products (see Figure 2) give rise to a host of organic and

Figure 1
Wood as a Chemical Raw Material

The tree is the source of many of the products we depend on each day: soaps, drugs, glues, fabrics and papers.

Source: *How Things Work: The Universal Encyclopedia of Machines.* London: Allen and Unwin, 1967.

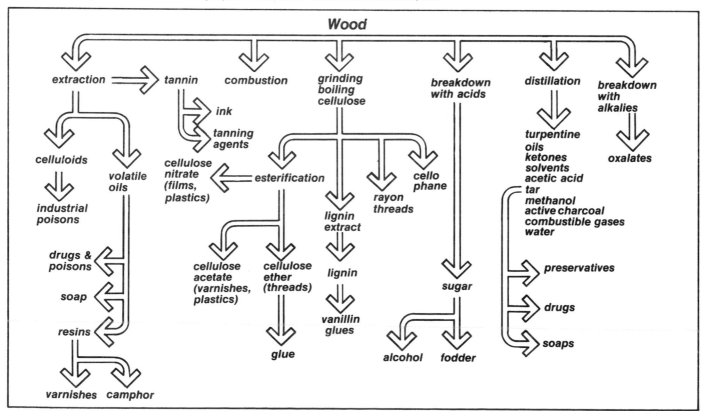

Figure 2
The Pulp and Paper Process

Source: Environment Canada (Water Pollution Control Directorate), *The Basic Technology of the Pulp and Paper Industry and its Waste Reduction Activities,* May 1973.

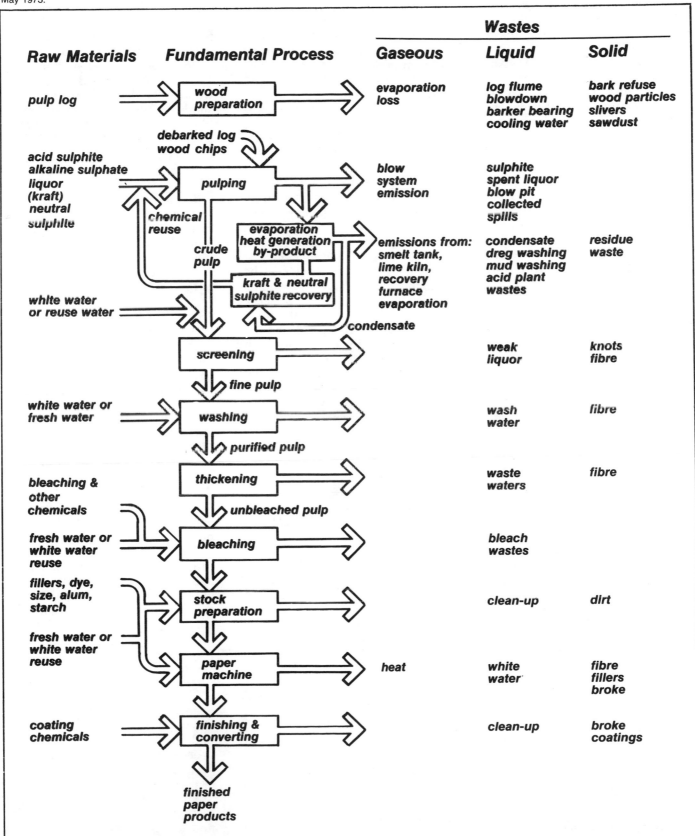

inorganic waste products.[5] The environmental regulations directed towards control of the pulp and paper industry are concerned primarily with BOD, suspended solids and, more recently, toxicity. Suspended solids are comprised of bark, wood fibres, dirt and other materials. Soluble organic materials, usually measured as five-day biochemical oxygen demand (BOD5) are decomposed by bacteria in the receiving waters which consume dissolved oxygen in the process. Dissolved solids are made up of dissolved salts and other inorganic chemicals.

There is a growing body of evidence on the effects of specific chemical toxins in the discharges of pulp and paper mills. Of concern, for instance, are the resin acid soaps. They are adsorbed on the gills of fish and other aquatic organisms where they interfere with the ability to take up oxygen.[6] Chlorine products, phenols and mercaptans are prime candidates for future specific discharge regulations. Table 1 lists the major liquid waste components of the industry and their effects.[7] Table 2 breaks down the effluents from each of the mill processes and assesses their impacts on the environment.[1]

Waste Emission Reduction

During the decade 1969-1978, production from Canadian mills rose from 54,300 to 63,922 tonnes, or 18%. The wastewater discharged during that same period declined substantially. Suspended solids decreased 53% in total and 59% when expressed as discharge per unit of production. Total BOD output dropped 14.3%, or 27% per unit of production.

Much of this improvement was due to mill modernization and conservation programmes designed to capture and use as much of the valuable wood fibre as possible. This second factor explains much of the improvement in, for instance, suspended solids loadings.

It is important to remember that despite these improvements, a great deal of work must still be done for the pulp and paper industry to achieve compliance with the federal emission regulations. Table 3 shows the percentage of mills that are in compliance with the discharge requirements.[1] These are mills which are not connected to municipal sewage treatment systems and dump their wastes (treated or not) into nearby water bodies.

Although the success rate varies greatly from province to province, almost 38% of mills have not met the BOD limits, more than 55% have not met the suspended solids requirements and nearly 70% have failed the toxicity test.

Progress by industry to meet the federal requirements has also been slower than expected. In 1975, it was projected that 90 to 100% of the pulp and paper mills would have solved their suspended solids pollution abatement problem by 1977. It can be seen that those forecasts are far from realized. By 1978, only 30.3% of Quebec mills were in compliance, 44.6% nationally.

The projections have been steadily revised downwards over the last five years. In all regions except the Atlantic, the compliance rate now projected (in 1980) for 1982 for suspended solids is less than the rate projected as recently as December 1975 for 1977.[1] The same situation holds true for BOD5 and toxicity.

In Ontario between 1975 and 1979, the average discharge of suspended solids per tonne of production decreased only 7.9% (from 62.6 to 57.7 kg). The BOD5 decrease is almost identical at 8.2% (19.5 to 17.9 kg). However, 9 of 29 mills showed increases in suspended solids per tonne of production and 15 mills increased the ratio of BOD to production.[1]

Despite the expenditures made on clean-up in Ontario ($83.5 million from 1975 to 1979 inclusive, according to the Canadian Pulp and Paper Association[1]), the aggregate improvements noted above appear to be very little.

The cyclical nature of pulp and paper markets and the relatively low rate of return on investment, when compared to other industrial sectors, make the long-term financing of the massive amounts of capital required a tricky and expensive proposition. Studies show that the industry in Ontario and Quebec may have to spend over $2 billion on modernization and pollution control over the next five years.

The melding of the proper technology, necessary financing and an appropriate level of regulatory enforcement can ensure

---

Table 1
The Environmental Impact of Liquid Wastes from the Pulp and Paper Industry

Liquid wastes cause the following damages and effects:

1. *Some constituents of wastewaters may be dangerous to human health. Residual mercury compounds are of particular significance;*

2. *Decomposition of organic materials can result in oxygen depletion in waters which threatens the survival of fish and other aquatic animals;*

3. *Suspended solids coat the bottoms of rivers and lakes and smother aquatic plants and animals;*

4. *Toxic substances kill aquatic organisms;*

5. *BOD5, suspended solids and toxic substances destroy fish habitats;*

6. *Fish may be tainted by chemicals. Residues of toxic materials such as mercury accumulate in fish tissues;*

7. *Colour, foaming, sludge deposits and odours impair the aesthetic properties of the receiving waters.*

Source: *Alternative Policies for Pollution Abatement: The Ontario Pulp and Paper Industry,* Ontario Ministry of the Environment, October 1976.

Table 2
Pulp and Paper Effluents: Their Sources and Characteristics

H = High   M = Medium   L = Low

Mill Source	Effluent Component	BOD	COD	Settleable solids	Colloidal solids	Dissolved solids	pH	Toxicity
Woodroom	Resin acids					M	M	L
	Barkchips	H		H				H
	Silt and Black fines	H			H			H
Groundwood pulp	Resin acids					M	M	H
	Cellulose fines	L			H			H
	Woodfines	L			H			H
Groundwood bleach	Zinc hydrosulphite		M					M
	Resin acid soaps					H	L	H
	Fatty acid soaps					H	L	H
	Inorganic sulphides and sulphates			H	M	M	M	M
	Organic sulphides			M	M		M	L
Kraft pulp	Lignin residues and derivatives				H			H
	Methyl mercaptan							H
	Alcohols		L					M
	Fibres	L		M				L
	Heavy metal ions				L	L		L
	Wood sugars and carbohydrates	M				H		L
	Phenol and derivatives (ketones)							M
Sulphite pulp	(Na) Sulphite			H	H	L	M	M
	(Ca) Sulphite			H	L	H	H	M
	(Mg) Sulphite			H	L	H	L	M
	(NH₄) Sulphite	H				H	L	M
	Resin acids						M	M
	Wood sugars and carbohydrates	H				H		L
	Phenol and derivatives (ketones)							M
	Lignin residues and derivatives				M			M
	Fibres	M			H			L
Chemical Pulp bleach	Chlorine and Chloroamines			L			H	H
	Organic dyes and colour surfactants					M		M/H
	Slimicides and Biocides					M		H
	Chlorinated lignins							H
	Resin acids							L
Papermaking Coating	Phenol and derivatives (ketones)	M		M				M
	Fibre particles	M			M			M
	Alcohols		L					
	Protein and starch adhesives	H			M	M		L
	Titanium dioxide					H		M
	Calcium carbonate				M			L
	Clay and talc					H		M

Source: Environmental Protection Regulation, Water Pollution and the Pulp and Paper Industry, The Economic Council of Canada, June 1980.

Table 3

Percentage of Mills in Compliance with Federal Discharge Requirements

Region	# Mills (1978)	BOD₅ 1975	1978	Suspended Solids 1975	1978	Toxicity 1975	1978
Atlantic	19	51	55	37	48	28	32
Quebec	50	36	49	19	30.3	9	12
Ontario	29	40	54	52	61	3.5	31
Prairies	7	79	84	38	71	50	86
Pacific	24	95	100	30	44	38	50
Canada	129	53.7	62.3	32.7	44.6	18.7	30.2

Source: Environmental Protection Regulation, Water Pollution and the Pulp and Paper Industry, The Economic Council of Canada, June 1980.

that future clean-up efforts are more satisfactory.

The most problematic operations are the sulphite and newsprint operations. Based principally in the Atlantic region, Quebec and Ontario (94% of Canada's sulphite pulp production), most of these plants are both old and small. Upgrading these mills to meet the federal guidelines would account for about 75% of the total required capital for cleaning up the whole pulp and paper industry. On the

basis of the average mill costs, that for a sulphite mill is about 2.5 times, and that for a newsprint mill nearly 1.4 times the average for all mills.[1]

There are also serious technical problems facing the small-scale pulp makers. According to a report by the United Nations Industrial Development Organization. There is no proven process for the recovery of cooking chemicals used in small-scale pulp making. This means that the black liquor containing as much as one-half of the

raw material feed and all of the cooking chemicals must be discarded. If chemical recovery were possible, dissolved organic matter could be burnt, and steam generated or recycled for cooking.[8]

The impetus for increased efficiency and competitiveness is causing re-evaluation in this slumping industry. Some large companies have decided to rebuild their pulping/bleaching process rather than resort to add-on waste treatment that would never offer a return on the investment.

Pollution Prevention Opportunities

1.

Canadian International Paper: Sulphonated Chemi-Mechanical Pulp

A newsprint mill facing tough environmental discharge regulations has two obvious courses of action available. Since its product is composed of chemical and mechanical pulp, it can choose to improve the strength properties of the mechanical pulp so as to reduce or eliminate the need for reinforcing chemical pulp with its attendant pollution problems. The second approach would be to improve the yield of chemical pulp

and thus reduce the BOD associated with the fibres lost through the chemical pulping process.

A research programme carried out by the Canadian International Paper Company (CIP) has utilized the first approach to develop an award-winning chemi-mechanical pulping process: Sulphonated Chemi-Mechanical Pulp (SCMP).

In the early 1970s CIP had decided to shut down the sulphite pulping operations at its Gatineau, Quebec mill and buy market Kraft pulp. When the price of Kraft pulp shot up, the firm needed to investigate ways of cutting their Kraft pulp consumption. Mechanical pulping was a

preferred option because of its low BOD discharges and high fibre yield, but the conventional mechanical pulping techniques did not produce a product of high enough strength to replace the reinforcing Kraft pulp. In 1972 and 1973, the CIP researchers studied the options before settling on SCMP and then began three years of trial runs at the Gatineau mill. Construction of a full-scale, 380-tonnes-per-day plant was started in 1976 and completed in July 1978. The $23 million project proved so successful that SCMP has been introduced at Abitibi-Price's Thunder Bay plant (160 tonnes per day) and is being planned at CIP's International

Paper Mill in New Brunswick and at another of its operations in the northeast United States.

The SCMP process is proving so popular because it offers advantages in pollution control, feed stock versatility, product quality, and energy conservation, in addition to being an economical alternative to Kraft pulp.

Soaking in a high concentration sodium sulphite solution (sulphonation) is the key to both energy savings and high fibre yields in the SCMP process. Wood chips are washed, presteamed and then cooked with a 12% sodium sulphite solution for 30 to 45 minutes at 140°C. The intermediate cooking temperature minimizes the loss of yield and brightness while the high Na_2SO_3 maximizes the sulphonation of the lignin in the chips. The spent cooking solution still contains high levels of NA_2SO_3 which is recovered to a great extent and re-used in the cooking.

The cooked chips are separated from the bulk of the spent liquor, pressed to about 50% solids to recover even more of the liquor, and refined to 300 to 400 mL CSF in two stages of atmospheric refining. The mechanical pump which reduces the softened wood chips to cellulose fibres takes only a second and therein lie great energy savings.[9]

The pressate is combined with the rest of the weak liquor, fortified with sodium hydroxide, and then passed through an absorption tower where sulphur dioxide is absorbed to bring the concentration back to 12% Na_2SO_3. The strong liquor is returned to the digester for cooking. An equilibrium level of dissolved organics is reached in continuous operation, but this does not have any detrimental effect on either the strength or brightness of the pulp.[10] Figure 3 illustrates the basic process which, at the Gatineau mill, employs a liquid phase cooking system.[10] A vapour phase process will also provide a high quality pulp as long as the chips are thoroughly impregnated under pressure. This technology is going to be used at the New Brunswick International Paper Mill.

Air emissions are also improved. Because alkaline liquor is used, no sulphur dioxide is given off.

If pollution abatement regulations require a greater level of control, it is possible to incorporate a more efficient sulphite recovery process into the SCMP system. An evaporation and crystallization operation has been developed which yields sodium sulphite crystals for re-use and a concentrated liquor for combustion.[10]

An important advantage of the SCMP process comes from the preliminary sulphonation step during which the wood chips are softened. The yield and optical qualities of SCMP pulp are close to those of other thermo-mechanical pulping processes, and its strength is similar to that of pulp obtained through chemical pulping, as are its fibre length and drainage properties. Table 4 summarizes these parameters and compares SCMP pulp with that derived from other systems.[10]

During pulping the fibres can be separated more completely and with much less damage. Microscopic photography shows the SCMP fibres are long and straight and the pulp is not filled with fines. Because the yield from the SCMP system is so high, there are fewer fibres lost in the process discharge, thus controlling BOD[11] (see Table 5).

At the Gatineau mill, newsprint production has increased while BOD in the discharge has decreased 72%, from 176 tonnes per day to 49 tonnes per day.[2] The pollution abatement is even higher when one considers the reduced need for sulphite-derived pulp that the SCMP has replaced. Pulp produced in a regular sulphite mill results in BOD discharges of about 500 lb per ton of production. The SCMP process cuts pollution to about 80 lb per ton BOD, or 84%.[11]

Trial runs at Gatineau and Trois Rivières proved that good quality newsprint could be produced using pulp just from SCMP

Figure 3
The SCMP Process

Wood chips from the presteamer are added to the digester unit where they are cooked at an intermediate temperature in a sodium sulphite solution before being passed on to the mechanical press. The used cooking solution is reconstituted and recycled back to the digester.

Source: "The Story of Sulphonated Chemimechanical Pulp," *Pulp and Paper Canada*, September 1981.

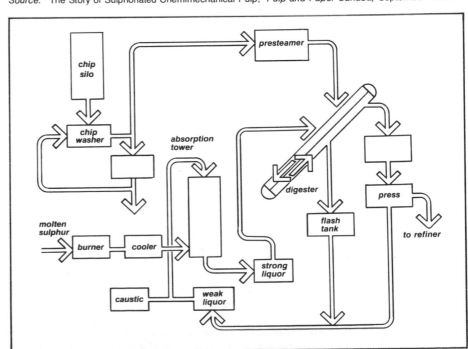

and stone ground sources. The low-yield, high-BOD-producing sulphite pulp could be eliminated entirely.

The SCMP process can also utilize a greater range of wood fibre sources. Because wood chips are used rather than logs, sawmill residues can be used in paper production, thus helping conserve the dwindling forest stocks. Hardwoods, which are regionally in great abundance, can also be used to replace the softwoods normally used in mechanical pulping operations. The SCMP system can accommodate up to 40% hardwoods in the pulp and both poplar and maple have been used in tests. At Gatineau, a 25% poplar mix was run without affecting newsprint quality.

The use of the SCMP process also results in substantial energy savings. Since the wood chips are softened prior to being broken up, 25% less energy is needed than in other refiner mechanical pulping operations.[11]

At present the SCMP process is being used exclusively to produce newsprint. According to its de-velopers, it also has the potential to supply pulp for the production of diaper fluff and other tissue products, packing materials, such as liner board and folding cartons, and even coated publication paper.

The SCMP system has been gaining recognition since its problem-free operation began at Gatineau. It won the Chemical Institute of Canada's 1980 Environmental Improvement Award. Its capacity to reduce pollution while increasing yield, saving energy and producing high strength pulp has earned the attention of people in the industry all over the world.

2.
Great Lakes Paper — Closed Loop Processing

The process that transforms a tree into bleached Kraft pulp requires large amounts of water and a steady supply of energy and chemicals. Besides producing a quality pulp to make paper, board or tissue, the operation also re-sults in the discharge of large amounts of wastewater containing, in part, more than half the weight of the original wood.[12] Normally, for each ton of pulp between 100 and 200 m³ of wastewater, with its load of suspended solids, BOD, toxic chemicals and colour contaminants, are produced.

"In the processes for conversions of logs to bleached Kraft pulp, four major effluents are normally formed. The logs are first debarked, commonly with large volumes of high-pressure water, producing an effluent high in suspended solids. The wood is chipped and then cooked at high temperature and pressure with regenerated sodium hydroxide and sodium sulfide. This process decomposes and dissolves the interfibre binding and when the pressure is rapidly released, free fibres are formed.[13]

"The spent cooking liquor is partially removed from the brown pulp by counter-current washing. Typically 92 to 98% of the spent cooking liquor is recovered, concentrated by evaporation and

---

Table 4
Typical Properties of Newsprint Pulps

	SGW	RMP	TMP	SCMP	SBK	HYBS
Yield on wood, %	95	95	94	92	43	65
CSF, mL	90	100	150	350	550	550
Breaking length, km	3.2	3.5	4.0	6.0	8.0	9.5
Burst index, MN/kg	1.3	1.5	1.7	3.4	6.0	6.0
Tear index, Nm²/kg	5.0	6.0	8.0	8.8	14.0	7.0
Apparent density, kg/m²	400	335	400	470	660	625
Wet web tensile at 20% solids, N/m	25	25	35	42	55	50
Brightness (Elrepho), %	59	58	56	56	70	50
Opacity, %	97	97	96	91	75	82
Long fibre, % (48 mesh, Bauer-McNett)	40	45	55	72	80	80
Fines, % (100 mesh, Bauer-McNett)	50	38	35	19	8	20

The SCMP process yields a pulp that compares favourably with other newsprint pulps in regard to strength, yield, brightness and opacity. SGW — stoneground wood; RMP — refiner mechanical pulp; TMP — thermomechanical pulp; HYBS — high yield bleached sulphite.

Source: "The Story of Sulphonated Chemimechanical Pulp," *Pulp and Paper Canada*, September 1981.

Table 5
BOD₅ of Newsprint Furnish Effluents

	Yield, % on wood	BOD₅ kg/ tonne
RMP	96	23-28
TMP	96	20-25[a]
SCMP	92	35-45
Low-yield sulphite	50	250
High-yield sulphite	65	150

[a] *Excluding steam condensate.*

Source:
"The Story of Sulphonated Chemimechanical Pulp," *Pulp and Paper Canada*, September 1981.

burned. However, some liquor is lost from the washing process, giving rise to up to 30% of the BOD discharge from the mill. Further, on evaporation of the spent liquor, volatile components are stripped out of the liquor and become concentrated in the condensed vapours or condensate. The methanol and malodorous sulphur compounds in the condensate contribute up to 30% of the BOD discharge of the mill.

"The fourth major effluent is produced on bleaching the highly coloured brown pulp. In the multi-stage bleaching process, the pulp is treated alternately with chlorine and/or chlorine dioxide and with sodium hydroxide. Washing is employed after each treatment. The effluent from the bleach plant has the largest volume and contains up to 50% of the BOD and most of the colour discharged from the mill."[13]

While much of the organic load resulting from the pulping operation has been utilized to some degree for almost a century, the wastes from the bleaching process are continually being wrestled with by pulp and paper plants around the world. In a modern mill the waste liquors from pulping are usually concentrated in an evaporator unit and used to feed a recovery boiler. The energy generated goes a long way to supplying all the heat and electrical power needed for pulping, bleaching, drying and chemical recovery.

The wastes derived from Kraft bleaching, however, are more exotic and not as amenable to simple solutions. They are rich in BOD, highly coloured, toxic and mutagenic. The bleaching process involves chlorination, oxidation and alkali extraction of the solid coloured materials produced from the wood during pulping, using chlorine, chlorine dioxide and sodium hydroxide, usually in at least five bleaching stages. The effluent from the bleaching and washing process is a large volume of dilute aqueous solution containing sodium salts, organic acids, other organic reaction products and sodium chloride.[11]

There are two alternatives to the operator who wishes to control, to the greatest degree possible, the

discharge of these pulping and bleaching wastes; expensive add-on wastewater treatment facilities, or internal process changes that strive to recycle all the polluted water within the mill.

The closed cycle Kraft mill concept was taken to heart by a University of Toronto professor in the Department of Chemical Engineering and Applied Chemistry, W. Howard Rapson, and his then-graduate student Douglas W. Reeve. The possibilities first presented themselves in 1965, and by 1967, the scientists were able to postulate the specific steps necessary to make the idea work. Years of research on bench-scale models and pilot studies finally culminated in March of 1977 when the new Great Lakes Paper "B" mill opened in Thunder Bay, Ontario. The 680-ton-per-day bleached Kraft mill incorporated all the necessary technology to make closed-cycle operation a reality.

At "B" mill, the bleach plant effluent is used to wash the unbleached pulp. The resulting load of dissolved organics enters the pulping liquor cycle and is burned

in the recovery furnace. The sodium chloride in the bleachery filtrate is removed from the recovery cycle by evaporation of the white liquor in a novel salt recovery plant and is used to reconstitute the required bleaching chemicals. Closed-cycle operation depends on six major process operations: counter-current washing; replacing most of the chlorine used in bleaching with chlorine dioxide; using the bleach plant effluent to wash the pulp and thus introducing it into the chemical recovery system; using a salt recovery plant to separate sodium chloride from the white pulping liquor and using it to regenerate new bleaching chemicals; establishing an efficient spill collection system; and steam stripping and recycling the contaminated condensates.

The result of the installation and fine tuning of this system at Great Lakes Paper has been the production of high quality pulp — strong, bright and stable — which is unusually clean. The mill has also been running at a substantially higher rate than its design capacity.

Figure 4
Bleach Plant Counter-Current Washing

Counter-current washing in the bleach plant is the key to reducing water use and saving energy at Great Lakes Paper. The bleach plant effluent is then used in the brown decker system to wash the unbleached pulp. This allows the bleaching chemicals to enter the chemical recovery system.
Source: "The Closed Cycle Concept Kraft Mill at Great Lakes — An Advanced Status Report," *Pulp and Paper Canada,* June 1979.

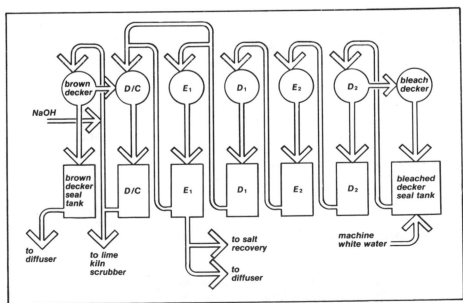

Each major process operation bears detailing. The first step is counter-current washing. It is used in almost every industrial sector concerned with waste. The result is a drastically reduced intake of fresh water and a more concentrated effluent stream. In the counter-current washing process, fresh water is introduced only in the pulp drying machine; the filtrate from each of the five bleaching stages is used to wash the pulp from the preceding one.[14]

Figure 4 shows a schematic of the bleaching process with counter-current water flow.[13] Filtrate from the E_1 stage is also diverted to the first stage brown stock diffuser and to the salt recovery plant where it is used for the dilution of the concentrated white liquor. The filtrate from the first bleaching stage, (D/C), is used in showers to wash the unbleached pulp in the brown stock decker, and in the lime kiln scrubber to purge calcium ions from the chlorination stage. This material is eventually recovered.

Since 1975, most Kraft bleacheries have converted their systems to counter-current jumpstage or complete counter-current washing processes.[15] Rapson has recently written, "This concept was regarded as impossible when I first proposed it but it is widely practised world-wide today because of (its) great advantages."[12] At "B" mill counter-current washing has helped to reduce the total water consumption from 20,000 to 4,000 gallons per ton of pulp (80%). The use of counter-current washwater is also responsible for saving the energy needed to keep the bleaching stages at 70°C (steam consumption is only 1 million Btu's per ton of pulp bleached[14]).

Secondly, about 70% of the chlorine normally used in the first stage of bleaching is replaced with chlorine dioxide. Chlorine dioxide was formerly used only in two later stages. The results are manifold; the pulp is stronger, whiter, cleaner, more stable; yield is increased about 1%; the high temperatures found in a closed system can be tolerated without a decrease in yield; the amount of sodium hydroxide used in bleach-

ing is cut by 80% for each equivalent of chlorine replaced.[14] Thus the amount of sodium chloride produced per ton of pulp is cut approximately in half, lowering the load on the salt recovery plant.

Third, the bleach plant effluent, with its load of sodium chloride and all its organic contaminants, is introduced into the brown decker system and used to replace fresh water for washing the pulp. This re-use also ensures that the spent bleaching chemicals enter the chemical recovery system and the organic contaminants are consumed in the recovery boiler.

Fourth, the spent pulping liquor and washing fluids containing the sodium chloride and the remains of the bleaching chemicals, are introduced into the chemical recovery process. Douglas Reeve and ERCO Envirotech Ltd. (Mississauga, Ontario) have developed the necessary equipment to remove the sodium chloride from the sodium hydroxide and sodium sulphide used in pulping. Their salt recovery plant entails evaporating the white liquor and capturing the almost pure salt.

The recovered sodium chloride is then used in the ERCO R-3 unit for generating chlorine dioxide. The R-3 unit eliminates the sulphuric acid waste obtained in other ClO_2 generation equipment. The ClO_2 is then used again in the bleaching process, thus closing the cycle. The ERCO R-3 system is now being used in over 60 plants around the world and was the winner of the Chemical Industry of Canada's Environmental Improvement Award for 1981.[16]

Fifth, an integrated and intregal spill detection and collection system has been installed at "B" mill. Four separate spill pits, ranging in capacity from 100,000 to 225,000 gal (U.S.), are available to collect and contain spills and overflows from separate operations in the mill. About 25% of the water pollution of a Kraft pulp mill arises from spills and washups.[12] If these releases are to be kept to the minimum, adequate precautions must be taken and plans developed that will allow spilled material to be returned to the system and/or the chemical recovery equipment.

Finally, a steam stripper removes 90% of the BOD_5 of the foul condensates from the flash heat double evaporator. Only 545 kg a day of BOD leave the plant from this source.[17]

In total, the effectiveness of the closed-cycle system has reduced BOD discharge from the mill to as low as 7.5 kg per ton. Operation in a semi-closed mode results in emissions of 15.4 kg per ton. This has eliminated the need for a secondary biological treatment plant. When Great Lakes was first planning the "B" mill, an elaborate system including large aerated lagoons was thought necessary by the Ontario Ministry of the Environment. The lack of available land, the need to build a long pipeline and the excessive costs involved prompted management to investigate the Rapson-Reeve alternative.[14]

According to Rapson, by avoiding the add-on biological treatment, the company also avoided "high power cost for aeration, high maintenance cost for aerators, incomplete destruction of organic matter and toxic chemicals, foam formation, slowed down fermentation in cold weather, fertilizer needs, the settling of sludge, dewatering of sludge and disposal of wet sludge by combustion or burial."[12] They also do not have to worry about increasingly stringent environmental regulation and the possible shift in focus from BOD and suspended solids to specific toxic chemical concentrations in the discharge. The rapidly accelerating cost of sludge disposal and the loss of landfill sites will be another care they will not have to face. The capital and operating cost of a single aerated lagoon is greater than that for the salt recovery plant in the mill.

While four years of operation have disclosed some minor corrosion problems in the closed-cycle system, the process has been refined and fine-tuned in the Great Lakes "B" mill until it now stands as a viable alternative to traditional chemical Kraft pulping.

The economics of closed-cycle Kraft mills are favourable in comparison to alternative biological treatment. While the Rapson-Reeve process increases the cost of the mill by 5%, traditional pollution abatement equipment would have added 10% to the capital costs. The closed-cycle system offers advantages in yield, energy conservation and reduced chemical purchases that should reduce the operating costs below those experienced by a "no-frill" mill (i.e., without pollution abatement equipment which would raise operating costs by about 5%). Biological treatment would also leave about 10% of the BOD, most of the toxic elements and all of the colour in the effluent discharge. These materials are likely to be addressed by future water quality legislation.[18]

3.
Technological Summary

While the work done by Great Lakes Paper and Canadian International Paper is praiseworthy, it is by no means the sum total of the efforts being made by the world pulp and paper industry. The list below is by no means exhaustive, but it does indicate the range of technologies and the variety of approaches that are employed to control pollution while improving mill efficiency.

Process	Company (Reference)	Effectiveness	Cost	Remarks
Black liquor recovery	La Rochette Cenpa-Vénizel plant (France) (18)	BOD reduced 91%; COD reduced 62%; suspended soilds reduced 90%		— new production process using monosulphate ammonium — new pulp washing unit, incineration — increased production — biological treatment
Magnesium bisulphate process	The European Cellulose Group — Strasbourg plant (France) (18)	Reduced BOD from 300 kg/tonne pulp to 45 kg/tonne pulp (85%)	energy savings	— switched from calcium bisulphate to allow recovery of cooking liquors; required pulpwashing unit, liquor evaporation unit, recovery boiler and recuperation unit
Oxygen bleaching	The European Cellulose Group — St.-Gaudens plant (France) (18)	Reduced colour in discharges by 50%		— also has biological treatment plant
Kraft pulp mill odour control	Russian pilot plant (19)	98% removal of hydrogen sulphide and mercaptans		— two-stage operation of jet scrubbers operated in series and activated coal catalytic oxidative adsorption process — spraying with black and white liquor
SCMP system	New Brunswick International Paper Co. (22)	80% reduction in discharge	$1.588 million	— closing high yield sulphite mill and installing sulphonated chemi-mechanical pulping plant (SCMP) by CIP; vapour phase cooking planned

Process	Company (Reference)	Effectiveness	Cost	Remarks
Closed process-water system	Gissler and Pass Waste Paper Mill (West Germany) (20)	Sludge (0.5% of paper production) is re-used in the paper stock	$11.3 per ton of paper	— key is trickling filter for partial removal of COD, BOD — nutrient content of circuit water is lower than most closed systems — components include: sedimentation cone, aerated buffering tank trickling filter plant, turbo-circulator settling tank, gravel bed, fine mesh screen
Sludge used as fibreboard	Russian pilot plant (19)	Sludge byproduct utilization		— 1978 process for making 100% paper mill effluent fibreboards used in construction
Closed water recycling system	14 Russian paper and board mills (19)	Fresh water consumption has dropped from 70 M³/ton to 7-8 M³/ton (89%)	No economical desalting technology has stopped complete recycling of water	— Excess effluent treated with aluminum sulphate at external plant and re-used — no intensified accumulation of mineral salts, biological growth — no substantial corrosion.
Wet oxidation sludge to recover filler materials	Biberist Paper Mill (Switzerland) (20)	BOD and COD reduced; sludge eliminated	$17,780 (US)/ton; payback in 6 yr	— recovers filler clay and energy from sludge
Thermo-mechanical pulping (TMP)	Bowater Mersey Paper Co. (Nova Scotia) (2,22)	BOD reduction and solids recovery system	$800,000; 9 tons/day reduction in suspended solids saves $300,000 over 3 yr	— 500 tons/day capacity plant — TMP process in place by 1983 removes need for sulphite use
Brown stock washer system	Reed Ltd. (Quebec City) (22)	BOD reduction	$24 million	— separate spent calcium base sulphite liquor from pulp fibres — new evaporators and equipment to spray dry the liquor at a lignin plant to produce lignin products for sale
New cooking process		Reduce SO₂ emissions		— modified cooking process and reduced SO₂ pressure in digester to alleviate SO₂ emissions from digester blows

Process	Company (Reference)	Effectiveness	Cost	Remarks
Recovery boiler Steam stripping Spill control	Abitibi-Price, 15 mills (22)		$140 million	— wet scrubber (teller) for the recovery boiler — foul condensate steam stripping system — primary treatment — black liquor spill control system
Oxygen bleaching (Modo-cil oxygen/ alkali bleaching)	Eddy Forest Products, Espanola Mill (Ontario) (23)	Reduction in chlorine consumption thus reducing toxics in discharge; bleaching capacity raised to 1000 tons/day	$225 million including modernization programme and lesser improvements at 3 Ottawa mills	— Phase 1 (1977) chlorine consumption at #1 bleach plant cut 50% to 100 lb/tonne — Phase 2 will cut chlorine use at #2 bleach plant from 150 lb/tonne to 100 lb/tonne — further reduction unlikely as too much oxygen in system degrades the cellulose — caustic soda use to increase plus small amounts of magnesium sulphate to stabilize pulp strength
Modernization programme		Capacity expanding from 621 tonnes/day kraft pulp to 840 tonnes/day		— 3 new digesters, new brown stock washer, kiln, recovery boiler, pulp machinery decausticizing unit
Recovery boiler	Macmillan-Bloedel's Harmac Pulp Division (Namaimo, B.C.) (24)	Capable of burning 4.8 million lb of black liquor solids per day; reduce odour and particulate emissions		— largest recovery boiler in Canada, supplied by Babcock and Wilcox — replace 2 existing units
Dynamic bleaching	Northwood Pulp and Timber (Prince George, B.C.) (15)	Bleaching effluent volumes reduced to about 15 M³/tonne pulp	$150 million (expansion and pollution control)	— includes 4 separate bleaching stages in a single tower; bleaching chemicals are displaced through the mat of pulp as it moves upwards through the stages — equipment supplied by Kamyr — double capacity from 750 tons/day
Counter-current horizontal belt washers	Ontario Paper Co.	Decreased BOD by 15-20 tons/day		— allows concentration and recovery of spent sulphite liquor solids to improve byproduct alcohol and vanilla production

Process	Company (Reference)	Effectiveness	Cost	Remarks
Protein byproduct	G.A. Serlachius mill (Finland) (sulphite pulp mill) (25)	Reduce BOD 40%; produce 1900 lb/hr. animal feed protein	$12 million	— process developed by Tampella (Tampere, Finland) as a more profitable alternative to biological wastewater treatment — continuous fermentation process can operate on wastestreams that contain a low level of fermentable substances
Alcohol pulping	CP Associates (Cincinnati, Ohio) hold patent (8)	Closed cycle for pulping chemicals is alternative to standard kraft process	just in prototype stage	— use of aqueous alcohol to pre-soak wood chips and later for cooking (in form of ethanol); alcohol is recovered by passing hot black liquor through flash drum and stripping off steam and alcohol under vacuum in a solvent recovery tower; condensed and recycled to fresh liquor tank — low molecular weight lignin in an aqueous sugar solution is drawn off the bottom and can be used for byproduct recovery or boiler feed
Extending delignification in pulping process (3 techniques)	Swedish Forest Products Research Labs (Stockholm) (8)	Reduce chlorine ion and chlorinated organics in wastestream (less lignin in pulp when it reaches bleaching, therefore less lignin to react with bleaching agents and carrying them into wastestream)		— (i) modify pulping to use high concentration of hydrosulphide and low concentration of alkali during initial stages — (ii) pulping at high sulphidity (measurement of sodium hydroxide and sodium sulphide content in kraft cooking liquor) — (iii) treating pulp with oxygen
SCMP	Canadian International Paper, (Gatineau, Que.) Abitibi-Price (Thunder Bay, Ont.) (2,9,10,11)	BOD decreased 72%; replaces need for sulphite/chemical pulp; no SO₂ air emissions; reduces wood requirements 10%	$23 million $4 million research investment has already paid for itself	— reduces BOD/SO₂ — saves 25% energy costs of TMP — 90% pulp fibre yield can entirely replace chemical pulp in newsprint production (SCMP has high strength) — can be used on wood chips and hardwoods

Process	Company (Reference)	Effectiveness	Cost	Remarks
Thermo mechanical pulping (TMP)	Bear Island Paper Co. (Ashland, Virginia) newsprint mill; capacity 500 tons/day (90% TMP, 10% purchased kraft) (26)	Uses less water than chemical pulping and effluent is easier to treat (1-1.5 million gal water/day); zero discharge by 1983 (mill effluent sprayed on 1800 acres of tree plantation)	High power costs (electric bill $1 million per month)	— wood chips are softened by pre-heating, allowing a 90% fibre yield (kraft process gives only 50% fibre yield) — TMP gives stronger pulp so does not require the 25 to 30% kraft or sulphite pulp that stoneground pulp does for extra strength — has back-up primary treatment (Union Carbide Unox system)
Rapson-Reeve closed cycle kraft mill	Great Lakes Paper (Thunder Bay, Ontario) bleached kraft mill, 680 tons/day (12,13,14,15, 16,17)	Water consumption reduced 80%; BOD reduced to 7.5 kg/ton kg/ton	50% cheaper than biological treatment; $8 million capital expense; operating costs could be negative	— counter-current washing in bleaching and using spent bleaching liquor to wash brown pulp — replace 70% of chlorine with ClO_2 in first bleach stage — NaCl removed in salt recovery plant and used to produce bleaching chemicals; white liquor recycled — intensive spill collection system — steam stripping of condensates — ERCO R-3 unit used to produce ClO_2 for bleaching
Thin film evaporator for black liquor	pilot plant study by International Paper Co. (New York) (29)	More water removed from black liquor before it is sent to recovery boiler; saves energy (fossil fuel consumption reduced 8.7%)	capital installed cost $6.2-8.8 million (for 750 tons/day bleached board mill; marginally attractive investment)	— concentrate black liquor to 90% solids (conventional evaporators achieve only 65% solids) — research has been discontinued

Conclusion

The pulp and paper industry is facing enormous pressures on every front. Antiquated mills require immediate modernization while both available capital and profits dry up in today's economic climate. Forest stocks are dwindling while operating costs escalate. On top of everything else, new environmental concerns require that great efforts (and expenditures) be directed towards controlling both air and water emissions. A pulp and paper firm will vastly improve its chances in the battle to survive if it can combine pollution control and increased efficiency in its update programme. Energy conservation measures that utilize wastes, new byproduct processing endeavours[30] (see Table 6) and innovative operating procedures that capitalize on recycling and re-use are all key steps in revitalizing the industry that helped establish this country as a strong and resource-abundant nation.

Table 6
Byproduct Processing of Spent Pulping Liquors

Fermentation	Chemical treatment	Other
Industrial chemicals	L.S. concentrates	Animal feeds
Chemical feedstocks	Furfural	Fertilizers
Chelating agents	Humus	Concrete additives
Food additives	Polymer additives	Yeasts
Methane	Absorbents for oil spills	
Protein		
Sulphite alcohols		

Source: "Pulp and Paper Industry Effluent Management," *Journal of the Water Pollution Control Federation,* June 1980.

FOR FURTHER INFORMATION

Associations

Canadian Pulp and Paper
Association,
1155 Metcalfe,
Montreal, Quebec.
H3B 2X9
(514) 866-6621

Pulp and Paper Research Institute
of Canada,
570 St. John's Blvd.,
Pointe Claire, Quebec.
H9R 3J9
(514) 697-4110

American Pulpwood Association,
1619 Massachusetts Ave., NW,
Washington, D.C.
20036
(212) 265-0670

Technical Association of the Pulp
and Paper Industry,
One Dunwoody Park,
Atlanta, Georgia.
30338
(404) 394-6130

Journals

TAPPI: JOURNAL OF THE
TECHNICAL ASSOCIATION OF
THE PULP AND PAPER
INDUSTRY,
One Dunwoody Park,
Atlanta, Georgia.
30338

PULP AND PAPER JOURNAL
(formerly CANADIAN PULP AND
PAPER INDUSTRY),
Maclean-Hunter Ltd.,
481 University Ave.,
Toronto, Ontario.
M5W 1A7

PULP AND PAPER CANADA,
Southam Business Publications,
310 Victoria Ave.,
Westmount, Quebec.
H3Z 2M9

FOREST SCENE,
Ontario Forest Information Service,
15 Toronto Street,
Toronto, Ontario.
M5C 2E3

References

1. Victor, P. *Environmental Protection Regulation, Water Pollution and the Pulp and Paper Industry.* The Economic Council of Canada, June 1980.

2. Hohol, R.S. "BOD Reduction, Effluent Control Examined at Quebec Conference." *Canadian Pulp and Paper Industry,* November 1980.

3. Ontario Ministry of Natural Resources. *The Ontario Pulp and Paper Industry — Status and Outlook.* April 1978.

4. *How Things Work: The Universal Encyclopedia of Machines.* London: Allen and Unwin, 1967.

5. Environment Canada. *The Basic Technology of the Pulp and Paper Industry and its Waste Reduction Activities.* Water Pollution Control Directorate, Environment Canada, Report No. EPS 6-WP-74-3, May 1973.

6. Tomlinson, George H. "Canadian Approach to Regulations for P&P and Thoughts for the Future." *Pulp and Paper Canada,* October 1979.

7. Donnan, J.A. and Victor, P.A. *Alternative Policies for Pollution Abatement: The Ontario Pulp and Paper Industry.* Ontario Ministry of the Environment, October 1976 (3 volumes).

8. "New Processing Routes to Paper." *Chemical Week,* March 12, 1980.

9. "Process Cuts Mill Pollution." *Forest Scene,* December 1980.

10. "The Story of Sulphonated Chemimechanical Pulp." *Pulp and Paper Canada,* September 1981.

11. Cummings, Christopher. "Award-Winning SCMP Process Reduces Pollution, Saves Energy." *Canadian Pulp and Paper Industry,* November 1980.

12. Rapson, W. Howard. "Industrial Recycling Conserves Energy, Protects Environment." *Waste Management (Canadian Consulting Engineer),* May 1981.

13. Rapson, W. Howard and Reeve, W. Douglas. "Non-Waste Production of Bleached Kraft Pulp." In *Non-Waste Technology and Production.* A Seminar of the United Nations Economic Commission for Europe, 1976.

14. Isbister, John A. *et al.* "The Closed Cycle Concept Kraft Mill at Great Lakes — An Advanced Status Report." *Pulp and Paper Canada,* June 1979.

15. "Pulp Companies Face $Billion Clean-Up." *Canadian Chemical Processing,* February 6, 1980.

16. "ERCO Industries Wins the Beak Environmental Improvement Award." *Chemistry in Canada,* April 1981.

17. "Great Lakes OK's Effluent-Free Idea." *Canadian Chemical Processing,* October/November 1978.

18. Fournier, Yves. "Common Policy Agreements in the Pulp and Paper Industry." *Industry and Environment (U.N. Environment Program),* December 1980.

19. Norrstrom, Hans. "Will Environmental Requirements and Energy Demand Limit the Growth of the Pulp and Paper Industry?" *Industry and Environment (U.N. Environment Program),* December 1980.

20. "Closed Cycle Wastepaper Mill Reduces BOD." *TAPPI: Journal of the Technical Association of the Pulp and Paper Industry,* April 1981.

21. Gosling, C.D. *et al.* "Wet Oxidation of Paper Mill Wastes to Recover Filler Materials." *TAPPI: Journal of the Technical Association of the Pulp and Paper Industry,* February 1981.

22. Freeman, H. "Industry to Spend Over $100M on Pollution Abatement." *Canadian Pulp and Paper Industry,* May 1981.

23. "More Oxygen Bleaching for Eddy." *Canadian Chemical Processing,* February 20, 1980.

24. "News Summary: Nanaimo, B.C." *Eco/Log Week,* January 30, 1981.

25. "Pulpers Turn Waste Water into Saleable Protein." *Chemical Week,* February 13, 1980.

26. "More Pulp with Less Pollution." *Chemical Week,* February 20, 1980.

27. White, John. "Pulping Liquor Recovery System Wins Ontario Energy Award." *Canadian Pulp and Paper Industry,* September 1978.

28. Sexton, E.A. and Wilkinson, E.G. "Spent Liquor Recovery at Ontario Paper." *Pulp and Paper Canada,* January 1980.

29. Andrews, R.S. and Roscoe, R.W. "Thin-Film Evaporation of Black Liquor to High Solids as an Investment." *TAPPI: Journal of the Technical Association of the Pulp and Paper Industry,* December 1981.

30. Grove, George W. "Pulp and Paper Industry Effluent Management." *Journal of the Water Pollution Control Federation,* June 1980.

Solvents

There's a change in the wind for solvent users. No longer content to pay good money to bury or incinerate spent solvents, a growing body of solvent users is exploring ways to breathe new life into these contaminated liquids.

With solvent costs and disposal costs locked in an upward spiral, solvent reclamation is shaping up to be an increasingly profitable prospect. But there is more to sensible solvent management than just recycling spent solvents. Some of the more prudent solvent users are appraising solvent losses and methodically improving housekeeping practices.

Mounting scientific evidence warns of health hazards associated with many solvents, particularly with chlorinated and aromatic hydrocarbons. Many of these solvents are doubly condemned because they also contribute to general air pollution through smog formation.

The impetus to restrict solvent loss to the environment comes from many fronts. Regulatory bodies in the United States have substantially upgraded emission levels to combat occupational disease and environmental deterioration.[1] For example, air pollution regulations proposed by the American Environmental Protection Agency would reduce degreasing operation emissions of organic solvents by 64% by 1985 from 1980 levels.[2] The adhesives industry is scheduled to reduce solvent use in adhesives by 50% over present levels.[3] Furthermore, the United States Resource Conservation and Recovery Act, which has no counterpart in Canada, makes the disposal of wastes such as spent solvents increasingly difficult and costly.

In Canada, solvent users are not under the same regulatory pressure. Nevertheless, some Canadian businesses are following the American example of minimizing solvent losses to the ambient air and dumpsites because they find it in their economic interest to do so.

It is important to stress the word *some*. Despite the vast potential to reclaim waste solvents, most industry spokesmen agree that only a portion of this resource is presently being tapped.

Solvent Use

In chemical jargon, the word solvent refers to any substance capable of dissolving another, and hence would include substances such as water. Industry, however, restricts the word "solvent" to mean an organic dissolving agent. Even so, organic solvents include hundreds of substances which belong to many chemical groups.

It is estimated that only a few dozen solvents are reclaimed at present (see Table 1). With the accelerating interest in solvent re-use, the number and quantity of solvents reclaimed is anticipated to increase in the future.[4]

Many different industries use solvents. The petroleum industry uses solvents to extract lube oils and waxes during the refining process.[5] Solvents are generally reclaimed on-site and used repeatedly in the refining process.

The plastics industry uses hexane, benzene and cyclohexane as a chemical medium in the manufacture of high-density polyethylene and polypropylene.[6] After polymerization, the solvents are reclaimed on-site and recycled back into the polymerization process.

Hexane and mineral spirits which are used in the manufacture of vegetable oil are reclaimed and re-used in the extraction process.

Table 1

Industrial Solvent Recovery

Industries that Reclaim Solvents	Commonly Recycled Solvents*
Adhesives application	Halogenated Hydrocarbons
Adhesives manufacturing	Fluorocarbons
Automotive	Methylene chloride
Chemical	Perchloroethylene
Dry cleaning	Trichloroethylene
Electronics	1,1,1-Trichloroethane
Electroplating	
Ink formulating	
Packaging	
Paint application	
Paint formulation	Hydrocarbons
Petrochemical	Hexane
Pharmaceutical	Benzene
Plastics	Toluene
Printing	Xylene
Rubber	Cyclohexane
Textile	Ethers
Vegetable oil processing	Mineral spirits
	Naphthas
	Ketones
	Acetone
	Methyl ethyl ketone
	Methyl isobutyl ketone
	Cyclohexanone
	Alcohol
	Methanol
	Ethanol
	Isopropanol
	Butyl alcohol
	Amyl alcohol
	Esters
	Amyl acetates
	Butyl acetates
	Ethyl acetates

*In addition, many proprietary blends of these listed solvents are recycled.

Source: Source Assessment: Reclaiming of Waste Solvents. U.S. EPA, 1978.

Similarly, the pharmaceutical industry is known to recycle spent methanol, butyl alcohol, methyl isobutyl ketone and acetate back into the extraction processes.[7]

Many dry cleaning establishments reclaim contaminated solvents on the premises. Another major generator of waste solvents is degreasing. The auto, appliance and furniture industries frequently use solvents to remove the protective grease layer from a metal part prior to assembly or painting. Solvents commonly recycled by dry cleaners and degreasers include methylene chloride, perchloroethylene, trichloroethylene and 1,1,1 trichloroethane.

The paint, adhesives and printing industries are large users of solvents in Canada. Unlike the United States, these Canadian industries are not under the same legislative gun as their southern neighbours. Although the trend is most pronounced in the United States, water-borne, high solids and powder coatings are emerging as viable substitutes to solvent-based products in both countries. But even with the gradual entry of alternative products into the marketplace, solvent-based paints, adhesives and inks still remain in widespread use.

Sources of Waste

The paint, adhesives and printing industries generate solvent wastes in two major ways — in the drying process and in the equipment clean-out process.

Vapour Emissions from Product Drying

In industrial painting, coated objects are dried in a hot oven to accelerate curing. A conventional solvent paint typically contains 60 to 80% solvent in the formulation.[8] During drying, all the solvent is evaporated. The larger painting facilities have on-site solvent recovery or incineration systems to control gaseous solvent emissions during the drying process.

The adhesives industry uses solvents in the manufacture of solvent-borne adhesives. The application of solvent-borne adhesives to a surface, as occurs in the manufacture of tape or in the packaging industry, results in the evaporation of solvent during drying of the adhesives. Some large users of adhesives such as tape coating operations use solvent recovery or incineration systems to eliminate solvents from the air to be exhausted outside the plant.

Similarly, printing establishments that use solvent-borne inks generate solvent emissions upon drying of the ink. Solvent recovery or incineration systems to control vapour emissions are rarely used by the printing industry because of the small scale of many printing houses.

Waste Liquid Solvents from Equipment Clean-Out

The primary source of waste liquid solvents in the paint formulating industry is from equipment clean-out and colour changes in the mixing tanks. Smaller establishments tend to send waste solvents to an outside recycler rather than reclaim solvents on-site. Paint applicators, printers and adhesives users also generate dirty solvent from equipment clean-out that is suitable for recycling on the premises or by an outside reclaimer.

Although some professional solvent recyclers have been in the business for more than 30 years, it is only in the last decade that the number of solvent reclaimers has increased significantly.[9] The excellent economics of solvent recovery and increasing costs of waste disposal are spurring even smaller businesses to investigate recycling options for their waste solvents. In some instances, the economics of the situation may point to investment in on-site recovery equipment. In other instances, a firm may choose to use a professional solvent reclaimer to clean and return the solvent for re-use.

The Solvent Recycling Industry

In Canada, there are only a handful of professional facilities which recycle spent solvent. There is no official Canadian association of solvent recyclers although some Canadian solvent recyclers belong to the American Solvent Recycling Association. The United States National Association of Solvent Recyclers estimates that in 1980, over 100 million gallons of waste solvents were recycled by approximately 75 small reclaimers across the United States.[10] Most recyclers are small local businesses with revenues that average $1 million per year.

Some companies send their wastes to recyclers who, for a fee, return a purified product. Firms which are reluctant to use recycled solvents may simply sell their dirty solvents to a reclaimer.

Solvent Purity Needs

Industries vary in their solvent purity needs. A solvent is pure if it is relatively free of water and contamination with other types of solvents. Depending on how a solvent is used, it may become contaminated with suspended and dissolved solids, organics, water and other solvents. Although it is technically possible to restore any waste solvent to virtually virgin purity, the reclamation process may be more costly than buying new solvent.

In many cases, waste solvents are restored to a purity that permits them to be re-used as cleaning agents. Unless specified, however, the reclaimed solvent will still be a mixture of solvents. The reclaimed product can be used to clean painting equipment and printing presses as well as or better than virgin solvents.[9] Complex fractional distillation can further separate out the various individual solvents from the mixture, but for many uses, this high level of purification is not necessary.

Wastestream Segregation

In general, it is most cost-effective to keep solvent wastestreams separate, both at the source of generation and at the recycling plant. Because each batch of solvent is contaminated to a different degree, the cost to restore it will vary accordingly.

The electronics industry, for example, uses very high purity solvents. Wastes from such industries tend to be so clean that they may be transferred as is for use in another industry with lower purity requirements such as industrial painters. It does not make economic sense to combine relatively clean waste solvents from the electronics industry with more contaminated solvents of the paint industry, and then set about unravelling the mess at the recycling plant.

In some instances, however, it may be feasible to combine waste solvents, but only if they come from similar uses and are reclaimed to a similar end use. Some commercial painters generate such small volumes of solvent that it may be necessary to combine them with waste solvents from other painters.

Sharing Liability

Industrial use of solvents falls into two major categories: use in product formulation, and use in equipment clean-out. Although exceptions do exist, purity requirements generally tend to be higher for product formulation than for equipment clean-out.

Use of a reclaimed solvent of unexpectedly poor quality in product formulation may result in a spoiled batch of product. Some solvent users argue that the risk of using reclaimed solvents exceeds potential benefits. One spoiled batch may wipe out months of savings earned through the use of reclaimed solvents.

Solvent reclaimers have a poor reputation in some industries which have had negative experiences using reclaimed solvent. Paint formulators have been known to complain about water in the recycled solvent which has subsequently ruined a batch of paint.[11]

It is in the interest of both the solvent user and the professional reclaimer to investigate ways of sharing liability in the event that something goes wrong. It has been suggested that all off-site vendors be asked to provide industry with a proper certificate of insurance.[12] This would allow a solvent user to place a damages claim if a reclaimed solvent failed to meet the performance standards advertised. The issue is not the purity of the reclaimed solvent, but product guarantee that the reclaimed solvent achieves the minimum purity negotiated prior to reclaiming.

Contracts between recycler and user, product guarantees and liability insurance should be designed in a manner that facilitates recycling. The intent is to protect the user and the conscientious solvent recycler from those entering the business to make a fast buck from a lucrative waste without ensuring the proper quality control.

Figure 1
The Solvent Recycling Process

The loss of solvent can occur at many phases of the recovery process because solvents are very volatile, even at room temperature.
Source: *The Chemical Process Industries*, McGraw-Hill, 1969.

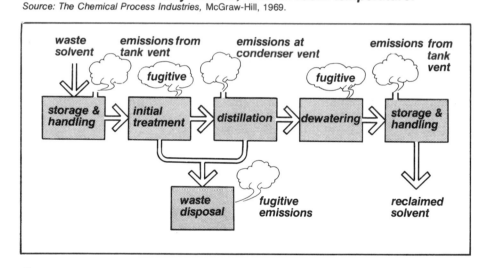

1.
The Solvent Recycling Process

Most solvent recyclers use the same basic process to reclaim solvents. The stages in the process include storage and handling, initial treatment, distillation, dewatering, waste disposal, solvent handling, packaging and final storage. Major pollutants emitted during the recycling process are hydrocarbons (solvents) and particulates.[13] Because solvents are very volatile, even at room temperature, the loss of solvents (known as fugitive emissions) occurs at many phases of the recycling operation (see Figure 1).

Good housekeeping practices can reduce emissions at each of these phases. This not only prevents solvent dollars from escaping, but also greatly reduces the movement of solvent vapours into adjacent neighbourhoods.

Storage and Handling

Solvents are stored before and after recycling in drums or tanks. Storage tanks that have a fixed-roof need venting systems to prevent excessive build-up of vapour pressure. Floating-roof tanks have lids which move on the surface of the solvent while forming an air-tight seal with the tank walls. Although not in widespread use, floating-roof tanks are superior to fixed-roof tanks because they allow only 1/20 as much solvent vapour to escape.[14] Fixed-roof tanks can be retrofitted with special conservation vents which limit fugitive emissions.

In the transfer of solvents, submerged filling of the storage tanks can reduce solvent emissions by 50% over splash filling.[14] The submerged filling technique minimizes the agitation and escape of aerosolized solvent.

Initial Treatment

Initial treatment of the waste solvent varies with the type of contamination. If solvent immiscible with water is contaminated with water and suspended solids, the water and solids are allowed to separate in a settling tank. Additional methods may include decanting, filtering, draining, settling or centrifuging.

Distillation

The solvent may then be processed further by distillation into its individual components (see Figure 2). However, if the recovered solvent mixture can be re-used without separation, and if the solvent is immiscible in water, distillation is not necessary and the solvent-water mixtures can enter the dewatering phase directly.

The purpose of distillation is to remove dissolved impurities in the solvent and to separate solvent mixtures. Where distillation involves heating and condensing the solvent, hydrocarbon losses from the exhaust stack may be significant. In a typical solvent recycling plant without control technology, hydrocarbon emissions from the distillation process make up almost 80% of the total plant solvent losses.[4]

Solvent vapours vented during distillation can be controlled by scrubbers and condensers. Counter-current vent scrubbers have demonstrated a 99% efficiency in controlling distillation vent gases.[4] In a counter-current scrubber, an absorbing liquid passes concurrently to the flow of vent gas through a packing medium and picks up escaping hydrocarbons. Afterburners and secondary condensers may also be used to control solvent emissions from the distillation stack.

Advances in modern technology make it possible to minimize the production of solvent vapour emissions during distillation by employing vacuum technology. Although it may be desirable to use vacuum distillation techniques at new installations, a more cost-effective way of minimizing solvent emissions from existing distillation units may be through solvent recovery via gas scrubbers and condensers.

The purity requirement for the reclaimed solvent will determine

Dewatering

The next phase is solvent dewatering. This is done by decanting (mechanical separation) or salting (passing solvent through a calcium bed which removes water by adsorption). Percolation through dehydrating agents such as anhydrous calcium sulphate or molecular sieves is the latest technology that permits solvent recyclers to achieve water levels in the purified solvent as low as 0.01%.[9]

Figure 2
Typical Solvent Recycling Process Using Distillation

In automatic recycling units, the sludge is pumped away as it is deposited. Rotating scrapers sweep the evaporator walls, keeping them clean and sending sludge to the bottom of the vessel where it can be pumped out. In manual systems, the still is shut down periodically to manually scrape off and remove the sludge.
Source: Brighton Corporation, Cincinnati, Ohio, 1982.

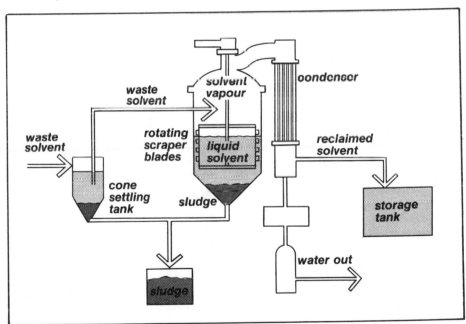

the number of distillations needed, and hence the cost. Companies with low purity requirements, such as those using solvent mixtures for cleaning purposes, may opt for a low-cost simple distillation process which yields a blend of clean, re-usable solvents. Clients with high purity needs may require fractional distillation to separate the waste solvent mixture into the various component solvents.

Although the major portion of a solvent can be separated from the wastewater, a small portion of the solvent tends to be soluble in water. The quantity of solvent that is discharged with the wastewater varies with the solubility of a particular solvent and the efficiency of the solvent-water separation process. Completion of a materials balance on the solvent inputs and the waste solvent outputs makes it possible to identify just how much solvent is escaping down the sewer with the plant's wastewater.

Residue Treatment and Disposal

The final stage concerns the disposal of materials removed from the waste solvents during initial treatment and distillation. Solvent reclaimers report that approximately 25% or less of the dirty solvent remains as a waste residue at the end of the solvent recovery process.[15] Typically, about half of this residue is unreclaimed solvent. Although it is possible to reduce the solvent content in the residue even further, most reclaimers choose to leave the residue wet enough to permit easy removal from the equipment. Depending on the source of the waste solvents, solvent residues (sludges and still bottoms) may include paint resins, inks, pigments, metals, detergents and other substances.

Because solvent still bottoms are designated as potentially hazardous wastes, their disposal is becoming increasingly costly. This has triggered further efforts to get better usage through resource recovery from waste solvents to further reduce the amount of residue requiring ultimate disposal. Two of the following case studies show how some innovative businesses are experimenting to put still bottoms back to work.

2.
Professional Solvent Recyclers

In Canada, most professional solvent recyclers are located in Ontario. Despite the potential to recycle waste solvents in Ontario, a high percentage of waste solvents is still incinerated rather than recycled.

A common cry among solvent disposers is that many solvents are too contaminated for recycling. Clearly, an integral component of any solvent recycling strategy is to ensure that solvent wastestreams are kept separate and free of unnecessary contamination.

At Anachemia Solvents (Mississauga, Ontario), incoming waste solvents are received in drums and in bulk. (1) Solvent processing to remove solid contaminants is done as a batch operation using a thin-film evaporator. (2) Elaborate piping systems direct steam (heat source) and water to the various distillation units. (3) A bubble-cap fractional distillation column is used to separate solvent mixtures with different boiling points. (4) The solid residue remaining after distillation is incinerated for heat recovery. (5) A variety of temperatures critical to processing is monitored by computer. (6) Laboratory analysis is undertaken to establish solvent yields, check purity, identify quantity of water present, and establish other parameters as needed. (7) A coded distribution system ensures accurate refilling of reclaimed solvent into the proper drums and tanks.

■ Canadian companies seeking out dumpsites for their hazardous wastes may find themselves knocking on the doors of Anachemia Solvents instead. Anachemia Solvents Limited (Mississauga, Ontario) is experiencing a steady growth in business as the recycling of volatile industrial solvents becomes more appealing to potential customers looking for disposal alternatives.[16]

"Twenty-five years ago when we started, we had a tough selling operation. It was hard to convince people that recycling solvents was viable when it was so easy to get rid of their wastes, but environmental factors have steered many people our way," says Jack McGregor, vice-president of Anachemia Solvents Ltd. "Companies run out of alternatives and give us a call."

Anachemia, one of the largest solvent recovery operations in Canada, reclaims contaminated

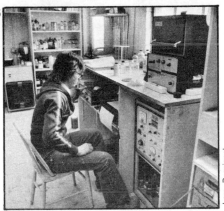

his company's service.

After a solvent has been processed by distillation, a solid residue is left. Anachemia takes advantage of this residue to fuel the distillation operation. McGregor estimates that 65% of the fuel required to run the distillation process is supplied by burning these leftover residues in a specially-designed incinerator, called a waste-heat recovery boiler.[16]

Although most solvents can be recovered, the company is careful in accepting solvents for treatment. To avoid causing local environmental damage or jeopardizing the health of their employees from noxious substances, Anachemia requires a sample of any material that is to be processed so it can be analyzed for acceptability. Benzene is one substance that Anachemia does not accept.

Large companies with heavy volumes of waste, such as Glidden, C-I-L and General Motors, are Anachemia's major customers, but Anachemia does business with small companies too. Small companies can pool their solvent wastes so that recycling a larger volume becomes more viable.[16]

■ Waste Reclamation (England) is a professional solvent recycling company established by Raywell Process Plants of Stratford, East London.[17] The Raywell company manufactures solvent recovery equipment that can recycle a wide range of organic solvents including chlorinated hydrocarbons.

Industries such as paint and printing ink manufacturers frequently use mixed solvents. Mixed solvents can be cleaned and returned to the customer in the same proportions as it left the customer. The company also offers fractional distillation services. Plans are underway to develop a plant to separate water from solvents such as acetone and ethanol by fractional distillation.[17]

■ Chemstar Ltd. (Stalybridge, England) entered the solvent recycling business in 1975 to service the "dirty end of the market — the soups of waste which no one else would touch", according to company management. Since then, the processing load has grown

solvents such as degreasing agents from metal shops, and lacquer thinners, vinyl coatings and exotic resins from paint and printing companies.

"In the car industry, when you are painting and you have to change colours, you clean your equipment in the same way you clean your paintbrushes at home," McGregor said. After they have been used, such cleaning solvents can be trucked to Anachemia's Mississauga plant where they are

recovered through a distillation process. Because different solvents have different boiling points, fractional distillation allows the separation of complex mixtures.

Solvents, or solvent blends, are returned to industries at prices substantially lower than the cost of new solvents. According to McGregor, customers find that they not only save on the costs of raw materials, but also reduce or eliminate disposal costs by using from 10,000 litres to 100,000 litres a week and a pre-tax profit of £100,000 in 1979. Accepting very dirty waste solvents has meant more frequent cleaning of gummed-up stills but it opened up an otherwise untapped source of supply.[18]

3.
Use of Residue as a Low-Grade Fuel

Solvent wastestreams vary in the type and degree of contamination. Solvents used to clean printing equipment are rich in waste paints. Recovery efficiency of waste paint solvents typically ranges between 75 and 85%.

In contrast, metal cleaning solvents or waste solvents from the packaging industry tend to have a small contaminant component. In such cases, solvent recovery efficiency may reach 90% and the volume of the residue generated is low. The following examples show how some recyclers are processing waste solvent residue for use as a low-grade fuel.

■   After 30 years in the solvent recovery business, Emory Hukill, president of Hukill Chemical Corporation (Bedford, Ohio) has witnessed the growth of the solvent recycling industry as a viable industry.

In earlier days when there were just a handful of recyclers, everyone was scrambling to get a reliable source of waste solvent. Says Hukill, "This started to change in the last five to ten years. The Environmental Protection Agency said no more dumping or throwing solvent down the sewers or in the fields. This has helped the solvent recycling industry substantially. Of course, there is the economic aspect as well. With soaring solvent prices, recycling becomes especially attractive."

Hukill Chemical is both a chemical distributor and a recycler. One quarter of the 43-person workforce is involved in solvent reclaiming itself, handling about 2.5 to 3 million gallons of solvent per year.

Hukill Chemical accepts a wide range of contaminated solvents including aromatic hydrocarbons such as toluol and napthol; oxygenated solvents such as ketones, acetones, esters and alcohols; as well as the widely used chlorinated solvents perchloroethylene and trichloroethylene. The processing method used is vacuum flash evaporation (distillation) and is accomplished with a Luwa thin-film evaporator.

Hukill Chemical run a custom operation in which they "launder" a batch of dirty solvent and return it to the customer. The cleaning fee is based on the volume, degree of contamination and residue disposal charges associated with each batch. In addition, some materials are purchased outright and sold as a blend.[9]

According to Hukill, the recycled product is almost always a mixture of solvents. Says Hukill, "The customer brings in a solvent that has traces of other solvents in it because there is always a pickup of solvents from the customer's own machinery." Although the reclaimed solvent does not meet commercial specifications for pure solvents, it does meet the specifications for blends.

In addition, Hukill's company can fractionate solvents to split them and get them back to their original purity. "In doing so, we can meet virgin specs but this is very expensive. It's not usually warranted or required."

What is the smallest batch size accepted? It depends on the value of the solvent, but generally they limit batch size to a minimum of five drums for custom recycling.

Economics favour recycling over other disposal options. Take the example of toluol, routinely used by paint companies for wash-up (see Table 2). The cost of virgin

---

Table 2

Economic Comparison of Incineration versus Reclamation of 1000 Gallons of Waste Solvent

If Incinerated		If Reclaimed*	
Incineration cost @ 40¢ per gallon	$400	Solvent reclamation @ 60¢ per gallon recycled	$480
		Residue disposal cost @ 30¢ per gallon disposed	$60
Total Incineration Cost	$400	Total Recovery Cost	$540
New solvent cost to replace 800 gallons of recycled solvent	$1,344	New Solvent Cost	0
Total Cost	$1,744	Total Cost	$540
		Savings compared to incineration alternative	$1,200

*Based on solvent recovery efficiency of 80%

Source: Hukill Chemical Corporation, 1981.

toluol runs at $1.68 per gallon (1981 U.S. dollars). Hukill typically charges 60¢ per gallon to reclaim the solvent and 30¢ per gallon to dispose of the still bottoms. In comparison, the cost of incinerating solvent runs at 40¢ per gallon.[9]

Based on a 1000-gallon batch, a customer would pay $1750 to dispose of dirty solvent and replace it with virgin chemicals. In contrast, based on a reclamation efficiency of 80%, the customer would save $1200 by having spent solvents recycled. These calculations do not include the cost of transportation.

At a time when most solvent recyclers are still wondering how to dispose of the 20% residue remaining from the recycling process, Hukill is well on the road to marketing a residue byproduct as a fuel supplement. "We try to close the loop by reclaiming the solvent, residue and the drums. When we used to have to dispose of residue, we also disposed of a lot of drums that the residue was put in. Now, even they can be recycled."

The residue is blended with other hydrocarbons to make it equivalent in terms of Btu's to No. 6 fuel oil.[10] The fuel supplement is then sold to the cement industry. Kilns at a cement company operate at about 3000°F which is a high enough incineration temperature to destroy stray halogenated hydrocarbons.

How do the economics of the experimental fuel programme stack up? "We're just breaking even with it," says Hukill. "Our fuel supplement is still in its infancy as a fuel. In the future we will be in a position to charge a higher price for it because of its acknowledged usefulness."

For Hukill, it is clear that economic considerations first drove him to re-evaluate his previous residue disposal practices. At a cost of $65 per drum to bury the residue, landfilling is the most expensive disposal option (see Table 3). At present, while the supplemental fuel programme is still in the experimental stage, most solvent residues are incinerated at a cost of $23 per drum. In the case of solvent residue which is rich in hydrocarbons and hence

Table 3

Cost Comparison of Residue Disposal Options at Hukill Chemical (1981)

Cost of Burying Residue	Cost of Incineration as is	Present Revenue from Fuel Sales
$1.16/gal	$ .40/gal	$ .15/gal
$65/drum	$23/drum	$8.50/drum
$696,000/year*	$240,000/year*	$90,000/year*

*These numbers are based on the assumption that 20% of the 3 million gallons of solvent handled annually result in residue.

Source: Hukill Chemical Corporation, 1981.

very burnable, incineration costs are substantially lower than for other hazardous wastes which burn less readily. Hukill is now offering advice to other recyclers who want to market their still bottoms and sludges.

Hukill Chemical is surviving the squeeze from increasing disposal costs for hazardo wastes. Says Hukill, "We always claimed solvent recovery was an economical thing to do, but we couldn't sell it in a big way in the early days. The Environmental Protection Agency calls dirty solvents hazardous waste — we call them feedstocks."

■ Resource Recycling Technologies Inc. (Madison, Tennessee) is a large company starting up a plant to convert waste solvents into a synthetic No. 2 fuel oil.[10] The solvent conversion facility will be operated by Chem-Fuel Inc. (Portland, Tennessee). Chem-Fuel, a subsidiary of Resource Recycling Technologies, will receive industrial solvents from eight southern states, resulting in the daily conversion of 40,000 gallons of waste solvents into fuel.

Solvents accepted for conversion include alcohols, ketones, glycols, acetals and aromatics, but not chlorinated hydrocarbons. The resultant fuel oil will sell for 10% less than the going price of standard No. 2 fuel oil.[10] The No. 2 oil product has a heating value of 142,000 Btu per gallon and sold for 90¢ (U.S.) per gallon in 1981.

Unlike solvent recyclers that custom-clean a client's batch of waste solvents, the Chem-Fuel operation is based on a mixed solvent stream. Mixed waste solvents are first filtered to remove solids, and the solvent is then subjected to vacuum distillation.

The still bottoms and filtered solids are incinerated. The clean liquid solvent from the distillation process then undergoes a low-pressure, low-temperature reduction reaction to produce the synthetic oil base. Some industry observers, however, question the economics of turning all the waste solvent into oil when many of the solvents are of much higher economic value than fuel oil.[10]

■ Hydrachem Corp. (Dallas, Texas), in conjunction with the United States Department of Energy, plans to build a plant to produce both recycled solvents and fuel oil. Spent solvents such as xylenes, toluenes and other aromatics will be accepted from the electronics, aircraft and metal-working industries.

Hydrachem will reclaim 20 to 25% of the waste solvent stream and recover 55 to 60% as substitute No. 4 fuel oil. No. 4 fuel oil has a heating value of 100,000 Btu per gallon and is worth 45¢ per gallon (U.S.) in 1981.[10]

The 20% residue from the recovery process will be pyrolyzed in the future to obtain a saleable, low-Btu gas. Current disposal costs for the residue hover at 50¢ per gallon.

4.
Use of Residue as a Low-Grade Paint

For those solvent recyclers that reclaim large amounts of waste solvents from the paint industry, the potential exists to turn the paint residue in dirty solvents into a low grade paint. With 20 to 25% of the waste solvent stream contaminated with paint pigments and resins, dividends from the recovery and re-use of paint may make this option more attractive than costly land disposal.

■ Five years ago, Chemical Recovery Systems Inc. (Romulus, Michigan) started experimenting with the re-use of pigment wastes in solvent residue. With employees numbering 20 or so, and annual sales at the $2 to $3 million mark, this solvent recycling company generates substantial volumes of residue.

Peter Shagena, president of the company, says that at present, all their residue is re-used in some manner, whether as a fuel supplement or as a source of pigments and resins for the paint industry.[19]

"I don't like landfill," says Shagena. "It's a direct cost to an operation like ours. If we didn't sell the residue as a valuable commodity, it would cost our customers $20 to $50 per barrel to landfill it."

The major portion of solvents reclaimed by Chemical Recovery Systems derives from the automotive industry. Subsequently, the still bottoms of Shagena's plant contain largely pigments and resins. Shagena custom treats the residue to meet a customer's specifications.

The customer usually is a paint formulator who makes the treated residue into a low-grade paint. Because the still bottoms contain a variety of pigment colours, the resulting mixture is rusty tan or greyish blue. According to Shagena, some paint formulators buying this residue can make new colours out of it, and hence substantially enlarge its re-use potential.

Customer specifications for the residue vary. "Some customers want less high boilers so we leave the residue in the distillation equipment longer to evaporate them off," says Shagena. "Others want it cut with a different solvent, or they want it filtered." The customer then does additional processing of the treated pigment sludge before it can be re-used as paint.

Payment received for the residue depends on what process the customer specifies. When Shagena sells the residue "as is" for use as a fuel, he charges 20 to 30¢ per gallon. With additional processing to meet customer demands, his residue sells in the neighbourhood of 50¢ per gallon.

Although there is some interest and assistance by the paint industry, Shagena concedes that it will be some time before paint sludge re-use becomes more widespread.

5.
A National Recycling Network . . . How A Large Company Does It

No matter how sound the technology or how satisfactory the recycled product, the success of any professional solvent recycling operation hinges on the availability of waste solvent and on a steady market to consume the recycled product.

Large companies that break into the business of selling recycled solvents can often secure a competitive edge over smaller companies. Large companies can usually offer a more reliable supply of recycled goods. Because of their size and volume of business, large companies tend to have a better distribution network to both collect wastes and distribute recycled products. Small solvent recovery companies are better suited to custom-cleaning of contaminated solvents.

■ There is a newcomer to the field of solvent recycling in the United States. But unlike its smaller competitors, Foremost - McKesson (San Francisco, California) is already a well-established $500-million-a-year chemical business geared to distributing solvents.[20]

The new feature in the Foremost-McKesson approach is that it hopes to offer a nation-wide recycling service. The company is moving fast on its goal of capturing 10% or $100 million of the United States solvent recycling market by 1986. The company purchased one recycling plant and has revealed plans to spend an additional $50 million to build six new facilities in the next two years across the country.[20]

Foremost-McKesson is banking on its position as the nation's largest chemical distributor to provide the edge in winning a big corner of the solvent market.

The company has a trump card in relation to the majority of smaller recyclers who tend to operate within a 200-mile radius to keep freight costs down. Because its business is already geared to trucking chemicals across the country, the company speculates that its trucks can haul spent solvent for recycling instead of returning empty from deliveries.

Company personnel predict that when Foremost-McKesson's facilities come on line and the firm can promote its recycling service as a permanent feature of its operation, the combination of dollar savings and security of supply will escalate the number of customers that purchase recycled solvent.

On-Site Solvent Reclamation

Environmental regulations prevent big companies generating large amounts of solvent vapour from simply exhausting them into the ambient air. By and large, industry has responded to these environmental pressures by burning its unwanted solvent.

The last decade has seen a shift away from simply burning waste solvents to recovering solvents for re-use. Pollution abatement equipment itself underwent a major re-design. Equipment previously designed to destroy waste solvents is slowly being replaced with equipment to recover spent solvents. Although the economics of the early 1970s may have favoured solvent recovery in only the larger outfits which could afford huge capital expenditures, soaring solvent costs in the mid-1970s made it everyone's business to invest in solvent recovery.

A pattern repeats itself in almost every industrial sector. A technology breakthrough in pollution control is made for a large company. The sheer volume of recoverable wastes points very quickly to a rapid pay-back on the relatively large capital investment.

As the pollution recovery technology becomes more refined and other markets open, the technology becomes scaled down to fit even small businesses. For example, most dry cleaning establishments recover and re-use spent solvents on the premises, even though they are usually only very small operations. An equipment manufacturer in Canada now produces a solvent reclaiming machine economic enough for use by relatively small printing and painting establishments.[21]

1.
Good Housekeeping

The volatile nature of solvents contributes significantly to both environmental pollution and economic losses. Solvents that escape into the atmosphere do so at the expense of the business using them.

A first step in any good housekeeping strategy is to identify and prevent unnecessary solvent emissions. Solvent inputs and waste solvent outputs should be compared routinely to estimate the quantity of solvents unaccounted for, and hence leaking unnoticed into the environment.

Solvent recovery equipment, even if it is fully automated, should be monitored frequently to calculate the solvent recovery efficiency. Process difficulties such as carbon bed contamination, fouled heat exchangers or high cooling water temperature may go undetected unless the recovery efficiency of the equipment is determined regularly. A drop in efficiency of only 1% can represent thousands of dollars lost in a year.[22] Identifying and correcting problems before they become an expensive headache will always save money in the long term.

■ Union Carbide knows the value of good housekeeping. But what is routine today was unheard of a decade earlier.

In the early 1970s, Union Carbide suffered from severe image problems. Its plant at Alloy, West Virginia was dubbed "the smokiest factory in the world" and its Anmoore plant was the target of a class action suit for environmental damages.[23] "We simply got tired of always being the bad guys in the press," said Fred Charles in 1976, then director of environmental affairs.

Since those days, the company has programmed its extensive computer bank with the details of hundreds of processes and products that make up the Carbide empire. This abundance of data permits Carbide to do materials balances at all of its plants. By keeping track of the raw materials used in a process and how much product the process yields, the company can calculate the concentrations of waste in the stack or in the effluent.

At one of its plants, a materials balance revealed an unexpected solvent loss. This led Douglas Bess of Carbide's Environmental Protection Branch to say,[23] "We had no idea that we had an extensive fugitive emissions problem. After doing a materials balance, we realized we were losing upwards to 20,000 pounds of material a day." By plugging up leaks, the company saved $2000 a day in lost solvents.

Now Union Carbide policy mandates a computer-assisted plant evaluation system to identify and correct pollution problems before they become expensive.

■ IBM, like Union Carbide makes use of computer technology to safeguard the environment.

Many of IBM's manufacturing processes such as polishing, machining and cleaning used in the production of magnetic discs require the continuous use of solvents. Solvents are also used in batches in the mixing of coatings.

The solvents are supplied from remote tank farms. Previously, solvent from the remote tanks was piped to a day tank just outside the plant building. According to Konrad Stokes of IBM, saturated vapour was released to the atmosphere via a vent in filling the day tank. Hence the tank actually became an emission source of hydrocarbons.[24]

IBM has since implemented a computer-assisted solvent control system to meter solvents as they enter the building, thereby eliminating the need for day tanks. The computer can shut off the line from the tank farm, warn the operator that excessive solvent has been used, and indicate that a check for leaks is required.[24]

Says Stokes,[24] "We have been able to eliminate the day tanks, their cost, and their contribution to pollution of our atmosphere without having to sacrifice the safety and convenience of our operations."

2.
On-Site Recycling of Solvent Vapours

Little more than a decade ago, most firms using solvent-based processing would not have thought twice about solvent vapours escaping out the company exhaust stack.

Industrial painters, printers and adhesives manufacturers using solvent-based paints, inks and adhesives may lose thousands of dollars worth of solvents during the drying phase unless solvent vapour recovery systems are installed.

If a business generates waste solvents in the vapour form, these wastes must be treated on the premises, or at least condensed into a liquid form. However, businesses that generate only liquid waste solvents may choose to send their spent solvents to an outside recycler. Businesses with on-site treatment needs include dry cleaners, industrial painters, and manufacturers of adhesive products. These industries all generate waste solvents in the vapour form.

Carbon adsorption units can be readily installed in an existing operation to trap solvents from vented solvent-laden air. Carbon adsorption is a proven technology that has been available to industry for several decades.

Carbon Adsorption

The activated carbon adsorption process is a time-tested technology that has been used in North America for over 40 years to recover a variety of solvents from solvent-laden air. Because solvent prices have increased significantly, the enhanced economics make it a viable control technology for even small shops in certain industries. Its cost-effectiveness for the low-volume spray painter remains dubious at this time, however, the economics are favourable in comparison to other pollution abatement options should they ever become mandatory. Off-the-shelf equipment can be readily modified to meet many

small business needs. Solvent-laden air is passed through a bed of activated carbon which acts as the adsorption medium. Because the major portion of the solvent is retained by the carbon bed, relatively clean air is exhausted from the system[25] (see Figure 3).

The next step is to desorb or strip the carbon bed of the solvent temporarily attached to it. This process of recovering solvent and freeing the carbon bed for re-use is known as desorption. It can be accomplished by several methods including: low pressure steam; a solvent that will remove the adsorbate; acidic or caustic wash and removal of carbon from the bed followed by thermal activation of the carbon at 1000°C; and indirect heating with a nitrogen purge.[26]

Steam is most often used in the desorption/reactivation stage of the carbon bed because it is relatively inexpensive, inert and easily condensed back to the liquid state. The resultant liquid contains water, solvents and other impurities.

Now the solvents may be recovered from the mixture through the same distillation or decanta-

tion procedure used by professional solvent cleaners and described earlier in this chapter. Or the liquid waste solvents may be sent directly to a reclaimer for outside recovery.

If a single solvent is present in the solvent-laden air, as is common among dry cleaners, the carbon adsorption process is relatively simple and cost-effective.

Industry spokesmen question whether the same economic feasibility exists for the industrial painting industry, another large generator of solvent emissions. Here, solvent vapour is emitted both in a typical spray booth and in the drying oven. Because there often is a mixture of solvents present, and because they are present at low concentrations in large quantities of air, the use of carbon adsorption as a recovery process is frequently viewed as uneconomical for the small operator.

This factor was a major influence in triggering the paint and adhesives industries to make increasing use of non-solvent coating systems.[27]

Some larger paint facilities view

Figure 3
The Carbon Adsorption Process

Solvent-laden air is passed through a bed of activated carbon which retains the solvent. In the desorption phase, solvent is stripped from the carbon bed and condensed to a liquid.

Source: "Disposal of Surface Coating Solvents," *Industrial Finishing*, February 1981.

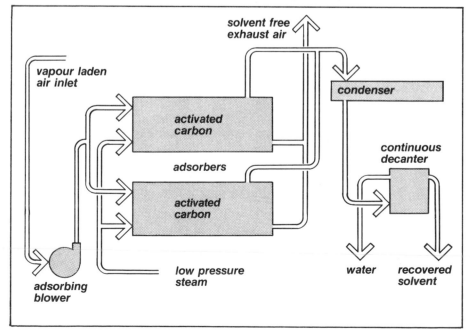

incineration as a more economical approach to reduce paint solvent emissions than carbon adsorption, especially when heat released during incineration is recirculated back into the process.[28]

■ For Shuford Mills (Hickory, North Carolina), a major American tape manufacturer, the installation of two costly carbon adsorption systems will have paid off in the long run. With a pay-back period of 4 years, and a 95% efficiency in the recovery of toluene,[29] company staff are pleased to have met air quality standards and put their accounts back in the black.

Shuford Mills uses millions of gallons of toluene each year to dissolve rubber and resins required to to put the "stick" on an assortment of tapes, including freezer, printable, packing, strapping and insulating tapes.

In 1967, the price of toluene hovered at 24¢ per gallon. In 1973, just prior to the oil embargo, the price had risen gradually to 35¢ a gallon. Four years later, toluene prices shot to $1.36 per gallon, close to a 400% increase.[29]

Shuford Mills installed its first carbon adsorption line in 1967 because, even at those toluene prices, solvent recovery looked promising. Four years later the equipment had paid for itself. In 1977, a second carbon adsorption system with a similar pay-back period was installed.

During the adhesive coating operation, toluene is heated to 280 - 400°F, resulting in a massive solvent vapour problem. In the recovery operation, the vaporous solvent stream is cooled to 80°F by a chiller before it enters the giant carbon adsorption units. After the adsorption and desorption phases in the carbon beds, the solvent passes through a heat exchanger which condenses the solvent in an energy efficient manner. Because toluene is not miscible in water, the solvent can be easily separated from the water through a simple decantation process. The solvent is then ready for re-use.

Nitrogen-Based Solvent Recovery

The recent focus on energy con-

Figure 4
Nitrogen-Based Solvent Recycling System

With an inert nitrogen atmosphere, solvent vapour can be safely concentrated to well above traditional oven levels, at which levels the solvent is recoverable by condensation. The oven exhaust is cooled with multiple heat-exchange stages. Solvent recovery reaches 99% efficiency.
Source: "Solvent Recovery System Saves Costs and Cleans Air," *Chemical Engineering*, March 10, 1980.

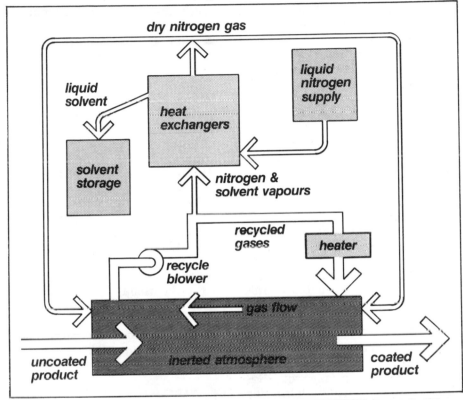

servation has triggered the development of a more efficient solvent recovery system. Available both for new installations and for retrofits, the system features a switch to an inert nitrogen atmosphere. Use of an inert nitrogen atmosphere permits solvent vapour to be safely concentrated above conventional levels. By eliminating the normal requirement for ventilation of the drying oven with atmospheric air, fuel is conserved.

Although the economics appear to be more promising than either carbon adsorption or incineration, the technology is relatively new. At present, nitrogen-based solvent recovery is primarily applicable to larger businesses because of the significant capital cost.

■ With years of research and development behind it, Airco Industrial Gases (Murray Hill, New Jersey) has set up shop to market

its new technology to recover solvents on-site. The system features a switch from a conventional carbon unit to one with an inert nitrogen atmosphere (see Figure 4).

Field testing of the prototype equipment occurred in a fabric-coating facility in Kenyon, Rhode Island. Test data compiled in 1979 indicated a 60% reduction in the heat energy required over the previous conventional system. Net operating cost savings were estimated at $7.75 per hour for the retrofit system.[30]

Installation of the first commercial Airco unit is underway at a magnetic tape facility in California. In the manufacture of tapes, the deposition of iron oxides on the magnetic tape requires the use of tetrahydrofuran. Tetrahydrofuran is one of the most expensive solvents in use, selling for over $8 per gallon or about five times as much as toluene.[31]

In a conventional drying oven, a constant source of new air is required to dilute solvent concentrations below explosive levels. This constant venting operation means that hot air is exhausted off continuously, resulting in substantial energy losses. By replacing the air with an inert nitrogen atmosphere, solvent vapour can be safely concentrated to levels much higher than in conventional air-dry ovens.

At these higher levels of solvent concentration, the solvent can be recovered directly by condensation. Solvent recovery efficiency may reach 99%. Airco cite energy conservation and cleaner stack exhausts as the major improvements of their system over conventional carbon adsorption units.

"The operational costs are absorbed by the energy savings in many cases, and hence solvent recovery pays for itself," says Davis Rieman, manager of solvent recovery at Airco.[31] "The value of the solvents reclaimed goes towards paying off the capital costs of the system."

Intended applications of the new technology include use in synthetic rubber, polypropylene, vinyl chloride monomer and pharmaceutical processing. Recovery units are available for smaller and medium-sized businesses as well. Modules are available to recover 45, 120 and 350 gallons of solvent per hour at an estimated pay-back of two years, depending on the price of the solvent.[31]

3.
On-Site Recycling in Small and Medium-Sized Businesses

Recent developments in the production of solvent recycling equipment have yielded commercially available units small enough for businesses generating low volumes of waste solvents. The simple heating and condensing systems remove impurities from the solvent wastestream, returning the same solvent or solvent blend to the user that generated

the wastestream.

The amount of time required to pay off the recycling equipment through dividends from the recovered solvent depends upon the value and quantity of solvent recycled. As transportation costs continue to escalate, even small-volume solvent users may find it more economical to recycle waste solvents on the premises than to truck them to a professional reclaimer.[32]

■ Some solvent users are thinking twice before trucking their solvents to an outside recovery firm, and well they should according to James Teale of J.M. Teale Associates (Woodcliff Lake, New Jersey).[33]

Teale reviews the problem encountered by a small printing company in the northeastern United States and offers a practical solution to its solvent shortage and accompanying disposal of solvent wastes.

In 1977, Teale was able to show the economics were in favour of on-site solvent recovery compared to conventional disposal methods and to recovery by an outside recovery firm.

Consider a new mixture of n-propyl acetate (10%) and ethyl alcohol (90%) purchased by a

small printing company for $1.75 per gallon. Every day, 150 gallons of the solvent mixture is used to clean ink from the press rollers and to dilute colour concentrates. Spent solvent resulting from the clean-up process contains 95% solvent and 5% residual ink. This material is stored in 5-gallon cans for trucking to incinerators.

Do the economics warrant on-

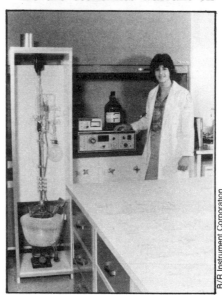

The B/R fractional distillation unit is suitable for the recovery of used laboratory solvents.

Installation of a single-stage batch-type distillation process for recycling contaminated solvents on-site.

site solvent recovery?

According to Teale, yes. He estimates that it would cost the company 36.7¢ per gallon reclaimed to recover the solvent. By not needing to purchase new solvent, the company saves $1.38 per gallon of solvent recovered. Payback period for a $7000 capital outlay is calculated to be about four months.[33]

■ The Histopathology Laboratory at the Toronto General Hospital (Toronto, Ontario) recently participated in a four-year solvent recycling demonstration. Waste xylene and chloroform were cleaned to 100% purity using a commercially available distillation unit. Contaminated isopropyl alcohol was restored to a purity of 99.7%. Under normal conditions, the hospital lab pays about $275 each week to purchase new xylene, chloroform and isopropyl alcohol. By reclaiming waste solvents on the premises, the lab is able to recover $180 worth of solvents each week which would otherwise require costly disposal off site.[34]

The solvent recovery system used is produced by the B/R Instrument Corporation (Pasadena, Maryland). Solvents are purified using a distillation column capable of processing up to 4 litres of solvent per hour. Applicable for research, industrial and clinical labs, the solvent recycling unit has been used to recover waste xylene, chloroform, isopropyl alcohol, methanol, hexane, toluene, methylene chloride, freon, acetone, coal tar, acetonitrile and others.[35]

■ The Brighton Corporation (Cincinnati, Ohio) is one of several manufacturers of on-site solvent recovery equipment. Their equipment has been on the market for 20 years. "That's allowed a lot of time for the technology to be scaled down to the needs of the smaller user," says Art Kinpell of Brighton Corporation.[36] The smallest unit available will automatically treat 7 1/2 gallons of solvent per hour. Such a unit is currently in use by a Chicago telephone book printer. Canadian installations include International Paint in Montreal, C-I-L in Toronto and Du Pont in Ajax.[36]

■ Canadian Lukens Ltd. (Rex-

This Brighton solvent recycling still has an automatic sludge disposal system. Sludge is pumped out continuously from the bottom of the cone.

Electrically heated boiler to the left of the evaporator provides heat for installations where 100 psi steam pressure is not available.

dale, Ontario) similarly manufacture on-site solvent recycling equipment to reclaim acetone and other ketones, alcohols and chlorinated hydrocarbons.[21] According to the manufacturers, the Lukens equipment is automatic, requires very little maintenance and is simple to install.

■ The Finish Engineering Company Inc. (Erie, Pennsylvania) manufactures on-site solvent recycling equipment in a variety of sizes. The Fin-E-Co Little Still reclaims solvents such as methylene chloride, acetone, MEK, toluene, xylene and many others having a boiling point of 160°C or less. The waste solvent is reclaimed in 15 gallon batches although clean solvent can be drawn off during operation. Recovery levels range from 80 to 95%, depending on the amount and type of contamination.[37]

■ From England comes an automatic solvent recovery unit the size of a filing cabinet. The Alida Packaging Group (Derby, England) reclaims 90% of their waste solvents using the compact Newgate Simms (Chester, England) recovery unit.[38]

At Alida, printing 20 million

Electrically heated circulating heat-transfer fluid system designed for distillation above 300°F.

Brighton Corporation

bags in a week results in 200 gallons of waste isopropyl alcohol. The recycling equipment can recover up to 30 litres of solvent per hour. Contaminated solvent is evaporated using an electrical oil heater in the centre of the regeneration container and condensed through an air-cooled condenser.

Reclaimed solvent is of high enough quality to be used in re-formulating ink, as well as in cleaning the presses. Alida estimates ink use to be 500 kg of ink per week, to which is added about 20% of the reclaimed solvent to adjust the viscosity.

The waste ink is itself 90% solvent. Reclaiming the isopropyl alcohol from the waste ink will save Alida £1.16 per gallon of solvent reclaimed. By salvaging solvent from the 45 gallons of waste ink generated weekly, Alida nets an annual savings of £2325.[38]

4.
Reducing Solvent Losses During Degreasing

Solvent degreasing refers to industrial cleaning processes in which organic solvents are used to remove grease, oil and dirt from a range of materials including metals, glass, plastic and textile objects. The automobile, electronics, appliance and metal working industries are the major users of solvent degreasers. Also involved in degreasing operations are the printing, chemical and plastics industries. Solvents commonly used in degreasing include trichloroethylene, 1,1,1-trichloroethane, perchloroethylene, methylene chloride, trichlorotrifluoroethane and Stoddard solvent.

In the United States, the Environmental Protection Agency is imposing standards to be effective by 1985 which will lower organic solvent emissions by 64% in industrial degreasing operations.[2] Country-wide compliance with these regulations is estimated to result in a total capital expenditure of $94 million. On the plus side, the investment in the solvent control and recovery equipment is expected to reduce the operating

expenses of the degreasing industry by $124 million *each year* through credits in recovered solvent. Reducing solvent losses from

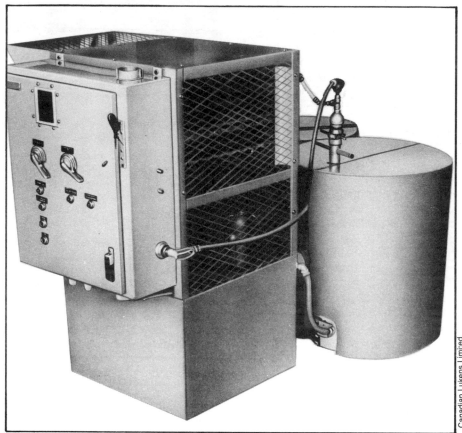

Small-scale batch distillation unit suitable for recovering common solvents such as acetone, alcohols, chlorinated solvents and Freons.™

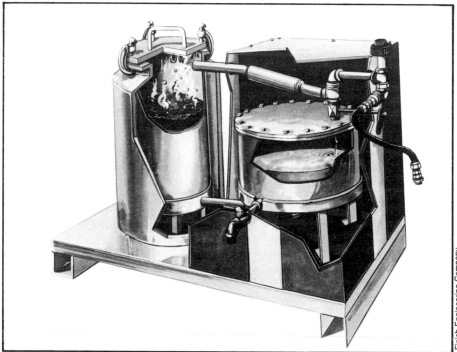

The Finish Little Still LS-15 can recover 75 to 100 gallons of solvent per week. The contaminated solvent is heated. Solvent vapours rise, pass through a water condenser, and exit as a clean liquid that gravity-flows to a storage tank.

degreasing operations can be a highly profitable venture.

The Degreasing Operation

In the degreasing operation, a solvent in a liquid or vapour state is used to remove grease, oil and dirt. Two types of solvent degreasing are room temperature degreasing, better known as cold cleaning, and vapour degreasing.

Cold cleaning refers to the degreasing operation in which a solvent at room temperature is sprayed, flushed or allowed to immerse the items to be cleaned. Cold cleaning is simpler and cheaper than vapour degreasing, although not always as effective in cleaning inner cavities.

In vapour degreasing, the solvent is heated to its boiling point, resulting in the escape of solvent vapours. The parts to be cleaned are then lowered into the vapour zone. The best cleaning action is achieved by vapour degreasing.

The degreasing process can entail batch or continuous operations. Batch operations are done in open degreasers while continuous operations are performed in conveyorized degreasers (see Figures 5 and 6).

In 1978, the United States Environmental Protection Agency estimated that 85% of the 30,000 degreasers in use in the United States were open-top vapour degreasing units.[39] An open-top vapour degreaser emits 10 to 20 times as much solvent as a typical cold cleaner, but less than half as much as a conveyorized degreaser.[40] In addition to evaporation losses, solvent is lost through drag-out of liquid solvent when clean items are extracted from the degreaser.

Minimizing Solvent Losses

Two major ways to cut evaporative solvent emissions are by upgrading the cleaning process and modifying the degreasing equipment.

Based on tests in degreasing shops, the Environmental Protection Agency concluded in a 1977 study that implementing any or a combination of four major emis-

Figure 5
Open-Top Vapour Degreaser

Open-top vapour degreasers are responsible for emitting large amounts of solvents unless special emission control systems are employed. The majority of degreasers in use are open-top vapour degreasing units.

Source: *Controlling Pollution from the Manufacturing and Coating of Metal Products, Vol. 2*, U.S. Environmental Protection Agency, 1977.

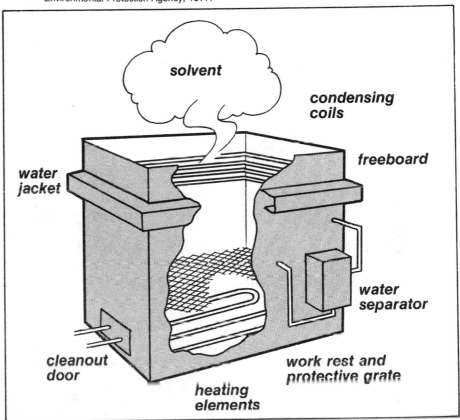

Figure 6
Conveyorized Degreaser

In a conveyorized degreaser, the objects to be cleaned are passed through a solvent spray or solvent vapour. Conveyorized degreasers result in twice the solvent loss as open-top units.

Source: *Controlling Pollution from the Manufacturing and Coating of Metal Products, Vol. 2*, U.S. Environmental Protection Agency, 1977.

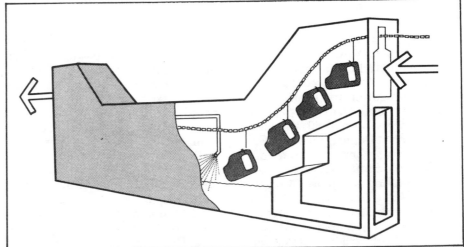

sion reduction techniques (see Table 4) substantially decreased solvent losses. Not only were solvent losses reduced, but economics indicated that each of these techniques netted a profit in most instances. Today's increasing solvent costs should only sweeten the deal.

Upgrading the Cleaning Process

Solvent losses due to drag-out can be reduced by regimenting good operating procedures.

Vapour degreasing emits the highest amount of hydrocarbon pollution and should be reserved only for those functions not accomplished by cold cleaning or non-solvent cleaning methods unless ample solvent recovery mechanisms are in place.

For open-tank systems, even though covers are part of the original equipment design, it is common for operators to leave the covers off when the system is at rest or is shut-down. Tests have shown that use of a tank cover during shut down periods reduces solvent loss from 25 to 50%.[40]

Equipment Modification

Equipment modification such as increasing the height of the degreaser freeboard has been demonstrated to reduce solvent losses by 25%.[40] The freeboard height of a degreaser is the height of the tank above the vapour level. Until recently, the accepted freeboard height was equal to one-half the width of the tank. Increasing the freeboard height to 75% of the tank width significantly reduces solvent losses from an operating degreaser.[41]

■ Being in the metal furniture manufacturing business meant that Pierce Industries Inc. (Walden, New York) required degreasing equipment on the premises to clean the metal furniture prior to finishing. Early in 1980, the New York State Department of Environmental Conservation advised Pierce Industries to upgrade the degreasing equipment to meet existing emission regulations.[41]

Two equipment modifications were made. The company installed a Detrex freeboard extension unit

Table 4
Effectiveness of Techniques Used to Reduce Solvent Emissions During Degreasing

Technique	Reduction in Solvent Loss	Profitability
Tank covers	25 to 59%	Generally profitable
Increased freeboard height	25 to 55%	Generally profitable
Refrigerated chillers	40 to 60%	Generally profitable
Distillation of recovered vapour	80% solvent reclaimed per year	Profitable above 350 gallons solvent

Source: Controlling Pollution from the Manufacturing and Coating of Metal Products: Solvent Metal Cleaning Air Pollution Control. US EPA, May 1977.

Detrex Chemical Industries Inc.

Detrex solvent degreasing tank with powered tank cover.

along with a powered degreaser cover. By simply pressing a button after degreaser use, the cover automatically closes from each end toward the center in a horizontal plane.

In the first six months of operation, solvent use dropped by 1650 gallons, which saved the company $6600 previously spent on new solvent purchases. Although the stimulus to reduce solvent pollution resulted from pressure to comply with the regulatory agencies, Pierce Industries now profits

from the compliance activity. The retrofit equipment was paid off in the first six months while future solvent savings add to the company's profit margin. Furthermore, by containing solvent vapour to an acceptable level within the retrofit degreaser unit, the company realized additional savings through avoidance of an external exhaust system to blow 4000 cubic feet of air from the plant every minute of operation.[41]

Installing Chillers

Another equipment redesign is to install a second set of condensing coils, also known as chillers, in the degreaser (see Figure 7). The condensing coils would create a cold blanket above the vapour zone in the degreaser and prevent the escape of vapours. Although such a retrofit will result in both capital and operating costs, the savings from the anticipated 40% reduction in solvent loss will more than cover the expenses incurred.[40]

■ Vapour degreasers are vital pieces of equipment to the Sealed Power Corporation (Muskegon, Michigan) in the manufacture of piston rings.

When Sealed Power installed Detrex freeboard chillers on seven of their degreasers, they were amazed at the drop in solvent use. The solvent concentration above the chiller units now averaged 55 ppm, well below the Occupational Safety and Health Administration's prescribed limit of 100 ppm (time-weighted average over an 8 hour day).

The company monitored the performance of two of the chillers over a four-month period to calculate the solvent savings. Projected savings in solvent costs for the two units was $17,688 in the first year.[41] This success prompted company management to purchase chiller systems for the remaining vapour degreasers.

Carbon Adsorption System

In those instances where the size of the degreaser is very large, or where degreaser use is frequent, a company may opt for a solvent recovery system rather than minimize solvent loss through installation of metal covers or chillers.

Solvent-laden air from above the degreaser tank is collected and pushed through a bed of carbon in the carbon adsorption recovery unit. The solvent is adsorbed onto the surface of the carbon and the clean air is recirculated to blow across the degreaser tank (see Figure 8). Solvent is stripped from the carbon and re-used in the degreasing tank.[42]

Figure 7
Open-Top Degreaser with Chiller

By retrofitting an open-top vapour degreaser with a second set of condensing coils, a cold blanket of air is created above the vapour zone, preventing the escape of solvent vapours.
Source: *Controlling Pollution from the Manufacturing and Coating of Metal Products, Vol. 2,* U.S. Environmental Protection Agency, 1977.

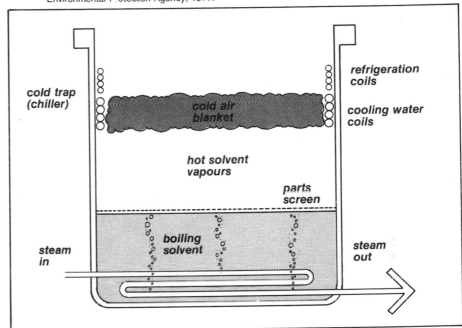

Figure 8
Vapour Degreaser with Solvent Recycling System

A closed-loop forced air system causes most of the solvent-laden air above the degreaser to enter the solvent recovery unit. Solvent is removed from the solvent-laden air and returned to the degreaser. The solvent-free air is recirculated above the degreasing tank.
Source: "Meeting Regulations by Saving Money in Vapour Degreasing," *Industrial Finishing,* November 1981.

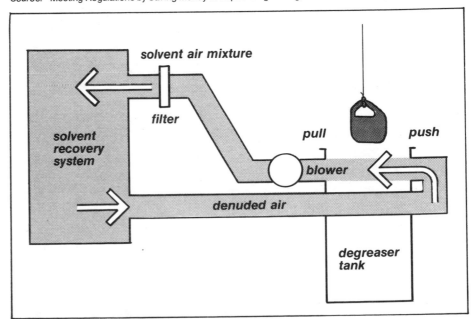

■ Halstead Industries (Scottsboro, Alabama) specializes in the production of custom-made heat transfer equipment. The operation at Halstead frequently involves the degreasing of large and unwieldy metal coils, sometimes extending more than 20 feet. The degreaser at Halstead is 30 feet long by 3 feet wide to accommodate long pieces of metal requiring cleaning. Because the degreaser is in continuous use, even a powered metal cover over the degreaser box would unnecessarily impede the degreasing operation.

Environmental regulations and solvent costs were uppermost on the vice-president's mind when he investigated upgrading the degreasing system. Shortly thereafter, an Econ-O-Solv carbon adsorption system was installed, along with a unique push-pull exhaust system to conduct solvent-laden air to the carbon adsorption recovery unit.

Since the installation, trichloroethylene concentrations in the air around the operator have dropped to 25 ppm, well below the Occupational Safety and Health Administration's limit of 100 ppm. Compliance with the regulatory agencies ultimately netted the plant an annual saving in excess of $25,000 in solvent purchases.[41]

Conclusion

Despite the widespread availability of solvent recycling technology and equipment, only a fraction of Canada's waste solvents are recovered for re-use. The rest are incinerated, landfilled or exported for disposal elsewhere.

Large companies have the financial and technical resources on hand to invest in on-site solvent recovery equipment. The capital cost of the recycling equipment is frequently paid off in two years or less because of the value of the large amounts of solvents that are recovered.

For smaller businesses, the total value of the solvents recovered is less, and the capital cost of the equipment is paid off more slowly. Nevertheless, an investment in recycling technology is just that — an investment. Eventually the recycling equipment will be paid off and any dividends that accrue from solvent recovery will net the company a profit.

Solvent recovery may have been marginal in the past for many of the smaller businesses. Now, with disposal and solvent costs spiralling, and disposal regulations tightening, it is everyone's business to maximize solvent re-use.

FOR FURTHER INFORMATION

Solvent Recyclers in Canada

Professional solvent recyclers generally clean waste solvents for a fee and return the purified solvent back to the customer. For those companies which choose not to use recycled solvents, waste solvents may be sold directly to most solvent recyclers.

Solvent recyclers vary in the types of solvents that they accept for cleaning. Contact your nearest recycler and ask what types of solvents, and the smallest batch-size, are accepted for recycling. Some solvent recyclers will permit companies to pool small quantities of waste solvents to make recovery economically feasible.

A&J Chemicals,
12 Nottinghill Road,
Thornhill, Ontario.
L3T 4X9
(416) 484-8838

Anachemia Solvents Ltd.,
3549 Mavis Road,
Mississauga, Ontario.
L5C 4T7
(416) 279-5122

Anachemia Solvents Ltd.,
P.O. Box 147,
Lachine, Quebec.
H8S 4A7
(514) 489-5711

Oakside Chemicals Ltd.,
R.R. #4,
London, Ontario.
N6A 4B8
(519) 681-1103

Van Waters and Rogers Ltd.,
62 Arrow Road,
Weston, Ontario.
M9M 2L9
(416) 741-9190

Van Waters and Rogers Ltd.,
2700 J.B. Deschamps,
Lachine, Quebec.
H8T 1E1
(514) 631-9451

Varni Colour Chemical Ltd.,
29 First St. East,
Elmira, Ontario.
N3B 2Z6
(519) 669-3318

Journals

Many excellent chemical processing and engineering journals exist that occasionally contain articles on solvent recycling technologies and applications. In addition, these journals carry numerous advertisements and new product information on solvent recycling equipment.

CANADIAN CHEMICAL
PROCESSING,
Southam Business Publications Ltd.,
1450 Don Mills Road,
Don Mills, Ontario.
M3B 2X7

CHEMICAL ENGINEERING,
McGraw Hill Inc.,
1221 Avenue of the Americas,
New York, New York.
10020

ADHESIVES AGE,
Communication Channels Inc.,
6285 Barfield Road,
Atlanta, Georgia.
30328

CHEMICAL WEEK,
McGraw Hill Inc.,
1221 Avenue of the Americas,
New York, New York.
10020

INDUSTRIAL FINISHING,
Hitchcock Publishing Co.,
Hitchcock Building,
Wheaton, Illinois.
60187

PROCESS ENGINEERING,
Morgan-Grampian Ltd.,
30 Calderwood St.,
Woolwich, London, England.
SE18 6QH

CHEMICAL ENGINEERING
PROGRESS,
American Institute of Chemical
Engineers,
345 E 4th St.,
New York, New York.
10017

CANADIAN JOURNAL OF
CHEMICAL ENGINEERING,
Canadian Society for Chemical
Engineering,
151 Slater St.,
Suite 906,
Ottawa, Ontario.
K1P 5H3

Associations

Although no Canadian association of solvent recyclers exists at present, Canadian companies can join the National Association of Solvent Recyclers (NASR) in the United States. This active association is knowledgeable about upcoming conferences, seminars and expositions, new technologies and equipment, and American legislative changes and regulations.

Membership in the association entitles a member to the NASR Newsletter and periodic bulletins on legislative updates. The association has recently completed a narrated slide presentation on solvent recycling for promotional purposes.

Contact: National Association of
Solvent Recyclers,
1406 Third National Building,
Dayton, Ohio.
45402
(513) 223-0419

The Canadian Waste Materials Exchange

The Canadian Waste Materials Exchange (CWME) is a country-wide information exchange designed to match waste streams with potential new users. For a small fee ($25) you can become a member of the CWME. Membership entitles a participating company to receive the CWME Bulletin, and to list wastes for exchange. The CWME Bulletin provides bi-monthly listings of waste solvents that are available and wanted. Both the quantity and the composition of the wastestream are identified.

Contact: Canadian Waste Materials
Exchange,
Sheridan Park Research
Community,
Mississauga, Ontario.
L5K 1B3
(416) 822-4111

References

1. Capone, S.V. and Petroccia, M. Guidance to State and Local Agencies in Preparing Regulations to Control Volatile Organic Compounds from Ten Stationary Source Categories. Prepared for U.S. Environmental Protection Agency, Research Triangle Park, North Carolina, September 1979.

2. U.S. Environmental Protection Agency. "Update: Organic Solvents." EPA Journal, June 1980.

3. "Packagers Bend to New Solvent Rules." Chemical Week, July 2, 1980.

4. Tierney, D.R. and Hughes, T.W. Source Assessment: Reclaiming of Waste Solvents. Prepared for U.S. Environmental Protection Agency, Industrial Environmental Research Laboratory, Cincinnati, Ohio, 1978.

5. 1976 Refining Process Handbook. Hydrocarbon Processing 55(9), 1976.

6. Formica, P.N. Controlled and Uncontrolled Emission Rates and Applicable Limitations for Eighty Processes. Prepared for U.S. Environmental Protection Agency, Research Triangle Park, North Carolina, 1976.

7. Shreve, R.N. The Chemical Process Industries. New York: McGraw-Hill Book Co. Inc., 1969.

8. Niemi, B. "How to Figure Potential Emission Reductions for High-Solids Coatings." Industrial Finishing, November 1979.

9. Hukill, Emory. Hukill Chemical Corporation, Bedford, Ohio. Personal communication, July 1981.

10. Berry, R.I. "Squeezing Spent Solvents to Yield Synthetic Fuel Oil." *Chemical Engineering,* February 23, 1981.

11. Heslin, M. Industrial Spray Painters Ltd., Weston, Ontario. Personal communication, November 1981.

12. Pojasek, Robert. Weston Designers/Consultants, Burlington, Massachusetts. Memorandum to the Business and Industry Association of New Hampshire, February 9, 1982.

13. U.S. Environmental Protection Agency. *National Emissions Report 1972.* National Emissions Data System of the Aerometric and Emissions Reporting System, U.S.E.P.A., Research Triangle Park, North Carolina, 1974.

14. American Petroleum Institute. *Manual on Disposal of Refinery Wastes: Volume on Atmospheric Emissions.* Washington, D.C.: American Petroleum Institute, 1976.

15. Wentlandt, George. Anachemia Solvents Ltd., Mississauga, Ontario. Personal communication, February 1982.

16. Wordsworth, A. "Solvents Recycled by Firm." *Probe Post* 3(3), September-December 1980.

17. "Recycling Boosts Profits and Saves Resources." *Process Engineering,* May 1980.

18. Kilpatrick, D. "Where There's Chemical Muck . . ." *The Sunday Times* (London, England), June 11, 1978.

19. Shagena, Peter, Chemical Recovery Systems Inc., Romulus, Michigan. Personal communication, July 1981.

20. "Aiming for a Solvent Recycling Network." *Chemical Week,* February 18, 1981.

21. Canadian Lukens Ltd., Rexdale, Ontario. Product literature on the Canadian Lukens Solvent Recovery System, 1981.

22. Cunningham, D.B. "Solvent Recovery: Improving Its Efficiency." *Adhesives Age,* December 1980.

23. "How Union Carbide Has Cleaned Up Its Image." *Business Week,* August 2, 1976.

24. Stokes, K.H. "Solvent Control System for Safety and Minimum Environmental Impact." *Journal of Environmental Sciences,* March/April 1980.

25. Drew, J.W. "Design for Solvent Recovery." *Chemical Engineering Progress,* February 1975.

26. Roobol, N.R. *et al.* "Disposal of Surface Coating Solvents." *Industrial Finishing,* February 1981.

27. Hamer, A.D. *et al.* "Computer Program Compares Economics of Solvent and Aqueous PSA Systems." *Adhesives Age,* March 1980.

28. "Incinerator Draws Energy from Pollutants." *Chemical Week,* January 2, 1980.

29. "Toluene Recovery at Shuford Mills." *Adhesives Age,* March 1980.

30. "Solvent Recovery System Saves Costs and Cleans Air." *Chemical Engineering,* March 10, 1980.

31. Rieman, Davis. Airco Industrial Gases, Murray Hill, New Jersey. Personal communication, August 1981.

32. Porrini, M. "Solvent Recovery and the Prevention of Atmospheric Pollution." *Industry and Environment,* No. 2, 1981.

33. Teale, J.M. "Fast Payout from In-Plant Recovery of Spent Solvents." *Chemical Engineering,* January 31, 1977.

34. Sparling, David. Western Scientific Services Ltd., Toronto, Ontario. Personal communication, December 1981.

35. B/R Instrument Corporation. *Distillation: Past, Present and Future.* B/R Instrument Corp., Pasadena, Maryland, 1981. (product literature)

36. Kinpell, A. Brighton Corporation, Cincinnati, Ohio. Personal communication, August 1981.

37. Finish Engineering Company Inc., Erie, Pennsylvania. Product literature on the Fin-E-Co Still, 1982.

38. "Isopropyl Alcohol Solvent Recovered from Waste Ink." *Environmental Pollution Management,* September/October 1980.

39. U.S. Environmental Protection Agency. *Controlling Pollution from the Manufacturing and Coating of Metal Products, Vol. 2.* Environmental Research Information Center, U.S.E.P.A., 1977.

40. Gerstle, R.W. *et al. Evaluation of Low Solvent Emission Degreasing Systems.* Presented at the First Annual EPA/AES Conference on Advanced Pollution Control for the Metal Finishing Industry, Lake Buena Vista, Florida, 1978.

41. "Meeting Regulations by Saving Money in Vapor Degreasing." *Industrial Finishing,* November 1981.

42. U.S. Environmental Protection Agency. *Organic Solvent Cleaners: Background Information for Proposed Standards.* Office of Air, Noise and Radiation, Research Triangle Park, North Carolina, October 1979.

Tanning

Much of the waste generated by a tannery is unnecessary. Resource recovery and re-use options are available, many offering an attractive financial return on investment. But tanning is an old and well-established industry. For many plants, the rearrangement of the process flow and the drainage patterns would be a major undertaking and although the present system of waste treatment is not close to optimum, it has been working relatively satisfactorily for years.

In any operation, there is strong pressure not to change something that seems to be working; tradition dies hard. It will take a combination of strict government effluent controls and a realization of the economic benefits of resource recovery over disposal to push tanneries into the next stage in their development.

Chromium recycling, salt recovery, byproduct manufacture, and protein and sulphide collection are employed by some firms. Unhairing solutions, tanning liquors and even bate may be held for re-use. The installation of holding tanks with their associated piping and pumps, and the correction of reagent concentrations after screening are the only requirements. The flow sheet for an efficient tanning operation should be replete with recycling arrows and byproduct sales potential. The money spent on hauling useful material to the dump can then find its way back into the investment capital of the firm.

Waste Sources and Conventional Treatment

Common pollutants originating with the tanning industry include chromium, sulphides, ether solubles, dyes, suspended and dissolved solids, and organic materials (see Tables 1 and 2).

The traditional effluent treatment system entails the collection of the wastestreams from each of the tannery processes followed by pH adjustment and, finally, clarification[1] (see Figure 1). In some cases, this treatment is sufficient to meet local sewer disposal regulations. Conventional treatment removes most of the solids and chromium and some of the other soluble material and BOD (biological oxygen demand). The mixing of the acid stream from the tanning process and the alkaline wastes from the hairburn stage achieves an effluent pH suitable for clarification and amendable to most sewer by-laws. However, this requires that the tanning liquors be held separately and released into the waste treatment plant at the same time as the hairburn dump.

In the face of stricter controls, some firms have opted for sophisticated treatment: activated sludge systems, trickling filters, or, if space is not at a premium, even lagoons or oxidation ditches.[2,3] An advanced waste disposal system allows a more complete scrubbing of contaminants from the wastewaters prior to discharge to the sewer, but it still is preoccupied with tail-end treatment. While the amalgamation of all the wastes from each wet stage in the tanning process offers some treatment benefits (in pH adjustment and precipitation of chromium salts by hairburn alkalines), it makes liquor recycling and chemical recovery extremely difficult.

Tail-end treatment also relies heavily on the availability of local landfill sites for the disposal of chromium-laden sludges. The addition of coagulants and other treatment chemicals adds to the heavy financial burden of sludge removal.

Table 1

Processing Sequence and Pollution Sources

Processing Area	Operation	Effluent Compounds
Slaughter House	curing	salt added
Hide House	trimming and sorting	
Beamhouse	soaking	dirt, manure, blood fat, salt removed
	unhairing	add lime, sodium sulfide to remove hair
	fleshing	flesh fat removed
Tanyard	bating	add deliming chemicals, enzymes to remove alkalines (from unhairing) and skin substances
	pickling	salt and acid added
	tanning	chromium salts, vegetable agents or synthetic tanning agents used
	wringing	water removed
	splitting and shaving	hide shavings
	retanning	same as tanning
	colouring	dyes
	stuffing and fat liquoring	liquid oils and fats added
Finishing	drying conditioning staking buffing finishing plating	dry operations

POLLUTION PREVENTION OPPORTUNITIES

1.
Soaking

As soon as possible after a hide has been stripped at the slaughterhouse, it is cured to prevent bacterial attack. This is most often done by covering the hide with salt. The salt removes the water from the hide and the dehydration prevents spoilage.

The hides are then shipped from the slaughterhouse to the tannery where they are stored in the hidehouse. There, the hides are split for ease of handling and the unwanted pieces are removed. The split hides, or sides, are then bundled in large packs usually weighing 5000 lb. Each pack is processed through the tannery as a unit. The batch processing of packs through the succesive tanning stages results in large variations in waste flow and waste characteristics during an operating day. Direct sewer discharge of these divergent wastestreams would not meet effluent disposal regulations, so bulk temporary storage facilities or individual treatments are necessary.

The packs then enter the second of the tannery's four main processing operations; the beamhouse, where dirt, hair and flesh are removed. The packs are first placed in soaking vats to restore their natural moisture. Rotating paddles move the hides around while dirt, manure, blood, fat and all the carefully applied salt are washed away. The lost salt in the washwater represents both a source of pollution and a lost process chemical.

Salt Recovery

Scientists with the United States Department of Agriculture have developed a process that reclaims up to 100% of the common salt used in curing.[4] The used hide-preserving salt is washed several times with a saturated brine that contains sodium hydroxide, sodium bicarbonate and alum. The saturated brine wash cannot absorb any more salt but it is quite capable of removing impurities from the preserving salt including calcium and magnesium salts and suspended colloidal materials. The wet clean salt is dried and returned to the slaughterhouse for re-use in curing. The used brine can be restored by adding calculated amounts of $NaOH$ and Na_2CO_3. The coagulating agent, alum, is also added.

Table 2
Relative Contributions to Waste Loading

Process	% of Water Use	% of BOD	% of Solids	% of Chromium	% of Sulphide	% of Ether Solubles
Soaking	18	18	30	—	—	25
Unhairing	24	45	40	—	99	50
Fleshing	2	5	10	—	trace	20
Bating	20	15	10	—	trace	trace
Pickling	5	4	1	—	trace	trace
Tanning		4	1	95	trace	trace
Wringing	1	trace	trace	5	trace	trace
Retanning	20	7	6	—	—	5
Colouring						
Fatliquoring						
Finishing and Miscellaneous	10	2	2	—	—	trace

Source: "Tanneries", In Control of Industrial Wastes in Municipalities, 1977.

Salt Substitution

Even though it is possible to reclaim salt, one of the main pollutants in tannery effluent, it may also be possible to avoid its use altogether. If the hides do not have to be stored for an extended period, replacement curing chemicals could be used.

■ Chemists at the Eastern Regional Research Centre (Wyndmoor, Pennsylvania)[5] substitute a mixture of acetic acid and sodium sulphite for salt. After the hides are soaked in the solution for ten minutes, they remain in good condition for up to 28 days. Leather produced from the hides has the same quality as that from conventionally treated skins.

Because no salt is used, the saline content in the tannery wastewater is reduced by 97%. For the small processor this may offer a real economic advantage. The researchers estimate that if all hides that are held less than 28 days were given the acid-sulphite treatment, the amount of salt in the wastewaters of American tanneries would be reduced by 75,000 tons. They further calculate savings of $50 million a year through curing chemical substitution.[5]

The acid-sulphite curing process has already been successfully used in a co-operative programme by the Research Centre and a commercial locker plant and hide dealer. It offers the greatest potential to the small slaughterhouse or locker operator who produces only a small number of hides which are picked up at frequent intervals.

Recovering salt or avoiding it are both equally effective at keeping it out of the sewer. The process favoured depends on individual capacities and needs of the operators.

2.
Fleshing

Fleshing entails the use of a machine with rotating blades that scrapes off unwanted flesh and fat. From 40 to 50% of the hide that enters the tannery ends up as solid waste.[6,7] Table 3 gives a breakdown on how these wastes are dispersed.

Byproduct Potential

Although raw and tanned collagens are not useful for making fine leather products, they are complex organic compounds with more potential than filling a space in the local landfill site or being washed into the closest drain. Limed split and hide scraps can be re-used as edible sausage casings; edible packing materials for food stuffs and gelatin food items; carriers of immobilized enzymes; sutures, dialysis membranes and artificial organs; hide powders for tannin analysis; poultry and animal feeds; and, collagen fibres can be used for absorbents and filtering materials.[7]

■ The Centre Technique de Cuir (CTC) (Lyon, France) has developed three commercial products made from fresh lime splits: Pancogen™ S, an acid-soluble collagen base for pomades, beauty creams and lotions; Collagen ST, a fibrous sterile collagen aid; and Collafilm™, for the cicatrization of open wounds and varicose ulcers.

Figure 1
Wastewater Treatment — Minimum
Source: "Tanneries," In *Control of Industrial Wastes in Municipalities*, 1977.

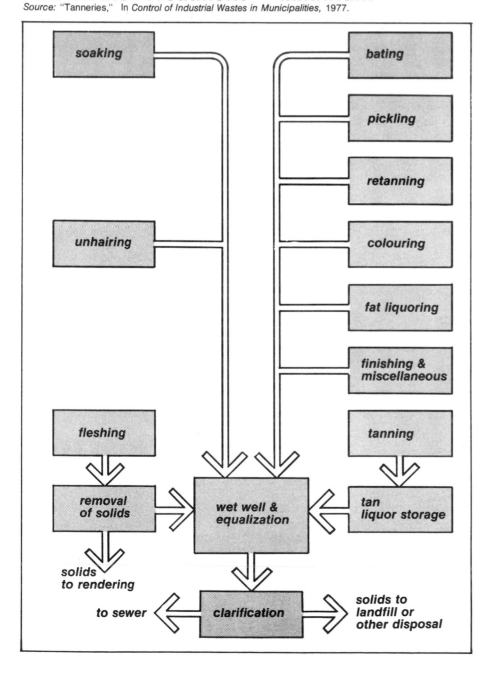

The CTC also advocates the use of 10% collagen dispersions as an agent in paper making. Added to the mixing head of paper making machines, the material aids fibre retention as well as improving paper quality. It is also a useful additive to collagen-rubber used in shoe sole manufacture.[6]

The CTC developed a unit, based on grease recovery principles used by other industries, to recover the fatty components and collagens found in fleshing and trimmings.[8] The system can handle from 1 to 3 tons of waste material an hour; the CTC pilot plant processed 1.5 tons of raw material an hour. To turn a ton and a half of waste into a saleable byproduct requires 700 to 900 litres of hot water, 1.5 tons of steam, 30 to 35 kw of electricity and 37.5 litres of hydrochloric acid. The yield is 100 to 150 kg of protein meal and 140 to 160 kg of grease. The system also recovers 1500 litres of wastewater.

The recovery process involves several steps. First, the waste is ground and transferred into a tank with acid and steam. The acid neutralizes the collagen pulp and allows the greases to be separated from the proteins.

The protein is separated from the rest of the material in a centrifuge and the remaining aqueous material is pumped to a vertical bowl separator where the greases are removed, again by centrifuging. The protein is dried by hot air in a conventional dryer, then ground, weighed and conditioned.

The grease recovered is used in the production of soaps, detergents and leather soaps. The protein is returned to the food chain as a poultry feed supplement. Tests on this material, a brown powder with a faint meat odor, show it is rich in trace elements including manganese, cobalt, copper, iron and zinc. Most poultry feeds are a mixture of grease, maize, soya, and mineral and vitamin blends. The reclaimed hide protein can replace up to 57% of the soya in a feed (15% of the total weight) provided a few synthetic amino acids are added (DL methionine and L lysine).

The German tanning journal *Das Leder* reports another system used to convert machine fleshing to animal feed.[9] The fleshings are treated with metal salts to precipitate sulphides and the pH is reduced to between 8.0 and 8.5 with sulphuric acid. Then the enzyme pronase is used to liquify the fleshings at 50 to 60°C and the fats and solids are removed by sedimentation and centrifugation. The remaining proteins have a high nutritive value and can replace other feed proteins in

---

Table 3
Solid Wastes from Tanneries in France-1979
(Hair Pulp-Chrome Tanning-Retanning-Wet and Dry Finishing)
Cattle Raw Hides Processed: 70,000 tons/year (38% Water Content) = 43,400 tons Dry Solids

Wastes	% Salted Raw Hides Weight	% Water Content	Tons of Wastes/ Year Wet Basis	Tons of Dry Solids Per Year	% of Raw Hides Dry Solids
Non-tanned wastes					
Wastes with hair	1.5	62	1,050	400	1
Fleshings	13.9	80	9,800	1,950	45
Splits-trimmings	4.8	75	3,400	850	20
Total	20.2	—	14,250	3,200	75
Tanned Wastes					
Chrome tanned splits	6.9	45	4,850	2,650	60
Shavings	6.5	40	4,550	2,750	60
Trimmings (finished leather)	4.7	18	3,300	2,700	60
Buffing dust	1.0	15	700	600	15
Total	19.1	—	13,400	8,700	195
Proteins in sludge	20.0	70	14,000	4,200	100
Total	20.0				
TOTAL	59.3		41,650	16,100	37

Source: "Improvement of the Mass and Energy Balances in the Tanning Industry", *Journal of American Leather Chemists Association,* Vol. 75, July 1980.

amounts up to 60%.

■ CWS Fellmongery Ltd. (Pontefract, Britain) treats sheephides and in the process produces an effluent rich in grease, fibrous matter and skin pieces, and highly alkaline. The control system the firm installed removes fats, suspended solids and other contaminants to the point that the resultant wastewater is well within the strict limits for sewer discharge laid down by the Yorkshire Water Authority. A series of screens removes large solid bits before the filtered effluent is pumped to a 50,000 - gallon balancing tank. Here, the wastewater is mixed and aerated by a positive displacement blower on three sides of a rectangular tank. This causes the scum to collect on the fourth side and the treated liquid is transferred to two settling vats. Finally, the effluent is passed through a second Vickerys Hydrasieve before the water is discharged to the sewer. The collected greases and organic material can then be sent to a rendering plant.[10]

3.
Unhairing

After soaking and fleshing, the pack moves on to a hairburn tank where a solution of lime and sodium sulphide dissolves the hair, epidermis and certain unwanted proteins. During the unhairing process, a certain amount of the lime and the sulphide are consumed while a fraction of the bath is retained in the hides as a result of alkaline swelling. Approximately 55% of the initial sulphide and 40% of the lime are removed from the hairburn tank in this manner. The remaining liquor is contaminated with degraded hairs in a dissolved or suspended state, residual salts from cured hides, and some fats. The contamination of the lime liquor may reach 3.2% of the fleshed weight.[6] If these liquors are to be re-used, the continued increase of the organic residues will have to be controlled to retain proper action of the lime and sulphide on the hair.

There are three major methods

for returning the sulphides and lime to the hairburn tank and keeping them out of the sewers: direct recycling, ultrafiltration and chemical absorption. The applicability of each system depends on a firm's economic resources, particular process and hide properties.

Direct Recycling

Sulphide recovery through direct recycling is the least demanding option in terms of equipment and capital expenditure. Upon completion of the hairburn, the residual bath is drained from the vessel (either paddle, drum or mixer). However, as much as 20 to 30% of the liquor may remain because it is impossible to drain the tank completely. It is necessary to rinse and flush the tank several times with an appropriate amount of fresh water. Eventually the volume of the spent bath water will amount to a little over 100% of that originally employed. The extra water will ultimately be lost again from the system during sludge removal.

The used bath is collected and transferred into an equalization tank where the grease is lifted off the top with a mechanical skimmer. The equalization tank is an open basin equipped with mechanical agitators which prevent the settling out of solids. It also contains a floatation chamber to maximize grease removal. The system has been developed in co-operation with the Italian Tanners' School in Naples and is in commercial use in a number of European operations.[11] Because North American hides have a higher grease content, the floatation chambers employed on this continent need to be somewhat larger than those used in Europe.

The main component of the recovery system is the hydrodynamic sedimentator which removes the protein, keratin and other suspended solids, as well as most of the lime. All this material is emptied automatically from the sedimentator by a time control valve in the form of sludge.

The purified bath water then overflows from the sedimentator

to a holding tank. In the holding tank the solution is agitated to prevent settling, heated to process temperature, and sampled to determine sulphide and lime concentrations. If the sulphide content needs to be strengthened, this can be done either in the holding tank or after the recovered bath has been returned to the hairburn vessel.

This relatively simple procedure has proven itself to be economically viable, effective for effluent control and an improvement in quality leather processing.

The recovery of the bath realizes sulphide savings of at least 50% and lime savings of 20% or more. From the reduction in chemical replacement costs alone the capital costs of the system can be amortized by a medium-sized tannery in two to three years. This time period is further reduced if the firm is able to reduce its waste treatment budget or eliminate sewer discharge fees, for the wastewater improvements are substantial.

Of the BOD produced from beamhouse operations, 70% can be eliminated by direct sulphide recycling. Since about 50% of the total BOD in a tannery's effluent comes from the beamhouse, total plant BOD is reduced by 35%. Similarly the total sulphide waste load is cut by 70%, suspended solids by 20% and pH by 1.5 to 2 units. The sludge generated by the hydrodynamic sedimentator is suitable for fertilizer. It has dry substance content of 30 to 40%, is rich in protein, and is free of any heavy metals. Although the water content of the sludge will contain some sulphide, this material should oxidize quickly when exposed to air.

Not only are valuable materials recovered and waste reduced, but the recycled liquors are more efficient in producing fine leathers. The returned bath is enriched with protein and amines which attack the hide softly and open the fibres up more effectively. The end result is a softer leather with a smoother grain.

■ The Centre Technique du Cuir (Lyon, France) has carried out studies to determine how often the hairburn bath waters can be re-used without affecting process efficiency.[6] They have developed a filtering system that removes solid waste such as pieces of hide and partially dissolved hair from the bath. A vibrating screen with a 1 mm mesh allows troublesome solids to be removed prior to each re-use cycle. The screen system also reduces the volume of waste sludge that would otherwise be produced by instituting a settling stage in the recovery system to remove organic solids.

The volume recovery of the hairburn bath (on average 85%) and the sulphide and lime recoveries (about 50 to 60%, respectively) are satisfactory, and fairly constant through repeated re-use cycles. In fact, control testing may be needed only once or twice a week. However, a quick and simple quality control test may be carried out on every batch if desired.[11]

However, the buildup of trace organics, if continued unchecked, could cause some problems, particularly solubilized keratin. The French team found, to its surprise, that the organic level continued to increase until the sixth or seventh re-use cycle at which time it leveled off and remained constant. They had expected a linear buildup of approximately 3.5 to 4.0 g/litre after each bath use but the maximum level encountered was 11.5 to 12.0 g/litre. From their experimental results, they were able to derive a theoretical model of nitrogen buildup which calculated the fresh water additions that are required to dilute the bath to the maximum allowable organic content. If there is no dilution of the hairburn liquor, the bath becomes too viscous to be effective in hide treatment.

The re-use of sulphide unhairing liquors has also been investigated by two American researchers.[12] In small scale trials, they showed their baths could be re-used at least 20 times and perhaps indefinitely. The only treatment they afforded the recycled liquors was temperature adjustment, and lime, sulphide and water replenishment. They noted that water from previous unhairing washes could be used to "top up"

the liquor. Fat removal would be necessary when the process is applied to a commercial operation. The researchers found fat would adhere to the drum with recycled fluids and cause greasy leather.

The bath could be used indefinitely, however even if it is discharged after every 20 cycles, there is an overall 20-fold reduction in water use and effluent sulphide, and a 7-fold reduction in effluent lime and protein.[12]

Further lime savings could be realized if their concentrations were reduced in the initial hairburn bath. According to the Centre Technique du Cuir[6], 3 to 4% lime (calculated on fleshed weight) is usually used in tannery operation. The CTC used only 2% lime liquors without observing any change in leather quality. From their 2% lime they recovered 1.2% and concluded any extra use of lime produces sludge which constitutes an unjustified charge on the effluent.

Ultrafiltration

Ultrafiltration (UF) is a recovery option that has found wide application in the automotive, electroplating, textile and food processing industries but is only beginning to be appreciated by tanners. While the technology is relatively new, the principle behind it is simple: membranes employed in the UF system will allow the passage of certain solvents such as water and dissolved matter of small molecular size through its small pores. Larger dissolved molecules cannot pass through.

When a spent hairburn bath is passed through the UF unit, water and the low molecular weight solutes such as salt, sulphide and some surfactants cross the membrane and are removed as the "permeate". Suspended solids, emulsified oils and other high molecular weight species are rejected by the membrane and removed as the "concentrate".

Although UF units come in a variety of configurations (see Figures 16 and 17 in the Waste Recovery Technologies chapter, the general principles of operation

are similar. The constant flow of fluid through the tube does not allow the buildup of filter cake on the membrane. High filtration rates can be maintained without the need for expensive maintenance and cleaning or the loss of permeate separation efficiency. A number of these tubes can be connected in series or in parallel to form a separation system with the capacity to process the wastestream from any sized unhairing bath.

■ The Abcor UF System has been recycling the hairburn liquor of an Italian tannery since 1977. After coarse screening to remove large solids, the spent fluid is collected in a holding tank. Here the temperature may be raised slightly to ensure the protein content of the bath is stable. The holding tank also allows the bath to be pumped to the UF process tank at a constant rate, avoiding any concentrated buildup in the membrane over short periods of time (see Figure 2).

The hairburn bath is fed continuously through the UF modules by a centrifugal pump. The permeate is removed to a storage vat and the concentrate is cycled back to the UF process tank for another trip through the system. Thus the concentrate is stripped time and again of its valuable load of sulphides and process water.

The complete processing cycle lasts one day, at the end of which the concentrate is removed for further dewatering, and the permeate, with its load of purified water and sulphides, is ready for re-use in the hairburn vessel.

Only about 5% of the sulphide in the spent bath is rejected by the membrane and thus missing from the permeate. On the other hand, nearly 80% of the protein is rejected and ends up in the concentrate. Again, the presence of limited amounts of organic pollutants in the recycled liquors seems to favour leather processing. A consultant to the Italian tannery writes, "The presence of moderate amounts of amines and amino acids, deriving from protein degradation, seems to favour the hair removal process, avoiding harmful derm swelling."[13]

The economics of ultrafiltration

Figure 2
Ultrafiltration System to Recycle Hairburn Liquor

The spent hairburn bath is fed continuously through the ultrafiltration modules. Sulphide molecules cross the membrane and are removed as the permeate which is re-used in the hairburn bath.

Source: "New Approach for Treatment of Spent Tannery Liquors," *Journal of American Leather Chemists Association,* November 1979.

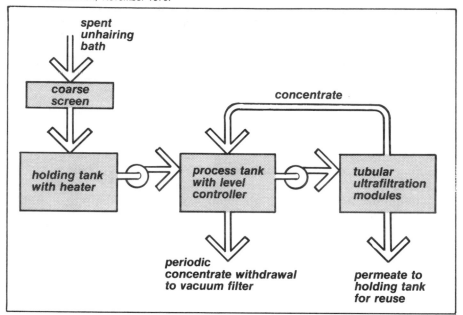

are extremely favourable. The recovery of process chemicals and water, and the avoidance of expensive waste treatment and disposal costs exceed both the capital, and the operating and maintenance charges of the UF system by a sizeable margin.[13] Table 4 outlines the costs and benefits of a modern UF processing facility. These cost figures are based on a tannery which processes 50,000 lb of hides a day (about 1000 hides), 260 days a year. Only the first dump, a 50% float by weight, is treated for recovery (3000 gallons per day with 3% sulfhydrate, 1% sulfide flakes, 4% lime — all based on hide weight). The UF system recovers 80% of the spent bath water (2400 gal per day) and the membranes have a replacement life of 3 years.

Since the membrane used can handle a flux rate of 40 gallons per square foot per day, 60 square feet of membrane area is needed. This would require a $40,000 (U.S., 1979) UF unit with a total installation and capital cost of $80,000.[13]

It can be seen from Table 4 that the total savings from resource recovery exceed the costs by $43.48 a day or $11,300 a year. The pay-back period of 2.9 years is calculated by dividing the capital cost of the system (without interest) by the total of the yearly net savings ($11,300) and the average depreciation per year ($16,000). If there is any potential profit in the resale of recovered protein as a byproduct animal feed, this could be added to the equation. The potential for sludge utilization is investigated more fully later in this chapter.

■ The Centre Technique du Cuir has also investigated ultrafiltration for hairburn recycling and has concluded that it offers promise for large beamhouse facilities although it cannot compete with direct recycling for small production units.[6] The CTC modified an existing UF model, fitting it with 48 membrane-carrying plates in grooved PVC with hidden joints which assure the leakproofness of the assembly. The membranes were obtained from Rhone Poulenc (France) and have a theoretical flux rate of 8000 litres

per day per metre squared.

The system is set up much like the Abcor process. In addition, a washing container is placed alongside the permeate tank in which the unit cleaning solutions are prepared (soda, acid surface active agents, detergents etc.). The entire system is under sophisticated electronic control and monitoring, and the control panel is placed under pressure to minimize corrosive attacks on the electrical components by the environment of the beamhouse. The cleaning of the UF unit requires special and precise washing techniques if membrane life and efficiency are to be protected.

Table 5 shows the average recovery results after processing the hairburn liquors through 14 cycles. It can be seen that 75% of the residual sulphide, 25% of the residual lime and 85% of the bath volume are retained for re-use; much of the remainder is trapped in the protein concentrate. The pollutants in the plant effluent are cut dramatically: sulphides by 90%, lime 69%, water 95%, chemical oxygen demand (COD) 77% and nitrogen 72%.[6]

The protein concentrates underwent further processing. Acidification treatment, using HCl to reach the isoelectric point of the keratin in the solution (isoelectric point being the point at which a molecule has neither a positive nor a negative charge, achieved by adjusting the pH from 3 to 6) was followed by settling and repeated washing to remove inorganic matter particularly calcium. Finally the protein is dried, ground and packed. For each ton of salted hides processed, the CTC recovered 10 to 12 kg of keratinous protein that could be sold as an animal feedstock supplement.

The CTC was able to conclude from its ultrafiltration work that, based on the current costs of sodium sulphide, lime, and protein meal, the costs of purchasing, installing and operating the unit could be written off only if the operator processed at least 40 tons of salted hides a day. This is a considerably larger facility than the one Abcor says would be cost-effective, although Abcor does not give any credit to byproduct protein sale (about $12.00 a day for their system).

The CTC calculates that for a daily input of 40 to 50 tons of hide, a liming float volume of 50 to 80 cubic metres, the protein recovery of 600 kg, and the need for 4m² of membrane for each ton of hide, the credits ($U.S. (1979)/ton hides) are:

Water + sulphide + lime	$ 3.00
Protein	.50
Waste treatment costs avoided	20.00
Total	$23.50

The costs of the system are:

Amortizing (5 years return time on $300,000)	$ 7.00
Running (energy, chemicals, maintenance)	5.00
Membrane (200m², 6-month lifetime)	8.00
Total	$20.00

Table 4
Projected Operating Economics for Ultrafiltering Spent Unhairing Baths

Item	Description	$/Day
COSTS Operating Labour	2 hr/day x $10.00/hr including overhead	$20.00
Power	70 kwh/day x $0.035/kwh	2.45
Membrane Replacement	60 ft²/3 yrs x $45/ft² ÷ 260 days	3.46
Maintenance	2 hr/week ÷ 5 days/week x $12/hr. including overhead	4.80
Cleaning Chemicals	200 gal/week x 8.33 lb/gal x 0.5% chemicals x $1/lb ÷ 5 days/week	1.67
		Sub total — $32.38
Depreciation*	$80,000 (max), 5 yr, straight line	61.54
		Total expenses — $93.92
CREDITS Sulfhydrate	1500 lb x 40% recovery x $0.16/lb	$(96.00)
Sulfide	500 lb x 40% recovery x 0.14/lb	(28.00)
Lime+	2000 lb x 20% recovery x 0.018/lb	(7.20)
Water	2400 gal/day x $0.50/1000 gal	(1.20)
Reduced Chemicals for Final Effluent Pollution Control or Reduced Sewer Surcharge	1% reduction in total plant effluent flow rate 50% reduction in sulfide loading $30,000/yr chemical cost assumed	(5.00)
		Total credits — $(137.40)
		Net daily savings — $(41.48)

$$\text{Payout Period (no interest charge)} = \frac{\text{Depreciable fixed capital investment}}{\text{Average savings/yr} + \text{average depreciation/yr}}$$

$$= \frac{\$80,000}{\$11,305 + \$16,000} = 2.93 \text{ years}$$

*Accelerated depreciation of pollution control equipment

+Rough estimate

Source: "New Approach for Treatment of Spent Tannery Liquors" *Journal of American Leather Chemists Association,* November 1979.

The application of accelerated capital depreciation allowed on pollution abatement equipment expenditures may defray the capital costs somewhat, but the major burden is the price of membrane replacement. There is cause for optimism. New membranes are developed and improved constantly. The six-month lifetime experienced by the CTC may be extended anywhere from two to five years. Such an increase in membrane dependability would put UF technology well within the financial range of small and medium tanners. Membrane technology has been rediscovered by the food industry to process wastewater and concentrate protein byproducts. Work with tubular and flat membranes will soon allow tanners to cost-effectively treat unhairing liquors and reduce the concentration of greases and surfactants in degreasing effluents.[14]

Chemical Absorption

In 1975, scientists at the Darmstädt Institute (Germany) began publishing laboratory results on a new, rapid, run-through process for unhairing which incorporated a sodium hydroxide column for recovering the sulphide from the hair removal sludge.[15] The process lived up to its favourable early reports in the pilot reactor of the Darmstädter system and was eventually incorporated in the recovery plant of the Blue Side Company (St. Joseph, Missouri).[16,17]

In the Darmstädter process, the hides are treated individually and sequentially sprayed with 10% Na_2S solution, fleshed and split, and then sprayed with a $NaClO_2$ solution which destroys any Na_2S that remains deep in the hide. Cleaning and splitting the hides prior to their entering the lime suspension removes 80 to 90% of the proteinaceous offal and opens them up more fully than the conventional beamhouse methods.

The process increases the line efficiency by reducing the amount of time required for making "wet-blues" from 2.33 to 1.75 days. The system also requires less process and washwater: savings of about 50% with fresh hides and 33% for salt-cured hides.[18] One of the most important benefits of the system is the opportunity for sulphide recovery.

The excess fluid and sludge produced are treated with hydrochloric acid and passed over two sodium hydroxide absorbers. Hydrogen sulphide is absorbed into the two columns until saturation is reached. When treated with NaOH, the NaHS is changed back to Na_2S and is ready to be used in unhairing operations again. Sulphide recovery is about 75%.

The residual decomposed hair pulp can be used in fertilizer as a slow-acting source of nitrogen.[19] The pulp can be filtered easily and the Blue Side Co. finds it unnecessary to centrifuge the sludge to further lower its water content.[20]

The cost of implementing the Darmstädter process in a new tannery is appreciably higher than conventional beamhouse treatment ($900,000 as opposed to $600,000 for a standard system consisting of 3 drums and capable of handling 800 to 1000 cattle hides a day). The tanner considering establishing or updating his facilities will have to consider whether the improved process efficiency, reduced chemical and water costs, improved waste treatment and eliminated disposal charges justify the added expense.

■ The recovery of protein from unhairing liquors is occurring in a commercial Japanese tannery with a capacity of $100M^3$ of effluent per day. The system used is essentially the same as the one outlined in detail above: precipitation of protein by acidification, concentration and dewatering of the precipitates, absorption of the liberated hydrogen sulphide into a sodium hydroxide solution and, finally, re-use of the recovered sodium sulfhydrates.[21]

4.
Pickling and Tanning

After the hides have been soaked, fleshed and unhaired, they leave the beamhouse and enter the third processing area of the tannery — the tanyard. It is in the tanyard that the animal skin is transformed into the leather products we are familiar with.

There are basically two major classes of leather; heavy leather, a hard and durable product used in the soles of shoes, belts and harnesses; and light leather, a soft and flexible material which is used in thousands of items from gloves to shoe uppers. The fundamentals of tanning are similar in the production of both these kinds of leather although the tanning of lighter leathers is usually shorter and simpler. Heavy leather offers more resistance to the penetration of the tanning agent.

Tanning turns a hide into a non-putrescible material, one that is resistant to bacterial degradation. Tannin is the compound that joins with the skin protein to form leather. Chromium salts are the most widely used tannins although vegetable tannins and synthetic tanning agents (syntans), like phenolsulphonic acid-formaldehyde, are also used.

Heavy leathers are largely tanned with vegetable tannin which adds weight and substance to them, imparting good wearing qualities, while light leathers may be tanned largely with mineral tanning agents.[22]

Vegetable extracts were the original tannins and their use dates back at least 12,000 years. They are obtained from the bark and wood of trees like the chestnut, quebracho, mimosa, mangrove and sumac, and the pods of a vast number of bushes. They are also a source of environmental contamination. Spent vegetable tanning solutions are responsible for a major portion of the organic content and almost all of the colour-causing material in the tannery effluent. The replacement of vegetable tannins with syntans would result in lower levels of residual colour in the wastewater.[23]

Chromium salts are of particular concern to regulatory agencies and are particularly toxic in the hexavalent form. In addition to the environmental impact, there is a strong financial incentive to recover the tannin from the operation's wastewater and re-use it in

Table 5
Ultrafiltration Mass Balance

Rawhide Processed = 1,180 kg at each cycle (average on 14 cycles)

	Volume l	Dry Solids kg	Sulphides kgS^{--}	Lime kg Ca^{2+}	COD kg O$_2$	Nitrogen kg N
Initial float	1,350	105	3.43	5.41	64	4.95
Ultrafiltrate	1,136	56.7	2.55	1.29	21	1.56
Concentrate	214	31.3	0.49	2.43	28	2.02
Membrane cleaning	70	17.0	0.39	1.69	15	1.37
% of recovery and pollution prevention (ultrafiltrate recycling)	84%	54%	75%	24%	33%	31%
% of recovery and pollution prevention (concentrate valorization)	11%	30%	15%	45%	44%	41%
TOTAL	95%	84%	90%	69%	77%	72%
Residual pollution (membrane cleaning, losses...)	5%	16%	10%	31%	23%	28%

Source: Vulliermet, B., "Improvement of the Mass and Energy Balances in the Tanning Industry," *Journal of American Leather Chemists Association,*

the tanning process. The waste characteristics of tannins[24] are listed in Table 6.

Organic Acid Pickling

Prior to the introduction of the tannin, the hides undergo bating and pickling. Bating involves the removal of the residual unhairing alkalines and the addition of bate. Bate is made of enzymes, similar to those found in the digestive system, which remove the skin substances that will not form leather. Bating takes several hours, after which the hides are washed and transferred to the pickling station.

Pickling prepares the hide for tanning. Since the chrome tanning compounds are not soluble in alkaline solutions, an acid condition must be created. Any number of acids may be used, but salt must also be added to prevent "acid swelling" of the hides.[1]

It is possible to reduce the effluent from the tanning baths by adjustments to the pickling process. Substituting organic acids for sulphuric pickling acids and using a low tanning float can substantially reduce the chrome levels in the effluent.[25] Organic acids are less strongly attracted to the protein in the hide and are therefore able to penetrate the lime/bated stock more quickly and facilitate a proper and rapid chrome fixation while reducing pickling time. The tanner will use about 20% less chrome and significantly reduce the amount of salt required. The shorter drum time also reduces the energy requirements.

A recycling process utilizing a low float procedure will result in an almost complete consumption of the needed chrome, and the effluent chrome levels will approach zero. The exhaust chrome liquors can be collected, refortified and re-used indefinitely. After the third re-use cycle, the chemicals in the bath reach equilibrium and

Table 6
Waste Components of Tannins

Vegetable tannins
Lime sludge, hair, fleshing tan liquor, bleach liquor salt, blood dirt, high BOD.

Chrome tannins
Lime sludge, hair, fleshing chrome, tan liquor, salt, blood dirt, lower BOD, higher in dissolved solids and smaller in volume than the vegetable tannins.

Source: Krofchak, D. and Stone, N. *Science and Engineering for Pollution Free Systems.*

there is no further buildup of any undesirable contaminants.

This simple process change requires only a minimum investment for a storage tank and pump system, although some modification of the present tannery equipment is required to facilitate the spent liquor recovery if recycling is intended. This cost-effective process change has the dual benefit of improving the tanning line efficiency and avoiding costly effluent treatment.

Chrome recovery from tanning liquors is of high priority to operators. The rising cost of chemicals coupled with increasingly strict discharge and sludge disposal regulations have provided the incentive for investigating a wide variety of recovery options. Companies and research institutes are gaining much experience with direct chrome recycling,[6,11,26,27] chemical precipitation,[11,28,29] new "low use" chrome compounds,[30] ultrafiltration[13] and incineration ash reclamation.[20,31] Each system offers specific recovery, economic and process advantages and must be evaluated with the specific operating conditions of each individual tannery.

The recycling process is simple, at its most basic requiring only a reliable filter. The purified exhausted chrome liquor can then be used as a pickling float for the next batch.[11] A hydrodynamic sedimentator can be used for filtering and since it cannot be clogged by grease, it is free of serious maintenance problems.

Direct recycling is most applicable when all the hides are being processed by the same kind of tannage; then all the baths can be mixed together. When a number of different baths are used, the recovery circuits become too complicated and another system may offer better results.[6] When possible, though, direct recycling offers a 95 to 100% chrome recovery rate and when coupled with lime reuse, can result in a potential economic saving of $30 per ton of hide each day. The recovery of residual products of lime and tanning floats can result in enormous chemical savings: 40 to 50% of the sodium sulphide, 50 to 60% of lime, 95 to 100% of sodium chloride, 20 to 30% of chromium sulphate and 20 to 30% of the auxiliary tanning chemicals. The plant's effluent undergoes a corresponding improvement with a reduction in suspended solids of 40%, BOD of 50% and toxicity of

80%.

■ The Gebhardt-Vogel Tanning Company (Milwaukee, Wisconsin) began direct chrome recycling in April 1975.[26] The stimulus for recycling was promising economics, not environmental regulation. The Milwaukee Metropolitan Sewer District had been accepting the plant's effluent without protest and were processing the sludge into a marketable fertilizer. Gebhardt-Vogel's recycling effort paid off. In 1979, the firm saved $50,000 (U.S.) in chrome tannin replacement costs.

The exhaust chrome liquor is pumped from the tanning drums through a hydrasieve into one of two 3900-gallon storage tanks. One tank has sufficient capacity to handle the spent bath from the firm's 6 hide processors. The second tank allows for an extra day's storage time and gives the liquor time to cool. The simple system — tanks, sieve, piping and pumps — cost $35,000 (U.S. 1975). Maintenance is restricted to draining once a week and flushing out the buildup of natural grease and chrome soap with several thousand gallons of warm water.[26]

As can be seen from Table 7, Gebhardt-Vogel have been able to make significant reductions in their pickling and tanning chemical requirements. Salt usage is cut from the standard 5.7% to only 3% and there are also savings in sodium formate, sulphuric acid and chrome. In 1979 these totaled:[26]

Salt	$11,000
Sodium formate	14,300
Sulphuric acid	1,250
Chrome	50,000

TOTAL $76,550

The chrome recycling system also reduced the chrome in the plant's effluent by 70%. Although this alone may not be sufficient to meet upcoming stringent water quality guidelines, it is a financially rewarding first step.

The management of Gebhardt-Vogel is pleased with the results. The 12,000 sides the company processes each week are producing leather equal in every respect to the leather produced before recycling was implemented. The system

has been trouble-free since it was brought on stream. Pollution abatement is netting more than $75,000 a year — a good deal for the Milwaukee firm.

Chromium Precipitation

Direct chromium recycling is now being practised in Australia, Europe, South Africa and the United States.[27] As a cost-effective recovery method which maximizes chromium utilization and flexibility, it is a superior technology, however some firms are opting for chromium precipitation. Although precipitation is more expensive, it can be used on all other chrome-containing water including the run-off from wringers, drippings from the hides on horses, etc.[11] For a firm facing stiff effluent controls, it may represent a viable option.

■ The Tannery and Footwear Corporation of India (Kanpur, India) uses lime to precipitate chromium from its spent tanning liquors.[29] The waste solution has a spent liquor concentration of 5125 mg/litre and a 70% chromium utilization efficiency. The addition of lime removes 98.2% of the chromium as chromium hydroxide. The precipitated material is separated by settling, filtering and redissolving in sulphuric acid to form chromium sulphate, which is then recycled. Filtration is done with a slow sand filter to remove 85% of the water.

The Indian company anticipates a 27% total chrome powder cost savings and has found the system to be an economical alternative to waste disposal. A shared re-use plant used by a number of local plants would further increase the economic viability of the process.[32]

Chromium Replacement

■ Rather than recycle or precipitate chromium, Granite State Leathers (Nashua, New Hampshire) combined improved low-float drums with a new tanning agent, Baychrome 2403, to reduce the chrome concentrations in their final effluent to less than 1 ppm.[30] Granite State also experienced a reduction in chrome requirements, savings in retanning, and lower water consumption.

The Baychrome 2403 tanning system requires changes to the traditional beaming and tanning process. An exceptionally good soaking is followed by thorough unhairing, a final wash and 90% deliming. Following a sulphuric acid pickle, 1.2 to 1.4% Cr_2O_3 is introduced into the large Vallero tanning vessels. Regular tanning makes use of 1.7 to 2% Cr_2O_3 (based on white weight). The new system requires a hide penetration with 0.9 to 1.0% of regular chrome liquor (38% basic) and then adding the remainder of the

Table 7

Bating-Pickling-Tanning by the Recycle and Regular Procedures

Steps	Recycle procedure	Regular procedure
WHITE WEIGHT	17,000 lb	17,000 lb
Wash before bate	450 percent, 90°F	450 percent, 90°F
BATE		
Drain	15 min, 6 rpm	15 min, 6 rpm
Add:		
Float	50 percent, 90°F	50 percent, 90°F
Ammonium sulfate	3 percent	3 percent
Liquid bate	0.2 percent	0.2 percent
Run	30 min	30 min
Add nonionic detergent	0.4 percent (recirculate)	0.4 percent (recirculate)
Run	45 min, 7 rpm	45 min, 7 rpm
Drain	20 min	20 min
Wash	150 percent water, 70°F	150 percent water, 70°F
PICKLE		
Drain	20 min	10 min
Add salt	3 percent (dry)	12 percent float, 75°F
		5.7 percent brine
Run	5 min	10 min
Add exhaust chrome	650 gal	—
Add sulfuric acid	1.5 percent, 2 feeds	1.65 percent, 150 gal 75°F
Run	15 min - 2 hr, 7 rpm	2 hr, 7 rpm
TAN		
Liquid	pH 2.6 - 2.9	
	Salometer: 46 -51 percent	
	Cr_2O_3; 0.025 - 0.035 lb/gal	
Drain	—	To 47 in. from base
Add sodium formate	1.5 percent (dry)	2 percent (dry)
Run	—	15 min
Add Waynetan 175	117 gal	145 gal
Run	2 hr, 10 rpm	30 min (recirculate)
Liquid	pH 3.6 - 3.8	
	Salometer: 61 - 65 percent	
Add sodium bicarbonate	0.75 percent, 128 gal, 90°F	0.75 percent, 128 gal, 90°F
Run (4 feeds)	15 min - 15 min - 15 min - 1 hr	15 min - 15 min - 15 min - 1 hr
	Recirculate to 120°F	Recirculate to 120°F
Add water	—	18 percent, 160°F
Run	—	1 hr
Add Tamol SD	0.25 percent, 25 gal, 120°F	0.25 percent, 25 gal, 120°F
Run	15 min	15 min
Liquid	pH 4.0 - 4.2	
	Salometer: 54 - 59 percent	
	Cr_2O_3: 0.07 - 0.09 percent	
	(To recycle)	
Drain		
Flood	1500 gal, 60°F	1500 gal, 60°F
Dump		

Source: "Chrome Recycling," *Journal of American Leather Chemists Association,* January 1981.

Cr_2O_3 (0.3 to 0.35%) in the form of Baychrome 2403. By lengthening the running time and adding a small amount of neutralizing agent, the chrome exhaustion rate is increased from 80% to between 90 and 95%.

The increased efficiency in chrome take-up results in a two-thirds reduction of chromium in the effluent. Spent chrome precipitates out as a result of alkalinity in the wastewater. In the past, the tannery had to treat its spent tanning baths with lime to obtain a chrome sludge. The company used to churn out 240,000 gallons of waste with a chrome oxide concentration of about 10 ppm. Use of the Baychrome 2403 has reduced water consumption to 130,000 gallons for the 2000 hides it processes daily and dropped chrome oxide to less than 1 ppm.

Chrome retention and retanning operations have also been improved. The first tanning wash results in about ten times less chrome being stripped out due to more permanent chrome fixation and has eliminated the need for chrome retanning. And although Granite State still has to deal with chrome contaminated sludge disposal, there are indications that this waste product may have a lessened environmental impact. With the higher pH of the waste, the chrome is somewhat better bound and less liable to leach out.[30]

The bottom line for all process changes has to be product quality. A high level of product quality and reduced chrome use were ensured through some process modifications. The large tanning vessels had to be equipped with 84-horsepower motors; otherwise, the low floats would not have tanned through the heavy parts of the hide. Retanning and colouring operations had to undergo some change due to the higher pH of the Baychrome tanning process, and the relatively high end temperature (140°C) causes a degreasing effect which results in a drier piece of leather. This and possible abrasion in the low float vessels require some careful handling, but leather of equal quality to that produced before the Baychrome system was installed is now being sold by Granite State.

The management of the company admit the changeover was a difficult affair and required considerable effort and ingenuity. But the results speak for themselves; less chrome in, less chrome out (and out to the dump). The savings also speak for themselves— $40,000 to $50,000 a year.

Vegetable Tanning

A lot of tannin recovery work has focussed on the chromium component. This effort is based on the amount of chromium used and its toxic nature. About 85% of leather is produced by chrome tanning. This results in 75% of the waste generated by the tanning industry being contaminated by potentially hazardous trivalent chromium. Vegetable tannins are less environmentally sensitive but their use is expected to decrease over the next five years.[33] However, it is worth discussing one available recovery option for those firms which will continue to use the organic material for the production of specialty leathers.

Ultrafiltration

Ultrafiltration was already discussed in some detail in connection with sulphide recovery from unhairing baths. For tannins, the process is virtually the same except for one major difference. The UF permeate is discharged to the drains and the concentrate is continuously recycled through the tubular membrane modules until the tannins are concentrated to the point they can be re-used. After the membranes are cleaned, a new batch of spent tanning liquor can be introduced to the holding tank and the cycle repeated.

The use of UF in two pilot programmes at American tanneries[13] showed tannin concentrations can be increased from 2.7 to 4.1%. This represents an 84% recovery rate.

An ultrafiltration system capable of handling 5000 gallons per day would cost about $75,000; installation would bring the total capital costs to $112,500, making the system the major expense in the tannin recovery project. Maintenance and labour would make up only approximately 15% of the budget.

As can be seen from Table 8, the daily operating expenses total $163.26, while the savings in tannin recovery and water re-use are $342.73. A firm using UF would therefore net $61,500 annually and recover its capital costs in a little over 18 months. Again, improvements in membrane quality and increased credit due to lower wastewater treatment costs would shorten the pay-back period.

Ultrafiltration offers a cost-effective way to recover vegetable tannins while improving effluent quality. Researchers in the field have achieved a spent liquor purity of 50% and are currently developing systems that yield a spent liquor-concentration of 70% (commercial purity).

Chemical Re-Use for Wastewater Treatment

As much as two-thirds of the chromium used in the tannery can leave the plant as waste. Between 10 and 40% leaves' as a liquid waste in the form of spent tanning liquors, washwaters and retanning baths, depending on the chromium re-use and recycling programmes that have been initiated. Another third is lost during trimming processes as leather scraps, scrappings and dust.

After leather has left the tanning vessel, it is passed through wringers to remove the excess water and passed onto a splitting and shaving station. Here, shaving adjusts the leather to a uniform thickness and a splitting machine uses a horizontal blade to slice the material.

Next, retanning, colouring, stuffing and fatliquoring imbue the leather with the softness, flexibility, water repellence, hue and other qualities required. Finishing operations, including drying, conditioning, staking, buffing and finishing, further prepare the leather for sale, but are, on the whole, dry processes.

Much of the waste chromium and leather scraps already play a role in plant wastewater treatment. Chromium at concentrations of about 150 mg per litre acts as a chemical coagulant to aid in the precipitation of soluble tannery wastes, precipitating up to 75% of the organics and 95% of the suspended solids. This leaves a residual chromium concentration of 20 to 25 mg/litre. The leather shavings, if added prior to precipitation, will absorb grease, oil, and between 50 and 75% of the colour and other potentially toxic compounds. Additional treatment reduces chromium levels to between 1 and 3 mg per litre. Some operators use tannery wastestreams to neutralize or concentrate other effluents. In the United States, some sewage treatment plants are not averse to accepting tannery chromium-laden effluents to aid in BOD, phosphate and suspended solid removal.[31]

Incineration

Yet even after the spent chromium solutions have been utilized as a waste treatment chemical, the operator will still be left with heavily contaminated chromium sludge to dispose. Some researchers propose that these chromium sludges could be incinerated and the resultant ash treated to recover the chromium, making use of the heating value of the waste.

■ One incineration system uses the Air Suspension Incinerator manufactured by Molten Salt Systems Inc. (Bristol, Rhode Island).[31] Low temperature burning (between 600°F and 1200°F) combined with small quantities of alkali and carbonates will yield a soluble hexavalent chromium product in the ash and virtually no insoluble trivalent chromium oxide. The sludge volume is reduced by 90% and the chromium is then available for extraction. Air quality

---

Table 8

Projected Daily Operating Costs and Credits for an Ultrafiltration System Recovering Spent Vegetable Tannin Light Liquor

Item	Description	$/Day
COSTS		
Operating Labour	3 hr/day x $10.00/hr including overhead	$30.00
Power	200 kwh x $0.035/kwh	7.00
Membrane Replacement	210 ft²/2 yr x $45/ft² ÷ 260 days	18.26
Maintenance	2 hr/week ÷ 5 days/week x $12.00/hr including overhead	4.80
Cleaning Chemicals*	400 GPD x 8.33 lb/gal x 0.5% chemicals x $1/lb	16.66
		Subtotal = $76.72
Depreciation**	$112,500 (est.), 5 yr, straight line	86.54
		Total expenses = $163.26
CREDITS		
Vegetable Tannin	2500 gal x 8.33 lb/gal x 4.1% tannin x $0.40/lb	(341.53)
Water	2500 gal x $0.50/1000 gal	(1.20)
		Total credits = (342.73)
		Net daily savings = $(179.47)

$$\text{Pay-out Period (no interest charge)} = \frac{\text{Depreciable fixed capital investment}}{\text{Average savings/yr + average depreciation/yr}}$$

$$= \frac{\$112,500}{\$46,662 + \$22,500} = 1.63 \text{ years}$$

*May not be required on a daily basis

**Accelerated depreciation for pollution control equipment

Source: "New Approach for Treatment of Spent Tannery Liquors", *Journal of American Leather Chemists Association,* November 1979.

control is ensured by molten salt scrubbing and a baghouse filter.

The chromium can be removed from the ash by acid leaching to give a 15 to 25% bichromate solution without evaporation. The chromium can also be reclaimed as a trivalent oxide paste by reduction with SO_2 at a pH of 4.5, or sugar at a pH of 2, followed by the addition of lime or a polymer to enhance flocculation.

■ Table 9 shows the cost of recovery of the chromium from ash in the sludge incinerator of the South Essex Sewerage District (Salem, Massachusetts). If leather shavings are used as a fuel source, the cost of oil is eliminated and chromium content in the ash is doubled.

The South Essex plant produces chromium-hydroxide floc which is separated by dissolved air floatation. A 30% chromium hydroxide paste is formed and sold to a chemical producer as a raw material for new tanning liquors. The economics of the incineration system have led some writers to call it the "ultimate solution" for tannery wastes.[31] Although it should not preclude investigation of some of the other alternatives already discussed, the value of any solid

leather waste and sludge make residual incineration an option that cannot be overlooked.

■ Jones and Beach Engineering Inc. (Stratham, New Hampshire) maintain that each wet ton of solid leather waste contains $34 worth of chromium and has a heating value of $10 (U.S. 1979). Sludges contain $57 worth of chromium and $3.50 worth of Btu's on a dry weight basis.

■ Conservation Technologies Inc. (Bristol, Rhode Island) note that a typical wet shavings waste will contain about 45% of dry solids which have a tested heating value in the neighbourhood of 7000 Btu per pound. This is a total of 6,300,000 Btu per wet ton. If converted to the equivalent in No. 2 oil at $1.00 per gallon, this energy value amounts to $45.00 (U.S. 1981) per wet ton of shavings.[20] The chromium (3% of dry weight) value of that wet ton of shavings is $34.81, for a total of almost $80.00.

Conservation Technologies Inc. has taken bits and pieces of combustion expertise from other incineration applications and combined it with chemical fundamentals to come up with a jet mill combustion unit. By fine grinding

and suspension firing in a turbulent jet chamber, oxidation is maximized and chromium recovery is enhanced. The increase in burn efficiency means residence time is reduced and a smaller combustion chamber is sufficient for a given loading rate. And because of grinding and complete burning, the resultant ash is remarkably uniform. This is important for it eases the chromium extraction process and reduces to the barest minimum the amount of potentially toxic material that is released to the environment.

Combining basic combustion principles and the latest technologies in coal and other fuel burning makes for a cost-effective way to treat a tannery's residual wastes and recover every last bit of resource material.

Byproduct Manufacture

Chrome-treated shavings undeniably have a high Btu value. They contain chromium which has a definite value if recovered, and they have nitrogen and protein value. It must be remembered, however, that above all else they are leather. Much time, effort and

---

Table 9

Estimated Annual Savings to be Realized by Recovering Chromium from Ash of Incinerated Tannery Wastes as an Alternative to Disposal

(Based on 20 tons of ash per day)

Item	Disposal without recovery of chromium	Chromium recovery by reroasting Using oil	Using shavings
Expenses			
Disposal	$150,000	$ 75,000	$ 75,000
Trucking	50,000	—	—
Fuel	—	40,000	—
Chemicals	—	75,000	100,000
Total expenses	$200,000	$190,000	$175,000
Savings			
Net value of recovered chromium	—	$250,000	$550,000
Net expenses	$200,000	—	—
Net savings	—	$ 60,000	$375,000

Source: "Chromium Recovery Through Incineration of Liquid and Solid Tannery Wastes — The Ultimate Solution" *Journal of American Leather Chemists Association*, January 1981.

expense (to say nothing of personal sacrifice on the part of the cow) have gone into turning skin into leather. If possible, waste materials should be used to manufacture new products that utilize and take advantage of the special properties of leather.

Some additional applications can be identified. Chrome shavings can be processed into gelatins for industrial use, leather board, electrodeposited piles, numerous composite materials,[7] thermal insulation, acoustic materials, cleaning or absorbent materials, and non-woven materials.[6]

■ The Centre Technique du Cuir (CTC) developed Dermonat™, a leather fibre product, which has been produced industrially since 1978 by Lincrusta-Sangiar. It is used as a support for coated fabrics used in ski and football boots and in an uncoated form as a lining material, and for seat covers. The CTC believed that past failures to make good synthetic leathers from waste leather fibres lay in the processes tried, not in inherent flaws in the raw material. They concentrated on a new process that did not rely on polymer-binding agents which masked the absorbent and flexible properties of the original fibres. They also looked closely at dry process technology so as not to affect fibre length.

First they analyzed available waste material to determine which ones would yield leather fibre with the best re-use potential. They found fibres were more likely to be acceptable when liming had been intense, tanning had been carried out with an excess of fixed chrome, and the fatliquoring was carried out with a fatty matter content from 3 to 8%. They eliminated waste trimming from goat and sheep skins and vegetable tanner leathers.

The re-use process that was eventually developed consists of granulation, defibrillation and mechanical "knitting". The leather fibres are mixed with synthetic fibres in a 2 to 1 ratio to form a non-woven textile composite material. This material is dyed and treated to minimize surface abrasion and fraying.

The equipment, available in modular form for a reasonable investment, allows the transformation of a waste product into a hygenic byproduct which maintains the flexibility and durability of leather.

The CTC has also started pilot plant production of SOL 300™, a chemical absorbent. Leather is capable of soaking up and retaining a number of organic liquids. When dried and ground, waste leather can be substituted for sawdust, for the containment and clean-up of spilled hydrocarbons, solvents, oils and other industrial chemicals. This leather waste byproduct may eventually end up in the landfill site, but not before helping to clean up some of the flotsam and jetsam of industrial processing.

■ Italian researchers advocate the use of trimmings and tanning sludges for the production of biogas. The organic and protein components of the waste can be transformed into a combustible gas by anaerobic fermentation. Using a "Totem" (total energy module obtained from Fiat) the biogas can be used to produce electric energy for plant use, and combustion heat can be reclaimed by a series of heat exchangers for operational process heat. The Totem exponents claim the total energy production of the system is 92% and turns a disposal problem into an economic advantage.[34]

Water Recycling

Water consumption in a modern tannery can be cut significantly by the implementation of many recycling, resource recovery schemes outlined previously. But further savings are possible by in-plant purification and re-use.

One plant that directly recycles unhairing and tanning floats has cut its water consumption by 10%. The first soaking floats make up another 25% of the total water use. Many firms find first floats too heavily contaminated by chlorides and organics to treat for re-use. With few exceptions, they are usually discharged. The remaining 65% of the wastewater can be reclaimed by either direct or indirect recycling.

The effluents to be recycled are collected in a central sump and passed through a rotary screen to remove the heavy solids. The solution is then pumped to a large equalization tank where a floation chamber is used to remove grease, hair and other material with mechanical skimmers. An aeration unit keeps material from settling out and supplies oxygen that may be needed for biological treatment. The pH of the equalization tank is maintained between 6.5 and 7.5.

The next stage entails the use of hydrodynamic sedimentators. After the adding of aluminum sulphate and a polyelectrolyte to promote coagulation and flocculation, the sedimentators remove the suspended solids, lime, sulphides, chrome and phenols. The resultant sludge must then be subjected to further treatment and may be suitable for fertilizer manufacture or incineration and chemical recovery.

The purified water may now be re-used in washing and soaking operations or further treated in a biological treatment tank to further reduce BOD. The microorganisms necessary for the treatment will develop after 3 or 4 weeks in the tank and will require no special attention. These microorganisms tend to develop a resistance to contaminants in the tannery wastewaters that permits them to function in a harsh environment. The final purified water can then be used in any plant operations. Because of its softness and consistency, recycled water may be better than new water from outside sources.

Sludge Handling

The control and recovery systems described in this chapter dramatically reduce the total waste load produced from a well run tannery. However, we have yet to achieve a closed system for tannery operation. Approximately 20% of the initial sulphides used will end up in the wastewaters requiring treatment, as will 25% of the lime and 15% of the chromium. Figures 3 and 4 offer a mass balance analysis that shows

Figure 3
Lime, Sulfide and Chromium Balances in Leather Production (Percentage Basis)

Source: "Improvement of the Mass and Energy Balances in the Tanning Industry," *Journal of the American Leather Chemists Association,* July 1980.

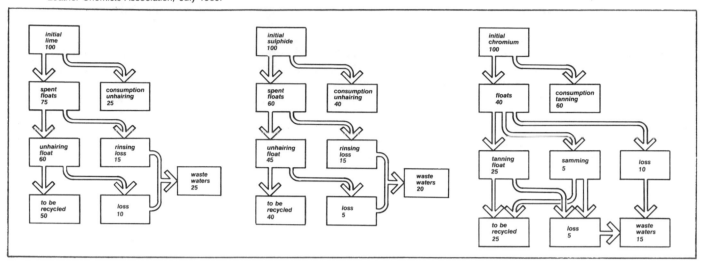

both the potential for recovery and the magnitude of the residual disposal problem.

Based on the work of the Centre Technique du Cuir (CTC), raw material re-use and byproduct utilization can reduce the levels of solid wastes and effluents substantially: water by 49%, greases by 20%, inorganics by 46%, collagens by 72% and keratins by 67%. Other advances described earlier would offer even greater improvements on these figures. Salt recovery and substitution, grease recovery from unhairing, fleshing and degreasing operations, water conservation programmes, spill containment plans, the development of new process chemicals and relatively simple modifications to tanning parameters such as time, temperature, pH and float length are all being tested and incorporated in some modern commercial plants. The refinement of ultrafiltration techniques will also aid in increasing recovery percentages and ensuring more of the hide is turned into useful consumer products.

Even with all these advances, tanneries will still have to deal with a sludge disposal problem. Incineration with chemical recovery and biogas production are two innovative options available. Another alternative to the traditional landfill is fertilizer production.

Tannery sludges have a high ion adsorption capacity, a property they can impart to light soils with poor adsorption qualities. These sludges are also high in nitrogen, calcium, sulphur, sodium, iron and chromium. Ammonium nitrate accounts for about 7% of the total nitrogen (composition of sludges varies widely and must be thoroughly analyzed prior to considering a land application programme) and accounts for the decomposition of the nitrogen compounds during sludge storage. Thus, when tannery sludges are added to the soil, they break down and release nitrogen, which can be used by vegetation.

From Table 10, it can be seen that potassium and phosphorus additions would be needed to supplement the higher nitrogen levels in the sludge. High sodium levels, found in sludges from those plants without a salt recovery programme, could prove deleterious to soils, though the high calcium component should do much to offset any potential hazard. Soil liming would also negate the sodium effects. Sulphur in moderate levels can benefit crops, as can chromium if present in very low

Table 10
Chemical Composition of Tannery Sludge
(% Dry Matter)

Element	Mean	Range
Total nitrogen	3.78	1.97 - 5.67
Ammonium nitrogen	0.25	——
Phosphorus	0.25	0.09 - 0.49
Potassium	0.09	0.04 - 0.21
Calcium	3.83	1.00 - 7.51
Magnesium	0.27	0.01 - 0.94
Sulphur	2.86	1.22 - 5.45
Sodium	1.39	0.13 - 6.37
Iron	0.95	0.001 - 12.52
Chromium	1.29	0.34 - 2.80

Source: "The Fertilizing Value of Tannery Sludges," in *Handbook of Organic Waste Conversion,* Van Nostrand Reinhold Environmental Engineering Services.

concentrations and deficient in the receiving soils.[35] However, the chromium content of the tannery sludge may in certain instances make it unsuitable for use on agricultural crops and limit it to non-farm markets such as landscaping, professional turf and sod nurseries.[36] A continuous monitoring programme would be necessary to check the accumulation of chromium in the soil and its uptake into vegetation. Liming is again helpful; it speeds up the decomposition of the sludges, particularly the fats contained in them, and reduces chromium solubility.

Sludge applications have increased the yield of corn, tall fescue, bush bean[33], barley, oats, buckwheat, potatoes,[35] soybeans and alfalfa hay.[36] They could be used in any situation where farm manure is employed (i.e., for those crops that respond well to organic fertilizers).

■ Polish researchers have been investigating the direct application of tannery sludges to agricultural lands.[35] Tannery wastewa-ter is made alkaline with milk of lime and coagulated by the addition of ferrous sulphate or aluminum sulphate. The water is partially removed using liquid separating plots or vacuum filters leaving a sludge containing 17% dry matter. Preliminary fermentation is carried out on the liquid separating plots and further decomposition occurs when the sludge is composted into piles. The result is a material that resembles damp, black earth.

The material is supplemented with mineral fertilizers and spread onto good wheatland soil — 7.5 tonnes of dry matter per hectare per year. The application resulted in increased yields of oats and tubers. The combined application of sludges and commercial fertilizers increased potato yields by 42%.

■ At the Firdaus Tanneries in Pakistan, wastewater has been used for irrigation purposes for years.[37] When the irrigated areas were compared to adjacent wastelands, it was found that the moisture content, water stable aggre-gates, water holding and cation exchange capacities, amounts of organic matter and exchangeable sodium were greater in the irrigated field. Researchers from the University of Punjab concluded that highly saline and sodic soils would reap the greatest benefits from tannery wastewater application. Disposal of the material on normal soils would likely create salinity problems.

■ The economics of making nitrogen fertilizers from tannery sludges have been studied at Thorstensen Laboratory Inc.[36] Organic nitrogen fertilizers make up 3.5% of the fertilizer industry's tonnage and account for 12% of its profits. Non-agricultural markets include golf courses, office parks, churches, high schools and government grounds. This is a $137 million market in the United States each year.

High-nitrogen sludge could be dried, crushed and screened to produce market quality fertilizer for about $52 a ton. This cost could be reduced if waste process heat from paste drying or other opera-

Figure 4
Mass Balance for a Tannery Operation

Source: "Improvement of the Mass and Energy Balances in the Tanning Industry," *Journal of the American Leather Chemists Association,* July 1980.

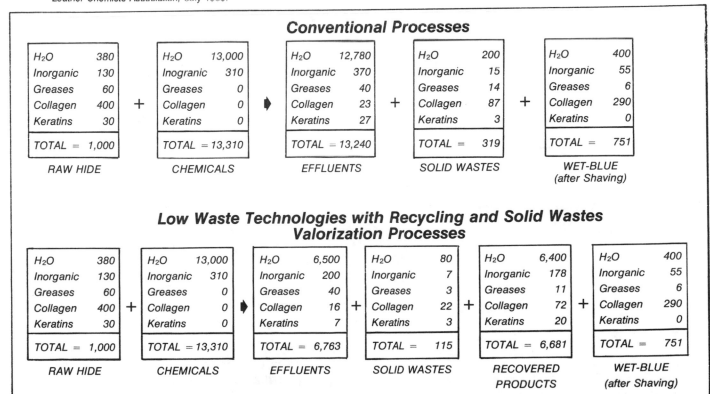

Conventional Processes

RAW HIDE		CHEMICALS		EFFLUENTS		SOLID WASTES		WET-BLUE (after Shaving)	
H_2O	380	H_2O	13,000	H_2O	12,780	H_2O	200	H_2O	400
Inorganic	130	Inorganic	310	Inorganic	370	Inorganic	15	Inorganic	55
Greases	60	Greases	0	Greases	40	Greases	14	Greases	6
Collagen	400	Collagen	0	Collagen	23	Collagen	87	Collagen	290
Keratins	30	Keratins	0	Keratins	27	Keratins	3	Keratins	0
TOTAL =	1,000	TOTAL =	13,310	TOTAL =	13,240	TOTAL =	319	TOTAL =	751

Low Waste Technologies with Recycling and Solid Wastes Valorization Processes

RAW HIDE		CHEMICALS		EFFLUENTS		SOLID WASTES		RECOVERED PRODUCTS		WET-BLUE (after Shaving)	
H_2O	380	H_2O	13,000	H_2O	6,500	H_2O	80	H_2O	6,400	H_2O	400
Inorganic	130	Inorganic	310	Inorganic	200	Inorganic	7	Inorganic	178	Inorganic	55
Greases	60	Greases	0	Greases	40	Greases	3	Greases	11	Greases	6
Collagen	400	Collagen	0	Collagen	16	Collagen	22	Collagen	72	Collagen	290
Keratins	30	Keratins	0	Keratins	7	Keratins	3	Keratins	20	Keratins	0
TOTAL =	1,000	TOTAL =	13,310	TOTAL =	6,763	TOTAL =	115	TOTAL =	6,681	TOTAL =	751

tions, or alternative energy sources, could be harnessed for the drying process. It might also be possible to avoid crushing and screening costs by selling the dried sludge in bulk to a dealer for future blending.

At present, 4% nitrogen fertilizers are being sold for about $32 a ton. If a tanner were able to offer a higher nitrogen blend byproduct, fertilizer sales could be an economic sideline. High disposal charges for sludges could also be

factored into the firm's operating costs. A tannery working 100,000 pounds of hides per day produces about 30,000 pounds of sludge. This sludge could cost $100 to landfill or $195 to produce 3.75 tons of dried fertilizer. If the

Figure 5
Resource Recovery/Re-Use Options

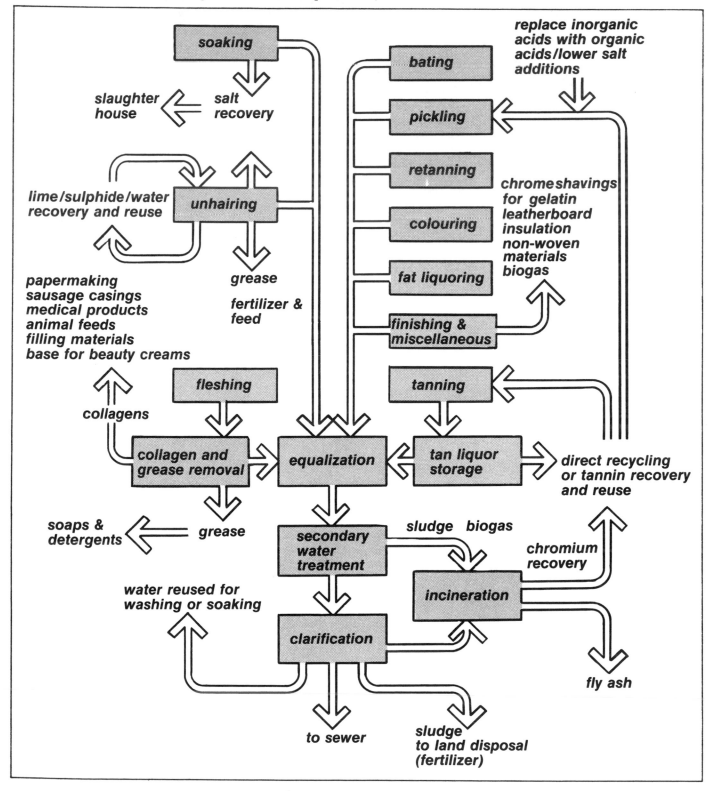

avoidance of disposal fees is considered as gross savings, then the fertilizer would cost only $25 a ton to produce. This byproduct could be marketed profitably within a 25-mile radius of the plant.

Conclusion

The simple flow sheet of the tanning process is ripe for renovation and addition. If the ideas presented in this chapter were instituted, the operation illustrated in Figure 1 could be amended to that sketched in Figure 5. A system emphasizing resource recovery and byproduct marketing would differ in only minor details from the traditional tanning plant. There is no need for radical restructuring or the purchase of major pieces of new equipment. The savings in process chemicals and disposal charges easily offset the necessary expenditures in short pay-back periods.

The advantages, however, are not difficult to see. Figure 5 illustrates them quite succinctly: more than 50% of raw hide that used to end up in the wastestream can now be recovered as can about 50% of the major process chemicals. The disposal of large amounts of toxic sludge can be economically replaced by the generation of byproducts and the recovery of chemicals.

FOR FURTHER INFORMATION

Associations

Footwear and Leather Institute of Canada,
Mart E — Eiffel 52,
Place Bonaventure,
Montreal, Quebec.
H5A 1B5
(514) 861-8277

Shoe and Leather Council of Canada,
Room 710,
1010 Ste. Catherine Street West,
Montreal, Quebec.
H3B 3R4
(514) 878-9337

American Leather Chemists Association,
Tanners Council Research Laboratory,
University of Cincinnati,
Cincinnati, Ohio.
45221
(513) 475-2643

Tanners' Council of America,
2501 M Street, N.W.,
Washington, D.C.
20037
(202) 785-9400

United States Hide, Skin and Leather Association,
Suite 302, 1629 K Street, N.W.,
Washington, D.C.
20006
(202) 833-2405

Journals

SOCIETY OF LEATHER TECHNOLOGISTS AND CHEMISTS JOURNAL,
Society of Leather Technologists and Chemists,
1 Edges Court,
Moulton,
Northampton, NN3 1UJ,
England.

WATER POLLUTION CONTROL FEDERATION JOURNAL,
Water Pollution Control Federation,
2626 Pennsylvania Ave., N.W.,
Washington, D.C.
20037

LEATHER SCIENCE,
Central Leather Research Institute,
Adyar,
Madras 600020,
India.

AMERICAN LEATHER CHEMISTS ASSOCIATION JOURNAL,
American Leather Chemists Association,
Campus Station,
Cincinnati, Ohio.
45221

References

1. Ontario Ministry of the Environment. "Tanneries." Chapter XI in *Control of Industrial Wastes in Municipalities*. Industrial Wastes Branch, Ontario Ministry of the Environment, 1977.

2. Panzer, C.C *et al.* "Improved Performance in Combined Nitrification/Denitrification of Tannery Waste." *Water Pollution Control Federation Journal*, September 1981.

3. Barber. L.K. *et al. Processing Chrome Tannery Effluent to Meet Best Available Treatment Standards.* U.S. Environmental Protection Agency, Office of Research and Development, Report No. EPA-600/2-79-110, July 1979.

4. Sehgal, P. "New Process for Reclaiming Used Common Salt." *Leather Science* 23 (1976). Abstract: *American Leather Chemists Association Journal* 76 (1981).

5. "Hold the Salt." *Agricultural Research* (U.S. Department of Agriculture), April 1977.

6. Vulliermet, B. "Improvement of the Mass and Energy Balances in the Tanning Industry." *American Leather Chemists Association Journal*, July 1980.

7. Okamura, H. *et al.* "Establishment of the Overall System for Utilization of Solid Byproducts and Wastes." *Hikaku Kagaku* 26 (1980). Abstract: *American Leather Chemists Association Journal* 76 (1981).

8. Centre Technique du Cuir. *A Pilot Plant for Processing Waste at the Technical Centre for Leather.* Pub. No. ID-2-74-300, Centre Technique du Cuir, 181, Avenue Jean-Jaures, 69342 Lyon Cedex 2, France.

9. Kerese, I. "Conversion of Machine Fleshings to Animal Feed." *Das Leder* 30 (1979). Abstract: *American Leather Chemists Association Journal* 76 (1981).

10. "Fellmongery Effluent Treatment Plant." *Environmental Pollution Management,* September/October 1980.

11. Spahrmann, J. "Direct and Indirect Recycling of Tannery Waste Water." *American Leather Chemists Association Journal,* November 1979.

12. Money, C. and Adaminis, U. "Recycling of Lime-Sulphide Unhairing Liquors." *Society of Leather Technologists and Chemists Journal* 58 (1974). Abstract: *American Leather Chemists Association Journal* 70 (1975).

13. Kleper, M.H. "New Approach for Treatment of Spent Tannery Liquors." *American Leather Chemists Association Journal,* November 1979.

14. Drioliand, E. and Cortese, B. "Ultrafiltration Processes for Pollution Control and Chemical Reuse in the Tanning Industry." *Desalinization,* July/August 1980.

15. Harenberg, O. and Heidemann, E. "Apparatus for Recovering Sulphides from Hair Painting Sludge and for Detoxifying the Waste Water." *Das Leder* 25 (1974). Abstract: *American Leather Chemists Association Journal* 70 (1975).

16. Flor, G. *et al.* "What Can Be Gained by a Continuously Operating Hair-pulp Reactor?" *Das Leder* 30 (1979). Abstract: *American Leather Chemists Association Journal* 76 (1981).

17. United States Environmental Protection Agency. Report EPA 600/2-77-03. Industrial Environmental Research Lab, Cincinnati, Ohio, December 1977.

18. Heidemann, E. and Dorstewitz, R. "The Present Status in the Development of the Darmstädter Run-Through Process." *Das Leder* 30 (1979). Abstract: *American Leather Chemists Association Journal* 76 (1981).

19. Dorstewitz, R. and Heidemann, E. "Hair Removal and Collection by a Rapid Run-Through Process." *Das Leder* 28 (1977). Abstract: *American Leather Chemists Association Journal* 74 (1979).

20. Terrel, G.C. "The Contribution of Innovative Combustion Technology to Chromium Recovery." *American Leather Chemists Association Journal,* August 1981.

21. Kubo, T. "Reduction of Pollution Effluents from Beamhouse Processes." *Hikaku Kagaku* 26 (1980). Abstract: *American Leather Chemists Association Journal* 76 (1981).

22. Howes, F.N. "Tanning Materials: Botanical Part." In Endres, H. *et al. Tanning Materials.* Stuttgard: Verlag Von J. Cramer, 1962 (5th. ed.).

23. Tomlinson, H.D. *et al.* "Removal of Color from Vegetable Tanning Solution." *Water Pollution Control Federation Journal,* March 1975.

24. Krofchak, D. and Stone, N. *Science and Engineering for Pollution Free Systems.* Ann Arbor, Michigan: Ann Arbor Science Publishers Inc., 1975.

25. France, H.G. "Recycle of Tan Liquor from Organic Acid Pickle/Tan Process." *American Leather Chemists Association Journal* 70 (1975).

26. Sharp, B.W. "Chrome Recycling." *American Leather Chemists Association Journal,* January 1981.

27. Davies, J.H. and Scroggie, J.G. "Theory and Practice of Direct Chrome Recycling." *Das Leder,* January 1980.

28. Navon, M. *et al.* "Treatment of Tannery Wastewaters: Reuse of Washing and Tanning Liquids." *Ingenieria Sanitaria,* October-December 1977. Abstract: *Pollution Abstracts* 10(1), 1979.

29. Arumugam, V. "Recovery of Chromium from Spent Chrome Tan Liqour by Chemical Precipitation." *Indian Journal of Environmental Health,* January 1976. Abstract: *Pollution Abstracts* 7(6), 1976.

30. Mayer, A.K. "Reduction of Chromium in the Effluent by Use of a High Exhaust Chrome Tannage with Baychrome 2403." *American Leather Chemists Association Journal,* January 1981.

31. Jones, B.H. "Chromium Recovery Through Incineration of Liquid and Solid Tannery Wastes — The Ultimate Solution." *American Leather Chemists Association Journal,* November 1979.

32. "Industrial, Municipal, Wastes Combined, Treated in One Plant." *Civil Engineering — ASCE,* December 1976.

33. Dawson, R. "Leather Tanning Industry: Sludge Problems Ahead." *Sludge Magazine* 1(5), 1978. Abstract: *Pollution Abstracts* 10(4), 1979.

34. Tombetti, F. "Recovery of Industrial Wastes, Hypothesis of Electrical and Thermic Energy Production at Low Costs: the 'TOTEM' in Tanning Industry." *Cuoio, pelli, mat. concianti* 54, 1978. Abstract: *American Leather Chemists Association Journal* 75 (1980).

35. Mazur, T. and Koc, J. "The Fertilizing Value of Tannery Sludges." in Bewick, Michael (ed.). *Handbook of Organic Waste Conversion.* New York: Van Nostrand Reinhold (Environmental Engineering Series), 1980.

36. Thorstensen, T.C. and Shah, M. "Technical and Economic Aspects of Tannery Sludge as Fertilizer." *American Leather Chemists Association Journal,* January 1979.

37. Sheikh, K. *et al.* "Wastewater Effluents from a Tannery: Their Effects on Soil and Vegetation in Pakistan." *Environmental Conservation,* Winter 1980.

Textiles

In North America's changing economic climate where energy, materials and water costs continue to spiral upwards, the textile industry is undergoing a gradual shift to minimize the quantity of wastes generated that require disposal.

Textile processing depends on the consumption of large quantities of water, energy and materials. The resultant volume of wastewater requiring treatment and disposal tends to be large. In the past when energy, material and water costs were low, the textile industry found it in its economic interest to use "end-of-pipe" abatement technologies usually designed to treat combined wastestreams from the entire plant.

The 1980s are expected to add a new wrinkle to disposal economics. Whereas sludge disposal costs were low in the past, the cost of disposing residuals is expected to increase dramatically as disposal technologies become more sophisticated and more costly.

While the 1970s marked a decade of research and prototype development, manufacturers of low-polluting equipment have been in hot pursuit. This has resulted in an influx of more efficient and less polluting equipment available to the textile industry.

Equipment is commercially av-

Table 1
Relative Size of Subsectors, Textile Industry, 1976

Subsector	Establishments		Employment	
	No.	%	No.	%
Man-made yarns and fabrics	89	9.0	12,477	16.4
Cotton yarns and cloth	22	2.2	8,947	11.8
Wool yarn and cloth	38	3.9	5,165	6.8
Man-made fibres	11	1.1	5,805	7.6
Carpet, mat and rug	32	3.2	7,060	9.3
Knitted fabric (P)	79	8.0	4,604	6.1
Auto fab. and accessories	20	2.0	5,557	7.3
Lino. and coated fabric (P)	17	1.7	3,272	4.3
Dye and finish (P)	74	7.5	3,757	4.9
Narrow fabrics (P)	38	3.9	2,171	2.9
Canvass products (P)	144	14.6	2,117	2.8
Fibre and felt	33	3.3	1,065	1.4
Cotton and jute bags (P)	22	2.2	681	0.9
Thread mills (P)	16	1.6	960	1.3
Cordage and twine	18	1.8	630	0.8
Embroidery, etc. (P)	90	9.1	1,307	1.7
Misc. textile industries* (P)	244	24.7	10,521	13.8
Total	987	100.0	76,096	100.0

(P) Preliminary

*Mainly home furnishings, such as draperies, curtains and bedspreads, non-woven.

Source: ITC Estimates based on Statistics Canada Census of Manufacturers, 1976

ailable that can recycle synthetic sizes, caustic soda, dyebaths, and oils used to lubricate knitting yarns. An assortment of highly efficient low-polluting machines is also available that gets more dye on to the fabric and less out with the wastewater.

Such equipment frequently requires a substantial capital expenditure, however the annual operating costs are low, especially when one takes into account credits gained through recovered materials, reduced energy costs and minimal disposal charges. On the other hand, conventional pollution abatement technologies tend to consume large quantities of energy and chemicals during the treatment process, and frequently result in a sludge problem. The operating costs compound over the years, as do the sludge disposal costs.

Textile firms which have invested in successful in-process recycling are doing so at an economic gain. Many advances in water re-use, heat recovery, in-process recycling and more efficient dye application are applicable to the smaller operator as well as the larger firm.

However, for the smaller company with limited financial and technical resources, a five-digit price tag on new equipment may seem prohibitive, especially when viewed in the context that much of the company's existing equipment is functioning adequately. Despite fears of high costs, the case studies that follow suggest that any company, no matter how small, would be prudent to investigate the long-term costs and benefits of upgrading existing operations.

Affordable, cost-effective improvements include low-cost housekeeping measures and minor process changes. In some instances, a significant expenditure on more efficient equipment may also prove to be highly profitable in the long term. By doing its pollution prevention homework, even a small company may find it is losing money by hanging onto old ways. This chapter identifies many success stories where firms have enhanced company profits by minimizing the quantity of wastes requiring conventional treatment and disposal.

Industry Profile

The Canadian textile industry is complex and diverse, composed of many subsectors whose activities include manufacturing the following products: man-made fibres and yarns; cotton and wool yarns; wool and man-made fabrics; knitted fabrics; hosiery and underwear; thread, cordage and twine; carpets, mats and rugs; and sheets, pillowcases, towels, blankets and bedspreads (see Table 1). The dyeing, finishing and printing of these products is another facet of the textile industry.

Canada's textile industry is concentrated in Ontario and Quebec, accounting for more than 90% of the industry's total employment in 1976 (see Table 2). In Ontario, there is a concentration of man-made fibre and yarn mills, cordage and twine mills, and auto fabrics.[1] In Quebec, there is a greater concentration of woven fabric mills, knitted fabric mills, and custom dyeing and finishing mills that process these fabrics.[1]

Based on 1976 census data, the textile industry was composed of 987 establishments which employed 76,000 people. There is a high degree of industry concentration in specific product areas such as in the production of man-made fibres, which is essentially a chemical process.[1] Generally, as production approaches the consumer level, the number of firms increases, probably as a result of lower investment requirements associated with smaller scale production.

Although 80% of Canada's textile establishments employ fewer

Table 2
Regional Distribution of Production of the Textile Industry, 1976

	Establishments		Employment	
	No.	%	No.	%
Quebec	434	44	39,570	52
Ontario	385	39	31,960	42
Western provinces	138	14	3,044	4
Atlantic provinces	30	3	1,522	2
	987	100	76,096	100

Source: Industry, Trade and Commerce (Canada) estimates, 1976.

than 100 people, this represents only 20% of the industry's total workforce.[1] Companies with more than 500 employees make up only 3% of the total number of textile establishments, yet they employ more than 30% of the industry.[1]

Process Descriptions and Wastewater Sources

Cinderella could not be happier. The flurry of activity among chemical engineers over the last decades has transformed the garment market from a subdued range of natural-fibre clothes to a dazzling and colourful array of polyesters, acrylics and nylons.

Although scientists are still unravelling the environmental impact of this transformation, one fact remains clear — the wastestream from the textile industry is changing in composition. The continuing influx of new products onto the industrial market has meant that a wastestream that may once have been homogeneous and biodegradable may have become heterogeneous and inert.[2] In the face of the changing composition of wastewater pollutants, it is possible that conventional biological treatment methods no longer can keep pace in adequately treating many textile mill effluents.[3]

The production of fabric from natural and synthetic fibres involves many different processes. These processes are frequently performed in different plants and result in different types of wastestreams. Fibres are combined into yarns which are then made into fabrics. The fabrics are processed further in a variety of ways known collectively as finishing.

Figure 1 shows the types of contaminants that occur in combined textile wastewaters. Fibres, also known as lint, are a significant part of the suspended solids in textile wastewater. Natural fibres such as cotton and wool will degrade if retained with the sludge in the treatment plant. In contrast, synthetic fibres remain inert for a relatively long time and may build up in the sludge of a treatment facility.

One dilemma in the textile industry concerns its complexity. The industry is segmented so that each subsector confines its plant operations to a component of the

Figure 1
Components of Textile Wastewater

Wastewaster

Solids	Substances Affecting pH	Substances Affecting Temperature	Organic Substances (imposing a BOD)	Nutrients	Colouring Matter
Fibres Insoluble impurities Resins Pigments Sizes	Acids Alkalis Salts	Dyeing liquors, Boiling-off baths, Cooling water, Direct steam	Dyeing/Printing chemicals, Detergents/ Surface-active agents, Finishing agents Sizes Solvents/ Solubilising agents Thickeners Greases/Waxes Fibre impurities Organic acids	Nitrogen compounds, Phosphorus compounds	Soluble dyestuffs, Dispersed dyestuffs, Pigments

Source: "Environmental Protection in the Textile Industry." American Dyestuff Reporter, February 1981.

entire textile manufacturing process.

One plant will impregnate the fabric with various chemicals during its particular process operations. The fabric might then be moved to another plant for further processing which frequently requires removal of these chemicals before the next phase of processing. Thus chemicals necessary for one plant's processing may become a costly nuisance in another plant. Some of the case studies that follow identify the co-operation possible between plants to ease recovery and re-use of chemicals previously discarded.

What follows is a brief overview of the processes and sources of pollution resulting from the production of cotton, wool and synthetic fibres. Specific processes at individual mills may vary considerably from site to site.

Although the natural fibres used by the Canadian textile industry are almost entirely imported[1], much of the processing of these fibres into finished fabrics occurs in Canada.

Cotton

Once the fibre is spun into thread, the warp thread is prepared for weaving with a wet process known as slashing. In slashing, the warp threads are impregnated with a synthetic or starch size to facilitate weaving by increasing warp strength and adhesion.

In North America, the principal sizing polymer used before 1960 was starch, which easily degraded biologically.[2]

As synthetics penetrated the textile industry and pure cotton fabrics were replaced with cotton-synthetic blends, new sizing agents, which are better suited to the needs of synthetic yarn, came into greater dominance. Polyvinyl alcohol (PVA) is the preferred type of synthetic size, although carboxymethyl cellulose (CMC) and polyacrylic acid are also used. Unlike starch, PVA and CMC are more resistant to biological degradation in conventional waste treatment. Some of the larger American textile mills are now recovering PVA for re-use as a sizing agent.

Once the fabric is woven, it is necessary to remove the sizing compound so as to ensure better dyeability in further processing. The removal of size is known as desizing and frequently occurs at another plant from the one where slashing and weaving occur.

The more common desizing operations are acid desizing and enzyme desizing, although in some plants, desizing is achieved simply through washing with a detergent. The acid desizing process uses a solution of dilute sulfuric acid to hydrolyze the starch and render it water soluble, whereas enzyme desizing utilizes vegetable or animal enzymes to decompose starches to a water soluble form.[4] The waste from the desizing operations tends to contribute the largest biological oxygen demand (BOD) of all cotton finishing wastes, approximately 45%.[2] In addition, desizing wastewaters frequently contain mildewcides, fungicides and other contaminants.[4]

The next process is scouring. Scouring is a process in which the natural impurities (wax, pectins and alcohols) as well as the processing impurities (size, dirt, oil and grease) are removed from the fabric by hot alkaline detergents or soap solutions.

By removing impurities, the scouring process tends to lighten the colour of the fibres to approach their natural colour. Scouring also makes the fibre more absorbent for subsequent bleaching and dyeing by removing the wax and other non-cellulosic components. Impurities are removed by washing with sodium hydroxide (also known as caustic soda), soaps and detergents, which results in an alkaline wastestream rich in these impurities.[4]

The cotton is bleached using oxidizing agents such as hydrogen peroxide.[2] When an oxidizing agent has done its job, it is broken down, however use of excess quantities means that some may end up in the process effluent.

Before cotton fabric is dyed, it frequently is mercerized (causticized) to increase its affinity for dyestuffs, as well as increase surface lustre. The process uses caustic soda and an acid wash. Increasing chemical costs have driven the larger companies to recycle caustic soda in the mercerization process.

The dyeing process can involve hundreds of different pigments, dyes and carriers, resulting in an effluent stream that may contain potentially toxic constituents.

Wool

The five major sources of pollution during the processing of wool fibres are scouring, washing after felting, neutralization after carbonizing, bleaching and dyeing.

The production of one pound of wool fibre produces 1.5 pounds of waste impurities[2], consisting largely of the dirt and grease present on the wool fibre. Wool scouring produces a strong industrial waste in terms of BOD. Up to half of the grease removed by scouring may be recovered by centrifugal separation of the grease stream. This crude grease is further refined to produce the useful byproduct lanolin.[4]

In felting, the fabric is impregnated with sulfuric acid, hydrogen peroxide and metal catalysts such as chromium, copper and cobalt. An estimated 10 to 25% of the felted cloth's weight is composed of process chemicals that are later washed out.[2]

Carbonizing of fabrics is a common finishing process which removes cellulose impurities by using a hot acid bath. After carbonizing, the acids in the fabric are removed by neutralization in a sodium carbonate bath and final rinsing.

Wool is bleached if white or light shades are desired. Bleaching of wool fibres may occur after the scouring process, or the wool fabric may be bleached after finishing. Bleaching is accomplished using sulphur dioxide, hydrogen peroxide, or brightening agents.

Wool may be dyed in fibre form (top dyeing) or after spinning (yarn or stock dyeing) or it may be dyed as fabric (piece dyeing).

Man-Made Fibres

There are two main categories of

Table 3

Textile Colourants and Potential Hazards

Dye Type	Description	Application	Potential Hazards
Direct Dyes (substantive dyes)	The direct dyes owe their fibre affinity to the formation of hydrogen bonds between the azo groups of the dye molecule and the hydroxyl groups in the cellulose molecule.	Direct dyes are suitable for dyeing cotton, paper and leather.	In the past, the most common direct dyes were the benzidine dyes. Benzidine dyes have since been linked to bladder cancer in people and are no longer in widespread use.
Naphthol Dyes (azoic dyes)	The naphthol dyes consist of two chemically reactive colourless compounds. Only with application to textiles is the coloured azo chromophore (colour imparting) compound finally produced. The reaction within the fibre pockets is a coupling of a diazonium compound with a phenolic compound.	Naphthol dyes are suitable for dyeing cellulosic fibres, acetate and triacetate.	Little long-term toxicological research has been done on the components of azoic dyes. Hyperpigmentation contact dermatitis has been observed in some workers handling fabric impregnated with 3-hydroxy-2-naphthol which is a common coupling agent.
Disperse Dyes	Disperse dyes are applied from near colloidal aqueous dispersions to fibres in which the dyes literally dissolve. The chromophore groups can be either of the azo or anthraquinone class. High temperatures and pressures are sometimes required for application.	Disperse dyes are used for hydrophobic fibres that repel water-soluble dyes such as triacetate, nylon, polyester and polyacrylonitrile.	As a class, only disperse dyes have caused widespread dermatitis from the finished dyed product. Specific dyes within this class have induced photo-contact dermatitis in employees of a dye manufacturing plant. Some dyes within this class have been identified as bacterial mutagens.
Acid Dyes	The chromophore group can be either an azo, anthraquinone or other chemical group. The dye-fibre affinity is due mainly to salt links between the sulfonic acid part of the dye and the basic amino groups in wool, silk and nylon fibres.	Acid dyes are used to dye wool, silk and nylon.	The acid class of dyes is predicted to be among the least carcinogenic of all the dye classes. The majority of food colourings are from this chemical group since they are highly ionized and not readily absorbed into the bloodstream from the stomach or intestine.
Mordant Dyes	Synthetic as well as natural dyes can be affixed to textiles by mordanting with metallic salts. Metal salts used to fix this class of dyes include chromium, copper, cobalt, aluminum, iron and nickel salts.	Mordant dyes receive relatively little commercial usage. They are frequently used for natural dyeing in arts and craft activities.	This class of dyes has not received extensive toxicological study. Some of the metal salts are corrosive and toxic.

Dye type	Description	Application	Potential Hazards
Basic Dyes	These dyes are called basic or cationic because the main dye chromophore is positively charged, with the negative charge residing in a single chlorine anion. This is the opposite situation of acid dyes. Basic dyes also encompass azo and anthraquinone derivatives with better fastness properties.	Basic dyes have affinity for protein fibres such as wool and silk, and for cellulosic fibres mordanted with tannic acid.	Basic dyes, like acid dyes, are highly ionized which make them less likely to be absorbed through the gastro-intestinal tract. Up to 90% of the food dyes from this class are recovered unchanged in the feces.
Vat Dyes	Vat dyes are usually first reduced with base to a colourless soluble leuco compound. The fabric is impregnated with the colourless form of the dye, and then oxidized to the coloured insoluble form either by air oxidation or by acid dichromate addition to the dyebath. Presolubilized vat dyes can be purchased in the reduced leuco form as alkali metal salts of the sulfuric acid ester of the dye.	Vat dyes can be applied to cellulosic fibres and some are suitable for wool and acetate.	Extensive toxicological study is lacking.
Oxidation Base Dyes	The oxidation bases refer to aromatic amines, diamines, or aminophenol compounds which are applied to fur, hair or textiles, and then oxidized with hydrogen peroxide to colour the material. The oxidized coloured products are complex mixtures of aromatic amines.	The oxidation base dyes are used to colour fur, hair or textiles.	Lab studies demonstrate that some of the oxidative type dyes are mutagens and animal carcinogens.

Source: "Textile Dyes are Potential Hazards" *Journal of Environmental Health,* March 1978.

synthetic fibres: cellulosics such as rayon and cellulose acetate, which are produced from cellulose and derived primarily from wood pulp; and non-cellulosics such as polyamid (nylon), polyesters, acrylics and modacrylics which are synthesized from petroleum distillates.

Unlike natural fibres such as cotton and wool which generate high BOD wastewaters due to the wax and grease impurities on the fibres, synthetic fibres are relatively free of these impurities, and

hence wastewaters are low in BOD.

The processing of man-made fibres presents other difficulties because these fibres tend to be hydrophobic, resisting water adsorption. In the absence of high temperatures and high pressures, fabrics such as polyester need carriers to take the dye into the fibre. Carriers used in polyester dyeing include substances such as methyl naphthalene, butyl benzoate, diphenyl oxide, perchloroethylene, orthophenyl-

phenol, biphenyl, benzyl alcohol and chlorobenzenes. High concentrations of carrier ranging from 0.06 to 0.4 pounds per pound of polyester fibre have been used at conventional dyeing temperatures.[4] Generally however, the amount of carrier used in conventional dyeing is at the low end of this concentration range. High-temperature and high-pressure dyeing techniques can significantly reduce or eliminate the need for carriers.

The current trend in dyeing is to

eliminate the use of dye carriers by altering the physical conditions during dyeing.

The processing of man-made fibres can be problematic because of electrostatic charge build-up. To facilitate weaving and knitting operations, antistatic mineral oils and other agents such as PVA, styrene-based resins, polyalkylene glycols and polyvinyl acetate are applied to the yarn. The use of antistatic oils and other agents yields a polluting discharge when they are later removed from fabrics during scouring or tentering. During tentering, the fabric is subjected to heat, resulting in haze-producing particulates in the tenter exhaust. Scouring generates a water-oil mix in the process wastewater.

Finishing

Most fabrics undergo a finishing process designed to give the fabric desired properties. Types of finishes used include permanent press finishes, fire retardants, soil release agents, oil repellents, abrasion-resistant polymers, germicide and fungicide chemicals.[2] Although some of these chemicals are readily biodegradable, many are not and may present waste treatment problems when they occur in the wastewater.

Textile wastewaters have been adequately characterized in terms of BOD, solids content and pH. However, the potentially toxic contaminants in textile wastewaters resulting from dyes, carriers and finishing agents have not received the same attention

because of the hundreds of chemicals involved.[5]

Pollution prevention depends on a knowledge of the types of pollutants that a plant generates. This points to the increasing need for the better characterization of industrial waste. Understanding which process streams contain hazardous wastes and which ones contain relatively innocuous biodegradable wastes will permit not only more complete waste treatment but also a more cost-effective one.

Description and Hazards of Dyes

Many textile dyehouses in North America are relatively low-volume operations that dye small batches of textiles in a variety of colours. The resultant wastestream from the dyeing process may yield a highly mixed waste effluent that contains dozens of different colourants, carriers and auxiliary chemicals. The cost of on-site waste treatment facilities may well be prohibitive for the smaller textile dyehouse.

Nevertheless, preliminary research in the last decade on the health effects of many of the chemicals used in the manufacture of dyes and carriers points to potential health and environmental problems of some of these materials.[6] Potential hazards are two-fold. One, in some of the smaller dyehouses, workers still weigh and mix dry dye powder with water, resulting in possible exposure of the skin to dye mate-

rial. A second potential hazard concerns the entry of dye agents into the environment through insufficiently treated wastewater from the dyehouse. In such instances, certain dye agents may be hazardous because of their inherent toxic properties, the sheer volume of their release, or their persistence in the environment.[5]

The dye and pigment industry in North America produces well over 2000 colourants and carriers. The volume and importance of organic dyes derived from petroleum and natural gas have grown substantially since the 1940s. Some dyes are derived from potentially hazardous materials such as acenaphthene, acrylonitrile, nitrotoluenes, nitrophenols, amines and p-toluene sulfonic acid.[5] Metals such as lead and mercury have also been used to make dyes and pigments, although their use is declining.

There are several classes of dyes. Dyes are usually grouped according to chemical structure and by dyeing procedure. Dye classes include direct, naphthol, disperse, acid, basic, mordant, vat and oxidation base dyes. Table 3 gives a brief description of each dye class and lists some of the potential hazards associated with each.[7,8] As dye hazards are identified, use of the questionable dye tends to be minimized or even discontinued. Research scientists in the field of dye hazard identification point to the enormity of the task before them in verifying the safety of the numerous dye substances currently on the market.

POLLUTION PREVENTION OPPORTUNITIES

1.

Housekeeping and Low-Cost Process Improvements

In the competitive battle to upgrade productivity and cut production costs, it is particularly difficult for the smaller company to consider the advantages of preventing pollution. But with increasing waste treatment costs, stricter pollution regulations, and escalating energy costs, priorities can be expected to shift.

A first step in any pollution prevention strategy must concern good housekeeping and low-cost process improvements. Although good housekeeping can refer to any of a multitude of process adjustments that curb waste, they all have in common a low capital investment with a rapid but significant pay-back.[9]

■ The Grace Finishing plant of Spring Mills (Lancaster, South Carolina) is one of many dyeing and printing plants whose good housekeeping practices have paid off. Although much of the impetus to improve plant processes resulted from an energy conservation drive, their continuing endeavour has put a big dent in pollution abatement costs. It became obvious to company management that the more the wastewater volume was reduced during processing, the less water there would be to undergo costly waste treatment.

The project at Grace involved several low-cost improvements including the installation of solenoid valves on each washer water feed line to automatically stop the water flow when the bleaching and dyeing ranges stopped. Flow indicators were installed to give the operators a means of accurately setting the flow rate for each washer. Then, flow rate standards were set for each dye type, cloth style and colour. With standards established and a means of

measuring flow rates provided, staff had the necessary tools to ensure optimum equipment efficiency. Steam and water consumption dropped 10%.[10]

At a total project cost of $50,000, management agrees that the investment had proven to provide a very good pay-back.

■ The success of this project prodded the Grace plant to launch another programme — reviewing the efficiency of all plant processes. As a result, scouring was restricted to medium and heavy dye shades for many styles of fabric, and low-energy dyes were substituted for the more energy-intensive dyes previously in use. In conjunction with other conservation measures, energy consumption dropped by 20% between 1973 and 1976. According to company staff, more than 10% of the savings resulting from process redesign were made without major capital expenditures.[10]

Another strategy to reduce the volume of wastewater generated involves improved wash design. Generally, the effectiveness of a

washing can be seen to increase directly with the volume of washwater used, but it increases exponentially according to the number of washings used. Thus, four washings of 2.5 gallons water per pound of goods is more effective than a single 10-gallon washing.[4] Removing as much of the liquid from the goods as possible by squeezing before adding the next rinse would further minimize the ultimate amount of wastewater generated during rinsing.

Another waste reduction option is to ensure that chemical mix amounts are carefully calculated and routinely monitored. In some plants, continuous bleach ranges are set up to use chemical formulations designed for the most demanding fabric style. This results in "overkill" or chemical wastage on lighter, more easily treated fabrics.[4] Good housekeeping practices advocate that the various fabric styles be segregated into groups, and that chemical formulations be adjusted to meet the needs of each group.

■ Automatic control equipment

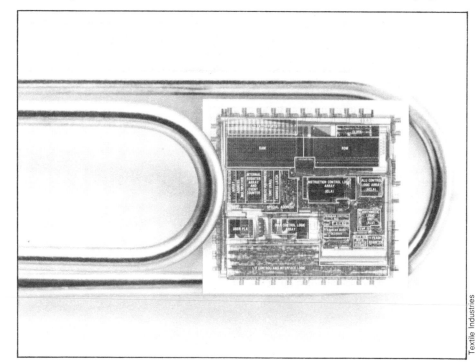

The microchip, also known as the microprocessor, is smaller than a paper clip.

designed to maintain chemical bath concentrations at predetermined levels has resulted in savings of 30% at the Dan River textile plant.[4]

The opportunities to improve process efficiency are great and will vary with every plant. But all housekeeping improvements can be assisted by an accurate accounting of raw materials introduced in a process compared with the sum of products and waste materials generated in the process. Taking care to do a materials balance can pinpoint sources of unnecessary waste and pollution.

2.
Process Control Through Computer Use

The "microchip revolution" is forging inroads into many facets of textile processing. The microchip, more commonly known as the microprocessor, is a very small processor with the essential components which characterize computer processors. Nowadays, a single chip, smaller than a paper clip, has the computing power of a large $100,000 room-sized computer of the 1950s, yet it costs only $10.[11]

By going miniature, the microprocessor is fast becoming an economic reality for even the smaller and medium-sized plants. While the cost of process controls covers a wide range, depending on the degree of sophistication desired, it is generally agreed that pay-back occurs within a few years.[12,13]

■ The Idhammar-Terema system devised by Idhammar Konsult AB (Tumba, Sweden) is a computerized preventative maintenance package based on the continuous monitoring of all mechanical, electrical and control equipment. Available internationally, the system has been successfully applied to more than 60 manufacturing installations in Sweden, Finland and Norway, including textile plants.[14]

■ To date, computerized process control in the textile industry has made its greatest penetration into

Figure 2
Schematic of Integrated Dyehouse Control System

Schematic of an integrated dyehouse control system which enables a dyehouse manager to sort and retrieve formulas, quickly and accurately create new dye formulas, and maintain tight control over the dyeing process.
Source: "Progress Report on Process Control," *Textile Industries,* July 1972.

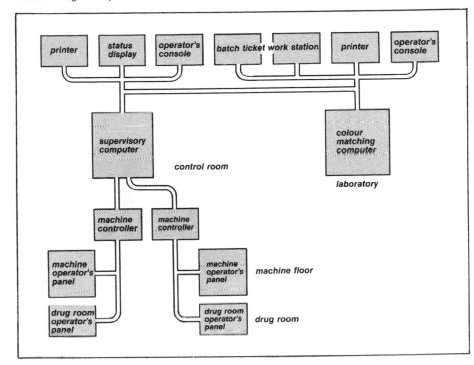

batch dyeing. An estimated 20 digital computer systems controlling dyeing operations exist in the North American textile industry.[11] Although Foxboro and Taylor were the main software suppliers just 5 years ago, the microprocessor market has since exploded to include more than a dozen new firms.

■ The Gaston County Dyeing Machine Co. (Stanley, North Carolina) provides a microprocessor-based dyeing machine control system with which up to 32 units can be controlled by one operator from one console. Gaston County are collaborating with Applied Color Systems (Princeton, New Jersey) who supply computer-based colour-matching and control systems to provide textile dyers with an integrated dyehouse control system[15] (see Figure 2).

The combination control package will enable a dyehouse manager to quickly and accurately create new dye formulas, generate production batch tickets, sort and retrieve formulas, keep track of production batch dye costs, and maintain tight control over the dyeing process and inventories of dyes and chemicals.

For the batch dyeing plant, the opportunities for increasing output, improving efficiency and minimizing pollution have never been better. Although modernization of the dyehouse through computer technology may require an outlay of considerable capital, the goal is often a realistic one.

■ Information Laboratories Inc., a Gaston County subsidiary, showed in 1972 that a 10-machine polyester dyehouse buying a 1200-D computer control system could save $8000 a month in reduced chemical, utility and labour costs. Despite a capital expenditure of $500,000 based on a 5-year amortization, the investment yields a 5-year net cash generation of $500,000.[16] Marion

Dyers (Gaffney, South Carolina) is one company which installed Gaston County's computer control equipment and substantially enhanced its dyehouse efficiency.

What does automation have to do with pollution? The microprocessor can automatically and precisely calculate new dye formulations, thereby eliminating human error and wasted batches. Both water use and wastewater generation are reduced by eliminating wastage, resulting in potential savings of thousands of dollars per year per machine. Reduced dyeing times and the possible elimination of some steps of the procedure also contribute to improved productivity and reduced operating costs.[12]

Although talk of computers still has the small businessman feeling for his pocket book, the trend among many software suppliers has been to accommodate the economic constraints of the smaller business.

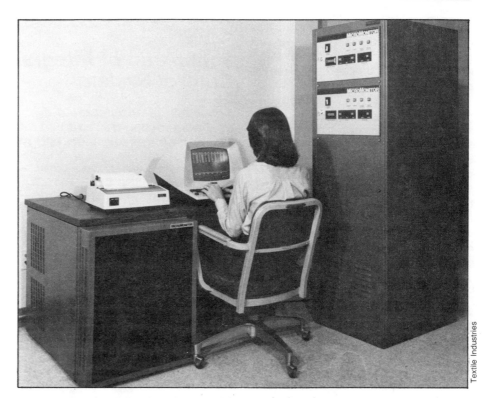

Microprocessor-based dyeing machine control system.

3.
Waste Recovery Versus Waste Treatment

No one can deny that pollution control costs money.[17] The question is, can pollution control be designed in such a manner as to become profitable in the long run? Although still in a minority, some innovative textile plants would answer this question with an unequivocal "yes".

Conventional waste treatment technologies such as biological treatment, chemical coagulation and carbon adsorption are routinely used to treat pollutants once they are generated. In simplistic terms, conventional technologies tend to consume resources and yield a sludge that requires further disposal. By turning a water pollution problem to a sludge disposal problem, wastes are relocated from the water to the land. Although such waste handling systems have enabled textile plants to meet effluent guidelines, this approach tends to be a drain on company profits.

Recognizing waste for what it is —a waste of materials and energy

— reducing and recovering these otherwise wasted resources can yield financial returns. Whereas conventional waste treatment technologies reinforce industry's perception that pollution abatement constitutes an economic loss, innovative waste recovery applications guarantee a financial return on investment in pollution prevention.

Not only is waste recovery becoming increasingly promising in terms of economics, but waste recovery applications tend to be more efficient in reducing polluting discharges.

In the past, resource recovery technologies suffered from economic and technological disadvantages compared to more conventional waste treatment. However, as waste treatment and sludge disposal costs spiral, and as chemical costs escalate, waste recovery is becoming increasingly promising economically. In many instances, technological advances in waste recovery applications result in greater efficiency in reducing polluting discharges than do conventional technologies.

Biological treatment may degrade potentially recoverable waste chemicals and produce a

biological floc or colloid which prevents direct recycle.

Chemical coagulation can be very effective at treating specific wastestreams containing pigments, latexes and phosphates. Commonly used coagulating chemicals include alum, lime, iron salts and organic polymers.[3]

In chemical coagulation, the waste process chemicals are combined with the coagulating chemicals and become locked in the sludge, making the use of separation technologies unfeasible.

Carbon adsorption is efficient in removing medium-sized organics, dyes and detergents from a wastestream. Chemicals with high water solubility or with very high molecular weights such as organic polymers are not efficiently adsorbed by carbon.[3] Carbon adsorption destroys many of the chemicals it removes from the wastestream when the carbon is reactivated at very high temperatures.[3]

Despite the general unsuitability of conventional treatment methods for recovering process chemicals from a wastestream, conventional waste treatment equipment currently in place can be modified and added to in order to permit the successful recycling of wastewater. Textile plants that have modified their waste treatment systems for water recycling are doing so at an economic and energy saving.

Waste Recovery

Unlike conventional treatment technologies such as biological treatment, coagulation and carbon adsorption, which contaminate or destroy potentially recoverable waste chemicals, separation technologies are proving to be a cost-effective way to recover select waste materials.

It must be recognized that many separation technologies represent leading-edge technology. Unlike more conventional technologies which have withstood the test of time, the newer recovery technologies have been known to present operational difficulties in some situations. Whereas conventional treatment technologies tend to be flexible in treating a range of waste types, separation technologies function best when wastestreams are segregated and predictable.

Implementation of waste recovery technologies frequently requires more than simple installation of off-the-shelf recovery equipment. It is common to alter waste collection and rinsing systems to match the needs of a particular separation technology. Yet despite these process changes, the economics of recovery technologies, where applicable, tend to be superior to end-of-pipe treatment.

Membrane systems are among the new technologies receiving attention from the textile industry. These systems include reverse osmosis and ultrafiltration.

Although there is some overlap in nomenclature, a reverse osmosis system is usually meant to refer to a unit operating at fairly high pressures capable of rejecting low-molecular-weight salts such as sodium chloride.

An ultrafiltration membrane system refers to lower-pressure units that can filter out colloids and polymers of molecular weights greater than 10,000.

Membrane technology has made remarkable strides in the last decade. Tailor-made resin membranes permit their application in many industrial sectors, and under many different conditions. Application of membrane technology to textile wastewaters has made it possible to isolate a product water of comparatively high quality and a concentrate water containing 80 to 95% of the chemicals present in the original wastestream.[18]

The chemical concentrate is suitable for re-use in the process which generated that specific wastestream. The ideal application of membrane systems would be to have one at each different process machine to recycle all products within the system. To date, membrane technology is commercially available for only select process wastestreams. The excellent separation abilities of many membrane systems permit re-use not only of process chemicals but also of the purified water remaining after removal of the process chemicals.

Table 4 compares the efficiency in removing pollutants from textile wastewaters when using different treatment methods. It is noteworthy that membrane systems consistently show the highest removal efficiency. Removal efficiencies are based on data collected from operating textile plants.

Unlike conventional treatment systems which typically combine various wastewater streams for ultimate treatment or discharge, waste recovery systems depend on a greater segregation of wastewater streams for their success.

Keeping wastestreams separate permits wastewater from a specific process unit to be recovered before it is contaminated

Table 4
Pollutant Removal Efficiencies of Different Treatment Methods Applied to Textile Wastewater
(shows percent removal)

	Biological	Alum Coagulation	Carbon Adsorption	Membrane Systems
BOD	70-95 %	50-70%	60-95%	80-98%
COD	30-70	50-70	60-95	80-98
Solids				
Total	5-10	5	10-30	70-98
Volatile	10-50	50	50-80	75-98
Suspended	30-90	80-98	60-90	95-100
Colour	10-80	80-90	80-98	95-100
Alkalinity	10-20	0-20	5	80-95

Source: "Waste Treatment Versus Waste Recovery." Textile Chemist and Colourist, November 1977.

Table 5

Potential for Conservation by Recycle in the U.S. Textile Industry

	Water Discharge (1000 kgal/d)	Dyes (1000 lb/d)	Auxiliary Chemicals (1000 lb/d)	Salt (1000 lb/d)	Process Thermal Energy 10⁹Btu/d
Industry Total	706	1291	594	581	784
Recycle Potential	635	129	489	481	352
% Recycle Potential	90%	10%	82%	82%	45%
Estimated Annual Savings (millions of dollars)*	$79	$95	$24	$3	$264

Based on unit costs of: water @ $0.5/1000 gal; dye @ $3/lb; auxiliary chemicals @ $0.2/lb; salt @ $44/ton; and process steam @ $2/10⁶ Btu.

Source: U.S. EPA. *Application of High-Temperature Hyperfiltration to Unit Textile Processes for Direct Recycle,* 1978.

---

with other chemicals from other processes. The water and energy (from the hot water) can also be recovered for re-use.

With the advent of commercially available membrane systems, water, chemical and energy recovery becomes an economic reality. As seen in Table 5, the conservation potential for the textile industry is enormous. The potential for water re-use is estimated at 90%, with salt and auxiliary chemical recovery predicted at more than 80%.

Membrane systems alone will not provide all the waste management needs of a textile plant, but in many cases, they will enhance pollution control efficiency while paying dividends on the investment.

4.

Water Recycling

On a world scale, the textile industry consumes a lion's share of water resources and is among the top ten industrial consumers of fresh water.[19] This enormous demand for water can be greatly alleviated by recycling process water.

For example, the total flow of the River Thames is already being used one and a half times before it reaches London Bridge, and some of its waters are being used several times, having been extracted, treated, used, discharged to sewage works, and then to the river repeatedly.[4]

The United States textile indus-

try, unlike its Canadian counterpart, has been under considerable pressure to meet ever stricter discharge limitations. Given the rising costs of end-of-pipe treatment for discharge to streams or of pre-treatment for discharge to sewers, it may well be cheaper to re-use wastewater rather than

---

Table 6

Effects of Process Modification on Water and Energy Conservation

Process Modification	Water Consumption (gallons/day)	Average Process Temperatures (°F)	Energy for Heating Water (million Btu/day)
1. No modification	346,000	165	274
2. Temperature increase and water reduction	194,000	195	202
3. Multiple use of water	158,000	195	165
4. Water recycle via ultrafiltration	43,000	195	45

Source: "Water Quality Requirements for Re-use in Textile Dyeing Processes." *American Dyestuff Reporter,* October 1980.

Figure 3
Comparison of Wastewater Recycle and Conventional Waste Treatment

applied to unit processes and/or to composite plant effluent.

Source: "Water Quality Requirements for Re-Use in Textile Dyeing Processes," *American Dyestuff Reporter,* October 1980.

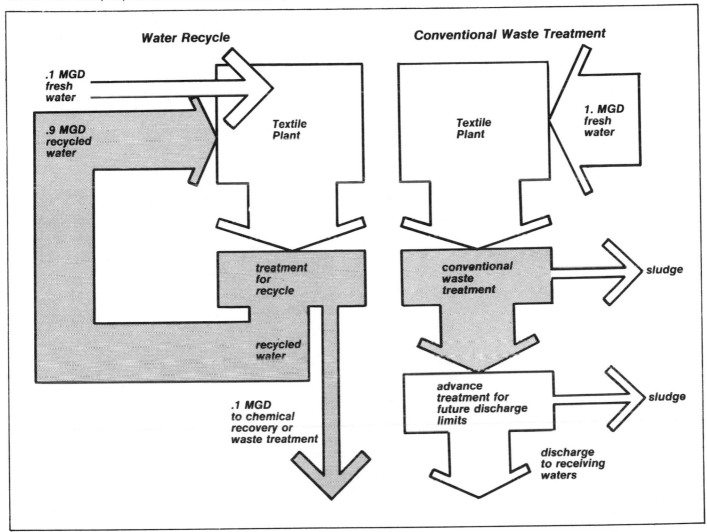

treat it for discharge.

Current wastewater recycling technology does not constitute a completely closed-loop system, but rather is based on maximum water re-use (see Figure 3). Water re-use efficiencies of 90% are attainable using separation technologies. In some instances, it is possible to take a relatively clean wastestream and use it in another process with reduced water purity requirements. Usually, water that is recycled for re-use has a limited amount of contaminants remaining in it. It is not uncommon to add a certain percentage of new water to the recycled stock so as to dilute troublesome impurities such as salts.

Sophisticated recycling technologies such as ultrafiltration tend to be more successful if applied to unit processes rather than to the composite plant effluent. Table 6 indicates that water recycle via ultrafiltration can slash both water and energy consumption by more than 85%.

For the few mills engaged in single process, single shade production, water re-use is a relatively simple matter since incompatible dyes and chemicals are not mixed in the recycle system. Most wet-finishing plants are more complex in that they may include both batch and continuous processing, and handle a variety of shades, dye classes and fibre types.[20]

To ensure that the wastewater re-use process is successful, it is important to take into account the following considerations.[20]

Process effluents most suitable for recycle must be identified. Although some process effluents such as exhaust dye baths may be difficult to treat for recycling, most of the water used in textile processing is for rinsing or washing, and requires relatively little treatment for recycling. In most cases, it is better to keep process waters separate to avoid unnecessary mixing of incompatible chemicals. Furthermore, by recycling process waters individually, it becomes possible to recover heat and process chemicals.

Not all process waters have the same water quality requirements. It may be cost-effective to rehabilitate recycled water only to the purity level required in its re-use function.[20]

■ When the Cannon Mills Company added a dye plant to its facility for continuous dyeing of towels and sheets, a system to segregate dye wastes from the other wastestreams was provided at the time. All the hot wastewaters were collected and channelled through heat recovery units. The heat recovered by these units saved the company $600 a day and delayed the construction of an additional steam plant for five years.

■ The Illinois Water Treatment Company (Rockford, Illinois) designed a recycle system to recover 80% of the water used in a dyehouse.

First, the dyehouse effluent was filtered through diatomaceous earth and then pumped to a continuous counter-flow carbon adsorption unit. Following carbon adsorption, the wastestream was put through an ion exchange system to remove salts added during the dyeing process. A special regeneration technique allows for recovery of sodium sulphate in a 15% concentration for re-use in the dyeing baths.[21]

Based on 1974 figures, the operating cost of the system was 60¢ per 1000 gallons of treated wastewater. A savings of $1.12 per 1000 gallons in recovered heat, water and select chemicals completely offset the operating cost. With a savings of 52¢ per 1000 gallons treated and a capital cost of 75¢ per gallon, the water recycle system pays for itself in five to ten years.[21]

■ Not all water re-use must be in-house. England has investigated the possibility of using the outfall from a domestic sewage plant for process water in industry.[22]

An English textile mill that dyes and finishes blazer cloth uses water directly from a neighbouring tertiary sewage treatment plant. Previously, the mill used 200,000 gallons of water per day at a cost of £200 per day. By using the new, cheaper water supply from the sewage plant, water costs will drop to £40 per day.[4]

■ The Foremost Screen Print Plant of Fieldcrest Mills (Stokesdale, North Carolina) had little choice when it decided to recycle 100% of its wastewater. Well water is limited and no other public water system exists.

Due to the nature of the screen printing processes which include the printing of towels, washcloths, sheets, bedspreads and blankets, thousands of gallons of wastewater, contaminated primarily with solvents and pigments, are produced daily.[23]

By recycling 175,000 gallons of water daily, the Foremost plant countered both its limited water supply and wastewater problems.

After primary treatment in an air flotation unit, the wastewater undergoes alum coagulation to trap pigments and other suspended solids. The dewatered sludge is incinerated and the clarified wastewater is chlorinated before storage in a 100,000 gallon tank.

The Foremost plant has made its processes virtually a closed-loop system, and still remains a highly competitive force in the textile printing industry.

■ Hollytex Carpet Mills Inc. (Southampton, Pennsylvania) was faced with a serious problem when it began to plan an east coast carpet manufacturing plant. Water usage and discharge was estimated at 500,000 gallons per day at the start, with expansion planned for 1 million gallons per day. Since the existing sewer capacity could not handle this volume of water, the municipality would have had to install sewer lines, leaving the carpet firm to pay the bill in the form of a sewer surcharge. In addition, the existing water supply was inadequate.[24]

Because the costs for fresh water and sewer charges were prohibitive, Hollytex chose a more cost-effective alternative — wastewater re-use. Since implementation of the water recycling system in 1960, the carpet company has been recycling 80% of its wastewater and discharging the rest to the

The dual-cylinder apparatus in the centre is Gaston County's ultrafiltration loop used in the recovery of PVC size.

Gaston County Dye Machine Company

sewer.

Impurities from the wastewater are removed on-site with a carbon adsorption unit which traps the dyes and other organic materials. Periodic burning of the carbon in a reactivation furnace destroys the trapped organics and restores the carbon to near virgin activity. Still in operation, the plant is now owned by the Stephen-Leedom Carpet Company.

■ Hoechst AG (Germany) recently has developed a solid liquid separation technology using flocculation and filtration with the aid of gravity. Unlike other solid-liquid separation systems, this one is reputed by the manufacturer to operate under reduced energy requirements.

The system can be used to separate polyester filaments from textile plant wastestreams prior to wastewater recycling. The Hoechst filtration system, known as the TSF process, is in operation at a textile mill in Syntheen, Germany.[25]

5.

Size Re-Use

Every year, millions of pounds of sizing chemicals are generated as a result of desizing operations.

Size chemicals, which are applied to warp yarn to protect them during the weaving operation, represent a valuable material that may be recovered and then re-used in the slashing operation.[26]

Spokesmen for the Canadian textile industry suggest that most Canadian plants tend to use starch as the predominant sizing agent. In the United States, use of polyvinyl alcohol (PVA) and carboxymethyl cellulose (CMC) are becoming increasingly prevalent.

To date, the recovery of starch has remained elusive, largely because starch, a natural polymer of glucose, is very degradable biologically. Because desizing waters are extremely high in BOD, on-site biological treatment to reduce BOD can add significant costs to plant waste treatment. Past American legislation calling for zero discharge of pollutants by

Figure 4
Carbon Tube Within Ultrafiltration Loop

The carbon tube membrane filter provides mechanical separation of the liquid stream according to molecular or particulate size. The membrane consists of an inorganic coating mechanically bonded to a porous carbon tube.

Source: Gaston County Dyeing Machine Company, Stanley, North Carolina.

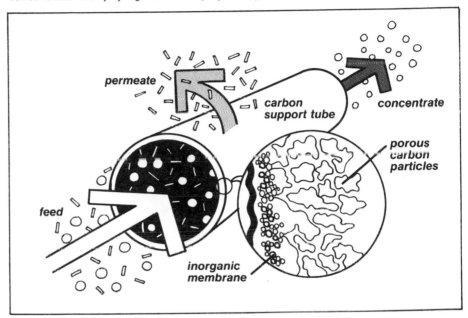

1985 has encouraged some textile plants to switch to synthetic polymers such as PVA. Compared to starch, PVA has a low BOD (5 day), but is also more difficult to degrade biologically. However, this very resistance to degradation has made PVA an attractive candidate for size recycling.

■ The J.P. Stevens Company, one of North America's larger textile companies, has been recovering PVA size for about seven years at its Clemson, South Carolina plant.

At the Clemson plant, the size recovery technique is based on ultrafiltration technology (also known as hyperfiltration). The technique was developed jointly by Clemson University, J.P. Stevens Company, Gaston County Dyeing Machine Company and the Union Carbide Corporation. Gaston County remain the distributors of this ultrafiltration equipment.

"Where chemicals can be re-used in the same process, the basic textiles produced cost less to make," says W.A. Sibley,[27] vice

president of manufacturing at J.P. Stevens. "Also, by re-using chemicals instead of spewing them into the environment, pollution is curbed and the communities where these techniques are employed benefit from the increased environmental protection."

According to Gaston County (Stanley, North Carolina), the heart of their ultrafiltration system is a carbon tube/membrane filter which provides mechanical separation of liquid systems according to molecular or particulate size. The membrane consists of an inorganic coating mechanically bonded to a porous carbon tube (see Figure 4). Both membrane and support tube possess a high degree of resistance to chemical and abrasion degradation, and tolerate wide pH and temperature ranges. Gaston County claims that tubes mounted in systems in operation for over 7 years exhibit no signs of wear nor loss of filtration efficiency. Molecules with diameters as small as 2 nanometers can be filtered out.

Figure 5
Ultrafiltration Loop™

The ultrafiltration loop through which the wastestream is circulated consists of two modules, each with hundreds of carbon tubes joined to form a continuous wall, leaving a more concentrated solution within the loop.

Source: Gaston County Dyeing Machine Company, Stanley, North Carolina.

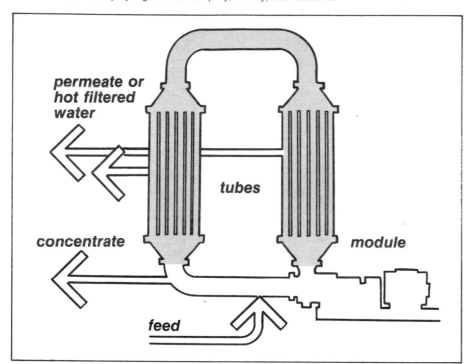

The Ultrafiltration Loop™ through which the wastestream is circulated, consists of two modules, each with about 1000 tubes joined to form a continuous loop. Water passes through the membrane and carbon tube wall, leaving a more concentrated solution within the loop (see Figure 5). A loop may be operated continuously or in a batch operation.

How do the economics stack up? Excellent, especially for the larger user, says Tom Grizzle, engineering product manager of Gaston County. Take a finishing plant that processes 50 million pounds of fabric a year. Assuming that PVA makes up 5% of the total fabric weight coming into the plant, about 2 million pounds of PVA are available for recovery. The capital cost of the recovery system is about $0.75 per pound of PVA recovered.

Operating cost ranges between $0.12 and $0.20 per pound PVA recovered. The real incentive to recover, claims Grizzle, is the

relatively high cost of PVA. At $1 per lb, throwing out 2 million pounds of waste PVA is like throwing $2 million out the window, each year. Grizzle estimates equipment pay-back at about 15 months.[28]

■ Spring Mills (South Carolina) is another large textile plant which uses membrane technology to recover PVA. Its Abcor System (Wilmington, Massachusetts) consists of a spiral-wound module attached to a perforated central permeate pipe. The module is a sandwich of two membrane layers back-to-back with a permeate conducting layer between them[29] (see Figure 17 in Waste Recovery Technologies chapter). PVA recovery from the wastestream is 96%.

■ The Riegel Textile Company (La France, South Carolina) has recently constructed a full-scale ultrafiltration plant for the complete recycle of textile wastewater and the recovery of heat. This facility was constructed under a co-

funding grant from the United States Environmental Protection Agency.[30,31]

Problems Facing the Smaller Operator

Many large textile companies such as J.P. Stevens own both grey (greige) mills and finishing mills, permitting good co-operation between the two plant types for size recovery. A grey mill refers to the plant where sizing is applied to the warp threads and the fabric is woven. At the finishing plant, the protective size is washed off in preparation for bleaching and dyeing.

"We have to make sure that what we are recovering is compatible with what we are putting on," says Clayton Mosley of J.P. Stevens. "If we were to use an assortment of sizes, recovery might become so complicated as to make the operation unfeasible."[32]

The smaller independent finishing plants that process a large variety of fabrics supplied by many grey mills have a more difficult time at present in attempting to recover size.

As one finishing plant executive explains,[29] "We process many different types of fabrics that are sized with different products. Often we are not told what warp size is used, even though we keep hounding the grey mills. This makes life very difficult."

Good co-operation is needed between grey mills and finishing plants to enhance the feasibility of size recovery among smaller facilities. An additional problem facing the small operator is the cost of transporting the recovered size from the desize plant back to the grey mill.

6.
Caustic Soda Recovery

Caustic soda recovery is not new technology. But it is an example of the cost savings and pollution avoidance possible when a company recycles what was previously thrown out.

■ When Canada's largest textile company, Dominion Textiles Inc.,

Abcor's ultrafiltration system used for the recovery of PVA sizing material is shown at the Spring Mills plant in Lancaster, South Carolina.

rebuilt its finishing plant at Valleyfield, Quebec, it was forward-looking enough to put in a caustic soda recovery system. Back in 1969 when the recovery system was installed, caustic recycling was hardly a breakthrough. It had already been a proven technology on the world market, but not in widespread use in Canada. In addition, the Valleyfield plant installed on-site waste treatment for the other process effluents.

Says Morris Davies, manager of plant engineering at Valleyfield, "In those days we were advanced in terms of pollution control."

What spurred the concern with pollution control?

"It's Dominion Textile's continuing attitude to be concerned about the environment. Furthermore, the writing was on the wall —it's just a question of time before we're forced into it. The United States is doing it, why shouldn't we?" says Charles Planzer of Dominion Textile's environmental group.[33]

At the Valleyfield plant, the cloth is scoured and bleached first to result in clean cloth. Then it is mercerized in a separate process by dipping in a 25% solution of caustic soda.

"We are successful in our caustic recovery operation because we keep the used caustic solution relatively clean and easy to recoup," says Davies. "In other plants, the bleaching and mercerizing occur together which makes caustic recovery problematic and uneconomical."

The washwater is also recycled. The dilute caustic-laden wastewater is concentrated back to 25% caustic in a Swenson double-effect vacuum evaporator. The excess heat generated in condensing steam for the evaporator is re-used to preheat the boiler feed water.

When a shortage of caustic hit the world market three years ago, Dominion Textile's caustic suppliers rationed the Valleyfield plant to 110 tons per month. This prompted another round of efficiency improvements, including the addition of more washers.

"There is no doubt that caustic recovery is economical," says Davies. "In just over a decade the cost of caustic has gone up five-fold."

Davies estimates that if his plant did not recycle caustic, they would be hounding their supplier for 300 tons of caustic every month, instead of the usual 90 tons.[34]

7.
Lubricant Recovery

For years, the blue haze surrounding the exhaust stacks of a tenter frame was just part of the textile landscape. This visible form of air pollution has caused the smaller knitting and finishing plants considerable grief.

In the manufacture of polyester fibre, the thread is coated with mineral oil or other substances by fibre producers to function as a lubricant. "Blue haze" is a hydrocarbon emission that results when the various oils on the polyester are subjected to the heat of a tenter. During tentering, the fabric is stretched over a frame in a hot oven so that it dries evenly without shrinking. Considerable heat is applied to the tenter to ensure rapid drying of the fabric.

Various methods may be employed to remove the lubricant before it becomes an air pollution problem. By removing hydrocarbon pollutants from the tenter exhaust, it is possible to use the exhaust stream to preheat cool air coming into the tenter drying oven. Alternately, the lubricant can be washed off the fibre prior to tentering and recovered for re-use or incinerated as an auxiliary heat source.

■ At four J.P. Stevens textile plants, tenter exhaust pollution has been turned into auxiliary heat for the drying process. In-house engineering efforts resulted in the development of the "autocondenser" which cleans up the exhaust stacks and recovers oil released in the process.

The autocondenser is a type of packed-column scrubber (see Figure 6) which has previously not been generally successful on oil mists because the hydrophobic oil droplets are not inclined to enter the falling waterstream. In the autocondenser, the scrubbing fluid is the oil itself.[27]

The hot oil gas stream is passed upward through a column packed with ceramic packing. Cold oil distributed over the top of the packing falls by gravity, countercurrent to the gas stream. As the gas is cooled, a mist is formed and

Figure 6
Tenter Exhaust Pollution Control and Heat Recovery

The autocondenser recovers the oils emitted from the tentering exhaust stacks to control hydrocarbon pollution. Excess heat is recovered and used to heat the plant's process water.
Source: "Recycling Saves," *American Dyestuff Reporter*, October 1979.

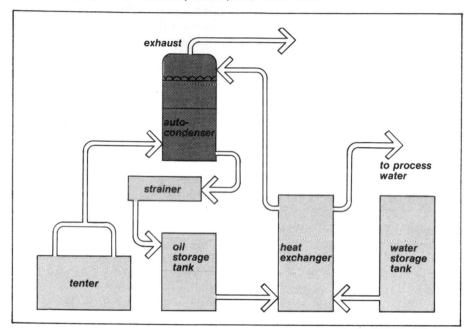

is absorbed by the falling oil. Some of the vapour passes into the oil stream without condensing. The oil is heated as the gas stream is cooled. This oil is then cooled in a heat exchanger and returned to the top of the column.[27]

The oil is collected and re-used to heat the plant and its boilers. Despite a capital investment of $260,000 for the four autocondensers at each of the four plants, company management does not have to look far into the future before the systems are paid off. In just five years, the recovery systems will have paid for themselves while having licked an environmental problem.

■ The Lumberton Dyeing and Finishing Co. (Lumberton, North Carolina) was dismayed to learn from state environment officials that their tenter emissions were above permissible levels. But with the help of FDW Energy Systems (Wallace, North Carolina), an environmental problem was turned into opportunity.

The FDW system is a counterflow heat recovery system applied to the tenters which functions to reduce hydrocarbon emissions as well as shave energy costs. The process begins by cooling the exhaust from the dryer stack from 230 to 190°F, thereby ensuring that most of the hydrocarbon pollutants are precipitated out. This resulted in particulate emissions well below permissible levels.

During fabric drying (heat setting), dryer exhaust is transferred to the entry end to preheat the incoming air (see Figure 7). Drying temperatures must be 350 to 380°F for effective drying. By preheating incoming air with previously exhausted heat, the company was able to pay off the $6000 conversion cost for each tenter within five months through savings on natural gas expenditures.

In addition to recovering heat and pollutants from the dryer exhaust, the company invested in a heat recovery system on the boiler stack to increase boiler efficiency. Sprayed water jets create a scrubbing action that lowers the stack exhaust temperature to 90°F and heats the cooling

water at the same time. The heated cooling water transfers its heat through a heat exchanger to heat up process waters for the plant's dyeing operations. Boiler efficiencies have increased from 75 to 90%, resulting in considerable savings in fuel costs.[35]

■ The Hanes Dye and Finishing Company (Weston-Salem, North Carolina) turned headache into opportunity.

"We more or less had to buy a mist eliminator for our exhaust stacks," claims Mr. Dobson of Hanes. "But we fast realized that the exhaust was too hot to go into the pollution abatement equipment directly. By recycling exhaust cooling water back to the boiler, the plant saved a lot of money."

The chairman of Hanes Dye and Finishing says, "Cleaning up our stacks was expensive, but in the balance, we have actually made money on our pollution control effort."[36]

■ Fiber Industries (Greenville, South Carolina) uses a different method to remove lubricating oil from its textile operations. Mineral oil is first washed from the fabric using water and detergents. Using commercially available membrane separation equipment, the oil and water are separated. The oil is concentrated, homogenized and used as a fuel to burn in the plant's boilers.[37]

■ One American fibre manufacturer recycles its costly proprietary mineral oil using a reverse osmosis membrane system. Previously, the sewered rinse had been causing excess loading on the local sewage treatment plant. Installation of an Osmo™ spiral-wound membrane module increased the concentration of soluble oil rinsewaters containing 0.1% oil to a level of 20% oil. The permeate subsequently contained such a low concentration of oil that it was suitable for recycle in the rinsing process. The concentrated oil fraction is suitable for re-use as a fibre lubricant in the company's fibre processing operations. According to Osmonics Inc. (Hopkins, Minnesota), the reduction in processing costs due to the oil recovery system resulted in a six-month pay-back on the equipment.[38]

Figure 7
Heat Recovery System on Tenter Exhaust

The heat recovery system is used to lower the temperature of the tenter exhaust from 230 to 190°F. The hydrocarbons in the cooled exhaust steam precipitate out and are easy to remove. In addition, a heat recovery system is applied to the boiler stack, lowering the exhaust temperature to 90°F and reducing total fuel costs.

Source: "Commission Finisher Racks Up Big Energy Savings," *Textile Industries,* November 1981.

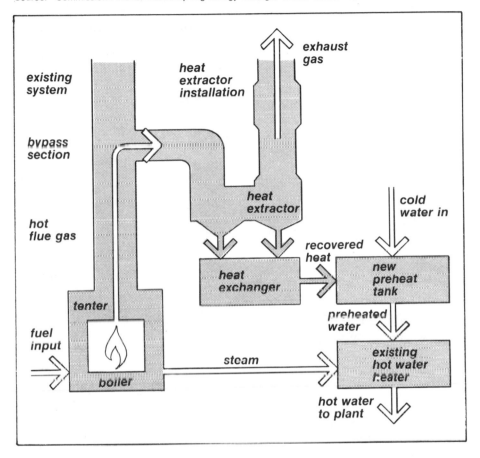

8.
More Efficient Dye Application

Fueled by rising costs and the threat of dwindling energy supplies and increased pollution control requirements, designers, dyeing specialists and equipment manufacturers are continuously improving dyeing efficiency. The recent accomplishments are good news to the industry, especially to the smaller dyeing plant. Two research thrusts are evident: taking the water out of dyeing, and substituting less hazardous dyes and dye carriers.

Although dry dyeing is not yet a commercial success, much progress has been made in significantly reducing water demands and wastewater generation in dye application. These improvements have permitted companies to cut energy, water and labour bills, and still increase dyeing outputs. In fact, it has put some companies' red ink into the black.

Two basic methods used in the colouring process are continuous (pad-fix) and batch (exhaust) dyeing. Continuous dyeing is used for long runs of a given fabric colour. Continuous processes tend to be more efficient than batch processes because of their continuous nature and the use of relatively small volumes of dye liquor that need to be wasted at the end of a run.

Batch processes, on the other hand, are generally very inefficient in their use of chemicals, water and energy. They also generate large volumes of wastewater. Many of the smaller dye establishments do custom work. Batch dyeing is generally the only economical method for small runs with many colour changes.

Many different types of batch dyeing processes are in use, including beck dyeing, jet dyeing, jig dyeing, package dyeing and beam dyeing.

In conventional batch dyeing, fabric is added to water in the dye beck (dye vessel). Auxiliary chemicals and dyes are added. The dye bath is heated, frequently to 200°F, until dyeing is completed. The dyebath is discharged to the sewer and the fabric is rinsed to remove incompletely fixed dye.

Atmospheric Beck Dyeing

In North America, the atmospheric beck remains the dominant machine used in dyeing. With modernization, however, most batch operators are opting for more efficient systems such as jet dyeing and low-liquor dyeing. One way of enhancing dyeing efficiency and cost-effectiveness is by reducing the dye-liquor-to-cloth ratio. Atmospheric beck liquor-to-cloth ratios of 20:1 are giving way to 5:1 ratios in new low-liquor dye machines.

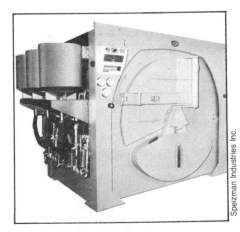

This Pellerin-Milnor 450-pound dyeing-extracting machine reduces chemical use by up to 60% and dyestuff use by up to 25% over conventional equipment.

Table 7

Cost Comparison of Low-Liquor Dyeing versus Atmospheric Beck at Spinners Processing

	Low-Liquor Dye Machine	Atmospheric Beck Dye Machine
Cycle load (lb)	1,600	1,100
Cycle time (hrs)	7	14
Pounds/week	22,000	7,600
Costs/pound (cents)		
Direct labour	1.36¢	3.95¢
Water	1.05	4.53
Steam	1.00	4.08
Electricity	0.42	0.21
Chemicals	2.00	9.50
Total	5.84¢	22.27¢
Weekly Costs per 22,000 pounds of fabric (dollars)	$1,300	$4,900

Source: "Low Liquor Dyeing Pays Big Dividends." *Textile World*, April 1980.

Difficulties in dyeing newer textured polyester doubleknits promoted an increase in the use of pressure becks.[4] Polyester fibres have a poor affinity for dyes, and hence generally require dye carriers to attach dye to the fibre. Since increased pressures allow the use of few or no carriers, the pressure beck is advantageous in reducing the strength of the wastewater.

■ Specialty Dyers (Concord, North Carolina) have beefed up the conventional beck design into a "superbeck". It handles double the capacity of knit goods at a time, and still saves energy and chemicals.[39]

At Specialty Dyes, their specialty is velour and terry fabrics, both of which have greater volume and area requirements than woven goods.

By increasing dye-liquor circulation, the superbeck can handle 100 pieces of goods instead of the usual 50, and still use the same amount of water as a conventional system. According to Specialty, dyeing temperatures are reached more quickly and heat throughout the machine is more even.[39] And quality hasn't dropped a notch.

Jet Dyeing

Jet dyeing is an advancement over beck dyeing because of its increasing dye efficiency, reduced water consumption and less polluting wastestream.

■ It has been four years since Gaston County (Stanley, North Carolina) came out with its low liquor Aqualuft™ dye machine. Although Gaston County has outfitted dyers for years with a jet dyeing machine based on a dye liquor-to-cloth ratio of 10:1, a 50% improvement over conventional becks, the new Aqualuft™ machine outdoes them all with its 5:1 liquor-to-cloth ratio.[40]

"Low-liquor dyeing is the way to go because it gets more dye onto the material and less out with the wastewater," says Edwin Crisp of sales engineering, Gaston County. "The energy crunch and environmental requirements are making low-liquor dyeing the preferred new technology of the batch-type operations."[41]

■ For Spinners Processing Company (Spindale, North Carolina), the first plant to install low-liquor dyeing, the Aqualuft™ system was found to pay big dividends.

"This machine represents one of the most significant energy breakthroughs in all of dyeing," says plant manager Clyde Henson.[42] "Not only is there a four-fold reduction in hot water requirements as compared to beck dyeing, but also a four-fold saving in steam needs."

More than 20,000 pounds of T-shirts are dyed in the Aqualuft™ machine each week, a big improvement in productivity over the atmospheric beck. Although the pioneer installation of the low-liquor dyeing system seemed chancey in 1977, Spinners now takes comfort in knowing that it is saving $3600 a week on dyeing costs (see Table 7).

■ Low-liquor dyeing has come to Canada. Harvey Woods (Woodstock, Ontario) uses an Aqualuft™ low-liquor dye machine to assist in the dyeing of 45,000 pounds of fabric a week.

"The minute you reduce the liquor ratio, the less effluent you have to deal with," says Jerry Maruschak of Harvey Woods. "Therefore exhausting most of the dye onto the fabric rather than disposing it into a sewer is the route to go from a pollution prevention point of view."

■ The Spencer Dytex machine, represented by Imtex Machinery Ltd. (Montreal, Quebec) is a combined dyeing/centrifuging machine capable of carrying out scouring, bleaching, milling and dyeing operations using low-liquor ratios and short process cycles. According to the manufacturer, the Dytex, which is manufactured in a range of sizes, cuts water consumption by 80%, chemical usage by 50% and dyeing time by 50%.[43]

As with most "new" techniques, the principles of present day jet dyeing have their roots in the past. Although the commercial application of jet dyeing may be a newcomer to the textile scene, the potential use of continuous jets of

Figure 8
The Millitron Process

Source: "Jet-Impregnation Methods for Dyeing and Printing Carpet Yarns and Carpet Goods," *Canadian Textile Journal,* April 1978.

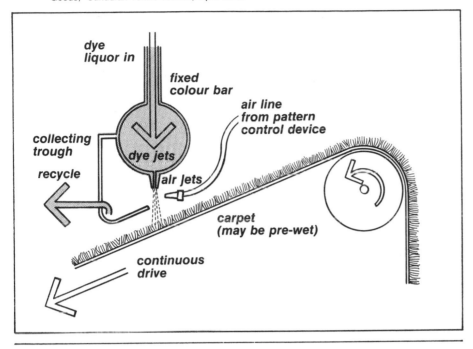

Figure 9
The OPI Process

Source: "Jet-Impregnation Methods for Dyeing and Printing Carpet Yarns and Carpet Piece Goods," *Canadian Textile Journal,* April 1978.

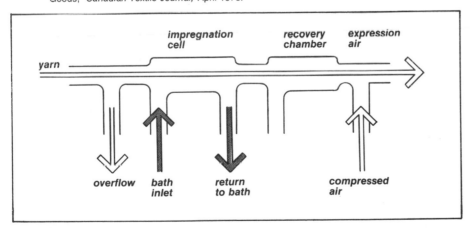

dye liquor onto moving fabric beneath the jets has been embodied in a number of patents throughout the 20th century.[44] New cost-cutting and pollution constraints have accelerated the refinement of jet dyeing principles.

■ Jet printing colour carpets is one commercial success of high-efficiency, low-pollution colour application. The Millitron Machine (Milliken & Company, New York, New York) uses continuous dye streams which are deflected by air jets.[44] A programmed magnetic disc controls the jets of dye liquor applied in spurts from individually controlled outlets, permitting colour to be applied in a predetermined pattern.

The dye liquor is kept in constant circulation by a pump. In the "no-print" position, the jet of dye is deflected by the jet of compressed air into a gutter and recycled[44], thereby significantly reducing waste pigment (see Figure 8).

■ Another newcomer to yarns and piece good dyeing is the OPI Process under license by Callebaut de Blicquy (France). The novelty of the process concerns the use of compressed air cells to impregnate and squeeze the yarn uniformly prior to dye being fixed by steaming[44] (see Figure 9).

Efficient dyeing of carpet fibre in yarn form is of prime interest to the woven carpet trade because it overcomes the costly hank winding-scouring-dyeing-rewind process.[44]

■ Another approach to dyeing comes from France. The process is based on the transfer of a mist of dye to fabric by electrostatic attraction. By maximizing the transfer of dye, polluting dye effluents are greatly reduced.[44]

Bump-and-Run

Management personnel who lament the high cost of pollution control equipment and modern machinery sometimes fail to recognize the savings possible through simple, low-capital modifications of existing processes. A case in point is bump-and-run.

Bump-and-run is the brainchild of Dr. Fred Cook (Georgia Tech. School of Textile Engineering) and Jack Toon (Piedmont Chemicals). Its discovery was prompted by the knowledge that the typical carpet beck-dyeing operation loses 45 to 60% of its total energy consumption through the exhaust stack. Much of the steam during conventional dyeing blows directly through the dye bath near the boil without releasing its heat.[45]

With the bump-and-run modification, the dye bath is "bumped" to the boil in the usual manner, however, after five minutes, steam injection is terminated and the dampers and openings are closed. The beck, which now resembles a closed kettle with no energy input, would drift or "run" during the remainder of the hold cycle.[46]

■ The first in-plant demonstration of bump-and-run at Salem

Carpet Mills (Chickamauga, Georgia) was a big success. Steam consumption dropped by 38% without any loss in dye quality. Based on the trial runs, implementation of the bump-and-run modification on the plant's 14 production becks is estimated to save the company a whopping $250,000 a year. The only capital investment required to incorporate the new procedure was a scant $50 each for a set of auxiliary timers on the 14 becks.[46]

9.
Dye Bath Recycling

At present, dye bath recycling is best suited for those operations that use a limited number of colours or that have large runs of a particular colour. Future developments in the area of dye bath recycling may see wider application of this environmentally sensitive technology.

For the smaller and medium-sized operator, it is unlikely that dye bath recycling will be possible for all colours dyed on the premises. However, the prudent operator may be able to schedule and sequence his jobs so that similar colours can be dyed in succession, enhancing the feasibility of recycling select dye baths.

Dye Bath Reconstitution

Reconstitution of dye baths by the textile industry resembles the reconstitution of processing solutions in the photofinishing industry. As the strength of the process bath diminishes, fresh chemicals are added to replenish the solution. The capacity for re-use is finite. Eventually the build-up of contaminants in the process solutions will interfere with the quality of the dyeing operation. Reconstitution of dye baths is a major step forward in minimizing dyehouse pollution because the volume of pollutants generated is severely curtailed compared to conventional dyeing in which dye baths are used once, then discarded.[47]

■ When the Adams-Millis Hosiery

Table 8
Materials and Energy Reduction in Dye Bath Re-use

	Conventional Dyeing	Re-Use Dyeing	Reduction
Energy (pounds steam per pound fibre dyed)	2.18	0.94	57%
Water (gallons per pound fibre)	4.08	2.31	43%
Chemicals (pounds per pound fibre)	0.0731	0.0475	35%
Dyes (pounds per pound fibre)	0.0058	0.0047	19%
Cost (cents per pound fibre)	5.25¢	3.28¢	37%

Source: Tincher, W.C. *In-Plant Demonstration of Dyebath Re-Use Applied to Nylon,* February 1979.

Company (High Point, North Carolina) decided to stop pulling the plug on their exhausted dye baths, they were not sure what to expect. However, since participating in an in-plant demonstration of dye bath re-use technology, the cost of energy and materials dropped one-third in their hosiery batch-dyeing operations.

At Adams-Millis, the spent dye bath is analyzed for the amount of remaining dye and chemicals, reconstituted to the desired strength, and re-used for subsequent redyeings. Dye bath analysis and reconstitution is computer assisted.

Although only one dye colour was involved in the re-use project, five different shades and two fibre types were used in the dye series, necessitating reconstitution to several different specifications. Even though both fibre types and light and dark shades were mixed indiscriminately in the run, no problems were encountered in dyeing a light shade following a dark shade.[48]

By reconstituting and re-using

dye baths an average of 15 times before discharge, significant reductions in dye (19%), chemical (35%), water (43%) and energy requirements were achieved (see Table 8).

According to Wayne Tincher of Textiles Engineering, Georgia Institute of Technology, "The Adams-Millis runs clearly demonstrate that dye recycling can be incorporated in a commercial operation with no loss in quality or productivity, with substantial savings in materials and energy costs, and at a relatively low capital cost."[48]

■ Reconstitution and re-use of dye baths have been extended to fabric and carpet dyeing using jet dyeing machines. Scientists from the Textile Engineering Department of the Georgia Institute of Technology have completed a pilot project in dye bath re-use for jet dyeing. Nomex Type™ 455 fabric was selected because large quantities of costly auxiliary chemicals are required to dye material, thereby giving a significant economic advantage for the re-use procedure.

The plant at which the demonstration was conducted dyes an average of 875 cycles per year on the jet machine. Approximately 30% of the cycles are black, 40% are yellow and 20% are blue. About 10% of the cycles are other miscellaneous shades.[49]

Select dye baths were reconstituted and re-used an average of ten times before discharge. Annual savings, expected to exceed $110,000 per year, far exceed the capital equipment costs of $15,000 for the analytical system, pumping system and holding tank.[49]

Savings are even greater when one takes into account reduced wastewater disposal costs. Conventional dyeing produced over 500,000 gallons of spent dye liquor per year. Recycling spent dye baths can shrink this volume to 140,000 gallons per year, a reduction of 72% in the quantity of potentially toxic waste entering the treatment plant.[49]

Closed-Cycle Dyeing

Closed-cycle dyeing, the ultimate in dye bath recycling, is still in the pilot stage. Because both dye baths and rinsewaters are re-used, wastewater effluents are virtually eliminated.

■ La France Industries (La France, South Carolina), in co-operation with the United States government, is installing a full-scale ultrafiltration system to its production range with the objective of demonstrating the practicality of closed-cycle dyeing. The continuous range at La France is used for dyeing, bleaching and scouring a variety of velour fabrics.

About 85% of the dyes are exhausted on the fabric. The remaining dye and most of the auxiliary components are removed by the washing process.

Ultrafiltration technology is used to concentrate the dye solution for re-use, and recycle rinsewaters for re-use. Residual dye liquor and ultrafiltration concentrates are reconstituted by adding the proper amounts of new dyes and auxiliary components' using a computer-assisted colour matching process.

All rinsewater and equipment clean-out wastewater during colour change is collected for recycle. These rinsewaters are usually highly coloured before entering the ultrafiltration unit. At least 97% of the dyes must be removed to avoid possible staining of new fabric during re-use.[50]

Despite a hefty capital cost of $400,000 in 1981 and an estimated annual operating cost of $31,500, the return on the investment is expected to be excellent. Total annual savings from the recycle project are pegged at $560,000 (see Table 9).

Craig Brandon, president of Carre Inc. (Seneca, North Carolina) and consultant to the La France project, emphasizes the importance of pollution prevention by keeping wastestreams separate. "One gets the best chance to recover chemicals if one doesn't mix in other wastestreams which will contaminate the stream that you are trying to recover a chemical from. The same holds for energy recovery. One gets the best chance to recover heat if one integrates a hot water wastestream back into the process, rather than by mixing it with another cold wastewater stream," says Brandon. "And with toxics, usually only one or two streams contain toxics. These require special handling which is usually made easier if the wastestream is small. There is no advantage to contaminating relatively innocuous wastestreams with toxic wastestreams."[51]

Indigo Recycling

With indigo prices hovering at the $10-per-pound mark, some indigo dyers are fast investing in ultrafiltration equipment to recover residual dye in the waste rinsewater. During application, 90% of the indigo is retained on the garment, with 10% potentially exiting down the sewer.

■ Cone Mills (Greensboro, North Carolina) and the Dan River Textile Company (Greenville, South Carolina) are two satisfied customers of indigo recovery systems. No recovery system is known to exist in Canada.

Installation of an indigo recovery system requires redesign of the rinse boxes to a counter-current rinse system. In doing so, the amount of water required in rinsing drops by 80% and results in an adequately concentrated feed for the ultrafiltration unit.

The porous membrane within the unit separates molecules on the basis of molecular size and shape. The size of the pores within the membrane is extremely small. According to Dorr Oliver (Stamford, Connecticut), manufacturers of an indigo recovery system, stretching the membrane from Miami to San Francisco would yield holes large enough to permit passage of a basketball. Indigo recovery is based on the fact that oxidized indigo will not pass through the membrane while water and most non-indigo solids will pass through the membrane.[52]

Table 9
Estimated Annual Savings Due to Recycle Project at La France Industries

Savings from reduced water use	$ 35,500
Savings from reduced energy use	254,000
Savings from reduced dye use	180,000
Savings from reduced auxiliary chemicals use	91,000
TOTAL ANNUAL SAVINGS	$560,000

Source: Brandon, C.A. et al. *Closed Cycle Textile Dyeing,* 1981.

Installation of Dorr-Oliver's ultrafiltration system which is used to recycle indigo dyebaths.

Exhausted dyebaths collect in feed tanks prior to ultrafiltration.

Fred Leonard of membrane marketing for Dorr Oliver, lists 1981 prices for the ultrafiltration unit at $300,000 (U.S.). Even so, based on a counter-current rinse flow of 30 gallons per minute and an indigo concentration of 800 ppm, the value of dye recovered from wastewaters is calculated to be $800,000. Annual operating costs are around $65,000.[52]

Says Leonard, "Industry tends not to spend money on pollution abatement unless to comply with some environmental regulation, or if there is money to be made in materials recovery. That's a fact of life." Dorr Oliver has no control over the former but certainly addresses the latter.

Greater commercialization of membrane separation systems may well see more businesses opting for materials recycling systems that promise both better environmental protection and reduced operating costs.

10.
Textile Waste Recycling

The recycling of textile waste has been an established practice for many years throughout the world. In the 1800s, England was well known for its "shoddy trade" in which rags were hand sorted and graded for re-use as coarse cloth suitable for heavy weather and work garments, and to pro-

duce flock fillings for saddlery and upholstery.[53]

In Canada, less than a decade ago, many garment manufacturers could expect to receive 5¢ per pound of waste cuttings from scrap dealers and fibre recycling companies.[54] Nowadays, many garment manufacturers are fortunate if they can give their scraps away.

The industry trend to synthetics, multicolours, permanent press and other special treatments, together with rising labour and transportation costs, has created technical and economic barriers to the use of cuttings from the garment and carpet trade.[54] Most manufacturers today resort to few options other than to dispose textile wastes at a landfill site.

Some recycling of pure cotton and wool scraps still exists in Canada, however, the increase in fabric blends, in which synthetics are mixed in with natural fibres, has made textile waste reprocessing both technically difficult and financially unattractive.

It is possible to reprocess thermoplastic waste fibres such as nylon, polyester and polypropylene by a melt process into chip and pellet form for injection moulding and extrusion. It is more difficult to regenerate this secondary material into fibre, except as a small proportion in a predominantly virgin polymer melt.

Sources of textile waste include the following:[53]

Man-Made Fibre Manufacture

Wastes are generated at the start-up and shut-down stages; during extrusion or spinning; and at the drawing, texturizing and quality control stages. At the manufacture stage, fibre wastes are easily identifiable by type and are generally most easy to recycle. Much of this waste may be reprocessed on the premises for re-use or taken to an outside recycler. Sub-standard filament fibre may be used directly in staple form to make non-woven textiles.

Textile Manufacture

Wastes result in the conversion of fibre into yarns, yarns into fabrics, and fabrics into finished products. Sources of waste include the manufacture of garments, home furnishings and industrial textiles such as carpets.

Because fabric waste from the garment and other industries tends to be heterogeneous, consisting of a variety of colours and fabric types, recycling into products of good commercial value is difficult and costly. Emerging technologies applicable to the recovery of heterogeneous wastes promise to change this.

Post-Consumer Waste

Post-consumer waste refers to textiles that have served a useful life. Wastes are generated by domestic, commercial, industrial and military sources, including uniforms, overalls and bedding. Due to the diverse textile types and sources of post-consumer waste, and to the small volumes of specific waste types, these wastes are generally the least economical to recover.

For those textile wastes that are recycled, new uses include cleaning cloths, towels, blankets, mattresses, toy and upholstery fillings and carpet yarns[55] (see Table 10). Figure 10 presents a flow chart of the movement of textile wastes from the generators to end-users.

It would be unfair to suggest that textile waste recycling has fallen by the wayside. Textile waste recycling is still a viable industry in Canada, however, the quantities of wastes, such as gar-

ment scraps, that are landfilled far surpasses what is recycled.

Based on a 1977 survey of 93 garment manufacturers by the Ontario Ministry of Industry and Tourism, more than 65% of the textile scraps generated were landfilled and the remainder were sold to scrap dealers. The 35% of the textile wastestream sold to dealers netted the companies generating them almost $2 million, whereas disposal costs for the non-recycled wastes cost $75,000. Although the textile industry faces some real barriers in the recycling of its waste, it is likely that even given current constraints, the potential to recycle textile wastes is greater than currently achieved. In the face of increasing disposal costs and materials prices, any textile manufacturer would do well to aggressively seek new markets for his wastes.

■ A major barrier in recycling waste blends containing natural and synthetic materials is that dye affinities vary for different materials. Contamination of wool fabric with as little as 1% polyester or acrylic fibres can cause serious problems in dyeing. Research in Japan (Toyobo) has produced polyester fibre that can be dyed in a one-dye bath process with wool using acid dyestuffs.[54] Introduction of such fibres into widespread commercial use would significantly enhance the economic feasibility of recycling wool-synthetic blends.

■ Kurt Salmon Associates (At-

lanta, Georgia) consult the apparel industry on improving textile utilization through low-capital-cost measures such as better planning and pattern layout. According to this company, about 17% of the fabric bolt ends up in the scrap bag. Companies which hire an expert to upgrade the utilization of textiles in the garment plant can add an additional 3 to 6% on their gross earnings.[56]

■ The Textiles and Clothing Technology Centre (Mississauga, Ontario) offers a computer-aided pattern grading and marker-making service to improve fabric utilization in the apparel industry. The fee-for-service operation is geared to assist the smaller apparel companies across Canada which currently use a manual process in grading and marking.

■ Industry observers speculate that in a carpet manufacturing plant, the total amount of scrap waste can reach 12%.[57] Syntex Chemie (Frankfurt, Germany) are actively engaging in carpet recycling research. Patents are currently available for a continuous reclamation process system known as the Lesti process. The reclaimed product has a variety of applications, particularly in the construction industry.

New uses of reclaimed waste carpet scraps include:[58]
• Insulating sheet for sound-proofing and thermal insulation.
• Prefabricated structural elements in housing and furniture.

Table 10

Some End-Uses for Reclaimed Man-Made Fibre Wastes

Synthetics

Impact polymer
Clothing: blended fibres for skirts, coats, suitings, etc.
Waddings: anorak, sleeping bag fillings
Carpet yarns
Non-wovens: felts, blankets, carpet tiles
Cleaning cloths
Mattress and soft toy fillings
Underfelt, linoleum, roofing felts

Cellulosics

Clothing: blended fibres
Upholstery and curtain fabrics
Flannelette sheets
Towels
Surgical: sanitary pads, cotton wool
Blankets
Insulation felts
Waddings: general fillings
Cleaning cloths, dishcloths
Underfelt, linoleum, roofing felts.

Source: "Textile Reclamation in Britain: Some Recent Impacts on a Traditional Industry." *Conservation and Recyling,* 1979.

Figure 10
Textile Waste Generators and End-Users

Source: "Recycling Man-Made Fibers," *Textile Industries,* December 1972.

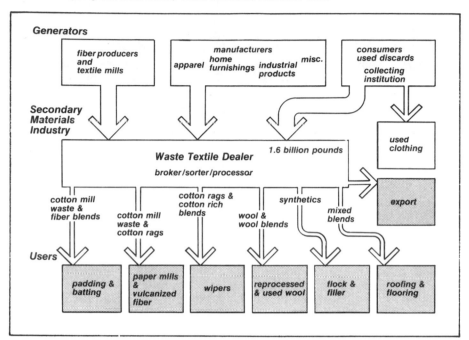

- Foundation slabs in road building.
- Covers for high-noise-level machinery.
- Building blocks, doors and partitions.
- Roofing material.
- Packing materials and pallet plates.

■ Czechoslovakia is active in converting waste textile material into wipers and other re-usable materials. Based on non-woven stitch-knitting technology, the technique mechanically interlocks recycled textile fibres into a non-woven fabric. The yarn used for the stitch-knitting makes up 3 to 35% of the total weight of the stitch-knitted fabric.

The advantage of this technique is that the textile production process is significantly shortened and hence economically attractive. When using man-made filament fibres in the warp, no spinning is necessary. By utilizing commercially available Arachne equipment, textile wastes can be transformed into a wide range of products including:[59]

- Industrial cloths such as packing cloths, insulating fabrics, filtering cloths and cleaning wipers.
- Home furnishings such as blankets, table cloths and backings for lineoleum and carpets.
- Outer wear such as coats, dresses and loungewear.
- Footwear and linings for the shoe industry.
- Bandages and other sanitary products.

The potential to recycle textile wastes is enormous. Difficulties in achieving this potential hinge largely on economic barriers. The current escalation in landfill charges and material costs may slowly steer the textile industry along a path of maximum recycling. Waste textile recycling will not move into high gear until the cost of landfilling wastes surpasses the cost of reclamation.

Conclusion

The challenges facing the textile industry in Canada are great. Competition from outside markets, where labour costs are low, threaten the survival of the textile manufacturing sector.

In the past, the textile industry, like many other industries, perceived pollution control expenditures to be an economic drain which further inflated product costs and hampered competition with cheap foreign imports.

As disposal and material costs continue to escalate, however, the economics of pollution control are beginning to favour pollution avoidance strategies and materials recovery rather than the conventional technologies that treat pollution once it has been generated.

Technological innovations in the 1970s are resulting in an increasing array of commercially available equipment and processes that promise to operate more efficiently, more cheaply and with less waste than previous systems. By eliminating unnecessary waste, both the environment and the company profit.

In many instances, even the small textile plant can profit through pollution prevention by relatively simple housekeeping and low-capital-cost process changes. Even greater savings are possible by installing more efficient, less polluting equipment. Although capital costs of such equipment may be substantial, buying new equipment is an investment that pays for itself in a few years through reduced disposal costs or material recovery benefits.

Large companies are usually in a better position economically to assimilate the capital costs of more efficient process machines and recovery equipment. Many of the large companies have technical experts permanently on staff to specifically address pollution control needs and possibilities.

The small textile plant tends to be less fortunate. Financial and technical resources are scarce. Although more efficient machines and recovery equipment may be commercially available for even the small operator, relatively large capital costs and the high cost of borrowing money make modernization more difficult to achieve.

The small operator in particular can benefit substantially from greater access to technical and financial resources to assist in its pollution prevention activities. Economic incentives such as well-placed tax breaks for expenditures on more efficient machinery and materials recycling equipment can do much to steer the textile industry along a path of pollution avoidance and recovery, rather than along the current path of treating pollution after the fact.

FOR FURTHER INFORMATION

Associations

Contact the following trade associations for additional information on pollution control technologies and equipment. These trade associations can assist you directly, or point you in the right direction for more information on commercially available recycling equipment, technology transfer programmes, technical experts in the field, existing tax breaks and other economic incentives, and upcoming regulations.

Encourage those associations which rank pollution control low on their priority list to direct more attention to pollution prevention. Preventing pollution can benefit both businesses and the environment.

The following list identifies primarily national associations in Canada and the United States. It is not uncommon for Canadian companies to belong to American associations. Contact the national associations and ask if a local chapter is in operation near your business.

Textiles & Clothing
Technology Centre,
2395 Speakman Drive,
Mississauga, Ontario.
L5K 1B3
(416) 822-4111

Canadian Textiles Institute,
Suite 1002,
1080 Beaver Hall Hill,
Montreal, Quebec.
H2Z 1T6
(514) 866-2081

Canadian Allied Textile
Trades Association,
135 Liberty St. West,
Toronto, Ontario.
M6K 1A7
(416) 535-2137

American Association for
Textile Technology,
1040 Avenue of the Americas,
New York, New York.
10018
(212) 354-5188

American Association of Textile
Chemists and Colorists,
Box 12215,
Research Triangle Park,
North Carolina.
27709
(919) 549-8141

Institute of Textile Technology,
P.O. Box 391,
Charlottesville, Virginia.
22902
(804) 296-5511

Textile Research Institute,
P.O. Box 625,
Princeton, New Jersey.
08540
(609) 924-3150

Northern Textile Association,
211 Congress Street,
Boston, Massachusetts.
02110
(617) 542-8220

Carpet and Rug Institute,
P.O. Box 2048,
Dalton, Georgia.
30720
(404) 278-3176

Journals

Numerous excellent publications are currently available in both Canada and the United States. The journals listed below frequently contain articles that relate to improving process efficiency, energy and water conservation, and waste recovery. These journals also carry an assortment of advertisements by manufacturers of recycling and other pollution abatement equipment.

CANADIAN TEXTILE JOURNAL,
Canadian Textile Journal
Publishing Co. Ltd.,
4920 de Maisonneuve Blvd. West,
Suite 307,
Montreal, Quebec.
H3Z 1N1

TEXTILE INDUSTRIES,
W.R.C. Smith Publishing Co.,
1760 Peachtree Road, N.W.,
Atlanta, Georgia.
30357

TEXTILE CHEMIST AND
COLORIST,
American Association of Textile
Chemists and Colorists,
Box 12215,
Research Triangle Park,
North Carolina.
27709

TEXTILE WORLD,
McGraw-Hill Inc.,
1221 Avenue of the Americas,
New York, New York.
10020

TEXTILE RESEARCH JOURNAL,
Textile Research Institute,
Box 625,
Princeton, New Jersey.
08540

TEXTILE PROGRESS,
Textile Institute,
10 Blackfriars Street,
Manchester, England.
M35 DR

INTERNATIONAL DYER, TEXTILE
PRINTER,
BLEACHER AND FINISHER,
Textile Business Press Ltd.,
91 Kirkgate,
Bradford, West Yorkshire,
England.
BD1 1TB

References

1. Department of Industry, Trade and Commerce (Canada). *A Report by the Sector Task Force on the Canadian Textile Industry.* 1976.

2. Porter, J. *et al.* "Water Uses and Wastes in the Textile Industry." *Environmental Science and Technology,* January 1972.

3. Porter, J. and Sargent, N. "Waste Treatment Versus Waste Recovery." *Textile Chemist and Colorist,* November 1977.

4. U.S. Environmental Protection Agency. *Environmental Pollution Control in the Textile Processing Industry.* Environmental Research Information Center, October 1978.

5. U.S. Environmental Protection Agency. *Potentially Toxic and Hazardous Substances in the Industrial Organic Chemicals and Organic Dyes and Pigments Industries.* Industrial Environmental Research Laboratory, March 1980.

6. Cook, F. "Textiles May Be Running Out of Acceptable Dye Bases." *Textile World,* November 1980.

7. Jenkins, Catherine. "Textile Dyes are Potential Hazards." *Journal of Environmental Health,* March/April 1978.

8. National Institute for Occupational Safety and Health. *Health Hazard Alert: Benzidine, O-Tolidine and O-Dianisidine Based Dyes.* U.S. Department of Health and Human Services, December 1980.

9. Suchecki, Stanley. "Troubleshooting in the Dyehouse." *Textile Industries,* December 1977.

10. Suchecki, Stanley. "Energy Conservation: Opportunities Still Unlimited." *Textile Industries,* October 1977.

11. Suchecki, Stanley, "Process Control: Where Are We Now?" *Textile Industries,* March 1981.

12. Turner, Robert. "Dyehouse Control: The Next Step Forward." *Textile Chemist and Colorist,* May 1981.

13. Collins, D. "Automation: Enter the Microprocessor." *Textile Industries,* April 1977.

14. "Preventative Maintenance Package." *Canadian Textile Journal,* November 1980.

15. "Technology: Dyehouse Control Systems." *Textile Industries,* November 1981.

16. "Progress Report on Process Control." *Textile Industries,* July 1972.

17. Royston, Michael. *Pollution Prevention Pays.* Oxford, England: Pergamon Press, 1979.

18. Brandon, C.A. and Porter, J.J. *Textile Technology Ecology Interface.* Presented at AATCC Environmental Symposium, Charlotte, North Carolina, May 1975.

19. Durig, Gottfried. "Environmental Protection in the Textile Industry." *American Dyestuff Reporter,* February 1981.

20. Goodman, G. and Porter, J. "Water Quality Requirements for Re-Use in Textile Dyeing Processes." *American Dyestuff Reporter,* October 1980.

21. Burke, D. and Palesh, C. "Wastewater Recycle for Dyehouses." *American Dyestuff Reporter,* October 1974.

22. Harker, R.P. "Recycling Sewage Water for Scouring and Dyeing." *American Dyestuff Reporter,* January 1980.

23. "Anti-Pollution Measures at Fieldcrest Mills." *American Dyestuff Reporter,* October 1979.

24. U.S. Environmental Protection Agency. *Wastewater Treatment Systems: Upgrading Textile Operations to Reduce Pollution.* U.S.E.P.A. Technology Transfer, October 1974.

25. "A New Textile Process for Solid-Liquid Separation." *Textile Industries,* July 1980.

26. Porter, J. and Black, D. "Water, Energy and Chemical Recovery from Desizing." *American Dyestuff Reporter,* December 1979.

27. Sibley, W.A., Jr. "Recycling Saves." *American Dyestuff Reporter,* October 1979.

28. Grizzle, T. Gaston County Dye Machine Company, Stanley, North Carolina. Personal communication, July 1981.

29. Suchecki, Stanley. "Energy Savings Through Warp Size Recovery." *Textile Industries,* October 1978.

30. Samfield, M. Consultant, Durham, North Carolina. Personal communication, May 1981.

31. Brandon, C. and Samfield, M. *Application of High-Temperature Hyperfiltration to Unit Textile Processes for Direct Recycle.* Industrial Environmental Research Laboratory, U.S. Environmental Protection Agency, 1978.

32. Clayton, Mosley. J.P. Stevens Company, Clemson, South Carolina. Personal communication, August 1981.

33. Planzer, C. Dominion Textiles, Montreal, Quebec. Personal communication, August 1981.

34. Davies, Morris. Dominion Textiles, Valleyfield, Quebec. Personal communication, August 1981.

35. Bowen, D.A. "Commission Finisher Racks Up Big Energy Savings." *Textile Industries,* November 1981.

36. Royston, M. "Making Pollution Prevention Pay." *Harvard Business Review,* November/December 1980.

37. Houseley, John. Fiber Industries, Greenville, South Carolina, Personal communication, July 1981.

38. Osmonics. "Textile Oil Reclamation and Water Re-Use." *Tech Bulletin No. 504.* Hopkins, Minnesota, Osmonics.

39. Richardson, B. "Super Beck Doubles Knit Dyer's Output." *Textile World,* January 1980.

40. Camp, J. "Low Liquor Ratio Piece Dyeing." *Canadian Textile Journal,* October 1979.

41. Crisp, Edwin. Gaston County Dye Machine Co., Mount Holly, North Carolina. Personal communication, July 1981.

42. Richardson, B. "Low Liquor Dyeing Pays Big Dividends." *Textile World,* April 1980.

43. "Combined Dyeing/Centrifuging Machines Popular for 'Small Goods'." *Canadian Textile Journal,* August 1980.

44. Dawson, T. and Roberts, B.P. "Jet-Impregnation Methods for Dyeing and Printing Carpet Yarns and Carpet Piece Goods." *Canadian Textile Journal,* April 1978.

45. Cook, F. *Energy Conservation Case Study: Bump-and-Run Implementation.* Atlanta, Georgia: Georgia Institute of Technology (mimeographed).

46. Cook, F.L. "Bump-and-Run: Touchdown for Batch Dyeing Processes." *Textile World,* September 1980.

47. Cook, F. "Dyebath Reuse in Batch Dyeing." *Textile Chemist and Colorist,* January 1978.

48. Tincher, W.C. *In-Plant Demonstration of Dyebath Re-Use Applied to Nylon.* Presented at Conference on Energy Conservation in the Textile Industry, Atlanta, Georgia, February 13-14, 1979.

49. Tincher, W. *et al.* Re-Using Dyebaths in Jet Dyeing. Atlanta, Georgia: Georgia Institute of Technology (mimeographed).

50. Brandon, C.A. *et al. Closed Cycle Textile Dyeing: Full Scale Renovation of Hot Wash Water by Hyperfiltration.* Seneca, South Carolina: Carre Inc., 1981.

51. Brandon, Craig. Carre Inc., Seneca, South Carolina. Personal communication, July 1981.

52. Leonard, F. Dorr Oliver, Stamford, Connecticut. Personal communication, July 1981.

53. Bromley, J. and Dunstan, R. "Textile Reclamation in Britain: Some Recent Impacts on a Traditional Industry." In *Conservation and Recycling.* Oxford, England: Pergamon Press, 1979.

54. Utilization of Textile Wastes Seminar. Sponsored by the Ontario Ministry of Industry and Tourism and the Ontario Ministry of the Environment, Queen's University, Kingston, Ontario, June 20-21, 1977.

55. Bajaj, J.K.L. "Recycling Man-Made Fibers." *Textile Industries,* December 1972.

56. Kurt Salmon Associates. *Better Utilization of Textile Wastes.* Presented at the Utilization of Textile Wastes Seminar, sponsored by the Ontario Ministry of Industry and Tourism and the Ontario Ministry of the Environment, Queen's University, Kingston, Ontario, June 20-21, 1977.

57. Wagner, Rolf. "Reclamation of Carpet Waste for Building Insulation." In *Conservation and Recycling.* Oxford, England: Pergamon Press, 1978.

58. Wagner, R. *Building Products from Carpet and Textile Wastes.* Presented at the Utilization of Textile Wastes Seminar, sponsored by the Ontario Ministry of Industry and Tourism and the Ontario Ministry of the Environment, Queen's University, Kingston, Ontario, June 20-21, 1977.

59. Palm, C. *Wipers from Waste.* Presented at the Utilization of Textile Wastes Seminar, sponsored by the Ontario Ministry of Industry and Tourism and the Ontario Ministry of the Environment, Queen's University, Kingston, Ontario, June 20-21, 1977.

Waste Exchange

Chicago is famous for its hog butchers. Its hog butchers in turn are renowned for their conservation-minded techniques. Every part of a slaughtered hog is used except the squeal, and, according to local lore, they are working on that.

Although Chicago hog butchers set a good example of minimizing waste by maximizing re-use, it must be recognized that materials differ in the economic viability of their recovery. Almost all materials are recyclable, but not all are economically recyclable.

As disposal costs rise, industry is responding by looking elsewhere for waste handling solutions. Two strategies are emerging in the struggle to cut costs. The first strategy is to employ on-site resource recovery technologies to reduce the quantity of wastes requiring disposal elsewhere. A second strategy is to transfer one industry's wastes to another industry for re-use.

The transfer of wastes from one company to another means that both companies can benefit economically from the exchange. The exchange of wastes offers income from an unexpected source as well as reduces the amount of money spent on disposal. In order for that transfer to occur, the two companies must know of each other's existence. This "matching" function may be accomplished by a waste exchange programme.

Waste exchanges are of two major types: information exchange and materials exchange. A waste exchange, whether it is an information exchange or a materials exchange, strives to match waste generators with waste users, thereby linking potential trading partners.

It has been common practice to ensure confidentiality on the types and amounts of wastes generated so as to obscure production rates and manufacturing data. Information exchanges routinely list a code number instead of the company name when publishing lists of wastes wanted and wastes generated.

Some industry spokesmen suggest that, except in a few instances, confidentiality in the listing of wastes is not imperative.[1] Some industry spokesmen go so far as to suggest that the coded listing system acts as a barrier, preventing one company from soliciting wastes directly from the generator. In response, some information exchanges use a confidential coding system only for those companies that request it, and list other wastes openly in conjunction with the company name and address.[2]

The utilization of waste materials from another company is met with skepticism by some companies which fear changing their established processes that have been proven successful over a long period of time. The lure of reduced material costs by using another company's wastestream may not be enough to counter a company's fear of making a costly mistake in processing unless potential savings appear to be substantial.

Fears about waste recycling may be allayed to a great extent by enlisting the services of a waste broker who has the technical know-how to advise business on the problems and benefits of using specific industrial wastes. Experts in the field of waste exchange note that smaller businesses tend to be more flexible than very large companies in accepting wastes as feedstocks. A common trend among waste exchanges is the movement of wastes from large firms to smaller companies.[3]

Another concern in using a recycled wastestream is the supply problem. Once a receiving company has adapted its processes to use a recycled product rather than a virgin product, the receiving company wants to be assured of a continued level of purity and quality.

Such constraints are relatively easy to meet when waste transfers are continuous rather than "one time only." One company may produce a waste continuously for years. The receiving company may use the recycled waste as a raw resource in its manufacturing processes for many years. In such a system, a profitable symbiotic relationship is established that can be expected to continue for a long time.

Waste generally recognized as having components of potential value include those having high concentrations of recoverable metals, solvents, alkalis, concentrated acids, catalysts, oils and combustibles (for fuel).[4,5]

Waste Exchange Types

Waste exchanges differ in whether they transfer information about wastes or whether they receive and handle actual waste materials. Four types of waste exchanges are discussed. They are: passive information exchange, active information exchange, broker-assisted materials exchange, and direct transfer.

1.
Passive Information Exchange

An information exchange functions as a clearinghouse in which the exchange agency regularly distributes lists of wastes generated and wastes wanted. Because the information is usually coded to protect the identity of the waste generator and the waste user, the interested parties must contact the clearinghouse and ask that their requests be forwarded to the appropriate company. Beyond these introductions, the clearinghouse plays no further role. The transfer itself must be negotiated by the waste generator and user.

The information transfer is passive in that clearinghouse staff do not go into the marketplace seeking business, but rather wait for generators to offer and users to request wastes.

Although it is important to measure the effectiveness of a waste exchange, data on the number of waste transfers can be misleading and must be interpreted with caution. The number of successful match-ups will vary with the value of the material listed, the volume, the frequency of waste generation and the number of years the exchange has been in operation.

In the first years of any exchange programme, the number of successful transfers will be particularly high. Match-ups initiated by waste exchanges soon become established avenues of exchange, eliminating the need to list these wastes. After a few years, the exchange lists materials with decreasing potential for transfer. Consequently, transfer efficiency based on the number of successful transfers from the total listing will be high in the early years of the exchange, and gradually decrease as the exchange matures. This trend is evident in many European exchanges and some of the older U.S. exchanges.[2]

Information exchanges have been in existence in Europe longer than in North America. Many American and other foreign exchanges which originally were begun and funded by government agencies are now operated by private sponsors such as Chambers of Commerce or trade associations.[2] According to the United States Environmental Protection Agency, the shift to non-government sponsorship of waste exchanges is expected to increase their effectiveness and efficiency in the long term, as well as avoid possible conflict of interest with the regulatory functions of government.[2] This viewpoint is not shared by the Canadian Waste Materials Exchange. Industry-operated waste exchanges may be inclined to focus on the profitable fraction of industry's wastes, thereby ignoring opportunities for developing new transfer routes for less lucrative wastestreams.

Canada has one national information exchange, rather than several regional exchanges as occur in the United States. The greatest benefit of a single national exchange is the reduced overall operating cost.

In its first four years of operation, Canada's Waste Materials Exchange programme achieved an efficiency of 15% successful transfers based on the total number of wastes listed.[5] In contrast, European exchanges have achieved transfers amounting to as much as 30% of their listings.[6] The average transfer efficiency of the older American waste exchanges is 10%.[6]

In Canada, 5000 companies or 12% of the total number of companies solicited have joined the materials exchange programme. In Germany, where participation in the national information exchange is a legal requirement of industry, the waste exchange programme is one of the most successful and has a membership of 700,000.[5]

The Canadian Waste Materials Exchange

The Canadian Waste Materials Exchange is operated by the Ontario Research Foundation. A small membership fee of $25 per year enables a company to list wastes wanted or generated. Confidentiality of the lister is maintained by coding the wastes. In addition, companies offering analytical, consulting, transportation, and disposal services may list themselves by company name for an additional fee.

The interest in wastes listed has been very high. Of the 1276 wastes listed in the bi-monthly bulletins over the first two years, 90% of the

Canadian Waste Materials Exchange

The letters of this map are used to identify the geographic region in which waste materials are available or wanted. The letter appears as the last letter in the waste code number.

Wastes are listed in the bulletin under 10 categories:

1. Organic Chemicals and Solvents
2. Oils, Fats and Waxes
3. Acids
4. Alkalis
5. Other Inorganic Chemicals
6. Metals and Metal Containing Sludges
7. Plastics
8. Textiles, Leather and Rubber
9. Wood and Paper Products
10. Miscellaneous

wastes were of sufficient interest to generate at least one enquiry.[7] The number of enquiries per listing is about five. Despite this high level of interest in some component of the wastestream, only 15% of the listings are transferred.[8]

Failure to consummate a transfer may be caused by the degree of contamination of the wastestreams in question. Future efforts to maximize transfers may require that the waste generating company undertake some upgrading of its wastes prior to exchange to eliminate certain contaminants.

Other major reasons for transfers not occurring are excessive distance between generator and potential users, and inability to reach agreement on acceptable economic terms.

The Canadian Waste Materials Exchange Bulletin lists ten categories of wastes for transfer. These are organic chemicals and solvents; oils, fats and waxes; acids; alkalis; other inorganic chemicals; metals and metal-containing sludges; plastics; textiles, leather and rubber; wood and paper products; and miscellaneous materials (see Table 1). Of these categories, the first two categories of wastes have undergone the highest rate of transfer.[8]

Twenty-eight percent of the organic chemicals and solvents listed, and 24% of the oils, fats and waxes listed have been transferred during the first two years of the national exchange programme. The exchange of other waste categories has been less successful.

An estimated 187,000 tons of industrial wastes are transferred annually via the Canadian Waste Materials Exchange programme. The replacement value of the 187,000 tons of wastes exchanged annually is estimated at $5.3 million per year (1981 dollars).[8] Almost 60% of the waste exchanges occur in Ontario, however, it must be remembered that Ontario generates about half the total hauled liquid industrial waste generated in Canada.

As of yet, only a minority of Canadian businesses participate in the national exchange programme. Because of the relatively few participants, the total amount of wastes that are transferred for re-use instead of being landfilled or incinerated remains small. In Ontario, for example, only 0.2% of the hauled liquid industrial waste was transferred via the Canadian Waste Materials Exchange during 1979 and early 1980[9] (see Table 2).

There can be little doubt that a

materials exchange programme has enormous potential in Canada. As the waste burial option falls into further disrepute, and as waste destruct systems spiral in cost, the waste recovery and exchange option will move into prominence.

The use of separation technologies permits the waste generator to concentrate even small amounts of contaminants from a liquid wastestream, thereby enhancing both the value and probability that the wastestream will be transferred to another industry. Good housekeeping practices such as keeping wastestreams as separate and pure as possible further enhance the maketability of a company's wastes.

As the number of participating companies increases, the economics of waste exchange can be expected to improve. By iden-tifying more sources of re-usable wastestreams, it is probable that participating companies will find trading partners closer to home. Minimizing transportation distances not only reduces the cost of the exchange, but it also significantly reduces the probability of accidental spills and associated environmental problems.

2.
Active Information Exchanges

Unlike passive information exchanges which simply list wastes generated and wanted, active information exchanges take a role in matching users with generators. Trading partners may be introduced through interviews and joint meetings between technical consultant, waste generator and waste user.

Alternately, active information exchanges may provide computerized matches of waste users and generators, or may offer an extensive range of information on upcoming technologies, expertise, facilities and regulations. Two examples of active exchange service are described below. They are only two of several active information exchanges currently in operation in North America.

Minnesota Association of Commerce and Industry Waste Exchange Services

The Minnesota Association of Commerce and Industry operates the Waste Exchange Service in co-operation with Technotec.[2] Technotec is a technology exchange service of the Control Data Corporation.

Table 1
Analysis of the Canadian Waste Materials Exchange Program
January 31, 1978 - December 31, 1981

Category	No. of wastes listed	Percent enquiries	Enquiries per per listing	Percent transfer
Organic chemicals and solvents	145	88	5.6	28
Oils, fats and waxes	88	94	6.7	24
Acids	47	91	6.3	13
Alkalis	60	100	6.2	12
Other inorganic chemicals	150	85	4.1	8
Metals and metal-containing sludges	208	92	6.1	12
Plastics	120	93	10.0	19
Textiles, leather and rubber	232	90	5.7	12
Wood and paper products	326	93	6.0	15
Miscellaneous	176	77	4.0	14
Total	1352	90	5.9	15.3

Source: R. Laughlin, Ontario Research Foundation, Mississauga, Ontario. Personal Communication, February 1982.

Unlike many of the passive information exchanges which rely on hand-maintained filing systems, the Minnesota Waste Exchange is based on computer listing. Firms wishing to obtain or dispose re-usable wastes submit a generic listing of the material available or sought. A computerized match is made between users and producers, who are notified of each other's interests.[2] The actual transfer, sale or purchase of materials is negotiated between the waste users and producers.

An advantage of computerized matching and direct notification is that a company wanting a specific waste need not spend the time reading through lists of wastes that are of no interest. Instead, a select list of candidate wastes may be brought to the attention of specific companies. On the other hand, proponents of providing industry with full lists of available wastes suggest that the educational activity of reading through lists may trigger good ideas for other waste uses.[8]

California Waste Exchange

The California Waste Exchange is operated by the State of California through the Hazardous Materials Management Section of the Department of Health Services. According to Carl Schwarzer, originator of the exchange programme, its purpose is to conserve energy and chemical resources by re-using materials which normally would be disposed, and to reduce the volume of materials going into landfill sites.[10] The waste exchange was started in 1976 as a pilot programme in the San Francisco Bay Area, to locate and identify the wastestreams of various companies with potential for recycle and re-use.

The California Department of Health offers free technical consulting advice to potential waste trading partners.[11] The sole function of the service is to bring the right parties together to ensure successful waste transfer. The trading partners are left to handle the transfer of wastes and funds directly without further involvement by the California Waste Exchange programme.

The approach is a highly active one, based on a careful investigation of many wastestreams from a variety of industries. The success of the programme is attributed to the use of the personal interview approach which identifies a potentially useful product that is presently being wasted, and uncovers potential consumers.[12] According to Schwarzer, personal interviews establish a relationship helpful not only in locating useful wastestreams, but also in convincing companies to explore the use of a wastestream in their own production line.

By becoming familiar with the effluents that various types of industries produce, patterns emerge. Table 3 identifies some of the successful waste transfer ideas initiated by the California Waste Exchange. In many of these transfers, two or more wastestreams are combined or "married" to facilitate the recovery of certain components by precipitation or concentration.

Once the technical consultant identifies a new link between waste generator and user, it is frequently possible to transfer the re-use technology to other companies of the same industrial type.

What appears to be a formidable task initially gains momentum as a growing stock of transfer routes are applied to an increasing number of companies.

The California Waste Exchange is unique in that it provides the business community with free advice in waste recycling. The free advice comes from experts with science backgrounds who take stock of wastes and devise uses for them.

According to Schwarzer, this free advice is well received. Industry has not only sanctioned the programme, but is gratified to learn that the state has instituted a programme to help solve its disposal problems.[11] The economic incentive is compelling. Not only do companies receive income from an unexpected source by re-using or selling wastes for re-use, companies benefit by spending less money on waste disposal fees.

Table 2
Disposal Methods for Ontario's Liquid Industrial Wastes
(1979 and early 1980)

Disposal Method	Percentage of Wastes Disposed in this Manner
Burial (codisposal in landfills with municipal refuse and other solid wastes	43%
Incineration	30%
Solidification	10%*
Export to the United States	8.6%
Dust Control (mainly oil wastes)	8%
Canadian Waste Materials Exchange	0.2%**

*Ceased operation April 1980

**Estimation

Source: MacLaren Inc. *The Siting of Facilities and the Management of Liquid Industrial and Hazardous Wastes in Ontario: Annex One.* November 1980.

Limitations

Although information exchanges play an important role in waste transfer, it is doubtful that information exchanges in themselves can ever realize the full potential of waste transfer.

A passive information exchange approach cannot identify reusable wastestreams unless a company first comes forward with this information. Many companies, particularly ones lacking extensive in-house expertise, may not recognize the re-use potential of their wastestreams, and as such, neglect to inform an information exchange of their existence.

Knowledge of wastes available does not ensure that a transfer of wastes will occur. Unless the waste generated is a very close match to what the user is looking for, it is unlikely that an exchange will take place via a simple listing system.

3.
Broker-Assisted Materials Exchange

In contrast to many information exchanges, materials exchanges play a much more active role in arranging transfers. Many of the American materials exchanges are profit-seeking firms, and as such can survive economically only by seeking transfer opportunities vigorously and completing them successfully.[2]

In a broker-assisted materials exchange, the two trading partners deal with each other only via a middleman — the broker. The broker is responsible for the physical transfer of wastes from generator to user, for the transfer of funds, and for any legal requirements. Typically, the broker's income results from commissions charged on completed transactions.

A broker dealing in hazardous waste usually has in-house expertise and facilities to analyse wastes. In some cases it may be possible to transfer wastes "as is" to a new user. More frequently, however, the wastes will require

additional processing or treatment. Waste brokers vary in the type and extent of waste reprocessing that they perform.

The broker and information exchange may exist side by side with mutual benefit. The broker must specialize in the most obviously transferable wastes. The brokers utilize the information just as primary potential users do.

Zero Waste Systems

Zero Waste Systems (Oakland, California), a materials-handling exchange, is a surplus chemicals dealer, and a consulting firm specializing in industrial processing wastes. As a small and innovative enterprise, it sees itself pioneering a new industry and offering the best model for a waste materials exchange.

Because of its highly trained staff of chemists and engineers, Zero Waste Systems has the know-how to handle surplus chemicals, collect industrial processing wastes, sell recycled and surplus materials and provide consulting aid in waste management and control problems. The firm takes possession of materials for recycle, and prepares them for specific market needs by processing them via distillation, recrystallization, electrowinning, grinding or simply repackaging.[13] Contract processors and other consultants are used as required to supplement the services offered by Zero Waste Systems.

Dr. Paul Palmer, company president and founder, is an outspoken critic of burying industrial waste in the ground. Most industrial garbage is still sent to the dump and buried, a method of disposal Palmer complains has "not changed substantially since the first cave man threw the first bone out on to the ground and kicked some dirt over it."[14]

According to Palmer, waste is something that is not wanted. There is nothing wrong with it other than it happens to be in the wrong hands. Zero Waste Systems sees its role as scavenging for industrial wastes and putting them in the right hands.[13]

The benefits of industrial waste

recycling are numerous. By matching an old chemical to a new use, some company obtains a cut-rate chemical. This means that one less chemical has to be synthesized from raw materials, saving energy. It also means that one less chemical ends up at the dumpsite. By being persistent and aggressive in identifying waste, and in finding appropriate matches, Zero Waste Systems can maintain a profit margin and still avert pollution and materials wastage.

The small company's history has its roots in scarcity. According to Palmer, the energy crisis made his business venture possible. By 1973, the oil embargo forced chemical suppliers to ration the amount of chemicals they distributed and companies realized they had to explore alternative sources of supply.[15]

Founding his company in 1973, Palmer realized he could make a profit collecting, purifying and redistributing chemicals that were previously consigned to the dumps. Although the energy crisis has relaxed somewhat since 1973, raw materials are again growing more scarce and more expensive every day. According to a federal study by the United States government, by 1985 industry will be dependent on foreign countries for much of the supplies of nine of the basic raw materials used, based on the current rate of depletion.[13,14]

A major assist to Palmer's operations comes from California's hazardous waste control law and regulations, which require generators to report in detail on all wastes sent out for disposal. Many plant managers prefer to sell or even give wastes to Zero Waste Systems to save themselves the cost and bother of lengthy wastes reporting.[13]

The company also serves the needs of companies which either choose not to or do not know how to transfer scrap wastes in small quantities. Companies with little or no technical skills in industrial chemistry may fail to recognize that they have significant wastes generated by their processes. By interviewing waste generators directly, Zero Waste Systems is able to identify wastes of re-use potential that may otherwise go un-

Table 3

Waste Re-use Routes Identified by the California Waste Exchange

Wastestreams	Re-Use Potential
• Spent diatomaceous earth filter cakes.	These wastes provide siliceous materials usable by cement manufacturers.
• Non-repulpable paper from a paper recycling company. • Tannery wastes containing proteinaceous materials.	Non-repulpable wastes can be biodegraded to make loam used in lawn preparation. By using phosphoric acid in place of sulfuric acid to neutralize the alkalinity of tannery wastes, tannery wastes in conjunction with biodegradable paper wastes provide a useful soil amendment.
• Pickle acid from galvanizers (contains 8 to 10% zinc sulfate as well as some iron salts). • Bag house dust from scrap steel processors (contains up to 25% zinc oxide). • Waste sulfuric acid.	Recovery of solid zinc-iron sulfate by a dehydration process is enhanced by mixing these wastestreams and concentrating the materials to be reclaimed.
• Steel pickle acid (contains 10 to 15% ferrous sulfate).	Used to treat hydrogen sulfide in steam from geothermal power generation. The resultant sludge consisting of iron sulfide and elemental sulfur is recovered for use as a soil amendment.
• Ammonia copper solution waste produced by printed circuit board manufacturers. • Caustic sodium sulfide waste from a refinery.	Recovery of metals such as nickel, copper, gold and silver from ammonia copper solution by combining with the sodium sulfide to precipitate the heavy metals.
• The semiconductor industry produces a large amount of acid stripper — a mixture containing 96% sulfuric acid and 2% chromic acid.	Waste acid stripper can be used for refining used crankcase oil.
• The production of silicon wafers in the Semiconductor industry yields a waste mixture called mixed acid etch. It contains 60% nitric acid, 20% hydrofluoric and 20% acetic acid. • The manufacture of acetylene from calcium carbide yields lime and calcium hydroxide.	Mixing of these wastestreams yields calcium nitrate, calcium fluoride and calcium acetate. Calcium nitrate is a valuable fertilizer. Calcium fluoride is useful in cement manufacture and as a raw material for hydrofluoric acid manufacture.

Source: C. Schwarzer. "Recycling Hazardous Wastes" *ES&T,* February 1979.

noticed.

Because most transfers occur within the San Francisco Bay Area, transportation costs are kept to a minimum, however, some waste exchanges are made over great distances when the economics of the transfer are favourable. Zero Waste Systems foresees a national network of regional waste exchanges, and greater reliance on data banks to store the technical procedures in waste re-use identified to date.

American Chemical Exchange

The American Chemical Exchange (Skokie, Illinois) functions as a profit-making materials exchange, acting as a broker between buyer and seller. At present, close to 90% of the transfers accomplished involve virgin surplus chemicals. Unless transferred, most virgin surplus chemicals suffer the same disposal fate as other process wastes. The rest of the transfers concern hazardous and non-hazardous waste materials. The list of non-virgin waste materials transferred is increasing yearly, but at a slow rate.

In 1980, the American Chemical Exchange charged a membership fee of $250 and a commission of 5% for virgin chemical transfers. The exchange handles about 100 deals per year as match-ups, representing a transfer volume of approximately 150 million pounds.[2] Like other materials exchange brokers, the company's small staff has extensive training in chemistry and business.

The Ohio Resource Exchange (ORE)

ORE, founded in 1979, is a profit-making exchange company that serves industry by marketing byproduct waste materials.[2] The company's forte is its willingness to deal predominantly in the transfer of potentially hazardous wastes. ORE cultivates both Canadian and American clients.

Unlike other materials exchanges, this small company functions truly as a broker. Working strictly on commissions, the company matches waste generator to user, but does not take legal title to or physical possession of the wastes.[16] To ensure a proper match, ORE arranges for the potential buyer to receive full disclosure and a representative waste sample from the waste generator.

Commissions are established on the revenue realized by the sale, plus the disposal costs avoided. For example, if the value of the transferred material is $2 per barrel, and its disposal cost is $50 per barrel, the exchange company's commission would be a negotiated percentage of the $52 combined cost.[16]

As with other profit-making exchanges, ORE stays in business by its active involvement in waste marketing. ORE points to many successes. It advised a paint manufacturer to add dispersants to sludges from paint mixing and to sell the sludge as a filler coat for cement blocks. For a glass company with stockpiles of unwanted waste silica sand that contained too much alumina, ORE found an outlet in a sand-blasting firm. ORE assisted a fish-processing company swimming in organic wastes by finding a fish food extender market for the company's fish sawdust waste.[16]

ORE publishes a catalogue of information about available and wanted wastes. Listings are free of charge. Exchange income is based on a commission charged for successfully completed waste transfers.

Shanghai Chemical Recycling Works

The Shanghai Donghai Oil and Chemical Recycling Works (Shanghai, People's Republic of China) built in 1958 for the comprehensive utilization of waste acid, oil and metal scrap, has recovered in the last 20 years more than 2.5 million tons of waste acid; extracted 8200 tons of chemical products of 30 varieties including copper sulphate, copper carbonate, nickel oxide and cobalt chloride; and refined 15 tons of silver and 6300 tons of oil from industrial residues, waste liquids and oils.[17]

Prior to the establishment of the materials recovery plant, 300,000 tons of waste acid were discharged annually from the industrial city of Shanghai. The rivers and farmlands were seriously polluted, and an indemnity of 10 million yuan was paid annually.

Prior to construction of the acid re-utilization component of the recycling facility, investigations were completed to fully assess acid consumption and discharge of waste acids. After an education phase of informing acid-utilizing companies in Shanghai on the benefits of recycling, recovery plant employees began re-utilization trials.

To win the confidence of the acid-utilizing factories, samples of processed waste acid were sent to individual companies for trial use. Because the factories were previously accustomed to high quality acids, they were not convinced that the recovered acids could ensure high product quality until test trials provided satisfactory results.[17]

Today waste acids discharged by 60 factories are processed for use by 300 factories. For example, the waste liquid discharged by pharmaceutical and titanium-white factories contain 15% sulphuric acid and a high percentage of iron with a few impurities. After it is retrieved and used by iron and steel plants in cleaning rolled steel, it is returned to pharmaceutical plants for making iron protosulfide for medical use.

The waste organic sulphuric acid solution containing 70% of the acid discharged by dye works and chemical works is sent to chemical fertilizer plants to make phosphate fertilizer. Weak sulphuric acid and hydrochloric acid solutions are transferred to paper, printing and dyeing mills to neutralize waste alkali solutions, and to make ammonium salt of humic acid, a chemical fertilizer.

Waste hydrochloric acid is first used by electroplating plants and metal drawing plants for cleaning their products, and is then re-used in the manufacture of chemical reagents such as magnesium chloride and calcium chloride.

The recovery and re-use of waste acids at Shanghai not only minimizes environmental pollution but it also saves resources and cuts costs. For example, one iron and steel plant which used to clean rolled steel with virgin sulphuric acid, saves 54,000 yuan a year by using recycled waste acid.[17]

4.
Direct Transfer

Some of the larger chemical companies which house a wide variety of chemical processes and their associated waste products have learned that byproduct recycling can be a highly lucrative endeavour. Initially, these companies set up special departments to maximize surplus and byproduct chemical recovery within the company's own multi-plant facilities. In some instances, chemical recovery became such a profitable venture that subsidiary companies were formed specifically to market the new-found wealth in chemical byproducts, surplus chemicals and process wastes.

Monsanto Chemical Intermediates

Monsanto Chemical Intermediates (St. Louis, Missouri) is a newly formed subsidiary of Monsanto Chemicals designed to market the millions of pounds of byproducts resulting from the parent company's chemical synthesis processes. According to Monsanto, these millions of pounds of chemical byproducts represent a potential market of $350 million.[18]

Rising chemical costs have made chemical recovery a shrewd investment for Monsanto, so much so that staff now refer to *byproducts* strictly as *co-products*. Previously, many of these materials were handled by incineration, by burning for fuel value, by deep well injection, or by placing them in landfills.

New life has been given to several chemical byproducts. Monsanto's nylon processes and styrene streams yield amine and nitrile streams. One new market for some of the amine streams is as corrosion inhibitors. The *bottoms* left after production of detergent alkylate can be used to make high molecular weight sulfonates, similar to the petroleum sulfonates that some companies manufacture as a primary product.[18]

Investment Recovery Group Union Carbide Corporation

Union Carbide (New York, New York) has been actively marketing surplus materials and equipment since it set up its corporate Investment Recovery Department in 1964. Recognizing the profitability of materials recovery, the department was expanded in 1971 to develop markets for damaged goods, off spec or obsolete products, byproducts and residues, spent catalysts, metallic wastes, slimes, sludges and flue dusts.[2]

Union Carbide operates both an internal materials exchange and an exchange for sales outside the company corporation. To promote internal transfers, a monthly list of surplus-available and surplus-wanted is circulated to every Union Carbide plant.

The majority of materials transfers are continuous streams including substances such as spent catalysts and various byproducts. About 30% are the result of plant accidents or faulty processing. For example, instead of disposing a bad batch of ethanol, Union Carbide sold it to a gasohol plant where it was re-used.[2]

Where existing markets are lacking for one of Union Carbide's wastestreams, in-house engineering, technical and marketing expertise is focussed on finding lucrative recovery and resale alternatives.

In 1973, Union Carbide's Surplus Products Group, which finds new markets for process byproducts and wastes, sold over 40 million pounds of materials, recovering almost $1.25 million in cash income and disposal cost avoidance. The Surplus Materials Group, which handles excess unused materials, and the Surplus Equipment Group generate an average income of $15 million per year. Every dollar spent by the Investment Recovery Group nets Union Carbide a return of $20 to $25.[2]

Virginia Chemicals

Despite its small size relative to other chemical companies, Virginia Chemicals (Portsmouth, Virginia) finds it in its economic interest to re-use many of its wastestreams. The Portsmouth plant employs about 200 people in the manufacture of such chemicals as alkylamines, zinc sulfate and sodium metabisulfite.

The scrubbers on the amine plants recover ammonia and recycle it back into the production process. Similarly, a tailgate scrubber on the sodium metabisulfite plant removes sulfur dioxide from the discharge gases and puts it back into the process. Process wastewater from the zinc sulfate plant is up-graded and re-used.[19]

For wastestreams where recovery is not feasible, the wastewater undergoes waste treatment. For example, acidic wastewater from the sulfur dioxide, sodium metabisulfite and other inorganic plants is collected and neutralized with slurried lime. Previously, mined lime was purchased for neutralization. Now, Virginia Chemicals uses lime slurries that are waste materials from an acetylene operation in Norfolk. Both companies benefit from the transfer.[19]

Diversey Environmental Products Limited

Turning environmental headache into opportunity, Dow Chemical (Canada) and Diversey (Canada) combined research efforts to transform steelmaker's waste dust into a valuable end product. Successful pilot studies resulted in the formation of a joint venture company by Dow and Diversey known as Diversey Environmental Products Limited (Mississauga, Ontario). In operation since 1974, the plant recycles and eliminates the need to landfill more than 10 million pounds of steelmaker's dust annually.[10]

At a steel making plant, electrostatic precipitators trap iron-rich dust from the process furnaces. The steelmaker's dust is trucked as dry cake to the Mississauga plant for recovery. The dry ferric oxide dust, also known as magnetite, is slurried and fed to a reactor along with anhydrous hydrogen chloride to produce ferric chloride (see Figure 1).

Ferric chloride is sold for use in water purification and waste treatment processes, and is particularly effective in phosphate removal from municipal sewage treatment plant effluents. Prior to production of ferric chloride at the Mississauga plant, ferric chloride was imported from Dow's parent company in Michigan and resold on the Canadian market.

In addition to providing the commercially useful ferric chloride product, the recycling process created a new market for hydrogen chloride. Hydrogen chloride is itself a waste product in the manufacture of chlorinated hydrocarbons. Anhydrous hydrogen chloride is transported to the Mississauga site, vaporized on-site, and fed as gaseous hydrogen chloride to the reactor (see Figure 1).[20]

This waste exchange effort not only earned Dow and Diversey an Environmental Improvement Award in 1977 from the Chemical Institute of Canada, but also earned these companies additional profits while contributing to environmental protection.

By mid 1980, Diversey Environmental Products encountered difficulties in obtaining a cheap and continuing supply of magnetite, and hence discontinued this particular recovery process. The company currently recovers waste pickle liquor (ferrous chloride) from the steel industry and transforms it into re-usable ferric chloride through

Figure 1
Recovery of Steelmaker's Dust

Ferric oxide cake from steel mills is transported to the ferric chloride recovery plant. The ferric oxide dust is slurried and fed to a reactor to which is added anhydrous hydrogen chloride. The resultant ferric chloride undergoes purification and is ready for use elsewhere. Aqueous effluents and run-off are contained in an on-site lagoon which also provides make-up water for the process. The vent from the reactor is scrubbed with water and the scrubber effluent is sent to the lagoon. The plant operates as a closed loop with no aqueous discharge. A relatively small amount of solid wastes is generated, which is disposed as landfill.

Source: "Ferric Chloride Process Wins CIC Award," *Chemistry in Canada*, Summer 1977.

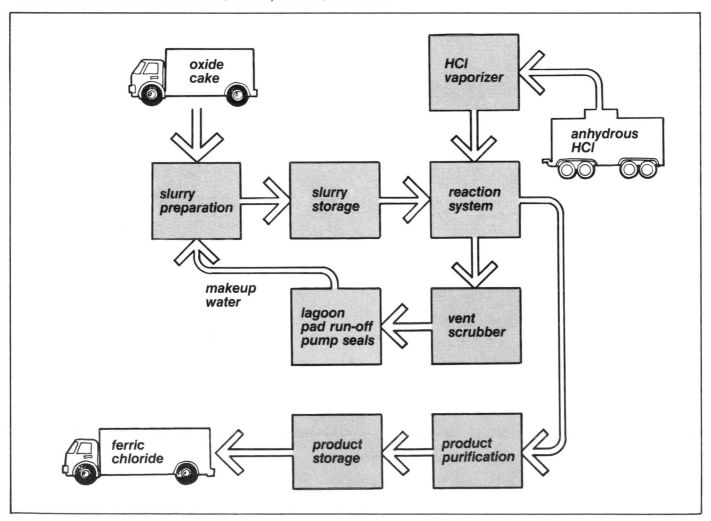

chlorination. The chlorine used in the chlorination process may itself be a byproduct from the production of caustic soda by the chemical industry. The ferric chloride product is sold to municipal sewage treatment plants.[21]

Conclusion

The sound management of industrial wastes necessitates careful attention to maximizing production efficiency, substituting less hazardous products and processes, and minimizing the generation of wastes at each individual company. Yet despite attempts to maximize in-plant waste reduction and recovery, it is probable that many companies will gener-

ate a wastestream of little or no value to its own operations. Participation in a waste exchange can benefit both the environment and a company's profit margin.

Present waste exchanges are hindered by many factors. Industrial participants are relatively few. Transport costs are high. Many potentially useful wastestreams go unnoticed, ending up instead at a landfill or incinerator. The waste burial option is still so cheap in Canada that the economics of waste transfer pale in comparison. And, despite a growing knowledge of waste transfer potential by experts in the field of waste utilization, this knowledge rarely reaches the smaller and medium-sized companies.

Another stumbling block hin-

dering widespread waste transfer and re-use concerns the purity requirements for materials used in manufacturing. No manufacturer wants to sacrifice product quality in exchange for somewhat reduced material costs. It is questionable, however, whether some of the high purity specifications for materials used in manufacturing and processing are really required. There is a need to re-examine specifications for materials to determine whether less pure feedstocks would be acceptable. A waste exchange can succeed only if ample markets exist for recycled materials. Re-examining purity specifications may well result in a larger market for reclaimed materials.

FOR FURTHER INFORMATION

Waste Exchanges in North America

Although an attempt has been made to provide up-to-date information on Waste Exchanges in North America, it is possible that new Exchanges have opened and others closed down in the meantime. Consult the nearest environmental government agency, Chamber of Commerce or appropriate industry association to identify new Waste Exchanges in your area. The U.S. Waste Exchanges are listed alphabetically by state.

Exchange	Address	Type of Exchange	Description
Canadian Waste Materials Exchange	Dr. Robert Laughlin Ontario Research Foundation, Sheridan Park Research Community Mississauga, Ontario L5K 1B3 (416) 822-4111	Information	Country-wide information exchange in operation since 1978. Wastes generated and wanted are listed in a bulletin for bi-monthly distribution.
Zero Waste Systems Inc.	2928 Poplar St., Oakland, California 94608 (415) 893-8257	Broker & consultant	Private for-profit company founded in 1973. Handles surplus chemicals, collects industrial processing wastes, sells recycled and surplus materials and provides consulting services in waste management. Circulates list of surplus materials to selecting mailing list. Main route is through personal contact in the region.
California Waste Exchange	Department of Health Services, Hazardous Materials Management Section, 2151 Berkeley Way Berkeley California. 94704 (415) 540-2043	Consultant	State Waste exchange started in 1976 as a pilot programme in the San Francisco Bay Area to identify and locate wastestreams of various companies with the potential to recycle and re-use. Uses technical know-how to find new uses for wastes on an industry by industry basis.
Georgia Waste Exchange	Georgia Business and Industry Association, 181 Washington St. S.W., Atlanta, Georgia. 30303 (404) 659-4444	Information exchange	A non-profit organization administered by the business community. In existence since 1976. Lists wastes 'wanted' or 'available' in quarterly publication.

Exchange	Address	Type of Exchange	Description
American Chemical Exchange	4849 Golf Road, Skokie, Illinois. (312) 677-2800	Broker	A for-profit materials exchange acting as a broker between buyer and seller. Handles transfer of payment and goods. Uses a computerized matching service in buying and selling surplus chemical inventories.
Environmental Clearinghouse Organization	3425 Maple Lane, Hazel Crest, Illinois. 60429 (312) 336-0754	Broker	A private for-profit organization that acts as both a waste broker and a consultant. Provides clients with waste surveys and waste management programmes.
Waste Materials Clearinghouse	Environmental Quality Control Inc., 1220 Waterway Boulevard, Indianapolis, Indiana. 46202 (317) 634-2142	Information exchange	Non-profit information clearinghouse. Wastes wanted and generated are listed in the Waste Materials Clearinghouse Catalog' for regular distribution.
Industrial Waste Information Exchange	Center for Industrial Research and Service, 201 Building E, Iowa State University, Ames, Iowa. 50011 (515) 294 3420	Information	Exchange is non-profit and operated by Iowa State University. CIRAS staff have worked with individual firms since 1964 to identify economical methods of waste re-use.
Industrial Waste Information Exchange	Columbus Industrial Association, 1646 West Lane Avenue, Columbus, Ohio. 43221 (614) 486-6741	Information	Non-profit information exchange service. Based on a relatively small number of listings.
Ohio Resource Exchange	ORE Corporation, 2415 Woodmere Dr., Cleveland, Ohio. 44106 (216) 371-4869	Broker	Private for-profit company functioning as a waste broker. Special emphasis on transfer of hazardous wastestreams.
Minnesota Association of Commerce and Industry Waste Exchange Services	Minnesota Association for Commerce and Industry, 200 Hanover Building, 480 Cedar St., St. Paul, Minnesota. 55101 (612) 227-9591	Information	A non-profit information exchange service in operation since 1972. Computerized match is made between users and producers who are notified of each others' interests. Sales and purchases negotiated directly between users and producers.

Exchange	Address	Type of Exchange	Description
Monsanto Chemical Intermediates	Monsanto Corp., 800 North Lindbergh Blvd., St. Louis, Missouri. 63166 (314) 694-1000	Materials transfer	This newly formed subsidiary of Monsanto Chemicals is designed to market the millions of pounds of byproducts resulting from the company's synthesis processes.
Midwest Industrial Waste Exchange	10 Broadway, St. Louis, Missouri. (314) 321-5555	Information	Functions as an information clearinghouse. In operation since 1975 as a non-profit service. Lists wastes regularly in publication entitled "Clearinghouse Catalog and News".
Industrial Waste Information Exchange	New Jersey State Chamber of Commerce, 5 Commerce St., Newmark, New Jersey. 07102 (201) 623-7070	Information	Operated and funded by the New Jersey State Chamber of Commerce as a non-profit information clearinghouse since 1978.
EnKarn Research Corporation	P.O. Box 590, Albany, New York 12201 (518) 436-9684	Broker	A private for-profit company in operation since 1977. Act as either consultants or brokers to assist in the re-use of surplus inventories and waste materials. Publishes listings in its "Industrial Materials Bulletin".
American Alliance of Resources Recovery Interests Inc.	AARRII, 111 Washington Ave., Albany, New York. 12210 (518) 436-1557	Information	Initiated in 1979, the exchange is a clearinghouse for information on industrial waste materials available or wanted.
Union Carbide Corporation	270 Park Ave., New York, New York. 10017 (212) 551-3661	Materials transfer	Union Carbide actively markets surplus materials and equipment, by-products and residuals. Transfers are made internally between different Union Carbide plants or externally to outside markets.
Oregon Industrial Waste Information Exchange	Western Environmental Trade Association, 333 S.W. 5th St., Suite 618, Portland, Oregon. 92704 (503) 221-0357	Information	A non-profit information service listing wastes wanted and wastes available. May include listings from British Columbia. Distributes listing bulletins regularly.

Exchange	Address	Type of exchange	Description
Tennessee Waste Swap	Tennessee Manufacturers Association, 708 Fidelity Federal Building, Nashville, Tennessee. 37219 (615) 256-5141	Information	Initially sponsored by the Tennessee Department of Health. Since then, taken over and managed by the Tennessee Manufacturers Association, a non-governmental organization.
Chemical Recycle Information Program	Houston Chamber of Commerce, 1100 Milam Building, 25th Floor, Houston, Texas. 77002. (713) 651-1313	Information	Non-profit information exchange sponsored by the Chamber of Commerce since 1977. Publishes inventory of waste chemicals for monthly distribution.
Information Center for Waste Exchange	2112 Third Avenue, Suite 303, Seattle, Washington. 98121 (206) 623-5235	Information	Operates as a passive clearinghouse for information transfer. In existence since 1977, it is sponsored by the Western Environmental Trade Association (Washington) — a non-profit labour/business association. It serves Washington, Oregon, Idaho and Western Canada.

Source: References 2, 7, 10, 14, 16, 18, 22, 23 and 24.

Associations and Journals

The following associations and publications provide additional information on waste exchange opportunities. Although the current emphasis is on the recycling of solid wastes such as metal, glass and plastics, an increasing amount of attention is is being devoted to liquid wastestreams.

Associations

Canadian Association of Recycling Industries,
Suite 602,
8 Colborne St.,
Toronto, Ontario.
M5E 1E1
(416) 362-4521

National Association of Recycling Industries,
330 Madison Avenue,
New York, New York.
10017
(212) 867-7330

National Solid Wastes Management Association,
Suite 930,
1120 Connecticut Avenue, N.W.,
Washington, D.C.
20036
(202) 659-4613

National Center for Resource Recovery,
1211 Connecticut Avenue, N.W.,
Washington, D.C.
20036
(202) 223-6154

Environmental Industry Council,
Suite 210,
1825 K St., N.W.,
Washington, D.C.
20006
(202) 331-7706

Trade Journals

RECOUP,
Venture Publications Ltd.,
223A McLeod St.,
Ottawa, Ontario.
K2P 0Z8

RESILOG,
Waste Management Branch,
Environment Canada,
Ottawa, Ontario.
K1A 1C8

MATERIALS RECLAMATION
WEEKLY,
Maclaren Publishers Ltd.,
Box 109,
Davis House,
69-77 High St.,
Croydon, England.
CR9 1QH

ONTARIO BULLETIN,
Ontario Solid Wastes Management
Association,
Box 10,
Kitchener, Ontario.
N2G 3X2

RECOVERY ENGINEERING NEWS,
ICON Information Concepts Inc.,
211 S. 45th St.,
Philadelphia, Pennsylvania.
19104

WASTE AGE,
Three Sons Publishing Co.,
6311 Gross Point Road,
Niles, Illinois.
60648

SLUDGE,
Business Publishers Inc.,
Box 1067,
Blair Station,
Silver Spring, Maryland.
20910

INDUSTRIAL RECOVERY,
National Industrial Materials
Recovery Association,
4 Stanley Park Road,
Wallington, Surrey.
SM6 0EU

RESOURCES
RECOVERY/ENERGY REVIEW,
Wakeman-Walworth Inc.,
P.O. Box 1144,
Darien, Connecticut.
06820

REUSE/RECYCLE,
Technomic Publishing Co. Inc.,
265 Post Road West,
Westport, Connecticut.
06880

CONSERVATION AND
RECYCLING,
Pergamon Press Inc.,
Maxwell House, Fairview Park,
Elmsford, New York.
10523

NCRR BULLETIN,
National Center for Resource
Recovery,
1211 Connecticut Avenue, N.W.,
Washington, D.C.
20036

References

1. Laughlin, R.G.W. and Golomb, A. (Ontario Research Foundation). *The Methodology for the Operation of a Waste Materials Exchange in Canada*. Prepared for the Solid Waste Management Branch, Environment Canada, January 1977.

2. U.S. Environmental Protection Agency. *Waste Exchanges: Background Information*. Office of Water and Waste Management, December 1980.

3. "Waste Materials Exchange." *Canadian Chemical Processing*, March 1980.

4. Terry, R.C. *et al*. "Waste Clearinghouses and Exchanges." *Chemical Engineering Progress*, December 1976.

5. Laughlin, R.G.W. "Waste Exchange." *Ontario Bulletin*, December 1980.

6. U.S. Environmental Protection Agency. *Industrial Waste Exchanges*. Office of Solid Waste, 1978 (fact sheet).

7. Lauglin, R.G.W. (Ontario Research Foundation). *Canadian Waste Exchange Program*. Prepared for presentation to the 2nd National Conference on Waste Management in Canada, Winnipeg, Manitoba, October 17, 1980.

8. Laughlin, Robert. Ontario Research Foundation, Mississauga, Ontario. Personal communication, February 1982

9. MacLaren Engineers, Planners and Scientists Inc. *The Siting of Facilities and the Management of Liquid Industrial and Hazardous Wastes in Ontario: Annex One — Need for Waste Management Facilities and Available Technologies*. Prepared for the Ontario Ministry of the Environment, November 1980.

10. Schwarzer, C.G. "Recycling Hazardous Wastes." *Environmental Science and Technology* 13(2), February 1979.

11. Schwarzer, Carl. Aerojet Energy Conversion, La Jolla, California. Personal communication, August 1981.

12. Smith, G. "Turning Wastes into Money." *The Globe and Mail* (Canada), January 12, 1981.

13. Palmer, Paul. Zero Waste Systems, Oakland, California. Personal communication, February 1981.

14. Siskind, L. "Recycling with a Valence." *San Francisco Examiner: California Living Magazine*, March 6, 1977

15. Lerner, S. "Recycling Vs Disposal." *Commonwealth Research Publication: Working Papers* 1(10), Summer 1978.

16. "Broker Aims to Profit from Trading Wastes." *Chemical Week*, February 27, 1980.

17. Ming, Chen. "The Recycling of Waste Acid, Oil and Metal Scrap of the Shanghai Donghai Oil and Chemical Recycling Works." In *Conservation and Recycling*. Oxford, England: Pergamon Press Ltd., 1980.

18. "They're Getting Gold from Dross." *Chemical Week*, February 4, 1981.

19. Long, Janis. "How Small Firm Copes with Federal Regulations." *Chemical and Engineering News*, May 18, 1981.

20. "Ferric Chloride Process Wins CIC Award." *Chemistry in Canada*, Summer 1977.

21. Coleman, Peter. Diversey Environmental Products, Mississauga, Ontario. Personal communication, April 1982.

22. Mackay, Bentley B. "Sow's Ear Becomes Silk Purse Thanks to St. Louis Matchmaker." *Solid Wastes Management*, August 1976.

23. World Association for Safe Transfer and Exchange. *Turning a Problem into a Profit*. Waterbury, Connecticut: W.A.S.T.E. (brochure).

24. Western Environmental Trade Association Inc. *WETA Memo*. Portland, Oregon: W.E.T.A., August 1980. (fact sheet).

Technology Descriptions

Waste Recovery Technologies

Resource recovery is the science of material separation — netting the process chemical from the wastewater, wresting the metal from the sludge, capturing the protein from the pomace, or separating the gold from the dross.

The key to the separation of substances is the understanding of their nature and their differences. Two compounds cannot be separated unless they differ in some chemical or physical manner. The knowledge of these properties is the domain of the chemist and the physicist. Their fields involve the analysis of how and why materials behave differently to external pressures. Scientists have developed extensive data on a wide variety of chemical and physical parameters. What they tell us about ionic charge, specific gravity, solubility, reactivity, size, shape and a host of other parameters form the basis of separation science.

Once the differences are known, the engineer can devise the equipment that utilizes that knowledge as the lever to pry materials apart. Because the chemists and physicists can supply him with a host of properties on which two substances will differ, the engineer's response can encompass an enormous range of technologies. Indeed, separation science is a field that has been called an inventor's paradise. Many commercially available separation technologies exist at present, however the future should bring an even greater array of recovery innovations.

This chapter is meant to present a brief overview of some of the separation technologies for which in-plant performance is a proven success. Other technologies applicable to waste recovery include filtration, centrifugation, flotation, anaerobic digestion, pyrolysis and wet-air oxidation. Because these technologies are used primarily for waste treatment or destruction at present, they are described in the Waste Treatment and Disposal chapter.

It should be noted that several of the technologies such as precipitation, filtration, anaerobic digestion, wet-air oxidation and pyrolysis described in the Waste Treatment and Disposal chapter are also suitable for resource re covery. Their description appears in the treatment and disposal chapter because these unit technologies are most frequently used in conjunction with destruct or landfill methods.

1.
Carbon Adsorption

Carbon adsorption technology has a long history, including the commercial use of activated carbon in the sugar industry for decolorization and as a filter in war-time gas masks in the early 1900s.[1] It was not until the 1970s that carbon adsorption technology gained prominence in the treatment of liquid industrial waste. At present, carbon adsorption technology is used predominantly to remove contaminants from a wastestream for further disposal through incineration or landfill. As recovery economics improve, greater attention is placed on the implementation of carbon adsorption technology for the removal, recovery and re-use of select wastestreams.

Waste Recovery Applications

The affinity of activated carbon for organics makes it a useful tool

in removing organic contaminants in wastewaters, particularly industrial contaminants such as select solvents and chlorinated pesticides that are resistant to biological degradation and may be toxic to a biological treatment process. Carbon adsorption is also

successful at removing gas-phase organics such as solvents from solvent-laden air.

Industries which treat segregated industrial wastestreams with activated carbon include the textile, pharmaceutical, dyestuff, resin, detergent, chemical, pes-

Figure 1
Carbon Adsorption System With Thermal Reactivation Cycle

Thermal reactivation destroys the adsorbed organic solutes in a furnace at temperatures around 900°C and with the introduction of steam. Carbon lost from the system is made up with fresh carbon. The use of afterburners ensures that organic compounds are destroyed. Scrubbers are used to remove particulates from the furnace exhaust.

Source: "Industrial Wastewater Treatment by Granular Activated Carbon," *Industrial Water Engineering,* January/February 1974.

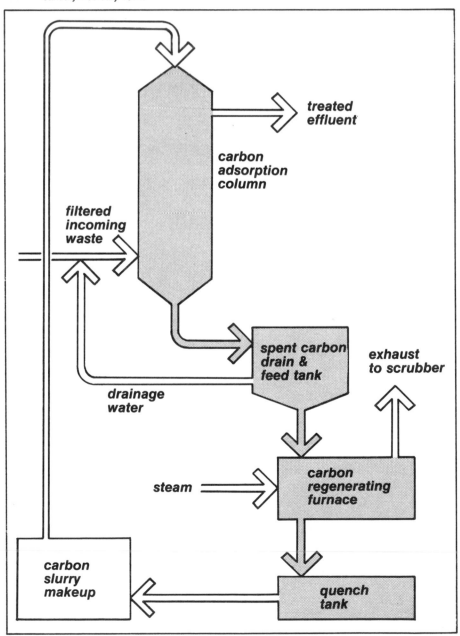

ticide and oil refining industries. Organic contaminants removed through carbon adsorption include dyes, phenols, polyethers, TNT, cresol, toluene, xylene, xylol, resorcinol, chlorophenols, chlorobenzenes and insecticides.

In general, carbon adsorption is suitable for the removal of organic contaminants with a high molecular weight, low water solubility and low polarity, however, exceptions do occur. Industrial wastestreams vary in the types of impurities that they contain. Some contaminants are easily removed using carbon adsorption, whereas other organic impurities show a poor affinity for the carbon. Long-chain organic soaps and other macromolecules such as certain dyes may be too large to reach a significant fraction of the carbon's internal pores, making removal inefficient.[2]

Activated carbon adsorption has been demonstrated to be feasible for the removal of low concentrations of certain inorganic compounds from aqueous industrial wastestreams. The following is a partial list of inorganic chemicals that can be removed by activated carbon: alkali metals from basic solutions, ammonia, arsenates, calcium hypochlorite, chlorine, chromium, cobalt, copper, cyanide, dichromates, ferric salts, gold chloride, hydrogen sulfide, hypochlorous acid, iodine, lead, mercuric chloride, molybdates, permanganates, selenium, sodium hypochlorite and zinc.[3,4]

Process Description

Carbon adsorption is a separation process which relies on the weak physical attractions between contaminant molecules and the charged surface of carbon. Typically, activated carbon is used because of its porous nature and high adsorption capacity. Adsorption is a suface phenomenon and is reversible. Heat, steam or solvent may be applied to remove the adsorbed contaminants from the surface of the carbon, thereby regenerating carbon for future re-use.

In decontaminating aqueous wastestreams, wastewater is pas-

Figure 2
Carbon Reactivation Options

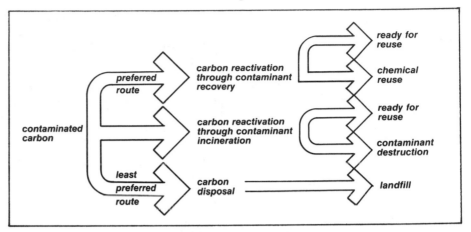

sed through a tank or column filled with activated carbon (see Figure 1). The contaminants are trapped in the pores of the carbon by surface attraction forces and purified water passes through the unit. As more and more contaminants adhere to the pore surfaces of the carbon, the adsorptive capacity of the carbon is exhausted.[5]

Three options exist for restoring capacity to the treatment system (see Figure 2). The preferred route from a materials and energy conservation aspect is to strip the carbon bed of its contaminants in a manner that permits recovery and re-use of these contaminants. This practice may be feasible if wastestreams are kept segregated and if relatively large quantities of select contaminants occur. Carbon adsorption systems have been used to recover solvent vapours generated during adhesives manufacture, textile finishing, printing, coatings application and dry cleaning.

Installations exist that chemically recover adsorbed phenol, acetic acid, p-nitrophenol, p-chlorobenzene, p-cresol and ethylene diamine from carbon used to decontaminate segregated wastewater effluents.

For wastestreams that contain a large variety of small amounts of contaminants, chemical recovery might not be feasible, however, the reactivation and re-use of the carbon bed may still be possible. In the second option, the contaminated carbon is incinerated in a furnace at around 900°C to destroy

the organic contaminants, thereby re-opening the pore spaces in the carbon material. Although the cost of on-site carbon regeneration processes may be prohibitive to the small operator, the smaller company should investigate the possibility of carbon regeneration elsewhere at an established facility.

The third option used in handling contaminated carbon is to bury it in a landfill site.

Environmental Aspects

The greatest environmental concern is associated with the landfilling of non-regenerated carbon impregnated with potentially hazardous material.

When the carbon is regenerated chemically by washing with solvents, acids or bases, potential impacts are associated with the handling of particular regenerants. The use of solvent regenerating agents requires proper controls to minimize fugitive solvent emissions.

Thermal regeneration of the exhausted carbon bed may yield air pollution during incineration, however, air pollution can be minimized through the use of control devices such as scrubbers and baghouses.

2.
Distillation

Distillation has been in widespread industrial use for many years in the petrochemical industry to purify chemicals or separate them from secondary byproducts. In recent years, distillation principles are applied with greater frequency to treat liquid organic wastestreams.

Waste Recovery Applications

Distillation is applicable to the separation of water-organic or organic-organic liquid mixtures where the boiling points of those liquids differ. In the case of simple purification of a contaminated solvent, distillation is used to separate the solvent from the contaminants. The purified solvent may be a single solvent type or a blend of solvents, depending on the composition of the wastestream. In addition to simple decontamination, distillation principles may be used to separate solvent blends into their constituent solvent types.

Many organic industrial wastes can be purified for re-use using distillation methods. Waste solvents can be distilled for re-use in cleaning equipment in the painting, printing, plastics, adhesives, electronics and other industries. Phenol recovery from aqueous solutions is achievable through distillation.[6] Methylene chloride can be recovered from polyurethane waste.[2] Ethylbenzene can be separated from styrene and recovered.[2] Waste oil can be re-refined to produce commercial grade oil with the aid of distillation.[7]

Process Description

Distillation is the boiling of a liquid solution and condensation of the vapour for the purpose of separating the components. The process utilizes the differences in the boiling points of the components as the means of separation. If the solution to be separated

Figure 3
Batch Distillation Unit

Contaminated liquid solvent is boiled in a still to evaporate solvent. Solvent vapour is condensed and may be collected as a liquid for re-use. If the desired product is the residual liquid in the bottom of the still, distillation proceeds until the "bottoms" concentration is at the required level.
Source: Unit Operations for Treatment of Hazardous Industrial Wastes, Noyes Data Corporation, 1978.

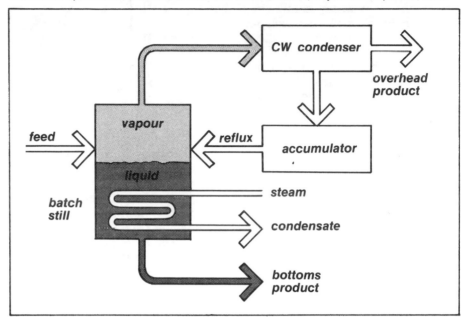

contains only two components, one component concentrates in the condensed vapour (condensate) and the other in the residual liquid. For solutions containing more than two components, the less volatile components concentrate in the residual liquid and the more volatile ones concentrate in the vapour or vapour condensate.

The complexity of the distillation process varies with the number of components in the wastestream and the degree to which separation is required. The simplest form of distillation is batch distillation. Batch distillation is a single equilibrium stage operation and is carried out in a still in which the heat source is a steam jacket or a heating coil. The solution is boiled and vapour is driven off, condensed and collected until the desired concentration of product has been reached. If the desired product is the residual liquid in the bottom of the still, distillation proceeds until the "bottoms" concentration is at the required level.

Small-scale batch distillation units are commercially available

for on-site reclamation of cleaning solvents such as those used in the painting and printing industries. These simple stills will remove impurities such as waste ink and paint from the cleaning solvent, however, they cannot separate the components of a solvent blend (see Figure 3). Most industries rely on solvent blends rather than a pure, single-type solvent for equipment clean-out purposes.

Those industries that require virgin-purity solvents, or precisely controlled solvent mixtures may choose to have their waste solvents undergo fractional distillation to separate them into component solvents. High-purity, single component solvents may be required by paint and ink formulators, and by hospital and science laboratories. There are many configurations that a fractional distillation unit may take. Typically, the fractioning column is a tall, cylindrical column which contains material or internal structures to maximize contact between the liquid and vapour (see Figure 4).

Figure 4
Fractional Distillation Process

Fractional solvent distillation is used to separate waste solvent blends into component solvents. During distillation, vapours of volatile solvents move up the distillation column while less volatile solvents still in the liquid form move down the column.

Source: Unit Operations for Treatment of Hazardous Industrial Wastes, Noyes Data Corporation, 1978.

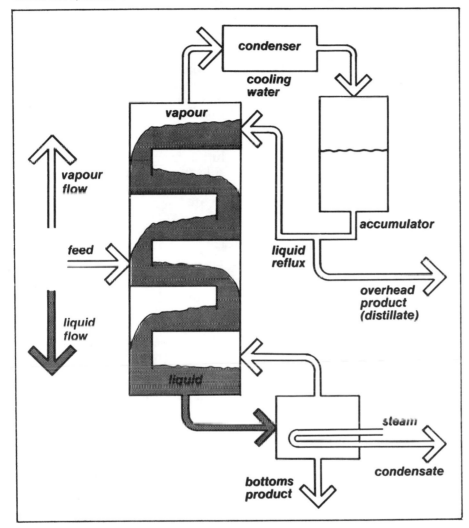

3.
Electrodialysis

Electrodialysis technology has been in commercial operation for more than two decades, however, its application was directed primarily to the production of potable water from salt water, or to the production of salt from seawater. Hundreds of electrodialysis units are in use throughout the world, many of which have been in service for more than 15 years.

Electrodialysis is used industrially to remove mineral constituents or contaminants from process streams that contain large amounts of organic products. Examples of industrial use of electrodialysis include de-ashing of sugars, washing of photographic emulsions, demineralization of whey, desalting of food products such as whey, and in the chemical industry for a variety of solution enrichment or depletion purposes.

The current attention to waste recovery is making electrodialysis a suitable candidate for many of industry's wastewater problems. Pilot operations using electrodialysis have been successful in the recovery of plating rinses, desalting of sewage plant effluent, sulphite-liquor recovery, and recovery of hydrogen fluoride and ammonium fluoride effluents from glass and quartz etching facilities.[2,8,9] Future research and commercialization may see more widespread application of this technology to on-site industrial waste recovery and re-use.

Waste Recovery Applications

Electrodialysis is widely applicable in the separation of an aqueous salt stream into dilute and concentrated streams. The purpose of the separation is to concentrate certain constituents in the wastestream for re-use, treatment or disposal. Typically, electrodialysis can separate a wastestream containing 1000 to 5000 ppm inorganic salts into a dilute stream that contains 100 to 500 ppm salt and a concentrated

Environmental Aspects

The treatment of waste organics by distillation does not create significant air and water pollution problems.[2]

The distillation of organic solvents requires the handling of large quantities of volatile and potentially toxic chemicals, however, emissions can be prevented by proper controls on tank vents and the distillation process itself.

Still bottoms are the residue remaining in the distillation unit after the volatile fractions have been vaporized and the useful, heavier fractions removed. Still bottoms may present a waste disposal problem because they contain impurities, tars and sludges, some of which may be toxic. The current disposal practice of landfilling these wastes is giving way to investigations in residue recovery as an auxiliary fuel, roofing material or low-grade paint, depending on the composition of the residue.

Figure 5
Electrodialysis

Cations in the feed water show the same behaviour as sodium (Na⁺) and anions the same behaviour as chloride (Cl⁻). Under the action of an electric field, cation exchange membranes permit passage only of positive ions while anion exchange membranes permit passage only of negatively charged ions.

Source: *Unit Operations for Treatment of Hazardous Industrial Wastes,* Noyes Data Corporation, 1978.

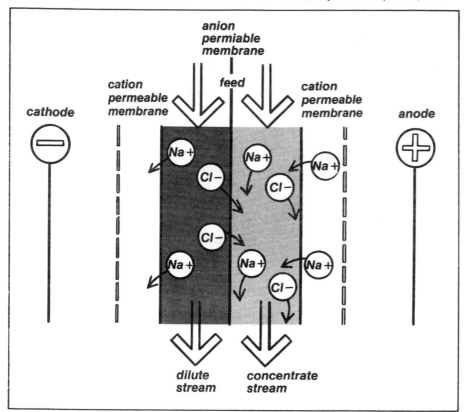

stream that contains up to 10,000 ppm salt.[2] Electrodialysis technology is currently in use in waste developer recovery by the photo processing industry.

Process Description

Electrodialysis, along with reverse osmosis and ultrafiltration, are known as membrane technologies because they depend on membranes to selectively retain and permit passage of specific molecules. Unlike ultrafiltration and reverse omosis, separation in electrodialysis technology is induced by electrical current. Special synthetic membranes based on ion exchange resins are used which are permeable only to a single-charge ion. The construction of an electrodialysis unit is such that anion membranes are alternated with cation membranes in stacks of cells in series. Under the action of an electric field, cation exchange membranes permit passage only of positive ions while anion exchange membranes permit passage only of negatively charged ions. This results in the concentration or dilution of salts in alternate compartments (see Figure 5). The life of separation membranes is frequently five years, however, this varies with the type and volume of wastewater processed.

The use of electrodialysis to recycle spent developer baths from photo processors is similar. Commercially available electrodialyzers consist of cation exchange membranes stratified alternately, with a pair of electrodes installed at both ends. By applying a suitable direct current voltage, anions and cations in the developer solu-

tion compartments are attracted toward the electrode of the opposite charge. In the case of developer recycling, only halide ions such as bromide must be accumulated and eliminated, leaving other ions in the developer undialized and ready for re-use once the solution has been replenished.[10]

Environmental Aspects

Like other membrane separation methods, electrodialysis must be used in conjunction with additional recovery or treatment processes. There is some concern that electrodialysis may cause air pollution from the small amounts of chlorine gas generated at the electrodes when chlorides are treated.

4.
Electrolysis

Electrolysis technology has been an important component in a variety of industrial processes over several decades. Its use as a waste recovery technology is also well established in many industries, and its significance as a recovery tool continues to grow as the costs of conventional disposal escalate. Examples of the use of electrolysis in industrial processing include the production of chlorine-caustic, metal refining and electroplating.

Waste Recovery Applications

Electrolysis is an important waste treatment and recovery technology. One of the major applications of this technology is in the recovery of heavy metals from wastewater. In the photo processing industry, silver is routinely recovered from spent fix through electrolytic means.

Electrolysis technology is applied to waste pickling solutions to recover metals.[11] In the copper industry, for example, waste pickling solutions are used to remove scale and oxides from freshly cast and hot worked copper metal. As the sulfuric acid bath accumulates

Figure 6
Electrolysis System

During electrolysis, oxidation or reduction takes place at the surface of conductive electrodes surrounded by wastewater. Metal ion present in the wastewater is reduced to metal itself at the cathode.
Source: "Heavy Metals Recovery Promises to Pare Water Clean-Up Bills," *Chemical Engineering,* December 22, 1975.

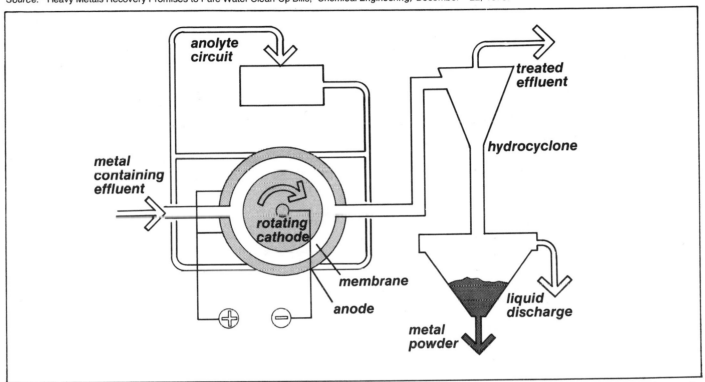

copper, it loses its effectiveness. By applying an electrolytic cell to plate the excess copper from the solution, copper is recovered, and the pickling bath retains its effectiveness over a longer period of time. Waste rinse solutions in which the metal ion concentration is very dilute may first undergo a separation or concentration process before the electrolytic recovery process is applied.

Another use of electrolysis in wastewater treatment is the oxidation of a dissolved species at the anode, such as in the destruction of cyanide. Electrolysis may be used indirectly to separate oil-water mixtures by generating tiny bubbles in a process known as electroflotation.[12]

Process Description

Electrolysis is based on the oxidation or reduction which takes place at the surface of conductive electrodes immersed in a chemical medium under the influence of an applied potential.[13] At the cathode (negative electrode) the metal ion is reduced to the metal itself ($M^+ + e^- \longrightarrow M$) (see Figure 6).

In the case of electrolytic recovery of silver by photo processors, silver is deposited on the cathode in the form of silver plate with a purity close to 99%. The cathodes are removed periodically and the silver is chipped off and sent elsewhere for refining. To enhance the migration of metal ions to the cathode, it is common to engineer the recovery chamber such that the cathode rotates continuously, mixing the incoming metal-laden wastewater.

Environmental Aspects

Electrolytic systems may generate a potential air pollution problem due to the formation of gases such as hydrogen and chlorine at the electrodes.[2] Chlorine emissions, if significant, may be controlled with scrubbers.

5.
Evaporation

Evaporation is a well-established waste concentration practice in widespread use throughout the industrial community. Some industries use evaporation technology to concentrate or separate wastes to permit re-use. Other industries use evaporation methods to dewater sludges prior to landfill disposal or incineration. Although evaporation is an expensive, energy-intensive process, it is used extensively in the treatment of hazardous waste because of the flexibility of the process and its proven success record. Evaporators have been used for many years in industrial recovery programmes and there are a number of systems available: rising film evaporators, flash evaporators using waste heat, submerged tube evaporators and atmospheric evaporators are all being used in commercial settings.

Waste Recovery Applications

Evaporation technology is widely used to separate water from inorganic solutions and slurries, though it is also used for concentrating sludges containing organic solvents. This technology is capable of handling liquids, slurries and sometimes sludges, both organic and inorganic, containing suspended or dissolved solids, or dissolved liquids where one of the components is essentially non-volatile.[2]

Evaporation is commonly used to dewater liquid radioactive waste to form a dry residue that is buried with other solid radioactive waste.[14,15] In the explosives industry, trinitrotoluene waste is concentrated by evaporation for disposal by incineration.[2] Some photographic chemical processing plants use exaporation procedures to dewater dye waste sludges.[2] In the pulp and paper industry, dilute "black liquor" is concentrated by heat from the steam recovery furnace prior to incineration for heat and chemical recovery.[16] Spent mash from molasses distillery processes is concentrated in a multi-effect evaporator and then incinerated for heat and chemical recovery.[2]

Waste types that can be handled by evaporation include heavy metals, radioactive materials, fluorides, chlorides, many hydrocarbons and halogenated hydrocarbons, amines, nitro compounds, explosives and dyestuffs.

Process Description

Evaporation is a physical separation process in which liquid is vaporized to separate it from a dissolved or suspended solid. Although evaporation resembles the distillation process, no attempt is made to separate the components of the vapour as in distillation.

Evaporators achieve resource recovery by distilling the wastestream until there is sufficient concentration of chemicals in solution for treatment, recovery or re-use. Because of their high energy requirements, evaporators are not used to concentrate highly dilute solutions. Water vapour

Figure 7
Evaporator System

Wastewater is boiled to drive off water. The distilled water vapour can be condensed and re-used. The remaining wastewater is concentrated enough to permit re-use or treatment.
Source: *Unit Operations for Treatment of Hazardous Industrial Wastes*, Noyes Data Corporation, 1978.

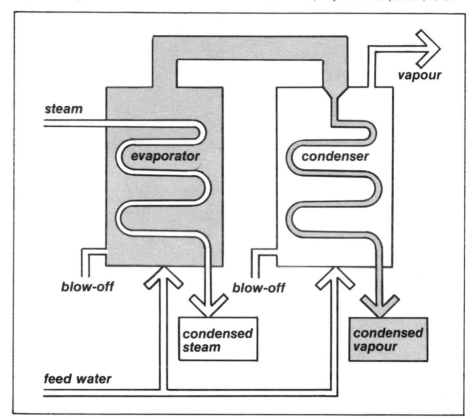

produced during the evaporation process can be condensed and re-used, or released to the atmosphere. Condensing allows the recovery of some of the heat used in the evaporation process.

Evaporation equipment takes on many configurations. The most common evaporator type makes use of metal coils, tubes or jackets to maximize the surface area of heat transfer. Evaporators have undergone numerous design changes in past years to minimize energy requirements. Many evaporators operate under a vacuum to reduce the boiling point of the liquid, thereby minimizing energy consumption[17] (see Figures 7 and 8).

A common industrial evaporator is the vertical tube evaporator consisting of a relatively small flash chamber above a vertical arrangement of tubes within a cylinder.[18] Operating on the same principle as a smoke

stack, the long tube evaporator gives high fluid velocity to the rising liquid and vapour within the tubes. The high fluid velocities promote high heat transfer efficiency between the evaporating fluid and the tube walls.

Another evaporator system is multiple-effect evaporation in which the vapour from one evaporator is used to provide heat for the next evaporator (see Figure 9). The significance of this design is that less energy is required to evaporate the same quantity of water compared with single-effect evaporators.[19] A company's decision on how many effects or evaporative stages to construct will be based on a trade-off between increased steam economy and the capital cost of additional evaporator equipment.

Another energy-conservative approach to evaporation is to use ponds exposed to the sun for concentrating brines or sludges.

Solar evaporation ponds are widely used in California for dewatering hazardous wastes prior to land disposal. This technology is not suitable for climates where precipitation rates are high. As solar collector technology develops, an increasing number of companies are experimenting with sun-derived heat to provide auxiliary heat to plant operations.

covery, treatment or disposal.

Despite the energy-conservative feature of solar evaporation ponds, numerous potential problems exist. It is critical that solar evaporation ponds be located on impermeable terrain and constructed in a manner that ensures full retention of the waste material. Failure to do so may result in groundwater and surface water contamination. Solar evaporation ponds must be restricted in the types of wastes they contain to avert the emission of noxious and potentially toxic vapours in the air.

Figure 8
Long-Tube Vertical Evaporator

The long-tube vertical evaporator is one of many evaporator configurations.

Source: Chemical Engineering Handbook, McGraw-Hill, 1963.

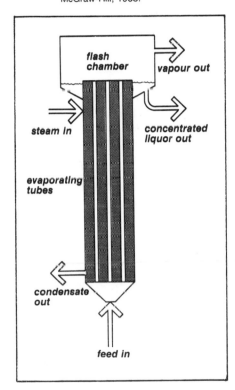

Environmental Aspects

Air pollution problems are minimal in evaporation processes in which the material being evaporated is water. However, if the material to be concentrated contains volatile organic compounds such as solvents, it is necessary to condense these vapours for re-

Figure 9
Multiple Effect Evaporator

By using several evaporators in series, the vapour from one evaporator can be used to heat the next evaporator and so on. The total heat consumption is less than for three evaporators functioning separately.

Source: Physical, Chemical and Biological Treatment Techniques for Industrial Wastes, U.S. Environmental Protection Agency, 1977.

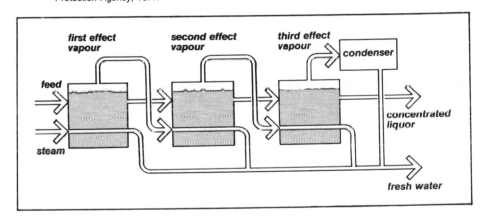

6.
Hydrolysis

Hydrolysis technology is as old as the making of soap. Known as saponification in the soap making industry, hydrolysis is the addition of alkali to hydrolyze heated fats to produce soap. A variety of hydrolysis reactions employing different reagents have been employed for years in the manufacture of organic materials. Although hydrolysis is not, as yet, widely used in the treatment of industrial wastes, the principles and equipment used in manufacturing applications are applicable to various waste treatment and recovery needs.

Waste Recovery Applications

Hydrolysis shows promise for the future treatment and recovery of industrial wastes. Some recovery applications in operation or demonstrated to be technically feasible follow.

Hydrolysis is used to recycle wastestreams in an organic chemicals plant.[20] For example, the manufacture of crufomate generates large quantities of wastewater and waste tar. Hydrolysis of the wastestreams yields an organic phase suitable for distillation and recycling, and an aqueous phase that may undergo biological treatment.

Another application of hy-

drolysis occurs in the treatment of acid sludge generated by the petroleum industry.[21] Hydrolysis of acid sludge yields a weak sulfuric acid fraction and a tarry acid oil layer. The recovery, concentration and re-use of the sulfuric acid portion can supply a refinery with more than half of its acid needs. The tar fraction can be recovered as an auxiliary fuel source.

The following applications of hydrolysis technology are technically feasible but not yet in widespread commercial use. Hydrolysis is suitable for the conversion of sludge to animal feed by converting activated sludge to a thick syrup which is high in protein, carbohydrates and vitamins.[22]

Hydrolysis processes can be used to decompose polyurethane foam waste to its constituent components to permit reprocessing into new polyurethane, or just recovery of the chemical components for resale.[23] Current research is demonstrating the feasibility of cyanide destruction through hydrolysis.

Hydrolysis is widely applicable to wastestreams from dairies, food industries, wool-scouring operations and antibiotics manufacture.[2] Hydrolysis of these wastestreams rich in carbohydrates may yield useful animal feed products.

Process Description

In general usage, hydrolysis refers to the decomposition brought about by water when hydrogen reacts with one component and hydroxyl reacts with another component. However, hydrolysis also refers to reactions in which water is not a reactant. For example, the addition of an alkali to solution and the subsequent formation of the alkali salt of an organic acid is known as hydrolysis. There are many classes of hydrolytic reactions. Most commercial hydrolysis processes operate at elevated temperatures and pressures to promote reaction.

Environmental Aspects

Despite the beneficial recovery aspects of hydrolysis, it must be recognized that certain hydrolytic reactions are capable of producing toxic byproducts. Use of this technology must be based on a clear understanding of the byproducts generated so that control measures may be initiated to avoid environmental hazards.

7.
Ion Exchange

Ion exchange technology has been in use since the late 1800s in water softening and sugar crystallization procedures. By the late 1930s, the discovery of synthetic ion exchange resins resulted in their application to hydrometallurgy, deionization of water, and uranium processing and extraction. Ion exchange technology is also well developed and in commercial use to recover metals from wastestreams generated by the electroplating industry.

Ion exchange technology can be employed to remove a wide range of inorganic and organic contaminants including all metallic elements when present as soluble species, anions such as halide, sulfate, nitrate and cyanides, acids such as carboxylics, sulfonics and some phenols, amines and alkylsulfates.[2]

Waste Recovery Applications

Ion exchange technology is well developed in the electroplating industry[2,24] to remove ionic impurities from rinsewater enabling re-use of the water. The impurities collected are suitable for recycling. This technology is gaining greater prominence among photo finishers to recover both water and silver from dilute waste rinsewaters.

Ion exchange technology is also employed to remove low concentrations of undesirable impurities from concentrated process streams. In such cases, the purpose is to recycle active materials while ridding the process bath of unwanted impurities. For example, in the cleaning of aluminum,[2,25] the phosphoric acid cleaning agent becomes contaminated with dissolved aluminum phosphate salts from the dissolution of the aluminum. Subjecting the contaminated cleaning bath to

Figure 10
Ion Exchange Nickel Recovery

Wastewater containing nickel ion contaminants is pumped through the cation exchanger where the nickel ions are retained by the resin. The wastewater then passes through an anion exchanger which retains anion contaminants. The purified water is ready for re-use. The cation exchanger is regenerated with sulphuric acid and a concentrated solution of nickel sulphate is eluted, leaving residual acid. It is possible to recycle the residual acid for re-use. The anion exchanger is regenerated with sodium hydroxide.

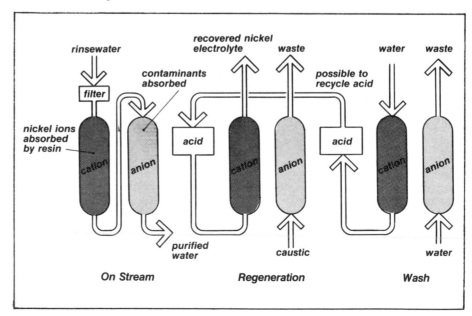

cation exchange ensures removal of the aluminum contamination and re-use of the bath.

Ion exchange technology is capable of separating organic materials and inorganic salts from industrial wastestreams. Highly saline liquid industrial wastes from food processing [26] have been desalinized by an ion exchange separation technique known as ion exclusion. In this type of separation, the sodium chloride is excluded by the resin while the non-ionized organic material can penetrate the resin.

Pilot demonstrations indicate that ion exchange is applicable to the recovery of chromium from cooling tower blowdown waters.[27] Ion exchange is also suitable for the removal of cyanide which occurs in some photo processing wastes.

Another promising development is the use of cation exchange technology to recycle metal pickling wastes.[28] Copper and steel pickle liquors, which result from an acid cleaning process, can undergo ion exchange to remove contaminants and permit re-use of the acidic cleaning solution.

Future research and commercialization of synthetic resins promise to extend the application of ion exchange technology to an even wider range of wastestreams.

Process Description

Ion exchange is a process for separating dissolved inorganic or organic substances from an aqueous liquid. This may entail the general or selective removal of heavy metals from dilute aqueous wastestreams, or the removal of select contaminants from more concentrated process baths.

The contaminant-laden liquid is passed through a bed containing a natural or synthetic resin. The resin exchanges ions with the inorganics in solution, resulting in the removal of inorganics from the solution and their attachment to the resin column (see Figure 10).

The wastestream is passed through the resin column until the ion exchange resin no longer effectively removes the contaminant. Once the resin bed is saturated

with contaminant species, it is necessary to regenerate the resin by rinsing the contaminants from the resin with a concentrated brine or acid solution. The resin is restored to its original effectiveness and the contaminants may be recovered and recycled.

To ensure the effective operation of the ion exchange unit, it is important to remove any suspended solids prior to exchange that might otherwise plug the exchange bed.

Environmental Aspects

Commercially available ion exchange units tend to be closed systems and as such present no major air pollution problem. Because the regenerant solutions may be strong acids and bases, proper handling practices must be followed to avert spills or discharges. Although the purpose of many ion exchange units is to recover select metals for re-use, those systems which use ion exchange to collect hazardous wastes for further disposal must do so in an environmentally acceptable manner.

8.
High-Gradient Magnetic Separation

High-gradient magnetic separation is a relative newcomer to waste recovery practices. Although not commercially attractive except in those instances where the recovered metal is of sufficient value to justify investment for its recovery, future research and development may enhance commercialization of this waste separation technology.

The predominant industrial use of high-gradient magnetic separation is in the purification of kaolin clay to remove a small unwanted magnetic fraction.[29] Another processing application is in the removal of impurities from iron and other ores.[30] Although magnetic separators capable of removing highly magnetic particles have

existed for some time, high-gradient magnetic separation extends the efficacy of magnetic separation to include particles that are only weakly magnetic.

Waste Recovery Applications

Pilot plant trials are underway to apply high-gradient magnetic separation to coal desulphurization, water purification and the removal of flue dusts in air streams from blast furnaces. Potentially treatable waste forms include aqueous and non-aqueous liquids, slurries and dry powders. Waste types not amenable to high-gradient magnetic separation include sludges, tars and gases. Wastes suitable for this separation technology should flow easily through a relatively open filamentary matrix or be finely divided.

High-gradient magnetic separation appears to be best suited for the removal of magnetic wastes present in low concentrations in a liquid wastestream. Paramagnetic elements and compounds are removable by magnetic separation. Non-magnetic suspended solids may be removed from a contaminated stream if they associate with a magnetic floc which can be added to the wastestream. Dissolved material in water may be removed by magnetic separation if it co-precipitates with a ferric hydroxide gel in a wastestream.[31]

Process Description

The interest in high-gradient magnetic separation technology is spurred by the fact that separation speed and efficiency is considerably enhanced over ordinary filtration methods, and at lower costs and energy requirements.

The high-gradient magnetic separation process makes use of fine ferromagnetic filament material containing 95% void space as occurs in compressed steel wool. Magnets capable of generating high-intensity fields are placed around the steel wool chamber. As the wastestream passes through the magnetic field in the chamber,

Figure 11
High-Gradient Magnetic Separation

1. **Magnetic impurities collect on the steel wool as the wastewater passes through the magnetic field.**

2. **The magnet is shut off and the steel wool is rinsed free of adherent particles.**

Source: *Unit Operations for Treatment of Hazardous Industrial Wastes*, Noyes Data Corporation, 1978.

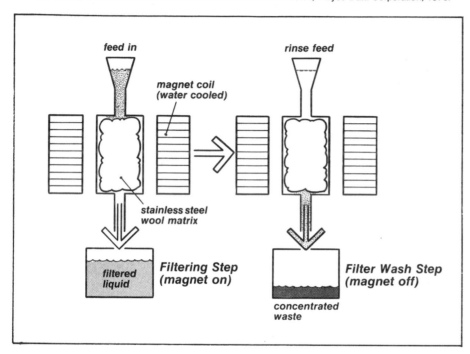

impurities collect on the steel wool matrix by magnetic attraction. Metals and other magnetic impurities may be recovered by shutting off the magnet and washing the steel wool matrix clean of the adherent particles (see Figure 11).

Environmental Aspects

From a materials and energy conservation aspect, the optimum use of high-gradient separation is as a separation technology in conjunction with material recovery. The separation process itself appears to generate no serious environmental problems. However, if material recovery is not designed into the installation, great care must be taken to properly dispose of the sludge collected by washing the filter free of its impurities.

9.
Solvent Extraction

Solvent extraction, a process for removing organic substances from aqueous or organic solutions, is used in both commercial processing and waste treatment. Commercial operations include the manufacture of lubricating oil from crude oil in which saturated paraffins are extracted with such solvents as phenol, furfural, propane and benzene; upgrading gasoline by separating aromatics from low-octane paraffins with the solvent diethylene glycol; the extraction of sulphur compounds from gasoline; the manufacture of fine chemicals and pharmaceuticals; and the refining of vegetable oils and fats.[32,33] Much of the solvent extraction technology currently used in manufacturing is directly applicable to the treatment and recovery of organics from aqueous wastestreams.

Waste Recovery Applications

Solvent extraction is applicable to the removal of organic compounds from aqueous and organic wastestreams. It is used in conjunction with other unit processes such as distillation or stripping to further purify selected solvents for re-use.

Although not in widespread use, solvent extraction has been demonstrated to be successful in the recovery of phenol and related compounds from aqueous wastes as generated by petroleum refineries, coke ovens and phenol resin plants.[34,35] The extraction process reduces phenol concentrations from 5% down to levels of a few ppm.

Extraction technology has also been applied to the recovery of halogenated hydrocarbons such as methylene chloride from an aqueous wastestream.[2]

An example of the extraction of a solvent from an organic wastestream concerns the reclamation of Freon™ solvents.[2] The wastestream contains oil, Freon™ and acetone. After distillation to separate the oil fraction, an extraction process is used to recover Freon™ from the remaining Freon™/acetone mixture. Many research projects are under way in the United States to investigate solvent extraction as a viable waste recovery process.

Process Description

Solvent extraction is the separation of select organic substances from a liquid solution by contact with an immiscible liquid. Separation of the liquid solution will result only if the original liquid solution distributes itself differently between the two liquid phases.

A solvent is added to the wastestream that does not dissolve in the wastestream. The mixture is agitated, enabling the added solvent to extract those organics in the original wastestream which have an affinity for it. Separation of the immiscible solvent from the wastestream is followed by distillation, stripping or adsorption to

Figure 12
Solvent Extraction of Wastewater

A solvent is added to wastewater to extract residual solvent in the wastestream. The solvent and solute undergo separation through distillation, stripping or adsorption.

Source: "Wastewater Treatment by Solvent Extraction," *Canadian Journal of Chemical Engineering* 49(6).

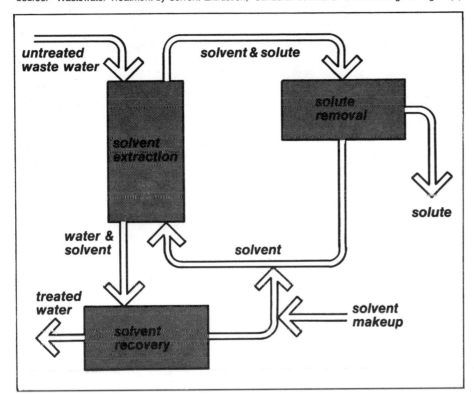

10.
Reverse Osmosis

Although the principle of reverse osmosis has been understood for centuries, it was not until the late 1950s that researchers built the first reverse osmosis units. In the short 30 years since its cumbersome prototype was developed, reverse osmosis technology has undergone a dramatic transformation to become one of industry's most trim, efficient and versatile waste treatment systems.

Waste Recovery Applications

Reverse osmosis is applicable to the separation of dissolved ionic and non-ionic components from water solutions. Typically, the concentration of incoming wastewater is in the range of 500 ppm to 20,000 ppm although solutions containing up to 10% of the dissolved component can be processed.[2]

The types of wastestreams suitable for processing are limited by the ability of the plastic membranes to withstand the destructive nature of a given wastestream. Although aqueous

separate the organic contaminants from the extracting solvent. The solvent extraction process yields a treated solvent-free wastestream and a re-usable solvent stream (see Figure 12).

Environmental Aspects

There is potential for solvent loss through fugitive solvent emissions, however, this loss is minimal if proper extraction methods are employed. Solvent extraction is usually conducted to achieve material recovery for resale or re-use, and as such does not tend to generate large quantities of waste requiring further disposal.

Figure 13
Reverse Osmosis Process

Wastewater is pumped under pressure through a semi-permeable membrane which permits the solvent (water) to pass but retains the dissolved components.

Source: *Desalting Handbook for Planners,* Bureau of Reclamation and Office of Saline Water, May 1972.

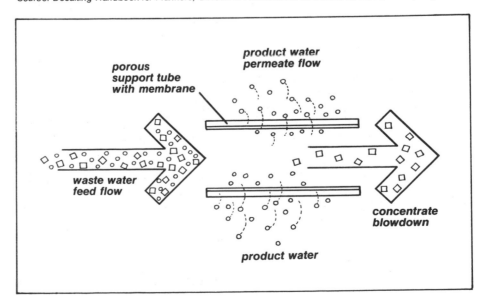

Osmonics Inc.

Osmonics Inc.

Front and back view of a reverse osmosis/ultrafiltration membrane separation system.

Figure 14
Reverse Osmosis Module

Reverse osmosis modules commonly consist of membranes wrapped around the permeate tube in a scroll configuration.

Source: Unit Operations for Treatment of Hazardous Industrial Wastes, Noyes Data Corporation, 1978.

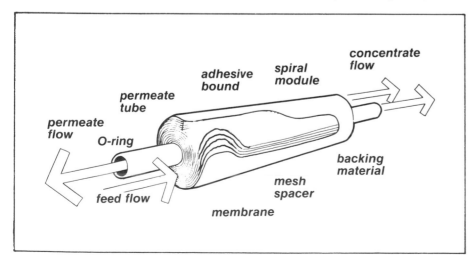

streams with dissolved organics may be processed by reverse osmosis, pure organic streams usually deform plastic membranes. Similarly, strong acids and bases cannot be fed to reverse osmosis units. Reverse osmosis is well suited to accept many ionic compounds, including heavy metal solutions.

Reverse osmosis is widely used in chemical processing, in the preparation of pure water for industrial manufacturing and processing,[36] in preparation of rinsewater for use in semiconductor and electronic manufacturing, for reclamation of electroplating chemicals and water,[37,38] and in sugar reclamation in the food industry.[2]

Process Description

Reverse osmosis is based on a semi-permeable membrane which permits only certain components of solution to pass, and a driving force to separate these components at a useful rate. High pressure pumping in conjunction with a semi-permeable membrane permits passage of the solvent, which is usually water, but not the dissolved components of a solution.

Reverse osmosis results in a concentration of dissolved components on the high pressure side of the membrane while the water passing through the membrane is relatively pure (see Figure 13). The concentrated stream is allowed to flow out of the system and is known as the blowdown stream.

Although cellulose acetate was commonly used as the membrane material in the past, some units today make use of nylon membranes which permit operation at high pH values. Reverse osmosis units vary in how the membranes are arranged to maximize the contact areas.

The reverse osmosis module shown in Figure 14 shows a scroll configuration which contains a high percentage of membrane area per volume and is very easy to replace. The membrane with a synthetic backing is wrapped around the permeate tube and sealed around the edges.

Environmental Aspects

Virtually no air emissions or solid wastes result from a reverse osmosis operation. The process yields two streams, one, a concentrated stream, and the other, a relatively pure water stream. It is common to recycle the constituents in the concentrated stream, however, if a concentrated stream containing potentially hazardous constituents is improperly disposed, serious environmental pollution may result.

11.
Ultrafiltration

Ultrafiltration, like reverse osmosis and electrodialysis, is a membrane separation technology. Ultrafiltration resembles reverse osmosis in that pressure is applied to a solution to force water across a semi-permeable membrane, however, unlike reverse osmosis, the passage of soluble material across the membrane depends only on its molecular size.

Waste Recovery Applications

Ultrafiltration is used to concentrate high molecular weight components of a waste solution for recovery or disposal, and to produce a decontaminated effluent for water re-use or discharge. The process is applicable to both homogenous solutions and colloidal suspensions which are difficult to separate by conventional filtration means.

Ultrafiltration technology is highly versatile and applicable to a wide range of industrial waste recovery needs. Some of the current commercial applications of ultrafiltration include the recovery of polyvinyl alcohol sizing from textile wastewaters,[39] paint recycling from an electrodeposition painting process, [40] the recycling of indigo from spent indigo dyebath as in textile dyeing,[41] protein recovery from cheese whey, [42] and the concentration of oil from metal machining, rolling and drawing.[43]

Other promising uses of ul-

Figure 15
Membrane Ultrafiltration Process

Wastewater is pumped under pressure to the semi-permeable membrane which permits passage of small molecules but retains the large ones.
Source: Unit Operations for Treatment of Hazardous Industrial Wastes, Noyes Data Corporation, 1978.

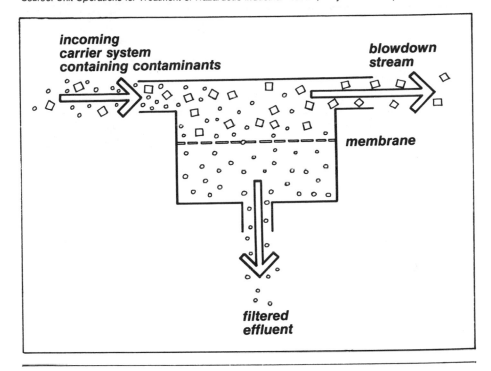

Figure 16
Fibreglass Reinforced Ultrafiltration Module

This diagram depicts another configuration for an ultrafiltration module. A membrane film is cast onto the inside of a porous fibreglass-reinforced epoxy support tube. The support tube is one inch in diameter by 10 feet long and fits into the permeate collection shell.
Source: Abcor Inc., Wilmington, Massachusetts.

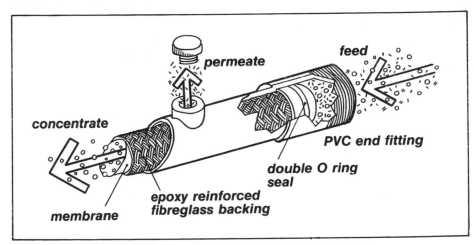

trafiltration technology include pulp mill waste treatment, industrial laundry waste treatment, protein recovery from soy whey, product recovery in pharmaceutical and fermentation industries, and sugar recovery from orange juice pulp.[2]

Process Description

Ultrafiltration of a wastestream results in two streams, one, a concentrated stream containing high molecular weight solute or colloids, and the other, a dilute water stream. A hydrostatic pressure is applied to the upstream side of a semi-permeable membrane.

High molecular weight species remain on the high pressure side of the membrane while water and small size molecules pass through the membrane (see Figures 15, 16 and 17). Ultrafiltration membranes come with various filter pore sizes for molecules ranging from molecular weights of 200 to 100,000. The membrane can be tailor-made as to what size of molecules it will allow to pass. Typically, suspended material and high molecular weight dissolved species such as colloids, protein, carbohydrates and synthetic resins are not able to cross the membrane. Low molecular weight solutes such as certain salts, sugars and organics can pass through the microporous membrane.

Ultrafiltration systems can operate under lower pressures than reverse osmosis systems and the typical membrane flux levels are 20 to 200 gallons/day/foot².

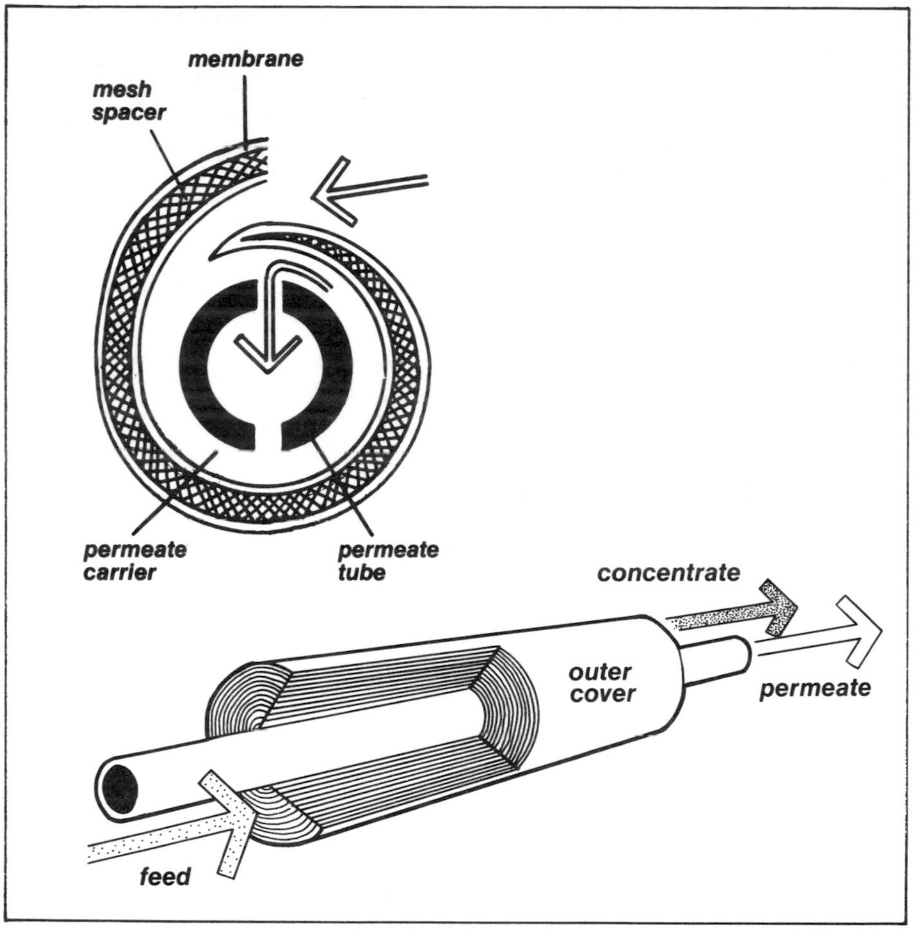

Environmental Aspects

Ultrafiltration is essentially a separation process. If hazardous constituents are present in the incoming wastestream, this technology serves only to concen-trate these hazardous constituents for further recycle or disposal. In some instances, even the dilute filtrate will require additional treatment prior to sewering or discharge into a body of water.

Figure 17
Spiral Wound Ultrafiltration Module

Cut-away (upper figure) shows the spiral wound layers wrapped around the permeate tube. Cross-section (lower figure) shows the build-up of layers in this scroll configuration. The permeate flow arrows indicate the flow of pure water that passes through the membrane and spirals through the permeate carrier to the permeate collection tube.

Source: Osmonics Inc., Hopkins, Minnesota.

FURTHER READING

Bridgewater, A.V. and Mumford, C.J. *Waste Recycling and Pollution Control.* New York: Van Nostrand Reinhold Co., 1981.

Cooper, W.J. *Chemistry in Water Reuse: Volume 1.* Ann Arbor, Michigan: Ann Arbor Science Publishers, Inc., 1981.

Krofchak, D. and Stone, J.N. *Science and Engineering for Pollution-Free Systems.* Ann Arbor, Michigan: Ann Arbor Science Publishers Inc., 1975.

Lund, H.F. *Industrial Pollution Control Handbook.* New York: McGraw-Hill Book Co., 1971.

Metcalf & Eddy, Inc. *Wastewater Engineering: Treatment, Disposal, Reuse.* New York: McGraw-Hill Book Co., 1979.

Sell, N.J. *Industrial Pollution Control.* New York: Van Nostrand Reinhold Co., 1981.

Sittig, Marshall. *Resource Recovery and Recycling Handbook of Industrial Wastes.* Park Ridge, New Jersey: Noyes Data Corporation, 1976.

Toxic Waste Assessment Group. *Alternatives to the Land Disposal of Hazardous Wastes.* Prepared for the Office of Appropriate Technology, State of California, 1981.

U.S. Environmental Protection Agency. *Treatment of Hazardous Wastes.* Proceedings of the Sixth Annual Research Symposium. Report No. EPA 600/9-80-011, 1980.

REFERENCES

1. Wherry, C.R. "Activated Carbon." In *Chemical Economic Handbook.* Menlo Park, California: Stanford Research Institute.

2. De Renzo, D.J. *Unit Operations for Treatment of Hazardous Industrial Wastes.* Park Ridge, New Jersey: Noyes Data Corporation, 1978.

3. Hasler, J.W. *Purification with Activated Carbon.* New York: Chemical Publishing Company Inc., 1974.

4. Nelson, F. *et al. Adsorption of Inorganic Materials on Activated Carbon.* Proceedings of 29th Industrial Waste Conference, Perdue University, 1974.

5. Hager, D.G. "Industrial Wastewater Treatment by Granular Activated Carbon." *Industrial Water Engineering,* January/February 1974.

6. Fox, C.R. "Remove and Recover Phenol." *Hydrocarbon Processing,* July 1975.

7. Weinstein, N.J. "Lube Oil: Re-Refining Schemes Compared." *Hydrocarbon Processing,* December 1974.

8. Leitz, F.B. "Electrodialysis for Industrial Water Cleanup." *Environmental Science and Technology* 10(2), February 1976.

9. Takenaka, H.H. and Chen, C.L. *Demineralization of Wastewater by Electrodialysis.* Prepared for U.S. Environmental Protection Agency, Report No. EPA-600/2-75-047, October 1975.

10. Taylor, Ray. Snook Corporation, Los Gatos, California. Personal communication, July 1981.

11. Warner, B. *Electrolytic Treatment of Job Shop Metal Finishing Wastewater.* Prepared for U.S. Environmental Protection Agency, Report No. EPA-600-2/75-028, September 1975.

12. Kuhn, A.T. "Electrochemical Treatment of Aqueous Effluent Streams." In Bockris, J.O. (ed). *Electrochemistry of Cleaner Environments.* New York: Plenum Press, 1972.

13. Ricci, L. "Heavy Metals Recovery Promises to Pare Water Clean-Up Bills." *Chemical Engineering,* December 22, 1975.

14. Goodlett, C.B. "Concentration of Aqueous Radioactive Wastes." *Chemical Engineering Progress,* April 1975.

15. Petrie, J.C. *et al.* "Vacuum Evaporator-Crystallizer Handles Radioactive Waste." *Chemical Engineering Progress,* April 1976.

16. Rosenblad, A.E. "Evaporator Systems for Black Liquor Concentration." *Chemical Engineering Progress,* April 1976.

17. Perry, J.M. (ed.) *Chemical Engineers Handbook.* New York: McGraw-Hill, 1963.

18. Reid, Crowther & Partners Ltd. *Hazardous Wastes In Northern and Western Canada: Technology Review.* Prepared for Environment Canada, December 1980.

19. A.D. Little Inc. *Physical, Chemical and Biological Treatment Techniques for Industrial Wastes: Volumes I and II.* Prepared for U.S Environmental Protection Agency, Report No. NTIS/PB-275-054, 1977.

20. Bailey, R.E. *et al.* "Process Changes in an Organic Chemicals Production Plant to Improve Yields and Decrease By-Products." In *Industrial Process Design for Pollution Control,* Vol. 4. New York: American Institute of Chemical Engineers, 1972.

21. Willem, R. *Industrial Wastes.* New York: Reinhold Publishing Co., 1953.

22. "SO₂ Hydrolysis Converts Sludge to Animal Feed." *Industrial Research* 12(10), October 1970.

23. Mahoney, L.R. *et al.* "Hydrolysis of Polyurethane Foam Waste." *Environmental Science and Technology* 8(2), February 1974.

24. Downing, D.G. *et al. Chemical Engineering Progress Symposium Series No. 90.* Vol. 64, 1969.

25. Church, F.L. "Bright Dip Breakthrough." *Modern Metals,* August 1963.

26. "Reduction of Salt Content of Food Processing Liquid Waste Effluent." *Water Pollution Control Research Series, No. 12060 DXL,* January 1971.

27. Chemical Separations Corporation. *The Chromix Process*. Oak Ridge, Tennessee: Chemical Separations Corporation, 1975.

28. Higgins, I. *Total Recycle Systems for Steel Pickle Liquor*. Presented to American Institute of Chemical Engineers, 64th Annual Meeting, San Francisco, California, November 1971.

29. Watson, J.H. "The Beneficiation of Clay Using a Superconducting Magnetic Separator." *IEEE Transactions on Magnetics* 11(5), 1975.

30. Oberteuffer, J. "Magnetic Separation: A Review of Principles, Devices and Applications." *IEEE Transactions on Magnetics* 10(2), 1974.

31. Okamsto, S. "Iron Hydroxides as Magnetic Scavengers." *IEEE Transactions on Magnetics* 10(3), 1974.

32. Kiezyk, P.R. and Mackay, D. "Wastewater Treatment by Solvent Extraction." *Canadian Journal of Chemical Engineering* 49(6), 1971.

33. Scheibel, E.G. "Liquid-Liquid Extraction." In *Encyclopedia of Chemical Technology* 8, 1962.

34. Witt, P.A. and Forbes, M.C. "Valuable By-Product Recovery by Solvent Extraction." Al ChE Symposium Series No. 124, Vol. 68, Winter 1971.

35. Kiezyk, P.R. and Mackay, D. "Screening and Selection of Solvents for the Extraction of Phenol from Water." *Canadian Journal of Chemical Engineering* 51, December 1973.

36. Westinghouse Electric Corporation. *Westinghouse Reverse Osmosis Systems — Pure Water for Industry*. Philadelphia, Pennsylvania (product literature B-160).

37. Robinson, G.T. "Plating Waste Treatment: In-Plant Ingenuity Pays Off." *Product Finishing*, August 1975.

38. Spatz, D.C. "Reclaiming Valuable Metal Wastes." *Pollution Engineering*, January/February 1972.

39. Brandon, C.A. and Porter, J.J. *Hyperfiltration for Textile Wastewater Treatment and Re-Use*. Presented to the Water and Wastewater Equipment Manufacturers Association Annual Meeting, March 1976.

40. Schrantz, J. "Fisher Body's New Painting Facility." *Industrial Finishing*, November 1979.

41. Leonard, F. Dorr Oliver, Stamford, Connecticut. Personal communication, August 1981.

42. Selitzer, R. "Crowley Begins Membrane Process of Cottage Cheese Whey." *Diary Field*, June 1972.

43. Weinstein, N.J. *Waste Oil Recycling and Disposal*. Prepared for U.S. Environmental Protection Agency, Report No. EPA 670/2-74-052, August 1974.

Waste Treatment & Disposal Technologies

The success of waste reduction and recovery should not detract from the need to adequately contain or destroy hazardous residuals. Even those companies active in industrial waste reduction, recovery and exchange generate a wastestream that requires disposal. Waste recovery and re-use operations can not recycle 100% of a company's wastestream. Recovery efficiency of a particular wastestream may be very high, but in the end, some residual waste generally remains.

In most instances in Canada, it is still cheaper for a company to dispose wastes by landfilling than it is to recover and re-use these waste materials. Those wastes that are recycled tend to be materials of high economic value such as semi-precious metals and select solvents. If waste disposal costs reflected the true costs of immobilizing wastes in perpetuity, it is probable that many of the wastestreams currently considered to be of marginal recycle potential would become economically feasible to recycle.

Two trends promise to steer industry along a path of greater waste reduction and recovery. One is the increasing value of raw materials, particularly the petroleum-based resources whose costs are spiralling. The second trend is the upgrading of legislation to end improper waste disposal practices. The upgraded disposal requirements result in higher disposal costs. Both these factors are anticipated to accelerate waste recovery and environmental protection.

Disposal of a drum of hazardous waste cost American businesses $3 to $100 in 1980 (see Table 1). Any business confronted with a large bill to dispose of a single barrel of hazardous material is sure to give the waste recycle option serious consideration when resource recovery technologies are estimated to cost $10 to $40 per drum.[1] The disposal of hazardous wastes cost Canadian industry an average of $6 to $24 per drum in 1980[2] except for highly hazardous wastes such as PCBs and 2,4,5-T, for which accepted disposal facilities are lacking. For the most part, Canadian disposal costs tend to be lower than those in Europe and the United States.

The cost of burying waste will rise sharply as secure chemical landfill replaces sanitary landfill in the disposal of hazardous wastes. Based on 1980 prices, the cost of disposing wastes in a secure landfill in the United States was 4 to 40 times the cost of burying non-hazardous wastes in a sanitary landfill.[1]

In Canada, in the absence of widespread secure landfill facilities, much of industry's waste is co-disposed in sanitary landfills at a low cost. With the anticipated construction of sophisticated treatment and landfill facilities in Canada, it is highly probable that disposal costs will escalate significantly to reflect more accurately the true costs of proper disposal.

The technologies described in this chapter are applicable to the treatment and disposal of residual wastes remaining after waste reduction, recovery and exchange options have been exhausted. No single disposal option can meet the needs of all wastes. Some waste disposal methods are suitable only to organics, others only to inorganics and metals. Each method varies in environmental risks, efficiency and costs. Table 2 summarizes possible environmental impacts. The following major categories of waste disposal are discussed:

1. Biological Treatment
2. Physical-Chemical Treatment
3. Thermal Destruction
4. Radiation Destruction
5. Land Disposal

1.
Biological Treatment

Biological treatment encompasses an assortment of technologies which use living organisms to decompose organic wastes into water, carbon dioxide and other simple organic and inorganic molecules.

Many conventional biological treatment processes have been in widespread use for decades by municipal sewage treatment plants and by industries generating wastestreams rich in biodegradable pollutants such as starch, cellulose, fats, oils and greases.

Industries using biological treatment processes include textile plants, tanneries, pulp and paper mills, refineries, breweries, petrochemical plants, steel companies and pharmaceutical plants.

Conventional biological treatment technologies such as activated sludge, trickling filter, aerated lagoons, waste stabilization ponds and anaerobic digestion have been the workhorses of the pollution abatement industry for years.

The application of biological treatment technologies to biodegradable wastes free of non-degradable contaminants yields a sludge suitable for composting and use as a soil amendment.

Although conventional biologi-

Table 1
Disposal Options: The Going Rate (1980) in the United States

	Price in U.S. Dollars	
	$/metric ton	$/drum
Sanitary Landfill	5-10	1-2
Secure Landfill		
Wastes which are not acutely hazardous, including sludges	20-90	4-18
Highly toxic, explosive or reactive chemicals	100-400	20-80
Incineration		
High BTU value, no acute hazard	50-300	10-60
Highly toxic, heavy metals	300-1000	60-200
Chemical Treatment		
Acids, alkalines	15-80	3-16
Cyanides, heavy metals, highly toxics	100-500	20-100
Resource Recovery	50-200	10-400
Deep Well Injection		
Oily wastewaters	15-40	3-8
Dilute toxic rinsewaters	50-100	10-20

Source:"Time for Decisions on Hazardous Wastes", Industry Week, June 15, 1981.

Table 2
Major Environmental Concerns of Various Waste Disposal Technologies

Waste Technology	Technology Type	Major Environmental Concerns
Activated Sludge	Biological	Disposal of sludge, particularly if contaminated with metals. Odours.
Rotating Biological Contactor	Biological	Disposal of sludge, particularly if contaminated with metals. Odours.
Trickling Filter	Biological	Disposal of sludge, particularly if contaminated with metals. Odours.
Aerated Lagoon	Biological	Disposal of sludge, particularly if contaminated with metals. Odours.
Stabilization Pond	Biological	Disposal of sludge, particularly if contaminated with metals. Odours.
Anaerobic Digestion	Biological	Disposal of sludge, particularly if contaminated with metals. Odours.
Composting	Biological	Adequate destruction of pathogenic organisms.
Landfarming	Biological	Danger of leachate migration.
Mutant bacteria	Biological	Possible development and escape of pathogenic strains.
Precipitation	Chemical Treatment	Disposal of sludge. Disposal of treated effluent. Safe transport and handling of reaction chemicals.
Solid-Liquid Separation	Physical Treatment	Disposal of sludge. Possible water pollution from residual contaminants in discharge stream.
Neutralization	Chemical Treatment	Possible air pollution, e.g. cyanide. Safe transport and handling of reaction chemicals. Additional pollutant loading of aqueous wastestream.
Chemical Oxidation and Reduction	Chemical Treatment	Safe transport and handling of reaction chemicals. Disposal of sludge. Disposal of treated effluent.

Table 2 (continued)

Waste Technology	Technology Type	Major Environmental Concerns
Chemical Dechlorination	Chemical Treatment	Safe transport and handling of reaction chemicals.
Liquid Injection Incineration	Thermal Destruction	Air pollution. Safe disposal of scrubber wastes. Transportation and handling hazard.
Rotary Kiln	Thermal Destruction	Air pollution. Safe disposal of ash and scrubber wastes. Transportation and handling hazard.
Fluidized Bed	Thermal Destruction	Safe disposal of ash. Transportation and handling hazard.
Multiple Hearth Incineration	Thermal Destruction	Air pollution. Safe disposal of ash and scrubber waste. Transportation and handling hazard.
Calcination	Thermal Destruction	Air pollution. Safe disposal of ash and scrubber wastes. Transportation and handling hazard.
Molten Salt Incineration	Thermal Destruction	Safe disposal of ash.
Plasma Arc Torch	Thermal Destruction	Air pollution. Safe disposal of ash and scrubber wastes.
Wet Air Oxidation	Thermal Destruction	Transportation and handling hazard. Water pollution unless wastestream treated further.
Cement Kiln	Thermal Destruction	Air pollution. Safe disposal of scrubber wastes. Transportation and handling hazard.
At-Sea Incineration	Thermal Destruction	Air pollution. Transportation and handling hazard.
Mobile PCB Destruction	Thermal Destruction	Air pollution. Transportation and safe handling of flushing solvent.
UV Radiation and Electron Beam Radiation	Radiation Destruction	Possible pollution from chemical intermediates.

Table 2 (continued)

Waste Technology	Technology Type	Major Environmental Concerns
Solidification	Physical-Chemical	Air pollution during use of monomers and catalysts. Solidification product vulnerable to weathering. Leachate migration.
Secure Landfill	Physical	Air pollution. Leachate migration. Explosion hazard. Safe handling and transport of wastes to site.
Retrievable Storage	Physical	Air pollution. Explosion hazard. Safe handling and transport of wastes to site.

cal treatment processes are environmentally benign with few negative impacts, their ability to adequately treat the effluents of some modern industrial processes is limited. Biological treatment systems do not destroy inorganics such as metals. Metal constituents and certain toxic organics can inhibit microbial decomposition or may accumulate unchanged in the sludge. Contaminated sludge must be dewatered and disposed of through incineration or secure landfilling. Segregation of wastestreams on the company premises permits the hazardous component to undergo special and cost-effective treatment while the biodegradable fraction is treated, composted and re-used as a soil conditioner.

Biological treatment technologies are summarized in Table 3. Most of these treatment methods are tried and tested technologies in existence for many years. The development of mutant bacteria to detoxify persistent chemicals is an emerging technology that is discussed in greater detail below.

Mutant Bacteria

The complexity and variety of industrial wastestreams has researchers sleuthing for "super bugs" able to degrade chemicals that defy traditional waste treatment. Thousands of strains of bacteria occur naturally in the environment. Bacterial strains differ in their ability to degrade specific chemicals.

There are two major approaches in the development of special pollution-eating bacteria. One approach, known as genetic engineering, makes use of recombinant DNA to modify the genetic information in bacteria. In genetic engineering research, genes responsible for degrading specific chemicals are spliced into other organisms to create new bacteria.

Despite the vast potential of creating versatile bacterial strains capable of detoxifying wastes, genetic engineering is viewed with concern. Genetic experimentation brings with it the fear that mutant bacterial strains may form that are hazardous to human health and environmental well-being.

A second approach in the development of special pollution-eating bacteria involves strain selection of mutant bacteria to concentrate selected characteristics into a new organism. Although selective breeding is less efficient than recombinant DNA in creating new microbes, it is perceived as less of a threat than genetic tampering.

Genetic engineering and selective breeding experiments have developed bacteria capable of detoxifying such resistant chemicals as PCBs, 2,4-D, 2,4,5-T, DDT, phenols, certain dyestuffs and oil spills.

Battelle Memorial Institute (Columbus, Ohio) is focussing on bacterial means of destroying DDT and 2,4-D. Researchers have transplanted the gene for 2,4-D degradation from a less active organism into a bacterium of the genus *Pseudomonas*. The resultant bacteria convert 2,4-D into harmless products such as carbon dioxide and water.[3]

Battelle researchers have identified a bacterium that attacks DDT by accumulating it inside the organism's cell. Although the bacterium does not detoxify DDT, it can be used to concentrate DDT residues in wastewater.

Dr. Chakrabarty, a researcher with the University of Illinois, has created a new strain of bacteria that degrades 2,4,5-T. A major drawback is the length of time required to destroy the waste. The bacterium takes 2 weeks to consume 1 mg of 2,4,5-T, however researchers are striving to cut the time required to 5 to 7 days.[4]

Chakrabarty has also identified a naturally occurring bacterium capable of breaking down PCBs and toluene.[4]

Research at SRI International (Menlo Park, California) is proceeding on bacteria that can inject and destroy the pesticide parathion, certain chemical intermediates and organic dyestuffs.

Table 3

Biological Treatment Technologies

Technology	Wastestreams Applicable	Description
Activated Sludge	Used for secondary treatment of dilute biodegradable wastestreams. Industrial applications include cannery, pulp and paper mill, refinery, brewery, steel plant, petrochemical and pharmaceutical wastes.	Micro-organisms break down dilute organic wastestream in a continuously aerated tank. Typical retention time is 6 to 24 hours. The wastewater is then clarified in a settling tank in which sludge is separated from the organic-free water. Treated water is discharged and a portion of the sludge from the clarifier is recycled back to the aeration tank to maintain a high microbial population. Major problem is the disposal of copious amounts of sludge, frequently contaminated with metals.
Rotating Biological Contactor	Biodegradable wastestreams.	Based on the same microbial decomposition principle as activated sludge systems. Equipment is designed to enhance the rate of waste treatment and to reduce the overall space requirements of the treatment complex. Microbial populations adhere to the slowly rotating discs which are in partial contact with the wastestream. The rotating discs carry a thin film of wastewater into the air where the efficient breakdown of organic wastes occurs. Sludge disposal is a concern.
Trickling Filter	Used for secondary treatment of aqueous wastes. Industrial applications include cannery, pharmaceutical and petrochemical wastes including oils, phenols, alcohols and sulfides.	Wastes are sprayed through the air to absorb oxygen and then allowed to trickle through a bed of crushed rock or other media that is covered with micro-organisms including bacteria, fungi, protozoa and sludge worms. A trickling filter system includes a final settling tank to remove biological residue sloughed off the filter media. Requires disposal of residual biomass.
Aerated Lagoon	Used for secondary treatment of aqueous biodegradable wastes. Industrial applications include textile, pulp and paper mill, cannery, refinery and petrochemical wastewaters.	Wastewater is retained in a large earthen lagoon containing a high microbial population. Mechanical aerators introduce oxygen into the pond and keep the wastewater well mixed. Unlike activated sludge systems which recycle sludge rich in microbes, sludge is not recycled in aerated lagoons. This necessitates a longer retention time, typically 2 days. Before the treated effluent is discharged, sludge is removed from the wastestream in a settling basin. The sludge requires periodic removal and disposal.

Table 3 (continued)

Technology	Wastestreams Applicable	Description
Stabilization Pond	Used to provide final polishing of treated wastewater. In other instances, used to partially degrade high-strength raw wastes prior to subsequent treatment.	Large shallow ponds are used to degrade residual contaminants in treated wastewater. Aeration is provided by the wind. Some stabilization ponds are deep enough to provide anaerobic decomposition at the lower levels. Stabilization ponds are not energy intensive, however land requirements are great and treatment time is long. Typical retention time may be 4 days. Sludge accumulates in the bottom of the stabilization pond.
Anaerobic Digestion	Used to treat sludges and high strength biodegradable aqueous waste. Industrial applications include high-strength food production and paper mill wastes.	Anaerobic digestion occurs in oxygen-free closed vessels heated to 35°C at which temperature bacterial decomposition is optimal. Microbial activity in the absence of oxygen results in methane gas, hydrogen sulfide, carbon monoxide and nitrogen. Sludge volumes are reduced considerably, and methane gas may be burned to provide process and plant heating.
Deep Shaft	Used for strong biodegradable industrial wastes such as brewery wastes.	In this aerobic process, the wastewater is oxidized in a 500-foot-deep shaft placed in the ground. There is good oxygen utilization because of better dissolution of the oxygen at the high pressures existing in the bottom of the shaft. Prior to oxidation in the shaft, the wastestream undergoes primary settling to remove sludge. Compared to other biological treatment methods, deep shaft treatment has a small land requirement.
Composting	Biodegradable sludges that are free of metal and other toxic contaminants.	Composting of biodegradable sludges may occur in the presence or absence of oxygen. Aerobic composting occurs more quickly and with less noxious odours than anaerobic composting. In aerobic composting, sludge is mixed with a bulking agent and turned periodically to ensure optimum oxygenation. Composted sludge is an excellent soil conditioner for agricultural uses. Sludges with moderate to high metal levels are unsuitable as soil conditioners and present a disposal problem.
Landfarming	Biodegradable wastes free of metal and other toxic contaminants. Industrial applications include meat packing wastes, organic chemical wastes and oily wastes from petroleum refineries.	Wastes typically are sprayed on top of a tilled field, and periodically ploughed to ensure ample aeration of the soil bed. Micro-organisms that occur naturally in the soil break down the organic wastes. Oily wastes from the petroleum refinery operations are applied at an average rate of 600 barrels per acre per year in southern U.S. climates.

Table 3 (continued)

Technology	Wastestreams Applicable	Description
Mutant Bacteria	Specific bacterial strains can destroy specific wastes including 2,4,5-T, 2,4-D, PCBs, phenols, fats and greases, ammonia, cyanide and other degradable compounds.	Select microbial cultures resulting from genetic manipulation and selective breeding are commercially available to treat specific waste components. A major difficulty facing industrial users of microbial waste destruction techniques is the variability of the incoming wastestream. Large fluctuations in pH, temperature and metal content of the wastestream will kill the bacterial culture and render detoxification incomplete.

Kenzo Tonomura, of the University of Osaka (Sakai, Japan), has isolated a strain of bacteria capable of degrading organic mercury compounds.[4]

The Chemical Engineering Department at Ohio State University is investigating cost-effective methods of removing phenol from a wastestream.

Established colonies of *Pseudomonas* bacteria can consume phenol at concentrations up to 300 ppm. Researchers at Ohio State demonstrated that the use of *Pseudomonas* bacteria in a semi-fluidized bed process can save up to 50% of the cost of conventional sludge processes for phenol removal.[5]

Several small companies are in the business of selling mutant bacteria to clean up wastewater, hazardous spills and digest solid wastes.

Major companies in the business include Polybac (Allentown, Pennsylvania), Worne Biochemicals (Berlin, New Jersey), Flow Laboratories Environmental Cultures Division (Englewood, California) and General Environmental Services (Cleveland, Ohio).[3]

The mutant strains sold by these companies can decompose materials such as aromatic hydrocarbons, fats and greases and ammonia. The mutants can handle thousands of time more material than their precursors.[3]

The use of mutant bacteria to mop up after chemical spills into the environment such as oil and toxic chemicals has been met with some reservation. Experts disagree on whether the use of mutant bacteria should be confined to a waste treatment facility, or whether new bacterial strains should be allowed to be dispersed directly into the environment.

2.
Physical-Chemical Treatment

Physical and chemical treatment processes are used to detoxify or reduce the volume of industrial and municipal wastes. These treatment procedures are applicable to most inorganic wastes such as metal-laden discharge waters, and to some organic wastes such as oil/water mixtures.

A large segment of industry's hauled liquid waste includes aqueous wastestreams which are contaminated in varying degrees with metals and other inorganics. Because of the dilute nature of many of these hazardous wastes, the volume and subsequent transportation costs are high.

Transportation costs may be curtailed by concentrating the hazardous component of the wastestream prior to transfer. Technologies applicable to the concentration of wastes include neutralization, filtration, precipitation, sedimentation, flotation, membrane separation, reverse osmosis and evaporation.

Many waste concentration technologies are directly applicable as materials recovery and water re-use techniques. Physical/chemical recovery technologies include ultrafiltration, reverse osmosis, carbon adsorption, electrolytic recovery, distillation and others. Recovery technologies are discussed in detail in the preceding chapter, Waste Recovery Technologies.

Provincial and local governments establish permissible levels of industrial discharge into natural water bodies and sewers. The level of contaminants in industrial process waters may exceed local guidelines and standards. In order to comply with permissible pollution levels, many industries truck their waste to a treatment/disposal facility. In other instances, an industry may chose to pre-treat its wastewater using an assortment of physical-chemical means, and then discharge the treated effluent in a sewer.

The physical-chemical treatment methods described are mostly conventional technologies. Many are currently in use by industries and sewage treatment plants receiving combined municipal-industrial wastes. Treatment methods described include:

Precipitation
Solid-liquid separation
Neutralization
Chemical oxidation and
  reduction
Chemical dechlorination

Precipitation

Application

Many industries generating wastewaters high in dissolved solids use precipitation, flocculation and sedimentation as consecutive processes to treat the same wastestream. This technology, in industrial use since the 19th century,[6] is used widely to treat wastestreams containing soluble metals and colloidal hazardous substances.

The iron, steel and copper smelting industries routinely use precipitation to remove metals from pickling wastes. Precipitation techniques are also used in the metal finishing industries to remove toxic metals such as cadmium, chromium, and nickel from rinsewaters and discarded plating baths. The electronic industry removes copper from spent etching solutions. The inorganic chemical industry removes metals from a variety of wastestreams, again using chemical precipitation methods.[7]

Process Description

Precipitation and flocculation are characterized by the addition of chemicals to a wastestream to enhance the separation of the suspended solids or dissolved solids fraction from the liquid component.

Wastewater which contains dissolved solids must undergo chemical change before the dissolved solids are changed to a form in which they can be physically removed from the wastestream. In some instances, a precipitating agent added to the wastestream reacts directly with the dissolved contaminants to form an insoluble product. The insoluble product then undergoes settling or filtration.

Many precipitation reactions depend on pH changes through the addition of chemicals to convert dissolved contaminants to insoluble products. Another method is to alter the temperature of the wastestreams to increase the precipitation of contaminants.

Some wastestreams contain extremely fine suspended solids not easily filtered by conventional means. In such instances it may be preferable to add a chemical agent to cause these solids to form an agglomerated mass. Flocculation is a process by which suspended particles are combined into larger particles or "flocs" that can be readily separated by gravity sedimentation.

An example of precipitation involves zinc chloride and sodium sulfide, both of which are highly soluble in water. When these two chemicals are combined, the zinc ions and sulfide ions combine to form zinc sulfide. Zinc sulfide is insoluble in water and may be removed from the wastestream by simple settling methods, leaving sodium chloride in the solution.

Most chemical precipitation processes used by industry today involve the addition of virgin chemicals including lime, metallic salt cations and sodium hydroxide. The use of virgin precipitating agents is both expensive and demanding of industry's supply of chemical resources. Instead of relying on solely virgin chemicals, some industries have learned to precipitate one wastestream with another wastestream. In the case of sodium sulfide precipitating out the zinc in zinc chloride to produce insoluble zinc sulfide, it is common to find separate zinc chloride and sulfide wastestreams originating from different industries. Matching the two wastestreams forms a zinc sulfide precipitate which happens to be a useful, saleable fertilizer.

Precipitation technology has been in existence for many decades. However, as the thrust for cleaner industrial discharges continues, it is questionable whether conventional precipitation technologies can meet the increasingly stringent emission requirements facing industry in North America.

Solid-Liquid Separation

Solid-liquid separation processes are simple, relatively inexpensive technologies designed to physically separate the solid and liquid components of wastestreams.

In treating liquid wastestreams, solid-liquid separation techniques are used to remove suspended and settled solids from the wastewater prior to discharge or further treatment. Solid-liquid separation processes will not remove dissolved solids from the wastewater, unless a precipitation process precedes.

In treating sludges for disposal, solid-liquid separation methods are used to remove excess water from sludges prior to ultimate disposal. Four major types of solid-liquid separation include:

Sedimentation,
Flotation,
Filtration,
Centrifugation.

Sedimentation

Sedimentation is a process in which material heavier than the wastestream settles out by gravity in a special tank or holding pond.

Chemical coagulating or flocculating agents may be added to help collect the particles together to speed settling in those wastestreams where solids such as colloidal particles remain finely dispersed in a liquid, making them resistant to rapid settling.[7]

Flotation

Dissolved air flotation is used to remove certain solids, greases and emulsified oils difficult to remove by simple sedimentation. Excess air is dissolved in the wastestream under pressure and then released to the bottom of the flotation tank at atmospheric pressure, resulting in the formation of many tiny bubbles. The solids in the wastestream are carried to the surface by minute air bubbles, and subsequently removed by skimming.

Flotation is used by the refining, meat packing, paint, poultry processing, paper milling and baking industries to achieve a 80 to 99% removal of suspended and floating solids.[7]

Filtration

Filtration is based on the movement of a wastestream through a filtration medium which functions to trap suspended solids while permitting the liquid component to pass through unchanged. In instances where water-soluble contaminants exist in the wastestream, it may be necessary to treat residual soluble contaminants after filtration.

Two major applications of filtration processes include the removal of suspended solids from a wastestream, and the dewatering and subsequent volume reduction of sludges.

Filtration technology has been in use for decades, and as such has witnessed the development of many technology refinements and variations. Filtration is used in conjunction with other treatment technologies. For example, it may be necessary to filter a wastestream to remove suspended solids before that wastestream can undergo further treatment such as ion exchange or carbon adsorption.

Filtration procedures differ in whether the filtered solids are trapped and accumulate on the surface of the filtration medium, or whether the filtered solids are entrapped within the pores or body of the filtration medium.[6]

Diatomaceous earth is an example of a filtration medium used to trap solids within the pores of the medium. Diatomaceous earth results from the gradual deposition of aquatic organisms known as diatoms on the bottom of a lake. Diatoms consist of silica shells with four tube-like projections. Diatomaceous earth, mined from old lake bottoms, is used as a filtration medium because of its excellent porosity.

Some oil recycling companies, for example, use diatomaceous earth to remove dirt and other particulates from used oil.

Other common filtration media are silica sand, garnet sand, perlite, carbon and various synthetic materials. Some of the more widely used filtration techniques are described in Table 4.

Centrifugation

Centrifugation is an alternative technique for dewatering sludges and for concentrating precipitated solids in a wastestream.

Two types of centrifuges are the sedimentation centrifuge and the filtration centrifuge.

Table 4

Common Filtration Types

Type	Description
Granular media filtration	Wastestream flows through a bed of granular material, either by gravity flow or under pressure. The filter bed may be regenerated periodically by back flushing the solids from the bed using a reverse flow of washwater.
Filter presses	Filter presses are used to dewater sludges or slurries. Fabric positioned over a porous metal plate forms the filtration medium. The liquid passes through the fabric under pressure. The solids become concentrated within the dewatering chamber, forming a dried sludge cake.
Leaf filter	Pressure leaf filtration is used to remove suspended solids. The filters consist of a series of frames over which a fabric filter cloth is stretched. A thin layer of filter aid material such as diatomaceous earth, perlite or activated carbon is placed on the filter fabric. Liquid passes through the filter media under pressure and is discharged through the pores of the leaf filter. Filter restoration includes periodic removal of the accumulated solids and clogged filter aid materials. With each clean-out, a new layer of filter aid materials is applied to each filter leaf.
Rotary vacuum filtration	Rotary vacuum filtration is used for the dewatering of slurries and sludges. Filtered cloth covers a drum-shaped steel cage. The revolving drum is partially immersed in sludge or a waste slurry. A vacuum applied to the inside of the rotating drum sucks liquid through the filter cloth, leaving a layer of relatively dry solids on the outside of the drum. As the drum rotates, solids are scraped off the surface of the filter cloth before the cloth is reimmersed in the slurry (see Figure 1).
Cartridge filters	Cartridge filters are used to remove solids from a wastestream with relatively low solids loading, as occurs in previously treated wastestreams. Although cartridge filters have only limited capacity to store solids, they are popular because of their convenience and ease of cleaning. Spent cartridge filters are replaced with new cartridges.

Source: Hazardous Wastes in Northern and Western Canada. Volume 2. Prepared for Environment Canada, December 1980.

A sedimentation centrifuge is used to accelerate the settling of solids in a wastestream. The wastewater is rotated rapidly in an enclosed chamber, resulting in the build-up of sediment on the inside wall of the chamber.

A filtration centrifuge operates on the same principle, however, in this instance, the rotating chamber composed of filter cloth permits liquid to move out through the cloth. Dewatered sludge collects on the inside of the filter cloth and is removed for disposal.

Neutralization

Application

Neutralization is in use in a wide spectrum of industries which generate acidic or basic wastewater[8] (see Table 5).

The purpose of neutralization is to prepare a wastestream for discharge into a sewer. Otherwise, if a company sent pulses of acidic or alkaline wastes into the sewer system, it is highly probable that bacteria responsible for wastewater decomposition at the centralized sewage treatment facility would be destroyed. In many instances, neutralization functions as just one step in a sequence of treatment processes.

Metal cleaning operations in which scale, oxides and other impurities are removed from metal surfaces by immersing them in inorganic acids such as sulfuric, hydrochloric or phosphoric acid result in an acidic wastestream known as pickling liquor.

Process Description

Neutralization is a common chemical treatment process in which an acid is mixed with a base in order to neutralize the wastestream to a pH approaching 7. Typically, mixing acidic wastewater with a base, or mixing alkaline wastewater with an acid results in water and a salt. Resultant salts that are insoluble in water form a sludge that must be eliminated prior to discharge of the neutralized effluent.

Most industries still use virgin chemicals to neutralize their wastestreams. However, as chemical costs increase and treatment costs spiral, some industries are saving themselves thousands of dollars by substituting another industry's wastestream to neutralize their wastes.

Figure 1
Rotary Drum Vacuum Filter

A vacuum applied to the inside of the rotating drum sucks liquid through the filter cloth, leaving a layer of relatively dry solids on the outside of the drum.
Source: Hazardous Wastes in Northern and Western Canada, Vol. 2, prepared for Environment Canada, December 1980.

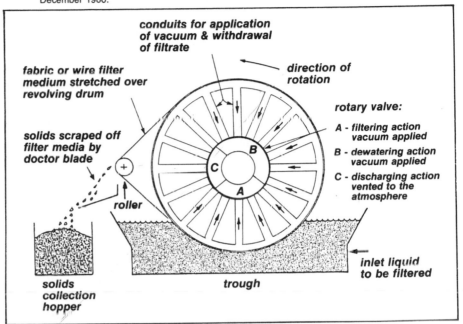

Table 5
Industries Using Neutralization

Industry	pH Range of Wastewater
Beverages	Acidic and Basic
Cement, Lime & Concrete	Basic
Dairy Products	Acidic and Basic
Fertilizer	Acidic and Basic
Fruits and Vegetables	Acidic and Basic
Grain Milling	Acidic and Basic
Industrial Gas Products	Acidic and Basic
Inorganic Chemicals	Acidic and Basic
Leather Tanning	Acidic and Basic
Metal Finishing	Acidic
Non-Ferrous Metals (aluminum)	Acidic
Pharmaceuticals	Acidic and Basic
Plastics	Acidic and Basic
Pulp and Paper	Acidic and Basic
Steel Pickling	Acidic
Textiles	Basic

Source: Pretreatment of Pollutants into Publicly Owned Treatment Works. U.S. EPA, October 1973.

Waste unloading docks at the Kommune-Kemi waste treatment facility in Denmark. Wastes are received in containers of all sizes and types at this treatment facility. Bulk storage of liquid wastes until time of treatment and disposal.

Rick Findlay

Rick Findlay

Rick Findlay

Alkaline wastes are neutralized by the addition of hydrochloric or sulfuric acid. Sodium hydroxide, calcium hydroxide, calcium carbonate and quicklime are used to neutralize acid wastes. Blending acid and alkaline wastestreams is often feasible because it eliminates the cost of purchasing neutralizing agents.[9]

Despite the promise of merging different wastestreams together to achieve neutralization, several caveats must be heeded. Wastestreams typically contain small amounts of heavy metals and other dissolved contaminants. Toxic components must be reduced to acceptable levels by precipitation, sedimentation and filtration before the neutralized effluent is released to a sewage treatment plant.

The successful mixing of wastestreams depends on full knowledge of wastestream constituents as well as a sound understanding of chemistry. It is critical that reaction products be predicted and evaluated prior to the physical mixing of the wastestreams. Otherwise, unexpected toxic gases may result. For example, the acidification of wastes containing sulfide or cyanide salts may result in the production of hydrogen sulfide or hydrogen cyanide gases.

Chemical Oxidation and Reduction

Application

Chemical oxidation is suitable to aqueous wastestreams containing inorganic and organic wastes. Typical hazardous waste constituents that can be detoxified by an oxidizing agent include cyanides, pesticides, phenols, aldehydes, aromatic hydrocarbons and sulphur compounds.

The electroplating industry is a significant generator of cyanide wastes. The cyanide in solution can be oxidized with chlorine gas or hypochlorite solutions, yielding nitrogen and carbon dioxide. Potassium permanganate and hydrogen peroxide have also been successful in detoxifying aqueous cyanide wastes.[7]

Process Description

Chemical oxidation processes depend on a chemical reaction to detoxify hazardous wastes. The hazardous wastestream is subjected to an oxidizing agent such as chlorine, ozone, sodium hypochlorite, calcium hypochlorite, potassium permanganate, hydrogen peroxide and nitrous acid. Chemical bonds are broken and the toxic material is converted into simpler, less toxic chemicals.[7]

In Europe, a cyanide destruction system in use acidifies cyanide waste to hydrogen cyanide. The hydrogen cyanide is then stripped from the wastestream in a trickle-flow counter-current packed tower (see Figure 2). Incineration of the off-gases yields water, carbon dioxide and nitrogen. Extreme precautions must be taken to prevent highly toxic hydrogen cyanide gas from escaping into the atmosphere during acidification and stripping.[6]

Joint research by Dr. Donald Sawyer of the University of California and Dr. Julian Roberts of the University of Redlands has resulted in another advance in chemical oxidation technology. The two California scientists discovered that a negatively charged form of oxygen known as superoxide could break down many chlorinated hydrocarbons (excluding PCBs) into relatively harmless substances.[9]

When an electrical current is passed through chemical waste in a solution, the oxygen content is transformed into superoxide. The halogenated molecules present in the waste solution are then converted to harmless substances such as carbonates. The process is not suitable for aqueous wastes. Bench scale studies have demonstrated the rapid degradation of chlorine compounds such as carbon tetrachloride, chloroform, methylene chloride and DDT.[9]

Chemical reduction is applica-

Figure 2
Daester-Fairtec Cyanide Destruction System

Cyanide waste is acidified to hydrogen cyanide. The hydrogen cyanide is then stripped from the wastestream in a trickle-flow counter-current packed tower.

Source: Hazardous Wastes in Northern and Western Canada, Vol. 2, prepared for Environment Canada, December 1980.

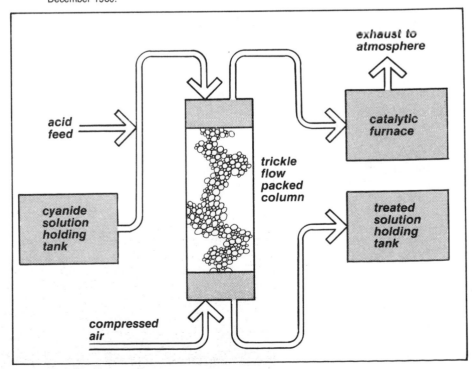

ble in the detoxification of metals in solution.

Chromium typically present in electroplating and tanning wastestreams as hexavalent chromium (VI) is highly toxic. In the reduced state, trivalent chromium (III) is much less hazardous and can be precipitated for removal.[6] Common reducing agents include sodium bisulphite, iron, aluminum and zinc compounds.

Chemical Dechlorination

Application

Chemical dechlorination is suitable to non-aqueous wastestreams contaminated with chlorinated organics.

Among the more common chlorinated hydrocarbons are polychlorinated biphenyls (PCBs), tetrachloroethylene (perc), chlorobenzene, pentachlorophenols, dichlorophenols, vinyl chloride (VC), methylene chloride, trichloroethane, carbon tetrachloride and an assortment of pesticides such as aldrin, heptachlor, 2,4-D and 2,4,5-T.

Process Description

Chemical dechlorination refers to a group of emerging technologies which can be used to strip chlorine atoms from highly chlorinated toxic compounds to produce a non-toxic residue.[7] A highly reactive chemical reagent is introduced into the chlorinated hydrocarbon liquid to chemically break apart the stable chlorinated molecules into simpler and less toxic constituents.

Proponents of chemical dechlorination cite many reasons why a chemical destruction system is superior to incineration of chlorinated hydrocarbons. Unlike incineration processes, there are no emissions from the totally enclosed chemical dechlorination systems.[7] The use of chemical dechlorination to detoxify transformer oils contaminated with PCBs ensures that they are not burned up and wasted, but rather cleaned for re-use. Unlike many incineration systems, chemical

dechlorination technology can be portable. By detoxifying wastes on-site, transportation risks and costs are eliminated.

A major concern with chemical dechlorination involves the hazardous nature of the chemical reagents employed. Extreme caution is necessary when handling the metallic sodium reagents. Given the high reactivity of sodium in water and air, it is critical that no air enter the reaction vessel.[7]

In 1980, the Goodyear Tire and Rubber Company (Akron, Ohio) used a proprietary process to treat 40,000 gallons of PCB-contaminated heat-transfer fluids. PCB levels were reduced from 82 ppm to less than 10 ppm. Goodyear uses a metallic sodium reagent called sodium naphthalene tetrahydrofuran to chemically destroy PCBs.

Sunohio Inc. (Canton, Ohio) has developed a chemical dechlorination process using a different reagent to destroy PCBs. In recent tests, Sunohio successfully reduced the concentration of PCBs in transformer oil from 225 ppm to 1 ppm.[7] Acurex Corporation (Mountain View, California) is another company striving for the commercialization of a chemical dechlorination process.

Despite the current preoccupation with PCB destruction, chemical dechlorination technology is anticipated to be directly transferable to the destruction of other chlorinated hydrocarbons such as pesticides.

3.
Thermal Destruction

Thermal destruction technologies are used to break down organic hazardous wastes into less toxic constituents, ideally CO_2 and water. Heat is applied to the waste in an enclosed chamber to cause the disintegration of the molecular bonds of the organic material. Equipment design varies according to whether liquid, sludge or solid organic wastes are destroyed.

Thermal destruction technologies are classified into two broad categories: incineration and pyrolysis.

Incineration

Incineration technologies are based on the combustion of wastes in the presence of excess oxygen. The products of incineration include water, carbon dioxide and ash. In addition, most incineration processes yield non-combustible residuals such as metal oxides and other inorganics. The non-combustible residuals may escape with the flue gases or may accumulate in the ash. The type and quantity of non-combustible residuals remaining after incineration depend upon the degree and type of contamination of the organic wastestream.

Pyrolysis

Pyrolysis technologies are based on the combustion of wastes in an oxygen-deficient environment. Organic wastes are broken down into a range of lower molecular weight, simpler organic molecules and an ash. Pyrolysis is of interest because it not only detoxifies organic wastes, but does so in a manner in which process end products might be recovered for re-use as chemical feedstocks or as a fuel.

Since the pyrolysis of some organics may yield products which are more toxic than the original waste, it should be used very carefully with well-defined waste feedstocks. Chlorinated materials, for example, would not be a good feedstock to a pyrolysis system.

Energy Content of Wastes

Rich Wastes

Organic wastestreams are differentiated on the basis of the energy content of the waste. Wastes are described as rich wastes or lean wastes. Rich wastes are those which are high enough in heating value to sustain combustion on their own, except for the ignition of the fuel. Wastes with a heat value of 7000 Btu per pound are characterized as rich wastes. Flame temperature must be at least 2000°F to ensure complete oxidation.[10]

Lean Wastes

Lean wastes are those below 7000 Btu per pound. Such wastes require additional fuel or an energy-rich wastestream to sustain combustion temperature.[10] Some organic wastestreams are considered lean because they contain a high water content. In such cases, it is advantageous to reduce the water content before incineration.

Organic sludges are characterized as having a high solids content, typically 20% or more by weight, and having sufficiently high heating value to support combustion. Disposal costs for incinerating organic wastes vary depending upon the additional heat required to burn them and on the ash content requiring further disposal.

Although landfill is still the cheapest and most widely used disposal method in North America, there are many thermal destruction technologies available to industry. Many of these technologies have been in use for many years, and as such are "proven" technologies. Emerging technologies that show great promise for specific problem wastes include the plasma arc torch, molten salt incineration, the wet air oxidation process and pyrolysis.

The following technologies are discussed in greater depth on the following pages:

Liquid injection incineration
Rotary kilns
Fluidized bed
Multiple hearth incineration
Calcination
Molten salt incineration
Plasma arc torch
Wet air oxidation
Cement kiln
At-sea incineration
Mobile PCB destruction

Liquid Injection Incineration

Application

Liquid injection systems are used to burn pumpable organic liquids. Wastes must be removed from the transport container and fed into the combustion chamber via a nozzle. This incineration system cannot dispose of drums or non-pumpable wastes.

Highly viscous wastes may be heated to an easily pumpable viscous state. Other methods of lowering the viscosity of the organic wastestream include emulsifying the waste or dissolving it in a lower-viscosity waste.[6]

Liquid injection incinerators have been used to destroy a variety of wastes including phenols, PCBs, still and reactor bottoms, solvents, polymer wastes, herbicides and insecticides.[7] They are generally unsuitable for burning organic wastes contaminated with heavy metals, high-water-content wastes, or materials with a high inorganic content.

In Europe, injection incinerators have been used to destroy halogenated organic liquids under carefully controlled combustion temperatures and residence times.[6] When burning halogenated organics, it is critical that appropriate gas scrubbing devices are used to trap escaping halogens such as chlorine.

Liquid injection incinerators are probably the most commonly used type of incinerator for hazardous waste destruction in North America. An example of a Canadian liquid waste incinerator is found near Sarnia, Ontario. Operated by Tricil (Corunna, Ontario), this incinerator destroys non-halogenated organic liquids. The absence of pollution control equipment on the Tricil liquid

Liquid injection unit for the incineration of liquid wastes. This unit lacks scrubber equipment for air pollution control.

Figure 3
Liquid Incineration

Liquid wastes are preheated and blended with other combustible materials as necessary. The wastestream is then injected in an atomized form into the combustion chamber.

Source: *Hazardous Wastes in Northern and Western Canada, Vol. 2*, prepared for Environment Canada, December 1980.

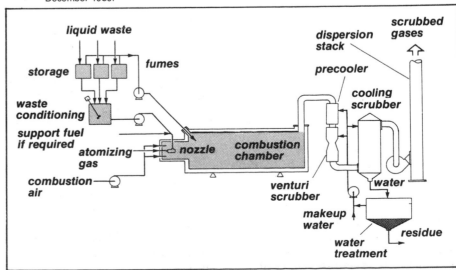

waste incinerator makes it necessary to limit the concentration of inorganics and halogenated organics present in the wastestream.[2]

Process Description

A typical liquid waste incinerator consists of one or more atomizing nozzles and a refractory-lined combustion chamber. The liquid wastes are usually pre-heated and blended to upgrade their combustibility and pumpability. The wastestream is then injected in an atomized form into the combustion chamber (see Figure 3). Complete combustion is obtained only if the waste is adequately atomized and mixed with air.

Typical combustion chamber temperatures range from 650 to 1650°C with exhaust temperatures maintained constant at 750 to 1200°C.[2] Incineration temperature and residence time of the incinerated waste vary with the needs of specific wastes to ensure complete combustion.

Rotary Kiln

Application

The rotary kiln offers greater flexibility than a liquid waste incinerator because of the wider range of wastes it can incinerate. A rotary kiln can be used to incinerate organic liquids, slurries, sludges, solids and even drummed waste.

Existing installations of rotary kilns include units operated at the following locations: Rollins Environmental Services (Baton Rouge, Louisiana; Logan, New Jersey; and Houston, Texas); Dow Chemical (Midland, Michigan); Eastman-Kodak (Rochester, New York); 3M (Minneapolis-St. Paul, Minnesota); GSB (Ebenhausen, West Germany); and KommuneKemi (Nyborg, Denmark).

Process Description

A rotary kiln incinerator uses a slowly revolving steel cylinder lined with fire bricks for the primary combustion chamber. The

A rotary kiln at the Ebenhausen waste disposal facility in Germany.

Scrubber system to capture potential air pollutants emitted during incineration of wastes in the rotary kiln.

cyclinder is mounted at an incline so that wastes fed into the high end of the kiln pass through the combustion zone as the kiln rotates. Liquid or solid waste is fed into the kiln via a sealed feed system. The slow rotation of the kiln causes solid wastes to tumble and break apart, thereby improving combustion efficiency.

Ash and non-combustible residues are moved along the cylinder and removed from an ash box at the low end of the cylinder.

Residence time for wastes ranges from seconds for gases to hours for solids, and combustion temperatures range up to 3000°F. In addition to the primary chamber, a secondary combustion chamber is normally used to provide the necessary retention time at controlled exhaust temperatures to ensure that organics are destroyed.[2]

The sizes of existing rotary kilns vary from units that burn a ton of waste per hour to units which burn eight tons of waste per hour. Some rotary kilns are equipped with boilers to reclaim heat energy.[7]

It is common practice to include a stationary after-burner unit after the rotating kiln to ensure complete combustion of the off-gases. Frequently, the after-burner is fueled with rich liquid organic wastes, and combustion occurs at temperatures of 1200°C or higher.[6]

The presence of inorganic contaminants and halogens in the wastestream necessitates the use of emission control devices such as scrubbers and electrostatic precipitators to remove metal oxides and halogens such as chlorine present in the exhaust gases of the after-burner.

Fluidized Bed

Application

Fluidized bed incinerators are well suited to burn certain kinds of sludge. At present, they are used primarily to dispose sludges from municipal wastewater treatment plants, oil refineries, and pulp and paper mills. Fluidized bed units cannot be considered for incineration of "as-received" drummed organics because fluidized bed in-

cinerators typically operate at much lower temperatures than rotary kilns or liquid injection incinerators, and hence are limited in the types of organic wastes that they can safely destroy. Some industries report burning organic wastes from pharmaceutical manufacturers, phenolic wastes, methyl methacrylate, old munitions, spent blasting abrasives containing organotin compounds, and an organic dye water slurry.[11] Fluidized bed combustion studies on chlorinated hydrocar-

bons (mainly polyvinyl chloride) have shown that chlorine can be neutralized by using a substance such as dolomite for the bed material.[12] In such instances, the dolomite bed acts as a catalyst to assist in the destruction of the chlorinated hydrocarbon, as well as trapping free chlorine from the destruction of the molecule. In general, however, there is only limited data on the use of fluidized beds as hazardous waste incinerators.

Examples of fluidized bed installations in existence for indust-

Figure 4
Fluidized Bed Furnace

Wastes are injected into the sand bed where combustion occurs within the fluidized medium. The sand is fluidized by forcing combustion air through a perforated plate under the sand.

Source: *Hazardous Wastes in Northern and Western Canada, Vol. 2,* prepared for Environment Canada, December 1980.

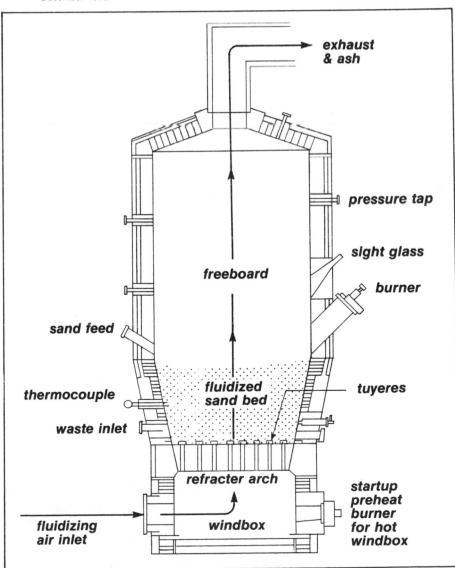

rial waste sludges include Papier Cascades Inc. (Cabano, Quebec) and two Amoco installations, one in Mandan, North Dakota and one in Maynard, Massachusetts. Other applications include the incineration of waste sludges from distilleries, packing houses and pulp and paper processes.

Process Description

The fluidized bed incinerator is a vertical, refractory-lined, cylindrical vessel which contains a bed of inert granular material such as sand. The sand is fluidized by forcing combustion air through a perforated metal plate under the sand. The upward flow of air through the sand bed results in a dense turbulent mass which behaves much like a fluid.

The wastes are injected into the bed where combustion occurs within the fluidized medium. Sand bed temperatures typically range from 750 to 870°C, and the bed acts as a large heat reservoir.[6] The heat capacity of suspended sand is several times greater than that of a gaseous stream at the same temperature. Heat is transferred from the sand to the waste. As the waste is incinerated, the exothermic heat of combustion is transferred back into the bed. Since the mass of the heated turbulent bed is much greater than the mass of the waste, heat is transferred rapidly to the waste material and destruction of the waste occurs in a few seconds.

The exhaust gases move up into the freeboard zone (see Figure 4), which functions at a lower velocity, allowing suspended particles to return to the bed and providing additional retention time for complete combustion.[2] The lower velocity freeboard zone also ensures that sand particles are not carried over with the exhaust gases. Ash from the incineration process is reduced in size by the bed motion and eventually is carried out of the combustion chamber with the exhaust gases.

Figure 5
Multiple Hearth Furnace

Rotating rabble arms and teeth push the wastes across the hearths to drop through holes. The waste cascades down to increasingly hotter hearths for burning.

Source: *Hazardous Wastes in Northern and Western Canada, Vol. 2,* prepared for Environment Canada, December 1980.

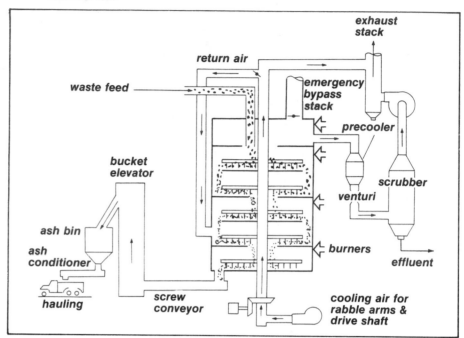

Multiple Hearth Incineration

Application

Multiple hearth incinerators are used to incinerate municipal sewage sludge. Because the operating temperature of multiple hearth incinerators tends to be much lower than those of rotary kilns and liquid injection incinerators, multiple hearth units are limited in the types of hazardous wastes that they can destroy. Some industries are currently using multiple hearth incinerators to burn tar and certain types of chemical sludge. These incinerators are also used to regenerate activated carbon systems and in ore roasting operations.

Process Description

A multiple hearth incinerator consists of a refractory-lined, circular, steel shell with multiple refractory hearths located one above the other[6] (see Figure 5). Sludge and other solid waste enters the incinerator at the top through a feed point. Rotating rabble arms and teeth push the wastes across the hearths to drop through holes. The waste cascades down to increasingly hotter hearths for further burning. Frequently, waste greases, tars and combustible liquid organics are injected through side ports to enhance combustion.

Calcination

Application

Calciners can be of various types including open hearth calciners, rotary kiln calciners and fluidized bed calciners. Calcination technology is commonly used in the production of cement, lime, magnesia, plaster, and in the smelting of sulphide and carbonate ores. Calcination technology lends itself to chemical recovery from hazardous wastes, such as mercury recovery from the roasting of mercury sludges.[7]

Process Description

Calcination is an energy-intensive, endothermic process used to recover metals and other non-combustible materials from waste sludges. Heat is applied to the sludge to drive off volatile and thermally decomposable inorganic components. The burning process results in a dry powdered or sintered solid product suitable for materials recovery, further processing or disposal.[7]

Calcination occurs typically at temperatures of 1000°C. Because the calcination process releases particulates in the exhaust gas stream, it is necessary to install emission control devices such as wet scrubbers, filters, cyclones, electrostatic precipitators or gas absorption equipment for proper control.

Molten Salt Incineration

Application

Molten salt incineration is an emerging technology that offers great promise in destroying some of industry's most hazardous organic wastes. The technology has proven itself in destroying waste pesticides and pesticide containers. Perhaps the most attractive feature of molten salt technology is that small-scale incinerators could be constructed as portable units that can be hauled to the source of the waste.

The molten salt destruction process was developed by Rockwell International (Canoga Park, California). Pilot scale facilities

exist in Idaho and Santa Susana, California.[13]

Anti-Pollution Systems (APS) has developed an alternative molten salt process designed for easier removal of ash and to avoid problems when water is introduced directly into the melt. APS has designed a portable molten salt unit that can be fueled with propane. This system has been used to combust tannery wastes so that chromium metal can be recovered. The unit also scrubbed hydrogen chloride and raw halogens generated from the combustion of aluminum chlorohydrate.[11] In another application of the APS process, textile manufacturing wastes containing acrylic residue are purified in a melt consisting of potassium and calcium nitrates.[11]

Process Description

Molten salt incineration is a relatively new method of destroying hazardous organic wastes which simultaneously scrubs halogens and other objectionable byproducts from the exhaust gases. Molten salts act as catalysts to permit complete combustion at temperatures below those of normal combustion.[14] For example, salt bath temperatures of 800° to 1000°C are adequate to destroy PCBs using molten salt technology. In contrast, conventional high-temperature incinerators require a temperature of 1200°C to destroy PCB wastes.[15]

Molten salt incineration is based on the injection of a mixture of waste material and air under the surface of a pool of molten sodium carbonate or other salt (see Figure 6). The hydrocarbons of the organic waste are immediately oxidized to carbon dioxide and water, and the combustion byproducts containing such elements as phosphorus, sulphur, arsenic and the halogens react with sodium carbonate. These byproducts are retained in the melt as inorganic salts rather than released to the atmosphere as volatile gases.[16]

Various types of salts can be used. "Neutral" salts include the metal halide salts. "Oxidative" salts donate oxygen while taking up hydroxides, oxide, chlorate,

Figure 6
Molten Salt Incinerator

Source: *Hazardous Wastes in Northern and Western Canada, Vol. 2,* prepared for Environment Canada, December 1980.

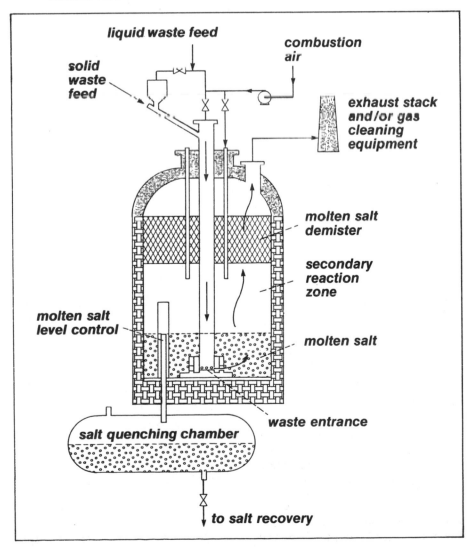

sulphate and nitrate byproducts.[6]

Any gaseous products that escape from the molten salt layer during the combustion of wastes are burned in the secondary reaction zone above the melt to complete the oxidation of combustible material. Combustion gases then pass through a de-mister which traps particulates in the off-gas stream for return to the salt bath.

As the inorganic products resulting from the reaction of organic halogens, phosphorus, sulphur and other compounds build up in the molten bed, it becomes necessary to regenerate or replace the molten salt.[17] Waste molten salt can be reacted with lime in an aqueous or molten medium to form a water-insoluble calcium salt residue.

Plasma Arc Torch

Application

Plasma arc technology is suitable for the destruction of both solid and liquid wastes. Liquid wastes can be pumped continuously into the plasma arc reaction vessel (see Figure 7). Solid wastes are first shredded and then deposited in the reaction vessel where they fall into the molten slag pool at the bottom. Excess slag is removed from the reaction vessel as necessary.

Resource Recovery Corporation (Raleigh, North Carolina) holds the patent rights to the plasma torch.[6] The Canadian subsidiary is the Canadian Resource Recovery Corporation (Montreal, Quebec). Although not in widespread use yet, several plasma arc units have been built and successfully operated in the destruction of liquid industrial wastes such as toluene and PCBs.[6] The capital cost for a plasma arc system that processes 16.5 cubic metres of waste per day is estimated at $500,000. Electrical energy costs are calculated at $20 per tonne of waste destroyed.[6]

Both American and Canadian governments are supporting further development of plasma arc technology as a means of hazardous waste disposal. Environment Canada, Ontario Hydro and the Ontario Ministry of the Environ-

ment are providing the Royal Military College (Kingston, Ontario) with financial assistance in the preparation of commercially available plasma arc systems that destroy PCBs.[18]

There are many reasons for optimism regarding this emerging disposal technology. The plasma arc system is relatively versatile in that it can handle both solid and liquid wastes.

Unlike incineration in the presence of oxygen, plasma arc pyrolysis generates a much smaller volume of gaseous end products than incineration. Only a small amount of gas is required to generate the arc, and the majority

of carbon in the feedstock can be converted to carbon black.[10] The reduced volume of exhaust gases from plasma arc pyrolysis reduces the size requirements for downstream gas clean-up devices. Hence process equipment can be relatively compact.

The most promising aspect of plasma arc technology is that it is suitable to both portable and small-scale installations. In the future, many of the larger companies might invest in on-site destruction units. The smaller businesses may be serviced by a travelling plasma arc unit.

Figure 7
Plasma Arc Reaction Vessel

Waste materials and air are injected under the surface of a pool of molten sodium carbonate, resulting in the immediate oxidation of the waste.
Source: *Hazardous Wastes in Northern and Western Canada, Vol. 2*, prepared for Environment Canada, December 1980.

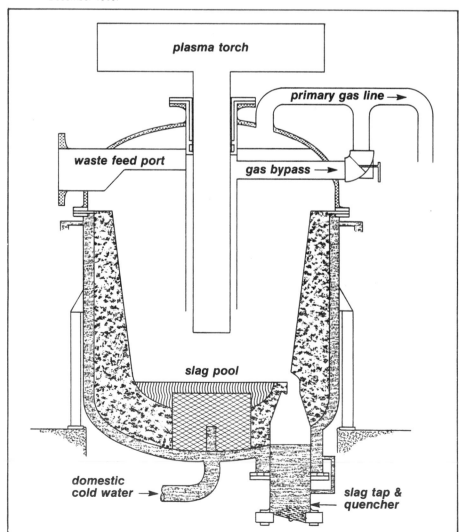

Process Description

Plasma torch technology grew out of the United States space programme. NASA scientists required a very intense heat source in their simulation experiments on the ability of heat shields to protect space vehicles upon re-entry into the earth's atmosphere. Plasma arc technology was developed for this purpose.[19]

A plasma arc torch functions to pyrolyze wastes into combustible gases by exposure to a gas which has been energized to its plasma state. A plasma is a gas consisting of charged and neutral particles, having an overall charge of zero, and exhibiting collective behaviour.[10] Plasma is characterized by a good ability to conduct electricity.

An electrical current is passed through a low pressure gas which activates the gas molecules into ionized atomic states. Plasma gas temperatures of about 50,000°K are achievable. As waste materials are fed into the plasma zone, the injected waste materials absorb energy radiated by the ionized gas molecules. This process occurs in the absence of oxygen.

The transfer of energy from the decaying plasma species to the molecules of waste material causes the breakdown of the wastes into atom and ion constituents. Plasma arc pyrolysis is based on molecular fracture rather than on chemical oxidation typical of incineration.[10]

Although plasma arc technology has been known for some years, commercializing the technology has taken a long time. The extreme heat generated by the plasma torch caused the plasma torch to destroy itself within minutes. Ongoing research has resulted in the construction of plasma arc torches that no longer destroy themselves and require relatively little maintenance.

Wet Air Oxidation

Application

Wet air oxidation technology is applicable to aqueous organic

Figure 8
Wetox Process

The wastestream is pumped into a multi-compartment reactor designed to agitate and aerate the waste. Reactor temperature ranges from 200° to 300°C and reactor pressure is equivalent to 40 atmospheres.

Source: *Hazardous Wastes in Northern and Western Canada, Vol. 2,* prepared for Environment Canada, December 1980.

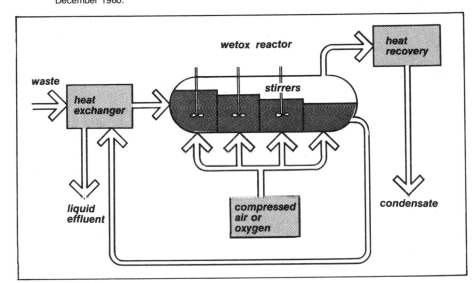

wastestreams containing approximately 1 to 20% organic material such as spent pulping liquor from the pulp and paper industry, paint sludges, food wastes and refinery sludges.

Process Description

Wet air oxidation achieves oxidation of water-borne organic wastes without prior dewatering. The normal oxidation process is accelerated by subjecting wastes to increased temperatures and pressures within a reaction vessel.[20]

The wastestream is pumped into a multi-compartment reactor designed to agitate and aerate the waste (see Figure 8). Reactor temperature ranges from 200 to 300°C[21] and reactor pressure is equivalent to 40 atmospheres.[6]

Typically, wet air oxidation achieves reductions in organic material in the wastestream of 75 to 90% as measured in terms of chemical oxygen demand (COD). It has achieved 99.9% and higher destruction of specific contaminants such as phenols, diphenylamine and pentachlorophenol. These materials are broken down to simpler molecules which are further oxidized.

Wet air oxidation works well in combination with a biological treatment system. Wet air oxidation breaks down toxic organics to simpler low molecular weight species. The biological system treats the effluent to destroy these compounds to a level at which the treated wastestream may be discharged.[22]

A major problem faced by biological systems is the disposal of sludge produced during wastewater treatment. The sludge resulting from biological treatment can be readily oxidized in the wet air oxidation process. Thus the two processes are symbiotic, each destroying what the other cannot. Figure 9 shows how the two processes might work in a situation when both concentrated and dilute organic wastestreams are generated.

Research into wet air oxidation techniques to destroy aqueous wastes is occurring at the Ontario Research Foundation (Mississauga, Ontario). The specific process under investigation at the Ontario Research Foundation is known as the Wetox™ process. Wetcom Engineering (Scarborough, Ontario) possesses the rights to market Wetox™ technology.

The Wetox™ process can be applied to the destruction of not easily biodegradable materials such as pesticides or substances that may create an air pollution hazard when incinerated in a conventional manner.[23] While the system destroys organic wastes, it can recover inorganic materials that can be recycled or removed for disposal. The process allows for the recovery of resources such as nitrogen converted to ammonia and sulphur converted to sulfuric acid. In addition to materials recovery, up to 60% of the potential energy in the incoming waste can be recovered from the oxidation of more concentrated wastes (generally for those wastestreams containing more than 5% organics).[18]

Cement Kilns

Application

At present, non-halogenated organics such as certain waste solvents and still bottoms from reclaiming operations are purchased routinely by some cement companies for use as a fuel supplement in the operation of rotary kilns.

There is interest in Canada, Sweden and the United States in destroying hazardous halogenated wastes such as PCBs in cement kilns. Test burns in these countries showed PCB destruction efficiencies exceeding 99.99%.

Process Description

In the production of cement, limestone is subjected to very high temperatures, hovering at 2600°F for several hours in a large rotary kiln. The solid material which results from the heating process is ground up and becomes the major constituent of cement.

One advantage of the cement kiln is the tremendous thermal inertia of the kiln and its contents. Even if the burner goes out, the kiln will remain at very high temperatures for minutes, even hours, allowing ample time to turn off the waste injectors.

Proponents of waste incineration in cement kilns suggest that incineration temperatures are

guaranteed to remain optimal and hence ensure virtually complete destruction of wastes. Failure to do so would interfere with the production of high quality cement.

Another advantage of burning chlorinated hydrocarbons in a cement kiln is that the alkalinity of the cement neutralizes the hydrochloric acid produced during the destruction of PCBs. Despite the obvious economic advantages of using an existing cement kiln to incinerate hazardous wastes, there are several drawbacks to this disposal option.

As with other centralized treatment facilities, the transportation of hazardous wastes to an incineration site entails the risk of spill and environmental mishap. When siting new waste treatment facilities, there is greater flexibility in locating such a facility remote from population centres. When using an existing cement facility, no such flexibility exists.

If cement kilns are remote from populated areas, and if the facility is upgraded specifically to handle wastes and capture air pollutants, the use of existing cement fac-

tories to incinerate wastes may be a cost-effective option for the disposal of hazardous wastes compared to building a new incinerator.

At-Sea Incineration

Application

Typical wastes incinerated at sea include pesticides and other halogenated organics.

At present there are two functioning incinerator ships. The Vulcanus, previously operated by Ocean Combustion Service BV, a Dutch subsidiary of the Hansa Shipping Line (Bremen, West Germany)[24], was sold to Waste Management Incorporated (Chicago, Illinois) in the latter part of 1980.[2] The Vulcanus, now equipped with a high temperature incinerator, is a former freighter whose waste storage tanks have a capacity of 770,000 Imperial gallons.

The Vulcanus specializes in the burning of halogenated organics. Its incinerator system can handle

Figure 9
Use of Biological Treatment and Wet Air Oxidation to Treat Both Dilute and Concentrated Organic Wastestreams

Wet air oxidation breaks down toxic organics to simpler low-molecular-weight species. The biological system treats the effluent to destroy these compounds to a level at which the treated wastestreams may be discharged.
Source: W. R. Laughlin, Ontario Research Foundation, 1981.

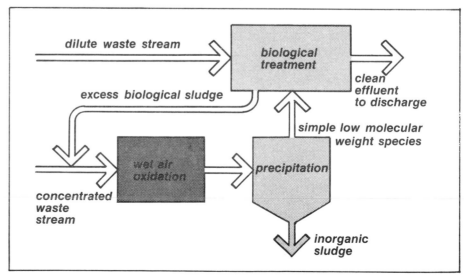

waste with a chlorine content as high as 70%. In 1977, the United States Environmental Protection Agency gave permission to have the Vulcanus burn more than 10,000 tons of surplus Agent Orange.[24] Agent Orange, a toxic herbicide contaminated with dioxins, was used as a defoliant during the Viet Nam war. Waste destruction efficiency of Agent Orange was reported to be 99.9%.[2]

The Mathias II is an incinerator ship owned and operated by Industrie Anlage (Berlin, West Germany).[24] Hazardous wastes are collected from several European countries for storage in Antwerp (Belgium). Wastes are then transferred to the Mathias II and incinerated in the North Sea. Mathias I, a prototype for Mathias II has been sold and no longer operates as an incinerator ship. A sister ship, Mathias III has been taken out of service for repairs.

Late in 1980, the Environmental Protection Agency and the Maritime Administration announced plans to push for the construction of a fleet of waste incineration ships to serve the North American waste market.[25] Financial assistance and loan guarantees are being considered to fund privately-owned American incineration ships. In the absence of private sector interest, the United States government itself may oversee construction of a prototype incineration ship.[25]

Process Description

The incineration of hazardous organic wastes on ships situated in the ocean has occurred since the early 1970s. Incinerator ships are ocean-going vessels that are equipped with a high temperature incinerator, such as a liquid injection unit.

The stimulus to burn hazardous wastes at sea has been two-fold. First, incinerating wastes at sea is much cheaper than burning these wastes on land. In 1979, at-sea incineration cost under $100 (U.S.) whereas the incineration of equivalent organics on land cost several hundred dollars.[24] The reason for the reduced operating cost of at-sea incineration com-

D & D's portable filtration unit used to pump PCB fluids from transformers into a container.

D & D's PCB destruction unit which is based on the design of a diesel engine.

pared to land incineration is the absence of pollution abatement equipment on ship incineration systems. Secondly, by burning wastes in the ocean, waste disposers are able to circumvent public opposition typical when siting incineration facilities on land.

Mobile PCB Destruction

Process Description

The D&D Group (Smithville, Ontario) has developed a mobile

PCB destruction unit based on the design of a diesel engine. Preliminary testing by the Ontario Research Foundation and Environment Canada in 1980 indicated a high PCB destruction efficiency.

If the unit is licensed for use in Canada, the D&D Group will be able to provide a complete on-site detoxification service. PCB-containing fluids are first drained from electrical transformers and hydraulic equipment. A solvent is used to flush and decontaminate the equipment. After cleaning, functionally sound equipment is refilled with a less hazardous substitute fluid.

Distillation methods are used to separate the solvent trichlorobenzene from the PCB mixture. Trichlorobenzene is recovered and re-used to flush and decontaminate PCB-containing equipment.[26] The final step in the PCB detoxification service is the destruction of PCBs in the mobile destruction unit.

4.
Radiation Destruction

Most waste destruction technologies based on radiation are new technologies or novel variations of established technologies.

Radiation destruction technologies depend on the energy of electron beam, ultraviolet (UV) or other radiation to provide the energy necessary to break apart molecular bonds in the hazardous material. The absorption of radiation at certain wavelengths causes the waste chemical compound to decompose or break down. In some cases, the incoming radiation functions as a catalyst to accelerate an otherwise chemical destruction of the waste.

Types of highly hazardous chemicals under scrutiny for destruction by radiation include dioxins, PCBs, pesticides, chemical warfare agents, explosives and propellants. One of the major advantages of radiation destruction systems is the energy efficiency of the waste treatment process, particularly in comparison to many of the incineration techniques.

Radiation destruction technologies described include:
    Photolysis
    Electron radiation
    Dehalogenation
    UV-assisted chlorinolysis

Photolysis of Dioxin

Dioxin is known to break down in the presence of UV light. As with any emerging waste disposal technology, the issue remains whether the degree of destruction is adequate.

In 1980, Syntex Agribusiness

Inc. (Springfield, Missouri) employed a specially designed extraction photolysis process to destroy 13 pounds of dioxin contaminating 4300 gallons of sludge.[27]

The dioxin-laden sludge discovered on Syntex's premises had been abandoned by a former pharmaceutical company manufacturing a hexachlorophene skin cleanser. The distillation residue resulting from the synthesis of hexachlorophene contained more than 300 ppm of dioxin.

I.T. Enviroscience (Knoxville, Tennessee) had designed a treatment process to destroy dioxin contaminants in sludge. In this process, the dioxin is extracted from the sludge using a common organic solvent. The extract is then exposed to ultraviolet light which breaks down the dioxin compound. The solvent is distilled for recycling within the process[27] (see Figure 10). The dioxin level in the residue was reduced from 343 ppm to less than 0.5 ppm. The 1980 cost to Syntex for the equipment and installation was $500,000 (U.S.).

Electron Radiation

Research at the Michigan Institute of Technology has revealed that electron beam radiation is highly effective in destroying water-dissolved PCBs and other toxic chemicals. The electron beam technology was not successful, however, in destroying PCBs in wastestreams high in lipid content. In pure water, a 10-kilorad dose produced almost complete PCB destruction. As the concentration of lipid increased in the wastewater, the effectiveness of the treatment was severely inhibited.[11]

Electron radiation of the persistent, urea-type pesticide known as Monuron resulted in almost complete destruction after exposure to 30 kilorads of radiation.[28]

Dehalogenation by UV Radiation

The Atlantic Research Corporation has developed a process for breaking carbon and halogen bonds in wastes.[11] Waste halogenated organics are dissolved in

---

Figure 10
Photolysis of Dioxin

Using the extraction photolysis process, 4300 gallons of sludge contaminated by 13 pounds of dioxin (343 parts per million) were detoxified to a dioxin level of less than 0.5 parts per million — a reduction of over 99%.

Source: "Destroying Dioxin: A Unique Approach," *Waste Age,* October 1980.

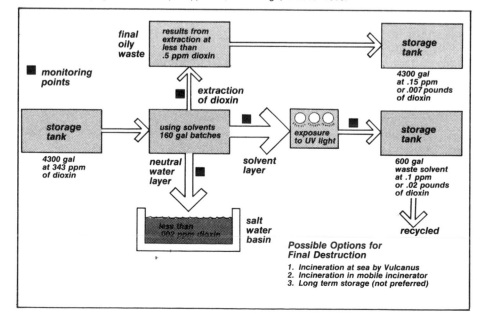

methanol and exposed to UV radiation and hydrogen. Cleavage of the carbon-halogen bonds results in the formation of free halogen ions. Research to date indicates that dehalogenation via UV radiation is applicable to kepone, PCBs, and tetrabromophthalic anhydride.[11]

UV-Assisted Chlorinolysis

Chlorinolysis refers to the destruction of hazardous wastes by exposure to chlorine at high pressure and low temperature, or at high temperature and low pressure. Depending on the constituents in the wastestream, chlorinolysis may result in the undesirable formation of hazardous reaction products such as carbon tetrachloride, carbonyl chloride and hydrogen chloride.[29]

Chlorinolysis in combination with UV exposure is observed to minimize the production of hazardous byproducts. Chlorinolysis catalyzed by UV light has been used to treat dilute concentrations of hydrazine in wastewater. No undesirable products were found in the wastewater at the end of the treatment process. Significant amounts of chlorinated contaminants remained in wastewater when processed by chlorinolysis without UV radiation.[11]

5.
Land Disposal

In recent years, the waste disposal industry has developed and made available better-designed methods of isolating and storing industrial wastes. The strategy is to encase the toxic material to prevent it from escaping into the environment.

It must be stressed, however, that there is an enormous difference between using land disposal to dispose of residuals such as ash, and using them as a primary disposal method. The difference is one of volume and waste type. If only the residuals are solidified and landfilled, the volume of wastes buried would be a small fraction of the total wastes treated. If solidification is used as a primary disposal method, this may result in the majority of the industrial wastes being put underground.

Waste encapsulation and solidification processes are still in the development stage. They have received only limited testing as to the full range of chemical and climatic interactions possible that could contribute to the movement of toxics from the containment site.

No single technology such as solidification or secure landfill can adequately manage all industrial wastes. Industrial wastestreams are composed of thousands of constituents, each with its own set of physical and chemical properties.

Some of the constituents will react with others. Some will degrade the containment structure over time. Carefully controlled lab experiments suggest that engineers can do much to ameliorate the destructive actions of the various wastestreams by keeping wastestreams separate, or by mixing in special additives.

Transferring carefully controlled lab experiments to a land disposal facility is another matter. Human error in analyzing wastestreams or in keeping certain constituents separate may result in accelerated leakage from the containment area. Given the lack of evidence on the long-term effectiveness of such technologies as solidification, the preferred management route is to exhaust all other waste treatment methods before resorting to land disposal.

Four developments in land disposal technology include:
Solidification
Secure landfill
Deep-well disposal
Retreivable storage

Solidification

Solidification is the fixation or encapsulation of waste to produce a solid end product. Fixation is based on the addition of an agent such as lime or cement to turn the waste into a concrete-like solid. Encapsulation is a physical process in which the solidification agent surrounds the waste particles and makes them adhere together into a mass. The main objective of solidification is to chemically and physically trap toxic constituents within the solid. Leaching of some constituents may still occur, but at a significantly reduced rate.[30] Solidification technology was developed for use in those instances where secure landfill was not available.

Solidification is an outgrowth of processes developed to manage low-level radioactive wastes. The

---

Table 6

Suitability of Wastes for Solidification

Solidification	Wastes Suitable for Solidification	Wastes Detrimental to Solidification
Cement-based	Toxic inorganics Scrubber ash and sludges	Organics Some anions
Pozzolanic	Toxic inorganics Scrubber ash and sludges	Organics Some anions
Thermoplastic	Toxic inorganics	Strong oxidizers
Organic Polymer	Toxic inorganics	Acidic materials Strong oxidizers
Encapsulation	Toxic and soluble inorganics	Strong oxidizers

Source: Toxic and Hazardous Waste Disposal. Volume I and II Ann Arbor Science.

most common solidification techniques include the following:

Cement-based
Lime-based (pozzolanic)
Thermoplastic
Organic polymer
Encapsulation

Solidification processes are compared in Table 6 with respect to the types of wastestreams suitable and unsuitable to particular solidification agents.

Cement-Based

Cement-based solidification processes use Portland cement and other additives such as fly ash and silicates to solidify inorganic wastes and sludges rich in metals. The high pH of the cement mixture tends to keep the metal ions in the form of insoluble hydroxide or carbonate salts.[31]

Common cement consists of calcium silicates and calcium aluminate which incorporate the waste into a rock-like mass during solidification.

Organics and some anions are not compatible with the cementing process and generally weaken the cement. Soluble ions such as chlorides, sulfates, sodium and potassium leach relatively easily from the solidified waste.

One factor contributing to the disintegration of the solid is seasonal wet-dry, freeze-thaw cycles, particularly for solidification products occurring above the frost line.[32]   The cement-based techniques are the most common of the solidification methods because they are generally the cheapest and easiest to use.[32] Major cement-based processes include the Terra-Tite, Petrifix, Terracrete and Sealosafe processes.

Lime-Based (Pozzolanic)

The term "pozzolanic" comes from Pozzuoli, a city near Naples where volcanic silico-aluminate calcium ash has been mined since before the time of Christ.[32] Lime is mixed with siliceous material and water to produce a very hard material known as pozzolanic concrete. Common additives are cement kiln dust and fly ash from

During solidification of wastes, the incoming wastestream is mixed thoroughly with the solidification agents in large tanks.

Disposal of liquid stabilized product on the ground at a Stablex facility in England.

Concrete-like blocks cast from Stablex product.

electric power plants, which are wastes in themselves.[6] Other additives are added if necessary to enhance the strength or impermeability of the solid.

Pozzolanic processes have been used to solidify sludges generated during sulphur scrubbing operations at coal-fired power plants.

IU Conversion Systems (Horsham, Pennsylvania) markets a process called Poz-o-Tec that converts flue gas sludge into a stable material that can be used in properly designed landfills, embankments, roads and parking lots.[32]

Solidified fly ash wastes from coal-burning power plants now underlie the Veteran's Stadium complex in Pittsburgh and some of the runways at Dalles International Airport near Washington, D.C.[33] Fly ash wastes resulting from the burning of coal are considered appropriate for use in construction projects because they are relatively low in heavy metal contaminants. Because sludges from the electroplating industry are very high in metal contaminants, this process is not appropriate for use in road construction.

The Dravo Lime Company (Pittsburgh, Pennsylvania) markets an additive known as Calcilox capable of solidifying flue gas sludges resulting from the combustion of coal.

Pozzolanic solidification suffers from similar disadvantages as cement-based techniques. Contamination with organic matter may result in organic decomposition after curing, resulting in increased permeability and reduced sheer strength. The solidified wastes are vulnerable to weathering from rain and ice if the resultant solids are not properly capped with clay in a secure landfill. Neither the cement-based nor the lime-based solidification products are completely impermeable to water.

Thermoplastic

Thermoplastic solidification makes use of materials such as polyethylene, paraffin, bitumen or asphalt to bind wastes into a uniform mass.

Unlike cement-based and lime-based solidification, thermoplastic techniques require that the waste be dry before it is mixed with the solidification agent. The solidification agent and wastes are mixed at temperatures ranging from 130 to 230°C in close to equal amounts. Cooling of the mixture results in solidification of the mass.

One advantage of thermoplastic solidification is that the resulting solidified waste is impermeable to water. Contaminant leaching is also lower than for other solidification processes, however, the cost is higher.

The Werner and Pfleiderer Corporation (Waldwick, New Jersey) have used thermoplastic solidification in more than 2000 applications in the chemical, plastics, food and nuclear industries.[32]

Organic solvents capable of dissolving the solidification agent are not appropriate for thermoplastic solidification. Other unsuitable wastes include those containing high concentrations of oxidizing salts such as nitrates, chlorates and perchlorates.[31] Wastes that are volatile at low temperatures present safety problems during the heating of the solidification agent.

Organic Polymer

Organic polymer solidification is based on the addition and thorough mixing of a small amount of monomer to the wastes. A catalyst is added, resulting in the linking of the monomers into a sponge-like polymer.

The sponge-like polymer traps solid waste particles while permitting much of the wastewater to escape. Current research is directed at minimizing the leachate problem.

Several polymer techniques are being investigated. The Teledyne Corporation (Louisville, Kentucky) has developed the urea-formaldehyde process. Washington State University is studying solidification with polyester resins, while the Dow Chemical Company is pursuing the use of polyvinyl chloride as the polymer matrix. Organic polymer techniques are suitable for toxic organics, but not for acidic materials and strong oxidizers.[32]

Other solidification processes suffer from the disadvantage of requiring such large volumes of additives that the resultant product is twice the size or weight of the original waste materials. This contributes significantly to materials and transport costs and landfill sites are filled up twice as fast.

Organic polymer processes require only small amounts of additives to solidify wastes. As little as 3% of the total weight of the final solid may be polymer additives.[32] However, if insufficient resin is used, the matrix will not trap all the wastes.

Other problems exist. The catalysts used in the urea-formaldehyde process are strongly acidic. Many metal ions are soluble in acidic solutions and insoluble in alkaline conditions. Strongly acidic polymerization catalysts redissolve precipitated metal ions, permitting them to leach out in water not trapped in the polymer matrix.[32]

Contamination of the wastes with corrosive materials such as strong oxidizers will result in gradual breakdown of the organic matrix. Both urea-formaldehyde and polyesters are unstable in corrosive environments.[6]

Surface Encapsulation

Surface encapsulation is a process in which wastes are coated with a water-impermeable sealant.

A system developed by TRW Systems (Redondo Beach, California) uses polybutadiene to bind toxic inorganics into small cubes. A thick layer (1 to 2 cm) of high-density polyethylene is fused onto the surface of the cube, encapsulating the waste into a seamless container.

The cost of resin encapsulation is high, partly due to the high costs of petroleum-based resins. As with any hydrocarbon polymer, degradation of the protective plastic coating is accelerated in response to contact with solvents, heat or UV radiation.

Surface encapsulation is a useful technology when applied to the interim storage of waste materials whose recovery is uneconomical at

Secure landfill at Gallenbach (Germany) showing deposition of incinerator ash and stabilized product.

Leachate collection well under construction within the secure landfill pit.

Particularly hazardous chemicals are stored in barrels and placed within a secure concrete vault inside the secure landfill at Gallenbach.

present. Drummed wastes may be encapsulated in their entirety.

TRW Systems are developing a system to encapsulate drums of wastes of unknown composition from abandoned dumpsites. Drums are left sealed and are not analyzed. The drums are placed in a fibreglass cocoon big enough to accommodate warped and dented drums. A layer of high density polyethylene is fused onto the surface and the drums are relocated.[32]

Disposal of Solidification Products

The solidification of inorganic wastes from desulfurization processes that are free of metal contaminants is a reasonable strategy in utilizing scrubber wastes. The solidified product, if free of toxic inclusions, can be used in the construction of roads.

The long-term stability of solidification products rich in metals is currently under debate. Proponents of solidification are seeking approval to place solidified wastes embedded with metals and potentially toxic inorganics in non-secure landfill sites.

Concerns regarding the durability of the stabilized material when exposed to physical and biological factors in the soil have regulators scrutinizing which stabilized wastestreams require secure landfilling.

Secure Landfill

A secure landfill is designed to receive chemical and other industrial wastes. Secure landfills differ from conventional sanitary landfills in the degree to which the site is engineered to diminish the migration of pollutants.

Secure landfill cannot substitute for other waste treatment technologies such as waste reduction, recovery, treatment or destruction. The many environmental problems and unknowns associated with landfill make it a disposal option of last resort, and certainly one whose use should be minimized in the face of more progressive technologies.

Environmental dangers are numerous. Although secure land-

Figure 11
Typical Secure Landfill Cell

The pit is underlain with a leachate collection system that pumps migrating liquids to a leachate treatment system. The pit is lined with a synthetic membrane, clay liner or both.
Source: *Need for Waste Management Facilities and Available Technologies: Annex One,* prepared for the Ontario Ministry of the Environment, November 1980.

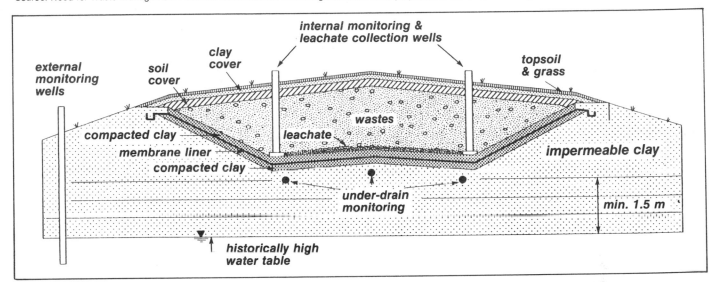

fill technology substantially reduces the migration of contaminants compared to previous systems, secure landfill is limited in types of wastes that it can confine.

The common disposal method is to co-dispose industrial wastes with municipal wastes in unlined pits. Depending on the geology of the region, existing landfill sites may be located in a natural clay deposit. However, some existing landfill sites are permeable to leachate movement.

There are many variations in the design of secure landfills. The simplest variation is a pit with a synthetic membrane or clay liner (see Figure 11). In some instances, where natural clay deposits are thick, no synthetic membrane is used.

The pit is underlain with a leachate collection system that pumps liquids to a leachate treatment system. The perimeter of the buffer zone contains a few monitoring wells which collect ground water for analysis of contaminants. Several years may elapse before a secure landfill is full. At closure, a layer of clay is deposited over the wastes to minimize water movement into the pit.

Some of the synthetic polymers used to line the landfill pit are vulnerable to disintegration by specific solvents and corrosive agents.[2] Based on research by the EPA, polypropylene appears to be one of the more versatile synthetic liners for secure landfill. Polyvinyl chloride and polyethylene liners have limited ability to retain acidic pickling waste and electroplating sludge (see Table 7).

Clay is mistakenly identified as a highly impermeable material. This perception is based on the poor ability of water to pass through clay. Water will penetrate clay, but at an exceedingly slow rate because of the nonporous structure of clay.

The permeability of clay is increased dramatically when penetrated by certain organics, acids and bases. Clay liners are dissolved by the infiltration of a chemical that dissolves the surfaces of the pores in the clay. Either organic acids or organic bases may solubilize portions of the clay. Acids have been reported to solubilize aluminum, iron, alkali metals and alkaline earths while bases will dissolve silica.[34] Since clay minerals contain both silica and aluminum in large quantities, they are susceptible to dissolution by acids and bases. The net result is that pore size increases and the

clay becomes more permeable.

Clay types differ in how much they swell or shrink when they become wet or dry. Montmorillonite clays undergo extreme swelling or shrinkage, depending on moisture content. Similarly, organic leachates can cause shrinking or swelling of clay liners.

Montmorillonite clays are reported to swell as a result of exposure to several forms of xylene, cyclopentane, alcohols, glycols and ketones.[35] A liner which has swelled and heaved may lose its integrity during heaving, or it may shrink later when water replaces infiltrated organic chemicals.[36] In either situation, the overall ability of the clay layer to stop the movement of contaminants is diminished.

Another factor that increases the movement of leachate through clay is the ability of certain materials such as sulphates to defloculate clay. Clay resists the movement of water because of the physical structure of the clay. Addition of certain chemicals causes the structure of the clay to change and become more porous.

Secure landfill sites are designed to be the final resting place for the full range of industrial wastes. The mixing of certain wastes may result in fires, explosions or the release of toxic gases (see Table 8).

These concerns have prompted the design of individual cells within the landfill, each of which would accept a different category of waste. The main landfill cell is divided by clay barriers into a number of subcells for specific types of hazardous wastes.[32]

Retrievable Storage

Retrievable storage refers to a secure system of long-term storing of wastes prior to recovery or destruction at a later date.

Waste storage permits certain materials to be recycled at a later date when recovery becomes more attractive financially. Another reason for storing wastes for easy retrieval is in instances where present technology is lacking to adequately detoxify or destroy select wastes. Chemicals currently in storage include PCBs and the restricted pesticide 2,4,5,-T.

Wastes are stored in drums, tanks, or ponds, depending on how hazardous or volatile the waste is.

In West Germany, the Kali & Salz Corporation (Kassel, West Germany) has been storing 40,000 tonnes of solid industrial waste per year in a salt mine since 1972.[2] Salt mines are considered suitable storage sites because of their dryness and geological stability.

Non-radioactive wastes are received from all over Europe. The solid wastes are placed in steel or plastic drums and arranged on wooden pallets. In some cases, drums are wrapped with additional polyethylene sheeting. Wastes are inventoried and systematically segregated into hundreds of different rooms within the underground salt mine.

Table 7
Compatability of Synthetic Liners with Common Industrial Sludges*

Industrial Waste

Liner Material	Caustic Petroleum Sludge	Acidic Steel-Pickling Waste	Electro-plating Sludge	Toxic Pesticide Formulations	Oily Refinery Sludge	Toxic Pharmaceutical Waste	Rubber and Plastic
Polyvinylchloride (oil resistant)	G	F	F	G	G	G	G
Polyethylene	G	F	F	G	F	G	G
Polypropylene	G	G	G	G	G	G	G
Butyl Rubber	G	G	G	F	P	F	G
Chlorinated Poly-ethylene	G	F	F	F	P	F	G
Ethylene Propyl-ene Rubber	G	G	G	F	P	F	G
Hypalon	G	G	G	F	P	F	G
Asphalt Concrete	F	F	F	F	P	F	G
Soil Cement	F	P	P	G	G	G	G
Soil Asphalt	F	P	P	F	P	F	G
Asphalt Membranes	F	F	F	F	P	F	G
Soil Bentonite (Saline Seal)	P	P	P	G	G	G	G
Compacted Clays	P	P	P	G	G	G	G

*P = poor, F = fair, G = good.

Source: *Need for Waste Management Facilities and Available Technologies: Annex One.* Prepared for the Ontario Ministry of the Environment.

At the Kali und Salz AG (Germany), wastes are stored underground in a salt mine. Incoming wastes are repackaged if necessary, and labelled for future identification.

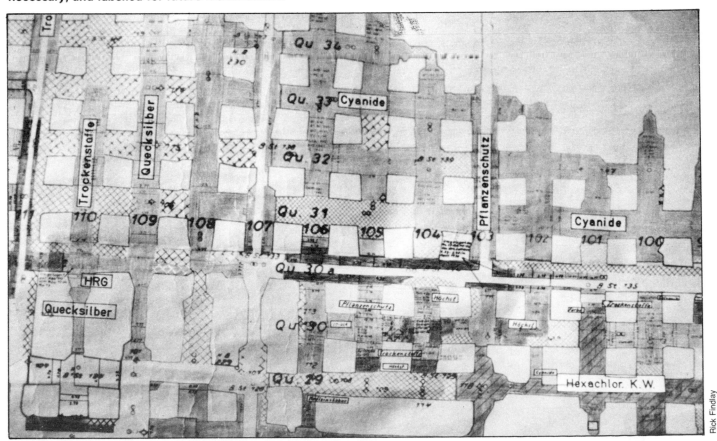

Wastes are catalogued and placed in designated cells in the salt mine. Maps are made to keep track of the location of these stored wastes.

The German system is designed to permit easy retrieval of wastes in the future. Elaborate records are kept on the composition, reactive potential and handling hazards associated with each stored waste.

A detailed map of the mine ensures that specific wastes can be located easily. A forklift truck is used to move drum-laden pallets into storage or out for recovery.

Table 8

Potentially Incompatible Waste Materials and Components

The mixing of a Group A waste with a Group B waste may have the potential consequence as noted.

Group 1: Potential consequences: Heat generation, violent reaction.

Group 1-A	Group 1-B
Acetylene sludge	Acid sludge
Alkaline caustic liquids	Acid and water
Alkaline cleaner	Battery acid
Alkaline corrosive liquids	Chemical cleaners
Alkaline corrosive battery fluid	Electrolyte, acid
Caustic wastewater	Etching acid liquid
	or solvent
Lime sludge and other corrosive	Liquid cleaning compounds
alkalies	Pickling liquor and
	other corrosive acids
Lime wastewater	Spent acid
Lime and water	Spent mixed acid
Spent caustic	Spent sulfuric acid

Group 2: Potential consequences: Release of toxic substances in case of fire or explosion.

Group 2-A	Group 2-B
Asbestos waste and other toxic wastes	Cleaning solvents
Beryllium wastes	Data processing liquid
Unrinsed pesticide containers	Obsolete explosives
Waste pesticides	Petroleum waste
	Refinery waste
	Retrograde explosives
	Solvents
	Waste oil and other flammable and
	explosive wastes

Group 3: Potential consequences: Fire or explosion; generation of flammable hydrogen gas.

Group 3-A	Group 3-B
Aluminum	Any waste in Group 1-A or 1-B
Beryllium	
Calcium	
Lithium	
Magnesium	
Potassium	
Sodium	
Zinc powder and other reactive	
metals and metal hydrides	

Source: Need for Waste Management Facilities and Available Technologies: Annex One. Prepared for the Ontario Ministry of the Environment.

References

1. Verespej, M.A. "Time for Decisions on Hazardous Waste." *Industry Week,* June 15, 1981.

2. MacLaren Engineers and Planners. *Need for Waste Management Facilities and Available Technologies: Annex One.* Prepared for the Ontario Ministry of the Environment, November 1980.

3. "It's Hard to Find Jobs for Industrious Bugs." *Chemical Week,* January 14, 1981.

4. "Building Superbugs for the Big Clean-Up." *Chemical Week,* July 23, 1980.

5. "Bacterial Bed Consumes Phenol." *Canadian Chemical Processing,* February 1981.

6. Reid, Crowther & Partners Ltd. *Hazardous Wastes in Northern and Western Canada, Volume 2: Technology Review.* Prepared for Environment Canada, December 1980.

7. Powers, P.W. *How to Dispose of Toxic Substances and Industrial Wastes.* Park Ridge, New Jersey: Noyes Data Corporation, 1976.

8. U.S. Environmental Protection Agency. *Pretreatment of Pollutants into Publicly Owned Treatment Works.* Office of Water Program Operations, October 1973.

9. Roberts, J.L. and Sawyer, D.T. "Facile Degradation of Superoxide Ion of Carbon Tetrachloride, Chloroform, Methylene Chloride and p,p'-DDT in Aprotic Media." *Journal of the American Chemical Society* 103(3), 1981.

10. Lombard, W.K. "Thermal Destruction of Industrial Wastes." In *Solutions for Industrial Wastes Disposal.* Proceedings of a Seminar sponsored by the Pollution Control Association of Ontario and the Ontario Ministry of the Environment, March 1981.

11. Edwards, B. and Paullin, J. "Emerging Technologies for the Destruction of Hazardous Wastes: Molten Salt Combustion." In *Treatment of Hazardous Waste.* Proceedings of the Sixth Annual Research Symposium of the Office of Research and Development, United States Environmental Protection Agency, March 1980.

12. Ragland, K.W. and Paul, D. *Fluidized Bed Combustion of Plastic Waste with Coal.* Presented at the Fourteenth Intersociety Energy Conversion Conference, Boston, Massachusetts, 1979.

13. Kapner, M. (Hittman & Associates). *The Economics of Hazardous Waste Incinerators.* Prepared for U.S. Environmental Protection Agency, 1980.

14. Greenberg, J.G. *Method of Catalytically Inducing Oxidation of Carbonaceous Materials by the Use of Molten Salts.* Pleasantville, New Jersey: Antipollution Systems, 1972.

15. Yosim, S.J. *et al. Disposal of Hazardous Wastes by Molten Salt Combustion.* Presented at Meeting of the American Chemical Society, Hawaii, 1979.

16. Freeman, H. *Molten Salt Destruction Process: An Evaluation for Application in California.* Prepared for the Toxic Waste Assessment Program, Office of Appropriate Technology, State of California (mimeographed).

17. Greenberg, J.G. *The Use of Molten Salts in Emission Control.* Paper presented at the 72nd Annual Meeting of the Air Pollution Control Association, Cincinnati, Ohio, 1979.

18. "Waste Treatment Processes Ready for Use." *Eco/Log Week,* December 12, 1980.

19. TRW Defence and Space Systems Group. *Destroying Chemical Wastes in Commercial Scale Incinerators.* Prepared for the Office of Solid Waste Management, U.S. Environmental Protection Agency.

20. Cardotte, A. and Laughlin, R. *Waste Destruction with Energy Recovery — The Wetox Process.* Presented at 29th Canadian Chemical Engineering Conference, Sarnia, Ontario, October 1-3, 1979.

21. "New Waste Processes Soon." *Canadian Chemical Processing,* February 13, 1981.

22. Laughlin, W.R. Ontario Research Foundation, Mississauga, Ontario. Personal communication, November 1981.

23. "System Developed to Destroy Wastes Harmful to Health." *The Globe and Mail* (Canada), September 14, 1977.

24. Maugh, T. "Incineration, Deep Wells Gain New Importance." *Science,* June 15, 1979.

25. "Washington Newsletter: Incinerator Ships Get Two Agencies' Backing." *Chemical Week,* November 5, 1980.

26. Drew, Thomas. D&D Group, Smithville, Ontario. Personal communication, September 1981.

27. "Destroying Dioxin: A Unique Approach." *Waste Age,* October 1980.

28. Trump, J. *et al. Destruction of Pathogenic Microorganisms and Toxic Chemicals by Electron Treatment.* Presented at the Eighth National Conference on Municipal Sludge Management, Miami, Florida, 1979.

29. "Emerging Technology of Chlorinolysis." *Environmental Science and Technology* 8(1), 1974.

30. Pojasek, R. "Stabilization, Solidification of Hazardous Wastes." *Environmental Science and Technology,* April 1978.

31. Pojasek, R. (Ed.) *Toxic and Hazardous Waste Disposal, Volumes I and II.* Ann Arbor, Michigan: Ann Arbor Science Publishers Inc., 1979.

32. Maugh, T. "Burial is the Last Resort for Hazardous Wastes." *Science* 204(22), 1979.

33. "Customized Waste Stabilization." *Waste Age,* April 1981.

34. Grim, R. and Cuthbert, F. *The Bonding Action of Clays.* Illinois State Geologic Survey Report of Investigation No. 102.

35. Barrier, R. *Zeolites and Clay Minerals as Sorbents and Molecular Sieves.* New York: Academic Press, 1978.

36. Brown, K. and Anderson, D. "The Effect of Organic Chemicals on Clay Liner Permeability." In *Disposal of Hazardous Waste.* Proceedings of the Sixth Annual Research Symposium of the Office of Research and Development, United States Environmental Protection Agency, March 1980.

Glossary

Adsorption   The process by which molecules, atoms or ions of solids, liquids or gases are retained on the surface of another solid or liquid. Contrasted with the penetration into the bulk of the solid or liquid which occurs in absorption.

Aerobic   Processes of biological activity occurring in the presence of free oxygen.

Afterburner   A device which performs afterburning, which is combustion in an internal combustion engine following the maximum pressure of explosion. An afterburner can be used to control emissions from an incinerator or distillation stack.

Aggregate   The sands, gravels and crushed stone used for mixing with cementing material in making mortars and concretes.

Anaerobic   Processes or biological activity occurring in the absence of free oxygen. For example, anaerobic bacteria get their oxygen by decomposing compounds containing oxygen.

Anion   A negatively charged ion, or ion that is attracted to the positive pole during electrolysis.

Anode   An electrode that attracts negative ions.

Atmospheric Beck Dyeing   Dyeing of textiles in a chamber called a beck, at atmospheric pressure. See also JET DYEING and LOW-LIQUOR DYEING.

Atomization   The breaking down of a liquid or meltable solid into drops ranging from 10 to over 1000 micrometers in diameter.

Atomized Paint   A spray of finely divided paint particles emanating from the nozzle of a spray gun.

Bating   In tanning, the cleaning of depilated leather hides by the action of tryptic enzymes.

Beamhouse   A place where the initial wet operations of tanning, involving soaking in water and solutions of alkali, are carried out.

Biochemical Oxygen Demand   See BIOLOGICAL OXYGEN DEMAND.

Biodegradable   That which is able to be decomposed by bacterial action.

Biogas   Fuel the source of which is biological waste material. For example, the organic and protein components of tanning wastes (trimmings and sludges) can be transformed into a combustible gas by anaerobic fermentation.

Biological Oxygen Demand (BOD)   The quantity of dissolved oxygen needed to satisfy the metabolic requirements of microorganisms living in water where there is a lot of organic material. Industrial effluents high in organic substances creates a high BOD in the receiving water, thereby reducing oxygen levels in that water. A measure of decomposable organic material, BOD is commonly calculated as the amount of oxygen (in mg/litre) used over a period of five days at 20°C. Also known as Biochemical Oxygen Demand. See also CHEMICAL OXYGEN DEMAND.

Biological Treatment   Waste treatment technologies including biological filtration, aeration, activated sludge, oxidation ponds, lagooning and anaerobic methods. Biological processes are classified by the oxygen dependence of the primary microorganisms responsible for waste treatment; there are aerobic, anaerobic and facultative processes. The living organisms decompose organic wastes into water, carbon dioxide and other simple inorganic and organic molecules.

Bleach   In photography, a chemical which oxidizes metallic silver to silver ion. Typical bleaching agents in the darkroom include ferricyanides, dichromates and permanganates. In textiles, bleaching removes the natural yellowish colouring of cotton fibre, rendering it white. Common textile bleaches are hydrogen peroxide, sodium hypochlorite and sodium chlorite.

Bleach-Fix   In photography, a chemical bath which both bleaches the silver of the image and fixes silver halide. Combined bleach-fixing baths are frequently used in the processing of colour prints.

BOD   See BIOLOGICAL OXYGEN DEMAND.

Boiler   A water heater for generating steam.

Bottom Ash   Residue from incineration that remains in the combustion chamber rather than being emitted with the effluent gases. (The latter is FLY ASH.)

Bottoms   See RESIDUES.

Brimstone   A common or commercial name for native sulphur.

British Thermal Unit (Btu)   A unit for measuring heat; the amount of heat necessary to raise one pound of water one degree Fahrenheit at its maximum density.

Btu   See BRITISH THERMAL UNIT.

Byproducts   Materials produced in making or doing something else; not the main product.

Cake   See RESIDUES.

Calcination   The process of heating to a high temperature without fusing, such as the heating of unformed ceramic materials in a kiln, or the heating of ores, precipitates, concentrates, or residues so that hydrates, carbonates, or other compounds are decomposed and volatile material is expelled. Calcination is used to recover metals and other non-combustible materials from waste sludge streams.

Capital Cost   The cost of new equipment and associated technical expertise to install the equipment or change the process.

Carbon Adsorption System   A device containing adsorbent material (e.g., activated carbon, aluminum, silica gel), an inlet and outlet for exhaust gases, and a system to regenerate the saturated adsorbent. The carbon adsorption system must provide for the proper disposal or re-use of all VOC adsorbed. Carbon adsorption has been long used to recover a variety of solvents from solvent-laden air.

Carbonizing   A finishing process in the textile industry used to remove cellulose impurities. The hot acid bath that is used is subsequently removed by neutralizing and rinsing.

Carcinogen   Any agent — biological, chemical, radioactive — that causes cancer. See also MUTAGENIC.

Carrier   Chemical used to speed up the textile dyeing process. Carriers are used to take dye into fibres that are hydrophobic (i.e., that resist water absorption) such as polyester. Examples are methyl naphthalene, chlorobenzenes, biphenyl, orthophenyl phenol and benzyl alcohol. When the dyeing operation is completed, these chemicals are discharged in the wastewater. Some are biodegradable, some are not. The need for carriers can be reduced by high-temperature and high-pressure dyeing.

Carry-Over   Unwanted liquid or solid material transferred from a processing bath, fractionating column, absorber or reaction vessel to the next phase in the processing sequence. In film processing, for example, carry-over refers to the chemicals adhering to the film as it is transferred from one process bath to another.

Catalyst   A substance that alters the rate of a chemical reaction and subsequently can be recovered unchanged.

Cathode   An electrode that attracts positive ions.

Cation   A positively charged ion, or ion that is attracted to the negative pole during electrolysis.

Centrifugation   A process widely used in industry which applies centrifugal force to separate liquids of different density and to thicken slurries or to remove solids. It is a technique for dewatering sludges and for concentrating precipitated solids in a wastestream. See also SOLID-LIQUID SEPARATION.

Chemical Coagulation   See COAGULANT.

Chemical Dechlorination   A group of technologies which can be used to strip chlorine atoms from highly chlorinated toxic compounds to produce a less toxic residue. See also CHLORINATED HYDROCARBONS.

Chemical Oxidation   A method of detoxifying hazardous wastes in which the wastestream is subjected to an oxidizing agent (e.g. chlorine, ozone, hydrogen peroxide). Chemical bonds are broken and the hazardous material is converted into simpler, less toxic chemicals.

Chemical Oxygen Demand (COD)   A measure of the quantity of oxidizable components present in water. Since the carbon and hydrogen, and not the nitrogen, in organic matter are oxidized by chemical oxidants, the oxygen consumed is a measure only of the chemically oxidizable components. COD does not necessarily correlate with BOD. See also BIOLOGI-

CAL OXYGEN DEMAND (BOD).

Chemical Waste Treatment   Treatment technologies including neutralization, coagulation, oxidation, chemical precipitation and electrochemical processes.

Chlorinated Hydrocarbons   Organic compounds in which one (or more) of the hydrogen atoms has been replaced by an atom of chlorine. Included are some of industry's most hazardous wastes, such as polychlorinated biphenyls (PCBs), vinyl chloride (VC), carbon tetrachloride and many pesticides.

Chlorinolysis   The destruction of hazardous wastes by exposure to chlorine at high pressure and low temperature or at high temperature and low pressure. Hazardous chlorinated reaction byproducts may result, but chlorinolysis in combination with exposure to ultraviolet radiation minimizes production of these byproducts.

Clarification   The purification of a liquid by clearing it of foreign matter.

Closed-Loop System   A process in which process byproducts and wastes are returned to the system for re-use in the same or in an alternate function. Unlike open-ended systems of the past, closed-loop technologies strive to maximize water, materials and energy recovery.

Coagulant   A material which, when added to industrial wastes, will combine with certain substances ordinarily present and form a precipitate consisting of more or less gelatinous floc particles and having the capacity to remove colloids from the liquids.

Coating   A paint, varnish, lacquer or other finish used to create a protective and/or decorative layer.

COD   See CHEMICAL OXYGEN DEMAND.

Coil Coating   See ROLL COATING.

Concentrate   In ultrafiltration, the suspended solids, emulsified oils and other high molecular weight species which are rejected by the separation membrane and removed as the concentrate. See also PERMEATE.

Condensate   The liquid product from a condenser used to liquify a gas. Also, a light hydrocarbon mixture formed as a liquid product in a gas recycling plant through expansion and cooling of the gas.

Condense   To change from a gas or vapour to a liquid.

Condenser   A device where vapourized solvent and water pass over water-cooled coil surfaces and condense.

Counter-Current Rinsing   A rinsing system designed to minimize the total volume of water required to rinse an object by using water from previous rinsings to contact the object at its most contaminated stage. Fresh water enters the process at the final rinse stage, at which point much of the contamination has already been rinsed off.

Deep Well Injection   A process for injecting waste under pressure in permeable underground strata.

Degreasing   The process of using solvent vapour or liquid to remove grease and oil from the surface of metal and other materials undergoing further finishing such as painting.

Dehalogenation   A waste disposal technology in which halogenated organics are dissolved in methanol and exposed to ultraviolet radiation and hydrogen. Cleavage of the carbon-halogen bonds results in the formation of free halogen ions. This technique can be applied to destruction of, for example, kepone and PCBs.

Deodorization   In dry cleaning, the process of reducing residual solvent in the clothing. The dryer door is opened slightly, then plant air is vented through the clothes in the dryer and exhausted. Solvent from the exhaust stream can be recovered.

Desizing   In the textile industry, the removal of size or sizing agents from textiles prior to finishing. See also SLASHING.

Desorption   A process by which a solvent temporarily attached to a carbon bed is removed from it. Methods used include the use of low-pressure steam; the use of another solvent to remove the adsorbate; the use of acidic or caustic wash; and removal of carbon from the bed followed by thermal activation of the carbon and indirect heating with an oxygen purge. The reverse of adsorption. See also ADSORPTION.

Developer   A chemical solution used to develop exposed photographic materials by reducing silver salts (e.g. silver halide) to metallic silver.

Dialysis   A process of separating solutes of low and high molecular weight by diffusion through a membrane. See also ELECTRODIALYSIS.

Diatomaceous Earth   When the shells of diatoms (a type of algae) are deposited, they form a type of earth that is light in colour, rich in silica, and porous. This deposit can be used to assist in filtering industrial effluents. Also known as tripolite and kieselguhr.

Discharge Liquor   See EFFLUENT.

Dissolved Solids   That fraction of the wastewater that contains ionic solids in dissociated form. Unlike suspended solids, dissolved solids cannot be separated from the wastestream using simple filtration methods. See also SUSPENDED SOLIDS.

Distillation   The process by which a liquid is heated to produce either gases or vapours which, in turn, are condensed into their respective liquids. In solvent recovery, distillation is used to remove dissolved impurities in the solvent and to separate solvent mixtures. Distillation takes advantage of the different volatility of substances to separate evaporable substances from non-evaporable ones. Distillation can be used only for the separation of substances the respective boiling points of which differ at least by 0.5 to 1.0°C, unless additives can facilitate the process (extractive distillation). There is a problem of the substance with a lower boiling point being contaminated with the vapour of the material with the higher boiling point, but this can be overcome to some extent by returning a portion of the distillate with the lower boiling point to the head of the column.

Drag-Out   Solution taken from a bath that adheres to the object being processed. See also CARRY-OVER.

Dross   Waste material, scum or impurity that comes to the surface of molten metals.

Dyeing   The application of colour-producing agents to material, usually fibrous or film, in order to impart a degree of colour permanence demanded by the projected end use.

Effluent   The liquid waste of sewage and industrial processing. Also known as discharge liquor.

Electrocoating   A dip method for applying a water-borne coating to metal by electrically coagulating paint solids onto the surface to be coated. Used largely for primers on automobiles and parts. Also used to apply finishes on some appliances. Also known as electrodeposition or electrostatic deposition.

Electrodeposition   See Electrocoating.

Electrodialysis   A system for removing unwanted particles from a solution by using an electric charge across a membrane. Electrodialysis, unlike ultrafiltration and reverse osmosis, is a membrane technology in which the separation is induced by electrical current. Cationic and anionic selective membranes are placed across the path of the current, allowing build-up of separate streams, one rich in ions and the other deficient in ions, but rich in colloidal and high molecular weight solutes. Reverse osmosis and ultrafiltration can remove 90 to 99 percent of the solute in one stage, while electrodialysis can typically remove 25 to 60 percent. The potential that has to be maintained between the anode and the cathode to maintain the passage of ions has to be continually increased as the purification continues. Electrodialysis has great potential for metal recovery, as regeneration and cleaning of the membrane goes on continually; there is no need for the unit to be shut down.

Electrolysis   A process which allows for chemical reactions to occur by passing an electrical current through an electrolyte solution.

Electrolytic Recovery   A relatively simple process in which direct current is passed through an electrolyte solution by means of cathode plates and insoluble anodes. This current flow directs cations to the cathode surface where a deposit is formed. The deposit increases in thickness as long as there are ample cations in the solution and an adequate current flow. This process is suitable for recovering metals from solution.

Electroplating   Electrodeposition of a metal or alloy from a suitable electrolyte solution. The article to be plated is connected as the cathode in the electrolyte solution. Direct current is introduced through the anode which consists of the metal to be deposited.

Electrostatic   Referring to the electric charge on an object.

Electrostatic Deposition   See ELECTROCOATING.

Electrostatic Painting   A coating application technique in which the spray nozzle is charged with one polarity, and the object to be coated with the other, so that spray is attracted to the object surface. Very high voltage at low amperage is used. Spray particles are attracted to the object by the opposite charge.

Electrostatic Precipitator   A device which removes dust or other finely divided particles from a gas by charging the particles inductively with an electric field, then attracting them to highly charged collector plates.

Emulsion   A liquid that is a mixture of liquids that do not dissolve in each other. In an emulsion, one of the liquids contains minute droplets of the other, which are evenly distributed throughout. In photography, an emulsion is a coating on a camera film, plate, etc., that contains the photosensitive agent.

Encapsulation   See SOLIDIFICATION and SURFACE ENCAPSULATION.

Enzyme   A protein molecule that acts as a catalyst and therefore affects the rate of a chemical reaction in a living organism. See also CATALYST.

Etching Solution   A solution which corrodes the surface of a metal in order to reveal its composition and structure.

Evaporators   Evaporators achieve resource recovery by distilling the wastewater until there is sufficient concentration of chemicals in solution for treatment, recovery or re-use. Because of their high energy requirements, evaporators are not used to concentrate highly dilute solutions, nor are they used on volatile mixtures. Water vapour can be condensed and re-used, or released to the atmosphere. Condensing allows the recovery of some of the heat used in the evaporation process. Evaporators have been used for many years in industrial recovery programmes and there are a number of systems available; rising film evaporators, flash evaporators using waste heat, submerged tube evaporators and atmospheric evaporators are all being used in commercial settings.

Feedstock   The raw material or chemical intermediary which is an essential input in a manufacturing process.

Fermentation   Decomposition of organic substances by organisms, especially bacteria and yeasts. Yeast, for example, decomposes sugar into ethyl alcohol and carbon dioxide.

Film   In photography, the term film is usually applied to the film base (which is flexible and transparent) and emulsion coating. See also EMULSION.

Filtrate   The discharge liquor in filtration. Also known as mother liquor or strong liquor.

Filtration   The use of filters (e.g. diatomaceous earth) to prepare wastewater for subsequent treatment processes or for direct re-use as highly clarified water. The filtration medium traps suspended solids in wastewater, and dewaters and reduces the volume of sludges. See also SOLID-LIQUID SEPARATION.

Finishing   In the textile industry, the treatment of a fabric that modifies its physical or chemical properties (e.g. permanent press finishes, oil repellents, fire retardants, fungicides).

Fix   See FIXATIVE.

Fixative   In photoprocessing, the process chemical that removes silver halide from the film, slide or print after exposure and development. Also known as fix, fixer or fixing agent.

Fleshing   The removal of flesh and fat from hides in a tannery.

Floc   Small masses formed in a fluid through coagulation, agglomeration or biochemical reaction of fine suspended particles.

Flocculant   A substance which will bring together fine particles of solids in a liquid to create floc.

Flocculating Agent   See FLOCCULANT.

Flocculation   A waste treatment process by which fine suspended solids are combined, by use of a chemical agent, into larger particles or flocs that can be readily separated by gravity sedimentation. See also FLOC, PRECIPITATION, SEDIMENTATION.

Flotation   A waste disposal operation used to separate solid or liquid particles from a liquid phase. Separation is brought about by introducing fine gas (usually air) bubbles under pressure into the liquid phase. The bubbles attach to the particulate matter, and the buoyant force of the combined particle and gas bubbles is great enough to cause the particles to rise to the surface. Particles that have a higher density than the liquid can thus be made to rise. The rising of particles with lower density than the liquid can also be facilitated (e.g. oil suspension in water). In wastewater treatment, flotation is used to remove suspended matter and to concentrate biological sludges. Once the particles have been floated to the surface, they can be collected by a skimming operation. See also SOLID-LIQUID SEPARATION.

Flue Gas Desulphurization Unit   Known more commonly as a scrubber. See SCRUBBER.

Fluidized Bed Incineration   A type of incineration which destroys organic wastes by thermal oxidation of the combustible material. Fuel particles are continually fed into a bed of mineral ash in the incinerator while a flow of air passes up through the bed causing it to act like a turbulent fluid. The amount of air available for combustion far exceeds that found in conventional burners and ensures more complete destruction of the waste material.

Fluorocarbon   A hydrocarbon such as Freon™ in which some or all of the hydrogen atoms have been replaced by fluorine atoms. Can be liquid or gas. Non-flammable and heat-stable. Used as a refrigerant, aerosol propellant and solvent. Also known as fluorohydrocarbon.

Fluorohydrocarbon   See FLUOROCARBON.

Fly Ash   Fine particulate, essentially noncombustible refuse, carried in the gaseous emissions from an incinerator. See also BOTTOM ASH.

Fountain Solution   A water-alcohol mixture used, in off-set lithography, to wet parts of the printing plate.

Fractionate   To separate a mixture in successive stages, each stage removing from the mixture some proportion of one of the substances, as by differential solubility in water-solvent mixtures. Fractionation may be used in solvent recovery to return solvents to their virgin purity.

Fugitive Emission   The loss of solvent vapour during various stages of a processing or recycling operation due to the solvent's high volatility.

Gasohol   A fuel which is a mixture of gasoline and ethyl alcohol (ethanol), commonly 10 percent ethanol to 90 percent gasoline. Larger percentages of ethanol necessitate minor engine adjustments.

Genetic Engineering   The intentional production of new genes and alteration of genomes (sets of chromosomes) by the substitution or addition of new genetic material.

Granulator   In plastics reprocessing, a device that reduces plastic scrap to a fine granular material suitable for reforming into new plastic objects.

Hairburn Tank   In tanning, the processing tank in which a solution of lime and sodium sulphide dissolves the hair, epidermis and certain unwanted proteins.

Halogenated Organics   Organic compounds containing chlorine, bromine, iodine or fluorine, but primarily relates to chlorinated organic compounds.

Hauled Liquid Industrial Wastes   Those wastes generated by manufacturing or processing operations which are hauled away from the place they were generated to another location for treatment and/or disposal. In Ontario, hauled liquid industrial wastes include industrial waste sludges, semi-solids and solid wastes.

Hazardous Waste   Waste that requires special precaution in its storage, collection, transportation, treatment or disposal to prevent damage to persons or property. There are no universally accepted definitions for the term hazardous waste, and each country defines the term with its own criteria. In a general sense, however, hazardous wastes include explosive, flammable, volatile, radioactive, toxic and pathological wastes.

Heat Exchanger   Any device that transfers heat from one substance to another. In industrial applications, heat exchangers are typically applied to hot wastewater streams or exhaust gases to retain heat otherwise lost from the plant.

Heterogeneous   Made up of dissimilar elements or parts.

High-Solids Paint   A paint developed to lessen the need for volatile organic solvents by increasing the proportion of solids. Includes catalyst systems (in two parts) that convert totally to film, and solution types made of pre-polymers, co-solvents and water.

Homogeneous   Made up of similar elements or parts.

Housekeeping   A low-cost, systematic review of the efficiency of existing in-plant processes as well as preventative maintenance to spot potential leaks and spills before they happen. It is a method of reducing the pollution load of a factory and concurrently reducing production costs. One method of good housekeeping is to maintain close control over factory operations, in order to avoid accidental spillages of process chemical baths and the preparation of too large a batch, the excess of which might be wasted.

Hydration   The process of combining with water; the incorporation of molecular water into a complex molecule with the molecules or units of another species.

Hydrocarbon   See ORGANIC.

Hydrolysis   A chemical process used to treat organic matter such as fatty oils. The reaction occurs at high temperatures and pressures in the presence of catalysts. Hydrogen ion or hydroxyl ion present in water react with a salt, an ester or an amide to produce an acid or a base.

Immiscible   Pertaining to liquids that will not mix with each other; e.g. oil and water.

Incineration   A waste disposal technology of the thermal destruction type. In incineration, combustion of wastes in the presence of excess oxygen produces water, carbon dioxide and ash, as well as non-combustible residuals. If combustion is incomplete, other organic byproducts may occur.

Industrial Brines   Aqueous solutions of inorganic compounds having dissolved solids contents of greater that one percent (10,000 ppm).

Inert   Lacking activity, reactivity or effect.

Initiator   A substance that begins a chemical chain reaction.

Inorganic Wastes   Wastes composed primarily of inorganic compounds but which may contain traces of organic contamination.

Ion   A particle with an electric charge.

Ion Exchange   A process for concentrating chemicals in a wastestream to enhance the possibility of effective treatment, or effect their recovery or re-use. The process is based on the exchange of one ionic species for another. The donating material is an ion exchange resin, a granular solid or organic beads which adsorb ions from the wastestream and release non-toxic ions of their own, such as hydrogen and hydroxyl ions. When the resin is exhausted, it is regenerated by another chemical that gives up the ions that were lost to the waste solution. This converts the resin back to its original form, and removes the adsorbed ions for further treatment or re-use. Anionic or cationic resins may be used separately or in combination depending on the nature of the wastestream. Ion exchange is particularly well suited for removing inorganic materials from liquid wastestreams. It is also used to reclaim metals from tanning and plating solutions and provide a source of deionized water for plant process uses.

Ion Exchange Resin   A resin, usually synthetic, that can combine or exchange ions with a solution.

Ion Exchange Technology   See REVERSE OSMOSIS and ELECTRODIALYSIS.

Jet Dyeing   A type of textile dyeing which is superior to atmospheric beck dyeing because of its increased dye effeciency, reduced water consumption and smaller wastestream. See also ATMOSPHERIC BECK DYEING.

Kieselguhr   See DIATOMACEOUS EARTH.

Kraft Paper   A strong paper or cardboard made from sulphate-process wood pulp; unbleached varieties are used for wrapping paper and shipping cartons.

Kraft Pulp   Wood pulp resulting from a pulping process in which sodium sulphate is used in the caustic soda pulp-digestion liquor. Also known as sulphate pulp.

Lagoon   A holding pit or pond for wastewater.

Landfill   See SECURE LANDFILL.

Lean Wastes   Organic wastes which require additional fuel or an energy-rich wastestream to sustain combustion temperature. Lean wastes have heat values below 7000 Btu per pound. See also RICH WASTES.

Lignin   A substance that, together with cellulose, forms the woody cell walls of plants and cements them together; a colourless to brown substance removed from paper-pulp sulphite liquor.

Liquid Waste   That waste which is in the liquid or fluid state under normal conditions, can be pumped and must be contained in a suitable vessel.

Liquid Waste Incinerator   An incinerator typically consisting of one or more atomizing nozzles and a refractory lined combustion chamber. The liquid wastes are usually pre-heated and blended to upgrade their combustibility and pumpability. The wastestream is then injected in an atomized form into the combustion chamber. Complete combustion is obtained only if the waste is adequately atomized and mixed with air.

Low-Liquor Dyeing   An alternative, less polluting type of textile dyeing compared to conventional beck dyeing. Low-liquor dyeing results in more dye on the material and less out with the wastewater. New low-liquor dye machines require only one quarter as much dye liquid as atmospheric becks.

Low-Waste Technology   A body of technologies that maximize processing efficiency, reduce pollution at source and maximize the re-use of process wastestreams in an attempt to control pollution in a most cost-effective and conservative manner.

Magnetic Separation   The separation of magnetic from less magnetic or non-magnetic materials by using strong magnetic fields. This technology is applicable to wastestreams containing heavy metals, since many of these waste metals are either ferromagnetic or paramagnetic. An advantage of magnetic separation is the relative purity and small volume

of metallic materials collected, giving recycle potential to the concentrated metallic product.

Maximum Allowable Concentration   See THRESHOLD LIMIT VALUE.

Membrane System   See ELECTRODIALYSIS, REVERSE OSMOSIS and ULTRAFILTRATION.

Mercerization   A process by which cotton and linen materials are increased in lustre and strength. This may result in a greater ability to absorb dyes. The material is treated with a solution of caustic soda which is heated to a controlled temperature. Afterwards, it is washed, neutralized and rinsed.

Metallic Replacement   In photofinishing, the settling out of dissolved silver from a solution as a sludge. A metal such as iron is brought into contact with the solution containing the dissolved ions of silver; the dissolved silver, present as a thiosulphate complex, reacts with the iron and settles out.

Molten Salt Incineration   Incineration based on the injection of a mixture of waste material and air under the surface of a pool of molten sodium carbonate or other salt. The hydrocarbons of the organic waste are immediately oxidized to carbon dioxide and water. The combustion byproducts may contain such elements as phosphorus, sulphur and arsenic. The halogens react with sodium carbonate. These byproducts are retained in the melt as inorganic salts rather than released to the atmosphere as volatile gases.

Monomer   A simple molecule which is capable of combining with a number of like or unlike molecules to form a polymer. It is a repeating structure unit within a polymer. Also known, in plastics manufacture, as the reactant. See also POLYMER.

Mother Liquor   See FILTRATE.

Muck Stripping   In the dry cleaning industry, the reduction of solvent holdup in the filter muck through air pressure or steam stripping. The dry muck may be sealed in a bag for disposal.

Multiple Hearth Incinerator   A type of incinerator used to dry and burn sludges that have been partially dried by vacuum filtration. It is a counter-current operation in which heated air and products of combustion pass by finely pulverized sludge that is continually raked to expose fresh surfaces. Such incinerators are used, for example, to incinerate municipal sewage sludge.

Mutagenic   Causing a change (mutation) in the DNA (deoxyribonucleic acid, the genetic "information") of a cell's chromosomes. A mutagen may also be a carcinogen.

Neutralization   The pre-treatment of acidic or alkaline industrial wastes, since most municipal sewage treatment regulations restrict the pH of industrial wastewater discharged to the municipal sewer system. Typically, mixing acidic wastewater with a base, or mixing alkaline wastewater with an acid, results in water and a salt. Resultant salts that are insoluble in water form a sludge that must be eliminated prior to discharge of the neutralized effluent.

Off-Site   A site other than the property owned by the company where the manufacturing or processing operations which generate the wastes are located.

Oil-Water Separator   A device which separates oil from water before discharge of wastewater, based on the fact that oil floats on water. The oil which is recovered may be dewatered and re-used, or hauled away for reprocessing.

On-Site   Within the property boundaries associated with the manufacturing or processing operations which generate the wastes.

Operating Cost   The ongoing cost of running machinery and processes, including energy, water, material and labour charges.

Organic   Any compound that contains carbon and hydrogen (or other elements substituted for hydrogen). An organic compound can also be called a hydrocarbon. They include both naturally occurring and synthetic compounds.

Organics   Short form meaning organic compounds, organic materials. See ORGANIC.

Ozone   Structurally unstable, allotropic form of oxygen (O_3) formed by electrical discharge in air. It is used as an oxidizing, deodorizing and bleaching agent and in the purification of water.

Paint Arrestor   Equipment used to trap paint spray drift. Common paint arrestors include the fabric filter type and the water curtain type.

Paint Overspray   That portion of the paint sprayed which does not adhere to the object. Paint spray guns vary in the quantity of paint that reaches the target object. Conventional spray guns have a transfer efficiency of 30 to 45 percent whereas electrostatic guns ensure that twice as much paint reaches the object. Paint overspray is also known as paint sludge or waste paint.

Paint Sludge   See PAINT OVERSPRAY.

Pay-Back Period   The time required to pay off the cost of new equipment based on the added income generated by installing more efficient equipment and processes. It is not uncommon for the pay-back period of recycling technologies to be two years or less because the value of the recovered materials or energy may be substantial. Once the capital cost of the recovery equipment is paid off, income generated through recovery contributes directly to a company's profit margin.

Example:

Capital cost of recycling equipment	$30,000.00
Cost to recover 1 pound of material	0.20
Value of 1 pound of material	1.00
Savings per pound through recovery	0.80
For a system recovering 300 pounds per week, the yearly savings are	$12,480.00
PAY-BACK PERIOD	2.4 years

In this simple example, 2.4 years are required to pay off the $30,000 invested in recycling equipment. It must be recognized, however, that this simple calculation of pay-back period does not include the cost of borrowing money which may add considerable time to the pay-back period.

Pelletization   Forming aggregates of about $^1/_2$ inch (13 mm) diameter from finely divided ore, coal or other substances.

Permeate   In ultrafiltration, the water and low molecular weight solutes that cross the membrane and are removed as the permeate. Typically, the high molecular weight fraction does not cross the membrane and is known as the concentrate. See also CONCENTRATE.

Photochemical Reaction   A chemical reaction that is affected or initiated by light, such as ultraviolet light.

Photoinitiator   Initiators which are activated by photons, thereby initiating polymerization. Examples: thioxanthones, acetophenone derivatives and benzoin ethers. See also INITIATOR.

Photolysis   The use of radiant energy (such as ultraviolet light) to produce chemical changes. For example, photolysis can be used to destroy dioxin.

Photon   A particle with no mass; the quantum of an electromagnetic field. Also known as light quantum, a photon carries energy, momentum and angular momentum.

Photopolymers   Any of a class of light-sensitive polymers which undergoes a spontaneous and permanent change in physical properties on exposure to light. Photopolymers can be used as a substitute for silver.

Phototypography   Any photomechanical process of engraving in relief that may be reproduced in connection with type on a printing press. Phototypography processes which are based on silver halide film produce large quantities of waste silver which can be recovered.

Physical-Chemical Treatment   Any one or combination of a number of unit operations commonly employed in the treatment of wastes and include: emulsion breaking, chemical precipitation, chemical oxidation, ion exchange, ultrafiltration, neutralization, solids removal and thickening, carbon adsorption, reverse osmosis, and electrochemical processes.

Pickling   A method of preparing hides for tanning by immersion in a salt solution with a pH of 2.5 or less. Also refers to the method of cleaning metal surfaces of scale with acids. Wastewaters from pickling processes are acidic.

Pigment   A solid substance which is used to give colour to other materials.

Plasma   A gas consisting of charged and neutral particles having an overall charge of zero and exhibiting collective behaviour. Plasma is characterized by a good ability to conduct electricity. See also PLASMA ARC TECHNOLOGY.

Plasma Arc Technology   A waste disposal technology in which a plasma arc torch functions to pyrolize wastes into combustible gases by exposure to a gas which has been energized to its plasma state. See also PLASMA.

Plastics Reprocessing   The process of converting scrap plastic to a useful material.

Platemaking   In the graphic arts industry, printing consists of making a plate or negative copy of the original material to be printed, then inking of the plate and application of the plate to paper or other materials.

Polymer   A substance formed by the linking of monomers (simple molecules) into giant molecules. See also MONOMER.

Polymerization   The linking of molecules (monomers) to form a more complex molecule (a polymer) having the same empirical formula as the monomers.

Pomace   The material remaining after juice or oil has been pressed out of a fruit, vegetable, seed or other agricultural product.

Post-Consumer Waste   Waste not from industrial processes, but of the industrial product itself after it has fulfilled its purpose or has served a "useful life". Recyclable post-consumer wastestreams from residential and commercial sectors include paper, glass, rubber, textiles, plastics and metals. Post-consumer waste is contrasted to in-plant (pre-consumer) industrial waste, also known as scrap. See also SCRAP.

Powder Coating   In the paint industry, a coating, prepared as a dry powder, which is placed on a surface and fused into a coherent film.

Pozzolan   A silica form that, when mixed with lime and water, will make cement. A finely ground clay or shale resembling volcanic dust found near Pozzuoli, Italy.

Precipitation   Precipitation requires the addition of a precipitating agent to react with the dissolved contaminants in the wastewater or the addition of a pH adjuster or a change of temperature, the result in all cases being an insoluble product which precipitates out. It is a waste treatment technology that may be used together with flocculation and sedimentation as consecutive processes to treat the same wastestream. It is used to treat wastestreams containing dissolved metal salts. See also FLOCCULATION and SEDIMENTATION.

Pyrolysis   A waste disposal technology of the thermal destruction type. Pyrolysis technologies are based on the combustion of wastes in an oxygen-deficient environment. Organic wastes are broken down into a range of simpler organic molecules and ash.

Radiation-Curable Coatings   In the paint industry, coatings containing no solvents; they are 100 percent solid. They are based on photochemical reactions such as the ultraviolet process or on the electron beam process or on thermal curing as in the infrared system.

Radiation Destruction   A waste disposal technology which depends on the energy of electron beam, ultraviolet (UV) or other radiation to provide the energy necessary to break apart molecular bonds in the hazardous material. The absorption of radiation at certain wavelengths causes the waste chemical compound to decompose. In some cases, the incoming radiation functions as a catalyst to accelerate an otherwise chemical destruction of the waste.

Reclamation   The recovery of a usable product from a waste following extensive pre-treatment such as distillation, chemical treatment, re-refining, electrolytic recovery, etc.

Recovery and Re-Use   Wastes are segregated and directed for re-use either on-site or off-site, and may include pre-treatment such as separation of organic and inorganic phases or separation of solids and liquids.

Refrigeration Solvent Recovery Unit   An alternative to carbon adsorption in the dry cleaning industry, to control solvent emissions from air otherwise exhausted directly to the outside. In the refrigerated condenser system, the solvent-stripped air may be returned directly to the dry cleaning machine, eliminating the need for external venting ducts.

Replenisher   Any concentrated process chemical added at frequent intervals to the depleted processing bath. For example, in photofinishing, a replenisher is a solution which is added to the developer solution as the developer is used and the concentration of developing agent decreases. The replenisher contains higher concentrations of developer, additional alkali and reduced concentrations of bromide.

Re-Refining   The process by which used cutting oils, lubricating oils, crank-case residues and oil compounds are recovered and refined again as commercial grade products.

Residues   The high-viscosity substances remaining in the bottom of a distillation unit, such as occurs from petroleum refining operations or after distillation of used solvents. The residues contain impurities and hydrocarbons. Also known as still bottoms or sludges. The term residue is also used in a more general sense to refer to any solid or semi-solid waste material generated by preliminary waste treatment such as precipitation, filtration or clarification. See also STILL BOTTOMS.

Resins   Usually polymers which are of a high molecular weight. Resins can be solid or semi-solid and can be either natural or synthetic in origin. In paint, a resin is the main ingredient which binds the various other ingredients together. It also aids adhesion to the surface.

Retrievable Storage   A secure system of long-term storing of wastes prior to recovery or destruction at a later date. Wastes are stored in drums, tanks or ponds, depending on how hazardous or volatile the waste is.

Re-Use   See RECOVERY AND RE-USE.

Reverse Osmosis   One of the three major membrane separation processes for wastewater treatment. The other two are electrodialysis and ultrafiltration. In reverse osmosis, the natural tendency of water to flow spontaneously through a semi-permeable membrane from a solution of low concentration to a solution of higher concentration is reversed by increasing pressure on the high concentration solution. This makes it possible to remove most of the dissolved minerals and organics as well as biological and colloidal material from water. The reverse osmosis membrane restricts the passage of molecules through it on the basis of their size and charge. Low valence molecules can pass through more easily than high valence ones. The reverse osmosis membrane is essentially non-porous. Molecules have to dissolve into the membrane and then dissolve out into the solution on the other side. Typical membrane flux levels are 2 to 15 gal /day/ft^2

Rich Wastes   Organic wastes which are high enough in heat content to sustain combustion on their own, except for the ignition of the fuel. Rich wastes have a minimum heat value of 7000 Btu per pound. See also LEAN WASTES.

Roll Coating   A coating application technique in which paint is delivered to a roll which rotates in the same direction as the flat object to be painted is moving, and essentially at the same speed. Very similar to printing, and often used for lithography or where designs are to be printed on the surface, as with wood graining of flat surfaces. Also known as coil coating.

Rotary Kiln Incinerator   An incinerator which uses a slowly revolving steel cylinder lined with fire bricks for the primary combustion chamber. The cylinder is mounted at an incline so that wastes fed into the high end of the kiln pass through the combustion zone as the kiln rotates. Liquid or solid waste is fed into the kiln via a sealed feed system. The slow rotation of the kiln causes wastes to tumble and break apart, thereby improving combustion efficiency. Ash and non-combustible residues are moved along the cylinder and removed from an ash box at the low end of the cylinder.

Runner   In a plastics injection or transfer mould, the channel (usually circular) that connects the sprue with the gate to the mould cavity. See also SPRUE.

Saponification   A chemical process used to convert plastics such as PET (polyethylene terephthalate) into its chemical components. Saponification is essentially the reverse of polymerization; it "unzips" the polymer into constituent chemicals which may be of resale value.

Scouring   The removal of grease and dirt from wool. Also, the cleaning of fabric before the dyeing step in order to remove the natural impurities (wax, pectins and alcohols) and the processing impurities (size, dirt, oil and grease). Normal scouring materials are alkalies (e.g. soda ash) or trisodium phosphate, often used in the presence of a surfactant.

Scrap   Any solid trim, cutting, or reject material which may be suitable for recycling as feedstock to the primary operation (e.g. scrap from plastic or glass moulding or metal working). See also POST-CONSUMER WASTE.

Scrubber   A device for the removal, or washing out, of entrained liquid droplets or dust, or the removal of an undesired gas component from process gas streams. Also known as wet collector.

Secure Landfill   A landfill designed to receive treated industrial wastes. It differs from a conventional sanitary landfill in the degree to which the site is engineered to diminish the migration of pollutants.

Sedimentation   The separation of suspended particles that are heavier than water from water by gravitational settling. It is one of the most widely used unit operations in wastewater treatment. Sedimentation basins are designed to produce both a clarified effluent and a concentrated sludge. See also SOLID-LIQUID SEPARATION.

Segregation   A system of keeping wastestreams separate that are generated by various processes within a single plant. Materials recovery is enhanced if wastestreams, which might contaminate the stream from which specific substances are to be recovered, are not mixed. The same holds true for energy recovery. Heat recovery is enhanced if a hot wastestream is recycled back into the process, rather than mixing it with a cold wastestream.

Silver Halide   A compound made up of any one of the halogen family (fluorine, chlorine, bromine, iodine) and silver.

Size   See SLASHING.

Sizing   See SLASHING.

Slashing   In the textile industry, a wet process in which the warp threads are coated with a size (either synthetic or starch). This increases their strength and smoothness, thereby preparing them for easier weaving. Size may be applied to the surface of the woven garment in order to fill the pores. Slashing is also referred to as sizing.

Sludge   A mixture of liquids and solids which flows under normal conditions and can be pumped using standard pumping equipment or vacuum equipment.

Sludge Cake   The material resulting from the drying of sludge on open or covered drying beds. Also, the dewatered cake from a vacuum-sludge filter.

Sludge Farming   A process whereby waste sludges are spread onto land and ploughed into the soil. Nutrients are added and the deposited sludges are turned at frequent intervals to ensure continuing bacterial decomposition of the biodegradable wastes.

Smog   Air pollution consisting of smoke and fog.

Soil Stabilizer   A chemical that alters the engineering property of a natural soil. It is used to stabilize soil slopes, to prepare for building foundations and to prevent erosion.

Solid Waste   Solid or a mixture of solid and liquid wastes which will not flow under normal conditions and which cannot be pumped using standard pumping equipment.

Solidification   The fixation or encapsulation of waste to produce a solid end product. Fixation is based on the addition of an agent such as lime or cement to turn the waste into a concrete-like solid. Encapsulation is a physical process in which the solidification agent surrounds the waste particles and makes them adhere together into a mass. The objective of solidification is to trap toxic constituents chemically and physically within a solid.

Solid-Liquid Separation   A group of simple, relatively inexpensive waste treatment processes designed to physically separate the solid and liquid components of wastestreams. These techniques are used to remove suspended and settled solids from liquid waste prior to wastewater discharge or further treatment. The processes will not remove dissolved solids from wastewater unless preceded by precipitation. In treating sludges, these processes are used to remove excess water prior to disposal. Four major types of solid-liquid separation are sedimentation, flotation, filtration and centrifugation.

Solute, Solution   See SOLVENT.

Solvent   The liquid part of a solution existing in a larger amount than the solute (the substance being dissolved). A solvent can dissolve or disperse other substances. In paints, a solvent is the volatile part of a paint composition that evaporates during drying. In industrial usage, solvent usually refers to organic solvent, and as such refers to the class of volatile hydrocarbons used as dissolvers, viscosity reducers and cleaning agents.

Solvent-Borne Paints   Paints in which the solvent is an organic compound. Solvent-borne paints typically contain 60 to 80 percent organic solvents.

Spent Liquor   The liquid effluent from the digestion of wood during pulping; it contains wood chemicals (e.g. lignin) and spent digestant (caustic, sulphite or sulphate, depending on the process used).

Sprue   A feed opening or vertical channel through which molten material, such as metal or plastic, is poured in an injection or transfer mould. Also, a slug of material that solidifies in the channel. See also RUNNER.

Sputtercoating   In the coatings industry, a process in which a thin metallic deposit is sandwiched between two organic coatings to give an object a metallic appearance.

Steam Distillation   See STEAM STRIPPER.

Steam Stripper   A distillation unit in which vapourization of the volatile constituents of a liquid mixture takes place at a lower temperature by the introduction of steam directly into the charge. Steam used in this manner is known as open steam.

Still Bottoms   In solvent recycling, the waste residue remaining in the bottom of the distillation unit during solvent recovery. In general, still bottoms refers to residue remaining in the bottom of any distillation unit. See also RESIDUE.

Strong Liquor   See FILTRATE.

Sulphate Pulp   See KRAFT PULP.

Surface Encapsulation   A process in which drummed wastes or treated solid waste cubes are coated with a water-impermeable sealant.

Suspended Solids   Fine, non-settling particles of any solid within a liquid or gas, the particles being the dispersed phase, while the suspending medium is the continuous phase. In industry, the suspending medium is usually plant wastewater, and suspended solids measures the total amount of solids separated by filtration of a wastewater sample.

Tailing   In photographic waste recovery, a secondary step carried out after most of the silver is recovered. It removes residual silver from the overflow fix.

Tannin   An acid obtained from the bark of some trees and from certain plants, used in tanning (also used in dyeing, in making ink, and in medicine). More generally, a tannin is any compound used to join with the skin protein to form leather. Chromium salts are the most widely used tannins, although vegetable tannins and synthetic tanning agents (syntans) are also used. See also TANNING.

Tanning   A process of preserving animal hides by chemical treatment (using tannins) to make them immune to bacterial attack, and subsequent treatment with fats and greases to make them pliable. See also TANNIN.

Tentering   During the many processes involved in textile finishing, the material is distorted and put out of shape. In tentering (generally the final step), the material is taken through a tenter frame (heated chamber), held to a desired width and dried, thus giving it the finished shape.

Thermal Destruction   A group of waste disposal technologies using heat to break down hazardous organic wastes into less toxic constituents, ideally carbon dioxide and water. The two broad categories of thermal destruction technologies are incineration and pyrolysis.

Threshold Limit Value (TLV)   The average concentration of chemical to which the normal person can be exposed without injury for eight hours per day, five days per week, for an unlimited period. TLV differs slightly from maximum allowable concentration in that threshold limit value is an average concentration. TLVs are set for purposes of government regulation and are subject to change pending further scientific data.

Thurmongery   The process of tanning animal hides.

TLV   See THRESHOLD LIMIT VALUE.

Total Solids   The sum of suspended solids and dissolved solids. See also SUSPENDED SOLIDS and DISSOLVED SOLIDS.

Toxicity   The capacity to produce biological injury.

Tripolite   See DIATOMACEOUS EARTH.

Ultrafiltration   Resembles reverse osmosis in that pressure is applied to a solution to force water across a semi-permeable membrane. Unlike reverse osmosis, the passage of soluble material across the membrane depends only on its molecular size. Ultrafiltration membranes come with various filter pore sizes ranging from molecular weights of 200 to 100,000. Ultrafiltration systems can be specific in what sized molecules it will allow to pass, by the use of a particular "molecular weight cutoff" membrane. Typically, suspended material and high molecular weight dissolved species such as colloids, protein, carbohydrates and synthetic resins are not able to cross the ultrafiltration membrane. Low molecular weight solutes such as salts, sugars and organics can pass through the micro-porous ultrafiltration membrane. Ultrafiltration systems can operate under lower pressures than reverse osmosis systems and typical membrane flux levels are 20 to 200 gal /day/ft ^{2}

Virgin Purity   The purity of a substance (e.g. a solvent) before it is used in industrial processes or after it has been reclaimed and stripped of process contaminants to original purity.

Viscosity   The flow resistance, or internal friction, of a fluid. The higher the viscosity, the more resistant the liquid to flowing.

VOC   See VOLATILE ORGANIC COMPOUND.

Volatile   That which evaporates rapidly.

Volatile Organic Compound (VOC)   A substance made up of carbon chains or rings, to which atoms of hydrogen and sometimes oxygen, nitrogen and/or other elements are attached. Volatile insofar as it evaporates readily.

Waste Audit   A thorough analysis of a company's processes and wastes to generate detailed information on the types and quantities of wastes that the company is generating. Completion of a waste audit identifies problem areas and provides baseline data from which to gauge the success of a waste reduction programme.

Waste Exchange   The transfer of wastes from one company to another. In order for that transfer to occur, the two companies must know of each other's existence. This matching function may be accomplished by a waste exchange programme or through a broker. A waste exchange strives to match waste generators with waste users, thereby linking potential trading partners.

Waste Paint   See PAINT OVERSPRAY.

Water-Borne Paints   Paints which contain substantial amounts of water with up to 80 percent of the volatiles being water. The polymers used to make the solids component can be dissolved, dispersed or emulsified. In industrial water-borne coatings, the paint formulations commonly contain 40 to 50 percent water, 10 percent organic solvents and 40 to 50 percent solids.

Way-Bill System   A waste tracking system in which a multi-copy shipping form follows the movement of hauled liquid industrial wastes from the site of generation to the site of treatment and disposal. The way-bill form specifies the type of waste being shipped, its chemical nature, volume, date and time of pick-up. The generator and the receiver of the hauled waste must each submit a copy of the way-bill to the appropriate government agency. In Ontario, the maximum penalty for failing to comply with the manifest system regulations is $2000. (A way-bill system is also known as a manifest system.)

Wet Air Oxidation   The process by which organic substances (e.g. sludge) may be oxidized under high pressures at elevated temperatures with the sludge in a liquid state by feeding compressed air into the pressure vessel. Combustion is 75 to 90 percent complete; some organic matter, plus ammonia, will be end products. Wet air oxidation technology is applicable to aqueous organic wastestreams containing one to 20 percent organic material.

Wet Collector   See SCRUBBER.

Whey   The watery part of milk that separates from the curd when milk sours and becomes coagulated or when cheese is made.

Zero-Waste Approach   An approach to waste handling that was intended to remove virtually all pollutants from a wastestream. Zero-waste technologies include closed-loop processing, maximizing re-use and transferring wastes as inputs into other business sectors. The term zero-waste has fallen into disuse and is currently replaced with the terms low-waste technology or maximum re-use. See also LOW-WASTE TECHNOLOGY.

Index